Diane

P9-DCM-208

OUR FATHERS

OUR FATHERS

THE SECRET LIFE OF THE

CATHOLIC CHURCH

IN AN AGE OF SCANDAL

David France

Broadway Books | *New York*

PRINTED IN THE UNITED STATES OF AMERICA

BROADWAY BOOKS and its logo, a letter B bisected on the diagonal, are
trademarks of Random House, Inc.

Visit our website at www.broadwaybooks.com

First edition published 2004.

Book design by Chris Welch

Library of Congress Cataloging-in-Publication Data

France, David, 1959–
Our fathers : the secret life of the Catholic Church in an age of scandal /
David France.—1st ed.
p. cm.
Includes bibliographical references and index.
1. Catholic Church—United States—Clergy—Sexual Behavior. 2. Child sexual
abuse by clergy—United States. I. Title.
BX1912.9.F73 2004
282'.73'09045—dc22
2003062973

ISBN 0-7679-1430-9

1   3   5   7   9   10   8   6   4   2

To Georgianne France and Jonathan Starch

CONTENTS

CAST OF CHARACTERS

THE VATICAN

John Paul II, supreme pontiff of the Roman Catholic Church, 1978–
present
    John Paul I, supreme pontiff, 1978
    Paul VI, supreme pontiff, 1963–1978
    Blessed John XXIII, supreme pontiff, 1958–1963
    Pius XII, supreme pontiff, 1939–1958
Cardinal Darío Castrillón Hoyos, prefect, Congregation for the
Clergy
Joaquín Navarro-Valls, chief spokesman for the Vatican
Cardinal Josef Ratzinger, prefect, Congregation for the Doctrine of
the Faith
Cardinal Giovanni Battista Re, prefect, Congregation for Bishops

AMERICAN BISHOPS

Cardinal Edward Egan, archbishop of New York, 2001–present;
bishop of Bridgeport, 1988–2001
Bishop Wilton Gregory, bishop of Belleville; president of the United
States Conference of Catholic Bishops
Bishop James Rausch, bishop of Phoenix, 1977–1981

Cardinal Roger Mahony, archbishop of Los Angeles, 1985–present
Bishop Thomas O'Brien, bishop of Phoenix, 1981–2003

ARCHDIOCESE OF BOSTON

Archbishops

Cardinal Richard Cushing, 1958–1970
Cardinal Humberto Medeiros, 1970–1983
Cardinal Bernard Law, 1984–2002

Auxiliary Bishops

Emilio Allue, auxiliary bishop, 1996–present
Robert Banks, vicar general, 1984–1990; auxiliary bishop, 1985–1990; bishop of Green Bay, 1990–present
Thomas Daily, secretary to Humberto Medeiros, 1971–1973; chancellor, 1973–1984; auxiliary bishop, 1975–1984; vicar general, 1977–1984; bishop of Palm Springs, 1984–1990; bishop of Brooklyn, 1990–2003
Walter Edyvean, vicar general, 2001–2003; auxiliary bishop, 2001–present
John McCormack, secretary for ministerial personnel, 1984–1994; auxiliary bishop, 1995–1998; bishop of Manchester, 1998–present
John Mulcahy, auxiliary bishop, 1975–1992
William Murphy, secretary for community relations, 1987–1993; vicar general, 1993–2001; auxiliary bishop, 1995–2001; bishop of Rockville Centre, 2001–present

Support Staff and Significant Boston Players

Father Robert Bullock, pastor of Our Lady of Sorrows, cofounder of the Boston Priests' Forum
Father John Connolly, secretary to Bernard Law, 1997–1999, 2001–2002

Father Charles Higgins, secretary for ministerial personnel, 2001–2002

Sister Rita McCarthy, liaison for sexual abuse victims, 1994–1997

Father Paul Miceli, secretary for ministerial personnel, 1994–2001; pastor of Immaculate Conception Parish, 2001–present

Donna Morrissey, secretary for public relations and communications, 2001–2003

Sister Catherine Mulkerrin, top aide to John McCormack and liaison for sexual abuse complaints, 1992–1994

Barbara Thorp, director, Office of Healing and Assistance, March 2002–present

PRIESTS AND NUNS

Joseph Birmingham (Boston archdiocese), Our Lady of Fatima Parish, Sudbury, 1960–1964; St. James, Salem, 1964–1970; St. Michael's, Lowell, 1970–1977; St. Columbkille's, Brighton, 1977–1985; St. Ann's, Gloucester, 1985–1987; St. Brigid's, Lexington, 1987–1989

Neil Conway (Cleveland diocese), various parish and chancery appointments, 1963–1985; St. John the Baptist, Akron, 1985; retired, 1985

Walter Cuenin (Boston archdiocese), various parish assignments, 1970–1993; Our Lady Help of Christians, 1993–present

Thomas Doyle (Dominican Order), professor and lecturer in canon law, 1978–1981; secretary-canonist, Vatican embassy, Washington, 1981–1986; tribunal judge, various dioceses, 1986–1990; Air Force chaplain, 1990–present

Gilbert Gauthe (Lafayette diocese), various parishes, 1971–1983

John Geoghan (Boston archdiocese), Blessed Sacrament, Saugus, 1962–1966; St. Bernard's, Concord, 1966–1967; St. Paul's, Hingham, 1967–1974; St. Andrew's, Jamaica Plain, 1974–1980; sick leave, 1980; St. Brendan's, Dorchester, 1981–1984; St. Julia's, Weston, 1984–1989; sick leave, 1989–1993; Office of Senior Priests at Regina Cleri residence for retired priests,

1993–1996; sick leave, 1996; clergy personnel office, 1997; defrocked, 1998

Jeannine Gramick (School Sisters of Notre Dame order), cofounder of New Ways Ministry, a national group advocating acceptance of homosexuals within the church

David Holley (Worcester diocese), 1962–1968; sick leave, 1969–1971; El Paso diocese, 1971–1977; San Angelo diocese, 1977–1984; unassigned, 1984–1987; Denver archdiocese, 1987–1988; unassigned, 1988–1993

Bernard Lane (Boston archdiocese), Alpha Omega House for troubled youths, 1971–1978; various parishes, 1985–1993; removed from active ministry, 1993; Office of Senior Priests, Regina Cleri, Boston archdiocese, 1996–1998; retired, 1999

John Lenihan (Los Angeles archdiocese), various parishes, 1969–2001; left priesthood, 2002

Theodore Llanos (Los Angeles archdiocese), various parishes, 1974–1994; unassigned, 1994–1997

Bob Nugent (Salvation order), cofounder of New Ways Ministry

Ronald Paquin (Boston archdiocese), various parishes, 1973–1990; unassigned or on sick leave, 1990–1998; hospital chaplain, 1998–2000

James Porter (Fall River diocese), 1960–1967; sick leave, 1967–1969; Crookston diocese, 1969–1970; unassigned, 1970–1974; left priesthood, 1974

Tom Powers (Boston archdiocese), various parish assignments, 1966–1993; St. John the Evangelist, 1993–present

Don Rooney (Cleveland diocese), various parishes, 1979–2002

Paul Shanley (Boston archdiocese), St. Patrick's, Stoneham, 1960–1967; St. Francis of Assisi, Braintree, 1967–1969; chaplain, Boston State College, 1969; minister for alienated youth, 1970–1979; St. John the Evangelist, Newton, 1979–1990; sick leave, 1990–1996; retired, 1996; assistant to the director, Leo House, a Catholic-affiliated hostel in New York City, 1995–1997

Dominic George Spagnolia (Boston archdiocese), St. Francis de Sales, Roxbury, 1964–1973; leave of absence, 1973–1993; St.

Edward the Confessor, Medfield, 1993; St. Mary's, Franklin, 1994–1997; St. Patrick's, Lowell, 1998–2002

John Whiteley (Jefferson City diocese), various parishes, 1967–1991; resigned from active ministry, 1992

Victim-Survivors, Litigants, and Advocates

Arthur Austin, Braintree, Massachusetts, poet who went to Paul Shanley for counseling as a college student

Barbara Blaine, Chicago attorney, founded the Survivors Network of Those Abused by Priests (SNAP)

Mary Scanlan Calcaterra, cofounder, Voice of the Faithful

David Clohessy, national executive director, SNAP

Maryetta Dussourd, Jamaica Plain, Massachusetts, mother of three and great-aunt of four abuse survivors, all members of the Geoghan 86

Jim and Mike Falls, southern California, brothers and litigants

Jackie Gauvreau, parishioner, St. John the Evangelist, Newton, Massachusetts, where Paul Shanley was pastor

Mary Grant, Long Beach, SNAP coordinator for southern California, litigant

Steve Krueger, executive director, Voice of the Faithful

Patrick McSorley, Dorchester, Massachusetts, member of the Geoghan 86

Joanne Mueller, Melrose, Massachusetts, mother of four victim-survivors, all members of the Geoghan 86

Jim Muller, cofounder and chairman, Voice of the Faithful

Leonard Muzzi Jr., Hingham, Massachusetts, member of the Geoghan 86

Jim Post, cofounder and president, Voice of the Faithful

Phil Saviano, Jamaica Plain, Massachusetts, founder and coordinator of SNAP's New England chapter

SURVIVORS OF JOSEPH BIRMINGHAM

Gary Bergeron, Lowell, carpenter
Tom Blanchette, Martha's Vineyard, independent contractor
Paul Ciaramitaro, Gloucester, owner/operator of mobile kitchen
Olan Horne, Salem, butcher
Dave Lyko, Dracut, letter carrier
Bernie McDaid, Lynn, independent painting contractor
Larry Sweeney, North Chelmsford, pharmacist

JOURNALISTS

Marty Baron, *Boston Globe* editor, 2001–present
Matt Storin, *Globe* editor, 1993–2001
Globe Spotlight Team: **Kevin Cullen, Matt Carroll, Thomas Farragher, Stephen Kurkjian, Michael Paulson, Sacha Pfeiffer, Michael Rezendes, Walter Robinson** (editor)
Kristen Lombardi, staff writer, *Boston Phoenix*

ATTORNEYS

Jeff Anderson, St. Paul, Minnesota, representing victim-survivors throughout the country since the early 1980s through Jeff Anderson & Associates
Mitchell Garabedian, Boston, sole practitioner
Roderick "Eric" MacLeish Jr., Jeffrey Newman, Courtney Pillsbury, Robert Sherman, David Thomas, for the Boston law firm Greenberg Traurig LLP
Wilson Rogers Jr., Wilson Rogers III, Mark Rogers, representing the archdiocese of Boston through the Rogers Law Firm
Constance Sweeney, Massachusetts Superior Court judge handling Boston suits

PART I

✦

"Thou Shalt Not"

Chapter 1

Before Orders

Late Summer 1953

WATERTOWN, MASSACHUSETTS — It was near midnight, uncommonly dark. Rain sheeted. A squally wind rattled the rectory's windows in their frames. Father Michael Logan rose from his reading to fasten the sashes, still in the cassock he'd fixed around himself that morning. Behind the rain-streaked glass, he was unsmiling, and utterly alone. Long seclusions, endless nights—these were the consequences of giving yourself totally and with undivided heart to God.

From the window he glimpsed a distressed figure down below as it dashed across the slick courtyard and into the church. The urgency of the man's haste, the terror that seemingly chased him through the night, made Logan anxious. He knew he must go down. Fingering the buttons on his cassock, he headed toward the church, making use of an interior stairway and private passage. He pushed into the darkened nave, through the thick, sweet perfume of ancient devotionals—beeswax, incense, and chrism.

Banks of vigil lights near the altar still flickered. Logan snagged one and lifted it high over his head to illuminate the pews. He called out, but no answer came. He moved slowly up the ambulatory into the velvet blackness, beckoning left, then right, until his torch seized upon the frightened eyes of a man he knew, Otto Keller, the church sexton, bent furiously in prayer.

"What are you doing here?"

Keller was disconsolate. He did not answer.

"Is something wrong?"

When Keller finally spoke, he was almost incoherent.

"No one can help me," he said. "You would hate me now."

Keller gripped Logan's sleeve and pulled himself up from his knees. The candlelight distorted his features.

"I must confess to you," he said. "I must tell someone! I want to make a confession!"

The strange demand of his declaration, its violent formality, unsettled the priest. Ordinarily, he might have advised such a man to confess during normal hours, on Saturday afternoon. The sacraments were governed by divine tradition, not whim; by priests, not parishioners. But this clearly was no time to withhold the possibility of absolution.

He led Keller through the darkness to an elaborately carved confessional box, and both entered, each through a separate door, into separate enclosures. Sitting, Logan removed a stole from a peg on the wall, kissed it hastily, and smoothed it around his neck. He hesitated briefly, said a small prayer, then drew back the curtain covering the grille that separated him from his supplicant, who whispered, "I confess to almighty God and to you, Father, that I have sinned."

Logan fixed his gaze upon a Bible. "When was your last confession?"

"I can't remember."

"Can you remember approximately?" he asked patiently.

Keller's voice shattered with grief. "I . . . I've killed Mr. Villette!"

Logan was thunderstruck. His head swung around, as though knocked wild by a fist, and nearly struck the mahogany wall. He was speechless. *Villette?* By awful coincidence, the priest had an appointment with Villette, a prominent insurance agent in town, the next morning. It was unimaginable that he would be dead, much less murdered. And the sexton? He had been working in the rectory for some time now, never giving the slightest indication of a villainous streak. What possible motive could he have?

Keller began to explain, his words leaking like poisonous gas through the grille. The confession of a murder. What could Logan do?

He knew what he could *not* do. He could not turn Keller over to the authorities, could not break the inviolable seal of the confessional, no matter how dark the threat of perdition. In fact he could not do anything at all on the basis of information he received in the confessional. This was a matter of great philosophical complexity, one of the prime credos dwelt upon in seminary. His only concern would be the penitent's soul.

Logan could not know what would happen tomorrow, that the police would come to suspect *him* for the crime, that a panel of jurors would ultimately conclude that depraved indifference drove the priest, not the sexton, to murder. Worse, they would base their conclusion upon the lying testimony of Otto Keller himself, a deception that Logan, ever bound by the confessional seal, could not contradict.

This was the risk priests took.

A stoic resolve hardened on Logan's young face as he leaned his ear toward the divider. "Go on," he whispered. There never was a more heroic gesture.

At least that was what Dominic George Spagnolia, seventeen years old and not an especially good Catholic, thought as he watched this scene unfold on the large movie screen. He had stolen into the theater to see Montgomery Clift star as the priest Logan in Alfred Hitchcock's *I Confess*. He was expecting a thriller, which the Keller killing certainly promised, but not the moral conundrum Father Logan was about to encounter. He never had imagined anything like the awful bind that tore at the priest's conviction, or the flooding bravery of a man who placed faith above self-interest, and doctrine over instinct. Most silver-screen heroes were swashbucklers and gun toters; Logan was a hero of a different sort. Spagnolia—"Spags" to his friends—felt as though he'd been jolted from a dream by a brilliant explosion. Later he would call this the work of providence. Right then and there, he knew he would become a priest. He would be a hero.

Spags watched Logan show up for his appointment with the insurance broker the next day as though he knew nothing. Nothing, that is, beyond the sanctity of the confessional, which he would guard at great peril. The secret. It was safe with him.

Fall 1953

ST. BENEDICT, LOUISIANA — Bernard Francis Law knew one thing about Louisiana, though he was twenty-two. It was much too small to contain him. Law was worldly at a young age. His father, first an air force flier, then a commercial pilot, led his family on a peripatetic life. Law knew six different homes before he was eighteen. He had been born in Mexico, raised in the Virgin Islands, schooled at Harvard—he was luminously intelligent, a polyglot, a natural leader, tall and handsome. When this young man drove fifty miles through the lonesome Florida Parishes north from New Orleans to arrive finally at the remote doorstep of St. Joseph Seminary College, he would have been tempted to exclaim in dismay as the locals do, "Shut my mouth wide open."

An only child, he was especially self-sufficient and kept his own counsel, but he wasn't a loner; just the opposite. He was personable, caring, inquisitive—a humble and obvious leader. At Charlotte Amalie High School, on the island of St. Thomas, the mostly black student body voted him senior class president, telegraphing respect and warm regard for their white classmate.

Law was raised a Catholic, though not of the rosary-thumbing variety. His mother had converted from the Presbyterian Church as a condition of marriage, and Catholicism was difficult to internalize in adulthood. The priesthood was nearly the last thing on Law's radar screen. In his generation, most future priests entered minor seminaries at age twelve or thirteen. But at twenty-one, in his senior year at Harvard, majoring in medieval European intellectual history, he came under the influence of Monsignor Lawrence J. Riley, a Benedictine monk whose Catholic faith was frenetic, almost evangelical. He proselytized in the manner of the Protestants among whom Law had grown up; he practiced "spread-the-word" Catholicism. Moved by his fervor, and drawn to his theological conservatism, Law prayed for a vocation, and it came the way it was supposed to, as a certainty. He selected St. Joseph in part because of its Benedictine roots.

It was smaller than he could have imagined, and much more cloistered. St. Joseph's lawns were dotted with silent floating apparitions, black-hooded monks, eyes blind in prayer. Harvard, this wasn't. But Law would make the best of it. He would spend two years here immersed in philosophy and prayer.

Spring 1954
CLEVELAND, OHIO — Neil Conway knew, beyond all of his confusing efforts to deny it, that he had just fallen hopelessly in love—quite inconveniently, to say the least, given that he was now fully committed to entering St. Mary's Seminary on Cleveland's East Side. No amount of prayer could still his hammering heart. He damned the affliction. He never saw it coming.

It had been prom night at St. Ignatius High School, and he had escorted another senior as a matter of grace and politeness. She was a nice girl, and as beautiful as he himself was handsome—and she was from a good family, as was he. The Conways were local legends, enormously wealthy, uniformly good-looking, well mannered, and exalted in the eyes of Cleveland's Catholic society. Neil's father, Timothy Conway, a grocery store executive and energetic fund-raiser for the bishop, was a Knight of St. Gregory, the highest papal honor extended to a layman. (He was allowed to call himself "Sir Knight of Gregory the Great Timothy Conway," though he never would; that was not the sort of man he was.) He belonged to seven private clubs, and for the summers sent his thirteen children to the family's 122-acre farm near Akron, on the hilly Western Reserve of the Connecticut Land Grant, while he remained in the nine-bedroom hilltop mansion in Shaker Heights, stoically alone save for a live-in staff of three.

Despite the servants and financial comforts, the demands were nonetheless a life-sucking drain on Neil's mother, Margaret Mary, who died of a "tired heart," as it was called in those days, when she had not yet crossed the threshold of old age and Neil, her second youngest, was only just twelve. That left to Neil's father the task of raising his baker's dozen, which he accomplished in the boot-camp style of Captain von Trapp before the arrival of Maria. An inscrutable and ghostly figure, he took to an unhappy routine, arriving from work at precisely 7:30 P.M., demanding a kiss from each of his offspring, and nothing more. Any child who interrupted this routine met with stinging belts and hands and shoes.

"I wasn't raised in a family," Neil liked to say; "I was raised in a large Catholic institution."

An emotionally complicated home life was a major motivator for many seminarians—a 1965 study found that a preponderance of them were from homes where parents exhibited definite psychiatric symptoms, 60 percent being alcoholics. By declaring a vocation to the priesthood, Conway brought great pleasure to his father. It was part of a campaign to win over his affections. Conway was also an equestrian star, renowned in local competitions, and played football well, even though he disliked it intensely, because this too pleased the old man.

But that was not the only reason he made up his mind to serve his church. Neil had a special relationship to God. He was prayerful and holy, and beginning at the age of fourteen, attended Mass every single day, despite the teasing of his siblings. He loved the church—the acoustics of the cathedral, the precise rituals, the way his thoughts would become a reverie above the gorgeous, undulant Latin liturgy.

He had not been at all interested in girls or sex, which made it easier. On the day he settled on his vocation, he swore off masturbation. If this was to be the consequence of his commitment, it would be a painless trade-off. He continued to accompany girls to various social events, like the prom, but they failed to knock him off his moorings.

But now, as in a dream, the prom music swelled and blurred into indistinguishable notes, and through the parting crowd the most dazzling pair of eyes, the fullest red lips, and purest white cheeks came floating toward Neil on the din of his throbbing heart. Those lips didn't stop until they pursed and planted against his—his mouth, his cheek? Even seconds later, he could not recall. All he knew was the soft deep heat of them, the way they scorched his heart. He was in love.

With a member of the football team.

Dislocated sensations sparked and exploded in his mind. Conway had never felt so emotionally vulnerable before, and nobody would have been more surprised than he that it was a boy, not a girl, who moved him. After planting the kiss, the young man stood back and giggled; the girls who were standing nearby giggled, too. Was this a cruel joke, a way to ridicule or shame him? He did not know. He should have felt shame. But instead Conway split wide open in a dreamlike grin. Afterward, for years to come, that was what he fixated upon. Even if he had enjoyed the peck, what kind of idiot would let the world know such a thing?

March 1954

VATICAN CITY — Pope Pius XII, a bookish and aloof pontiff, and not especially well liked, was profoundly interested in theological scholarship. He issued more papal encyclicals than most of his predecessors, on subjects ranging from the Blessed Virgin Mary's veneration to the exact hour at which Mass should be celebrated. His church was an interior one, a papacy of the mind and soul. Matters of world affairs were nearly inconsequential compared to his belief in God and heaven.

He had had the misfortune, however, of trading his cardinal's hat for the pontifical tiara at the opening bell of Hitler's march across Europe. The world clamored for him to become engaged in the war, but he buckled when he might have led. Even when evidence surfaced about Hitler's persecution of the Jews, Pius remained deplorably silent. He never publicly addressed Germany's anti-Semitism. On the grounds of neutrality, he had refused prominent rabbis who pleaded for his intervention to help stop the deportations, and rejected American entreaties to exercise his moral leadership.

In his defense, Pius had felt he was advancing a spiritual course to peace. For instance, late in August 1942, Andrej Septyckyj, a Ukrainian churchman, wrote begging the pope to denounce the killing of more than two hundred thousand Ukrainian Jews. The pope wrote him back, failing again to address the atrocities. Instead, he quoted Psalms and advised Septyckyj and his compatriots to "bear adversity with serene patience."

This approach did nothing to slow the genocide. Historians attributed tens of thousands of deaths to "the silent pope." Half a century later, his successors would offer an unqualified apology for the church's indifference.

In the years after the war, Pius did find his voice to fight evil. But the subject was not genocide or world war. It was instead a threat to priests and the priesthood itself, coming from the most cunning place: "the wiles of evil and the enticements of passion." Now, in March 1954, in the middle of the postwar baby boom gripping the West, he wrote and issued his most famous and lasting encyclical, *Sacra Virginitas*. Addressing himself to "Our Venerable Brothers, the Patriarchs, Primates, Archbishops, Bishops, and other Local Ordinaries in Peace and Communion with the Apostolic See," the pope acknowledged that threats to chastity would be one of the most devilish problems facing the clergy. He cast lust as a power emanating from outside, an animal impulse that pitted the corporeal body against the soul, the province of the Lord. He called upon those that would serve the Lord to carry on an operatic battle of soul over body.

For this, he offered a number of helpful suggestions. Pray to the Virgin Mary. Receive the Eucharist often—because celibacy may be a gift to God, but God's gift back is the power to sustain it. Sounding a practical note, Pius promoted a technique he called "flight and alert vigilance," and he spelled out the many ways to elude temptation. Stay out of movie theaters, he commanded. Pay attention to what is barred by ecclesiastical censorship, and heed it. Avoid novels, especially those on the Vatican's *Index of Forbidden Books*. Run from modern amusements of all types and publications that might be obscene, tempting, titillating, or otherwise wrong. For the young seminarian, he wrote, lock-and-key cloistering was advisable for maintaining innocence and thwarting carnal drives. Why taunt peril? "What gardener would expose young plants, choice indeed but weak, to violent storms?"

Years later, when scandal buckled the American church, theologians would look back and see the problem inherent in this approach. By casting celibacy as a fragile rarity in a world of temptation, it placed sexual *action* out of the hands of the actor, condemning him (or empowering him) to fail from time to time. Perfect celibacy was God's victory; it did not belong to the priest. On the other hand, sexual decadence was the work of a cunning Satan, not the failing of a flesh-prone human. The priest merely wafted on the smoke of their primordial battle.

And the dimpled youths who sat on laps, and teenagers stretched out in beds? *They* were the dark temptations who called the sinners away from grace—brilliant Lucifers, *sed ipsi per se facti sunt mali:* by their own deeds made evil.

October 1954
LOS ANGELES, CALIFORNIA — Dale Jennings helped lick closed over a thousand plain-paper envelopes containing *One* magazine, the first publication in the country that treated "homophiles" (that was the preferred term) as an essentially unique cultural minority, not merely a collection of deviants and anomalies. Outside of stern legislation and bathroom graffiti, homosexuality was almost never written about. The entire gay canon consisted of just fifty-nine nonfiction books and 213 novels and plays, most of them far from sympathetic. Jennings and a small group of classically educated men in Los Angeles stood alone in opposition. This was all there was of the organized homosexual underground. They had launched the magazine—with an academic, almost scientific, tenor—to chart medical, political, and cultural news affecting them.

The rest of the country was hardly receptive to their message. At the urging of Senator Joseph McCarthy, who inveighed against "those Communists and queers" he believed were infiltrating government, the State Department launched an internal investigation in 1950. Its final report, "Employment of Homosexuals and Other Sex Perverts in Government," concluded that the potential for blackmail made homosexuals unsuited for government work. Dwight Eisenhower responded with Executive Order 10450, making "sexual perversion" grounds for dismissal from government positions. Purges, which had been steady in civil service jobs, increased tenfold. Companies with government contracts followed. The Red Cross announced a nonhomosexual policy as did many private sector businesses. At the height of the Cold War, more people lost their jobs on suspicion of being "sexual perverts" than did alleged communists.

Many landed in prison. The physical act of sex between two men was illegal in every state, punishable by imprisonment and fines (sex between women was largely unnoticed by lawmakers). In New York and elsewhere, it was against the law even to sell a drink to a homosexual, and if two men were present together on a dance floor without a woman nearby, they were subject to arrest. In Iowa, suspicion of homosexuality was enough to get a person committed under state "sexual psychopathy" laws. Across the country, only a few hundred men and women voluntarily made their homosexuality known. Gay rights, not only unheard of, had never entered the public's imagination.

By the fall of 1954, the *One* publishing company had about five thousand names on a mailing list. It was to these people that the October issue was being shipped. The issue contained no discussion of sex, and there were no graphics or photographs of a suggestive nature. The lead story, titled "The Law of Mailable Material," explained the many ways *One* editors capitulated to postal inspectors, including a ban on lonely hearts ads and fiction in which characters held hands or brushed knees. Such content would surely trigger postal censorship. "There is one extreme school of legal thought which would say that *One*, merely by its existence, is illegal. That line of reasoning goes as follows: Homosexual acts are made crimes in every State of the Union. *One* is published specifically for homosexuals. Therefore, *One* is a magazine for criminals, their edification and guidance. It is therefore illegal. This is, however, too extreme a view for 1954. There is no indication from any quarter that such a view will ever be taken. . . ."

The author couldn't have been more mistaken. The October issue never made it any farther than the Los Angeles postmaster, who impounded it and declared its contents "obscene, lewd, lascivious, and filthy."

February 2, 1960
SUDBURY, MASSACHUSETTS — One by one Cardinal Richard Cushing ordained the 1960 graduates from St. John's Seminary in Brighton, seventy-five promising, fresh-faced men dispatched to the far reaches of the archdiocese, one of the largest crops of new priests in Boston in years. It was an especially platoonish group, most having studied and worshiped side by side for over a decade under austere circumstances.

Almost every aspect of life at St. John's was regulated. No radios or newspapers were allowed. Seminarians were not permitted off campus except in the most extraordinary circumstances, and then only with specific approval, plus an escort and a strictly enforced time of return.

When not in class they were virtually locked inside their dorm rooms. Being caught in another seminarian's quarters was grounds for dismissal. Even talking was circumscribed. St. John's adhered to the practice known as "grand silence," common in seminaries. No one was to speak a word between night prayers and morning Mass, nearly half the day. If the seminarians wished to socialize with one another, or compare notes on an issue of theology, they were allowed to do this only during the few minutes following each meal that were set aside for constitutionals. Even then, seminary rules established what topics could, and couldn't, be taken up. The lives of the apostles were approved subjects. So were the commandments, but not all of them. The fourth and the sixth commandments—the "sex commandments," regarding adultery and child rearing—were explicitly off limits.

Of special concern to authorities were "particular friendships," as any overt bondings between two young men were called. It was policy in seminaries to prepare the young men to have no attachment to anything but their church, into which they would channel a volitional love. This relationship was to be an exclusive one. They were dissuaded from relying on human beings for the succor they might find through prayer. Some students circumvented the rules by gathering in the jakes—the communal toilets—for a smoke and a bit of social chew, but if they were found out, grave notations were placed in their records. Too many of these "strings" would prevent them from advancing to the next year of study.

The class of 1960 never complained. Rather, they approached their ordination day with sterling piety and devotion. John Cotter, Bernard Lane, James Foley, Eugene O'Sullivan—all were eager, vibrant, and above all obedient men. But Paul Shanley and John McCormack stood out among the others. They showed remarkable leadership qualities throughout many years of study, and both enjoyed the innate attributes of charisma, good looks, and boundless energy.

But when it came to fidelity, no one matched Joseph Birmingham. Conservative and even-tempered, bright-faced and as tall as a movie star, Birmingham typified the ideal qualities of a parish priest. Cardinal Cushing had the perfect assignment for him. Our Lady of Fatima in Sudbury, a farm community west of Boston, had one elderly pastor running its many programs. He needed somebody who could shoulder many responsibilities immediately—the Catholic Youth Organization, altar boy programs, CCD (the Confraternity of Christian Doctrine, as catechism classes were called), Boy Scouts. In mid-February, Cushing made the assignment, naming Birmingham the curate, or assistant pastor, at Our Lady's.

It was only a few weeks later when Birmingham arrived at the Blanchette home as a dinner guest. Young Tom Blanchette didn't make it to the dinner table, owing to the flu. Before leaving for the night, Birmingham went upstairs to bless the youth. He sat on the edge of the bed.

"Where's it hurt?" Birmingham asked pastorally.

"My stomach," said Tom.

Birmingham began rubbing the sore area, but without further delay he slid his hand into Tom's pajamas. Tom froze. As time clicked by, much as he tried, he could not find the courage to say no to a priest, despite his burning shame. That night he was thirteen. He would turn fifteen before Birmingham stopped touching him like that.

One Friday Afternoon, 1961
Louisville, Kentucky — Father Louis E. Miller nodded at his students as they filed out of the sixth-grade classroom one by one. But he snagged Timothy Baker, an altar boy, and would not let him leave. "Stand over here; that's right," he said. Doing what he was told, Baker moved to the back of the classroom at the Holy Spirit Catholic School, where Father Miller, the curate of the adjoining church, was a regular visitor. He did not know why he had been picked to stay after class. But every Friday one boy or another would be instructed to stay behind—a special catechism lesson. Usually they wouldn't emerge for thirty minutes or more.

Catholic school enrollment had reached an all-time high in Louisville. Throughout the country, a Catholic school boom was under way. There were now thirteen thousand primary and secondary facilities under the church's aegis, with a combined student head count topping 5.25 million—a record—comprising nearly 15 percent of all school-aged American kids. Recruitment was not always without subtle coercion. One eighth-grader in public school in Breese, Illinois, recalled going into Mass one sweltering Sunday, and coming out the side door enrolled in Mater Dei, a Catholic school that had suffered underenrollment. When he objected, his mother explained she had no choice. After Mass the priest had taken her aside and told her—falsely, it turned out—that there was a canon law requiring children to attend Catholic schools if they were available. "If you don't, you don't get the sacraments," she said. "We didn't know anything about this until Father told us at Mass."

Most Catholic parents, though, would never consider secular education. For one thing, Catholic schools were extremely rigorous, rivaling other preparatory school training, usually at a fraction of the price. Parishes underwrote much of the overhead through collections, and nuns—who comprised 76 percent of the schools' workforce—toiled in poverty according to their vows, requiring only token stipends for their living expenses. More pressing was the growing concern in Catholic America that the secular world was becoming entirely too permissive in the second half of the century. The sexual revolution loomed. Organizations from the American Medical Association to the Department of Health, Education, and Welfare had endorsed talking to children about specific sexual functions and even birth control. Catholics saw parochial schools as a bulwark against this sort of moral decay. Discussions of sex, if they happened at all, would remain in the language of Bible passages; the act was to be avoided till marriage, and practiced then within tight limits unmatched in most other cultures, ethical systems, or religions.

Catholic schools were not especially happy places. Loneliness and alcoholism ran endemic among the nuns and priests who ran them, as studies would show. Laughing and running and prank playing could be met with stiff reprovals in a Catholic classroom, ranging from swipes with rulers to threats of eternal damnation—not just for the accused but for his entire extended family.

As Timothy Baker knew, disrespecting a direct order was too much of a risk. Father Miller closed the classroom door and pulled the drapes over the windows, darkening the room. He turned toward the boy— Miller's was a kind, young face, and it balanced a delicate pair of wireless spectacles. Timothy would have no reason to grow concerned, even once the priest locked the door.

"Get undressed, son," he said. "It's time for sex education."

October 11, 1962

VATICAN CITY — Starting before dawn, tens of thousands, or perhaps hundreds of thousands, of the faithful jostled in the corralled perimeters of St. Peter's Square, stretching their necks in the morning air for a glimpse of the march of bishops, the largest in the history of the church, that would mark the opening of the historic Second Vatican Council. Their presence was a testament to the vision of Pope John XXIII, who aimed to modernize and rejuvenate the ancient church. Anticipation jolted through the crowds. Under a cold sun, at precisely 8 A.M., the magnificent bronze doors of the papal palace clanged and swept open onto the square to reveal a seemingly infinite stretch of miters, balanced atop two thousand heads, eight abreast, all the way up the stairs of Bernini's baroque Scala Regia. Silently the bishops streamed through the square and into the magnificent St. Peter's Basilica, followed by the Sacred College of Cardinals, resplendent in their crimson finery. Finally, the pope arrived, enthroned uneasily on the gilded *sedia gestatoria*—balanced on the shoulders of twenty-four footmen clad in red uniforms—looking rather timid on his throne and, as one observer noted, "gradually warming to the mild acclamation of the overawed crowd, and gently smiling and quietly weeping as he was carried undulantly forward, blessing the onlookers."

Little had been expected from John's papacy. He was elected in 1958 at age seventy-seven with the express hope he would be a throne warmer, a man of little initiative who might help heal the church following Pius XII's many controversies by producing none of his own. No great intellect, an uninspired theologian, John seemed just the man for the job. Throughout his prepapal career, he had been an unexceptional prelate, serving passably on the political margins of the church, first in the remote outpost of Bulgaria, then as an envoy to France at the end of World War II, at that moment a thanklessly messy assignment.

John seemed to surprise even himself when, less than three months into his papacy, he declared his plan to consider the church's future in a time of modernity. The idea seized him suddenly—an inspiration, he felt sure, of the Holy Spirit. He saw how science and technology had recast human existence in one brief century. He worried about declarations among leading theologians that pitted religion against the modern world, as though they were in disharmony. Summing up that belief, the philosopher Mortimer Adler had said, "The greatest enemy of Christianity is man's self-confidence. The more power he has, the less religious he becomes." As a result, church teaching had been highly suspicious of any trend that impinged on its claim to total authority, from psychiatry to genetics to space science, now in its thrilling infancy. At a time when Catholics were becoming more educated, this was an increasingly alienating stalemate.

He called his Vatican Council an "aggiornamento," an updating. But the word, by suggesting incremental change, did an injustice to what he had in mind, which was a complete overhaul of the concept of Catholicism, integrating its ancient doctrine into a postindustrial world. Bishops greeted John's idea with unmitigated enthusiasm, especially in the West. Science and religion, John believed, were not adversarial disciplines, but perhaps had ways of informing and challenging each other. This was a revolutionary view, one most theologians compared in seismic power to Luther's theses on reform. The council—the first in the church in nearly a hundred years—would meet for four months a year, for four years, to discuss twenty propositions, or schemata, in total.

It was hard to anticipate the interest that greeted this initiative. The faithful monitored the happenings as though this were the Catholic World Series. Daily news bulletins were read in parochial schools, and synopses handed out regularly at Mass. American Catholics had been feeling increasingly penned in by their church's theological strictness.

Divorce was a reality now throughout America, even Catholic America, and yet the priests, cleaving to their medieval precepts, routinely ostracized the divorced and sometimes even their children, refusing them baptism and confirmation even if the broken marriage had been marked by violence. It seemed spiteful, especially to the children. What guilt did they bear? It was not *their* sacramental marriage that had dissolved.

Many liberal Catholics were wondering if they hadn't outgrown their beloved church. With relief and joy, they realized that wasn't true, that the church was growing along with them. Even the old guard, which embraced orthodoxy and tradition—and generally regarded change with suspicion—was enthralled. It was a time of great hope.

Sensing how momentous this event would be, reporters from around the world converged to chronicle every turn like they were covering a political convention. Their presence would also help Catholics to see their church as less autocratic and strictly hierarchical; it would become apparent that their teaching authority, their "magisterium," was hammered out and conceded in lively debates, not handed down on a lightning bolt from God.

No one was more thrilled by the radical potential of the council than Father Anthony Massimini, a scholarly young cleric from South Philadelphia. To his surprise, he was called upon to play a role—to serve as Latin translator throughout the gathering for a delegation of American church leaders headed by Archbishop Paul John Hallinan of Atlanta. Because the proceedings would take place entirely in the church's ancient tongue, a small army of such interpreters were needed, including Massimini's good friend Father Bill Leahy, a student of scripture at the pontifical Biblical Institute.

When he arrived breathlessly at the stone escarpment leading to the basilica, looking out at the sea of the faithful, Massimini was overcome with the knowledge that he was witnessing a tremendous historical moment. Seeing his opportunity, Massimini stole into the line of bishops and drifted alongside them into the basilica's main door, flanked by a regiment of Swiss Guards. Nothing prepared him for the awe that overcame him when he entered St. Peter's, made over with bleachers to accommodate the prelates.

But he did not find a church at peace with the future. The dynamics of the opening days of Vatican II were politically intense and threatened to ignite open battles within the church. The pope and his bishops seemed to be on a collision course with the insular and powerful Roman Curia, a revered cabinet of mostly Italian prelates. Through the "congregations," or curial offices, they defined and micromanaged nearly everything in the Catholic universe. They set rules for the seminaries that trained new priests, for the bishops who governed the priests, and for the faithful to whom the priests attended. Curial offices determined what gospel interpretations were sanctioned, and ruled on all ecclesiastical and liturgical matters. On sex and love, they had plenty to say. Their word was not open to appeal. As the journalist and historian Robert Blair Kaiser wrote in *Time* magazine, *"Roma locuta est; causa finita est"* had been the Curia's traditional pronouncement in deciding Catholic affairs around the world: "Rome has spoken; the matter is settled."

No single group was more stunned by the pope's plans for the council than his curial servants. Few people alive cared less for the march of modernity. When they learned of his plans, they told Pope John XXIII it would not be possible to organize such a massive synod by 1963, as he had demanded.

"All right," the pope replied, "we'll have it in 1962."

When the pope rose with his opening address inside St. Peter's, it was not yet clear if he had won the day.

In these modern times, he began, some men of the church saw only prevarication and ruin—but not him. Human existence had changed profoundly. Human thinking must change with it. He banished the prophets of gloom. It was right to teach a new understanding, he declared. He called upon his council fathers to exercise "holy liberty" in their deliberations—in other words, there would be no restrictions. The church was not an embalmed relic of a glorious past, he said. It was a dynamic organism, nurtured by the Spirit of truth and light. The council must throw open the windows of the church and cleanse it with fresh air, to prepare it for a world with unimagined responsibilities and complexities, a modern world of educated men and women with ambitious and grand expectations.

As a show of his own faith, Pope John XXIII then retired to his third-floor palace to monitor the proceedings via closed-circuit TV cameras, thus allowing the assembled bishops to interact directly with the Vatican insiders. From the very first utterance it was clear the Curia had no hope of prevailing. Cardinal Achille Liénart, of Lille, in France, being the seniormost prelate on the globe, was the first to speak. He rejected the curial plan to divide into committees headed by congregation prefects. "This is a council of bishops," he declared in Latin, "not a council of the Roman Curia!"

Massimini and Leahy whispered the English translation of his remarks into the ears of their respective clusters of American bishops, who seemed as stunned as their young interpreters at the high-stakes gambit. By acclaim, the bishops gained the initiative, agreeing with Liénart that they would man their own committees and determine their own agendas. The Curia had been trounced, and every major council document adopted over the next four years would reflect a brand-new attitude toward the church—a democratized, lay-empowering, free-world church.

But before long, Leahy began to hear the talk among curial functionaries. He heard them concede loss at the council. But they didn't care. When all the bishops go home, they swore, they would take back the church and do as they always had. Who could stop them? The gearshift of power remained in their grip.

Summer 1962

TAMPA, FLORIDA — "You're an extraordinarily intelligent young man. Such an agile mind for a kid of your background. So bright."

Father Norman Rogge was always flattering Bob Swart, who was an awkward fourteen-year-old nervous about entering tenth grade. Perhaps Bob needed the ego stroking more than most. He was just becoming a man. It was the summer he was taking driver's education. His body was changing. He was puzzled about who he was in the world, what role he would play. His parents were terrifically ordinary—already he could see that. He felt different from them, more ambitious. And something else. Bob suffered from utter terror that he might be homosexual. The dread flashed in and out of his mind, as it did for most boys at his age. But his preoccupation got worse one day in the summer. When he accompanied his mother to a local department store, he ducked into the rest room and was mortified to be propositioned by a man standing at the adjoining urinal. Heart pounding, palms damp, he fled the room.

What he felt, he knew, was *curiosity*. Did that seal his fate?

He made his confession and asked Rogge's advice.

The father bemoaned the presence of homosexuals in public rest rooms. He comforted the boy. He demanded that something be done.

"You must let me call the police," he said.

Bob knew homosexuals were sinners. He agreed to let the priest break the confessional seal to tell the authorities what he had seen. But the police who arrived at the priest's office to take Bob's statement made a strange proposal, which, it seemed to Bob, the priest had anticipated. They proposed installing a camera in the store's toilet to capture the offenders. But they needed Bob Swart to help flush out the prey. So that he would understand it clearly, they made themselves very plain. Bob was to show the men his penis—erect, if need be—and not desist until the men took hold of him.

"You'd be doing such good," Rogge encouraged. "You are helping God and your country by getting rid of these people."

Throughout the summer and into the school year, that is exactly what Bob Swart did. With police officers standing outside the door, he made himself available for the compromising approaches of a dozen men. Afterward, the police always delivered the boy to Rogge's church, not his own home. And the priest made an invariable command.

"I need to check you for damage," the priest said. His examination would not be complete until Bob Swart climaxed.

It was nearly winter before Bob finally told his mother, who naturally confronted her church. She called Rogge to her home and laced into him. But he warned her in sonorous bursts against bringing scandal upon the church. Whether she believed in hellfire or not, she did not make a formal police report, and the matter was allowed to slide off into memory, never spoken of again.

For the boy, however, it would remain a significant emotional burden. He never thought of his encounters with Rogge as sex or abuse, only sin. Mortal sin. He did not enjoy it, despite his trigger responses—a teenager's mechanical capacity. He didn't hate it either, though. He just kept pondering something he couldn't ask: Why was Father bent on prosecuting men for doing what he himself so patently enjoyed? His mind always brought him around to the only plausible answer. If he was sinning with the priest, it was nobody's fault but his own. Priests were not capable of sin. Whatever evil lived inside of Bob was so vile it was consuming them both.

Spring 1963

BRIGHTON, MASSACHUSETTS — For six days and nights, hunched in prayer, Spags thought about sex. The next morning, he would be called upon to give God the most remarkable gift a man can proffer, foreswearing the radical glory of sex, the most mysterious of all the mysteries. He prayed for the *gift* of celibacy, that is, for the power to really mean it. Castration would be easier. That would involve a single decision that, once made, he could never be tempted to rescind. Celibacy had to be reinforced over and over. Every morning he awoke to evidence of the challenge. Sex demanded his attention. Could he possibly deny his appetites for the rest of his life? When the dean asks him if he is ready for this, what will he say?

When he vowed to become a priest, this was not the sort of heroism he had in mind. This was Spags's second-to-last year at St. John's Seminary. Technically it had not been necessary to pledge celibacy as a condition of entering, because there were no conditions under which he might have been allowed sex anyway. Chastity was the assumed fact of life for any unmarried Catholic. Even masturbation was strictly forbidden. Catholic theologians considered self-pleasure to be a mortal sin, pretty near the gravest on the depravity scale—like murderers and blasphemers, the unrepentant masturbator would be denied a place in heaven. This was not entirely out of step with contemporary American folklore, which believed that masturbation led to numerous health complications. Graham crackers and cold cereal were developed specifically as tonics to keep boys from spending time in carnal solitude and, as a result, keep them healthy.

By virtue of being single, a seminarian was expected to be chaste before ordination. Even after beginning his ordination cycle—after receiving clerical tonsure and the minor orders—there existed a possibility that he could change course, marry, and engage in licit intercourse. Now that possibility, for Spags and his class, was ending. Tomorrow, they were to be ordained subdeacons and obliged to lifelong celibacy, which they believed was a more perfect state than matrimony—they had been taught that sexual denial increased their bond with Christ and his church.

Despite many frustrations at St. John's, Spags never seriously doubted his commitment to the priesthood. Yes, the quality of teaching was awful, and this disappointed him. There was no library. The school couldn't get accredited as a university, so his diploma was useless in the secular world. Even critical areas like homily writing were given short shrift, forcing the students to find their own voices as sermon makers. This frustrated and embarrassed Spags. Boston was the third-largest diocese in America, serving 1.8 million Catholics. It was also a hub of higher education in the United States. The seminary, he felt, should do better.

What he found hardest to adjust to was the severe restrictions on his liberty. The grand silences, the constant scrutiny by teachers, the rule against leaving campus—it was, as William Minichiello, Spags's classmate, later complained, "totally unrealistic training for anyone that was expected to be a leader of people the next day after you were ordained." Meanwhile, the world outside St. John's was undergoing a tremendous transformation. Moral doctrines that had girdled America in the fifties were being challenged and redefined and in some cases jettisoned. Amazingly, Spags and his fellow seminarians were kept in the dark about these changes, forbidden by their instructors from listening to the radio and reading secular newspapers.

In its totality, St. John's was about as fertile a place for human growth and development as a minimum security prison. Obediently but unhappily, Spags kept to himself. The other seminarians seemed to adjust to the tight strictures with less difficulty, Spags thought. Paul Shanley, John McCormack, and Joseph Birmingham, who had graduated with the class of 1960, had been remote and distant personages to

Spags. Paul Mahan, closer in age, had always greeted Spags with a pleasant wave, if little warmth. But hollow salutations were the métier of John Geoghan, a senior this year whose high-pitched voice could pierce buildings. Geoghan was a munchkin whom others called, without affection, "Jolly Johnny." His violations of grand silence blew through the campus like a dust bowl gale.

Fellow seminarians knew Geoghan was unusual—"He's not a regular guy," they would say, which was the searing brand they gave to anyone who appeared overly effeminate or who, to use another euphemism, "never dated girls." Even the administrators had trouble liking Geoghan. The rector, Monsignor John Murray, had him temporarily expelled a number of years before.

"First of all," he wrote in his decision, "he has a very pronounced immaturity, not entirely evident in casual meeting, and is a little feminine in his manner of speech and approach. Scholastically, he is a problem. To be sure, he received passing grades in most subjects, but I still have serious doubts about his ability to do satisfactory work in future studies. In his favor are the following good qualities: a very fervent spiritual life, industry, determination to succeed, happy disposition, obedience, docility, interest in and regard for others, and respect for his contemporaries. Perhaps maturity will bring this young man the qualities he needs in order to be successful in his quest for the priesthood."

Geoghan's uncle, a powerful monsignor, also noticed psychological difficulties. However, he blamed the seminary.

"I have just learned that he has not been well for several months, sleepless, and without appetite. Evidently Seminary officials were unaware of it," the monsignor fired back to St. John's officials. "When John entered the Seminary I was not concerned over his well being there. I had complete confidence in the Seminary. Now, however, I am terribly concerned about him. He had always been a happy, well adjusted boy with total Catholic education, and a good home. After three years in Diocesan Seminaries, he is now sick, unhappy and appears to be wrestling with his soul. . . . Whether or not you permit, or John chooses, to continue in the Seminary means nothing to me. Now my concern is that he returns to good health and saves his soul."

After a year away, the boy was readmitted and managed over time to adapt more wholesomely to the rigors of prepriestly life, at least in the assessment of Spags, who felt alone in his cultural alienation. He wondered if his background in public education—after all, he had joined the seminary system only at age eighteen—put him at a disadvantage in adjusting to the monastic constraints. Every other seminarian he knew had left the world of freedoms when he was twelve or thirteen. Their expectations of autonomy, even their very characters, were bent and gnarled, he thought.

Spags would like to have had more opportunity to talk about his adjustment troubles. Each week, he met with his spiritual director, primarily for the purpose of confessing. There were no therapists or counselors on campus—if you asked to see one, you were "clipped" and sent back to the lay world. Psychology was anathema to Catholic teaching. In Catholicism, only the sacraments can steady the spirit. "There are no more disintegrated people in the world than the victims of psychoanalysis," Bishop Fulton J. Sheen said in 1947. On the other hand, confession, Sheen believed, "gives you the standard of Christ, the perfection of personality."

Especially on matters of sexual drive, the one enormous struggle they all faced, the seminarians were left to their own devices. The subject was cordoned off like a crime scene, to be milled around and gawked at but never approached. For Spags, this had the unintended consequence of making sex sexier, a succulent and mysterious thing too deliciously outré to mention. Matters relating to reproduction and marriage in moral theology textbooks, for instance, were rendered *in Latin*, as though in some sort of secret code to be pored over intensely. Spags had never once masturbated. This required a great struggle of the will and prayer, but temperance always triumphed. He wondered if this meant he was especially headstrong, or just a lot less hormonally charged than his peers. He would never know—the closest Spags ever came to discussing it came during his annual evaluations, at which point his spiritual director would frankly inquire, "Any issues with celibacy?"

Honestly, Spags answered, *"None."* He still believed in the hero priest.

He knew what he was doing was right. Just to see the young semi-narians move purposefully across the great dells and fir-covered hills of St. John's, kicking at the hems of their cassocks—men like himself preparing for a lifetime of sacrifice in service to others—stirred in Spags a tremendous sense of devoutness. Now, after his prayerful retreat, he did not feel at all apprehensive about the decision he would face in the morning. It was what one did to become a priest, and he wanted nothing more. His family was not as sanguine—he was the only Spagnolia son, and his father would have liked the line to carry on. But despite being lapsed Catholics who had not attended Mass in twenty-five years, his parents supported Spags's decision.

After supper, the dean who led the retreat called together his young men to impart the knowledge they would need in order to survive as celibates in an increasingly sexualized world. He was a corpulent man with a deviated septum who preached his message as though he were addressing throngs in St. Peter's Square, making what he had to say markedly more horrendous and shocking.

Their path would be a torture, he shouted. Their nights, long with battle. Temptations would tear and torment, a physical ache like nothing else, crashing and receding and crashing without end.

"Gentlemen!" he called, snapping his hands in the air. "There will be days. *There will be days!* When your *whole* body. Will *feel.*" He looked around ominously, half rising in his chair. "Like one e-*long*-ated penis! *Stretching!* To penetrate *the vagina!* Of some! Young! Woman!"

Spags could not believe what he was hearing, and to keep from laughing bit his lip so hard it bled.

May 18, 1963
CLEVELAND, OHIO — As Neil Conway prepared himself for ordination, his only regret, his deepest sadness, was that his late mother could not be with him, would not receive the traditional winding cloth women who replenish the priesthood carry to their coffins, a token for the judgment jury to know of their eternal contribution. The Cathedral of St. John the Evangelist was overflowing with Conways. This was an exalted

occasion for them all, as each by way of Neil's ordination would earn the highest reverence before God. Dressed conspicuously in black tails and white gloves or long evening gowns, they filled the front pews of the church.

In compliance with the laws of the church, Auxiliary Bishop Clarence E. Elwell beckoned the future priest toward the altar by calling his name as if in song.

"Nilus Patricius Conway!"

Conway lifted his head. The light of the candles glinted off his wide black eyes.

"Adsum," he said. "I am here. I come to serve."

Tremulously approaching the altar, he knelt and then prostrated himself face-first onto the white marble rostrum, prostrate before God in absolute submission. Over his still body the bishop and his priests and the swell of choristers rhythmically summoned the saints from the ages to guide and assist Conway throughout this tremendous commission.

"Holy Mary, Holy Mother of God, Holy Virgin of Virgins," they sang. "St. Michael, St. Gabriel, St. Raphael, all you holy angels and archangels, all you holy orders of blessed spirits." They called to Peter, Paul, and Andrew, to John, Thomas, James, the most pious souls who walked the earth in the last two thousand years.

"All you holy men and women, saints of God!"

"Make intercession for us!"

"Be merciful!"

"Spare us, O Lord!"

At the very crescendo of fervency, Bishop Elwell locked a hand beneath the young Conway's alb-draped arm, lifted him to his knees, and placed his large soft palms upon the man's head, just as hands had been laid on his own head, and on the head before his, and so on in succession back to Christ. A silence swelled in the room. Conway listened to the roar of his lungs sucking and blowing, and saw how his breath was in syncopation to the bishop's. No words were spoken, no hymns sung.

In silence, they prayed that a miracle might pass through those hands and transform Conway mysteriously and ontologically into Christ's vessel on earth—consecrate him *in persona Christi,* as St.

Thomas wrote. Not only Christlike, but an instrument of Christ, wired directly *to* Christ. Different in his very being from an ordinary man. Holy, blameless, and unstained. "A man chosen and set apart from the midst of people," in the elegant words of Pope John XXIII, "and blessed in a very special way with heavenly gifts—a sharer in divine power, and, to put it briefly, another Christ."

Ordination conferred no special rights upon a priest, only responsibilities. He was imbued with enormous ecclesiastic powers—to celebrate Mass, to remit sins, to administer the sacraments, and to direct the people of Christ in matters of faith and morals according to the canons of the church, the teachings of the Holy See, and the word of the bishop or archbishop.

In exchange, the new priest proclaimed unwavering obedience to the bishop who stood over him, the successor of the apostles. It was a virtue to show obedience to him, as he obeyed the pope, the successor to Peter, to whom Christ entrusted his church. A priest would pass down that wisdom to the obedient faithful, relying perfectly upon the commands of his superiors. This was the obedience of legend, as of a young child to his parent, whom he obeyed even in the battlement of his own heart. In the old story, a boy observing his first ordination nudged his father and asked why the bishop was hunching above the man splayed out on the floor. "Shhhh," the father whispered, "this is where they remove the backbone."

Neil Conway had no reservations. In his nine years at seminary, he had made accommodations to its procrustean life. He believed wholeheartedly in the church's authority and wanted only what the church believed he should have.

He would become one of twenty-two new priests in Cleveland this year, one of the biggest crops in the diocese's history. This was a time of celebration for the church. This year Catholic integration reached a new pinnacle, a process spurred on by the significant role Catholics played in the Second World War. No segment of America was a bigger participant in the baby boom. Today there were 45.6 million Catholics. Nearly one in five Americans was Roman Catholic—among them the president of the United States of America. New churches were springing up all over the country. This required more priests than ever—

58,632 of them, including Conway, the largest concentration of Roman Catholic clergy in any nation except Italy.

Bishop Elwell raised his arms high in triumphal exaltation. *"Tu es sacerdos in aeternum, secundum ordinem Melchizedek,"* he proclaimed. "You are a priest forever, in the order of Melchizedek!"

Conway clenched closed his eyes and prayed as he never had before—for true piety, for uncommon virtue, for the ability to forget who he had been before this moment but could never remain, that is, a man who once was struck by love.

Late June 1966

ROME — When she first entered the bright meeting hall of the Pontifical Spanish College of St. Joseph, Patty Crowley felt a certain self-doubt about sitting among some of the most eminent and respected Catholic thinkers of her time. Besides herself and her husband, there were fifty-six in attendance: priests and monsignors, medical researchers and theologians, lay experts in sociology and demography. Just five were women, only two of them married.

They had gathered here at the request of the pope to hammer out a Catholic proposal on the use of birth control, a burning controversy among the faithful. The Pontifical Commission for the Study of Population, Family, and Births—informally known as the Birth Control Commission—had already met four times over the past three years. In this, their final marathon session, they seemed headed toward a nearly unanimous position: it was time for the church to change. But as if to thwart their progress, the Vatican had suddenly downgraded them from commission members to advisers, and put in their place a panel of fifteen bishops. It was to this group of men that she was getting ready to speak.

Patty Crowley was a Chicago housewife who, together with her husband, Pat, had helped found the Christian Family Movement to assist Catholic couples striving to live according to church doctrine. Members of CFM, which had affiliates in sixty-one countries, backed the governing rule of thumb, "The more children the better," but within limits. For most of the august gathering Crowley had remained relatively silent. But in these closing days, she felt compelled to represent ordinary Catholic women the world over, praying her words would reach the pope's compassionate ears.

Pope John XXIII had not lived long enough to see through his grand plan for church reforms—he died of stomach cancer on June 3, 1963, Pentecost Sunday, when three of Vatican II's four annual summits had not yet taken place. Upon his death he was declared one of the most beloved leaders in church history, "the good pope." He would have been a hard act for anybody to follow. But when the sacred conclave of cardinals gathered later that month in the Sistine Chapel, they elected a quiet and nervous man who had been a career administrator in the Vatican's Secretariat of State—Cardinal Giovanni Battista Enrico Antonio Maria Montini, the archbishop of Milan—as his successor. He chose as his papal name Paul VI, naming himself after Paul III, who restored the Catholic faith and prestige following the Reformation. But he was considerably less nimble than his namesake. He thought too narrowly and personally and darkly—he was a man, according to a *New Yorker* article, "obviously torn by doubts, tormented by scruples, haunted by thoughts of perfection, and above all dominated by an exaggerated concern—some called it an obsession—about the prestige of his office as pope."

Paul VI had the power to cancel the Vatican Council. In fact, the first Vatican Council had been interrupted by the Franco-Prussian War in 1870 and never again resumed. But although he was not nearly as enthusiastic about the process as his predecessor, Paul attached himself to John's great project in his first address to the faithful, and went on to preside as facilitator over the most profound redefinition of the Catholic Church ever carried out. By the end of Vatican II, four major "constitutions" for the church were adopted. The impact was widespread and immediate, noticeable at every level of Catholic life. Fish was no longer the mandated Friday supper. Liturgy would now be said in the vernacular by a priest who turned around and faced the parishioners, rather than in a language only he understood, muttered into the altar as a private affair between him and God. The laity was no longer considered the passive beneficiary of Mass, but an integral element in the reconstituted church.

Priests "were not meant by Christ to shoulder alone the entire saving mission of the church toward the world," the council fathers declared. "As sharers in the role of Christ the Priest, the Prophet, and the
King, the laity have an active part to play in the life and activity of the
Church."

No aspect of Vatican II was received more ebulliently. For the first
time in two thousand years, the subjects had a voice in managing the
fortresses. They were invited to form parish councils to advise priests
on all matters; they were invited to join finance councils to confer with
their bishops on economic affairs. Lay Catholics rejoiced.

But the most stunning change was the view the fathers took on doctrinal issues, which historically had been divined by the pope from
God, and handed down as inflexible rules to the faithful. In a document
they called *Lumen Gentium,* the council fathers for the first time allowed that the laity, through their collective sense (their *sensus fidel-
ium*), played a role in determining truth. "The entire body of the
faithful, anointed as they are by the Holy One, cannot err in matters of
belief," the fathers wrote. "Thanks to a supernatural sense of faith
which characterizes the People as a whole, it manifests this unerring
quality when, 'from the bishops down to the last members of the laity,'
it shows universal agreement in matters of faith and morals."

Some took this to mean that the laity's consent was now necessary
at every turn. But as the Notre Dame theologian Father Richard
McBrien wrote, the council was "hardly engaged in some form of reckless innovation." They were not, that is, creating a church based on
the principles of democracy. The laity were to perform a *consultative*
role. Priests, who no longer were unerring shepherds, were still in
charge of the show, as their bishops were over them, and the pope
most of all.

As a symbol of this unbroken hierarchy, Paul VI removed two subjects from the table at council deliberations, reserving them to his own
deliberations and pronouncements. Both had to do with sex.

The first, priestly celibacy, eventually would become the subject of
his first major encyclical. Some theologians had argued that lifting this
long-standing ecclesiastical requirement was overdue—it would stamp
out the perennial problem of scandalous lapses and resolve "celibacy

psychosis," a syndrome in which priests grow aloof and cold to human kindnesses. With change in the air, priests around the globe were beside themselves with hope. Many of Christ's apostles had married, they figured; perhaps now, with the church's windows flung wide open, they could too. Paul promised a hasty deliberation. So far, no word had come of his findings.

The other subject was birth control. Without interruption, the church had opposed contraception at least since the third century, when it condemned the tinctures, douches, and vaginal packs (fruit wedges, vinegar, dung) that were popular at the time as "magic" and "witchcraft." Thomas Aquinas called contraception a more serious sin than incest, and many in the church agreed with him. Even coitus interruptus was grounds for damnation. But in recent years several developments had made the matter much more pressing for Catholic families. Around 1930, thanks to improvements in industry and technology, cheap and effective prophylactics became ubiquitous. The Church of England voted three-to-one to allow condom usage that year. But Pope Pius XI went the other way. Procreation was the supreme and only goal of sexuality, he felt, and any sex act that precluded that eventuality was therefore morally sinful and "intrinsically indecent."

His successor, Pope Pius XII, reluctantly gave the official Vatican imprimatur to the rhythm method—whereby couples engaged in sex only during the woman's infertile periods—which he called the only contraception "compatible with the law of God." Catholics were not thrilled. As a birth control technique, it was exceptionally complex, frustrating, and faulty. It required a woman to keep a daily record of her basal temperatures and cervical mucosal viscosity (doctors dispensed special tape, like litmus paper, for this purpose). When followed precisely, this method reduced her sexual availability to about one week each month—while doing little to reduce her chances for conception. Efficacy rates in studies were as low as 14 percent.

"For God's sake and in his name," one woman wrote to *ACT,* the magazine published by Crowley's Christian Family Movement, "would the Church please review its attitudes on marriage, childbearing and related areas? We need help now or an awful lot of us will fall down under our crosses."

Overburdened by children, and sinking into poverty as a result, Catholic women clamored for the right to plan their families. Pope Paul VI had considered this subject too volatile to be debated in open Vatican II sessions before the assembled lay media. So he appointed a small panel of doctors and social science experts—all men—to his Pontifical Birth Control Commission to grapple with the science and theology. The group met in utmost secrecy in 1963 and twice more in 1964, gradually expanding to include church officials, theologians, and women. Their deliberations took them to the deep waters of human philosophy. If procreation was the sole aim of the marriage act, they wondered, what should they make of the fact that conception does not occur following most sexual encounters? Was it a sin every time conception failed? Were infertile couples inherently sinful?

Some commission members argued that love, not offspring, was what separated human sex from bestial sex. All creatures procreated, some even mated for life, but only humans could love each other. Wasn't human love an essential, not secondary, end of marriage? Around this point of view, the panel began to coalesce.

For this final marathon session, which had begun in April and would end late in June, Crowley arrived bearing the results of a larger-scale survey of three thousand married Catholics gathered from her organization's chapters around the world. Most were at the end of their patience. "These questionnaires," Crowley told the gathered bishops and lay experts, "were not filled out by disaffected Catholics, those who may be discouraged, disillusioned or disenchanted, or whose personal problems within marriage may have caused them to drift apart from each other and from the Church. Naturally, we do not presume to judge the success or happiness of a marriage or the quality of a person's Christianity. Yet if you were to ask us to select on the basis of outward appearances men and women who are indeed happy, who are committed to pursuing Christ's work on earth, who love the Church and look to her for guidance, these are precisely the couples we would select."

Having established the faithfulness of her subjects, she then laid out their responses. Some 32 percent said rhythm had failed them utterly, despite repeated (even obsessive) efforts. Almost 80 percent said it had harmed their marriage by injecting tension and destroying spontaneity.

Crowley continued. "Is there a bad psychological effect in the use of rhythm?" Almost without exception, the respondents said yes, she explained. "Does rhythm serve any useful purpose at all? A few say it may be useful for developing discipline. Nobody says that it fosters married love. Does it contribute to married unity? No. That is the inescapable conclusion of the reports we have received," she said.

She looked around the room and hoped the men would understand what she was saying. "We think it is time that this Commission recommend that the sacredness of conjugal love not be violated by thermometers and calendars. Marital union *does* lead to fruitfulness, psychologically as well as physically. Couples want children and will have them generously and love them and cherish them. We do not need the impetus of legislation to procreate."

These voices from the pews swayed the commission members to the conclusion that the church's teachings on love were essentially antisex. As the historian Garry Wills wrote in *Papal Sin,* "The more the assembled members looked at the inherited 'wisdom' of the Church, the more they saw the questionable roots from which it grew—the fear and hatred of sex, the feeling that pleasure in it is a biological bribe to guarantee the race's perpetuation, that any use of pleasure beyond that purpose is shameful. This was not a view derived from scripture or from Christ, but from Seneca and Augustine."

The panel of laypeople voted thirty-five to five in favor of change. When it was their turn to vote, the bishops overseeing the deliberations were nine in favor and three opposed, with three abstaining. They would report their landmark opinion to the Holy Father for his deliberation.

As she closed the folder on her prepared comments, Patty Crowley felt a rightful sense of pride in accomplishment. In a very fundamental way, she had lent her voice to the church of modernity. The church would change. Of this there was no doubt. Two years would pass, however, before the pope reached his decision.

July 1966

ATTLEBORO, MASSACHUSETTS — A woman and her teenage son arrived
at the Shrine of Our Lady of La Salette, desperate to tell the pastor
their disturbing story involving a dashing priest, Father Paul Shanley,
who ordinarily worked at St. Patrick's in Stoneham, a far-north suburb
of Boston. It was unusual that the pair had sought out the pastor of this
church, so far from their home, but he greeted them fraternally and
took detailed notes.

The son, who did not wish to be identified publicly, first met Shanley during confession over the summer. He did not say what he had
confessed. However, sometime later Shanley summoned him to his
rectory to talk about sexual impulses and explain what he called the
"theory of the lesser of two evils." "He said I should consider spending
the night with him there and if I felt the need to seek out sexual relief
from girls, I should contact him and that the lesser of two evils would
be for him to masturbate me and for me to masturbate him," the boy
said. For this procedure, the boy was encouraged to use any pretext
necessary to get permission to accompany Shanley to his cabin in the
Blue Hills south of Boston for the weekend. "He said he had put himself at risk and would take responsibility for that, in order to save my
soul."

Having his reasons, the youth reluctantly succumbed to the priest's
blandishments. He was not a toddler or even an especially impressionable young man. He was sixteen, the age of consent. But he could not
explain why he had consented. Yet shortly after arriving at the cabin,
just 150 yards off Route 128, the encounter began.

He never saw Shanley under such circumstances again. Nonetheless, in the weeks that followed, he began making lewd remarks about
Shanley in earshot of his mother, who eventually coaxed the sordid history out of him.

He recalled the address and gave directions for how to find the
priest's cabin. At the end of the driveway, he remembered, was a plaque
that read, "Owned by Fr. Paul Shanley, St. Patrick's Rectory." He gave
the phone number. It all checked out.

Shanley had boasted of bringing other teenagers to his cabin at least one weekend each month, the youth reported, providing two names. "I don't know if this is going on with them or not," he said.

The priest at the Shrine of Our Lady of La Salette, Father Arthur Chabot, wrote this all down in a sloping cursive, on church letterhead, and forwarded it to the Boston archdiocese. This missive, with its well-sourced presentation, did prompt the diocese to approach Shanley. He forcefully denied everything.

"That," he said, "is a mixed-up family."

For the powers that be at the chancery—the vicar for clergy, the personnel director, the regional auxiliary bishop, and even the cardinal archbishop, Richard Cushing—this was sufficient to quell suspicion. Monsignor Francis Sexton wrote "accepted as true" on Shanley's denial letter. But his assignment at St. Patrick's was imperiled by the allegation nonetheless. Should news of it reach parishioners, a grave scandal would follow him and the church.

Shortly, Shanley was transferred to St. Francis of Assisi Rectory in Braintree, about as far away from Stoneham as you could get in the diocese. As at St. Patrick's, he was given unrestricted access to young and impressionable teenage boys. In fact, he was put in charge of youth programs. The young priests always were.

Summer 1967

Hingham, Massachusetts — Anthony Muzzi was wide awake in his bed in a pitch-black room doing battle with an emotion he could not comprehend. Was it humiliation? Rage? Self-hatred? Was it pleasure?

He heard the whispering. "How does it feel? What do you think about when I'm doing this?"

Father John J. Geoghan was the new priest at St. Paul's, a big job in this teeming parish, located in a large Italian Catholic town south of Boston. He gravitated to youth programs, shouldering the responsibility energetically. He was always taking parish children for ice cream or drives in his car to Paragon Park and Nantasket Beach, sometimes knocking on doors with no other purpose than to visit the parish's little ones.

He had taken a special liking to the two Muzzi boys, and as a result of this friendship, which was the envy of the other mothers in the neighborhood, he was a frequent guest for lunch or dinner, or just dessert, or for a dip in the backyard pool. The Muzzis considered it a tremendous honor when he accepted these kindnesses, as if Jesus Christ himself had walked through their door for a slice of pie and coffee. Besides, he was extremely affable. His high-pitched rollicking laughter filled the Muzzis' simple home with unbounded energy.

From his bedroom upstairs, which he shared with his kid brother, Anthony, a boxy and self-assured thirteen-year-old, had overheard the infectious chortles—and heard the priest announce, "I'm going up to bless the children." Anthony was not quite a child; he was nearly fourteen.

His ears snapped wide at the sound of the bedroom door opening and closing, and the creak of the priest's knees at his bedside, the long in-and-out of the priest's encroaching breath. He was able neither to flinch nor scream as Father Geoghan's fingers spidered beneath his blankets and unknitted his bedclothes. Terror struck him. He played dead.

But his body betrayed him, and that made him feel complicit in this shocking act. Geoghan's fingers worked and worked. Could this be a test of his soul? If so, would Father refuse him absolution for this grievous sin—the sin, a mortal sin, of adolescent weakness? "How does it feel?" he heard in the darkness. It felt shameful, like flesh in conflict. Guilt and disgust multiplied in his mind. Years of religious education class had taught him about prevailing over temptation, but he was powerless now. The physiology of adolescence was too primal.

When it was over, Father Geoghan rose and retreated, leaving Anthony Muzzi alone in a darkness that had never been more absolute. What hope was there for salvation now?

In the years to come, as Anthony Muzzi grew into a strapping and barrel-chested teenager, he never told another living soul what he knew about the elfin priest. He continued going to church, and comported himself admirably at school throughout. All the while, Geoghan never left him alone. He could not keep track of the number of nocturnal visits, which always involved him pretending he was asleep. There were

even encounters when he was clearly wide awake. One afternoon, after Geoghan had coaxed him into his car, the priest demanded he remove his pants.

"Your mother asked me to make sure you are developing normally,"
Geoghan said.

He asked himself, How did I let this happen?

He could never say no. Why not? He had no idea. And that flummoxed him. More and more he was trapped in this thing, delivering
himself again to Geoghan's hands, soon fifteen years old, then sixteen,
but still with no voice of his own. No teacher or bus driver could trap
him like this. It was not what he wanted, it was never what he wanted.
It made him sick to his stomach. But it never stopped. Just the opposite, it got more brazen over time. Once, as Muzzi sat between his
cousin Ralph DelVecchio and Geoghan in the front seat of the priest's
car, Geoghan brushed his hand into Muzzi's lap and gave his genitals a
squeeze. Muzzi would have done anything to keep his cousin from
learning this secret.

Nobody suspected a thing, least of all Muzzi's devout mother. Even
Muzzi never suspected that Geoghan had moved from his bed to his
brother's, then next door to his cousin Lenny Muzzi's bed, then down
the hall to his cousin Roland, then across the street to fumble Ralph
DelVecchio. He cycled among the cousins from 1967 to 1974.

Finally Leonard Muzzi Jr., Anthony's uncle, caught the priest one
night as he stood over his son's bed in the pitch dark, with his hand in
Roland's pajamas. Muzzi threw the priest down the stairs and swore
he'd kill him if he ever returned. Inexplicably, and this said a great deal
about Geoghan's character, he did not disappear in shame. Rather, he
returned to masturbate the cousins again. Muzzi entered his house
one afternoon to find the priest forcing his crying children to sit on his
lap.

That time, Muzzi threw Geoghan out again and telephoned the pastor of another church in Hingham and told everything he knew to the
priest in charge. Leonard Muzzi Jr. demanded the priest be removed,
kept from smearing his filthy hands on another child.

Still nothing happened. Geoghan remained at the parish, apparently
immune to punishment. Nobody knew why.

June 24, 1967, Feast of St. John the Baptist
VATICAN CITY — Pope Paul VI addressed his long-awaited encyclical on
the sex lives of priests, titled *Sacerdotalis Caelibatus* and translated into
many languages, to "the Bishops, Priests, and Faithful of the Whole
Catholic World."

> Priestly celibacy has been guarded by the Church for centuries as
> a brilliant jewel, and retains its value undiminished even in our
> time when the outlook of men and the state of the world have un-
> dergone such profound changes.
>
> Amid the modern stirrings of opinion, a tendency has also been
> manifested, and even a desire expressed, to ask the Church to re-
> examine this characteristic institution. It is said that in the world
> of our time the observance of celibacy has come to be difficult or
> even impossible. . . .
>
> There are also some who strongly maintain that priests by rea-
> son of their celibacy find themselves in a situation that is not only
> against nature but also physically and psychologically detrimental
> to the development of a mature and well-balanced human per-
> sonality. And so it happens, they say, that priests often become
> hard and lacking in human warmth; that, excluded from sharing
> fully the life and destiny of the rest of their brothers, they are
> obliged to live a life of solitude which leads to bitterness and dis-
> couragement.
>
> So they ask: Don't all these things indicate that celibacy does
> unwarranted violence to nature and unjustifiably disparages hu-
> man values which have their source in the divine work of creation
> and have been made whole through the work of the Redemption
> accomplished by Christ?

Reading the encyclical in rectories around the globe, hundreds of
thousands of priests sucked in their breath, awaiting his verdict.
Mandatory celibacy, foreign to most human cultures, was a relatively
new institution in the Catholic Church. Over the centuries, many
priests and bishops had been married, and quite a few more consorted
openly with women, and sometimes even with men. Even the Vatican
sometimes seemed to rival Plato's symposia. Thirty-nine popes had

had wives. Pope Julius III, advised for appearance's sake to end a fling with a young teenager named Innocent, instead made him cardinal and installed him prominently in the Vatican as secretary of state. But it was not until 1078 that Pope Gregory VII elevated priestly celibacy, always practiced by various monastic orders, to the status of church law. Historians argued over why—whether it was indeed an effort to compel priests to vouchsafe undivided fealty to their flocks or simply a way to keep priests and their potentially endless heirs from becoming too heavy a financial drain on the enterprise. The practice had been the subject of fierce opposition, and steady defiance, ever since. The priests knew what Martin Luther once said was true, that perpetual celibacy was for most a twisting burden that caused "either a constant burning or unclean pollutions." No research had specifically identified sexual abstinence as causing the crime of sexual abuse. In fact, most sexual crimes, including those against youth, were committed by noncelibate men. But priests, especially after Vatican II, saw a clear hypocrisy to the system. Priests who importuned a sexual partner through coercion or outright assault could be forgiven by their higher authorities while those who fell hopelessly in love could not.

Would now be the time to reevaluate the sacred nature of clerical celibacy?

Not at all. Not only did Paul VI tighten the screws, he underscored the ecclesiastical justification for the practice. Celibacy was the necessary—and exclusive—avenue for serving God, he declared.

> The consecration to Christ under an additional and lofty title like celibacy evidently gives to the priest, even in the practical field, the maximum efficiency and the best disposition of mind, mentally and emotionally, for the continuous exercise of a perfect charity. This charity will permit him to spend himself wholly for the welfare of all, in a fuller and more concrete way. It also obviously guarantees him a greater freedom and flexibility in the pastoral ministry, in his active and living presence in the world, to which Christ has sent him so that he may pay fully to all the children of God the debt due to them.

Father Anthony Massimini, who had returned from his service to the Vatican Council to take up a teaching position in the theology department at St. Charles Seminary in the archdiocese of Philadelphia, was crestfallen. In a stroke, the euphoria he had felt over his Rome experiences had become undone. To close off discussion like that, he felt, was in contravention of the spirit of Vatican II, which he felt applied here: if priests were no longer to be seen as godlike, what right did Rome have to impose this penalty for their service?

In response, he joined up with his friend Father Bill Leahy and began lecturing in area churches on the thwarted reforms of Vatican II. Leahy, who had saved all the original draft documents from the Council, would publish them in a book. To their surprise, not all American Catholics were receptive to their message. In fact, a number were overtly hostile to it, picketing the pair, interrupting their presentations, cursing at them and their families. They wrote letters of complaint to Massimini's bishop, who eventually removed him from his teaching post and silenced him for a year.

"Why? What am I saying that's wrong?" he protested when the verdict came in.

"It's just that you're pushing us," the bishop said.

"Pushing us? That makes no sense. I'm just—"

"Pushing the *laity*."

"The laity *have* to get involved—in public schools, not just Catholic schools, in *every part of life*. We can talk to school boards, to politicians, corporate leaders, and say, 'There is another way to operate, there is a *Catholic* way. That is what we learned in *Lumen Gentium*. This is our obligation.' "

His feelings about his church never quite recovered afterward. Nor did Leahy's. He was also fired from the St. Charles Seminary faculty with these words: "Your idea of the church is not the same as ours." A professor at a Catholic college asked him to fill in there for a term, and he agreed, but the authorities stopped him immediately upon learning of his troubles at the seminary. Like Massimini, he felt like a pariah. Leahy, who loved his church and had been one of its rising stars, slid into darkness, loneliness, and alcohol.

Fed up, Massimini soon announced his resignation and married a beautiful and intellectually wily woman named Mary. It used to be almost unheard of for priests to reject their stature. Until recently, it wasn't even possible for a priest to reenter the lay life except under extreme circumstances—transformation by ordination was considered irreversible. A trickle became a stream—in 1967, 576 American priests renounced their priesthood, twice as many as the year before. The church had never faced such a flight. Pope Paul VI called them "Judases."

But his celibacy encyclical burst open the dams. In 1968, 1,023 priests would lay down their Roman collars, followed by 1,526 in 1969, 3,500 in 1970, 4,500 in 1971. By 1980, over twenty thousand American priests would abdicate, most leaving and marrying right away, some openly embracing the precepts of the free-love generation. In a landmark survey of those departing clerics that sociologist Father Andrew Greeley undertook for the National Conference of Catholic Bishops, the overwhelming majority (63 percent) admitted they left for a particular woman. One-third specifically cited the pope's reaffirmation of celibacy as the last straw. Asked to say what they least liked about the priestly culture they had left behind, 79 percent called it "psychosexually unhealthy."

In Cleveland, Neil Conway—now in his fifth year as a priest—paid no attention to the encyclical on celibacy. It was not a watershed of any sort for him anyway. In the long dark loneliness of night, he did not dwell on visions of domestic bliss, of loving brides and children underfoot. In his blurry viewfinder there was no happy alternative future. Evidence was multiplying that he was a homosexual. This realization might have filled him with dread, had he fully grasped it. The condition did not allow for happiness, at least not in his culture. It did not allow for domestic comfort. All he really knew was that he had no possibility of ever experiencing love. He was left empty. He had begun to drink heavily. Flailing around in his rectory bed on fitful nights, he literally was not capable of imagining anything different for himself, not even when the fragmentary images of faces and bodies began to populate his dreams. In the psychosis of his terrors—in his delusion—he would say to himself, What is *he* doing here?

July 29, 1968
CHICAGO, ILLINOIS — The phone rang shortly after 4 A.M. Patty Crowley's husband, Pat, dragged himself up on an elbow to answer it. Any

parents' first fear must have been for their children—in the Crowleys' case, four biological children, one adopted daughter, fourteen foster children, or any of the sixty foreign students who had stayed with them over the years. Rubbing the sleep from her eyes, Patty could hear her husband huff a few assents.

"I don't believe it," he said when he hung up the phone. The caller was an Associated Press reporter from New York City. The pope, he said, had issued his long-awaited birth control encyclical, on which Patty had lobbied so diligently.

"He rejected the commission's recommendations," Pat told his wife.

After years of anticipation, *Humanae Vitae* was handed down in Rome just a few hours previously. Instantly it would become the most famous papal encyclical—its Latin title familiar to Catholics and non-Catholics alike—and the most disastrous for the church in modern times. Pope Paul VI, it turned out, had been swayed by curial insiders who argued a tautology: The church could not have imposed such a grave burden on its faithful for so many centuries in the name of Jesus Christ if those burdens were not given down by Jesus Christ himself. No member of the commission, not even the pope, had the power to alter the teaching. Paul wrote: "The Church, calling men back to the observance of the norms of the natural law, as interpreted by its constant doctrine, teaches that each and every marriage act must remain open to the transmission of life. . . . Consequently it is an error to think that a conjugal act which is deliberately rendered sterile and thus is intrinsically dishonest could be made honest by an otherwise fertile conjugal life."

A global backlash would be immediate. Within weeks the national bishops' conferences from fourteen countries, including the United States, pronounced themselves disappointed. According to a Gallup poll in August, 72 percent of American Catholics opposed every aspect of *Humanae Vitae*. So did more than half of all priests, and by 1970 only 14 percent said they would deny absolution to a Catholic who persisted in using birth control.

And use it they did. Although oral contraception was almost universally rejected by Catholics in the mid-1960s, by 1970, 66 percent of

Catholic women of childbearing age were swallowing the pill. By 1980, that figure jumped to 94 percent, while the use of rhythm dropped to just 4 percent by 1988. Sterilization techniques like vasectomies, expressly banned by the pope, rose 500 percent in the thirteen years after 1965, far outpacing the growth among Protestants.

For the first time ever, a definitive papal encyclical went entirely ignored. The fact that Paul's doctrine had not been accepted, or "received," by the faithful was interpreted by some theologians to mean the teaching was not valid, and certainly not infallible. The laity had declared itself wiser on the subject than their supreme pontiff. Paul VI was despairing. He was seen crying around the Vatican grounds. "Through some crack in the temple of God, the smoke of Satan has entered," he complained. He never recovered from the shock of being disavowed, and in the remaining years of his lonely papacy he did not deliver another encyclical.

This tremendous breach would be no easier on the Catholics who were forced by their conscience into disobedience. Many would stop going to confession altogether, such was the crisis of their faith—they could not truthfully seek absolution for an action they did not intend to halt. Even men who served on the pontifical commission with Patty Crowley slid into doubt and, in at least one instance, agnosticism. Church attendance figures in the United States, which had stood at 75 percent of all Catholics in 1963, would tumble to a low of 40 percent in 1990.

"The pope rejected the recommendations," Patty Crowley's husband said. "The reporter wanted to know our reaction."

Patty blinked back her disbelief. Finally she said, "Why did we ever go to Rome in the first place?"

Fall 1968
SALEM, MASSACHUSETTS — Bernie McDaid pulled his small white surplice over his head, and the neck of it seemed to catch on his nose and ears, and the tangle only got worse despite his efforts, the way it sometimes did with pajamas, and he could hear Father B.—Joseph Birmingham—laughing and walking toward him. Birmingham had recently

been transferred to Salem from Sudbury, part of routine priestly rotation. He took special interest in the parish's many young kids.

The humiliation. To be an eleven-year-old altar boy at the 6:45 A.M. Mass who could not free himself from his own surplice.

The priest's large hands caught him in the armpits, and that made Bernie laugh in oboe peals, the reedy sound of puberty. A tremendous surge of self-esteem rose up and colored the boy's face—this moment of levity shared with a priest, a bonding with a revered man. Bernie's father never tickled him—he was bone tired from his shifts on the pile driver, an immigrant's lasting exhaustion. Bernie pleaded through his giggles:

"Please stop, Father, that tickles!"

Rather than halting, Birmingham ran his fingers down Bernie's rib cage one excruciating ridge at a time, making Bernie buckle and crack, even when Birmingham said something like "Tuck in your shirt, young man," and began snagging the tails of his white dress shirt and jamming them back inside his slacks. The very idea of a priest behaving so genially was mind bending. Really, Bernie couldn't believe his blessing.

Suddenly, though, without any particular timidity, one of Birmingham's hands was on the wrong side of Bernie's underwear. An error? When Birmingham wrapped his whole hand around his genitals, Bernie figured this was a taunt. A dangerous, thoughtless escalation. His flesh caught fire with shame. The young man froze. The priest, he realized now, had him pinned against a wall, and he could feel the weight of Birmingham grinding against him.

The assault was especially disorienting. He had just entered puberty, a period of great mystery and embarrassment, especially for Catholics inculcated in a culture of sexual ignorance and guilt. As Garry Wills once pointed out, "Nuns were reluctant to speak about sex except in vaguely threatening language. Priests were mechanically judgmental in the confessional."

"Father, it tickles," he complained. He knew he should twist away, but he was unable to rally his body in revolt. The one thing he knew was that he could never use his arms against a priest.

"Does that feel good?" Birmingham asked.

Bernie could feel the heat of the words on his neck. He shook his head *no*, and that was the truth. Good God, he was inside the sacristy of St. James Parish, as dauntingly sacred a church as was ever built. The altar was literally paces away. Of course it felt awful. It made him want to vomit.

Obviously this was a test of the kid's fitness to serve Christ.

"Don't you think you might like other boys?"

"No, Father," Bernie insisted. "I like girls, Father."

Later in 1968

BRAINTREE, MASSACHUSETTS — The parish office at St. Francis of Assisi was located in the back of a peach-colored colonial building with sloping shoulders, off Washington Street, and Father Shanley, who lived upstairs, kept the curtains of his first-floor den stitched tightly closed. He hammered angrily at a typewriter. A timid young man knocked on the doorjamb. Rail thin and tall, he was almost without color at all except for the pink of misery that limned his satiny eyes.

The young man introduced himself—Arthur Austin, twenty, a Boston College junior, a devastated Irish Catholic son of Braintree. His mother had grown concerned because he cried all the time these days, he said, and because he neither slept nor ate, and in two weeks' time he had dropped over twenty-five pounds. He suffered panic attacks and a psychosomatic rash, which spread across his arms, back, and chest. No intervention had helped him. A family friend insisted: "See Father Paul. He's wonderful with the young."

Austin knew of Shanley's reputation at St. Francis, a parish near his own. He even had heard of Shanley's nightly drives into Boston to work with the alienated youth on the streets. There was almost nothing else he could do but seek out Shanley. Who else could he tell the truth to? He had fallen in love with another young man—tender, lyrical, passionate love—and after three blissful months, had been summarily, bruisingly dumped.

Nobody knew about the homosexual affair during its flowering, much less about its staggering collapse. Heartsick, Austin was no longer sure of anything, and afraid of everything. Was he a homosexual? Was this a passing phase, a starter affair, a stepping-stone that would still lead toward heterosexuality, or a lonely sinful path to which he had been condemned? Having sinned, he loved it—"like God reaching into my heart and completing me," he said rather floridly. Having loved it, was he now doomed to exist in the wilderness, the way lepers teemed in the margins of the Bible, never allowed home from the sunburnt desert plains?

Tommy is gone, he said between keening sobs, emotionally spent in his bitter terror. *Father Paul, I am in pieces.*

He had never spoken of another man this way before. Nor had he heard anybody else say anything similar—there were no gay consciousness-raising groups, no known periodicals, no role models to guide him. There was something truly, deeply wrong with him, and there had been for a long time, he was sure. Most psychiatrists would have agreed. The *Diagnostic and Statistical Manual* of the American Psychiatric Association ranked same-sex attraction as a mental illness alongside other "deviations," like pedophilia, sadism, transvestitism, and exhibitionism—desires that sufferers cannot quell "even though many find their practices distasteful." Commonplace treatment modalities ran from aversion therapy to electric shock treatment and lobotomy. (In addition, lesbianism was sometimes treated with "beauty therapy," on the theory that lessons in coiffure and maquillage could render the stoniest women marriage-ready.)

Shanley regarded Austin through intense black eyes from across the paper-crowded desk. He pushed the fingers of one hand through his long black hair. Austin could not read his reaction. Damnation? Pity? It would be one or the other; a priest's replies were rarely ambiguous.

"How big is your penis?"

Austin's mind reeled. He must have misunderstood the priest.

"How big was Tommy's?"

Accepting that the priest must have some theologically sound reason for inquiring, Austin answered him.

"Did he come in your mouth?"

Despite his embarrassment, Austin again dutifully answered.

"You loved it, didn't you!"

Of course he did, to his everlasting shame. He would not be in pieces otherwise.

He braced for the irrevocable judgment. But it never came. Shanley was upset at a way of thinking, not a way of behaving. He launched into a stern and confusing sermon on situational ethics and contextualism. Every behavior, every so-called sin, he said, had to be dealt with separately and anew, within its own framework. That was the job of the priest, measuring and weighing, the work of the philosopher. It was not always clear going. Sometimes a contemplated action has both good and bad effects, was both moral *and* evil, but was not wrong in itself and was thus permitted. In other words, an action was not judged simply by motive or by consequences, but by a delicate moral puzzle connecting the two.

Was it morally right to love Tommy? Did that dent the clear moral evil of homosexual copulation? Emphatically, Shanley said it did. "Don't be poisoned by the heresy of Jansenism!" he declared. Perdition was not the predestined assignment of ordinary humans, as the theologian Cornelius Jansen once argued. Grace and virtue are right here, through our own means, Shanley told Austin. You've got to learn to understand your own body, and the way God intended for you—*you, Arthur Austin*—to enjoy it, he said.

Confused but relieved, Austin gave the father the wide-eyed look of thanks. Unloved by Tommy, loathed by the world, condemned by God—perhaps he was wrong about the whole thing.

"Tell you what I'll do," Shanley ventured. "I can tell you're a sensitive guy. I know, because I'm a sensitive guy too. We are kindred souls." He leaned forward and laid out his offer: For the sake of healing and clarity, Shanley would make his *own* body available for experimentation and discovery. He would absorb and deflect the moral dangers and protect the young man's soul. "I will take the moral responsibility for your actions," he said. "It is better for you to come to me than to be doing it in an alley somewhere with somebody off the street."

A non-Catholic might not have understood how profoundly appreciative Austin was at that moment, rescued from the fiery battlefields of moral warfare into the safe haven of grace. Austin was two decades old, an adult by every measure. He was not much younger than the priest. But in the matter of knowing his wrecked sexuality, he was as vulnerable and ill-informed as a child. Somehow he felt this was true: it was either Paul Shanley's body and salvation or back-alley sex and ruin.

Grateful for the priest's selfless generosity, he went home to pack his bags. The next day they drove together to Shanley's Blue Hills cabin. Austin removed his clothing and lay down on a musty mattress in a drafty room. Thus, the practicum began. His senses ran an obstacle course, from the smell of mildew and sweat, the sound of dead leaves lashing at the window, the racking pain of the priest inside him. He wept, not knowing why. Afterward, Shanley chucked him on the shoulder.

"You can call me Paul," he said. "You don't have to say 'Father Shanley' anymore."

Early 1969

BOSTON, MASSACHUSETTS — Father Spags was crumpled on the floor of the welfare office on Washington Street, his arms knotted to the people on either side. His legs were contorted and laced into a tapestry with scores of other legs—a mat of humanity that covered the floor and spilled out the door down the long dingy hallway. He was screaming at the top of his lungs.

"Hell no! We won't go! Hell no! We won't go!"

Spags loved the pageantry of protest. It always choked him up. He saw himself as a soldier in a robe-wearing army of warriors who, armed with the doctrines of the Second Vatican Council and their moral unimpeachability as Catholics, were committed to changing the world. He loved the energy, the spirit of life it infused in demonstrators, the pugnacity of it. He had to drop to his knees laughing during an antiwar rally a few weeks before when he read a banner that said, "Fighting for Peace Is Like Fucking for Chastity!"

"I love it!" he howled. "That's the best slogan I've ever heard!"

Right out of St. John's, Spags had been assigned to a wealthy suburban parish, which many of his classmates would have considered a plum assignment. Any priest serving there could become a rich man— in those days, at least in Boston, priests got to keep the collection plates from Easter and Christmas, which could mean $50,000 a year, an immense amount at that time. It was customary to tithe some back to the archbishop, but most priests with bulging bank accounts bought cottages on the Cape, which was why the beaches swelled with pasty round men in shorts and black socks during high season.

But Spags was caught up in the spirit of the times: antiwar demonstrations, social justice activism, civil rights. He hung out with the radical priest-brothers Daniel and Philip Berrigan; he visited fellow priests in jail for crimes of conscience. In March of 1965, he had driven to Selma to join the thousands-strong civil rights march to Montgomery, through gauntlets of fear, hate, and riot horses. He got to hear the Reverend Martin Luther King Jr. preach, something he would never forget, and to sleep in the tension-ridden campgrounds that moved with the march every night, surrounded by believers and not a few celebrities.

Upon his return, he had enlisted in the black freedom struggle, which he knew was concerned with more than civil rights, touching on every aspect of human expression in a modern world. He petitioned Cardinal Richard Cushing to reassign him to Roxbury, a black ghetto and one of the most destitute parts of the city. Cushing, himself a disciple of Dr. King's who once called upon Boston Catholics to "love all men and especially love Negroes, because they have suffered so much for lack of love," said yes in a minute. He named Spags parochial vicar in charge of education at a hardscrabble Roxbury parish, St. Francis de Sales.

As the expression went, "You don't live in Roxbury, you survive in Roxbury." Poverty was ubiquitous, racial anger was pervasive. Boston was one of the most fiercely segregated cities in the country, made that way by an educational system that kept the poor minorities ignorant and politically powerless. Because police squads played a lamentable role in black communities, and because the cops were mostly Irish Catholic, there existed a great deal of hostility from blacks toward the church. (In the whole country there was a paucity of black Catholics and even fewer black clerics—no more than fifty, up from three in 1930.)

Though he was Italian, not Irish, Spags hardly had an easy intro-

duction to Roxbury. But he persevered gamely, and steadily won a measure of acceptance and even admiration with his straight-talking blue-
collar wisdom and his strange folksy aphorisms. He would say things
that made people howl, like "The only good movement is a bowel movement," when it was so patently clear that he was as committed to social
change as they were.

Acquaintances from seminary had been seized with a general
malaise in their first years outside, adjusting awkwardly to their role as
neither fully human nor quite angelic, "a kind of marginal man," in the
words of Catholic sociologist Father Joseph Fichter. Not Spags and a
few others in the diocese who had taken over inner-city ministries.
They thrived in their radical vocations, and supported one another
through the Association of Urban Priests, which they created to compare notes on their pastoral concerns. Paul Shanley was one of the
founding members. More than any other men from St. John's class of
1960, he was the ultimate new cleric, dubbed "the hippie priest" by local editorial writers for his work on the sidewalks of the Combat Zone,
off Boylston Street, and the benches and hideaways inside the Boston
Common. Though officially assigned to Boston State College to minister to the Catholic students there, he spent most of his evenings on the
streets, tending to the most marginalized. A nearly cultish reputation
followed him.

Spags's ministry, though no less radical in the traditions of his
church, was decidedly parish based. He dedicated his ministry to Roxbury's children even though most who went to St. Francis de Sales
grammar school were Protestant, and 98 percent were black. In order
to educate his children, George Spagnolia needed to feed them—they
were coming to class in the mornings malnourished and sluggish. A
movement calling itself Mothers for Adequate Welfare had recently
opened a Roxbury chapter, and the women in the neighborhood seized
upon the opportunity to demand adequate resources from the state to
put food on the tables for their children. The group also railed against
a growing tendency among legislators to use welfare as a way to impose social controls—specifically by limiting the number of children
recipients could have. It struck the women as patronizing, humiliating,
and unacceptable. "Ain't no white man going to tell me how many ba-

bies I can have, 'cause if I want a million of them, and I can have them, I'm going to have them," declared Doris Bland, the group's telegenic chairwoman. "And ain't nobody in the world going to tell me what to do with my bod, 'cause this is mine and I treasure it."

This particular day, the MAW troops had taken over the Washington Street office to demand increases in the Aid to Families with Dependent Children. Spags joined the sit-in, the only Caucasian among them. Spags led the group in prayer. Afterward, as he milled about the packed room, he bumped into a brother priest from the chancery. He had not expected to find another priest in the crowd, and he was happy. Spags greeted him with ebullience.

"What are you doing here?"

"The cardinal heard about the sit-in on the radio, and that there was a priest among them," the man said.

"Really?" Spags could not imagine news traveling so fast. Notoriety pleased him.

"Eighty-five percent of the people working in this office are Catholic," the priest interjected sternly. "And they told me they'd never go anywhere where you say Mass. You're not a priest as far as they're concerned."

Cut cold, Spags didn't know what to say. He thought, Is this the new church, the one invigorated with the promises and obligations of Vatican II?

Then the man reached up and snatched the Roman collar from Spags's neck, spun around, and left the building. For the first time in his life, Spags was speechless.

June 28, 1969

GREENWICH VILLAGE, NEW YORK — When the police arrived, it was in the first hour or two of Saturday morning, the peak of the night at the Stonewall Inn, a dark and smelly hole in the wall on Christopher Street. Like other bars in the gay ghetto, this one had no windows, or more accurately, the ones that it had were encased in plywood and painted black to keep the outside out and the inside in. Homosexuals could not chance being spotted. Even suspicion of homosexuality was enough to cost a man or woman their job or home, or custody of their children.

There was a consensus about homosexuality's unacceptability, even among many gays. Although there were by now accepted estimates of the size of the homosexual population, between 5 million and 15 million, no locality in the nation had a gay rights ordinance. No known gay person served in any elected position or sat on any courtroom bench, none entered a corporate boardroom or a public classroom. There was not one openly gay police officer or sheriff or prison guard. For that matter, very few bus drivers or florists or musicians had come out either. On the public stage, homosexuals did not exist except in the unmasking, which produced hapless images of disgraced men being dragged out of a sleazy bar or public toilet or into courtrooms or police wagons or jails. Suicide was a common reaction to being revealed— even to oneself. Among gay teenagers, the manifestation of their sexual differences and the isolation that entailed produced an attempted suicide rate at least twice as high as among straights; gay youth accounted for nearly one-third of all suicides.

Even in the most ordinary gay bar, roustings were familiar and routine. A man or woman whose existence touched in any way upon the homosexual milieu was likely to have a police record as a result. This was a fact of life in the gay ghetto. The Stonewall Inn operated without a license because in New York City it would never be allowed one. This gave police the opportunity to push through the door regularly to carry out routine shakedowns.

Tonight was no different. Eight detectives entered the Stonewall shortly after 1 A.M., and closed and locked the door behind them. Patrons were interrogated individually, their identifications checked and double-checked, before being allowed to leave. Outside in the sticky summer night a crowd formed, as usual. At first, the spectators imparted an aura of camp and spectacle. When various old faces appeared from inside, they drew applause or hoots. Some freed patrons milked their moments of acclaim by strutting out like stars.

"Hello there, fellas!" one of them called as he walked with a lisp, as the expression went, through the squalid doorway. "I gave them the *gay power* bit, and they loved it, girls!"

When a police wagon arrived suddenly, it stilled the hilarity along the sidewalk. Cops waded into the crowd and nabbed three men wearing women's attire, and hustled them through a gauntlet of angry catcalls and taunts into the van. Statutes declared it was not legal to cross-dress, not even in jest, "without an apparent masquerade party in progress." The bartender and doorman were loaded inside the van, too, and it sped off.

Immediately after this, an officer emerged from the Stonewall dragging a reluctant woman toward a patrol car parked on the curb. It wasn't clear what he wanted with her—but that too was business as usual. She put up a fierce struggle and, breaking loose, raced inexplicably back through the bar's door. She might have gotten away had she broken toward the subway. Instead, the officer recaptured her and stuffed her bodily and loudly into the cruiser. Deputy Inspector Seymour Pine ordered the driver to take her to the Sixth Precinct, a few blocks away. The crowd grew restless. Some were tossing pennies and dimes into the air so they would fall on the policemen's heads and shoulders.

"Hurry back," Pine said to the driver.

Seeing the woman twist and buck in the vanishing cruiser angered the swarm. "Pigs," people yelled. The coins got bigger, nickels and quarters, flung with increasing venom at the police. A beer bottle, and another, sailed overhead. In timid surges, the line of protesters moved toward Pine and a few other officers at his side.

"Let's get inside," Pine said, almost amused. "Lock ourselves inside, it's safer."

But the minute the Stonewall door ratcheted closed, a brief and incendiary moment of full-scale riot broke out. Cobblestones, torn from the street, were sent through the plywood windows. The door bulged with the pressure of the crowd behind it, and for a second it seemed as though the gays were in pursuit of the police, a complete paradox. Gay people had never stood up to the police before. Up to this point in history, there had been fewer than a dozen gay rights protests. Called "Reminders," they were somber annual affairs begun in 1965 outside the White House and Independence Hall in Philadelphia, and attended by a few dozen picketers in suits and dresses, intent upon reminding everyone that not all citizens were equal under the law.

Inside, the police were growing anxious. A side door bucked and pounded, at times threatening to give way. An officer yelled, "Get away from there or I'll shoot!" Other officers trained their pistols on the pulsating doors and windows, proclaiming: "We'll shoot the first motherfucker that comes through the door!"

The crowd did not stop. A group of men used an uprooted parking meter as a battering ram to charge the bar's main entrance. Through splintered planks covering one of the windows, a hand reached in and poured lighter fluid on the floor, then ignited it with a flared match. Pine pointed his gun at the figure, but did not fire. A curtain of smoke rose in the room. Chants were ringing through the crowds:

"Liberate Christopher Street. Liberate Christopher Street."

Just then the scream of sirens announced the arrival of reinforcements. Instantly a line of officers in riot gear appeared, sweeping the angry throng across Sheridan Square and down Seventh Avenue, where they dispersed, and the evening's chaos came to an end.

The clash that came to be known as the birth of the gay rights movement, memorialized in books and movies, had lasted forty-five minutes. Though no articles made the next morning's papers, news of the brief and bracing contretemps traveled fast through the ghetto. By Saturday evening, a brimming river of gay New Yorkers flowed down toward Christopher Street, where the legends of the night before were being spun. It was hard to imagine what this transition foretold; surely no one predicted the type of integration that would come to the whole country by the century's end. But everybody in the streets then knew the Stonewall Riot marked the end of something awful and the beginning of something full of promise. For the rest of the weekend, Greenwich Village was like Oz on the afternoon Dorothy's house flattened the Wicked Witch of the East. Disbelief and wonderment caroled in the air. Celebrities of the underground culture arrived in droves to drink it in. The Beat poet Allen Ginsberg pushed his head inside the Stonewall and was stunned at what he saw.

"You know, the guys there were so beautiful," he said on the sidewalk outside. "They've lost that wounded look that fags all had ten years ago."

Winter 1969

ELLICOTTVILLE, NEW YORK — Father Neil Conway hung between sleep and waking, rocking restively in an ice-cold bed at the foot of the Holiday Valley Ski Resort, a day's drive east from Cleveland. Anxiety consumed him.

He was thirty now and well regarded back home as a charismatic, soulful, and intellectually expansive priest. A social activist priest, a priest *of the world,* his concerns were tangible, but his homilies were poems that moved ordinary parishioners to contemplate the heavens, the despairing to embrace hope. Women clamored to have him perform their marriage and baptize their children.

News of the birth of the gay rights movement had not reached him. It was safe to assume the news had not yet reached anyone in Cleveland, and perhaps no single member of the Roman Catholic clergy anywhere else in the country; these were men who viewed "copulation with an undue sex," to quote St. Thomas Aquinas, as purely abominable. Catholics weren't alone on this point. Leaders of every other major religion, and nearly all the minor ones, classified homosexuality as sinful or inappropriate or diseased or wrong. Anyway, what would Stonewall have mattered to a priest in the Bible-thumping Midwest? Conway didn't think of himself as gay. In fact that word "homosexual" had never traveled through his brain. It was not a word one *thought.*

As a seminarian, he was mostly able to keep his sex drive contained and detached. He knew his fellow students struggled, too. But their daily labor was different from his. They fought the sacramental temptations of marriage and family making. Conway fought disgrace. Obviously, he could not wed another man, even if he allowed himself such a thought, which he did not, for he knew it was an evil in the eyes of his church. Perhaps he suffered an affliction particular only to him. He did not even rightly know what that affliction was. He knew no gay person, man or woman. (Or so he believed. He would learn a favorite uncle was gay only years later, after old age claimed him and perplexed family members arrived in New York to empty his apartment. A brother would also come out.) Resisting homosexual love could not be made into a martyr's offering to God; in Catholicism it did not even exist.

There had been a moment on the eve of his ordination when this torment bent Conway away from grace. Two times in his senior year, only days apart, he had "incidents" with fellow seminarians, with whom in the throes of hormonal fevers he engaged in mutual masturbation. The weight of the sinfulness crushed him. He thought he was dying. He knew he was mandated for hell, not for the priesthood. It was official church law, promulgated by the Vatican's Sacred Congregation for Religious on February 2, 1961, that homosexuals were not to be ordained: "Advancement to religious vows and ordination should be barred to those who are afflicted with evil tendencies to homosexuality or pederasty, since for them the common life and the priestly ministry would constitute serious dangers."

When he had seen what he had done and that it was bad, Conway sought out a distant priest (this could not be discussed locally) to confess these "particular friendships," in the only language he knew. "I perpetrated one of them," he said, claiming moral responsibility, "and the other one perpetrated me." To his stunned relief, the priest absolved his sin, assuaged his guilt, and prodded him back to the straight and narrow.

Naturally, men slip and sin, as Neil Conway had. Sins against chastity, if they have been confessed and regretted, are forgiven—the principal of *absolution* has always been the basic tenet of Catholicism. Even men who murder can be returned to a state of grace and be raised to orders.

"This doesn't automatically ruin your chances in the priesthood," the unfamiliar priest told Conway. "Just take care it does not happen anymore."

For many years thereafter, his will and prayer would hold him fast, first as a parish priest and later as a rising star in the chancery, as aide to the bishop overseeing social justice programs for the diocese. He eliminated any conscious recognition of his splintering drives. He existed, or half existed, on a separate plane.

Much later, this would be diagnosed as "dissociative disorder." Doctors would tell him he failed to integrate his fundamental sexual drive into his personality, a growth phase attained by most people in adolescence.

That cold night at the Holiday Valley Ski Resort his foundation wall crumbled. As his eyes fluttered open in the darkness of the hotel room, he discovered—that's the way it seemed to him—he discovered his hand on the young man who had accompanied him on the ski weekend, a high school senior, and he could not, no matter how hard he prayed, remove that hand from the petrified boy's genitals.

Chapter 2

After the Summer of Love

Fall 1969

Salem, Massachusetts — Compared to many other priests ordained in 1960, Joseph Birmingham was a throwback to an earlier mold. He was not driven to the social justice work of Paul Shanley, or called to work with unruly children like Bernie Lane, or ambitious about leadership in his church, like John McCormack, one of his best friends from seminary and now his cocurate at St. James in Salem, who openly coveted a bishop's crosier. Birmingham's only aspiration was to be a good parish priest. But in his first assignment, at Our Lady of Fatima in Sudbury, he did not stand out in the minds of many, except in the abruptness of his departure. He arrived in Salem in 1964 and immediately fashioned his ministry around the parish teens.

More precisely, teen boys. He directed the altar boy program and set up a youth drop-in center in the church's basement. He also ran a self-styled afternoon chaplaincy, tooling around in his gold Plymouth Fury to collect boys and take them to ball games, movies, or the beach. Girls were never invited.

His temper was as legendary as his generosity. Not wanting to set him off, the boys always accepted his attentions. At first they felt charmed, even Bernie McDaid, who despite that weird vestry encounter carried on as an altar boy, while the assaults continued on a nearly weekly basis. He never said a word. In the neighborhood, he was thought to be one of Birmingham's favorites. In the spring and early summer of 1968, he was still climbing in the Plymouth Fury full of kids whenever the priest beckoned. He was perfectly powerless to stop. The outings were always the same. After a stop at the ice cream store, Birmingham would drop the kids off one at a time, selecting one to drop off last. That one would receive the business end of Birmingham's hands. Often, but not always, it was Bernie.

It slowly occurred to Bernie that he and Father B. were in some sense dating. Now he could see it. There were always supposed to be two altar boys serving the quarter-to-sevens, and every morning Birmingham made an excuse for why only Bernie was on hand. The other boy either had called in sick, or was called out of town, or had failed to show, Birmingham would explain—a prelude to priestly fumblings in the sacristy, or in the rectory bedroom next door, or the priest's private shower. Surely Birmingham was lying. Bernie began to call in sick himself. After a while, he got wise about the car rides, too, and at the very first stop he and all the boys would leap out of the door. As the summer progressed, they stopped getting in the car altogether. When the enormous gold vehicle turned the corner at Hathorne Street, the boys dove into hedges to hide. "Tell him we're not around," they would yell to neighborhood girls, like Donna Rediker, forcing her to lie to a priest.

Even as the boys huddled in fear of Birmingham, they never admitted to what had happened to them, what was continuing to happen over and over. Not even when Bernie McDaid's mother caught them evading the curate. "Get out there! It's a *priest,*" she hollered. "What are you *doing*?" Dutifully, Bernie pulled himself out of the bushes and slid into the front seat to endure his violations. He always wondered who else was aware of Birmingham's patterns. Once, sitting tensely in the Plymouth, he passed Father John McCormack studying them from an upper window. Surely McCormack knew, he thought, and that added to his shame.

When Father Birmingham blasted through the door to Sister Martha's eighth-grade classroom at St. James's School, all the children stood and sang in concert chorus: "Good morning, Father B.!" The way Birmingham loomed in that doorway, enormously tall, zestful, and handsome, sent electricity through the room. He wore distorting thick glasses that magnified his dark, puzzling eyes. His face was wide and engaging, his mouth always parted in a dreamy smile that put on display the gap between his two front teeth and amplified an approachable demeanor. He nodded a return greeting to the students.

Bernie McDaid was eighth-grade class president. He rose to his feet with the others. But his guts were in his throat. He kept his head down. "He run outta places to get us," he thought. He knew the routine. Everyone did. A student would be called away for pastoral counseling. "Please, God, please don't let him see me," he prayed. If Birmingham called one of the other boys, Bernie would be so relieved he would laugh sinisterly at the poor doomed kid. They all would, that's how widely held—though never shared—this secret was.

Through his dread, he barely heard the priest call his name. Bernie did not respond. He let the words to a song written by Bobby Abraham, a classmate, blare in his head, a song they sang out loud at recesses, in the cafeteria, to and from school, the unofficial school anthem.

> Father B.
>   Is a queer.
> This is
>   What I hear.
> Uh-huh, uh-huh,
>   Dada doo duh-dah.

Sister Martha, whose face was stretched in frustration, was calling him. *Did you hear Father? Go!*

Bernie moved woozily from behind his desk. He thought about fleeing, though he knew he would not. He was thirteen now, a very young man, still too young to disobey a priest's order. He was snagged by Father Birmingham's glowering eyes. The priest had crossed to a doorway in the back of the room. Guidance conferences were held in the cloakroom, an airless interior passage between the two seventh-grade classes on one side of the building, and the two eighth-grade classes on the other. Coats and lunch boxes lined the tight perimeter, and in the middle sat two small chairs for private meetings, usually with Birmingham, presumably on matters of encouragement or discipline.

Crossing the classroom in grudging discontent, Bernie sensed the anxious eyes of his peers following him. What consumed the girls was jealousy. Father B. never once called a girl to a guidance conference. They were numbed by the mystery of the summons. What occupied the boys was knowledge. Some of the boys sniggered and sneered at Bernie's peril. Others grew ill.

When Bernie finally reached the doorway and disappeared inside, Birmingham turned over the sign on the door to read "Private," and closed it behind them.

"Sit," he said, turning to the boy. "I want to talk to you today."

Birmingham always wore black suits for church business, but on the days when he crossed the parking lot to visit the parochial school he donned a long black robe, fastened closed with a score of buttons. It lent a flare of academe to his arrival. Bernie McDaid could see his hands scratching inside the robe's deep pockets.

He sat down.

"Now, son," Birmingham said, eyes narrow, "how many times did you masturbate this week?"

Bernie wanted to lie. The desire was almost cellular. To save himself, he needed to lie. But he believed in hell, he believed in shame. There wasn't one time when Birmingham touched Bernie that he hadn't objected in every twist of his heart. This was not a question of a boy taking a man's pleasure. It was never sex. Bernie McDaid stayed put because he didn't know how to run away from a priest. Of all the dozens of times, though, he never felt more trapped than in this room. On the other side of that unlocked door was his entire human universe, whose eyes would inspect him for corruption, whose ears were bent for his moans.

Bernie couldn't lie. He thought about not answering in any way, defiance by inaction. But he saw only one option. He told the truth about his acts of self-pleasure.

"How much did you ejaculate?"

He told.

"What were you thinking about? What was going through your mind?"

A bizarre interrogation commenced, as always, and the questions merged with demands, which became declarations whispered in his hot ears when Birmingham pinned him against the wall of coats and rummaged around in his underpants.

"You like this." He gripped Bernie's wrist and bent it toward him, forcing the teen to touch him back.

"I like girls."

"One day you will like this."

So he let Birmingham knock him against the row of coats, all the while Bobby Abraham's childish lyric filling his angry ears.

Every night
   at ten
He blows us
   again!
Uh-huh, uh-huh,
   Dada doo duh-dah.

Child abuse and the sexual exploitation of minors was not the exclusive domain of the Catholic priesthood. Such crimes plagued American childhoods. Surveys showed that 22 percent of the nation's adults—44 million people—had been subjected to unwanted sexual touching before they reached eighteen. Girls are three times more likely to be sexually molested than boys, mostly by men they know intimately: father or stepfather, uncle or brother. Many fewer men report a history of molestation, and as they enter puberty, the likelihood of being sexually manhandled by an adult diminishes.

But in the realm of the Catholic Church, sexual violations seemed to take a different course. According to estimates, 80 to 90 percent of the alleged abuse by priests targeted teen boys. This was not only a dark trend of modern life. As far back as the second century, long before there were words to describe the specifics of homosexuality or child abuse, Catholic Church leaders had sensed this was a problem perhaps unique among them. According to an extensive study of the literature by Father Thomas Doyle, penalties for *sodomia* first appeared in official literature as early as 177 A.D., when a Bishop Athenagoras declared abusive priests to be foes of Christianity and excommunicated them. Historians have interpreted this as a reference to clergy who molested boys and young men. If such abuse of power had not been commonplace, no one would have thought to legislate against it.

Over the years, in its wisdom the church increased the penalties, with each new amendment suggesting an upswing in sexual behavior against minors. In 1179, for example, offending clerics were sentenced to a monastic life; in the mid–sixteenth century, Pope Pius V, writing under the heading *Horrendum,* condemned offending priests to the total loss of "offices, benefices, privileges" and dispatched them to the secular courts for punishments, which at the time ranged from fines to castration and death.

The modern church had also been moved several times to condemn clergymen who defile minors, whether male or female. The Code of Canon Law, first promulgated in 1917 and revised in 1983, condemns priests who exploit minors (canon 1395), who abuse their power (canon 1389), and who solicit sexual favors while hearing confession (canon 1387). Official penalties remained stiff. A curial document called "Instruction on the Manner of Proceeding in Cases of Solicitation," published in 1962 and sent secretly to the world's bishops, gave lengthy directions for trying an accused priest and spelled out punishments ranging from suspension of duties to excommunication and defrocking (officially called "laicization," or "reduction to the status of a layman").

Rome was totally unprepared for the generation of clerics who entered seminary in the buttoned-up 1950s and reemerged in the 1960s to find a transformed America. Bishops across the country began noticing a massive upsurge in reports of their sexual inappropriateness. They blamed the influence of rock 'n' roll, flower power, and the sexual permissiveness in secular life. They saw their errant priests as victims of a tempting society, men who succumbed to moral failure, to sin, not crime or psychiatric disorder. More prayer is what they believed would solve the problem.

At this particular time, psychology was not promoting effective solutions either. The discipline had theories for treating pedophilia—defined as a sustained sexual attraction for preadolescent children—with everything from psychotherapy to castration. But grown men who fixated pathologically on having sex with teenagers (as opposed to those who simply found them alluring, a much larger category) represented an uncharted population. This was precisely where most priest predators fell. The typical target of a priest's sexual interest was fifteen or sixteen, according to the historian Philip Jenkins, while in the general population the average age of child abuse victims is substantially younger—seven to ten, according to David Finkelhor, director of the Crimes Against Children Research Center at the University of New Hampshire.

Such priests later would be called ephebophiles, after the Greek word *ephēbos,* which described a youth in early manhood, when he trained in gymnastics and the military arts, usually naked, in preparation for full citizenship. Ephebophiles appeared to be gender-specific. Men like Humbert Humbert, driven to madness by his obsession with the golden-haired teen Lolita, would not be tempted by a boy, just as Birmingham—like Conway and the others—were attracted solely by males in adolescence.

Homosexual ephebophilia was a growing issue in the priesthood. But why? Again, psychology was at a loss. Homosexuals generally were no more likely than heterosexuals to molest minors, experts agreed. Rather, all available data showed that the percentage of child abusers who are openly gay was considerably less than expected, approaching zero. From every study of homosexual men since the 1950s, it was agreed that homosexuals were psychologically indistinct from heterosexuals. Yet these studies all involved men (and women) who had traveled the long road to self-identify as gay. There had never been an effort to study the consequences of a life lived in the closet. What did it do to a man's mind to turn it against itself in lockstep authority with every last institution in the civil and ecclesiastical worlds? To convince him that he could not hope for physical love or companionship, which even birds and fish enjoyed? That his primal instincts were unspeakably rotten?

Even stranger, what did it do not only to condemn him to a lifetime of self-disavowal, but to put him in a job that obliged him to condemn others just like himself? For what other choice did he have but the priesthood? It alone allowed him to remain unmarried, without courting suspicion or feeling forced to leave town. It turned his debility into empowerment. Overnight he went from hated minority to beloved community leader.

In addition, it put him closer to the God, whose elusive forgiveness and forbearance, whose love, he craved perhaps above all else.

November 1969
SALEM, MASSACHUSETTS — "I'm sick of Birmingham," Bernie McDaid spat.

He had called together his council: Bobby Abraham and two other boys stood with him on his family's small front lawn under a late-afternoon sun. Though his grades were adequate and he got into trouble no more than the other students, Abraham had been ejected from St. James's Parish School. The group had no doubt about why. Father Birmingham had heard about his little ditty from a nun, who overheard the boys singing it to the tune of "Louie, Louie." Birmingham confronted Bobby. He demanded to know the name of the author, and in a moment of sheer but fleeting bravado, the thirteen-year-old took the credit.

"What would *you* call what you do to us?" Bobby seethed.

No one had ever confronted Birmingham before. Outraged, he demanded an apology, which, in total capitulation, Bobby offered, asking God's forgiveness for "imagining such things," he later told his friends.

Was it coincidence that Birmingham threw him out of school a few weeks later?

"Pure retaliation," Bernie said. He took a chance and spoke more directly than he ever had before about the torment they were all experiencing. "He run outta places to get us—the church, his car, now *school*," he said. "We gotta tell somebody what this pervert is up to."

"Tell who?" one of the others wondered. Accusing a priest was tempting the fates. Few parents could be counted on to believe them.

"It's your word against a priest."

"Maybe your dad, Bernie."

William McDaid was—unlike a lot of the other Irish immigrants in Salem—almost moderate in his churchiness. Bernie thought it might work.

"Maybe," he said, "if we all go in together."

"Strength in numbers."

"We stick together."

"Okay," Bernie said.

They turned and marched inside, where William McDaid sat in an armchair, attentively.

Delicately and indirectly, but leaving no room for misunderstanding, Bernie made it plain to his father what Joseph Birmingham was up to. As he spoke, his father sat mutely, and when he was done explaining, William McDaid looked into each boy's eyes. Still he would not speak. The silence had the boys on edge. They did not know whether to expect an explosion of anger or tears of despair.

A week or so later, McDaid put his son in the car. They drove to Danvers and parked outside a white building alongside the stately St. Mary of the Annunciation Parish church. Father Patrick Kelly, the pastor there, was a regional personnel manager for priests in the northernmost reaches of the archdiocese.

When William McDaid returned to the car, he was flushed and businesslike. "Don't worry, son," he said. "It's taken care of. He's going to be leaving soon. He's going to be getting help."

It was the first indication Bernie had that his father had believed them. Every morning thereafter, from Thanksgiving to Christmas, Bernie and his pals went to school expecting to find the priest had been removed. But every day he was still there, eerily clueless to his unmasking. Bernie wondered, *Who could be protecting Father B.?*

January 12, 1970
SALEM, MASSACHUSETTS — Even when life was progressing expectedly, Bernie McDaid's mother, Anne, was a nervous and shy woman.

But in the two months since her husband took on Father Birmingham, she had been wracked by terrors. Her God was a vengeful god, her church was a reign of potentates. What fate awaited the ordinary immigrant who had the nerve to challenge a priest? She took the fact that Birmingham had not been punished as convincing evidence that going against him was a huge mistake. Every morning that he returned to celebrate Mass plunged her deeper into a chasm of doubt. Though she had done nothing, she felt guilty, as though she and her family should slink from the church and rid it of the shame they represented.

Bernie's own tailspin came on suddenly. He went from being named class president in the fall to becoming a total reprobate by winter. His grades collapsed. He had become a chronic truant. He stopped cutting his hair. At home he was incorrigible and frequently inebriated. Worse than that was his caustic rejection of the Catholic Church in general. In the garbage one afternoon his mother found his acceptance letters from St. John's Prep, Bishop Fenwick, and St. Mary's in Linden—three of the most rigorous schools in the Catholic system. They even had offered scholarships, yet he ripped them up and announced he was going to attend public high school.

Timid as she was, Anne decided she could no longer sit idly by. With a girlfriend at her side for support, she walked the few blocks to St. James's School to see Sister Grace, the principal. Maybe a woman, even a celibate one, would recognize the harm done to a child and help speed along the priest's removal.

It was a wise move. It turned out Sister Grace had not been informed about the allegation lodged against Father Birmingham. She was outraged that nobody had informed her. She swore to have him out of the school, even if it meant removing him herself.

January 17, 1970
BRIGHTON, MASSACHUSETTS — As head of the archdiocesan personnel office, Father John J. Jennings managed the whereabouts of the 2,258 priests (and indirectly, the 5,718 nuns) serving the vast Boston archdiocese. This was no easy business. His spiritual territory spread

over 2,465 square miles and included 360 churches and 150 schools, in addition to 28 hospitals and nursing homes. To ease his immense burden, he employed a network of regional deputies assigned to satellite offices—the archdiocese was divided into "deaconates," each with a mini chancery; those were divided up into "vicariates," and so on. He and his regional deputies were part matchmaker between priest and parish, part coach, and part bartender, hearing out priests' career complaints, their idle gossip, their pastoral boasts and disappointments.

Too often, he also heard directly from the parishioners. This was a difficult aspect of the job. You wanted the people in the pews to respect and love their priests. It was their obligation to obey them. The sheep had no say over who was appointed their shepherd. That authority belonged exclusively to the cardinal. Jennings's job, when complaints came in about this or that priest, was to remind the parishioner of this hierarchy as firmly as needed: if you love the church, you will love the priest.

He did not, therefore, relish hearing that a parishioner in Salem was fomenting a kind of corporate discord, which is exactly the news that his morning mail seemed to bring—in the form of a letter from Father Patrick Kelly, his deputy in the northern region.

REGISTERED MAIL—SPECIAL DELIVERY
PERSONAL
Archdiocesan Personnel Office
Chancery Building
2121 Commonwealth Avenue
Brighton, Mass. 02135
   Attn: Rev. John J. [Jennings]

Dear Father:

I write you concerning a Brother Priest, about whom I had phoned you for advice on two occasions (around last Thanksgiving and again, on last Tuesday morning). You recall that our telephone conversation did not identify the Priest.

The problem presented was one of a "rumor of possible homosexuality"—and the rumor concerns Father Joseph E. Birmingham (class of 1960), presently stationed at St. James' Parish in Salem. The reason why I bring this name to your attention now will become apparent as I spell out my knowledge of the case, and the action I have taken regarding it.

The rumor first came to my attention around Thanksgiving time by way of a St. James' parishioner. This man indicated that the rumor was knowledgeable among the youngsters (boys and girls) at St. James' School, and among some of the parents. He also indicated that the problem surfaced about two years ago—but subsided shortly thereafter.

Having heard this, I phoned you to find out if the Personnel Office had any definite mode of action in such cases. We deliberately refrained from identification of the priest involved. Following our conversation, I visited Father Birmingham in his Rectory, indicated the existence of this rumor, and pointed out the following: He would either have to trace the rumor out and put an end to it—or, in the event that the rumor had any foundation in fact, he should consult with a psychiatrist. I offered my own service in making contact with a psychiatrist for him, should he feel that this would make things easier for him. As I expected, he denied any foundation in fact, and assured me that he would study the matter thoroughly.

Last Monday night (12 January), Sister Superior of St. James' School phoned me. She had been visited by my informant's wife and one/or several other wives. (It was from the informant's wife that she learned that the subject was discussed with me some 5 or 6 weeks previously.) Sister was deeply troubled, felt that she had an obligation to act, and didn't quite know where to turn. I scheduled a meeting at her convent on Tuesday morning, and discussed the matter with her and another Sister for about an hour and a half. Her "research" seems to point out that the rumor is founded on facts—and that these facts have occurred even since I spoke to Father Birmingham at Thanksgiving time—indeed, as recent as within the past two weeks. I suggested that, on behalf of the Sister, and in view of the fact that I had been earlier approached on the subject, I would discuss the matter with the Pastor of St. James' Parish.

It was at this time that I made my second phone call to you, and pointed out my intended visit to the Pastor. Again, no names were mentioned. In our conversation it came out that, since you are presently working on a list of proposed transfers to become effective within the next few weeks, it would be also possible to transfer the priest in question—as a normal routine matter—if his name were presented to you. I felt that such presentation should come from the Pastor, rather than from me.

My visit to the Pastor took place Tuesday afternoon. I told him what I have just spelled out above. The Pastor indicated that he would send a letter immediately to the Personnel Office, requesting a transfer of Father Birmingham—feeling that, as I do, Father's effectiveness in the Parish would decline in proportion as the rumor may spread. All the more reason for a transfer if the rumor proved true in fact.

And so, the matter stands. No doubt the Pastor's letter has already reached your Office. For this reason, I mention the name of the subject-priest—so that you can identify my phone calls with the Pastor's letter. It will also give you an up-to-date survey of what I have tried to do in this case. I feel that I am not betraying Father Birmingham since I had confronted him first with the situation— and now that several weeks have passed, the situation does not appear controlled. . . .

Respectfully,
(Rev. Patrick J. Kelly)
(Annunciation Rectory, Danvers, Mass.)

It was interesting that Kelly had chosen the phrase "rumor of possible homosexuality" when what indeed was being rumored—not just rumored, but formally alleged by various parishioners over several years—was a pattern of sexual assaults by a church leader and school official against his objecting students, a grave breach of professional conduct and a crime. In Massachusetts law, the sentence for "unnatural acts" with a consenting minor under age sixteen was five years to life. (Noncoerced sex with underage males was not criminalized until 1974, when statutory rape laws were amended from "intercourse with a female" minor to "intercourse with a child.") But alerting the police was never contemplated.

It was not the first official complaint to the chancery about Joseph Birmingham. Before becoming parochial vicar in Salem, Birmingham had spent four years at Our Lady of Fatima in Sudbury, an assignment that came to an end when Howard McCabe and Frank Taylor, two active parish members, brought their sons to the Brighton chancery and coaxed matter-of-fact testimony out of them in the vast formal conference room. It was a scene guaranteed to intimidate: Jennings was there, as was then-chancellor Monsignor Francis Sexton, the chief financial officer for the archdiocese, along with a number of other officials. Father Birmingham himself was seated at the long stretch of table.

Michael McCabe, who had a thirteen-year-old's cocky confidence, was not easily intimidated. He spoke plainly. "He'd come up behind you, rub your shoulders, make you calm, and then slip his hand beneath your underwear," he told the men. "It didn't seem wrong, and that's what's so weird about it."

Birmingham specifically denied the boy's account. Being careful not to call him a liar, he suggested the child was mistaken.

"It was a spontaneous gesture of grabbing him around the waist," he offered.

Monsignor Sexton turned to the boy. "Were the father's hands inside your pants, or around your waist, son?"

"Inside my pants," Michael said. "Inside my underwear!"

All eyes returned to Birmingham. He shrugged.

"I don't remember, honest to God," he said.

Without pronouncing a formal ruling of guilt or innocence, Sexton accepted the two boys' appraisal of events. He told the parents that Birmingham would be transferred to the care of a competent Catholic psychiatrist, and kept away from boys.

What really happened was a different story. Birmingham was thrown a farewell party in Sudbury, attended by the mothers of scores of boys he had trapped in sexual situations over the years. They made their kids go, too. Tom Blanchette was there. He never once told about the hundred times he had been summoned into Birmingham's bed, sometimes two or three times in a single afternoon. Unbeknownst to him, his four brothers had identical experiences. In the years to come Blanchette would realize that literally every teenage boy around his age had been ensnared by the priest, and perhaps two hundred succumbed to him in Sudbury. Except for the McCabe and Taylor boys, none spoke up.

After the send-off, Birmingham had bypassed therapy and gone directly to Salem. At the chancery, everybody seemed to believe that a change of venue had fixed everything. It occurred to no one to tend to the McCabe and Taylor boys, or to see if there were others. Nobody suggested warning the new parents in Salem, whose sons began falling prey immediately.

Now Jennings was looking at a request to transfer Birmingham one more time. History had shown that transferring him did not chasten him. It didn't address his psychology or behavior. It didn't train him to see the emotional damage done by initiating unwilling young men in sex, or the psychological damage caused by forcing on them an activity entailing damnation, or the damage done to their faith. It didn't address the legal aspects in Massachusetts at the time.

Jennings had a parochial vicar position open at St. Michael's in Lowell. Without agony or rancor, he moved Birmingham there. On the regular Sunday in February when announcements for priest reassignments were routinely made each year, Father B. would tell his parishioners he was leaving St. James. It was to appear as ordinary as a promotion, with one exception. Birmingham would not say exactly where he was going. When pressed, he might intimate his new parish was north of Route 128, the state highway that roughly forms a beltway around Boston, but nothing more.

As he was the last time, he would be treated to a soldier's send-off, with coffee, cake, and tears. "The best priest St. James has ever had is leaving," one of the church stalwarts, Mary Elaine McGee, would tell him there. "I mean it."

Mid-January 1970
BOSTON, MASSACHUSETTS — *No work of God is done after nine.* Paul Shanley remembered the aphorism they were all taught in seminary and thought, *That was another time.* In a world at war, in a country

split violently along ethical and ideological lines, in a city rocked by student unrest and youth disaffection, being a priest meant being constantly vigilant, on hand to catch a soul when it tumbled, even when it was tremendously cold outside, even now, when it was 3 A.M. Wearing his trademark jeans and a heavy parka—bare-necked, no hint of his station—Shanley slouched against a window in the Combat Zone and studied the mingling assemblage of freaks, castoffs, runaways, soldiers, druggies, prostitutes, hustlers, and refusniks, the assorted denizens of the night. His long dark hair fell on his shoulders. A forgotten cigarette smoked between his fingers.

The Combat Zone was Boston's white-hot center of venery, the collection of cross streets near Chinatown where thirty peep show marquees, crackling and buzzing like smoldering trash cans, called the youngsters to gather. They shouted out to Shanley, slapped his hand, took the money he folded in their pockets. He would say, "Your mother is worried, call your mother," or, "Don't do anything you don't want to do."

Tonight it was quiet. He circled through the lobbies of the Greyhound and Trailways terminals, then on to one of the two areas known as meat racks—flesh peddling never slowed for cold snaps. The girls and boys were starting young, marketing their bodies when they were not yet old enough legally to drink. Shanley did not scold them or preach to them. That was not how he defined his ministry. He tried to get kids to be safer about doing whatever it was they were going to do anyway. For instance, he made it his business to help them get tested and treated for syphilis and the clap, letting them use his name at the public clinic if necessary to protect their anonymity. He never told gay kids—the streets were suddenly crawling with them—to go back home. Instead, he listened sympathetically as they unloaded woeful stories of family explosions that ended in their rejection. Pregnant girls would present themselves to him for help and counsel. He knew the girls' menses—that was the level of his integration in the Combat Zone.

He helped these kids find shelters, and tended to their spiritual well-being, reminding them about God and decency. Mostly he showed them total acceptance, something they no longer expected from a figure representing an establishment they felt was out of step. He brought Mass right into their crash pads (he had to laugh when the bishops issued a rule that Mass could not be celebrated on a tabletop that had been used for food preparation—"Jesus of Nazareth would have been unable to have the Last Supper under that restriction!" he thought) and tried to keep them from danger betweentimes.

After stopping in the all-night Waldorf diner on the edge of the Public Garden, Shanley paused on the sidewalk outside to appraise the world around him. Oliver Wendell Holmes called Boston "the thinking center of the continent," but in the dead of night in the inner city it was more of a *feeling* center, a pulsing commotion of humanity—a discordant, antiestablishment mass that Fidel Castro called the "guerrillas in the field of culture." Ever since fall, when news broke of the My Lai massacre, the sentiment against the government had never been more raw among the 250,000 students scattered over sixty local colleges and universities. They staged strikes and sit-ins, shut down campuses, and moved out into the streets. Caught up in the spirit of resistance, all sorts of kids flocked to Boston. This year, the city would play temporary home to tens of thousands of dislodged kids under seventeen who rejected all convention and ruled the night.

Anticipating the influx, Cardinal Cushing appointed Shanley to a half-time "ministry to alienated youth," the first and only priest in the nation to have such a job. On their behalf, he was a vaunted crusader for leniency from the police, understanding from parents, and acceptance from society. Paul Shanley was a new breed of priest, as handsome and uncompromising a crusader as you'd find in any movie.

He had a way of identifying with the runaways, throwaways, and freaks. He hated "adult" culture as much as they did—the racism and hawkishness of the establishment. Even his own leaders rankled him, in small and large ways. Authority, he felt, was an elemental evil. He and the young people had this belief in common. He hoped they were building toward a better society.

Nothing seemed to shock him, least of all drugs, which they used with impunity. Marijuana arrests were up tenfold since 1965 and heroin use had increased 45 percent in the past year alone—Boston had the highest rate of drug penetration in the nation. He taught himself the geography of the shooting galleries so he could find his way to overdose victims. Some he cajoled into rehab, when the spaces came open. He knew discreet doctors who could treat a bad trip. If a youngster didn't know how to handle her hypodermic needles, he would even show her the way.

And sex—Shanley was an unabashed prosex priest. He encouraged it for recreation, endorsed it premaritally, accepted those who commodified it, and disagreed with most ordinary restrictions—including monogamy, which he believed was unnatural, and his own sworn celibacy, which he simply disregarded. Through these years, he continued seeing numerous other men whom he had met first as a counselor, especially Arthur Austin, with whom his liaisons stretched over six years.

Most of this was unknown to Cardinal Cushing, or if it was, he left no evidence to attest to it. But being a pacifist himself—not to mention an avuncular social drinker, outgoing, and a self-assured fixture in the larger fabric of Boston life, according to the historian Thomas H. O' Connor—he saw the modern church could no longer exist in a nonsecular ghetto. The cardinal took to heart the words of John XXIII, who said the church must go to where the people are. Increasingly, that was not in the pews.

Out here, Shanley thought, in a nation at war, embracing free love was the least offensive thing a Catholic could do.

March 1970, Holy Week
SALEM, MASSACHUSETTS — It was after eleven at night when Mary Elaine McGee, known by her middle name, awoke to the clatter of somebody leaning on her doorbell. Apprehensively, she slipped out of bed to discover her sister pounding distressfully on the door.

"Winnie, what is it? What's wrong?"

"I was just at Anne McDaid's house," Winnie said tightly. "She called me because Bernie was acting out again and she was scared. Wanted me to talk to him—her husband wasn't home. Something happened to him, Elaine. *With Father B.* Mary told me. That's why he left St. James."

Elaine's heart raced. She had known Birmingham nearly all her life. They were in the same class at St. Mary's High School. She thought she'd never met a more pious man. She never had a misgiving about sending her boy Matthew off with him to go bowling or play tennis.

"Bernie was drunk. Elaine, he's just thirteen years old and tied in knots. I said, 'Bernie, what's got into you?' And you know what he said? He said, 'Go ask Matthew.' He said, 'Go ask Matthew. Matthew knows.' "

As though she'd heard a gunshot, Elaine bolted into her son's bedroom. Snagged out of bed, he stood up confused and groggy, facing his mother. He looked so small to her, just twelve years old, so impressionable.

"Do you have something to tell me about Father B.?" she asked.

"Oh, Mama," he exploded. "I'm so glad you know!"

Elaine did not sleep that night, so sick was she with grief and anger, which through some alchemy felt almost exactly like fear. She thought about her father. She could tell her mother about this, but she could never tell her father. It would push him off the deep end, she thought, and who knew what he might do then? He might kill Birmingham in rage.

Or maybe he wouldn't. Maybe he wouldn't believe her at all. More likely he would say to her, "You watch your mouth about the church," unable to hear the truth. She would not tell him.

In the morning, Elaine drove shakily to St. James School, determined to tell the sister superior. Sister Grace had only to glimpse Elaine to know what had happened.

"Oh, my God," she said, "don't tell me he come to Matthew, too."

"I thought I was bringing you news you didn't know."

"I went down to Boston the minute I learned. I said, 'As long as I am superior of the school, that man would not be around any children here again.' "

Elaine's legs started to shake uncontrollably. She felt herself going to pieces. How many children had he bothered? she wondered. Sister Grace did not know exactly. Quite a few, she suspected.

"Lucky I didn't know this on that Sunday he left," Elaine said. "I'd have killed him."

Her thoughts careened to Birmingham's new parishioners, the mothers of sons somewhere north of Route 128. She could not bear the idea that they might one day feel as bad as she did now. Were they informed? she wondered.

They were not, said Sister Grace bitterly. When she heard about the transfer she had objected intensely, but Monsignor Jennings told her it was none of her business, she said. "He called me a 'meddling female.' "

Elaine was disgusted. If the welfare of children was not the business of a school principal, whose business was it? "I'm going down there," she heard herself declare.

April 3, 1970
It took Elaine McGee more than a week to get everything in motion. She resolved not to travel to the chancery alone, reasoning that if someone as fearsome as the sister superior was patronizingly dismissed there, she would need an army at her side. The day after Easter, she called a meeting at her house, attended by a dozen fathers and mothers. They agreed that Birmingham could not simply be set loose on another parish. If somebody mentioned the possibility of going to the police, it was not done in seriousness. Everyone knew the policemen were all Irish. They would never go against the chancery. Besides, they agreed, the church will come around and do the right thing.

Five mothers were nominated to represent St. James Parish. Elaine McGee, the most voluble among them, was tapped to head the group. Anne McDaid and Winnie Morton were to be delegates. So would Judy Fairbanks, who lived across the street from the McGees and had two young daughters at St. James grammar school. The last member of the entourage was the mother of another boy molested by Birmingham.

That Friday, April 3, they drove their station wagons to Brighton for a chancery meeting with Monsignor Jennings. They had made certain to let everybody know they were not coming in anonymously or timidly but as a formal delegation from their community. At the reception desk they each signed in, using their names, their parishes, their husbands' names, and their husbands' places of work. This last entry was Elaine's idea. Because her husband was a public school teacher, a profession also responsible for the safety of kids, she felt this gave her additional credibility.

Awaiting their meeting in the reception area, Elaine took note of the tarnished and shabby furnishings. *No wonder they're always begging for money for the bishop's appeal,* she thought. *They need some new furniture in here!* But when a nun ushered the ladies into the building's inner sanctum, it was a different scene entirely: Lavishly polished mahogany panels lined the walls. Light glinted off the rich patina on antique furniture and the gilded picture frames that lined the main hallway. Never in her life had Elaine seen such spectacular, intimidating opulence.

Monsignor Jennings motioned for the women to sit on chairs arrayed before his expansive desk on a hand-tied Tibetan carpet. Elaine gestured to have her sister tuck in on her left and Judy Fairbanks on her right. "Make sure I don't lose control," she said under her breath, "because if I lose control we'll screw the whole thing up."

After introductions, she got right to the point. "Our main concern is, number one, we want Father B. to have psychiatric help."

Jennings held up a hand. "We wouldn't agree to something like that," he said.

"We want his new pastor to be notified that this problem exists. That way he can keep an eye on him."

"We wouldn't agree." He scowled.

"Three, not to have any contact with young children. If he has to be around them, put him in with the high school kids, and they'll probably knock his block off if he tries something funny."

Jennings shook his head as though to say the entire matter was out of everybody's hands.

"Why can't you have psychiatric treatment for him?" one of the women interrupted.

In its wisdom, the church had done what would be done. "It's not in the cards," he said.

The women pressed their agenda, futilely visiting and revisiting the group's three goals. Ultimately Jennings signaled the end of his patience. "Ladies," he exploded. He raised a scolding finger at Elaine. "You must be very careful of slander."

Elaine climbed to her feet, tugging against her sister's efforts to restrain her, insane with anger. If the desk had been any narrower, she knew she would have slapped the monsignor's face. In her mind, his collar had disappeared and he was no more noble than any common man. She raised her own finger back at him.

"Jesus, Mary, and Joseph," she said, "where do you think my husband would be if he pulled this shit? If he pulled this shit he'd be in jail. He'd never be able to have another teaching job in his life. Furthermore, if this archdiocese doesn't have enough money to send Father B. for psychiatric care, I don't know what religion is if it doesn't even take care of its own. And if you can't afford it, I suggest you people hock this Oriental rug!"

She kicked at the rug with the toe of her shoe, then turned and stormed out of the room. With the ladies in tow, she headed directly over to see Father McCormack at the local office of Catholic Charities, where he had recently been named area director. She knew McCormack well from his time at St. James. If anybody would move decisively to protect the children, she knew, it would be John McCormack. His new office was just two blocks from her house.

Telling him about Father Birmingham, she had a feeling that he already knew about the priest's predilections. Though he professed surprise, there was something in his eye, a deadness, that betrayed knowledge, she felt sure. What did he do? He put his hands on her forehead and he blessed her.

"That's it?" she said. "A blessing? That's all you can do about this? A *blessing*?"

She didn't know where to turn next, or how to free herself from her own escalating horror, which played havoc on her blood pressure and invaded her dreams. She begged her doctor for something to induce sleep. "It hit me," she said. "It hit me like a ton of bricks. And you know who I blame? Joe Birmingham is a sick man. Jesus, Mary, and Joseph— I blame McCormack, I blame Jennings. Those two. I blame those two."

She would never set foot back inside a Catholic church. She would even withdraw her son from St. John's Preparatory, where he was expected to begin his freshman year in the fall. "I don't know if you're harboring the same type of men at your place or not, but I can't take that chance," she explained. The administration refused to refund her $500, and that became the last penny the Catholic Church ever got from her or her family.

Even so, it did nothing to assuage her guilt and bitter self-recrimination. Over the following year, she was back and forth to her doctor for high blood pressure and anxiety. She wasn't sleeping. Her doctor said he had never seen such profound stress in such a young woman. Before the year was through, she would suffer a massive stroke that would freeze the right side of her body and close one of her eyes. She was thirty-seven years old.

August 1970
Roxbury, Massachusetts — This was what it was like to run a parish in the ghetto, Father Spags thought. You have a rambling church that sat nearly empty, save for a few old doting Irish ladies, while your parochial school teemed with non-Catholics, every one of them black, all refugees from the worthless and perilous public school system, seeking help at the hands of nuns, all white. Just when everybody seemed to be getting used to the arrangement, the city redevelopment authority came along and claimed your buildings for some ostensibly noble public purpose (something called the Campus High School Project, but it would probably turn out to be a boondoggle), forcing you into a scattered diaspora. Services at the old Ruggles Street Baptist Church. Classes at the former Cabot Street Nursing Home, discomfiting to your students, let alone your faculty of nuns. Now came word the Boston Redevelopment Project was about to demolish the old nursing home.

"Talk about friggin' Job," Spags said.

Cardinal Cushing, like Spags, believed that education of the poor was a valid mission of the American church, perhaps its only valid mission today. He gave his word that St. Francis de Sales would rebuild the grammar school on an empty parcel the church owned nearby. The archdiocese could scarcely afford it. But this was Cushing's way—he was one of a generation of church leaders (including Francis Spellman in New York and John O'Hara in Philadelphia) committed to building vast social service empires. But Cushing fell ill in the summer months and was forced to step aside for medical reasons in September 1970. Bishop Humberto Medeiros, selected by the pope to assume command of the Boston see, was Cushing's opposite, an intensely self-controlled man with little of his predecessor's warmth or charisma. Complicating matters was the fact that he was also not from Boston, and not even from Ireland, which would have been even better—but hailed from *Portugal*, by way of the backwater diocese of Brownsville, Texas, both as far away from Irish Boston as you could get.

Many rude awakenings would follow his ascension. But Medeiros's first came when he saw how badly off financially the archdiocese was. Cushing's profligacy was legendary; tightfistedness became Medeiros's distinction. His priests chafed loudly—Medeiros had the temerity to end the practice of allowing pastors to keep their big holiday collection-plate offerings. This money, he ruled, belonged to the archdiocese (he committed it to retirement facilities for clergy members). In addition, he levied a new yearly tax on parish collection receipts, called the Archbishop's Stewardship Appeal. It was all part of his centralizing management plan, which was not unlike others exercised by bishops around the globe. He would organize the archdiocese into forty separate agencies, all of which reported directly to him as corporation sole, the single shareholder in an enormous enterprise that, had it been private, would have been ranked among the Fortune 500.

Medeiros cancelled or postponed building programs across the city, including the St. Francis de Sales School in Roxbury, which lacked only a signature on a construction contract. Through chancery channels, Spags pressed for an immediate groundbreaking. If the snow fell without a foundation in place, that meant the new school would not be completed before the old one was razed, and where would that leave his 173 students?

Reflexively—Spags was not a man to think before talking—he declared he would not eat until the paperwork was signed. "You have to go on the offensive," Spags told friends. "You learn that quickly when you live in a black community." He added: "And I'll camp on the lawn of the cardinal's residence until His Eminence changes his mind!"

Being a priest of his word, even if that word spilled out in fury, Spags set up a pup tent on the sloping green lawns outside the enormous three-story stone Italianate mansion on Commonwealth Avenue in Brighton where Medeiros now lived with his staff of nuns and priests in attendance. Emboldened by Spags's animated convictions, Roxbury moms made his one-man protest into an event, taking the Green Line to the end of the rail to stand vigil with him, singing hymns and reading scripture into the night. As the days stretched to weeks, they allowed their children to camp out with Father Spags in his tent. Their vigil even made the local papers, accompanying an incongruous quarter-page photograph of Spags—chubby and pale in heavy black glasses, a patchy mustache, and a thin shawl of hair wrapping around the back of his head—wedged into his tent next to two grinning teenagers in Afros.

Watching the bivouac's population accumulate on his lawn, the cardinal felt powerless and angry. Even if he could spare the money, the mechanics and logistics of the deal seemed to overwhelm him. "As far as I'm concerned, I wish the school was built already," he mumbled one afternoon, standing at his window. "If I have to go out and sell pencils . . ."

When reporters asked, Medeiros expressed his admiration for Spags: "I wish I had a thousand like him." But he did not know why Spagnolia was waging such a public challenge to his authority. Spags owed him total obedience. He had sworn an oath.

"Oh, my brother," he said to Spagnolia one morning on his way across the parking lot to work, "why are you doing this to me? I do not know. But I will accept it for the love of Jesus."

"Well," Spags said to him, "I'm doing *this* for the love of Jesus. Where does that leave us, Your Eminence?"

He ended his vigil on the day a representative from the chancery conveyed to him the cardinal's change of heart. The budget was rejiggered; there would be a school at St. Francis de Sales in Roxbury after all.

Later in 1970

LOWELL, MASSACHUSETTS — The old mill town, hard on the Merrimack River an hour's drive north from Boston, was America's first industrial city, built by Irish immigrants in 1822 around a grid of more than six miles of canals and dams; a flood of French Canadians followed. But the textile industry had repeatedly fallen on hard times, and by the time the Civil War broke out, most manufacturing had migrated to the South. A brief resurgence after World War I dried and cracked into the Great Depression, and the city never recovered significantly thereafter. Almost nothing worth celebrating had come out of Lowell, with the exception of its native son Jack Kerouac, Lowell's self-described "strange solitary crazy Catholic mystic."

For 170 years, Lowell had remained a Catholic ghetto. To Olan Horne, it was also a prison.

Olan was the kind of twelve-year-old who could tire just about everybody, a nonstop talker, overly dramatic, and self-satisfied. It was how he coped with his home life. A family member was regularly raping him. Olan kept this a secret for years, and would not have mentioned it at all if it weren't for the arrival to his parish of a young, charming new priest. Olan didn't trust Father Birmingham right off. But Birmingham had built a youth drop-in center in the basement of St. Michael's—just as he had in St. James in Salem and Our Lady of Fatima in Sudbury—and spent many afternoons talking to the young men who gathered there. He seemed genuinely to understand their issues and concerns.

When Olan Horne blurted his confession, the relief for having said it was immense—he felt a burden drain from him like an infection.

"Did you blow him?"

Olan answered.

"How big was his penis?"

He answered again.

"Did you get an erection?"

"What?"

"Let me see your penis."

"What?"

"If I stroke your penis, I can tell if you enjoyed it, I can tell if you have a natural response."

Mortified, Olan sat still as the priest examined his genitalia. He clamped his eyes shut. He was sure his responses were not natural in the least, in this chair, with this man, inside the church. A victim of abuse at home, and now at church. He could hear Birmingham volleying questions about homosexuality, and because he prayed for his own salvation he answered every question as honestly as he could.

He pleaded, "I'm getting real close."

"You're doing real well," Birmingham said. "You're okay."

December 1970

ST. ALBANS, VERMONT — "Across this great country, you adults don't reach out to the kids. You *killed* some of them in Guilford last year. Yes, you did! Those kids, my kids, your kids, *burned* to death in their commune. Because the fire engines couldn't get in to the conflagration. Because the road was purposely neglected. *Left unplowed!*" Paul Shanley's vitriol reached a fever pitch. That fire, at the rambling and filthy Johnson's Pastures Commune, had killed four people and cast a spotlight on the thriving commune movement, which had staked its claim in Vermont as a land of self-sufficiency, unfettered freedoms, and alternative families. To the unqualified dismay of the locals, over the past two years hundreds of disaffected kids from all over the nation had descended on Vermont's ramshackle small towns to snap up inhabitable farmhouses as temples for contemplating Utopia, smoking lots of pot, going topless, and living in squalor.

Concerned and confused by the influx of "dirty, unwashed, filthy beggars who won't do a day's work," as the *Vermont Sunday News* called them, a citizens' group in St. Albans had turned to Father Paul Shanley for advice. His hippie ministry in Boston had become full-time under Medeiros, who, feeling the young lacked "the solace of Christ in an increasingly impersonal world," officially named Shanley "minister to alienated youth on the streets," the only such apostolate in the American church. Immediately he became a nationally recognized authority on youth culture. He was asked to speak so frequently he had required a full-time secretary to organize his engagements.

His remarks always spun on his strident defense of the longhaired kids against their opponents, whom he accused of wanton prejudice. "The New Niggers," he called his flock. "We will one day stand accused of the same intransigent, irrational and unjust, therefore unchristian re-action to the New Nigger as will our forebears for the original nigger."

It had been a difficult year in America, one of the bloodiest periods of unrest since the Civil War. Indeed, the country seemed to be coming apart. One million students staged a nationwide general strike for civil rights and against the Vietnam War, the largest ever; they paralyzed 411 campuses. The backlash was fierce. Demonstrators were gassed by Washington, D.C., police for distributing leaflets; panicky governors dispatched national guard riflemen to over a dozen campuses. They bay-oneted seven students and reporters at the University of New Mexico, fired birdshot into rallies in Buffalo, and one sunny afternoon in May shot and killed four student protesters at Kent State University in Ohio.

If St. Albans's parishioners had hoped for comforting remarks from the famous street priest, their hopes were quickly dashed. He was as strident and messianic as a televangelist. He called for legalizing mari-juana. He blamed the federal government for pushing kids to use heroin by making pot scarce. He called all parents "hawks, racists, haters of the poor," and held them responsible for the runaway problem in the first place.

"The kids run away from a hypocritical and sick society, from a world they never made and want no part of," he said. "The kids have been ha-rassed by police; so have the social workers who try to give them a square deal. The police have planted drugs to make arrests; they've beaten them, intimidated them into terror."

Who were these people he represented? To him, they were the glo-rious future. "They seek the mystical and the spiritual—things that we have purged from our national religion," he said. "Street kids are among the most spiritual I've ever known."

The young listeners in his audience affirmed him. He was their prophet-priest, giving words to their generation's torments. They ap-plauded rowdily. But the older audience members had never heard such fervor. Most did not know what to make of the world Shanley painted. A few found his remarks downright irresponsible, as though he were incit-ing kids to drop out with his message of revolutionary detachment. These listeners wrote letters of protest to the local paper and petitioned Archbishop Medeiros down in Boston to reel in his radical reverend.

Medeiros had heard similar complaints before; he knew Shanley suffered from a stridency on this topic. He did not have a clear thought about the matter. As much as anybody in America, he was suspicious of the free-love youth movement, the Black Power ghetto organizing, the Weathermen, NOW, SNCC, SCLC, SDS—"these unfortunate phenomena of our society" he called them. But Paul Shanley was his ambassador to them, and would remain so. Medeiros could not afford to clamp down on the energetic priest and risk another defection. Between 1960 and 1970, the Boston archdiocese had suffered a steep slide in admissions to the seminary, from 418 a year to just 220 this past fall. Armed with a sense of the church's vulnerability, Shanley did not back down.

November 1971

ROME — Internationally, the priesthood was in perilous decline. In an effort to get a handle on the massive priest exodus and the shrinking seminary population, the Vatican commissioned Dr. Conrad W. Baars, a Catholic psychiatrist from Rochester, Minnesota, to study what was being called "the crisis in the priesthood." He delivered his report to church leaders attending the 1971 Synod of Bishops, called together to reexamine priestly life, especially celibacy. What he found said more about the priests who remained than those who had left. Drawing on his study of fifteen hundred Catholic priests and religious in the U.S. and the Netherlands, he discovered a unique and psychologically troubled cohort of men: uniformly distant, difficult, self-doubting, and markedly immature:

> In general, we estimate that 10–15 percent of all priests in Western Europe and North America are mature; 20–25 percent have serious psychiatric difficulties, especially in the form of neuroses and chronic alcoholism, or a combination of both; and 60–70 percent suffer from a degree of emotional immaturity which does not prevent them from exercising their priestly function, but precludes them from being happy men and effective priests whose fundamental role is to bring the joy of Christ's love and to be the appointed affirmers of men.

The cause, he postulated, was something his Dutch colleague and coinvestigator Dr. Anna Terruwe called "frustration neurosis." She first diagnosed it in pedophile priests and called it, in a personal meeting with the pope back in August 1969, the urgent subject of study for the church of our day. In her observation, priests tended to suffer from a weak sense of self-worth and powerlessness brought on by their removal from society and estrangement from the basic social unit, marriage. This resulted in an extraordinary kind of *self*-estrangement, or the creation of men whose basic humanity went so unaffirmed that they had become estranged from their own nature, as a penguin raised in a zoo among chickens would know nothing of icy migrations.

When coupled with the power and authority bestowed upon priests, Baars and Terruwe warned, the consequences of leaving such widespread confusion unaddressed—even unacknowledged—was dire.

> More often than not the priest comes from a "fine Catholic home," a strict one with little emotional love. Spurred on to develop his character, train his will, and grow intellectually, his emotional growth lags behind. Neither minor nor major seminary were capable of closing this "maturity gap" through authentic affirmation, and trained—the word is used deliberately—him to function without the benefit of the emotional life. The consequences of this unbalanced formation have been largely disastrous.
>
> In our clinical practices we have seen many priests with obvious identity problems. Priests who were uncertain in their attitude toward life, felt unloved, lonely and depressed, and whether they realized it or not, awkward in their interpersonal relationships. Psychosexual immaturity expressed in heterosexual or homosexual activity was encountered often. Many experienced difficulties in matters of faith, or suffered from severe scrupulosity, while a growing number of them seriously considered leaving the priesthood. Virtually all of them were non-affirmed men, suffering from a severe to moderate frustration with or without an associated obsessive-compulsive neurosis or chronic alcoholism.

The report was distributed in French and English to the 209 bishops who attended the 1971 synod. However, not content with these findings, in the United States the National Conference of Catholic Bishops commissioned its own survey, in two parts. The first, titled "The Catholic Priest in the United States: Sociological Investigations," undertaken by Andrew Greeley, confirmed that American clerics were remarkably unhappy and conflicted. The second, by the psychiatrist and former priest Eugene Kennedy, reproduced Baars's clinical insights. But it went a step further and put priestly sexuality under the microscope. Its findings were stark.

"For whatever reasons, these priests have not resolved the problems which are ordinarily worked through during the time of adolescence," Kennedy wrote in the report, titled "The Catholic Priest in the United States: Psychological Investigations," which he based on examining 271 priests. "Sexual feelings are a source of conflict and difficulty and much energy goes into suppressing them or the effort to distract themselves from them. Most report that their education about sexual development was negative or non-existent; many report no normal developmental social experience."

The American bishops did with these studies what they had always done with bad news about their priests: they found high shelves and deep drawers to slip them into. Though the problem was clearer, the solution was no more tangible than ever before, and the future no less grim. How could the church forge its campaign to stem the sexual awakening of America when its priests, bound by the prescribed church doctrine, had become twisted sexual distortions of men? So quietly that they went nearly unnoticed, some American church leaders suggested to the Vatican that modern times might merit a newer model of sexual morality, for the clergy as well as the laity. It took Cardinal Franjo Seper, a Croatian, to declare to the bishops in Rome: "I am not at all optimistic that celibacy is in fact being observed." In Spain, 60 percent of priests were sexually active. In South Africa, the figure was approximately 45 percent, and similar numbers had been confirmed in Ireland and Australia. By one estimation, based on fifteen hundred American priests interviewed by Richard Sipe, a psychotherapist and former Benedictine monk, 40 to 50 percent of all U.S. priests were sexually active—furtively, without the attendance of romance or responsibility, the most detached sort of sexual expression. The very kind they preached against.

Summer 1972

BOSTON, MASSACHUSETTS — Paul Shanley had gradually lost interest in his freaks, communards, and assorted dropouts. As they became less politically defined and angry, their countercultural stance was morphing into an unattractive culture of its own. Many turned to transcendentalism and the Ouija board, he'd noticed, and some openly dallied with devil worship. A heroin epidemic burned through Boston, and the kids—now accompanied by a large number of despondent Vietnam vets—were in trouble deeper than a solitary priest could reach, though he did what he could to expand treatment facilities and outreach programs.

The inheritor of the youth culture, and the next great street movement on the horizon after civil rights and opposition to the war, was much more challenging to the church: gay pride. In the three short years since the Stonewall Riot erupted in New York, there had been an incredible explosion of militant gay activism throughout the country. Homosexuality went from being nearly invisible to being aggressively *apparent*. Schoolteachers, nurses, and lawyers came out of their closets. Soldiers openly declared their identities and fought expulsion in the courts. More than five thousand men and women took to the streets in New York City in June 1970 to mark the first anniversary of Stonewall; those numbers doubled and tripled year after year as men and women shucked their shame and declared, if only for a day, that they were proud to be gay. An infrastructure of movement groups had flourished. The Gay Liberation Front, which took its inspiration from the Marxist National Liberation Front of Vietnam, was meanwhile holding "nude-ins" and distributing leaflets with messages such as "Do you think homosexuals are revolting? You bet your sweet ass we are!" The more mainstream Gay Activist Alliance lobbied for the enactment of fair employment and housing legislation, the repeal of sodomy laws, and an end to police entrapment and harassment. Across the country, there were now close to eight hundred new associations engaged in the struggle.

Especially in Boston, closet doors were splintering open. Staging that city's first gay protest in June 1971, organizers drew almost two hundred people to a march and rally, which ended with a "closet-smashing" spectacle in Cambridge Common. Now there existed a gay health clinic, a gay bookstore, and gay student organizations at Harvard, MIT, Tufts, Northeastern University, Brandeis, and the University of Massachusetts, all formed over a two-year period. Even high schools were experiencing the aggressive rejection of the closet. In the spring, the first gay youth group in the nation had formed in Boston—High School Gays United—to bring together "all Homosexual high school students, and gay people under 18 years of age, female and male . . . to give them the security they need and the assurance that there ARE others like themselves who are fighting the same battles."

After the long decades and centuries in which they were suppressed, homosexuals had finally joined together in a community whose critical mass was large enough, angry enough, and politically skilled enough to refuse being denied. As the historian John D'Emilio wrote in his book *Sexual Politics, Sexual Communities*, "For the first time, gay men and lesbians had substantial resources not only for naming their sexuality but for finding a gay subculture in which they could take a place."

It also raised eyebrows among nongays. *Time* magazine took note of the wild developments in a cover story called "Sex and the Teenager," in which experts debunked growing fears that everybody was suddenly gay. On the contrary, because of the new sexual freedoms teens enjoyed, they would be *less* likely to become homosexuals, the magazine argued, "because there are fewer sexual taboos today, the teenager is more likely to find the heterosexual pathway." (Incensed that homosexuality was presented as a reaction or choice, not as an immutable condition like one's race or gender, gay activists protested at *Time*'s New York City offices.)

Quietly at first, but more boldly every day, Paul Shanley changed the focus of his ministry from "disaffected youth" to "sexual minorities." He set himself up as a counselor and sex expert, advertising his services in alternative papers:

GAY? BI? CONFUSED?
Call Father Paul

He began to write rambling newsletter dispatches on the repression of the homosexual, and openly questioned some long-held aspects of the Catholic magisterium about homosexual sins. He spoke prolifically and stridently on the subject, animatedly detailing the dreadful statistics about the tendency of young homosexuals to commit suicide and the frequency with which they are banished from their own homes by confused and intolerant parents.

"Kids—average age 15—are leaving home to come to Boston's gay scene," he told the *National Catholic Reporter.* "Out in suburbia there's no one they can talk to about their sexual confusion."

Shanley was not the only man of the cloth delivering these messages, but he was the only Roman Catholic priest doing so.

Most Christian opposition to homosexuality was based on what was commonly referred to as the "seven biblical passages" (some say four or eight) that seemed to condemn same-sex relations. The two clearest, from Leviticus, were incontrovertible: "You shall not lie with a male as with a woman; it is an abomination" and "If a man lies with a male as with a woman, both of them have committed an abomination; they shall be put to death; their blood is upon them." To fundamentalists, this was a literal verdict. Other interpreters, for their part, pointed to the passage following, which condemns philanderers to death as well, to suggest that Leviticus should be taken with a grain of historical salt.

The Catholic Church had a uniquely complicated history of thought on the subject. Over the centuries, numerous popes had been homosexuals, some quite openly. Julius III, John XII, and Benedict IX were practicing orgiasts. Pope Boniface VIII (1294–1303) was alleged to have called same-sex activity, in which he apparently indulged, "no more a sin than rubbing your hands together." The renegade antipope John XXIII (the first John XXIII, who ruled in the fifteenth century) was tried and convicted in 1415 for persisting in acts considered morally detestable, despite repeat warnings. Paul II, who adored fine clothing and would collapse in tears when called upon to perform official duties, was known widely as "Our Lady of Pity."

Given his national standing as defender of the youth, Shanley was invited to deliver his message all across America. His advocacy had taken on a libertine bent, and sometimes tended toward rhetorical excesses. But he was fluent in Kinsey and in Masters and Johnson. Perhaps 20 million Americans were gay, and even more were bisexual. Suicide was the number one killer of gay teens. Sex between men or between women was *not* sinful; the sinner was the one who would condemn their love.

"I don't think sexual activity among members of the same sex is so much the problem," Shanley argued. "It's what society says and does about it. We have kids being given shock treatment for having interest in persons of the same sex! To me, that is like giving shock treatments to people who have become afflicted with the disease of adolescence. It is absurd."

Often his lectures prompted letters of protest to archdiocesan officials back in Boston. In one particular incident, following a radio interview, Archbishop Medeiros himself was moved to sit down and scratch out a note of grave concern.

"Dear Father Paul," the archbishop wrote in February 1973. "It has come to my attention that a number of good people have become very disturbed about some statements which they assert you made on a recent radio program. It is claimed that you expressed views contrary to the doctrine of the Church on several points of morality, stating, for instance, that such acts as masturbation and homosexuality are not morally evil, and that the church will change its teaching in regard to such matters.

"If such allegations are true, I must express deep concern and disapproval. I cannot understand how, in conscience, you as a Catholic can justify the causing of scandal among the faithful. Especially in regard to young people, whose welfare I had hoped was a genuine concern of yours, to express such erroneous and dangerous views can have no effect other than to lead these children of God astray in matters of faith and basic morality. As a Catholic priest, you have the obligation to preach and teach the doctrine of the Catholic Church in matters of faith and morality. To do otherwise seems to be nothing short of a betrayal of your calling. As the shepherd of the faithful in this archdiocese, for whose spiritual welfare God will hold me accountable, it is my duty to make it clear to you that, if the complaints made against you are true, you must desist."

Shanley was not one to be taken to the woodshed on questions of morality. He fired back a snide retort. "The greater portion of violence visited upon Gays comes from the Christian (in Boston read Catholic) community. Just as young Catholics in my boyhood felt it an act of piety to beat up a Jew on Blue Hill Avenue or stone a Protestant church, so today's Christians think they do God a service when they beat up a fag. If you have the purity of angels, and the abortion-less, monogamous church-blessed marriage; if you have the faith of Peter and the education of parochial schools; if your speech be devoid of four letter words yet you have no charity toward homosexuals then . . . tinkling brass . . . sounding cymbals . . . *Catholic, but hardly Christian*. Have you ever received any mail from any of these critics protesting what *we* are doing *to* homosexuals, or is their concern only about what homosexuals do? There are degrees of sin. Please God I am found among the latter rather than the former, if it must be one."

When it came to high-handedness, Shanley was a fearless adversary and a formidable foe.

Word of Shanley's showdown reached the other members of the Association of Urban Priests, and they were in awe of Shanley for tangling with Medeiros. Some wrote letters on his behalf, as did dozens of community leaders—including a high-ranking official with the Commonwealth Department of Welfare. Some privately speculated that Shanley was gay—among their numbers many undoubtedly were. For everybody's sake, they hoped Shanley would prevail. In him they saw a theology that melded sexual identity with Catholic morality. Of course, they assumed he was chaste. And if not—if he had somehow found the wherewithal to transcend the theological controls on gayness and enter onto the conjugal plane—they assumed at the very least that he was comporting himself in an ethical way.

Fall 1972
SALEM, MASSACHUSETTS — After turning his back on his Catholic school scholarships, Bernie McDaid went on to a very short and disastrous stint in public school. He favored pot, Seconal, and methamphetamines over scholarship. In his freshman year, he missed ninety days of class. And on the day in tenth grade they told him not to return, he had swallowed eight Seconals, nearly a fatal dosage, then fell asleep in the cafeteria after resting his groggy head comfortably, if alarmingly, on a pillow of mashed potatoes.

His parents tried everything. They sent him to Ireland and Scotland so that his grandparents could help mold him. While he was away, they moved from Salem to Peabody, thinking the shock of new surroundings would break his downward spiral. He refused to go to Peabody High. So his father showed him the door. He was sixteen.

He found a job as a parking lot attendant at a bingo hall, for $15 a week, but rather than getting better, his circumstances deteriorated. Now he was hanging out in an expanding drug scene populated mainly by demobilized GIs back from Vietnam, who taught him how to inject speed, rob, deal, trespass, and brawl. He was arrested fifty times. He hurt people sometimes for fun. He was not capable of identifying with others.

He never thought back on Father Birmingham. What he thought about was his own sexuality. What in hell did it mean that a part of him enjoyed what the nasty priest had done?

Spring Semester 1973
LOWELL, MASSACHUSETTS — Gary Bergeron lived in Lowell, just a few miles north of Route 128; attended St. Michael's, a large, ornate church; and was enrolled in the adjoining parochial school. His whole family was enlivened when Father Birmingham became their parochial vicar. He was a priest in perpetual motion, darting to his cottage on the Cape, or skiing up north, or swimming or playing tennis, and he never went alone. Parents loved him. Children loved him. Bergeron was an exception. At eleven, he had no interest in leaving town with a priest for

the weekend, not even one as fun-loving as Birmingham, and he turned down many entreaties. He didn't know why—not until the day Birmingham entered the community health club and found Bergeron in the shower. Without so much as a hello, he walked up to the kid and grabbed hold of him as if he were shaking his hand. Birmingham was that brazen. Even a suspicious kid stood still in his shame as the priest caused him to ejaculate.

A few days later, Birmingham was in the health club again. This time, Bergeron tried not to be so vulnerable. But the priest was a walking repertory of small talk, pulling Bergeron out of his shell in stages. *Are you good at sports? Which? How much do you weigh? Really? Get on the scale.*

He got on the scale.

No, no, no! Not fully clothed.

He peeled off his outer layers. He just didn't know why he did it. It was as though some alien force had entered his body and taken over the controls.

The skivvies, Gary. You got to take your skivvies off, because they account for a couple of ounces.

A prisoner of war didn't know more torture than what forced Bergeron to remove his own underwear against his will. The humiliation, the powerlessness, the lost interior struggle—more than the various acts of unwelcomed masturbation, that was the violation, that was what Bergeron would remember for years.

His brother Eddie would focus on something else, the sense of suffocating that overcame him the first time Birmingham touched him, a Thursday in seventh grade—the feeling that water was flooding his lungs, the panic of not being able to breathe.

June 5, 1973

Roxbury, Massachusetts — Father Spags had returned to his rectory from morning Mass, as he had every day, to put on a large pot of coffee. He looked at the can of coffee granules pessimistically. The world wouldn't care if today, for once, he accomplished nothing. For the first time in his life, he put down the coffee can unopened. Instead, he grabbed a bottle of vodka and poured himself a screwdriver. Then he

made another. Then he made a pitcher of them and slid into a chair
with a newspaper. It was seven-thirty in the morning.

The past few months had been wretched ones for Spags. It started
when the parish council at St. Francis de Sales called a special meeting to discuss the problem of race. Parish councils were the main tangible innovation of Vatican II dealing with the role of laymen in
temporal church affairs. Selected by the pastor, and subject to the approval of the bishop, parish council members served as community advisers in the management of nonspiritual business. In practice, it was
often little more than an honorary position. The priest remained the final authority.

Like everything else in Roxbury, the parish council at St. Francis was
something of an anomaly. Because Catholics were such a small part of
the parish constituency, in the spirit of ecumenism the archbishop had
allowed the parish council there to be multidenominational, a very unusual arrangement. The president was a Baptist. In itself, this did not
cause problems. But at this extraordinary meeting, council members
had demanded that something be done about the racial imbalance at
St. Francis School, where every nun and priest and faculty member was
white and every student was black. The other Roman Catholic church
in Roxbury, St. Joseph's, staffed its school with black nuns. They demanded integration.

Spags allowed them to conduct a personnel search and agreed to
hire a well-qualified black religious brother from Washington, D.C., to
be his principal. The honeymoon lasted only a few weeks. Spags disliked the administrator's style, his high-handedness with the nuns, his
get-tough approach to the children. When Spags heard he had struck a
student, he fired him summarily and the parish council voted to back
his decision. But opposition came from an unexpected place—black
nuns from St. Joseph's marched over to protest the termination. They
demanded a meeting with the white nuns, which ran into the night. As
word spread, parents and students joined the summit. By the time a
student ran to fetch Spags at 11 P.M., a large crowd had formed.

When he entered the school meeting room, he was informed that
the black nuns and the white nuns were of one mind. They agreed it
did not make sense to have an all-white Catholic educational faculty in

Roxbury. Their solution was stunning. Down to a nun, Spags's entire staff resigned in defiance, as though they held him responsible for their whiteness.

"While you're playing your funny political games," Spags bellowed, "who suffers in all of this? The kids! Their parents sitting right here don't know what the hell is going on. Most of them are not Catholic. They see this scandalous behavior going on—it's just awful!"

He thought he had never seen such hatred as what was burning in the eyes of the black nuns. He was not capable of fathoming their grievances. Racial rage baffled and frightened him. Economic and educational initiatives—these things liberated a community, he thought, not black power wars fought on the razor-sharp shoals of identity politics. He addressed the white nuns directly before stalking out of the room.

"Sisters of St. Francis School, I'm sure you did what you felt you had to do. Now, I must do what I must do. School will be closed for one week. When we reopen, it will be with an entirely new faculty."

Since then, on top of his duties celebrating morning Mass, visiting the sick and dying, and tending to the homebound, Spags was filling in as an eighth-grade teacher, serving as the school coprincipal, and functioning as its administrator at a time when public funds for inner-city schools were evaporating.

He was not a drinker. Alcoholism was one of many priestly disorders Spags was immune to. But on this morning he had reached the end of his goodness and he allowed himself a boozy debauchery. His pitcher of screwdrivers was empty by 10 A.M. when the telephone rang with a call from the chancery demanding he come immediately to a meeting with Cardinal Medeiros.

He panicked. Pulling out the large thirty-cup coffeepot used for church gatherings, he began a campaign to sober up, which was more or less effective. He was able to drive himself from Roxbury to the residence in Brighton, and appear steady on his feet at the cardinal's gilded meeting room.

"Oh, my brother, before we talk I know you have nothing to apologize for," Medeiros began sadly. He motioned for Spags to sit, and across the dark conference table slid him a copy of a letter he'd received from the Office of Black Catholics, which called for Spags's removal from St. Francis de Sales. If Medeiros refused, it continued, the group, which was founded in 1970 to promote integration in the church, promised a campaign denouncing the way blacks were treated in the archdiocese of Boston.

"I have to do something about this," he said. "Any job you want in the archdiocese you can have, but I must remove you from St. Francis."

The news struck him hard. He was beginning to think there was no institution in the world that was worthy of his faith, not Mothers for Adequate Welfare, which had deserted him the minute Spags's own troubles began; not the Association of Urban Priests, whose members were too embroiled in their own struggles for survival to come to his aid; not the church itself, which buckled at a political threat. He remembered the movie *I Confess,* in which the stoic cleric held principle above all else, including personal safety. What had become of idealism?

He rose to leave. When the cardinal extended his hand in condolence, Spags rejected it.

"Your Eminence," he said, "there are enough empty signs and gestures in this world without you and me adding to it."

When he reached his rectory in Roxbury he knew what he had to do. Spags typed out a resignation from the priesthood.

Sunday, September 2, 1973
LOS ANGELES, CALIFORNIA — Organizers had expected fifty people to attend, seventy-five at the most, but literally hundreds descended upon the Hollywood Holiday Inn for the first convention of Dignity, the new organization for gay and lesbian Catholics. They walked through the lobby wearing a look of wonderment, stunned at the turnout. Nationwide, Dignity claimed 432 members. Nearly every one of them had shown up. They came from as far away as Boston, but for many the journey was much more arduous than a three-thousand-mile trek. Their pasts were a dark purgatory of condemnation and rejection. Only through a forceful act of will—which went against their own instincts as sons and daughters, as brothers and sisters, as Catholics—had they

come to accept their orientation as innate and immutable. Homosexuals, unlike any other minority, are born in exile from their own kind, left to discover the truth about their essence in a hostile climate. For many here, they had reached their people only now, on this Labor Day weekend, in a windowless room off North Highland Avenue in the Hollywood Hills.

When they went to confession later, if they had sexual partners they would not seek absolution for loving them any more than a married Catholic would confess to conjugal happiness. As a sign of how quickly things were changing, among Dignity's ranks were twenty-five priests and four religious brothers, including the founder, Father Patrick Nidorf, an Augustinian from San Diego. For their part, the priests would not withhold absolution. The gay, as the straight, would be judged upon their comportment in love, as in life.

Father John J. McNeill, a bearded and intense Jesuit priest from New York City who was the conference keynote speaker, could not believe how things had changed in a few short years. His remarks would be carefully constructed—a theological argument to suggest that the homosexual might be able to reach ethical goodness *through* homosexual love, not despite it.

"As far as I can ascertain, this is the first convention of Catholic homosexuals in the history of the Church," he said. "Consequently, we are the inheritors of the suffering, anguish and even torture of literally millions of our homosexual brothers and sisters over the centuries. These sufferings continue today. There is no need for me to dwell at length on what that suffering and anguish has been, for there is probably no one here who has not had his or her share." He studied his prepared remarks. Now would be the time to say it, the moment to reveal who *he* really was, a man who had suffered too. But he could not. No priest had ever come out of the closet before. It would be another twenty years before he would break that barrier.

October 1973
BRIDGEWATER, MASSACHUSETTS — Will McLean dialed the number for the priest from the ad in an alternative weekly. It was his last hope. For

years he'd been haunted with sexual fears—menaced by his own desires for his best friend, a man who, like himself, was a college junior. The ad read, "GAY? BI? CONFUSED? Call Father Paul." He thought that "confused" hardly captured the awful strife inside his head. Try *at wit's end*. Everything he had done to deny his urges had failed spectacularly. McLean loathed himself, despised his weaknesses. He had just vowed to turn himself over to the church, and there was the ad. Coincidence? He didn't think so. This was the end of the road. Savagely depressed and suicidal, he had no other hope.

He dialed. He would do whatever the father told him to do in order to exorcise this evil occupying his mind and soul.

But when McLean showed up for his appointment with Paul Shanley, at a small office he kept in an apartment building on Beacon Street, it was immediately clear things were not going to work out the way he had imagined. Shanley did not look like any priest McLean had ever seen before—in jeans, long hair, and sitting beneath a poster on the wall that actually read, "How Dare You Presume I'm Heterosexual?" McLean, a college junior, had never knowingly met a homosexual before, much less a homosexual priest. At college there were a few guys who appeared manifestly gay, but none would declare themselves. Mere supposition was enough to keep McLean away from them—and them away from one another. The fear of discovery was universal.

Here was an overt homosexual—a sage, a guide, a priest.

"First," Shanley began his stirring introduction, "I don't care what your parents told you. I don't care what your pastor told you. Forget everything you've learned, or thought was true. *Gay is good*."

God, he said unequivocally, had no bone to pick with sexual orientation, and nor should the church. God made gays; would God foul his world by making something flawed? Don't be ridiculous! Gay is *part* of the plan. We already know that to please God, man must express himself as intended, each to his own tune. Same with the gays. Sex is no sin when it is between men, any more than it is between a man and a woman.

McLean, a psychology major, felt sure he would never hear anyone endorse homosexuality, much less a priest. He was scandalized, and said so.

Shanley grew impatient. "You've listened to too much propaganda," he snapped.

"This is never going to work out for me," McLean said. "I might as well kill myself. I'm never going to be happy."

"You will," Shanley declared with confidence. "You will meet somebody, and you will be happy."

There simply was no logic to this, McLean thought—if gay people were regularly settling down in happy couples, where was the proof of this domestic happiness? You never saw them going about their business in Boston. You never saw them resting a head in a boyfriend's lap on a sunny day in the Common, or holding hands in church. You never saw a gay couple portrayed in movies or novels, and certainly not on TV.

"They're in San Francisco," Shanley told him. "They're building a world there where gay people are making relationships openly. And in Greenwich Village in New York City. Even here, in places." A bourgeoning gay community was growing in the South End. There was a newspaper, *Gay Community News,* as well as bars and community groups, headquartered there.

"You don't have to buy into the patriarchal, homophobic, woman-hating society," Shanley snapped. His tone tilted toward impatience. "You will find somebody, and you will love him. And you will be happy."

"Maybe I'm not even gay," said McLean, a former altar boy from St. James in Medford. "I mean, I've never had sex with a guy before."

"So? Try it."

This conversation was not going the way McLean expected at all, but that was fine by him.

"Go to the bars," Shanley said. "Do you know where the Art Cinema is? It's a gay porno theater. Go there."

"Father, I couldn't do that," he said. Anonymous sex in public places held no allure for him. He feared being dragged out of the closet. "If I ever saw one of the gay guys from college there, I'd die."

"Tell you what I can do," Shanley said. "What we could do sometime, if you want to try being with another man? We could try that here."

"We could *what*?"

"I'm willing to help you with this. We could do some massage. We could get naked. And you could feel what it was like to be with another guy."

McLean leapt up and bolted for the door. This was not at all what he had in mind.

But on the drive back to Bridgewater State College, he could not stop thinking about the proposal. If it solved the riddle, he thought, what's the harm? Hell could not claim somebody who followed the orders of a priest. A week or so later he returned to Shanley's Beacon Street pad. The sexual performance was perfunctory and clinical. He felt terrible about the whole thing. He left the priest's apartment seconds after.

But over the next year and a half he returned for several more "counseling sessions." After each encounter, he felt incrementally better about himself. By his senior year in college, his war with himself was over. He could think about his homosexuality without feeling suicidal. He even began an affair with the classmate of his dreams. For all this, he credited Shanley. It took a priest to give back what the society—and his own church—had taken away, the privilege to know his own heart.

1970s

Littleton, Massachusetts — The name Alpha Omega hung outside one of the area's stately old homes, amid pristine rolling grounds and a large swimming pool. Its tranquil appearance was deceptive. The house was a residential center for troubled teens, operated by the archdiocese on contract to the state's Department of Youth Services—in effect, a minimum security prison for male juvenile offenders. These were troubled kids. Of the fifteen or so residents, ages fourteen to seventeen, most had stolen cars, perpetrated assaults, or committed crimes with guns. Nobody clocked time there voluntarily.

But Father Bernie Lane, who founded the home in 1970, did what he could to make it a palatable alternative to state-run facilities. The boys wandered freely around the rambling building. With good behavior they earned various privileges on a steep ladder of rewards. The "special boys," as Lane called them, were transferred out of the crowded dormitory into private bedrooms. Swimming pool time was earned or squandered each week.

By and large, Alpha Omega was an orderly place. Lane's boys were highly motivated. If they failed at Alpha Omega they were sent back to the dreaded Roslindale Detention Center, a lockdown facility where conditions were harsh. In comparison, this was like summer camp. With a major exception.

The therapeutic program Lane developed for his charges, who served between three months and several years, was novel. With no special training in juvenile reform, he modeled Alpha Omega after his understanding of the encounter groups then popular, which were believed to instill empathy, sobriety, and conflict resolution skills by freeing one's emotions. The boys were encouraged to express their innermost feelings in daily sessions.

As part of this exercise, Lane routinely ordered the youths to remove all of their clothing. Look at one another's bodies, he would command, arranging them in pairs of two. Get closer, he would say, face-to-face, squeeze together till there is no air between the bodies at all. This, Lane explained, would help them repair their relationships with their fathers, and thus extinguish their desires to act out in malicious ways.

None of the other therapists or employees of Alpha Omega ever reported these nude encounter sessions to authorities. It took eight years for one of the boys to mention the strange goings-on. And he might not have said a thing if he hadn't earned the highest reward offered by Lane, a weekend trip to his lakeside retreat in New Hampshire. There, he told authorities, Lane led a private workshop in massage, masturbation, and mutual ejaculation, describing these as essential skills for his eventual married life.

When confronted by DYS officials, Lane did not deny a thing. "It was therapeutic," he said. "And the kids were being honest with each other."

DYS reported these findings to the state licensing agency, Office for Children. An investigation was begun. Leaders from the Boston archdiocese, in a meeting with regulators, agreed to remedy the situation by pulling Lane out of Alpha Omega. He was immediately stripped of his title as director and given responsibilities in a local church instead. As was usual, the state deferred to the archdiocese. They reissued a license for the program.

Lane's replacement as director would be Father C. Melvin Surette, a part-time counselor there who considered Lane a good friend and mentor. He would run the program without alteration—including the one-on-one weekend getaways and regular nighttime visits to the bedsides of the special boys. When time had passed, he invited Lane to return to Alpha Omega to celebrate Mass. Some of the boys later complained they were passed between the two.

June 1974

HINGHAM, MASSACHUSETTS — *Terrific,* Joanne Mueller thought. Father Geoghan had just phoned to see if she needed him to drop by. As usual, Mueller was desperate to see him. Since her husband left her four years ago, Geoghan often helped out with the kids, giving them baths or putting them to bed. She would not have survived without his generosity and selflessness. That, she said to herself, is what being a parish priest was all about. So many other St. Paul's mothers also needed the assistant pastor, and since being transferred to the parish in 1967, with great fanfare, he had not seemed to let anybody down. But he treated her family specially. Once, he even celebrated Mass in her family's backyard, a tremendous honor. He let the boys wear cassocks and help out. She felt extremely lucky.

Unlike some of his classmates, after ordination Geoghan did not commit himself to ministering to the marginalized or isolated, but instead fashioned his apostolate in the model of the old-fashioned parish priests, always at the hospital in emergencies, hearing confessions no matter the time of night, teasing out solutions to complicated family problems. Moms, especially those whose husbands were absent—whether called away by death, alcoholism, or second jobs, or from simple lack of interest—adored him for the attention he paid to their children. He loved kids, and when he came by in his car to fetch them for ice cream, or dropped by long after they'd gone to bed to slip into their quiet rooms and offer a blessing, they seemed to love him, too.

Mueller called to her children that Father Geoghan would be there momentarily. But something unexpected happened. Her youngest son became totally hysterical, screaming and throwing himself to the floor. "I don't like him," he cried. "Don't let him come by."

"What?" she asked him. "What do you mean? What are you saying?"

"I just don't want him touching my wee-wee," he said.

She was mortified. This could not be true. How could she not have suspected? She called her other sons to the room. All four of her boys, now aged five to twelve, began to cry. One at a time, they told the same story.

"My God," she demanded, "why didn't you tell me?"

Tears burned red on the face of her oldest boy. "Father said it was like a confession. Confessions are secret, there's a seal on the confessional."

It was inconceivable to her that a priest, so like God—*this* priest, before whom she had knelt, from whom she begged absolution, a priest whom she had loved like her own father, to whom she had entrusted her young boys over and over—had visited such evil upon her children.

The truth pried open her dizzying mind; the betrayal did violence to her thinking. Geoghan might be just a few blocks away. She was not at all prepared to confront him. She had to leave the house immediately. Though she had no clue where she would take them, she ordered the kids into the car. She thought of Father Paul Miceli at St. Mary's in Melrose. He had her oldest sons in the altar boy program there. She sped through the frantic night to his rectory.

Luckily she found him in, and she unloaded her story at his doorstep. Policy at the time would have required him to take several steps. First, he should notify the pastor of the parish in which the suspected priest served, and then he was to contact the chancery office immediately.

Father Miceli showed appropriate concern for the children's well-being. Any priest guilty of such sins would not be tolerated in the priesthood, he told Mueller. "Joanne, this is a terrible, terrible thing. It's a disgrace. Let me take care of this. Will you trust me and let me handle this? It will never happen again."

As Mueller was leaving with her boys, he extracted from her a promise to keep this a secret, for the sake of the boys and for the health of the church.

Within weeks, John Geoghan was removed from his post and the parish. Miceli explained that he had been isolated in a mental hospital, forever out of the reach of small boys. "He will never do it again," he said.

Reassured, Mueller was grateful that the matter was resolved so cleanly. She had not wanted to report Geoghan to the police or to alert other mothers to the dangers; she wanted this devastating history simply erased.

But the truth was that Miceli had not told Geoghan's supervisor, or his own, or anybody at the chancery or any other church official. Rather, he spoke to Geoghan himself, and suggested he stay clear of the Mueller boys. It was pure coincidence that the vicar for clergy reassigned Geoghan to St. Andrew's in the Forest Hills section of Jamaica Plain, a grand Gothic church facing Parkman Playground. Only a few weeks after his arrival there, eleven-year-old Richard William Stokes was playing in the park when a priest with a chirpy voice introduced himself warmly. In the same playground Geoghan befriended Ronald Oreto and John MacClean, both eleven, and Joseph Hayes, twelve, who was playing Wiffle ball one glorious summer morning. In the vestry, the adjoining cemetery, or the parking lot, all four boys were wrestled, groped, molested, kissed, and disrobed, sometimes repeatedly, sometimes while the priest himself stood exposed before them. Three more boys that fall, four kids the next year, three the year after, and so on. For myriad reasons, these boys believed the priest when he said it would not be right to share their secret. No child made a report. Or if they did, the people to whom they complained—sibling, parent, priest—said nothing to anyone else, or spoke only to another person unwilling to act, and the truth was entombed in their many ears.

Late Summer 1974

It was after eight on a Sunday morning when Mary Elaine McGee's husband shook her awake and said, "Read this." On doctor's orders,

Elaine slept late on Sundays now to keep her blood pressure low. She reached for his copy of the *Boston Herald American* and sank into an article about a mysterious assailant who had nabbed a twelve-year-old Chelmsford, Massachusetts, boy, blindfolded and bound him with duct tape, then brutally raped him. The boy had leapt out of the moving car and run blind and naked through a suburban neighborhood, where he was discovered. Due to the dramatic circumstances of his captivity, the victim could offer only a limited description of his attacker: a white man in his forties, well built, over six feet tall.

"Oh my God," Elaine said. "Birmingham to a T."

Within the hour, she was seated at the local state police barracks a quarter mile from their new home, telling everything she knew about Father Joseph Birmingham. How the mothers of Salem had pieced together his patterns of predation, how they confronted Father McCormack at Catholic Charities and even Monsignor John Jennings, head of clergy personnel at the chancery in Brighton. How Birmingham was then transferred "somewhere north of Route 128"—she thought she had heard that the parish name begins with an *M*—and how, despite their tearful insistences, the chancery officials felt it was inappropriate to warn anybody there about Birmingham's notorious past.

"This is how naïve I was," Elaine McGee said. "I thought the church would handle it and take care of it. And I was thinking about Birmingham's mother, who was a very old lady. This would have *killed* her. She didn't need to know this. I felt sure Boston would do the right thing. That's how dumb I was."

The local police barracks wired Elaine McGee's report about Birmingham's supposed role in the kidnapping and rape case to Ray McKeon, the sergeant from Chelmsford in charge of the criminal bureau. A Roman Catholic himself, Sergeant McKeon doubted McGee's story quite thoroughly. But lacking any other leads, he set about the task of trying to find a church beginning with an *M* in the dozens of towns north of Route 128, one of the most densely Catholic parts of the country.

Luck alone explained what happened next. The very first phone book he plucked arbitrarily from a pile was for Lowell, the first church his finger found was St. Michael's, and the man who answered the telephone there was the man himself, Joseph Birmingham, who agreed, though quite discourteously, McKeon thought, to a meeting at the Chelmsford police station the following evening at seven. Pushing his luck, Sergeant McKeon made an odd request.

"Would you do me a favor? I know it sounds silly, Father. But wear civilian clothing—don't wear your Roman collar. And when you get here, go right up to the desk and ask the dispatcher for directions to the Drum Hill Traffic Circle—about a hundred people ask him that every day—then go take a drink of water."

At the appointed hour the following evening, Sergeant McKeon placed the twelve-year-old rape victim in a corner chair in the busy precinct to see if he could make a positive identification. Right on schedule Birmingham came in and did as instructed. To Sergeant McKeon's relief, the boy did not recognize him. No Boston-area cop had ever arrested a priest before, he was told, and few experts on law enforcement nationally could recall a priest arrest in the history of the country. Thank God, he thought, he would not enter the history books this way. He greeted Birmingham like an old academy chum.

"What's this all about?" Birmingham demanded.

"I'll tell you, Father. We have a tragic case, maybe you saw it in the papers. We had a boy molested, kidnapped, taped up, and raped, really very brutally. We had reason to believe you could be involved, which I know seems—"

"Wait a minute right there," Birmingham interrupted. "Do you know who you're talking to? I'm a Roman Catholic priest! You should be *ashamed* of yourself for even *suggesting* this to me. You're suggesting I would do something that evil, something that bad?"

Sergeant McKeon was staggered by the comeback. In fact, he *felt* ashamed. But in the local hierarchy of high-handedness, a Lowell curate did not have swatting rights over a Chelmsford sergeant in his own station house. Not a curate whose parishioners down in Salem had accused him of sexual assault.

"I'm gonna tell you something, mister. I know your MO," Sergeant McKeon came back. "I know what you did in Salem to them boys. We know *all* about your record. Believe me, if that boy had identified you out there, you know where you'd be going? Down that corridor to cell number one, my friend."

"I'm over all that now," Birmingham said, still dismissive of the officer.

"Over what?"

"I had a problem with that in Salem. But I'm over that now. I'm cured."

"You're *cured*? What did they do?"

"They sent me to St. Michael's."

"Wait a minute. Did they tell your pastor at St. Michael's what you are up to?"

Birmingham shook his head no.

"How did you get cured?"

"I cured myself."

Sergeant McKeon could not be sure Birmingham was his rapist. But he was disgusted at his church for hiding this man. There was nothing he could do about it. He could not arrest Birmingham for his crimes in another jurisdiction. So after alerting his counterparts in Lowell that the new priest in town was a confessed child abuser, Sergeant McKeon was forced to let Birmingham leave.

"Get outta here," he said. "You're stinking up the place."

Chapter 3

Gay Is Good

June 3, 1974

Dayton, Ohio — One of the first things Brian McNaught noticed as he approached the registration table, the port of entry for the first-ever National Conference on Gay Ministry, was the joyous expression of *arrival* on the faces of the men and women streaming into the Bergamo Center. His face shone no differently. This was the first national gathering of theologians and priest activists hoping to reform church teaching on homosexuality. McNaught, a popular columnist for the diocesan newspaper back in Detroit, was among the few self-declared homosexuals in attendance. He recognized the people whose work had made them famous—or infamous—in Catholic gay circles. Striding through the door were the legendary street priest Paul Shanley and Father John McNeill, whose writings on gay ministry had help spawn this meeting. Across the room were Sister Jeannine Gramick, an outspoken nun in the order of the School Sisters of Notre Dame, and her ideological counterpart, the conservative moral theologian John Harvey, who was deeply suspicious of the church's outreach to gays.

In the half decade since the Stonewall Riot, gay activism had become a full-bore revolution. The biggest strides were in the realm of medicine, which had first described homosexuality as a disorder about a hundred years earlier. Research, however, had consistently shown that homosexuals were identical in all personality components to heterosexuals, consistently scoring within normal ranges. At its meeting this June, under the weight of unanimous empirical data and gathering political storms, the APA voted to declassify homosexuality as a mental illness. As a clinical entity, then, homosexuality ceased to exist at that moment. In essence, the psychiatric establishment had come around to embrace the views of Sigmund Freud, who, in a 1935 letter to a distraught mother, called homosexuality "assuredly no advantage, but it is nothing to be ashamed of, no vice, no degradation, it cannot be classified as an illness."

Statistics showed that depression, alcoholism, and suicides especially during teen years persisted. But the APA now no longer considered them a symptom of one's sexual deviations. Rather they were seen as the result of social condemnations of one's true and natural self, the mind bedeviled by prejudice, hostility, and repression. They called this "ego-dystonic homosexuality," a condition marked by distressful plagues of doubt about self and "a desire to acquire or increase heterosexual arousal." Psychoanalysts lobbied hard for this classification. It justified a course of therapy designed to change homosexual orientation, even if such an orientation was no longer considered wrong. "Reparative" or "conversion" therapy gained new popularity, but was soon found to be ineffective—one's sexual orientation was as immutable as race or gender, the medical establishment concluded—and harmful. In fact, such therapy produced the very symptoms that were used to justify it, the APA concluded. By 1986, even this last vestigial diagnostic category would be reconsidered and all mention of homosexuality would be gone from the diagnostic literature.

This year, 1974, was also a powerful year of reckoning for Catholic homosexuals. Under pressure from Dignity leaders, who worried that some parish priests were contributing to the mental health problems of homosexuals, a committee of the National Conference of Catholic Bishops had published a guide for priests on how to counsel gays in the confessional. While still instructed to warn against gay sex, a priest now no longer had to prohibit gays even from socializing with one another, which had long been the case. "A homosexual can have an abiding relationship with another homosexual without genital sexual expression," it concluded. The fraternizing rules were eased further for lesbians, who presumably didn't feel the same "need for physical expression" as gay men. Women were now permitted to live with one another, chastely, if they wished. "Some Catholic women do maintain such a relationship," the directive said. "The emotional reward which they derive from such a relationship more than compensates for the lack of genital expression."

It was a small but significant step forward, followed by a huge leap in March, when the National Federation of Priests' Councils, a kind of clerical senate, adopted what amounted to a gay rights plank:

> BE IT RESOLVED that the National Federation of Priests' Councils hereby declares its opposition to all civil laws which make consensual homosexual acts between adults a crime and thus urges their repeal; and
> BE IT FURTHER RESOLVED that the NFPC also express its opposition to homosexuality as such being the basis of discrimination against homosexuals in employment, governmental services, housing and child rearing involving natural or adoptive parents.

Among gay Catholics, there was a sense of forward motion. McNaught was sure that acceptance by his faith was assured. He didn't feel his homosexuality in his genitals, he felt it in his heart, the way heterosexuals did, the way Catholics did their faith. His longings were *human* longings. His religion taught him that physical and emotional love were gifts from God. That's the way he intended to experience them, not in bars or parks or bathhouses, but in sacramental union with another.

In his next column for the weekly *Michigan Catholic*, McNaught opened by quoting from Paul Shanley's lengthy speech to the gay ministry conference.

> "Gay is not good," states Fr. Paul Shanley. "Gay is best! . . . Gay is best for gays. Straight is best for straights. Bi is best for bis," the 20-year veteran of street ministry declared. For the Catholic homosexual, Fr. Shanley's statement, coupled with numerous recent articles by theologian Gregory Baum, Jesuit Fr. Peter Fink, Sr.

Jeannine Gramick SSND, and a host of others, must be music to the ear. . . . Sexual expression is a sacramental gift, which, when used as an expression of inner love, is raised to the divine level. All men are given the gift. All men are challenged to express it divinely.

Perhaps he was naïve to expect his readers to immediately recognize the truth of these words. Later he would admit he'd been carried away by the thrill of his own enormous enlightenment. His column touched off a tornado of controversy. Dozens of angry letters poured into the editor, a chancery appointee. Subscriptions and advertising contracts were canceled. The diocese issued a statement saying that his column was theologically wrong—in effect, gay is *bad* for gays. The *Detroit News,* sensing the aroma of controversy, did a story about Dignity's campaign against church teachings, quoting McNaught—which ended his tenure as a popular speaker at father-daughter communion breakfasts and senior luncheons, and led to the cancellation of his column and his termination at the paper.

Fired. Not even for being gay, for he wasn't entirely out of the closet, but for believing in the rightness of homosexuality. Articles appeared everywhere, including the *New York Times* and the *Los Angeles Times.* Father James Baker, a prominent conservative columnist, called him a heretic.

When Paul Shanley heard, he jumped on an airplane and flew to Detroit. Sister Jeannine Gramick flew in from Brooklyn, where she was based at the time. A hundred people descended upon the archdiocese and joined McNaught in a hunger strike to protest his ouster. Shanley was concelebrant at a Mass in solidarity. When news reached the Detroit archbishop, he called the parish priest to demand he cancel the Mass. He refused, but the telephone call gave greater urgency to the protest, which spilled out of the church and wended its way to the steps of the chancery, with all the passion (if none of the broad support) of the civil rights march on Selma, Alabama.

McNaught's sacking would become one of the first great employment rights skirmishes for the nascent Catholic gay movement. He never got his job back—but that almost was beside the point. As he listened to Father Shanley's inspirational homily, Brian McNaught looked around and knew he was standing on the doorstep of a brand-new era.

For Sister Jeannine, the Detroit protests were a watershed. Paul Shanley was everything she wished she were, dynamic and unafraid, a crusader for the downtrodden, a visionary and leader. Obedience was the only thing required of her when she first entered the School Sisters of Notre Dame, as an eighteen-year-old from Philadelphia. She demanded more from the religious life than that. Opportunity presented itself in 1971 when she attended a home Mass near the University of Pennsylvania campus for a young man named Dominic, who had left the church in despair over his sexual orientation. She had never met a homosexual before. For years Dominic tried to turn around his heart, but could not. He wasn't emotionally unbalanced, wasn't "arrested" or "inverted" or any of the other attributes she had accepted as true, she thought. He had just as many faults and gifts and was as intelligent and witty as any heterosexual person she'd ever met. Being gay, he told her, was simply an innate attribute, like being left-handed—and just as morally neutral.

What was more, he did not feel alienated from God. In fact, after his long struggle with his church he came to feel that his love for God, and God's for him, was intact. What had ruptured was his relationship to his church.

That's what motivated her to attend the Ohio conference, which confirmed her feelings; Paul Shanley motivated her to activism. She adopted his faith that church teaching, the revered magisterium, would change. It had changed in the past. The church used to teach that collecting interest on a loan was a grave moral transgression, that slavery was a necessary evil, and that Jews were bad. When the wrongheadedness of those positions became laughably clear, the church was confident enough to reverse itself.

Gramick modeled a new national ministry around her convictions. She offered public speeches on the acceptability of gay orientation. She held workshops for parents of gays, who needed permission to love their children. She did not even reject gay couples but looked the other way when they discovered their mutual love. Her goal was peace and reconciliation—to bridge the divide between gay Catholics and their priests, to let them return to their family of faith as who they are.

Almost from the start, the highest-ranking members of the Vatican Curia were taking notice.

December 29, 1975

VATICAN CITY — In the first six years of the modern gay movement, no global institution came under more pressure than the Catholic Church. The magisterium had not changed its position on the evil of homosexual sex, not in one single nuance, since about 1400. It did not intend to do so now. Holding against the riptide of activism, the Vatican issued a document called *Persona Humana*, or "Declaration on Certain Questions Concerning Sexual Ethics."

One small subsection dealt with ministry to homosexuals. The authors, officials from the Vatican's Congregation for the Doctrine of the Faith, felt that "observations in the psychological order" represented a trend to "judge indulgently, and even to excuse completely, homosexual relations," and that this was a deplorable development. They granted that homosexuality now appeared innate. But that was not to say it was God-given:

> In the pastoral field . . . homosexuals must certainly be treated with understanding and sustained in the hope of overcoming their personal difficulties and their inability to fit into society. Their culpability will be judged with prudence. But no pastoral method can be employed which would give moral justification to these acts on the grounds that they would be consonant with the condition of such people. For according to the objective moral order, homosexual relations are acts which lack an essential and indispensable finality.

As defined elsewhere, the essential and indispensable finality of all sexual acts must be conception. Certain nuances had been adopted since the deliberations of the Birth Control Commission. Couples who could not conceive whether because of old age or medical complications were allowed genital relations—they were not held culpable for their infertility.

Gays, however, were: "In Sacred Scripture [homosexual relations] are condemned as a serious depravity and even presented as the sad consequence of rejecting God. This judgment of Scripture does not of course permit us to conclude that all those who suffer from this anomaly are personally responsible for it, but it does attest to the fact that homosexual acts are intrinsically disordered and can in no case be approved of."

Reception was mixed. Many theologians were relieved to have in hand their church's response to gay liberation and modern psychological thought. But others, with minds open to the simplest aspirations of homosexuals—that is, to love and to be loved—were disturbed by the trap this locution put them in: though recognizing homosexuals as "incurable," the church counseled them to overcome their permanent infliction. "It's like they're saying we can be birds," one gay Catholic complained, "but we can't fly."

The document, which carried force of official church teaching, reiterated the church's dim views on premarital sex, masturbation, and the "unbridled exaltation of sex" in books, plays, songs, and movies. It called upon parents to cut no slack if they saw their children living in relaxed constraints, and commanded artists and writers to produce wholesome work. Bishops and priests were exhorted to vigorously enforce these time-honored teachings. "It will especially be necessary to bring the faithful to understand that the Church holds these principles not as old and inviolable superstitions, nor out of some Manichaean prejudice, as is often alleged, but rather because she knew with certainty that they are in complete harmony with the Divine order of creation and with the spirit of Christ, and therefore also with human dignity."

Perhaps it was perfect coincidence, but intersecting with the delivery of this doctrine came a further decline in the priesthood. In 1967, American seminaries had had an enrolled student body totaling 37,383. In 1975, that number had dropped by half, to just 16,928. The slide would never be reversed. By the 2002–3 school year, enrollment would bottom out at 5,598, and according to accepted projections, there would be half as many priests per parishioners in America as in 1975.

It was particularly bad in Boston. In 1960 the seminaries in the archdiocese had produced more than seventy-five new priests. This year they had produced eleven. Cardinal Humberto Medeiros considered the decline in vocations to the priesthood "a grave danger for us and a source of profound sadness for the Church."

Sometime in 1976
MANCHESTER, NEW HAMPSHIRE — A reticent parish priest, exhausted by his interior battles, reached a conclusion he could no longer deny: as a priest, he was a menace. He knew there was something wrong with him, though exactly what was unclear. For the past five years, he had repeatedly provoked sexual incidents with teenage boys. Nobody ever caught him or brought him up on charges. But he knew that what he was doing was wrong, and that he could not stop.

Making an appointment with his superiors, he described his demons in detail. It was imperative, he said, that he be removed from proximity to boys. He pleaded for psychiatric help.

Alarmed church leaders sent him for an evaluation right away, but for whatever reason, they deemed the priest fit to work. Over his objection, he was returned to an assignment that required direct and regular contact with teenagers, and his request for ongoing therapy was denied.

September 23, 1977
ROCHESTER, NEW YORK — As usual, Paul Shanley began his exhortation at full speed. "Homosexual acts are not sinful, sick, or a crime nor are they immoral. What has been done to gays by the straight community calls out for vengeance from heaven! Gay persons aren't angry enough! They should become more angry at society!"

Shanley was now among the most sought-after Catholic speakers. With his provocative swagger, he could hold a large hall in this thrall for hours. Three of his most controversial speeches were now available on cassette tapes: *Straight Talk About Gays, Counseling Parents of Gays,* and most recently, *Changing Norms of Sexuality*, the edited version of a Fidel Castro–like nine-hour seminar blending scripture, natural law, and a survey of theological opinion with his own posturings about coming out of the closet (for), gay marriage (against), gay adoption (why not?), machismo (the root evil), petting and masturbation (morally harmless). Despite a steep price tag of $28.95, the three were heavy sellers. Meanwhile, Anita Bryant had just begun her campaign to roll back gay rights ordinances being adopted sporadically across the country. Her "Save Our Children" message polarized the nation, and increased Shanley's popularity.

Tonight's gathering at Becket Hall, cosponsored by Dignity and Integrity, the Episcopalian gay group, drew a large and eager crowd. The diocese of Rochester considered this a must-see event, and encouraged all priests, interns, and pastoral assistants throughout the diocese to attend. A smattering of Church traditionalists also participated and took keen notes. They patrolled their parishes like fifties-era Red hunters. Any indication the church might lift its perfect condemnation caused great concern.

"Straight people cannot tell the truth about sex," Shanley declared. "They spend all their time worrying about the bedsores of gays!"

The crowd laughed. But not Dolores Stevens, a Rochester laywoman who sensed she had stumbled upon heresy in its purest form.

When the meeting was over, Stevens called an acquaintance, Jeanne Sweeney, to tell her what she'd heard. Sweeney, a registered nurse and the wife of a physician, was a well-known letter writer to local periodicals, mostly on the subject of abortion, which she vigorously opposed. She was also a decorated belligerent in the wars against immorality. Hearing the woman's report, she was aghast. She asked for a written summation of the Shanley talk.

Among the passages Dolores Stevens wrote were these:

> He stated celibacy is impossible, therefore the only alternative is for gays to have sex with different persons whenever they want to.

> He spoke of pedophilia (which is a non-coerced sexual manipulation of sex organs including oral-genital sex between an adult and

a child). He stated that the adult is not the seducer—the "kid" is
the seducer, and furthermore the kid is not traumatized by the act
per se, the kid is traumatized when the police and authorities
"drag" the kid in for questioning.

He stated that he can think of *no* sexual act that causes psychic
damage—"not even incest or bestiality."

Jeanne Sweeney forwarded this transcript to an official in the north
region offices of the Rochester diocese, Father Bernard Dolan, seeking
clarification on official teaching. Father Dolan gave her query some attention. A dispute arose over the accuracy of Dolores Stevens's notes,
which diverged in key points from a news account of the address published in the *Rochester Courier-Journal*. The Rochester chancery called
a meeting on November 4 to investigate. *Courier-Journal* reporter John
Dash attended, as did two of his colleagues, various diocesan officials,
Sweeney and Stevens, and Monsignor George Cocuzzi, the official liaison to Dignity. They all agreed that Shanley's talk was "frank." But they
disagreed on Stevens's assertion that he was promoting bestiality or sex
with children.

Nevertheless Sweeney demanded that Monsignor Cocuzzi alert Paul
Shanley's superiors in Boston about his "frankness." He refused outright. Sweeney then wrote Father Dolan again at the north region office
demanding that *he* inform the Boston archdiocese, but he also refused.
So she wrote Cardinal Medeiros herself, on November 17, 1977, with
a provocative carbon copy to the president of the National Federation
of Catholic Physicians' Guilds.

When the letters arrived at the Boston chancery in Brighton, they
joined an expanding file folder chronicling the many Paul Shanley controversies. Hundreds of letters brought this or that sentence of his ministry to the administration's attention. Newspaper clippings were
carefully glued to paper and mailed in. A dozen or more of the faithful
had simply folded up the leaflets for his audiocassette series and forwarded them to officials. A network of eyes and ears gathered up information and reported it up the chain of command. But there were
other notes as well, from government officials, nuns, social workers,

moms and dads, tearful thanks for the goodness of Shanley's ministry, "a true Gospel witness to the life and teaching of Jesus Christ."

Cardinal Medeiros had asked Auxiliary Bishop Thomas Daily, his vicar general and second in command, to handle the "Shanley problem." Daily had many rogue priests to manage, but none as stubbornly cutting-edge. To an old-school cleric like Daily, Shanley's lack of ideological obedience seemed almost pathological. Now he was purportedly mentioning lust for animals and minors, if this woman's report could be believed, and to Daily those were merely variations on a theme. But he was not prepared to take any responsibility for it.

"I am grateful to you for your letter and for the information which is enclosed," he wrote back to Sweeney. "The position of the Archdiocese of Boston is that while Father Shanley enjoys the faculties of the Archdiocese of Boston, he alone must be held responsible for any statements regarding homosexuality."

October 14, 1978
VATICAN CITY — The cardinal from Krakow, Karol Wojtyla, was a long shot for the papacy when Paul VI, the self-doubting pope, died, not unexpectedly, on August 6, 1978. At the gathering of the Sacred College of Cardinals, positioned in thrones along the perimeter of the Sistine Chapel, the required two-thirds majority converged in favor of the patriarch of Venice, Albino Liciani, who was elected the 263rd pope. He selected the name John Paul after his two immediate predecessors. But he became better known as the September pope—he dropped dead from a heart attack on September 28, just thirty-three days after his installation.

At the next conclave, Karol Wojtyla was not expected to do much better. Just fifty-eight years old, he was extremely young by papal standards. Though he spoke Italian well, there had not been a pope selected from outside Italy in nearly five hundred years. In addition, at a time when passions among the cardinals still lingered for the liberalism of Vatican II, ideologically he was also among the most conservative branch of the church. Having suffered under a succession of totalitarian regimes in Poland, he was a virulent anticommunist—a divergence from Paul VI's policies, which included efforts to reconcile East and West. In other ways Wojtyla's vision for the church diverged significantly from Paul VI's, sometimes more liberal, sometimes less. He favored democracy aggressively, but warned that the free market could be rife with economic inequity; he opposed totalitarianism, but was dismissive of the liberation theology movement in Latin America; he was critical of the spiritual drift he had seen among the faithful and was resolute in his belief that Catholics in a time of modernity needed to redouble their obedience to church leaders. There was concern in the Sistine Chapel in October that Wojtyla represented an effort to unravel Vatican II.

On Sunday, October 14, the secret deliberation began in earnest. One hundred and eight cardinals penned their candidate's name on a piece of paper, folded it, and carried it one at a time to the altar, where after raising it above their heads to show they had voted, they slid it into a chalice. The votes were counted and when no clear majority emerged, as tradition required, the ballots were sewn one to another then set on fire, the black plumes of smoke signaling to the faithful outside in St. Peter's Square that the church remained in interregnum. Several ballots later, Wojtyla's fortunes were ascendant, thanks in part to the advocacy of Cardinal Josef Ratzinger, a Bavarian prelate who shared his ultraorthodox ideology, especially his opposition to communism. Late the next day, Wojtyla became Pope John Paul II, on the eighth tally. Historians credit Ratzinger not only for delivering German votes but luring over the American bloc, with help from conservative Polish-American Cardinal John Krol from Philadelphia.

In his homily the following day at St. Peter's Basilica, the new pope promised a papacy that would be faithful to the Second Vatican Council. But he would soon show himself a firm leader and a hard-liner on Catholic doctrinal policies. He drew a firewall against the ordination of women and for the defense of family life, rigorously opposing birth control, divorce, and abortion, which he considered "a veritable 'slaughter of the innocents' on a worldwide scale."

And seeing what chaos ensued following Paul VI's encyclical *Humanae Vitae,* John Paul II took to heart the lesson of indirect leadership. Many of the faithful and even some priests had chosen to disregard church teachings, especially on sexual matters, in favor of their own consciences. His papacy would be a strict one. His deputy in this undertaking would be Josef Ratzinger, whom he appointed prefect of the Congregation for the Doctrine of the Faith, the most powerful of the nineteen main offices that make up the Roman Curia, and also the most feared. Centuries earlier, under its previous name—the Holy Office of the Inquisition—it condemned to poverty scientists like Galileo, whose theories sounded unholy. Under Ratzinger, its main function would be to defend the magisterium from the many challenges of Catholic thinkers. He would use his enforcement powers aggressively, especially—as the journalist and historian John L. Allen pointed out in his biography, *Cardinal Ratzinger*—to mute feminists and gay rights activists who called upon the ancient church to acknowledge new liberties in a modern world.

Among clerics who thought that Vatican II had been only a beginning, that future liberalizations might soon bring a married clergy or female priests, or allow gays to marry or straights to divorce, or that condoms might be permitted even in the desperate war against HIV and AIDS, the election of John Paul II not only dashed those hopes. It made having them into an act of heresy.

Winter 1978

PHOENIX, ARIZONA — Over and over, Mark Kennedy, who was ten, his mother, Doris, and his father, Jack, had told the story of the boy's unwanted sexual encounters, each time earning a higher audience. Now they sat in a grand light-drenched room across a long table from the diocesan vicar general, Father Thomas J. O'Brien. They had expected this time to see their bishop, James S. Rausch.

"When can we get in to see him?" Doris asked through light sobs. She had never heard of O'Brien, Rausch's closest friend and longtime deputy. She felt the matter of an abusive priest was grave enough to merit a meeting with the head of the diocese. "Bishop Rausch has to be informed about Patrick Colleary."

"I can assure you I will be able to take care of this," said O'Brien firmly. "Father Colleary will be transferred. He will not be allowed near your boy again."

Jack Kennedy felt the priest should be sentenced to some form of punishment for his crimes. O'Brien disagreed. At the very least, remove him permanently from ministry, Jack Kennedy argued. O'Brien grew ill-tempered. The church forgives sinners, he said. The matter would be handled in the grace and wisdom of the loving church. What, Jack Kennedy wanted to know, would the church show in grace and wisdom to his son Mark, shivering at his side? "My boy should be in counseling," he said.

O'Brien, who would go on to lead the diocese as bishop, disagreed. "In our experience it is best to *not* mention these matters again. Any sort of talk therapy would only reinforce the incident in the little fellow's mind."

The Kennedys stammered their frustrations but O'Brien interrupted. "I trust you have not told anybody about this grave scandal."

"A few people," Doris admitted. She went down a short list. "Not many—"

O'Brien thrust a finger toward her and thundered, "You shouldn't have done that!"

Sacra Congregatio
Pro Doctrina Fidei

November 14, 1978
His Eminence
Humberto Cardinal Medeiros
Archbishop of Boston
2121 Commonwealth Avenue
Brighton, Massachusetts 02135
U.S.A.

Your Eminence,

    The attention of the Congregation for the Doctrine of the Faith has been called to a series of tapes about homosexuality produced for public distribution (e.g., "The Changing Norms of Sexuality," . . .) by Father Paul Shanley, a priest of the archdiocese of Boston who describes himself as assigned to full-time ministry to homosexuals under your authorization.

The contents of these tapes contradict Catholic moral teaching and recommend unacceptable pastoral practices.

May I ask you to inform this congregation of any steps you have already taken or intend to take in regard to the spread of these erroneous ideas and in regard to the position of Father Shanley.

With cordial best wishes for Your Eminence, I am

Sincerely in Christ,

Franjo Cardinal Seper

BRIGHTON, MASSACHUSETTS — In his enormous chugging empire, Cardinal Medeiros's attentions were a precious commodity thinly divided among a sprawling infrastructure of priests, nuns, parochial students, hospital employees, theologians, and politicians, but not one of them demanded more attention than Paul Shanley. Mainstream and conservative Catholics opposed everything he stood for, and spared no effort denouncing his progay espousals in deliberately phrased fulminations against heresy.

These detractors were thorough and obstinate. If Medeiros tended not to answer their complaints—frankly, lengthy letters from other parts of the country did not compel him to immediate action—he was sure to hear from the same writer again. He took to using a special rubber stamp on those communications: "Not Acknowledged at Cardinal's Residence." This was a signal to Bishop Daily to craft some sort of nonresponsive circumlocution: "His Eminence passed your letter to me; I will be sure to convey your concerns to His Eminence."

Crank mail from the faithful was one thing. Formal proceedings from the most revered and feared of the Roman Curial offices was quite another. In his lengthy response to the CDF regarding the Shanley condemnation, Medeiros, casting himself as a lone guardian of goodness in a libertine age of moral decay, declared that the burgeoning gay community was among the most serious challenges to American Catholicism in some time. He feared it was infiltrating the priesthood itself. He had recently conducted an extensive but so far secret campaign at St. John Seminary to "turn back the number of homosexuals who, for many reasons, are being drawn towards the sacred priesthood," he wrote. In the coming few years, he expected that his graduating classes would be seriously small. Such was the price of vigilance.

Meanwhile, what could Medeiros do with Shanley? Confronted, the man always denied he was undermining church teaching; challenged, he always went to the secular press. He was incorrigibly progay! "I believe that Father Shanley is a troubled priest and I have tried to be understanding and patient with him while continuously affirming—both privately to him and publicly to my people—the Church teaching on sexual ethics." Medeiros promised the Congregation for the Doctrine of the Faith that he would do what he could to temper Shanley. "Please pray for Father Shanley and for all our young people whose souls are attacked constantly by voices which distort and scandalize."

Then Medeiros summoned Shanley for a stern talking-to. He demanded that Shanley stop going around saying Medeiros appointed him to a "ministry for sexual minorities." In fact, he was still assigned to minister to "alienated youth," and though Shanley boasted of being the only full-time shepherd to gay sheep, he was no such thing. Medeiros instructed him to stop saying Mass for gays or blessing gay unions, and forbade him from expressing his own opinions on the morality of homosexual acts.

Feeling bitterly betrayed, Shanley leapt to the offensive. He had his old colleagues from the Association of Urban Priests send individual petitions to lift the ban on his gay ministry. He called his regular contacts in the media and fed them inflammatory lines about Medeiros turning his back on gays. "He says homosexuals don't need any special help from priests because all priests are trained to deal with homosexuals in the confessional," he told the *Globe,* knowing how ridiculously out of touch his boss would seem. He called the *New York Times* and the Associated Press, which wrote stories about Shanley's sidelining. Medeiros was leading a purge with homophobic overtones while pretending to care about homosexuals, Shanley warned. "If that means that gay people are welcome, it's like saying 'Niggers' are welcome, too."

He waged his guerrilla campaign for months, drafting support from across the country. Academics and liberal intellectuals were solidly behind him. Gay people wrote desperate letters of protest in his behalf. One mother told a *Globe* reporter that Shanley was the most heroic cleric she and her family had ever known. "This beautiful man gave me back my son," she said. "I felt he was dead when I found out about my son's homosexuality. God sent him to me when I didn't know where to turn, to help me understand. People like me need him." People still flocked to him for counseling. Shanley turned them away, saying he could not speak to them without written permission from the cardinal. By the dozens, they wrote Medeiros letters detailing the sort of roiling desperation that existed among Catholic homosexuals, their friends, and their families, begging access to Shanley's message.

In the mounds of mail, which by April 1979 would become a burden to the secretaries who filed it away, Medeiros read nothing but defiance. He decided to throw a net over Shanley and bring him indoors, to domesticate him, to remove him from the stream of trouble he always created.

> Dear Father Shanley,
>
> I am writing to inform you that I am ending your appointment to the Ministry to Alienated Youth and am appointing you as associate pastor of St. John the Evangelist Parish in Newton. The effective date of these actions is April 15, 1979. The special ministry you had undertaken to homosexuals was ended when you last visited me.
>
> It is understood that your ministry at St. John Parish and elsewhere in this Archdiocese of Boston will be exercised in full conformity with the clear teachings of the Church as expressed in papal documents and other pronouncements of the Holy See, especially those regarding sexual ethics. The pastoral ministry of priests can hardly be effective apart from the healing and saving truth of Christ proclaimed by His Church, even when "the saying may be hard."

Nearly apoplectic, Shanley threatened to expose Medeiros's antigay seminary purges. With the media fascinated by gay rights, he knew how bad that would appear. The papers would compare it to the discredited policy to exclude blacks from the priesthood, he promised; there would be demonstrations in the streets.

But with the CDF scrutinizing him, Medeiros was not about to buckle. "I reject completely your accusation that I am inflicting punishment on homosexuals and their families," he fired back. "I shall pass over in amazed but laughable silence the threat you invoke against me concerning further public pronouncements, this time about our seminary. I urge and direct you to take a parish assignment, as many of our priests do in this time of such great need, where you will be out of the limelight and involved in the ordinary, everyday work of a priest, work seen only by a few, unnoticed by the media, but dear to the heart of Christ."

Chapter 4

Falling Apart

August 1979

Jamaica Plain, Massachusetts — Believing that Father Geoghan had massaged and groped her son's buttocks and genitals, a local woman who gave her name as Mrs. Coveny went to the local police precinct to file a formal complaint. She had a large family, and was accustomed to coming to its defense. Because her allegation involved a Roman Catholic priest, it was directed to the attention of the chaplain of the police department. The disposition of the case was left up to him. No other information was reported back, either to the police officials or to the complainant. That is to say, she had no idea what became of her allegation or what became of the priest. Of course, she assumed that everything would be handled appropriately.

August 17, 1979
Most Rev. Thomas V. Daily
2121 Commonwealth Ave.
Brighton, Mass. 02135

Dear Bishop Daily:

I write in respectful recognition of your known concern for the well-being of a brother priest and your faithful adherence to the virtues of justice and charity.

It has been called to my attention that a Mrs. Coveny of Walk Hill St., Forest Hills, has made serious charges of a moral nature against Fr. John J. Geoghan, associate pastor here at St. Andrew's. It is also my understanding that Fr. William Francis, Chaplain of the Boston Police Dept. has reported this matter to you.

These charges are completely false and do not bear even a scintilla of truth. Fr. Geoghan is an outstanding, dedicated priest who is doing superior work at St. Andrew's Parish. He is a zealous man of prayer who constantly gives of himself in furthering the cause of Christ in this area. His good works are countless and I thank God daily that he has favored and blessed me with his priestly presence.

The Coveny family is emotionally unstable, psychotic, revengeful and spiritually barren. Their reputation in the community is poor and in my judgment they are people of low character whose presence presents an ever-threatening danger. I do not discount the possible hand of the devil where they are concerned and prudence dictates that they should be carefully avoided. Only recently I was the victim of an unprovoked assault by ROBERT COVENY (approx. 19 yrs. old) whose mind allegedly has been altered by drugs. Knowing that the Courts would do nothing, fearful of an implied threat to set fire to church property and not wishing to find myself on the front page of the *Boston Globe,* I have let the frightening incident pass. I predict that it is only a matter of time before Robert commits a violent criminal act against some person in this community.

Members of the Coveny family have seen fit to harass the priests at St. Andrew's over the years and I believe that a check of the Police files will reveal that charges similar to those made against Fr. Geoghan were made by Mrs. Coveny against a previous pastor. Like the present existing charges, they too were totally untrue. I suppose my turn will be next. As Shakespeare once said, "Be thou chaste as ice and pure as snow, thou shalt not escape calumny."

I presume that Fr. William Francis, after proper investigation, has by now informed you that the charges made against Fr. Geoghan are completely false. I regret that for some unknown reason he did not consider it necessary or important enough to discuss this matter with the pastor of the parish. Fr. Geoghan was very open about the whole matter from the very beginning.

The past week has placed a terrible strain on Fr. Geoghan and a lesser man would not have been able to bear up under it. The slow poison of calumny has a deadly affect upon the spirit. I now ask you in your priestly goodness to *personally* assure Fr. Geoghan that his record is clear and inform him that he still enjoys the blessing of a good priestly reputation—a reputation which is rightfully his. Only you, as Chancellor of the Archdiocese, can dispel the lingering doubts that are understandably in his mind, restore his confidence and bring peace to his mind and soul. There are calumnies against which even innocence loses courage. I feel sure that you will be happy to comply with my respectful and reasonable request.

Well, I'm off to Kennebunkport to fatten up a body that is already too fat *(bonum diffusivum sui)* and to take out my many frustrations on a little white golf ball. It keeps me at least half sane in these crazy, difficult times—

Wishing you all the best, always—

In Christ

Father Frank Delaney

Pastor, St. Andrews

August 23, 1979

Brighton, Massachusetts — Bishop Daily was sympathetic to the pastor's request on behalf of his curate. As far as he was concerned, a priest was too vulnerable to charges of a moral nature. Reassuring Geoghan with a brief letter was the least he could do as vicar general, he felt. He would have done it for anybody. So by return mail he wrote to the associate pastor at St. Andrew's acknowledging that the scurrilous charges leveled against him were "proven to be irresponsible, totally false, made by a woman who is well known and without credence in the community." He invited Geoghan to pay him a visit at the chancery, if he liked, so that Daily could reassure him in person. "I am sorry that you were disturbed," he concluded.

A *Summer Night, 1979*

PHOENIX, ARIZONA — A cute but strung-out seventeen-year-old farm boy named Brian O'Connell was patrolling a main thoroughfare hoping to turn tricks to pay for his heroin habit when his luck improved and a dark Mercedes pulled up alongside him. A middle-aged man with square, thick glasses made his acquaintance. Money was discussed, a deal was made. Circling around to the passenger side, O'Connell opened the door and slid in next to his benefactor, who said his name was Paul.

It was not until they perched awkwardly on a motel bed under an unflattering light that Paul seemed vaguely familiar to O'Connell. But his childlike qualities—he wanted to hold hands and giggled as though he were a sixth-grader—made identification difficult. O'Connell took a camera from his bag and photographed the two of them through the mirror, as the older man brushed a kiss sweetly on his head.

Several times in the following weeks, Paul would call O'Connell at home and arrange further liaisons. These were essentially cash transactions for O'Connell, who went from smoking heroin to shooting it in a fast descent and was always short on funds. Once, sitting alone in the car while Paul paid for a motel room, O'Connell rifled the glove compartment for anything of value. What he found instead shocked him, and explained why he thought he'd recognized this man before. His name wasn't Paul at all. It was James Rausch, and he was bishop of the diocese of Phoenix.

When he returned to the car, O'Connell confronted him. "I'm only relieving stress," the bishop explained. O'Connell accepted the explanation. Their arrangement would not be altered by this wrinkle.

Christmastime 1979

JAMAICA PLAIN, MASSACHUSETTS — He looked like a little holy altar boy, that's what Maryetta Dussourd thought when she first met Geoghan at the parish adjacent to hers. She was not well-to-do. Her husband, Ralph, worked long hours, to little financial effect, leaving her and her three sons—and the four boys of her niece, whom she was raising—

scraping to get by. She claimed he drank copiously, which aggravated an already hot temper and careless libido, making a miserable situation intolerable. She was a wretched woman who cried easily and often. She tried in an almost constant fervor to give praise to God for "both trial and joy," as St. Thérèse of Lisieux had advocated. On any given week she attended services at three separate churches. Saying the rosary sustained her. She was an adherent to the charismatic renewal movement, Roman Catholicism's answer to hands-shaking, tongues-speaking Pentecostalism. Whatever she tried, despair kept winning out. Until she befriended Geoghan.

She had attended his prayer services for about a month before he asked to come to her modest apartment for supper. He wished to meet her family. Maryetta's dream had come true: a priest, God's earthly presence, had made her home blessed. By his affable presence, the household was transformed. If Bing Crosby had been sitting at her table, she could not have been more starstruck.

Thereafter, he came over nearly every single evening for the next two years. She was ecstatic. She loved Geoghan the way she loved God and her church, with an overflowing, aching love. He was her best friend. She called him, simply, Father. And she had no reservations when, night after night, he excused himself from the TV room after dinner to offer his blessings to the children in their rooms. Sometimes these ministrations would take the span of three television programs before Father returned to the den. He loved her children that much. Once when he was out of town for a diocesan prayer retreat he missed them so badly that he drove back in the middle of the night just to see them.

"I feel so comfortable with your family. I love those children," he told Maryetta. The seven boys and one girl were ages four to eleven. There was only one other family he'd ever felt that way about, he said.

He was referring to the Muzzis, but she would not know that for decades. Her boys couldn't tell her what was happening to them; they knew she was too much in the priest's thrall to hear them out. Instead they told her sister, Marge Gallant, who broke the news to her.

"Your friend John Geoghan touched them while they were at your house," she said. "Talk to your children. Talk to your husband and get back to me immediately." She wanted the police and the church involved.

Terrified that it was true, Maryetta's mind rewound history. She recalled a night not long ago when Geoghan arrived near midnight and asked to sleep on the sofa—he had been "driving around" and felt it was too late to make the trip back to his quarters. In retrospect, this struck her as preposterous. The drive was not the least bit arduous. Obediently, she had stretched sheets over her sofa. Later in the night, she thought she had heard him tiptoeing past the doorway of the converted dining room where she and Ralph slept at the head of a darkened hallway. Nothing lay down that corridor but the two kids' rooms—six of the seven boys shared one room; the only daughter shared her bedroom with the youngest cousin.

A door squeaked. Footfalls receded. Maryetta knew he had entered the boys' room. She shook her husband awake. They listened for Geoghan to reemerge, and in time he did; they watched his shadowy silhouette retrace the length of the hallway past their door. It was almost impossible to grasp now what she felt at that moment. *Invulnerable*. Blessed with a guardian priest.

But in the morning when they mentioned his midnight stroll, Geoghan smiled at them blankly. "Oh, no," he said, "I didn't do that."

Ralph was appalled. A Baptist, he had agreed to allow his children to be raised as Catholics and attend religious instruction courses mysteriously called CCD—everything about the religion struck him as outmoded and silly. But honesty was a presumed clerical requirement. He pressed the point, but again Geoghan denied visiting the boys.

"Father, we saw you coming out of the room."

His smile never faded. "I went to bless the children."

Geoghan's easy lie drew Maryetta's and Ralph's attention equally, and they focused suspicion on the priest. But even as their thoughts turned dark, neither suspected sexual abuse. It was beyond their imagination. An alcoholic, they thought—most priests were drunks in their experience. For the next several nights, the Dussourds timidly attempted to dissuade Geoghan's visits. One evening, they turned off all the lights and pretended to be away, but he knocked and knocked until Maryetta, her heart breaking, relented and cracked open the door.

"The children are asleep, Father, and Ralph and I could really benefit from some time alone."

"When you send away a priest," Geoghan said brightly, gently pushing through the door, "his blessing will go with him!"

Now, Maryetta's mind was a blinding storm of hysteria. Doing as her sister instructed, she called Ralphie, her eldest, into the room. Geoghan had taken a particular interest in Ralphie—over the summer he took the boy for a weekend at his own mother's house. Something bothered the boy about what happened that weekend, but she had brushed the incident away. Now she found it difficult to speak through her fear.

"Ralphie," she said. "Ralphie, when you went to Father Geoghan's to stay over at his mother's house, when you came back the next day you wouldn't talk about it, and for the next week you wouldn't talk about it, and the week after you wouldn't talk about it, and you stiffened up on me and got very, very scared." She took a breath. "Can you tell me if something happened there?"

Reluctantly, he peeled back the layers of that one long night spent fending off countless advances without success, at one point demanding to be taken home so loudly that he awoke the old woman. The memory made him shake uncontrollably. His mother held him tight, bathed him with her own tears.

"Why didn't you tell me? Why didn't you tell me this?"

He pulled away from her and stood near the door as though he were planning to flee. His small hand was wired on the doorknob. A storm sprayed from his eyes.

"He told me you would never believe me! You loved the church too much to believe me! I'm sorry. I'm sorry I hurt you, Mommy!"

What would happen to a church-loving woman forced to confront such news? There was a good chance that she would find herself torn impossibly between two powerful allegiances. On one side was the defiled innocence of her child, whom she could not have loved more, whose suffering was her suffering. On the other was the everlasting church, to which she had sworn obedience and faith, whose total goodness was her solace and hope, and which offered her the only future she could accept, the reward of heaven. Believing the boy would have to mean discrediting the church, for its flaws must be many if it had bestowed upon a wicked man the high prestige of the priesthood. To disbelieve the boy, to see him as a liar bent on besmirching the church, would be to imagine him as Satan's helper, possessed by grievous evil. The conflict in her soul was almost poisonous enough to kill her. Catholics who fall from faith land hard. According to a massive study of Catholics in the Netherlands, suicide rates increase dramatically among those for whom Catholicism loses its strength and hold, such is their despair. Geoghan seemed to know this intuitively or he would not have put the warning to the boy in such terms—*she loved the church too much to believe him.*

Maryetta could not find the strength to talk to her other children. She asked her husband to meet with Danny, Edward, and Margaret. It was a serious mistake, she could tell immediately. A loathing overcame her husband that would drive him from her and their victimized sons (the daughter was not touched by Geoghan). She sat in the other room weeping while her husband exploded with anger at the boys.

"How could you do this to me? How could you do this? You know what it's like to be a man! Are you some kind of pervert? What is wrong with you?" Danny, the second oldest, wept and pleaded. He was nine years old.

February 9, 1980
Jamaica Plain, Massachusetts — By the time Maryetta Dussourd could breathe calmly enough to speak, weeks had passed. During that time, memories took on different meanings. She remembered a remark Geoghan made about the other family he had loved: one night, he had said cryptically, the father accosted him as he was blessing the children, chased him down the stairs and out of the house, and said, "If I ever see you again I swear I will kill you." This was a story she had heard him tell for years, plain as a confession. But rather than provoking suspicion, the sad tale refused to yield to her understanding. She felt pity for the priest.

And what had she been thinking the day she took her children to the

Southern Jamaica Plain clinic and the family's longtime nurse, out of the perfect blue, showed grave concern about the priest and her children? "There are two boys downstairs who were both friends of John Geoghan's, and they are getting psychiatric help," the nurse confided. "For setting their bedroom on fire. To get away from him. Have you had any problems with Father Geoghan?"

"Oh gosh, no," she said. "I love that priest very much! We all do. My husband is helping him raise money for his baseball league!"

She had dismissed the conversation as utterly incomprehensible, so totally unreconciled with reality that it didn't merit another thought.

Finally she made an appointment with her pastor, Father John Thomas, and managed to tell him everything. "That first family was in Hingham," she said. These must have been the Muzzis. "I don't know the name. There was another family. He used to talk about visiting a Greek family, that included two boys, on Walk Hill Street. He would take the children out for rides, watch TV with them, and spend time in their bedrooms. He told me that they told him to not visit anymore and suddenly moved." That was the Coveny brood, though she did not know their name, either.

By her count, there were at least fifteen children molested, including her own. Immediate and decisive action was necessary, she said, to keep her husband from marching down the aisle on Sunday, as he continually threatened, and punching Geoghan senseless.

Thomas took her allegations very seriously. Because Bishop Daily, the vicar general, was away for several weeks, he would have to confront Geoghan himself, a prospect which made him uneasy. He invited the priest to his own rectory for dinner, and posed the question to him almost casually. Geoghan's reply was chilling. "Oh well, it was just two families," he said, adding that he did not think this posed a problem for his apostolate.

Thomas reported his shocking confrontation to Daily upon his return to Boston. Daily reached Geoghan on the telephone and demanded to hear the admission of repeat "homosexual activity" himself.

He admitted to having molested the seven boys over a period of more than a year; he never once touched the Dussourd girl, Margaret.

"I feel very badly about it. I am ashamed." He hung his head. "I have been very open with my confessor, my spiritual director, about this, this problem. I asked about professional psychological help. But he told me to hold off for now."

Daily knew he had a big problem on his hands.

February 12, 1980

Dear Father Geoghan:

I am writing to inform you that I am ending your appointment as Associate Pastor at Saint Andrew the Apostle Parish in Forest Hills and I am placing you on Sick Leave. The effective date of this action is February 12, 1980.

I shall remember you in my Masses and prayers, Father John, that your recovery may be swift and complete.

I take this occasion to ask for a remembrance in your Masses and prayers. Please notify the Office of the Chancellor, and Reverend Gilbert S. Phinn, Personnel Director, that you have received this letter.

Invoking the Blessing of Christ, the Eternal High Priest, in our mutual priestly endeavors, I am

Sincerely in Christ,

Most Reverend Thomas V. Daily

Vicar General

Daily had handled cases like this before. His plan was to hustle Geoghan in to see a therapist and then, depending on what the professional opinion was, either give him some time off or move him immediately into a distant parish. The transfer would be a necessary precaution to keep the scandal contained. Geoghan accepted his suspension magnanimously, and vanished from St. Andrew's without a farewell. Parishioners were told he needed a rest. Even the other priests at St. Andrew's were told nothing of his derelictions.

Father Thomas dropped by the Dussourd apartment to inform Maryetta about the status. He undocked a chair from the kitchen table and sat down. "It was agreed that Father would be removed from St. Andrew's. He will go for treatment," he said. He advised her quite firmly to keep the matter to herself. It was a necessary precaution against stigmatizing the boys.

"Is there anything else your family wants?"

"They should be in counseling," she said. She was remembering the children who had set their home on fire. "My husband still wants the police involved, he still feels the same way. My sister Marge is broken up about this—she spent years in the convent, you know. She loves her priests and clergy very much. But she also believes the police should be involved."

The priest was resolute, which frightened Maryetta. She knew that a terrible family fissure was imminent if the church failed to mollify them. If forced to choose between family and church, Maryetta knew she would rather perish. "We have to have a chancery meeting," she pleaded. "If we don't get a chancery meeting, the whole family will . . . legally we'll have to do something. With the press and everything."

"You must think of his mother. She's very, very old."

Geoghan's mother? What she thought about Geoghan's mother was how unconscionable it was she lay in her own bed while Ralphie screamed out in the adjoining room. She must have known about her son's dreadful proclivities.

"Both families have problems," Thomas said. "The Catholic Church is bigger than you are. And probably, nobody would believe you. Can you really afford legal counsel?"

He leaned forward. "Maryetta, you are a sinner. What Father Geoghan did was also a sin. The difference is that we are talking about his career, for which he sacrificed for many years. You do not want to jeopardize that. You believe in forgiveness, don't you? Shouldn't you forgive him?"

She was feeling torn between her loyalty to her church and the escalating demands from her family. She had not even had the nerve to tell her brother Jack what happened. She knew how it would crush him—he had been a seminarian through high school. "I want to be loyal to the church," she said.

"Think about the people who go to Mass every Sunday, who send their children to CCD, the elderly and religious."

"I don't want to go to the police, Father," she mewled. "I love Father Geoghan. I don't want to hurt his mother. I don't want to hurt the congregation. I'm at the center of this. I just, I should have seen the signs. I'm the one guilty for all of this. But my husband is hysterical."

The Dussourds never got their chancery meeting. Around their home, Geoghan was not mentioned again. They trusted that matters had been taken care of by the cardinal or his vicar general. But there were many things the vicar general did not do. Because he wanted the matter kept private, which he thought was the priest's right, he did not report Geoghan's behavior to the church personnel committee. He did not tell the police a crime had been committed, believing, wrongly, that priests enjoyed immunity under the law. He never reopened the allegations Mrs. Coveny had brought, although she was so obviously the woman Dussourd mentioned—how many others on Walk Hill Street would have brought charges against Geoghan?—or those brought by the Muzzi family in Hingham. As a result he never dispatched a priest to talk to their children, nor expressed sympathy or compassion toward them in any way. Even the Dussourd children, to whose violation Geoghan had blithely admitted, were left to endure their traumas alone.

For the next year, Geoghan lived at his mother's house in West Roxbury, under the medical ministrations of a general practitioner named Dr. Robert Mullins, who was the Geoghan family's next-door neighbor, and Dr. John H. Brennan, a psychiatrist with no experience in sexually deviant behavior—other than his own history of abusing a patient. Despite their lack of credentials, both men eventually pronounced Geoghan "cured," and that was good enough for the archdiocese.

On February 25, 1981, with the blessing of every member of the hierarchy of the archdiocese of Boston, Geoghan was placed back into ministry as an assistant pastor at St. Brendan's in Dorchester. The pastor there—who was not informed of Geoghan's past—was relieved to have him. Geoghan was not told to keep away from children. In fact, the pastor gave Geoghan responsibility for the altar boys and CCD classes.

July 1981

Newton, Massachusetts — From the minute he got to St. John the Evangelist—pronounced by parishioners in the French manner, *St. Jean l'Évangéliste,* to distinguish their church from all the other institutions named St. John in the archdiocese—Paul Shanley was eager to get out. He felt caged in this extremely upper-middle-class and all-white enclave whose territory bordered the chancery office in Brighton and allowed Medeiros and Daily to keep a close eye on him. He longed for his lecture halls full of fans, his counseling practice, late nights in the field, the sharp attention of newspaper editorialists.

For Jackie Gauvreau, a lifelong St. Jean's congregant whose mother worked as a secretary at the parish office, the feeling was mutual. She had a bad feeling about the former street priest, and Gauvreau never doubted her feelings. It began on the hot afternoon she first arrived at the rectory with one of the toddlers she frequently baby-sat—she was almost pathologically dedicated to children, but being unfortunately divorced and living at her mother's again, she was destined to be the perpetual adoring nursery maid. She wanted the child blessed by the new parochial vicar. That's one of the things she did with her day. But Shanley bellowed accusingly down the stairs, "What is that child doing in my rectory?"

"I don't know," Gauvreau wisecracked. "Didn't this all *start* with a child?"

What kind of priest hated children? No warmth seemed to emanate from him whatsoever, at least not for the families of St. Jean's. In plain contrast, he doted on the so-called castoffs who followed him to Newton and sometimes pitched filthy tents in the churchyard, always extolling their mysterious virtues in his homilies and making everybody feel somehow personally guilty for their misunderstood circumstances.

She thought to herself, From this day on, I'm on my guard.

"You know those records I loaned you? I need them," she said now in contemptuous revenge. "Would you please bring me them?"

Stomping off in protest, Shanley retrieved the albums. Parish life degraded him in so many ways. A celebrated intellectual cited in footnotes in history books—silenced, placed in effect under house arrest, condemned to the strange scrutiny of Jackie Gauvreau and her mother, permanent fixtures on the first floor of his home, where the parish offices were located. They came with the building. It was more theirs than his. They demanded more from him than suffering forbearance.

He mistook this for perverse infatuation. You'd fall in love with a lamppost, he thought bitterly, if it had pants on it.

Paul Shanley's attitude about parish ministry did not improve over the ensuing two years. He managed his sacramental duties without flair, administered his parochial school passably, and with considerable effort kept the parish books in relatively acceptable order, while the church's aged pastor tended to his failing health. Most of the time he spent sequestered on the upper floors of his rectory, where, it soon became clear, he had installed a friend, Dale Lagace, a willowy layman who came and went with rodentlike stealth. This was cause for much demanding interrogation from Jackie Gauvreau, Shanley's tireless inquisitor. Her zeal gave Shanley chronic diarrhea. Lately he spent a great deal of time preoccupied with his health, which deteriorated in little projects of self-obsession. He was now fifty, dispirited, angst-ridden about his confinement, and desperate for peace.

He soon barred Gauvreau from visiting the parish office. Undeterred, she would stand on the sidewalk and call out for her mother at the reception desk, and the two defiantly carried on full-throated conversations through the opened doors and windows. He put in for various transfers until Father Phinn, the archdiocesan director of personnel, conveyed an unequivocal message from Medeiros: stop filling out applications and start doing the job you have. Shanley took out all his frustrations on Gauvreau, banishing her even from the church's adjacent sidewalks except during Mass.

Gauvreau would not have called Shanley this July afternoon, would not have pleaded for his help, if she saw any alternative.

One of Gauvreau's "kids" had appeared at her door in serious trouble. Danny Quinn was rugged and powerful, a sixteen-year-old who often made mistakes, occasionally while brandishing a firearm. As a result, for some time now he had been a ward of the juvenile court, in residence at a Division of Youth Services work farm. But he had escaped. There were many reasons he took this action, the principal one being he wanted to see his girlfriend, who was pregnant with his baby. He made it as far as Gauvreau's, where he proposed to hide out. Determined to return him to DYS, she ordered him into her station wagon, only to find it would not start. It took some hard convincing before Shanley agreed to run the errand himself. Watching them drive off together, Gauvreau had wept miserably about the decision she had felt forced to make.

A half hour later, Danny was at her door again, flushed and out of breath.

"Son of a bitch told me I could sleep with men and women, and then grabbed my nuts," he blurted out.

"Run that by me again?"

"Right when I got in the car, he started talking really strange, he told me I would never amount to anything because I was in the DYS program. Putting me down. And then we didn't get three quarters of a mile from here and the guy started talking about—he said it was all right to have sex with boys and girls, and *he* had had both, which really caught me off guard! My aunt's a nun! We're all wicked Catholic. I looked at him and the guy put his hand on my groin! *What the hell?* I turned around and pushed his hand away. He grabbed my arm. I jumped out of the car and took off out of there."

"Come in here and sit down," she said, walking to the parlor. "He said that to you? He said you could sleep with men?" Gauvreau had nothing against gays, only hypocrites and Shanley.

Danny nodded. Gauvreau noticed his hands and legs were trembling. She asked if he was hurt, and he said no.

"I'm gonna call him," she said, partly as a challenge. When she hung up the phone she was ashen. "He told me he did it."

Danny wasn't surprised.

"But he was *sooo* cocky. Danny, he said he did it! He said, 'Prove it.' "

After telling her mother and a cousin about what Father Shanley had admitted to her, Jackie Gauvreau placed a call to Father Joseph F. McGlone, a priest at nearby Corpus Christi, who directed her to

Father Arthur Calter, a member of the church's personnel board, who referred her to Father Michael F. Doocey, a cardinal's representative in the vicariate that included Newton, who agreed to a meeting. She was surprised when she arrived at the appointment that Paul Shanley wasn't there. "He doesn't have to answer the accusation?" she wondered.

She told what she knew and what she had heard, and because she felt the reception was a chilly one she was not surprised in the following months when nothing seemed to happen to her nemesis. Frustrated, she called the chancery—anonymously, because she didn't want to risk her mother's position at St. Jean's. This was a discouragement. She left a dozen messages for the director of clergy personnel, but never got a returned call. Now when she called she would be put on hold interminably. A woman of extreme determination, she never hung up herself, but sat there in her parlor imagining flashing yellow buttons on overtaxed phones in a chaotic colossus. Sometimes thirty minutes or more could pass. And then the imagined receiver would lift just slightly and fall back to its cradle, cutting her off.

Leaning forward, Gauvreau would dial again, reaching the same singing voice each time.

"I'm calling to talk about a priest who molested a child," she would tell the receptionist, then sink again into the dead air of hold.

When not balancing a telephone on her neck, Gauvreau regularly stationed herself on the sidewalk outside St. Jean's Rectory, arms folded, grunting antagonistically at church staff as they came and went. "Sisters, how could you go in there?" she called after a trio of nuns one afternoon. "He is the epitome of evil! He molested a child!" They scuttled past, ignoring her the way a couple kissing or a public urinater is ignored.

Gauvreau didn't care. The more her church ignored her, the more she committed herself to obnoxious proclamation—even snarling at the priest at the very moment she received weekly communion from him.

Ultimately, Paul Shanley told her she was no longer permitted to attend services at St. Jean's. He reiterated the message through his friend, another Boston priest, named Father Jack White, who poked his head out of the rectory one afternoon and almost comically commanded: "Begone! You, begone from here!" This she took right to her area bishop, and he instructed Shanley to lift the ban. One cannot simply banish a woman from her territorial parish.

Reluctantly, Shanley apologized. "The bishop told me to apologize, and to welcome you back to St. Jean's," he said obligingly.

"Tell them you're a child molester, and I'll accept your apology," she said.

She left him almost no choice. The next time Gauvreau showed up at the rectory to collect her mother, Father Shanley fired the woman.

"Do you realize what he just did? He fired you because I came into the churchyard. He can't do that!"

"He's a priest, Jackie."

"You're an American citizen!"

One of eleven children from a devout family, Mary Bernadette Gauvreau didn't blame the priest, she blamed her daughter, whose allegation she wasn't entirely inclined to believe. Nor was anyone else. Jackie's social standing was in disarray. She knew what was being said about her. Fellow communicants whispered, "Unrequited love," which made her laugh. The choir with which she had blended her voice since she was a little girl asked her to take her talents elsewhere. She did find another church, but even there she labored against a terrific disapproval of her whistle-blowing, which finally came to a head one Saturday night when the choir director invited her for a surprise outing.

"What should I wear?" Gauvreau wondered. "Where are we going?"

"To a church," she said coyly.

"Are we singing?"

"No."

"What are we going to do?"

"I'm taking you to a healing priest, Jackie, so you can get over your hatred of Paul Shanley."

"You go to hell!" Gauvreau snapped.

"At this point," the choir director said with a miserable sigh, "I don't want you around my children, because I don't think you're mentally stable."

July 24, 1982

Jamaica Plain, Massachusetts — "I saw him." Maryetta Dussourd stared at her son in disbelief, then dread. "I saw him," he said. "I saw Father Geoghan."

Thoughts of Geoghan had never stopped haunting her the past two years. The memory of his offenses permeated the small apartment like a noxious gas. The boys had begun showing signs of serious disturbances in school. Maryetta prayed every day for some help from the church, and for a calmness to revisit their home. Neither came.

"Where did you see him?"

"Brigham's." A few friends had gone there for ice cream.

"He was at Brigham's?"

"Yeah. With some kid."

"Was he in a Roman collar?"

"Yup."

Anger flooded her. A fresh church? A fresh child? Who was monitoring this man? How could they have allowed him to be out on the street, untethered, sitting at the very ice cream parlor where he had won over her children's trust?

And what of her own son? What memories might flood his mind following this unwelcome encounter? Again she wept in disbelief and pain.

When she told her husband, Ralph, he went crazy. He spoke disparagingly about Auxiliary Bishop Daily, who had let them down, and a church that would let this happen. He promised to harm Geoghan if he ever bumped into him. "I'd like to punch the man out—right on the altar, in front of the whole damned church! He belongs in jail," he bellowed. "Not Brigham's."

Enraged, he demanded a meeting with Daily. Maryetta was sick with apprehension about confronting her church this way. Too emotional to speak for herself and fearing that her husband might offend the hierarchy, she invited her sister Marge Gallant and sister-in-law Fran Dussourd to join them on the day Daily consented to meet. Ralph exploded rather ineffectually. There was something about the presence of a bishop, with his unflappable face and imposing ecclesiastical ring, that never ceded control. Then Daily spoke. He was not pleased with them, and made his feelings about their challenges plain. Geoghan had been assigned to St. Brendan's and in the wisdom of the church hierarchy—which was the only supreme wisdom, he reminded them—because he was deemed no danger to anyone. (For his own safety, he recently warned Geoghan to stay out of Jamaica Plain, and certainly avoid Brigham's ice cream parlor.)

As she sat listening, Maryetta noticed that her skin was cold to the touch. She began to tremble, as if her blood had gone to ice.

Weeks later Geoghan was still at St. Brendan's. Seeing how this continued to tear at her sister's faith, Marge Gallant wrote a scathing letter to the cardinal himself, demanding in the language of Catholicism that he take action.

"Our family is deeply rooted in the Catholic Church. Our great-grandparents and parents suffered hardship and persecution for love of the Church. Our desire is to protect the dignity of Holy Orders, even in the midst of our tears and agony over the 7 boys in our family who have been violated. We cannot undo that. But we are obligated to protect others from this abuse to the Mystical Body of Jesus Christ. It was suggested that we keep silent to protect the boys—that is absurd since minors are protected under law, and I do not wish to hear that remark again, since it is insulting to our intelligence. . . . Father Damien the leper went after a child molester once and beat him up. His cause was held up because of it—now the curse of Damien is in the Vatican. I am praying to him now to bring *this* cause to Jesus Christ. Father Damien would not sit on his fanny. He would act. My heart is broken over this whole mess—and to address my Cardinal in this manner has taken its toll on me, too. May God Almighty, Father, Son, and Holy Spirit, have mercy on all of us."

By return mail, in a letter signed by His Eminence personally next to a small cross he'd drawn, came Medeiros's reply. "While I am and must be very sensitive to a very delicate situation and one that has caused great scandal," he wrote, "I must at the same time invoke the mercy of God and share in that mercy in the knowledge that God forgives sins and that sinners indeed can be forgiven. To be sure, we cannot accept sin, but we know well that we must love the sinner and pray for him. I take great comfort in noting these thoughts in your letter to me and at your compassion for Father. Please be assured that I am speaking to the priest in order to find the most Christian way to deal with the problem with him and at the same time remove any source of scandal for the sake of the faithful. With every good wish, I am devotedly yours in Our Lord."

They care more about the sick priest than the poor children, Marge Gallant thought angrily. When she read the letter to her sister, it sent a chill up Maryetta Dussourd's spine. She wrapped her arms tight against her chest. She was still icy cold. Blood never seemed to flow normally through her veins again.

December 14, 1982
NEWTON, MASSACHUSETTS — Paul Shanley had asked his superiors for permission to seek a restraining order against Gauvreau—in fact it was the telephone company's suggestion when he complained of her many harassing calls—but after deliberation at the chancery they advised against it. Instead, in his morning mail, Paul Shanley received a brief note from Bishop Daily.

> Dear Paul:
>
>   I'm sorry to learn of the harassment you suffered from a woman. . . . As Father Ryan suggested, I'm not so sure a restraining order would be helpful. For us here at the chancery office, we stopped harassing calls like that from the use of the tape [machine]. It is rather an impersonal situation but we feel it does screen out calls that are from demented people and people we cannot help over the phone. The other recourse is not to speak at all when she calls but merely to leave her hanging until she hopefully gets discouraged.

June 30, 1983
SCHRIEVER, LOUISIANA — Father Gilbert Gauthe, pastor of a rural parish serving Cajun farmers, entered the office of his old friend Monsignor Alex Larroque, vicar general for the Lafayette diocese. Larroque had

sounded stern when he called for the meeting, Gauthe thought. He worried there was trouble with his bookkeeping.

"Gil," the monsignor said. "We have a problem."

Gauthe did not show a reaction.

"It's with young boys," he went on. "Lots of young boys, Gil. The bishop is very angry with you and wants you out of the parish right now."

Gauthe had been an ordained priest for a dozen years. For most of that time, at the very least since 1974, when Gauthe had admitted abusing kids in New Iberia, Bishop Gerard Frey knew about his predilections. In 1976, after two fathers complained that he had inappropriately kissed their small boys, Bishop Frey ordered Gauthe into psychotherapy. But he had never suspended or censured Gauthe in any way.

Nor did he monitor his progress in therapy. In 1977, when the pastor job opened at St. John Parish in the small village of Henry, Bishop Frey did not query the therapist. Rather, the bishop had asked Monsignor Richard Mouton, whose job it was to investigate allegations against priests, if any new incidents had occurred. Though he had spoken neither to altar boys, parents, laypeople, or other priests familiar with Gauthe's habits, Mouton gave Gauthe his approval.

More complaints had followed. In April 1980, St. John parishioners wrote Frey a letter anonymously complaining that Gauthe spent more time with young boys than adult parishioners, and regularly took children out of class early for weekend sleepovers, all to the detriment of his priestly ministrations. For the bishop, this rang no warning bells, and because it was unsigned, he dismissed the letter as unreliable and unworthy of concern. He subsequently even named Gauthe the diocesan chaplain for Boy Scouts.

Under various church canons, Gilbert Gauthe could have been defrocked in 1974. He could have been reported to police and thrown in jail. He could have been stopped after molesting just one child. Instead, by his own admission, he sexually exploited "thirty-five, thirty-six, thirty-seven" boys, some of them later hospitalized for depression, rectal bleeding, or suicidal ideation.

A few days before Gauthe's meeting with Larroque, the father of three boys who had spent nights at the rectory in Henry went with a lawyer to demand that Gauthe be removed from the parish immediately. Now more than ever before, Gauthe's behavior threatened public scandal, one of the gravest misdeeds a priest can commit. The bishop was no longer prepared to forgive, Monsignor Larroque said.

Feeling utterly forsaken, Gauthe was afraid, and began to cry. "I—I need some help," he said. "I think there are places you can send me?"

Larroque pushed a crisp sheet of paper across the table toward him. It was his formal suspension. "Get out of Henry within twenty-four hours, Gilbert," he said.

Roy Robichaux was the father who had brought the charge, first to his attorney, and then to the chancery. He sent his children to a psychiatrist, too, later explaining he was concerned that having been subjected to oral sex and anal penetration they might now risk becoming homosexuals. No such correlation existed, according to all accepted research. Though he expected the diocese to foot the therapy bill, it did not immediately volunteer. Rather, Robichaux's attorney was made to ask several times before the commitment was made. The boys continued in therapy for some time, but the diocesan largesse did not. Church officials soon determined that Robichaux and the other parents were best handled by hired attorneys, and treated as litigants to be thwarted, not as communicants to be courted with pastoral concern.

Robichaux also asked the vicar general to canvass the parishes where Gauthe had served and alert other parents, so that they might get their sons into treatment. On this point, the church was resolute in opposition. Out of concern for appearances, the official explanation for Gauthe's hasty departure would be "medical reasons." So Wayne and Rose Sagrera, who believed everything in the Bible and the Baltimore Catechism, were not immediately apprised. They had no reason to suspect anything when their son Craig fell into a major depression so debilitating he was hospitalized, at age eleven. Robichaux's ten-year-old son, Pete, also landed in a psychiatric hospital the following summer, when local psychiatrists deemed his health in serious jeopardy.

The church did almost nothing to see to the well-being of these boys thereafter besides offering a one-time cash settlement in exchange for their silence. Abandoned and isolated, the families no longer believed their church was forgiving, loving, or caring. "Evil," Rose called it. "It has very little concern for individuals."

In the meantime, though, Father Gauthe would remain well cared for. The day he was removed from ministry, the church arranged for him to stay at an out-of-the-way motel for a few nights, to shield him from any potential violence. Soon, they answered his prayer and they found a place to send him: the House of Affirmation in Massachusetts, a church-affiliated facility for sexually predatory priests. The facility was the flagship of a large network of such places, including a number of other Houses of Affirmation, as well as independent church-affiliated institutions in Toronto, Montreal, and Hartford, and holistic hospitals operated by the congregation of the Servants of the Paraclete, an order of priests and brothers, in Jemez Springs, New Mexico, in St. Louis and Dittmer, Missouri, and in Straud, England. Each of these facilities had one curious paradox: they were staffed largely with priests and nuns—celibates, that is, who struggled to confront some of the most complex manifestations of sexual expression.

Their existence was kept a closely held secret. It would not look right. It might even suggest that the priesthood had a unique problem with sexual deviance. What other profession operated its own clinics for pedophiles, ephebophiles, and sexual predators? But several hundred priests had graduated from these precincts, most all of them deemed safe to place back in ministry. There was even talk about using church coffers to buy an island in the Caribbean for treating and, when needed, warehousing problem priests.

Gauthe stayed at the House of Affirmation for almost a year before his doctors deemed him fit to resume ministry. The Lafayette diocese made arrangements to transfer him out of state for a fresh start in Gulfport, Mississippi. But first, as an added precaution, they shipped him north to the Institute of Living in Hartford, Connecticut, another treatment facility for troubled priests, specializing in psychological assessments—plus art therapy, needlepoint, and regular Mass. The cost was $9,000 a month, footed by the diocese.

Late 1983

NEWTON, MASSACHUSETTS — Nearly seventy, Cardinal Medeiros suffered from diabetes and hypertension, which aggravated a congestive heart condition. He died in September 1983, the morning after open heart surgery. As second in command, Bishop Daily was appointed to fill in temporarily. Canon law obliged him to not initiate any new policies but to follow the course of the man he replaced. When the infirm pastor at St. Jean's in Newton finally died, Daily elevated Father Paul Shanley to administrator, in keeping with what he felt were Medeiros's wishes. The formal title of pastor would soon follow. This was the pinnacle position for a parish priest, putting him in charge of all financial matters, the rectory administration, all policy decisions, and other matters pertaining to the pastoral care of the people of the parish.

Among the first things Paul Shanley did was to move the parish office out of the rectory and into the church next door. He cited "doctor's orders." Having people camped out on his first floor aggravated his nerves, he alleged. Watching the office equipment move out of the rectory, Jackie Gauvreau suspected the worst; she frequently told anyone in earshot that he had discharged the sentries so he could commit his crimes unhindered. That's not to say she never entertained self-doubts. From time to time she felt terrible guilt about what she was doing. What if Shanley were innocent? But then she remembered his voice egging her on: *Prove it.* He did it, she told herself. He did it and he *said* he did it.

Then at Mass one Sunday morning late in the year, as she sat defiantly in her usual spot, she heard Father Shanley addressing a personal matter.

"There's a woman in this parish who is out to get me," he said flatly. "She is out to destroy me. She wants to sue me. She will stop at nothing."

She didn't have to look up to know that in that instant she was despised, that her persecution of Shanley had thoroughly galvanized the parish in his fervent defense. She felt physically unsafe. But she raised her head anyway, hoping to project a look of peaceful serenity, in that way fools sometimes do. She would not buckle to rank intimidation.

She rose for communion as usual. She glowered at him as usual. When it was time to reach out to one another to express peace, she did that, too, and the first person to approach her was the priest himself.

"Touch me and I'll knock you on your ass," she said.

Chapter 5

Secret's Out

October 18, 1984

SCHRIEVER, LOUISIANA — The Gilbert Gauthe case was not destined to be contained. Despite assurances from the Lafayette diocese that the problem was under control, on October 18, 1984, a grand jury indicted Gauthe on thirty-four counts of aggravated crimes against nature, immoral acts, producing child pornography, and aggravated rape—one of the victims he had penetrated was younger than twelve. No cleric had been prosecuted so prominently before. Media attention at first was cautious: it took Barry Yeoman, a reporter for the weekly *Times of Acadiana,* to break the story, two weeks later. The dailies followed, and instantly the Gauthe story went worldwide. The unfolding revelations were stark and unseemly. It now appeared that nearly a hundred boys and young men had been sodomized.

The parents of Gauthe's victims were greeted neither as heroes nor as victims by their fellow churchgoers. Far from it. But at least they felt that their suffering would produce lasting change. Roy Robichaux consoled himself and his children with this belief. Light had been forced into the darkness. For the first time since this generation of priests unleashed a wave of sexual crimes against adolescent and preadolescent kids, mostly boys, the secret was at last out in the open.

The wickedness of molesting minors was being exposed and explored as never before. Around the country, lawmakers had begun increasing penalties for crimes involving the sexual exploitation of kids. Women's magazines and daytime television talk shows detailed the sometimes lifelong struggles of the survivors. Simultaneously, researchers sought to understand what caused people's sexual appetites to turn to minors.

They found it was surprisingly common among men. Using a device called a penile plethysmograph, researchers determined that as many as one in three heterosexual men were physically aroused by images of nude prepubescent girls. This didn't mean they were all pedophiles. Psychiatrists defined true pedophilia as the recurrence of such thoughts over a period of six months or more. Most would never act on the impulse. Many pedophiles were aroused by boys and girls indifferently, and most were also sexually attracted to other adults. The condition was believed to be the result of serious emotional disturbances.

When the child was well into teenage development, the context of attraction in most cases was cultural and aesthetic rather than pathological. Simply put, teenagers were alluring. Turn to any magazine and you would find evidence in advertising and fashion that teens were prized for their beauty and sexual bearing. What overcame Elvis Presley when he took Priscilla Beaulieu as his fourteen-year-old girlfriend was stormy infatuation. Same for Zeus, who was "set on fire" at the sight of the boy Ganymede. Most sexual attractions to teenagers derived from simple lust.

Most, but not all. Like pedophiles, many people who were attracted to adolescents were believed to be driven by a nonromantic and compulsive force beyond their control. This made them more likely to devise effective techniques for gaining young people's trust, coercing them into sex, and assuring their silence. This unique class of sexual predators had not been studied extensively—researchers tended to merge them in with true pedophiles. However, results of several small studies that considered ephebophiles separately suggested they shared an underlying neurobiological abnormality with pedophiles and other patients with serious psychosexual disorders. Priests were no different, according to Leslie Lothstein, who as director of the Institute of Living in Hartford, Connecticut, had treated four hundred priests for molesting minors. Scanning their brains, he discovered they suffered mild to severe frontal lobe dysfunction, manifesting as impaired verbal fluency, attention deficits, poor impulse control, poor judgment, problems sequencing and organizing thoughts, and a tendency to "perseverate," or cling to inappropriate mental operations.

It was unclear what might have caused this phenomenon. Head traumas as well as organic brain disorders such as schizophrenia can trigger frontal lobe dysfunctions. Many researchers hypothesized that early childhood abuse could produce similar results. There appeared to be a correlation between a history of being sexually abused and a history of being an abuser. About half of all adult child molesters reported being molested as children themselves, in contrast to 27 percent for women and 16 percent for men in the general population, according to a *Los Angeles Times* poll. The problem with the "abused abuser hypothesis" was that there was no evidence to prove causality. What it might instead demonstrate was that sexual abuse was endemic in parts of American society.

The statistical correlation was less apparent among abusive priests—20.8 percent reported having been initiated into sex as youths by an adult, according to a study by Thomas Haywood and colleagues at Rush–Presbyterian–St. Luke's Medical Center in Chicago. In another study, of seventeen priests under treatment for sexual compulsions with minors at the Institute of Living, 29 percent reported a history of being sexually abused. However, 53 percent were physically abused, and 35 percent had experienced otherwise traumatic childhoods—all theoretical triggers to frontal lobe abnormalities.

Perhaps sensing their lack of impulse control, these men entered the priesthood in disproportionate numbers, searching for external regulations for their sexuality and intimate relationships. Or maybe for some people, predisposed by childhood trauma, a well-meaning effort to live chastely simply backfired spectacularly. Whatever the cause, these men tended to construct complex justifications for their sexual misbehavior. Some argued they were preparing the youths for marriage, protecting them from sin, or showing them love. Some priests told Lothstein they didn't view having sex with young men or boys as being a violation of celibacy, which they tended to define narrowly as being unmarried—the word comes from the Latin *caelebs*, "alone" or "single"—but not asexual. Women, in their estimation, were the real threat to celibacy.

January 25, 1985
Washington, D.C. — Father Tom Doyle's stomach turned every time a new communiqué crossed his desk about the situation in Louisiana. As a canon lawyer stationed at the Vatican embassy in Washington, Doyle had encountered sexually inappropriate clerics before. Recently, he had worked on the cases of two bishops who had been accused of sexual impropriety—both were already dead. He'd heard of other priests who touched kids. But never had he heard of a man like Gauthe, whose appetites were insatiable—and whose supervisors had messed up so badly.

"What a goddamn nightmare," he thought. "How in hell could they be so *stupid*?"

Many of Doyle's contemporaries suffered from a blindness to children, but not him. His Irish-American family was vast and tended to gather in frequent and legendary reunions, dominated by sixty cousins and countless nieces and nephews, whose innocence, it seemed to him, was the very reason for Catholicism. To think of them being defiled by anybody disgusted him. The details of the Gilbert Gauthe case were especially egregious—Gauthe had told the victims he was doing God's work when he forced himself into them. Doyle prayed every morning—as was the practice of the embassy's staff—that those children had not lost their faith.

But Doyle was a company man. His future depended upon it. Many men who had held his important diplomatic post had been elevated to bishop and given a diocese to run. This fact was never far from his mind. It was a time of great conservative shifts in the church under John Paul II. A Republican, an air force reservist, and a lifelong NRA member, Tom Doyle's time had come, and he knew it. He attacked the Gauthe problem aggressively. As part of his research, Doyle called down to St. Luke Institute, an ecclesiastical hospital in the Maryland suburb of Suitland, opened in 1981 by a priest psychiatrist named

Father Michael Peterson to diagnose and treat that bundle of psychiatric disorders that seemed to strike priests more often than laypeople, especially alcoholism and sexual compulsivity.

Doyle dispensed with formalities. "So tell me about pedophilia, Mike. Are they all queers?"

"First of all," said Peterson, "don't use that kind of language. Secondly, that isn't the issue at all."

It was an open secret that the priesthood was full of gays. A random-sample survey of eighty priests nationwide conducted by the Johns Hopkins University Medical School, in Baltimore, had found that 38 percent self-identified as homosexual or bisexual. Given the perils a gay priest risked by answering honestly, that number was considered low. A more accurate way to measure the phenomenon was to ask priests their opinions on the prevalence of gays, because they could answer without betraying any self-knowledge. Those figures were considerably higher: priests believed their ranks were 48.5 percent gay. That figure dovetailed with a survey of seminarians in 1984, over 50 percent of whom had responded affirmatively to the statement "The male body sometimes attracts me."

But that alone could not explain the phenomenon. Proportionately, there are no more pedophiles or ephebophiles among gays than among straights. In fact, all available data showed that men and women who lived openly as gays accounted for less than one percent of sexual assaults on minors. But Peterson, who was already a clinical psychiatrist when he entered seminary at age thirty-two, had treated scores of sexual offenders at St. Luke. He saw the problem as being profound in the church. Also, Peterson was gay—a fact almost no one knew. He lived in a secret culture that never spoke its name. Like the overwhelming majority of priests in his position, he did not molest boys. However, he was a clinician, and loath as he was to admit it, Peterson knew a lot of these offenders were homosexual—twisted and diseased, manifestly troubled, men engaged in criminal behavior, but technically homosexual.

What did it mean that this subset of priests were so different from other gay men or other sex abusers? Nobody knew exactly. There had been no effort to study them. Peterson, who shared his insights with Jason Berry for the landmark book *Lead Us Not into Temptation*, chose to leave the matter unaddressed. "My impression when I came in as a clergyman," he said, "was that priests are ill prepared for everyday life, especially for their own problems. Before Vatican II, priests were supposedly perfect. We were not supposed to have sexual feelings. So suddenly, in the last few years, sexual abuse of children has emerged as a national issue. Let's put it in some perspective. Most pedophiles are parents: this seems to happen mostly in families. It's difficult to get good data, though, because so much of it is unreported. We've only begun to get a true picture. Imagine you're a bishop and someone says, 'This priest molested my boy.' He thinks, *I can't believe it*. It's that kind of milieu."

Peterson believed these men could be cured. He agreed to mail Doyle some relevant medical literature.

A week later, Peterson called and asked for a meeting. Ray Mouton, an attorney hired by the Lafayette church officials to defend Gauthe, was in town. He had some observations about the Lafayette diocese that Peterson felt Doyle needed to hear.

They met the following day, January 25, 1985, at the Dominican House of Studies in Washington, D.C.

The problem in Lafayette, Mouton said, was bigger than Gauthe. At least eight other priests in the diocese had been caught, moved, and caught again. Mouton had learned this in the course of preparing his case. This put him in a tight spot. Mouton was hoping to bargain with the district attorney for leniency for Gauthe, perhaps lengthy confinement in a hospital setting. If the DA learned about the other cases, he knew, Gauthe's chances were nil. He would be forced to stand trial, which the diocese wanted to avoid, and the scandal would surely explode wide open.

Peterson specifically felt the embassy and the Vatican should know about the cluster of cases there. But he also told Doyle for the first time that there were dozens of similar cases in dioceses around the country. Some of these men were such frequent recidivists that they were well known to priest psychiatrists across the country. With the explosion of publicity surrounding the Gauthe case, he was worried the other situations would soon make headlines as well.

The next few weeks would validate his concerns. In February, an el-

derly boozer in Providence named Father William O'Connell was arrested on charges of child sexual abuse, and his bishop admitted privately he knew of the problem since at least 1978. Then a hailstorm of
lawsuits in Orlando, Florida, revealed that a Father William Authenreith's similar crimes had first been reported in 1976, but he was transferred to another parish, then a school, then another parish, and so
forth, which allowed him to molest a dozen more boys. Newspapers revealed that Monsignor Rudolph Galindo of San Diego had begun a relationship with a young Vietnamese boy, upon whom he lavished
expensive vacations and $10,000 in gifts. A religious brother in Cleve-
land, priests in New Orleans, Baltimore, Portland, and New York—the
revelations flared everywhere.

In Boise, Idaho, Father Carmelo Baltazar, who had been kicked out
of three dioceses and a navy chaplaincy for abusing, among other
teenaged boys, one who was connected to a dialysis machine and another in double-leg traction, was finally arrested for fondling a kid he
met in a psychiatric facility. Along the long trail of his abuse, many allegations had been lodged against Baltazar, and none of them were
heeded. After handing down a seven-year sentence to the priest, Judge
Alan Schwartz said what was on many people's minds: "I think the
Catholic Church has its atonement to make as well. They helped create you." But the Boise bishop, Sylvester Treinen, shrugged off the suggestion: "I've felt all along we've done everything we can do. We've been
prudently careful all along for years. No matter how well you take care
of your car, no matter how safe your car is, you're still going to have an
accident now and then."

Thanks to an overly respectful relationship between the church, the
courts, and the media, none of these cases made more than brief appearances in the press. Doyle, concerned that a larger picture of abuse
within the church might soon materialize, took this information directly
to his boss, Archbishop Pio Laghi, the Vatican's ambassador in Washington. Laghi did not have any direct supervisory powers over the
American prelates, but he did exercise great influence. He hastily
arranged a series of meetings and at Doyle's suggestion appointed
Cleveland's Auxiliary Bishop A. James Quinn to monitor all legal aspects of the Lafayette case. With Laghi's blessing, Doyle, Peterson, and

Mouton volunteered to create a churchwide policy for dealing with sex abuse, similar to policies adopted by the Boy Scouts of America, the American Medical Association, and other professions that deal extensively with children.

April 24, 1985
VATICAN CITY — "I have a sense of being loved and accepted," an exhilarated Bernard Law told the crowd that had gathered in the large stone courtyard at the historic North American College in Rome on the occasion of his elevation to cardinal. Boston mayor Raymond Flynn, former Massachusetts governor Edward King, and state Senate president William Bulger were among the many dignitaries who had accompanied Law to Rome for this historic moment. Under a glorious sun, they lined up four deep and snaked past a shimmering reflecting pool to arrive, incongruously, upon an aged Oriental carpet, laid out beneath the newest American cardinal so his feet would not tire during the long reception.

In the two decades since his ordination, Law had enjoyed a prominent career. His first posting was a short stint in Jackson, Mississippi, as editor of the diocesan newspaper, where he made headlines—and drew death threats—for his editorials advocating civil rights. Coming to the attention of the U.S. hierarchy, he was tapped to run the national Bishops Committee for Ecumenical and Interreligious Affairs, before being named bishop at the young age of forty-one. For eleven years he was a well-regarded bishop of a small diocese, Springfield–Cape Girardeau, in Missouri. More a thinker than a pastor, he had never clocked a day as a parish priest, unlike most other church leaders. What fascinated him about his vocation was not the ordinary intricacies of diocesan life, but political and global affairs.

Like Medeiros before him, he was an outsider when the pope called him to serve in Boston. His appointment was looked upon with some suspicion, but he quickly won over the hearts of the archdiocese with his affable charm on the day he stepped from the plane at Logan Airport.

"After Boston," he said to applause, "there is only heaven."

Simply by arriving in Boston, he was now an archbishop, a recognition of the regional role the metropolitan Boston see played for the church. The head of the Boston church was charged with supervising other dioceses in Massachusetts, Maine, New Hampshire, and Vermont. In addition, he would regularly be consulted on the appointment of U.S. bishops. But being named to the College of Cardinals was a greater honor, symbolizing the pope's faith in his religious orthodoxy and loyalty to Rome. His elevation came with unusual haste at a time when John Paul II was keen to remake the church in America and elsewhere in a more conservative mode. Fate had given the pope a great opportunity: not only was the Boston job open, so were the cardinals' seats in New York and two other archdioceses. Not since the Vatican created the first American territories in 1808 had a pope enjoyed such a sweep of influence in this country. He selected men who shared the keystones of his vision: ambivalence about Vatican II and an almost single-minded opposition to abortion, which Law considered the "primordial darkness of our time, the cloud that shrouds the conscience of our world."

At the consistory ceremony in St. Peter's Square earlier in the day, twenty thousand pilgrims had stood under a hot sun to witness the solemn elevation, in which John Paul told his new cardinals their posts would require them to be both "wise as serpents and innocent as doves."

Law's office had given out over fourteen hundred tickets for the afternoon reception; guests included leaders of Boston's Jewish and Protestant communities, over a hundred Boston-area priests, and sixty members of Law's extended family. Even his high school English teacher had flown to Rome. The crush of admirers was so great that some waited two hours to express their congratulations to the man now in charge of the fourth-largest but most significant Catholic city in America. As he greeted and sang with them, Law stood in a red skull-cap and a red-piped cassock with a wide red sash pulled across his large middle, the emblems of his new status. He could not have felt more positive for the church he was inheriting. "This is the strongest moment for the church since the Reformation," he told his celebrating fans.

June 1985

WASHINGTON, D.C. — Doyle, Peterson, and Mouton worked quickly on their proposed manual for handling abuse allegations, hoping to get a working copy into the hands of the bishops as they gathered for their semiannual convention, this year scheduled for Collegeville, Minnesota. Their draft consisted of four main parts, covering civil law, canon law, criminal law, and insurance and medical considerations. Among the key proposals were the immediate removal from the pulpit of a priest accused of sexual misconduct, pending investigation; the creation of a national team of experts to help in that investigation; and a fundamental challenge to bishops who viewed such priests through the prism of sin alone, rather than psychology and law.

Doyle was to write the chapter on canon law. Initially his main goal was to provide practical advice on containing the various individual scandals. But the more he read about the phenomenon, talked to experts, and learned about how commonly offending priests were transferred from parish to parish and sometimes diocese to diocese to cover the trail of their sickness, the more he was convinced that the illness was within the church, not the priests. The hierarchy, he felt, needed to fling open the sash and clean house in public. The scope of the problem was daunting. By his estimate, more than a hundred thousand Catholic children in America were victims of clergy sexual abuse.

A huge number of these were bound to resort to civil courts, he believed. The litigation costs and damage awards could total more than a billion dollars. Doyle immediately grasped that the stakes were larger than that. Aggressive legal defenses against claims would cast the church in a terrible light, he warned. What the church needed to do was tend to the wounded, not battle them in courts.

> While the welfare of the priest offender is considered very important to the church officials, the welfare both at the time of the abuse and well into the future of the victims is most important and should be given a priority. . . . Sexual abuse of a child by a cleric, especially a priest, can have a devastating effect on the child's short- and long-term perception of the church and its clergy. How

will the child be able to perceive the clergy as authentic, unselfish ministers of the gospel and the church as the body of Christ?

With their manual completed, the group's next challenge was to convince American church leaders to endorse and implement it. The bishops' semiannual meetings were political labyrinths. Each bishop ran his diocese autonomously, answering only to the pope. They were loath to intervene through policies or resolutions in one another's domains.

Doyle had wrangled promises from a number of bishops to support the manual at the upcoming meeting. Auxiliary Bishop William Levada from Los Angeles and Auxiliary Bishop A. James Quinn from Cleveland, who had both offered their opinions during the drafting of the document, were on board. Specifically, Levada promised to introduce it on the agenda for the Subcommittee on Research and Pastoral Practices. Bernard Law chaired the committee. Taking every advantage available to him, Doyle buttonholed the new cardinal, whom he had met on several occasions, one evening after a state dinner at the embassy. Law acknowledged Doyle's concerns. He promised to create a special ad hoc subcommittee to review its findings at Collegeville.

But by the time the bishops held their final Mass and left Collegeville for home, the manual was already long forgotten. Nobody said a word to Doyle, Peterson, or Mouton about what happened there. Archbishop Laghi was likewise in the dark. When Doyle called Quinn, Levada, or Law, his calls were not answered. He telephoned the headquarters in Washington for the bishops' conference, and was put through to Mark Chopko, the group's general counsel. Chopko reported that the manual had been given some attention in the committee. However, the conference was powerless to bind bishops to any uniform plan, he said. Further, in the opinion of several bishops the manual suffered from various content flaws; it would cost too much to maintain a national response team; and frankly it seemed to be a vulgar bid for prominence on the part of the three authors, he added. As a result, the manual was not shared with the full body of bishops. What was prepared and circulated to them instead was a compendium of statute of limitations laws around the country, so that the bishops might better calculate their legal vulnerability.

"Moron," Doyle thought.

By this time, fifteen more cases had been reported in the papers. Doyle knew of yet fifteen more. He told a friend, "Sometimes I feel ashamed to be a priest."

August 1985

SUITLAND, MARYLAND — A van from the airport approached the spartan concrete block building that housed St. Luke Institute on a steamy, unbearably hot southern afternoon. Neil Conway gazed out the window at the unmarked building and although he could see from the architecture that this had once been a convent, he knew he was going to hell. Anxiety buzzed through his body like a disease, and he could hardly breathe. He had been expecting this day for the past two weeks. Back home in Cleveland, Conway had been bringing communion to the sick in the hospitals when, at his parish rectory, a nun entered his bedroom to tidy up, as was her morning obligation. There she discovered a teenage boy named Michael Doyle tangled sleepily in the priest's bedsheets. Wearing a habit did not preclude having an imagination— just the opposite. She assumed the worst. But when she queried the boy he was adamant that nothing untoward had transpired between him and the priest. He had been helping Father at the rectory the night before, he said, and they had allowed the evening to get by them, so rather than traveling home through the darkness, he had crashed at the rectory.

Even so, overnight guests were forbidden, especially underage ones. She left the room and telephoned her unallayed suspicions to the vicar for clergy at the chancery, Father Albert Tesek. Later in the morning, Conway had barely returned to the parish when he was summoned to meet Tesek and Auxiliary Bishop Gilbert Sheldon, supervisor of all priests in the Akron parishes within the Cleveland diocese. Conway had no inkling why he was called to the summit. He was about to leave for a two-week vacation to attend a family wedding in Washington State. Perhaps, he thought, there were administrative problems surrounding his absence.

Conway walked into the bishop's office and fell low into a chair. He was no longer the handsome young priest ordained in narrow white robes. He was forty-eight years old, ruddy, overweight, and unkempt. The bite of alcoholism had robbed his face of exuberance and awe; his eyes no longer glinted with the infectious knowledge of his church. It had been a long time since he inspired anybody to a greater self. For too many years, he had slogged half distracted through his performance of the sacraments.

The bishop got right to the point. "We have a report," he said, "of inappropriate behavior. *Genital sexual* behavior." The words shocked the priest. Nobody before had given voice to what Conway did to his motionless teenagers. In his fright, Conway could barely recall his boys except in a fuzzy montage. Over the years there had been eight, he knew that for sure. Each affair was like a little marriage, lasting months or even a few years. But the precise course of events—how each encounter began and how each ended—those facts would evaporate instantly from his conscious mind. He only twice felt guilty for what he'd done, both times in the fleeting blurry interval between sleep and waking.

Although the bishop offered no specifics, Conway knew he meant Michael. Conway had assiduously courted Michael over a period of months. Handsome and wild, he had few adult role models in his life. Those were the young men Conway learned to approach with his solicitous friendship and support, his patient advice, cultural instruction, flattery, even love. The ones who needed him allowed him to need them back.

He had cultivated Michael's affection with gifts and invitations to Wetmore, the Conway family farm; he had drowned him in attention and concern. In exchange he asked little, almost nothing. When night fell, there would arise some excuse requiring them to tuck into the same bed. Michael would fall asleep immediately, or appear to do so. Conway would do the same. But at some point in the night, the priest would snap awake amid the exploding realization that his hand had slipped into the boy's nightclothes. Never once did he recall putting it there. But even after the fog of his self-delusion cleared he was unable to retract it. He didn't consider it sex.

Cornered, Conway acknowledged sexual activity, but not with

Michael. Twice he strayed from his vows, he confessed, both times with adults. For approximately four years, he said, he had carried on a school-boy fling with a female parishioner with whom he shared a love of horses. At first worried he would not be able to perform, he sought the support of a psychotherapist, Mel Allerhand, who talked him through his fears. His breakthrough came one morning after a long canter through the farm, in a clearing under a warm spring sun. The first thought that entered Conway's mind was relief—perhaps he was not gay after all. Nevertheless, for the better part of a decade he'd also had reg-ular and perfunctory sexual encounters with a fellow diocesan priest. He now considered these trysts "complications," not emblematic of his sexual fate. The human mind showed a profound capacity to give no weight to evidence it rejected on wishful principle. Thanks to the grace-ful allowances of the woman parishioner, he was, as he liked to whisper to his mirror reflection, "a man's man."

And what about the young men, the eight quiet teenage boys? Some-times he thought he understood why he objectified them as sexual be-ings. He loved them. They were his best friends—really his only friends. But that was only a small part of the truth. Holding their gen-itals in his hand, he felt as though he had seized upon an unreachable part of himself, some aspect that had become so alienated from him it was no longer part of him. Michael's body was his own lifeless form, which he could not pleasure, could not even touch; Michael's sexual re-sponse was *his* sexual response at one remove. Through the boy, as through a fogged pane of glass, he thought he witnessed the purity of his own youth, an undefiled capacity for love and romance, even lust, even joy.

He sat before the bishop in robes of shame. He knew what he had to do. He offered the most heated and teary, you-wound-me-deeply-sir denial his vocabulary could produce. He would never, *ever* court such scandal, he said, would never endanger the church, which he loved.

The bishop seemed to accept his refutation. "Go on your family trip," he told Conway grimly. "We will talk to the boy. If all goes as it should, there will be no further discussion."

But something happened to Conway as he drove west across the country, and then east again. Perhaps it was a conversion of the sort

Catholics often talk about. Conway knew he had to come clean, to integrate his various selves. To stop troubling the boys. No boy had complained, either to him or to anybody else—at least not in words. But he knew they had not been consenting parties. Always they would mount some gesture to let him know the touching could not continue—like the kid on a ski trip who said without much ceremony, "I'm going to sleep on the floor from now on"—and it would break the priest's heart.

"This young man, Michael, backed you up," the bishop told Conway when he returned. "However, we are going to send you to a Catholic therapeutic facility for evaluation anyway. St. Luke, in Maryland. If you have no objection." Conway already knew of St. Luke's reputation as the place they sent you for drug and alcohol problems, and sexual indiscretions.

"I need to go to St. Luke," he interrupted. His voice was an encroaching storm, thunderous and abrupt. "Not for evaluation. For treatment! I cannot stop. Each one, when he got old enough to show signs of resistance, I did stop. But I found somebody new, didn't I? I started that wheel rolling again."

Conway feared for his own psychiatric stability. Something inside him was about to blow. "Please," he said, "let me take treatment. Let me take it right away. I cannot go back to my parish. Please help me fix myself."

That was one week ago. Now a priest in Roman garb and a female doctor in a lab coat swam through the heat toward the van, opened the door, and greeted their patient. Slowly, Conway unfolded himself into the humid morning and headed through the glass doors to embrace his possible resurrection. He vowed to approach psychotherapy as openly and faithfully as possible, to give it every chance to realign and to heal him. Catholics were notoriously stubborn psychotherapy patients— there was a well-established inverse relationship between frequency of confession and benefits from talk therapy. Conway would be different. His soul, he knew, depended upon it.

The first week inside the compound was consumed with evaluations and other tests. Conway admitted his offenses often. He was diagnosed with manic-depression, sexual compulsivity, chemical addiction (he entered AA), and homosexual ephebophilia, an obsessive sexual attraction to adolescent boys. The female therapist in charge of his care was not gentle. On their first meeting, she had rifled through his bags, distrusting his claims he had not tried to smuggle in any contraband liquor or pornography (she found nothing). "You and I are going to be working with each other for at least six months," she said, "and I know all the tricks you are going to try to pull. The minimizing and denying, that sort of thing."

"I will not!" Conway yelped, like a small boy. "And if I do, *please God* tell me so that I stop! I *want* to get rid of this thing!"

She looked at him with what seemed like disgust, or perhaps pity. Sizing up the situation, he concluded that she would be the bad cop. Maybe there would be no way to please her.

"Are you gay?" she asked.

This caught Conway completely off guard. Nobody had ever asked him before. His mind was conditioned to abstraction on the subject. "Straight," he said. Hearing the word, though, he knew it wasn't true. A panicky crisis followed. It was not as though Conway had been an anti-gay priest—on the contrary, he privately counseled homosexuals to ignore the strict teachings of the church and live in love and acceptance. Such postures were an essential part of his brand of liberalism. But beneath that stance, he did not see homosexuality as an acceptable orientation; he saw it as a freaky flaw of nature, unacceptably neither male nor female.

"My God," he thought, "I'm not really a man! I'm only *part* man. My priesthood is a sham! I've been portraying myself as a man, hiding behind this collar, and look at what I really am!"

Were homosexual priests more libidinous—and therefore less likely to live in chastity? Not according to two significant surveys. In one, 16.2 percent of straight priests reported being sexually active, versus 10.7 percent for gays; another, a random survey of eighty American priests by Gerard McGlone, a Jesuit priest and psychology fellow at the Johns Hopkins University Medical School's Department of Psychiatry, found that nearly one-third of heterosexual priests were sexually active, while fewer than one-fourth of the homosexuals were. There was at

least one suggestion that the opposite was true: an unpublished dissertation studying priest sexual behaviors, undertaken through the Institute for Advanced Study of Human Sexuality, found that in a sample of
fifty gay clerics, all but two—96 percent—were sexually active. This
striking disparity might reflect selection bias. Nothing was known
about how the men were chosen, but one data point suggested they
could have been recruited from inside gay bathhouses or STD clinics:
on average, they claimed to have had 227 different sexual partners. To
be sure, it could also be argued that the other surveys underreported
the behavior of homosexual priests, who would see a disincentive in revealing intimate details. Gays did seem to be among the most comfortably hypocritical priests. In one survey of sexually active gay priests, 88
percent said they would sign up for a celibate priesthood all over again,
given the chance.

October 1, 1986
VATICAN CITY — The deliberations of the Sacred Congregation for the
Doctrine of the Faith were always opaque, so its prefect, Cardinal Josef
Ratzinger, had given no indication what sort of thought process went into
his second major pronouncement on the subject of gay rights. Called
"Letter to the Bishops of the Catholic Church on the Pastoral Care of
Homosexual Persons," it was presented at a papal audience for John Paul
II's approval and, once granted, was "ordered to be published." Trans-
lated copies were to be delivered to every bishop on the globe.

Acknowledging that the church had come under a great deal of internal pressure to lift its call to chastity for gay Catholics, the letter explicitly and permanently declared the magisterium would not change.
Homosexual orientation, Ratzinger wrote, even if the person was totally
celibate, was unquestionably a "tendency" toward an "intrinsic moral
evil," not something that could be lobbied into acceptability. Any priest
who thought otherwise was doing a great disservice to the homosexual,
who needed acute pastoral care, not acceptance. "Special concern and
pastoral attention should be directed towards those who have this condition, lest they be led to believe that the living out of this orientation
in homosexual activity is a morally acceptable option. It is not."

Ratzinger felt that the trend among some priests to disregard this long-held edict was a grave threat to the church and to traditional Catholic families. He saw it as the work of anti-Catholic agitators. To counter this effort, Ratzinger declared that all gay ministries like Dignity were in conflict with official teaching. He ordered them banished from Catholic facilities all over the world.

"All support should be withdrawn from any organizations which seek to undermine the teaching of the Church, which are ambiguous about it, or which neglect it entirely," he wrote. "Such support, or even the semblance of such support, can be gravely misinterpreted. Special attention should be given to the practice of scheduling religious services and to the use of Church buildings by these groups, including the facilities of Catholic schools and colleges. To some, such permission to use Church property may seem only just and charitable; but in reality it is contradictory to the purpose for which these institutions were founded, it is misleading and often scandalous."

Within weeks, nearly seventy American Dignity chapters were forced out of the parishes where they had been praying, sent knocking on the doors of other faiths for shelter. Lost in the national purge were the hopes of many gays and lesbians that their church would one day welcome them and their families.

Sometime in 1986
BOSTON, MASSACHUSETTS — Eyes closed merrily, head oscillating on the end of his long neck, Cardinal Law was savoring the efforts of the Our Lady Help of Christians choir, knowing that they—and he—were under the scrutiny of television cameras and any number of Bostonians tuned to the live broadcast over channel 7. His many obligations required him to dash from one end of his massive archdiocese to the other, running through a blur of hospitals and schools, construction sites, government offices, press conferences, fund-raisers, and choral affairs. These were the endless obligations of a prince of the church, which he adored. To accomplish them, he had authorized the acquisition of a helicopter, making him perhaps the only religious leader in the nation immune to the turbulence and occlusions of rush hour.

But despite the ubiquity his advanced means of transportation allowed him, almost from the start of his reign Law maintained an unusual aloofness. He was there, but he was not. A symptom of this was his cabinet-based system of governance, which placed a powerful cordon of auxiliaries between him and his flock. News of the day-to-day came to Law filtered through their reports on Tuesday mornings. Critics, among them his own rank-and-file priests, accused him of an imperial hauteur. Meanwhile, he surrounded himself with Boston's leading citizens in political, business, and religious spheres. He befriended Governor Michael Dukakis and Vice President George H. W. Bush, who had made him a regular visitor to Capitol Hill. John Paul II had selected Law to sit on an exclusive Synod of Bishops to rethink key aspects of church teachings, a plum assignment that ramped up speculation that he had set his sights on becoming the next pope, the first from America.

He denied this, naturally—even a man of his ambitions knew there would not soon be a pope from the New World. However, through 1986 he spent so much time abroad that he was said to be the only American prelate with a foreign office. He led a pilgrimage to Poland with Catholic and Jewish participants, visiting Catholic shrines and Auschwitz, the former Nazi extermination camp. And in the fall he made a diplomatic turn to Nicaragua, torn by war and further divided by a staunchly anticommunist Catholic leadership out of sync with the aspirations of the nation. The timing had political designs. Eugene Hasenfus, an American mercenary and pilot, had been shot down over the Central American nation while covertly delivering arms to the U.S.-backed rebel group known as the Contras. Captured and tried, Hasenfus admitted he was a CIA contractor, an admission Washington had disavowed. The Reagan-Bush administration was in a bind. It had not yet admitted to covert support for the anticommunist rebels, so it could not intervene on Hasenfus's behalf. In his visit with the socialist president Daniel Ortega, Law asked for a pardon for the flier, which was granted before Christmas. Whether Bush sent Law as his emissary or Law went as a lone pastor, as he told reporters, was not important—he had shown his mettle in delicate global affairs.

When the singing was done, Law circled hastily through the cramped WNAC-TV studio, reeling off quick congratulations and smiling dutifully into Instamatics. Unbeknownst to him, he was under tight observation from the back of the risers by a pair of patrolling eyes belonging to Jackie Gauvreau. He and his entourage poured out of the studio and through the hallway to the door, a course slowed by the cardinal's courtly willingness to allow men and women to bend and kiss his ring. Gauvreau waited for her opportunity. When Law bid his farewell and walked with his driver toward his car, she broke into a jog and planted herself in front of him on the sidewalk.

"My name is Jacqueline Gauvreau," she huffed. "I come from St. Jean l'Évangéliste in Newton. The priest there, Paul Shanley, is a child molester."

Law took her hand. "I will look into it," he said.

Five years had passed since Gauvreau began trying to alert the hierarchy to Shanley's behavior. Her patience and perseverance had finally paid off. "Thank you," she said. "Oh, thank you!"

Summer 1986
WASHINGTON, D.C. — Little by little, Father Tom Doyle had begun to notice he was being sidelined. As secretary-canonist for the Vatican embassy, he was the person who had been consulted by bishops and cardinals on questions of canon law and its interface with the American legal system. Increasingly that work was being done by others in the office. To his surprise, he discovered that secret correspondence had been exchanged about sex abuse cases in Pennsylvania, in which the Vatican's ambassador, Pio Laghi, was investigating ways to skirt allegations that fell within the statute of limitations. Angrily, he again argued against using legal loopholes to dodge liability.

"The most important part of this whole thing is acting like Christians and taking care of the victims, and they've never done that," he thought. "It's a big fucking mess because of this. They see these people as the enemy and the only reason anybody has ever sued the Catholic Church in my experience is they are so completely frustrated—they try to get help and they finally wake up and see that they are the enemies and they go to the only place that will listen to them and help them find justice, which is the civil court system."

Late in 1985, he and his coauthors had copied the ignored manual and mailed it to every bishop in the country. At least each bishop would have the choice to follow it or not. And in May 1986, Doyle and Ray Mouton, who settled the Gauthe criminal matter when his client pleaded guilty and got twenty years in prison, had accepted an invitation to address a meeting of the Canon Law Society, in Morristown, New Jersey. Doyle was typically overheated. "This issue is hopping all over the country," he said. "This is the greatest problem in centuries . . . the worst situation that the Catholic Church has had to deal with since the Inquisition."

A man of principle never expects to be fired, much less unceremoniously. Now, an embassy official told him his office space would be needed by another appointee. That was it. His access to the corridors of power was gone. Any hopes he had of being named a bishop were ended. As a member of the Dominican Order, he was left to beg his superior for some meaningful assignment, which would eventually come in the form of a military chaplaincy, first at Grissom Air Force Base in Indiana, then at Lajes Field in the Azores, about as far away from church politics as a person could arrive.

Early 1987

LOWELL, MASSACHUSETTS — When the mother of a fifteen-year-old learned that her parochial vicar, Joseph Birmingham, had been abusing him, she called the chancery and reached, through perseverance and good luck, Auxiliary Bishop Robert Banks. He agreed to look into her suspicions and called Birmingham to his office for a talk. Birmingham did not deny it. "There had been some difficulty," he said.

Banks suggested it would be helpful for Birmingham to resign from St. Michael's in Lowell and seek assessment and therapy. After so many years of open abuse of children, the swiftness and immediacy of the confrontation must have surprised him. Reluctantly, he agreed. He tendered his resignation then and there and packed for the Institute of Living, in Connecticut.

March 25, 1987

Hartford, Connecticut — Evelyn Necochea, a fellow in clinical psychology attached to the Institute of Living, was the lead member on the team assessing Father Birmingham's progress in therapy. This was a patient with great promise, she felt. The resistance he displayed at the beginning of his stay had diminished, and what she called "a solid therapeutic alliance" had been established. Now he was attending three individual psychotherapy sessions and three therapy groups each week, and once a week he participated in a clergy support group and a workshop aimed at increasing his self-awareness. Twice weekly he also participated in a program that specifically focused on sexual issues.

His expression of shame and remorse was quite genuine, she felt. She strongly believed that, with time, he would come to understand both the impact of his actions on the young men and the triggers that caused him to "act out." What led her to believe this was his unique history. According to what Birmingham had told her, he had only twice displayed a behavioral problem—the previous occasion was seventeen years ago.

So when she sat down to write a formal report on Birmingham to his supervisor—his old classmate and friend Father John McCormack, whose rise in the church now saw him serving as secretary for ministerial personnel—she was extremely positive about his prognosis.

> The question uppermost in everyone's mind, including Father Birmingham's, is "what is the risk of his acting out in this manner again?" It would be unwise to say with 100 percent certainty that it will not happen again. However, I believe the risks of another occurrence are minimal. . . . Father Birmingham does not fit the usual profile of someone who is likely to frequently act out in this manner. His behavior is episodic and the last episode was 17 years ago. . . . The possibility for an interim placement in a church where the vicar is in need of temporary assistance seems appropriate. The idea of Father Birmingham serving as a hospital chaplain also seems appropriate.

When McCormack received the clean bill of health about his old classmate, he did not think to correct some of its inaccuracies, not even the assertion that Birmingham had abused only two young men in seventeen years. McCormack knew otherwise. He had personally fielded a half dozen complaints. Birmingham's personnel file detailed a dozen others. Since he'd shared a rectory with him when both were assigned to St. James in Salem, McCormack might have entertained even deeper suspicions. He did not. He was glad his old friend was coming home. When next he saw Birmingham, McCormack inquired about his struggles. "I'm wondering, you know, how you're handling that," he asked.

"I'm clean," Birmingham replied.

That was good enough for him. He cleared the way for Birmingham's reinstatement. On September 18, Cardinal Law invited Birmingham to a meeting to review his progress. They spoke of Birmingham's health, which was precarious; doctors had diagnosed cancer, telling him he did not have much time left.

Confident he was beyond risk, Law reassigned Birmingham to ministry, this time as pastor of St. Ann's Church, in Gloucester.

There was only one problem. One of the St. Ann's parishioners had heard a troubling rumor from a colleague who recalled a Father Birmingham being taken out of ministry in Salem after drawing molestation charges. Concerned for his young son, the parishioner wrote a letter to the cardinal asking, "Is this the same Birmingham who abused children in Salem? I'm concerned about . . . a priest possibly molesting my son."

Law passed the letter to McCormack, who wrote a curious return letter: "I contacted Father Birmingham and asked him specifically about the matter you expressed in your letter. He assured me there is absolutely no factual basis to your concern regarding your son and him. From my knowledge of Father Birmingham and my relationship with him, I feel he would tell me the truth and I believe he is speaking the truth in this matter. From my perspective, therefore, I see no need of your raising this question with your son."

Law thought this response was appropriate. Rather than answering the question *Was Birmingham a known child molester?* it slyly addressed the letter writer's concern for the future safety of his child while making it *seem* as though he were denying the priest's history. Deft and effective, he thought.

Sometime in 1987

NEWTON, MASSACHUSETTS — After chasing down the cardinal and alerting him to Paul Shanley's past, Jackie Gauvreau was a changed woman. She rejoined the choir at St. Jean's. If pressed to admit it, she would say she wanted a front-row seat to the demise of her nemesis. But she wasn't gloating, not openly at any rate. She knew that her fellow congregants held priests in extremely high esteem, and she saw no reason to disabuse them of that simply because of one cleric's lousy track record. She left them their beliefs, and was impressed by her own benevolence. She was grateful to have her church back.

For some reason, though, as the weeks and months unfolded, Shanley's anticipated demise never happened. Nobody called her to investigate her complaint. Danny Quinn, who said he had been groped, said he'd never heard from anybody either. Paul Shanley persisted at St. Jean's.

That was why, when she looked up from choir practice one afternoon and saw Cardinal Law in the back of the church nave, she pushed her way to the aisle and ran after him. She followed Law down a flight of stairs and tapped him on a landing, gripping his arm.

"Do you remember me? My name is Jacqueline Gauvreau and I told you about Paul Shanley?"

His face telegraphed impatience. "See my bishops," he said, before spinning out the door. "That's why I have them."

Summer 1987

GLOUCESTER, MASSACHUSETTS — On a Monday evening halfway between ninth and tenth grades, traditionally an interval of significant personal growth and social maturation, Paul Ciaramitaro was washing the dinner dishes at St. Ann's Rectory, his part-time job. An earnest and responsible youth, he kept carefully to himself. Among his high school classmates, no one was more bashful or remote. He came alive only in hockey season. On the ice, nearly hidden in his helmet and padding, he was a star. His coach once said that if he had fifteen Ciaramitaros on his team, nobody could beat them.

But off the ice, unmasked, the first thing you noticed about Paul was his profound disfigurement. He suffered from a rare genetic disorder called tuberous sclerosis, which caused benign tumors to erupt all over his body. Hundreds of them, as small as a grain of sand and as large as a golf ball, crowded around his internal organs. Already he had been forced to undergo heart surgery to correct a related condition, subaortic stenosis, which had restricted his blood flow and threatened his life. He was in danger again now. An aneurysm in his kidney was causing internal bleeding and throbbing pains. Kidney failure was a hallmark of tuberous sclerosis, and the principal cause of death.

But the most apparent manifestation of his condition sat right on his face. Literally hundreds of scarlet lumps encased his nose and cheeks in a carapace of tumors. They were uncomfortable, and required frequent surgeries. But the worst aspect was how insecure they made him, especially around girls. He could go weeks without talking to a girl. Just knowing a girl was looking at him caused him excruciating discomfort. It was nearly impossible for him to return the glance.

As he stood washing the dishes, the pastor walked up behind him and started massaging his kidneys. This was Father Joseph Birmingham. He had arrived here directly following treatment at the Institute of Living, though no one in the parish was given warnings, least of all Paul, who was fifteen. He was employed as the rectory assistant, answering phones several afternoons a week and serving supper on Mondays. In kindness or pity, throughout the summer Birmingham had invited Paul to Red Sox games and for swims at the beach, and Paul felt extremely blessed. Birmingham also had a nice way of rubbing his lower back. It was the ameliorative heat of his hands that Paul liked, the hands of a priest on a sick boy.

This time, as Paul worked on the dishes, the massage took on a strange character. Birmingham was whispering in his ears.

"Did you know any gay people?"

"What? No."

"Are you gay?"

"No, I'm not gay." The question galled him.

"It's okay, you know. Be quiet, shhhh. Don't say it to anybody."

"I'm not!"

"Do you masturbate? Because you know, that's okay now. But it would be better for you to confess it to me, not any of these other priests, because they don't all understand."

It was the same interrogation technique Birmingham had used over the decades with Tom Blanchette, Bernie McDaid, Olan Horne, and Gary Bergeron. Paul Ciaramitaro was no less vulnerable than they had been. He never had masturbated. Even the word was alien to him. He answered honestly, certain there was no alternative. There was no fifth amendment in Catholicism.

Birmingham kept working his thumbs into his kidneys, spinning strange questions off his thick tongue.

"If I said, come away with me for the weekend, what would you bring to sleep in?"

"Pajamas."

"No!" he exploded. "No, you wouldn't! You'd wear underwear. Big boys wear underwear. Say there's only one bed. Where would you sleep?"

"I'd let you have the bed."

"No, no, no, no, no!"

Paul was feeling blunt terror now. But as spooked as he was he did not think to flee, not even when Birmingham whispered conspiratorially for him to scoot upstairs for a more thorough massage. Paul followed him into the rectory's upper floors, a sanctum where laypeople were never allowed. Birmingham's private quarters consisted of a dark-paneled two-room suite. Books lined the walls. A hand-hooked Oriental rub hugged the floor. With a sudden flurry that left Paul no time even to wonder what was happening, Birmingham snapped the teen's shirt over his head, slid him onto the sofa, and straddled him, working his hands over his strong back. Paul's mind went white when he felt the hands creep toward his backside and begin to massage his buttocks. He heard the Velcro give way on the waistband of his slacks. Birmingham was now masturbating Paul, who was so stupefied by this turn of events that he could not formulate an objection. Out of respect for the priesthood he did not instantly recognize just how weird this was. He froze.

"Shhh, be quiet," Paul heard. *"It's okay if you're gay."*

He genuinely was *not* gay! His fantasies were pure matriarchies.

"Do you want me to show you how? Do you love me?"

He felt the priest's penis rubbing against his backside, felt the priest's hand gripping his genitals, felt the burning pain in his kidneys. He was suffocating in his degradation. When Paul ejaculated, it was the first time in his life. He had no clue what had happened to him. He mistook the semen for sludge from his diseased kidney, forced out of him under the terrible deadweight of the priest on his back.

"I'm bleeding," he pleaded. He kicked Birmingham off him, twisted on his clothes, and ran out the door.

The Following Sunday, 3 P.M.

Although he was expected to work the afternoon and evening shift at the rectory, Paul lingered conspicuously around home. He was tired of the deceit of the last few days, when his mother would drop him off at St. Ann's and pick him up a few hours later, unaware that he'd spent the time strolling the neighborhood in total botheration, without a clue what he could do. Quitting his job would entail explaining why, and there was no way he could speak about what Birmingham had done. But returning to work was also out of the question. How long could he keep up the charade?

Only his brother seemed to be onto him, goading Paul about how late he was going to be. With scant provocation, Paul lashed out, and their violent scrape was overheard by a neighbor, who broke them apart and peppered Paul with questions. Primed by an explosion of high-profile child molestation cases in the media, the neighbor began to suspect the worst.

"What is it, Paul?" he asked. "Something happened. What's wrong? Why can't you go to St. Ann's?"

Paul said nothing. "Come talk to me about it sometime," the man invited, "if you'd like."

It took several days before Paul took up the invitation and confided everything. The neighbor helped relate the story to Paul's mother, who despite being a devout Catholic had no trouble believing her son, to his relief. Not the type to let something like this go unspoken, she packed Paul in the car and they drove to see Auxiliary Bishop John Mulcahy, the administrator for their region, to immediately level a formal complaint against Joseph Birmingham.

Mulcahy did not betray any hint that others had complained about Birmingham, but he acted decisively. He bypassed John McCormack and went to his superior, Auxiliary Bishop Robert Banks, who had recently been named vicar general. Banks called Birmingham to the carpet and asked him for the truth. Birmingham confessed.

Acting with the urgency of a wartime paramedic, Banks yanked Birmingham out of St. Ann's Church in Gloucester. This was the new policy after the Gauthe debacle—*decisive, surgical action, no room for misinterpretation.* He ordered Birmingham immediately to Lexington, where the first blood was spilled in the American Revolution, a beautiful historic town with musty museums, manicured parks, cloistered schools, and with more than twenty houses of worship—none more vital than St. Brigid's Church, with six thousand parishioners, and eighty-one baptisms this year alone. But he did not send him there for treatment or legal counsel; he did not even send him there for spiritual intervention. Bishop Banks sent Birmingham there to work as parochial vicar, hoping that Paul Ciaramitaro would forget all about him. There were several restrictions placed on Birmingham in Lexington—he was not to work directly with youth groups, for example—but no one there would be forewarned about the priest.

With his molester gone, most people assumed Paul's life would return to normal. That was not the case. He reeled from Birmingham's implications about his sexual orientation. He lusted after women, he knew that. But Birmingham must have seen something that was still opaque to him. Why would he have importuned him so insistently? Paul had ejaculated with a man. That was proof of something. But what? His brain became a chamber of recrimination. Nothing was less acceptable than homosexuality, not even tuberous sclerosis—a life-threatening disease was at least morally neutral. He saw homosexuality as an inexorable character flaw.

Despite the revolutionary fervor of gay rights advocates, few Americans disagreed with him. In polls, they were only slightly warmer to gays now than they were fifteen years before. Two-thirds considered homosexuality morally wrong, according to an ABC poll. And 43 percent believed being homosexual was morally wrong even for people who were sworn to abstinence—they believed it was sinful just to *think* gay. The AIDS plague, now five years old and devastating the gay community, was doing no favors for its public image. Violence against gays was on the rise; one in four gay men and lesbians in recent surveys said they had been physically assaulted because of their sexual orientation, and as many as 92 percent reported being subjected to verbal abuse or threats. Even in youth culture, long a reservoir of encouragement for gays, 75 percent now considered homosexuality utterly unacceptable, according to a *Rolling Stones* poll.

For years to come, Paul Ciaramitaro's doubts and fears would harass him. To banish them, he would turn to drugs and liquor, the last thing his troubled kidneys could handle. One would fail, and he would have to have it removed. With pain consuming his remaining kidney, he would begin now to experience regular epileptic seizures, a symptom of his disease. He needed to talk to somebody about his demons. But no representative of the church ever came to him with an offer of assistance.

March 29, 1988
WASHINGTON, D.C. — Ministering to gays had been a difficult sojourn for Sister Jeannine Gramick. On the one hand, she felt utterly invigorated by the work, which she pursued zealously. Above all, she considered herself a bridge builder. In 1977 she had joined up with a Salvatorian Order priest named Robert Nugent, who was conducting a similar ministry. They formed New Ways Ministry in Washington, D.C., a social justice center working for reconciliation between the church and the estimated 5 million gay and lesbian Catholics. Gramick walked a fine doctrinal line, preaching compassion while remaining careful not to cross official church teachings. For instance, she made it a point never to talk about gay sex, which she would be forced to condemn. Some considered this coy and dishonest—gays wished she would be more overt in declaring their relationships licit, while some church leaders pressed her to be more rigorously opposed to gay unions.

Washington's archbishop, James Hickey, soon to be named a cardinal, was especially quick and constant with his suspicions, and as New Ways operated from offices in his territorial district, his scrutiny carried some weight. He had accused the ministry's leaders of "studied ambiguity," that is, preaching a message that allowed gay people to hear what they wanted to hear. In 1980, certain that Father Nugent was likely to be too lenient on gays in confession, Archbishop Hickey refused his request for faculties in the diocese; that meant he was not able to hear confessions or preach there. At Hickey's urgings, the Vatican then began an investigation to determine if Nugent and Gramick were misleading the faithful with their "ambiguous stand on the morality of homosexual activity."

Simultaneously, Hickey pressured their religious superiors to withdraw them from his archdiocese—he wanted their kind out of his neighborhood. His objections prevailed. Rome blasted New Ways as "the occasion of much controversy and concern." Under threat of disciplinary action from their superiors, and facing an order from the Congregation for Religious and Secular Institutes, a Roman curial office, Gramick and Nugent were forced to withdraw from New Ways in 1994. However, both interpreted their instructions very narrowly. They could continue their work, but not under the New Ways aegis. "I can still be a nurse, you can still be a doctor," Gramick reasoned with Nugent, "but we can't work for this hospital any longer."

Gramick became a well-known and popular lecturer, preaching that the church, in its wisdom, was sometimes wrong—but God, who created both gays and straights, never was.

From 1984 to 1988, she spoke in hundreds of lecture halls, to thousands of gay and lesbian Catholics, their relatives and friends. All the while, she was dogged by those who felt sure her agenda was wickedly heretical. The Vatican had received hundreds of sharp letters rebuking her. Cardinal Law banned her from speaking in Boston, and Archbishop McCarrick did likewise in Newark. Ordinary Catholics objected in person as well. Once, as she led a retreat in West Palm Beach, a member of an orthodox lay group called Roman Catholic Faithful broke into the facility, loudly prayed the rosary, and refused to leave.

Little could surprise her now, she thought. But then, on a cool day in March, she was called to a meeting in Baltimore at the motherhouse for her religious order. Sitting at a round table, Gramick listened to her general superior recount the details of a letter she'd just received.

Archbishop Vincent Fagiolo of the Congregation for Religious and
Secular Institutes noticed Sister Patricia Flynn, General Superior
of the School Sisters of Notre Dame, and Father Malachy
McBride, General Superior of the Society of the Divine Savior,
that a Commission would be established in the United States "to
render a judgment as to the clarity and orthodoxy of the public presentations" of Sister Jeannine Gramick and Father Robert Nugent
"with respect to the Church's teaching on homosexuality."

Nobody, in the immortal words of *Monty Python's Flying Circus,* expects the Spanish Inquisition.

Late November 1988
LEXINGTON, MASSACHUSETTS — A chill in the air, fog smearing his windows, Tom Blanchette drove west of Boston to Lexington. He had an
appointment with Joseph Birmingham. It had been twenty-five years
since Birmingham's going-away party in Sudbury, where they last
spoke. Although he had experienced several intense periods of trauma
and flux in his life, Tom was pretty sure Birmingham had nothing to do
with it. He always thought back on the sex, though, which began when
he was thirteen and ended when he was fifteen. He never wanted it,
never sought it out, and it still made him angry. He had to concede,
though, that he had never said no either.

"It's like that Simon and Garfunkel song about the whores on Seventh Avenue. I must admit I took some comfort there," he thought. "In
the act of abuse there is a pleasurable experience. I admit that I enjoyed that, but I never solicited it. I never wanted to engage in that. I
didn't feel shame. Or guilt. It was just weird. I wanted it to stop. But
after it went on for a while, I felt like now I'm a participant. How could
I ever explain it to anybody that I had laid naked in Father B.'s bed over
a hundred times? I knew what my sexual desires were. It wasn't like I
understood that as homosexuality. Although one would have to say that
I was engaged in homosexual activity, I had no word for it. All I knew
was I didn't like it. But I saw him every Saturday and every Sunday, because I worked in the church; I saw him at least one night a week for

CCD classes, and at least one night a week he was at our house for dinner. Every time we were alone he pursued sexual activity. For two years I would say we had sex two or three times a week, sometimes two or three times in a day."

Until he was in his twenties, he had never mentioned a word of this history. One morning he and a friend were reminiscing about their teenage years when Birmingham's name came up. "That bastard," the friend said. "He queered me."

"Fuck," Tom said, "I thought I was the only one!"

Tom then polled each of his four brothers, who admitted it had happened to them, too. They told their mother, who called her friends one by one and got the same answer about their boys. In the span of a week or so, Tom and his mother had compiled a list of nearly twenty-five victims. But Tom's father, a devout man, could not stand to hear about it. He demanded that in his house the subject of priests and sex would never be broached again. Curious as he remained, Tom did as his father instructed, and put the history out of mind.

But now he was starting to think that the silence policy had not been especially helpful for him. For one thing, in all these years he had not been able to develop a lasting relationship with a woman—at age forty he remained doggedly single. Even a stable place to live was too much of a commitment for him. He moved at least once a year. The bite of alcohol snuck up on him. He joined AA and began his twelve steps in earnest. The fifth required him to sit down with people in his life and forthrightly detail where he had done them wrong. The correlative to this principle was often put this way: "We're only as sick as our secrets."

He knew he had to find Birmingham. The priest was now at St. Brigid's Rectory, in Lexington. Reached on the phone, Birmingham agreed to a visit, and on this frigid early-winter day Tom headed to see him with some trepidation. Sitting in an armchair in his parlor, Birmingham was wide open and encouraging, which impressed Tom.

"I've had some experiences in my life and I've realized that some of the difficulties were a result of the relationship that I had with you," Tom began.

"I played sports in high school—I was a type-A personality. I went to college for a year at Merrimack, but I never settled down there. After that I decided I wanted to go into the army, so on Labor Day 1967, in the middle of the Vietnam War, I enlisted. And I did very well in the army. They gave me an appointment to the United States Military Academy. I went there for a year, too, but I decided I didn't want a military career, so I went to the University of Massachusetts and graduated there. I actually went to work for a guy I went to high school with in Sudbury, and ended up selling Monroe shock absorbers with him for years."

Birmingham listened scrupulously.

All those years, he said, he never attended Mass.

"I started being a little introspective after my dad died in 1981, and sort of had a spiritual awakening—I was living in Akron, Ohio, at the time. So I started to attend a little Episcopal church out there, which was very beneficial for me. The liturgy, you know, is fairly similar. I sort of felt a disregard for the Catholic Church. But the liturgy was familiar. I'm a basic Christian believer. I'm naïve enough to believe that the promise that Jesus Christ made is true."

Narrowing in on his main message, he was determined to speak without distemper.

"You know," Tom said dexterously, "what you did to me and my brothers, and all the other boys in Sudbury, that was wrong. You had no right to do it. And I don't think anybody has ever told you that before."

Fixed on Birmingham's face was a doleful expression. Perhaps it was grief.

"Now let me tell you *my* story," the priest said.

"I've had a very difficult life myself. Unlike you, who comes from a large family, I was an only child and both of my parents have died. I've had a lot of personal difficulties and recently some medical ones. I seem to be troubled with a lung disorder that defies diagnosis—nobody can seem to figure out what's wrong with me. I've been removed from ministry for sexually abusing boys. I'm not allowed to say Mass. I'm sort of under house arrest here. I can't leave the grounds unless accompanied by two adults. I can't have any contact with kids. I was up in Gloucester and they took me out and put me in a treatment facility in Hartford, Connecticut. I still go there one day a month. I'm seeing a psychiatrist in Boston."

Tom was relieved to learn that Birmingham's secret was out in the open and that he was being kept away from children. He was impressed at the man's apparent efforts to overcome his demons. Yet he thought Birmingham's presentation was lacking one aspect, evidence that he acknowledged the harm his sexual predations may have caused. Getting there would have to remain Birmingham's private journey—Tom Blanchette was here to talk about the harm that *he* had wrought, his fifth step to recovery.

"Having said all this brings me to the real reason I've come here," Tom said. "The real reason I've come is to make amends to those I have harmed. Now, I know I didn't do outright harm to you. But I've come to ask you to forgive me for the hatred and resentment I've felt toward you for the past twenty-five years."

Oddly, this seemed to infuriate Birmingham, who rose menacingly to his feet. Turning the palms of his enormous hands to the heavens, he bellowed, "Why are *you* asking *me* for forgiveness?" Perhaps he understood it after all.

Overcome, Tom began to sob. "Because," he tried to say, "the Bible tells me to love my enemies and to pray for those that persecute me."

Slowly Birmingham slid back into his chair, and in gratitude or disgrace he began to weep as well.

April 18, 1989
Arlington, Massachusetts — Several months later, when Tom Blanchette heard that Father Birmingham was probably dying, he was overtaken by a desire to see him once more. He drove to St. Brigid's in Lexington, but a priest there redirected him to a hospital in Arlington, nearby. Tom made it to the ward after 9 P.M. Peering into the priest's room, he could see Birmingham propped up in a chair, breathing ponderously through a mask. He scarcely recognized the man. Once a baronial 220 pounds, Birmingham at the relatively young age of fifty-five now weighed little more than eighty. He clung to the edge of the chair like a small child in a large dinghy. His hair was gone, his sight half lost to whatever consumed him.

Attending him was another priest, who, spotting Blanchette at the door, steered him back out into the hallway.

"He really didn't want visitors," explained the priest, Larry Kelly, an army chaplain with the rank of full colonel who had graduated from the seminary with Birmingham in 1960. "He has had twenty-three chemo treatments, which burnt away some of his esophagus. He really can't talk. Cancer in the lungs. Pneumocystis carinii pneumonia. He's in a lot of pain, on morphine."

"I've come all this way, Father. It would just take a couple minutes."

Reluctantly, Kelly capitulated. "Take a minute, no more."

Entering the darkened room, Tom knelt next to Birmingham's chair and took his papery hand. Silently for a while, he prayed. Soon Birmingham turned toward him and though he did not speak, he seemed to telegraph recognition through his fluttering eyes.

"Father, it's Tommy Blanchette from Sudbury," he said. He never called himself Tommy. Nor had anybody else, ever. What reflex motivated him to make himself diminutive now? Embarrassment colored his cheeks, but Birmingham did not notice. "I've come to visit you, Father. Is it okay if I pray for you?"

Birmingham nodded. Beneath the heavy clear plastic breathing apparatus, he seemed to mouth the word "yes."

Tom clamped his eyes shut. "Father, in the name of Jesus Christ I ask you to heal Father Birmingham in the body, the mind, and the spirit." He moved one of his hands over the priest's gowned chest. His fingers measured the rattle of Birmingham's lungs, and the woozy beat of his heart.

The priest's eyes closed, and the two men sat this way and allowed the moments to accumulate and the sadness to brim their hearts.

"Father," Tom said, "forgive him his sins through the shed blood of Jesus Christ, that he too might have eternal life."

Birmingham seemed asleep again now. Tom Blanchette gathered his hollow frame up in his arms and carried him to his bed, with Kelly's help. He smoothed a blanket over Birmingham and through the stream of his own tears he wished him good night.

"I'll come back and see you tomorrow if you like," he said.

But Joseph Birmingham did not have a tomorrow—he passed away just a few hours later.

Birmingham's cause of death was listed as cancer. However, if what Colonel Kelly told Blanchette was true—that Birmingham also suf-

fered from Pneumocystis carinii pneumonia—it was likely he also suffered from AIDS, as PCP is an HIV-related pneumonia. Even for non-
priests, an AIDS diagnosis carried a heavy stigma. Children with the
disease had been burned out of their homes, mothers threatened with
imprisonment. Prominent lawmakers and commentators discussed
quarantining or branding known carriers. Men had lost jobs as lawyers,
stockbrokers, hairdressers, police officers, and ministers.

Meanwhile, the epidemic was raging among priests in silence.
Church officials kept this matter under keen observation. They had no
way to know how many priests were among the estimated 1 million
Americans living with HIV. Perhaps a hundred priests had died to date.
Dr. Jon Fuller, a director at Boston Medical Center's Clinical AIDS
Program who also happened to be a Jesuit priest, began a specialty
treating infected Catholic clerics. He suspected the death toll among
priests was much higher.

So did Dr. Joseph Barone, a New Jersey–based psychiatrist and
AIDS expert. Starting in 1983, Barone worked as the lay director of an
AIDS ministry at the North American College in Rome, the preeminent seminary for Americans studying for the priesthood. At first, he
aimed his ministry at nonclergy. But sensing that his own seminarians
were at high risk for the disease, in 1987 Barone established an underground AIDS testing program. Lending the students false names, he
drove them himself to clinics to get them tested in secret. His hunch
proved accurate. One in twelve tested HIV-positive, a staggering plurality.

"The tragedy is many of them have been so duplicitous and so closeted," he told a reporter from the *Kansas City Star*. "They didn't realize
what they were doing, not only to themselves, but to other individuals,
because of the exponential transmission rate."

Of the notorious St. John's Seminary class of 1960, Birmingham
was among the first to die, and his passing was noted especially by
John McCormack, who more than anybody else knew the scope of
Birmingham's sexual crimes. He would not reveal what he knew—any
more than he would say what he knew about Paul Shanley, Bernard
Lane, Eugene O'Sullivan, or any of his classmates who stood accused
of fondling juveniles. There were plenty. No class from St. John's—

or anywhere else in the country—was as miscreant as the class of 1960. Before reaching the age of retirement, nine graduates in a class of seventy-five men would stand accused. It was accepted that about fewer than 4 percent of the general population acted on a sexual interest in minors. In the class of 1960, the figure was 12 percent.

Cardinal Law presided over Birmingham's funeral, eulogizing in poetic strains a man whom he had personally removed from regular parish work and who died in spiritual limbo. The cardinal did not allude to the harm he had visited upon his flock. Rather, he praised Birmingham's service, his faith, and his pastorate.

Several of the altar boys Birmingham had molested attended the funeral, hoping that by seeing the priest's embalmed body they might finally be released from their anger. The cardinal's eulogy confused them. A funeral was no place to settle scores, they felt, but nor was it a place for the most powerful prelate in America to sanitize and glorify a disastrous life. In generosity, Tom Blanchette simply assumed the cardinal didn't know what had transpired—perhaps these matters were handled in the lower ranks, by deputies or regional bishops. Following the service, Blanchette approached the cardinal in the church as he was sipping from a cup of tea.

"Your Eminence," he said, "I've never met you before. I'm Tom Blanchette from Sudbury. I knew Father B. in the 1960s."

Law showed that he was pleased.

"And have you maintained a friendship through the years?"

"No, we have not. But I went to see him a year ago, and I was with him the night before he died."

"Oh, wonderful, wonderful," Law said, grabbing and holding Blanchette's hands in his own.

"Cardinal," Tom said discreetly, "there will be a number of young men in this archdiocese in need of counseling in the wake of their relationships with Father Birmingham."

Law's blue eyes ran to ice. "What are you driving at?"

"Father Birmingham sexually abused me and my four brothers and dozens of boys in Sudbury. And I know he continued in that behavior in the last twenty-five years because he told me that himself."

"You must believe me," Law said commandingly, "you must believe me when I say that as soon as I heard about this, I removed him from ministry."

This admission surprised Blanchette, who could not understand why Law had presided at an elaborate ceremony if he knew how cunning and intractable Birmingham's problems had been.

Law asked, "How did this happen to you, Tom? Did you ever tell anybody when it was happening?"

"No, not till years later. And when we started talking about it, my father put an end to the conversation. He didn't like to hear such things about priests."

"Did you discuss this with Father Birmingham?"

Tom related his experiences to the cardinal in detail. "I believe I was appointed by God to go to see him and kneel before him at his deathbed in proxy for all the boys that he had sexually abused. Cardinal, the church has abrogated its responsibility not only to the people by moving bad priests around but to the priests for not holding them accountable. I know that pedophilia is an epidemic in this diocese."

The good rapport that existed between the two men vanished. "Would you go see Bishop Banks?" Law instructed coolly, his hands still tightly gripping Tom's. "Bishop Banks is handling this situation. I want you to go see Bishop Banks. We are offering counseling through Catholic Charities."

"I have the capacity to pay for my own therapy, thank you."

"May I pray for you?"

Tom nodded as Law placed his hands on the younger man's forehead. After a few moments, he opened his blue eyes. All traces of antipathy were gone from them. Once again he gripped Tom Blanchette's hands in his.

He said, "I bind you by the power of the confessional never to speak about this again."

Did the cardinal really think he could shut him up that way? It was the same thing his father had tried. Blanchette thought of all the many teenagers whose lives were altered all because the secret remained a secret. He was not about to shut up.

November 21, 1989

NEWTON, MASSACHUSETTS — Mostly, when Paul Shanley was not performing marriages or elementary school graduations, neither shepherding his flock through life's course nor blessing their souls upon death, he busied himself with doctor visits for the thirty-three ailments that plagued him—from allergies to prostatitis to an unspecified injury brought about by excessive squat exercises, requiring surgery—and the attendant bills, each of which seemed to require at least a pair of written requests for reimbursements. He was weary. Little energy remained for his old quixotic campaigns. When Sister Gramick was called to account by Rome, when the progay clergymen warhorses were twisting under the scrupulous attentions of Cardinal Ratzinger, he did not reach out to them or protest in any way, such was his exhaustion.

Ten years had passed since the days of his activism, and aside from an occasional invitation to speak, which nostalgia compelled him to accept, he was no longer a militant in the trenches but something of a stately parish priest whose thoughtful and kind homilies had helped fill pews at St. Jean's. He still believed in the rightness of physical love irrespective of sexual orientation, and he still enjoyed a following among the more liberal-minded Catholics. But he no longer leapt into a skirmish, no longer woke each day with a passion he once said "turned black-and-white into Technicolor."

But then the Vatican announced that all newly appointed pastors would have to sign a loyalty oath, affirming, among other things, the exclusively male priesthood and the unquestionable authority of the pope and bishops.

Nobody found acquiescence more difficult than Paul Shanley. He came out swinging, as in the old days, delivering inflaming lectures to his personnel directors about modern ethics and social justice. But the more he fought, the sicker he felt—eye trouble, pain in the knee, back, and hip, a hernia—and the more pathetic his complaints seemed. Cardinal Law never went in for the kind of tensions that bound Shanley and Medeiros together. He didn't have the stomach for hand-to-hand combat. He didn't respond to Shanley's challenges, which seemed only to further dishearten the priest.

In the end, Law determined to send Shanley into a sort of hybrid retirement state, though he was fifty-eight, starting with a year of sick
leave and reflection. Should he decide at that point to toe the line, he
would be lavishly welcomed home; otherwise, his service to the church
would reach its end. Undoubtedly other priests had refused to sign and
either stayed on as associate pastors or slid into disappointed retirement. Not Shanley.

"Your Eminence," he wrote, "thank you for your third patient, kindly
attempt to reconcile my conscience with the new oath. I agree with you
that I have to stop wrestling with it now to devote full time to recover-
ing my health. . . . As I told you, I feel haunted by and pulled into com-
plicity with historical abuses which the oath endorses, betrayed by this
new definition of pastor, abandoned after 38 years, shattered and de-
moralized not only by the oath but by the reaction to it (most priests
counsel perjury!). This has had an inevitably adverse effect on my already precarious health problems and I feel relieved to be laying down
the pastoral office."

He asked for $400 to buy an airline ticket for San Bernardino, Cali-
fornia, where Shanley hoped to spend his medical sabbatical beneath a
warm sun. He received a heartfelt send-off from his parishioners, and
right after the first of the year headed west with an official letter of introduction to present to the local bishop—a *celebret* attesting to his
good standing in Boston—so that for a bit of extra money he could
serve as a supply priest, that is, a stand-in to say Mass when local
priests weren't able.

As the Catholic Church entered the 1990s, whatever patina of heroism or moral allure the priesthood had once enjoyed in popular culture
was lost to history. The institution seemed in danger of vanishing. For
every priest, there were now twelve hundred Catholic faithful. By contrast, in the Lutheran Church the ratio was about one to five hundred,
and it was one to three hundred for Episcopalians. Both churches had
accepted women as clergy members. The scarcity of Roman priests was
only getting worse. Ordinations were down 86 percent over the peak
years in the mid-sixties, and seminary enrollments had withered. In
1968, there were forty thousand seminarians studying around the na-

tion. In 1990, their number stood just over eight thousand. Younger men were staying away—94 percent of high school seminaries had been closed in the past thirty years. Today's dwindling class of seminarians heeded the calling after college and sometimes well into their first careers.

Many now were not virgins, but sexually experienced and integrated men for whom sex was neither a mystery nor something to be feared. Many, too, were gay. This had become officially acknowledged in recent years. Following the eruption of the Gauthe case in the mid-eighties, American seminary directors reconsidered the way sexuality and celibacy was discussed among their students. A significant outgrowth of this reevaluation was new policies that called for one-on-one "priestly formation," in which faculty members helped mentor seminarians through all aspects of their spiritual growth, including their efforts to embrace celibacy. This required frank discussions about their sexual struggles. Many were tempted by men rather than women, it turned out.

Was this a problem? Not as far as the National Conference of Catholic Bishops or the National Catholic Education Association were concerned. So long as seminarians were chaste—and not frequenting gay bars or publicly identifying as gay—they met every requirement for the priesthood. It was unclear if their numbers began to proliferate following this change in policy; certainly the overall number of priests did not increase. But just by making this an acceptable topic of conversation in seminaries, something remarkable seemed to happen. The frequency of priests "acting out" with children plunged. The bishops never commissioned another psychological study of their priests to see why this was so. Father Robert Silva, president of the National Federation of Priests' Councils, was not convinced younger priests were any healthier or more sexually integrated overall. But a tremendous pressure had been taken off priests—especially homosexual priests—by letting them talk through their struggles. "It's paying off," Silva said. "If they're not developing more of a mature self-knowledge, they are at best developing the skill to contain the impulses."

The new openness was not greeted positively by everybody. Many heterosexual seminarians, in fact, felt their increasingly visible gay counterparts began to overdefine seminary culture, making it over as a "finishing school for a certain kind of homoerotic identity," as the historian Mark Jordan said—asexual, but nonetheless flamboyant and clubby. Discomfited by being in the cultural minority, some heterosexuals began complaining about what they started calling "pink palaces." They suffered from what the author Father Donald Cozzens called a "feeling that they don't fit," and the alienation tended to destabilize their sense of vocation. Most seminary directors were admitting they lost a number of heterosexual seminarians to this culture clash each year.

But the net effect seemed to have been overwhelmingly positive. As future data would show, adherence to celibacy among all priests was on the rise. More to the point, the new generation of priests were not attacking teenagers or minors like their predecessors. Reports of abuse began dropping off for priests ordained in the mid-1980s, and steadily declined every year after. But there was much damage yet to emerge.

Chapter 6

Confrontation

November 6, 1989

ANAHEIM, CALIFORNIA — In the middle of the third ring of the phone, a middle-aged woman sang, "Good afternoon, St. Boniface Church."

"Yes, I would like to speak with John." The caller's voice was tight, rushed. "Father John Lenihan."

"May I ask who's calling?"

"It's Mary."

"Mary? Last name?"

Mary thought she would be nervous, but she was not. She was more frightened the last time she spoke to him. Now she felt only rage.

"Mary Grant," she said, almost seething.

While waiting on hold, she breathed loudly into the receiver.

"Father John," he announced.

"Yes, John," she said. "This is Mary Grant."

"Uh-huh," he said, instantly suspicious. He read her mood quickly.

"I'm calling because I need to talk with you about a couple things. Um, the last time we talked a year ago about what happened when I was in your youth group, I thought I had resolved it but I didn't. I saw an article about you in the newspaper and I was just minding my own business reading the newspaper and there was a big photograph of you and about your church and it just brought all this back. About what happened."

In the dozen years since they first met, Lenihan had become a beloved citizen in Anaheim, handsome and influential, much chronicled in the local paper.

"I need to ask you something, and that is, why did you molest me? I need to know *why* you did that."

"Do you want to hold on for a minute?" he interrupted. He flicked the hold button without waiting for her answer.

He was back in a moment, seizing the offensive. "Okay, now you have to listen."

"I'm listening." Her sarcasm was plain.

"Okay, first of all, I never, ever thought in that term. Never. Because I never would have thought of it as a molestation situation. That's not the issue at this point, because I know you have a different point of view on it."

"Tell me again your point of view. I need to know."

"What happened was that I developed a strong feeling of . . . of *affection* for you because, um, I guess I was going through maybe the same kind of growth thing that had never taken place in my life up to that point. I had come through a system of, you know, Irish farm background. All-boys high school. All-boys seminary. I never had a date in my life. I had never gone out with a girl. I had never had a dance."

How touching, she thought. Mary Grant was disgusted. She had been fourteen! He had been thirty-two! He was the priest who led her *youth group*.

Also, back then he very directly told her about another girl, whom she did not know but whose life she had thought of often in therapy this past year. She did not for one minute buy his claims to virginity.

"You never touched a girl," she challenged.

"I never touched a girl at that point in my *life*, and, you know, I just didn't maybe understand what was going on inside *me*, because . . . I thought what had happened was I was falling in love."

"And how did you show your love? I mean, I need to understand." She was leaping all over him.

"Okay, I thought I was showing my love by caring, in terms of being supportive on the family situation. The physical stuff, I don't know how that even got going."

"You don't remember the first time it happened?"

"Ahhhh," he said, stonewalling her.

"You don't remember when you told me you wanted to touch me because you've never touched a girl there before?" It didn't make sense that he would say both things, this and his intimation about other girls, but that's the way she recalled it. She recalled the words, and so much about the words from back then made no sense in retrospect.

"Yes, that comes back," he agreed. "Yes."

"Okay, and that you never got to touch a girl and that I got to be the *lucky one*."

"Oh, no," he said. This attribution appalled him. "I didn't—I *hope* I didn't—use the term 'lucky one.' I did not. Oh, no. No, no. I didn't, didn't say *that*. Oh, no, gosh, I didn't say that, I *certainly* didn't say *that*."

"And you also wanted to show me because you wanted to have intercourse with me also, when my mom was gone, right? Do you remember?"

"No, that second part, no. I would never. I had never, ever, ever planned on having intercourse with you."

She was haunted by the Thursday afternoon in 1977 when she was home sick from school and he dropped by on his day off to cram his fingers inside her, saying, "This is to prepare you for intercourse."

"But when you came over to my mother's house," she demanded, "what happened then? I need to know that you remember that."

"Well wait a minute now. You're jumping me." His voice grew child-like, the way she remembered him. "Okay," he continued. "What happened that day as best I can remember was that you were sick at home from school and your mom was working. And I came over because it was my day off, I wanted to see you, and I wasn't dressed clerically, stuff like that." His voice thickened. "I wanted to hold you, I guess."

"And then what happened?"

"Well, what happened was an awful lot more than that," he said.

"Tell me, I need to hear it."

"Do you really?"

"Yes, I do."

"Okay," he said, "what happened was we went into your bedroom—"

"My mother's bedroom."

"All right, whatever, your *mother's* bedroom. And, ah . . . I took your panties off and I kissed you, you know, whatever that term is, between your legs."

"And didn't you pull yours down and . . ."

"No."

". . . and want to have intercourse?"

"No, no. I can tell you why I know that specifically. I never did, and I know why. Because when I went away afterward, because I had been holding you so tight and I had white pants on, the pants were stained with some of your, um, *juices,* and I was—no, it was an emphatic truth I had never unbuckled my pants or anything like that. You never saw my, my *physical parts,* and I never did unzip my pants, no. I am emphatic about that. I knew enough to know what was wrong."

She remembered most how heavy he was, how when he ground himself into her it pushed her breath out. But had he raped her? It was a blur. Maybe not. Had he *tried?* She remembered crying, "Please don't," and he rolled off her saying he would wait, kissing away her tears.

"What about the others you told me about? The other girls you were involved with? Why did you talk about them? Why did you . . ."

"What other girls?"

"Your other girls, the other girls you were involved in . . ."

She thought she remembered that Ann was the name of the girl before her. Lori Haigh came after. He admitted to Mary that he'd gotten Lori pregnant when she was sixteen, then took her for an abortion himself. There must be others.

He was not about to admit anything now, not in an edgy conversation like this one. "Now, see?" he said. "Now you've changed the situation."

"Well," she said, "I also remember you talking about Ann and about other girls."

"By the way, by the way," he interrupted. "Let me say something here."

She was pissed. "What?"

"What are you doing? Why are you doing this?"

"What do you mean? I need to know the truth and I need to hear the truth from you."

"Are you trying to just tape me and frame me or something?"

Mary Grant's heart jumped. She glanced across a desk and made eye contact with Detective Jack Jessen, who was listening in on the conversation spinning through the tape recorder. Throughout the police station, cops were trying to keep down the noise of ringing phones and crackling radios. She had already cleared her first hurdle. Even without acknowledging penetration, the oral sodomy he described constituted statutory rape. Problem was, because it took place a dozen years earlier, the statute of limitations had passed. There was no way to prosecute him for his crimes against Mary. So her challenge would be to get him to confess to more recent assaults—within the past decade—that might yield prosecution. The police had pushed this point.

Jessen gave her an encouraging look. But she was on her own.

There was a time when Mary Grant had believed that her priest loved her. That was before Mary ran away from home, and from her priest, when she turned sixteen. Lenihan tracked her from California to Missouri and begged her to come back. She refused. But her life spiraled downward. She got pregnant at seventeen with another man and fled that relationship at eighteen with her baby, into a decade of depression and emotional failures. Only last year did it occur to her that Lenihan had been her *abuser,* not a lovelorn suitor who made her feel so uncomfortable. Now Mary Grant tried to imagine what an ordinary adolescence might have been like—to innocently answer a ringing phone without hearing her priest whisper through the wire, "I'm stroking myself."

"I was what, twenty-two years old the last time I talked with you, and you were telling me about other girls, you know, and last year . . ."

"Why is that, why is that a big—"

"What about your vows that you made?" She raised her voice. "You're living a lie, because you're putting on a façade to people that you are celibate and you are living a holy vow before God when actually you're spending your time running around, messing around with little girls—

for all I know *little boys*—and women or whatever. It doesn't really matter, before God it's all the same, because it's living a lie, hypocritical
lie . . . And the people in your congregation are going to suffer because
of it, because of all these secrets that you've kept and all the responsibility that you've placed on me for what you did, for the sexual abuse
that you placed on me, and the guilt, the responsibility. How can you
live with yourself when you know you're living a lie, John? I'm concerned about you because I want to forgive you for what you did. That's
my *whole idea*—reconciliation in my life and so that I can get through
this crap and go on . . . I need to know that. *God* needs to know that.
How can you keep living this lie?"

Silence. He was playing dead.

"Can you answer that?"

"There's no point in my talking to you. I've got nothing to say."

Fall 1990
St. Louis, Missouri — David Clohessy was slouched next to Laura
Barrett, sharing popcorn. It was her second major relationship, his first.
They lived together, though her mother was not so keen on the
arrangement and his parents, strict Catholics still living in Jefferson
City, were scandalized. This is what had become of so many Catholic
kids, living by their own rules of morality. For David, morality meant
working for almost no money at Acorn, the national community organizing outfit; for Laura, whose own Catholic background was less encompassing, it was advocating for housing solutions for homelessness.

The movie they chose, because not everything about them was dissident or earnest, was *Nuts*.

Nuts told the story of a violently impulsive, high-class call girl, played
by Barbra Streisand, who in the course of standing trial for a murder
came to grips with a childhood clouded by incest. Almost imperceptibly at first, a parallel movie began to play in the darkness of Clohessy's
mind. A hum of conversation. A fractured image. The figure became
Father John Whiteley, who had been his friend through childhood—
who had taught him so much about social justice and activism. Always
smiling. Preaching. Setting up pup tents, holding open the screened

front door. Climbing on top of him. Squeezing their nakedness together.

These visions unspooled with all the clarity and vibrancy of a druggy memory. He recognized them as his own. It was all very familiar. He had known these things once before. Somehow they had withered and almost vanished, and only as he was watching Streisand's story did they reanimate, like a fish frozen in a pond suddenly freed by the arrival of spring.

Father Whiteley had used him from the time he was twelve till after he turned sixteen years old. David Clohessy had somehow forgotten.

March 14, 1991

SAN BERNARDINO, CALIFORNIA — At the end of his year on sick leave, Paul Shanley was not keen to return to Boston. Here, serving as a substitute curate at St. Anne's Parish, he was able to wear the collar while remaining ideologically uncompromised. Life was restful. His old friend Father Jack White, also on sick leave, had likewise relocated here, and the two were able regularly to make the drive down to the resorts of Palm Springs, ideal for his allergies. He wished he had more money, and he still "lurch[ed] from medical problem to medical problem," as he wrote a friend. But on the whole his strangely composed life as an "archdiocesan-sick-leave-weekend-supply-priest" was suiting him nicely.

If he returned to Boston, where the matter of the oath still pended, he was guaranteed a storm he didn't feel strong enough to weather. He put in for a yearlong extension. John McCormack was not a firm taskmaster with his old friend. He thought the request was reasonable. But he was also eager to reduce costs. He proposed a slight change in status: since Shanley was already working part-time at St. Anne's, why not go on salary there as a curate, since they were eager to hire?

The hypocrisy struck Shanley as unacceptable—why would his cardinal allow him to take a permanent assignment in California without having to swear his allegiance to Rome, but not in Boston?—and plunged him into a wild display of contrariness. "Not only am I reluctant to disturb the status quo that is working well," he wrote back, "but your plan would also violate the same principles that landed me here. I must protest the oath. Had I enough strength, I would be doing it from the rooftops because it is ultimately destructive to my church. . . . Again I tell you: Do the decent thing. Allow me, quietly, to retire, or put me on permanent disability. Remove the unpredictability and my health will return. This is cruel and unreasonable punishment."

His sick leave was extended indefinitely. As far as anybody in Boston knew, Shanley was living a decrepit life periodically interrupted by surgeries and allergy shots and requests to perform baptisms. However, being free of the Boston archdiocese, the strict mother against whom he had spent his life rebelling, Shanley was surprised to see his malaise lift, however slightly. But that wasn't the whole truth about why he had stayed. The previous December, he and Father White had invested in Cabana Club Resort, a small four-room guesthouse in the Warm Springs neighborhood of Palm Springs, which catered to gays.

Not only would he still minister to gays, in defiance he also made up their beds.

November 9, 1991
GLOUCESTER, MASSACHUSETTS — Paul Ciaramitaro felt as trapped in his memories of Birmingham as he had in his arms. The crazy images of his demeaning encounter never left him alone, not for a moment. As he got older, he grew even more self-conscious about his facial deformities. He saw more clearly over the years how Birmingham had used his tumor-wrapped face against him, isolating him, removing the last vestiges of his confidence. Girls were an abstraction now. He was a virgin, except for Birmingham. Though he occasionally attended counseling, he was unable to forestall his mounting rage.

On the day he turned nineteen he visited a lawyer. He wanted to know his legal rights. Knowing his parents would not approve, he never told them. It was his first unilateral step as an adult. He knew it would be momentous. Up to this point, he had done everything the church had expected of him: served at the altar, attended Catholic schools, studied the catechism. Now he had something to ask in return: restitution.

The lawyer thought he had a chance and agreed to investigate.

In a few weeks the attorney had sent a demand letter to church officials. In turn, Bishop Mulcahy paid a call on his mother, furiously condemning the move. The idea of a screaming bishop terrified Beatrice Ciaramitaro, but this one in particular had her undone. Mulcahy had become her personal counselor following her son's abuse, and now he threatened to cut her off.

That afternoon when Paul returned home from work, she demanded her son end his legal claim. "They've made up some form for you to sign," she shouted. "You're going to sign that piece of paper. And you're not going to sue the archdiocese."

The release waived his rights ever to sue the church for any claim related to Birmingham.

"What if I don't sign?" he asked defiantly.

"You're out of the family."

She would sooner abandon her son than her church.

What could he do? He lived in his parents' home. He relied on them for the food he ate. Without their health insurance, he would not have access to medical care. Without medical care he would surely die. He could not fight it. He signed. He signed a release that gave him no therapy or future rights—in fact, it took away one fundamental right. He was everlastingly bound to secrecy, enjoined from mentioning Birmingham again, in exchange for his mother's love.

Summer 1992

BOSTON, MASSACHUSETTS — "I don't see what the point is."

Phil Saviano, a soft-voiced man whose career and happiness had been savaged by disease, was at his doctor's office, sweaty and too weak to pull on his own clothes without extreme effort. No AIDS drug had helped him. His weight, which was meager to begin with at 160 pounds, had plunged to 130 and was dropping further. He could not absorb nutrients; food spilled right through him. That was the least of it. He had come through two bouts with Pneumocystis carinii pneumonia, and a painful parasitic infection called cryptosporidiosis, which began in the intestines and migrated to his gallbladder where, besides causing brutal pain, it was within striking distance of the liver. That would be the death of him.

Or perhaps the death of him would come from the fact that his body was purging calcium, and nobody could figure out a way to stop it. He was so deficient in the mineral that his legs twisted into painful cramps. The spasms could reach the heart muscle eventually, and kill him in an agonizing second. Every week, sitting at the hospital getting infusions of liquid calcium dripped into his veins, he thought about how that might feel.

Phil was forty years old, on permanent disability from his job as a publicity agent. His life was finished, and he knew it.

He asked his doctor for a large bottle of Seconal, the means to take his own life. He wanted finally to master the virus, to destroy it even if that meant destroying himself. Not right away. He wasn't suicidal in that morbidly depressed way he was as a senior in high school, when he tried to take his life. He did not have any immediate plan to swallow himself into the endless night. But he was dying, sooner rather than later, and he wanted to slip away in a pharmaceutical coma rather than in the clutching panic of a heart seizure or the suffocating, drowning death by pneumonia.

"I will give you the Seconal," his doctor said, "but on one condition. You have to give AZT one more try."

"That's ridiculous! You and I both know what will happen. I'll be on it for four weeks, and then have to stop."

The drug treated him badly the last time he took it, causing such daunting anemia that he was rushed in for transfusions twice. But AZT was still the only medication available to fight AIDS.

"The activists are calling it no better than rat poison. I just don't see the point," Saviano said weakly.

But the doctor was resolute.

"The dosage is much lower now than when you were taking it. It is helping other people."

Saviano was too weak to argue. "Fine," he said. "I'll try it."

Another patient might have gone home and flushed the AZT down the toilet. But Saviano was still Catholic enough to be a man of his word. That night, he slid the bottle of Seconal—"my parachute"—in his bedside table, and popped one of the tiny white-and-blue AZT capsules in his mouth.

This time was different. The pills did not make him anemic. Instead, they worked the way they were supposed to. His T-cell count crept up instead of down. The diarrhea abated somewhat. His appetite returned and he began to look a little less like a concentration camp victim. This was no reprieve, he knew. He was not making plans for the future. He still could not leave the house often.

"Maybe I'll see another Christmas," he thought.

May 1992

Westport, Massachusetts — Eric MacLeish was fulfilling a promise he made to Margot, who had suffered through the worst travails of being a young wife and mother whose husband had gotten completely carried away by his career. As a young attorney at a large firm, his year had been a blizzard of appointments, court appearances, depositions, and briefings that stretched into the night. It had paid off. He had taken on a hard-to-win sexual abuse suit, and actually won it. His clients all said they had been abused as children by James Ridell, a sort of neighborhood pied piper in rural Washington, Massachusetts. The jury awarded $1.4 million, one of the largest sex abuse verdicts in the state's history. It put MacLeish in league with the big earners.

To celebrate, he detached himself from his office and went on vacation, finally spending time with his year-old daughter. Westport was a beautiful inland fishing village located on the western end of Buzzard's Bay. The pristine beaches, one of the premier birding locations in New England, were wide and warm and close at hand.

MacLeish, though, wasn't the leisure type. Too hopped up with adrenaline to ignore his office altogether, he snuck in calls to his assistant, Beth Anderson, the way other men stole glimpses of ESPN. One afternoon Anderson told him about a possible new case. A man named Frank Fitzpatrick had called to say he was sexually assaulted by a priest, Father James Porter, in Fall River, a hard-knocks city ninety minutes due south of Boston. At the time, he was twelve. For years he had put it out of mind, but in 1989 he began pestering the church for accountability, without satisfaction. They wouldn't tell him where Porter was, in the priesthood or out, or even whether he was still alive. He was told to "leave it in the hands of the Lord." On his own, Fitzpatrick—a private detective, it turned out—tracked down the defrocked priest in Minnesota, where he lived with his wife and children. Fitzpatrick notified police, who did nothing.

Frustrated, he placed an ad in his old hometown newspaper that read, "Do You Remember Father Porter?" His misery needed company.

Six other victims called him, Anderson relayed. "They want to sue."

"You're shitting me," was MacLeish's response. Though he had been raised high Episcopalian, it was almost inconceivable to him that a Catholic priest had done this. Or that anybody would want to sue the Roman Church. "These people must be mentally ill. Molested by a *priest?*"

"You need to go meet them," she said. Fitzpatrick now lived in North Attleboro, which was near MacLeish's vacation cottage. "They have gone everywhere. They did everything—police, the DA's office. They have gone to a journalist who mysteriously died in a car crash," she added conspiratorially. *"A single-car accident."*

He wasn't sure what intrigued him more, the possibility that their story was real, or that it wasn't.

MacLeish had grown up as a child of privilege—his father and namesake was the famous television commentator Roderick MacLeish (Eric was the son's nickname), and his great-uncle was the Pulitzer-winning poet Archibald MacLeish—but with little domestic tenderness. At eight he was dispatched to a prestigious English boarding school, which as far as he was concerned was little more than a torture chamber set in an ancient mansion. The matrons were casual in their cold heartlessness and the headmaster's cruelty included regular canings that left marks still visible on MacLeish's backside. But it was the French instructor the students dreaded the most. He invited them to his rooms at night and pawed them with impunity. MacLeish managed to escape his attentions, once after throwing a punch; most boys were not as lucky. Thinking back on those years, it was impossible for MacLeish to not feel his anger simmer anew, the kind of anger that worked like a charm on a jury.

He headed out for North Attleboro.

Fitzpatrick, now forty, struck MacLeish as entirely credible. He had gathered eight others for the meeting, men and women from parishes in and near North Attleboro, whose alleged abuse began when they were in the fifth grade. Their stories also had the ring of truth. Fitzpatrick knew the law well. Though there was a ten-year statute of limitations for sexual assault in the state, or ten years from the age of majority in the case of children who suffered abuse, the commonwealth of Massachusetts allowed for the clock to stop if the suspect left the state. Father Porter moved from Massachusetts in 1967, he learned, so the statute had not tolled.

Fitzpatrick had even called his priest on the telephone and got a taped confession, which he played for MacLeish.

"Do you remember me in particular?" Fitzpatrick asked.

"No," Porter said. He scratched around in his memory, but it was no use. "I don't remember names."

"I have one question," Fitzpatrick said. "Why did you do that kind of thing?"

Porter laughed out loud. "I don't know. Who knows?"

"I mean, actually," the priest continued, "I've got to look back, how fortunate I was I didn't get creamed—*creamed*—by parents, the law, anything else. . . . It's funny how things worked out. Marvelous!"

Fitzpatrick told MacLeish he took the tape and the documents he had collected over to the Bristol County district attorney, Paul Walsh. He got back a letter declining to prosecute, in part because of "the difficulty effectively prosecuting a thirty-year-old offense."

"You are our last hope," one of them said to MacLeish. "If you don't take our case, we are going to pack it in—we just have nowhere else to go."

He knew his wife wouldn't be happy.

They would have to take on the Fall River diocese aggressively, he told them. Because of its proximity to the powerful Boston archdiocese, he knew this could become a big media story. If a large group of them agreed to appear on television, he believed they could win a lot of money. "The pocketbook," he told them, "that's the place to get them."

Thursday Evening, May 7, 1992

BOSTON, MASSACHUSETTS — Fitzpatrick was the first to sign up to go public about Porter. He simply was not going to feel responsible for his own abuse ever again. The others were more hesitant. Two more agreed to show their faces—Patty Wilson and Judy Mullett; five would talk anonymously, in silhouette. Joe Bergantino, the special I-Team reporter at WBZ-TV Channel 4 in Boston, told their sad stories.

"We want him to know that he hurt us," Frank Fitzpatrick told Bergantino. "We don't want to let him get away with this."

Everything Fitzpatrick had wanted in life was his already: a good income, a terrific marriage and family, a top-flight reputation in his field. But he was constantly vulnerable to ambushes by sadness or anger, and almost always he wanted to cry. In therapy, on antidepressants, he was unable to find the source of his troubles until 1989, when he revisited the memory of his abuse. He remembered being taken to Porter's parents' house in Revere and eating something there, a foul-tasting mincemeat pie, that sent him floating into sleep. When he awoke, the priest was crushing him with his body weight, penetrating him. His memory dovetailed with several other victims' recall. Perhaps they had been drugged by the priest, he speculated.

Joe Bergantino's report alleged that Porter molested child after child, in one parish after the next. But in the most dramatic part of his reporting, Bergantino reached Porter on the telephone. Like Fitzpatrick, he taped the call. The priest seemed almost excited about talking, his voice devoid of guilt, shame, or fear.

"Do you have a recollection of how many kids you actually molested?" Bergantino asked.

"Oh jeez, I don't know," Porter answered.

"Would one hundred be right?"

"Well," Porter hesitated, "let's put it anywhere, you know, from fifty to a hundred, I guess." He said this with a kind of playful diffidence, like a kid making a stab at a long-forgotten baseball score.

Bergantino couldn't imagine how he could have gotten away with such an extensive serial crusade against children. How many other priests, he wondered, knew he was abusing little boys and girls?

"Father Annunziato, Father Booth, Father Connolly—I mean, Bishop Connolly, bless him, when he was alive. They were wonderful people."

Bergantino knew what he was sitting on. Never before had a priest gone public with his mea culpas. The reporter and a crew caught the next plane for Minnesota. They caught up with Porter and his wife as they strolled along a quiet suburban road on a cool sunny day, pushing a toddler, one of four Porter children, in a stroller.

Obviously returned to his senses, Porter refused to talk more.

So for his broadcast on May 7, Bergantino played the shocking audiotape of his phone call as a kind of voice-over for the visual footage of an old and almost slovenly gray man in a baseball cap, darting with his baby carriage left and right, spinning full around, doing everything he could to avoid the unblinking scrutiny of the camera's lens.

The broadcast rocked Boston and, especially, southeastern Massachusetts, where it was simulcast on local radio affiliates. Dozens of other Porter victims heard the indifferent voice of their attacker while they were cooking supper, driving their cars, or in one case over the phone from a sister back home. Many called Bergantino the next morning, like Steve Johnson, who had never forgotten what happened to him thirty-seven times, and was infuriated by "the nonchalance, the admitting," he said.

All week calls like that would roll in, not only to Bergantino but to every reporter in town. Porter was the story of the season, the first abusive priest to get headlines in the most Catholic city in America. Then something unexpected happened. The tremulous voices on the telephone were now mentioning other priests too, a countless number of them, priests who had committed the most egregious sorts of violations in patterns almost identical to Porter's routine. Over and over, using their popularity as a guise, citing religion as their weapon, threatening any little child, whether in first grade or senior year, with purgatory for telling.

"My God," Bergantino said to himself, "what on earth could we be dealing with?"

After he had hung up the phone on the night of Joe Bergantino's first call, James Porter called his wife and children together at the dinner table for a family meeting. "I molested some children," he told them. Until that moment, his children hadn't even known he was a priest. Nobody was more stunned and confused than his wife. She demanded details, and he acknowledged brushing up against a number of altar boys' rear ends. "I had a thing for butts," he said, and she accepted that as best she could.

Besides, thirty years had gone by since then. He was cured, he said. There was nothing to worry about. Porter believed the statute of limitations was on his side. But the TV report launched police probes in three states as well as a national furor: a cover story in *Newsweek* and an endless stream of hammering segments on *Prime Time Live* and CNN, in the *New York Times,* and especially in the historically deferential *Boston Globe.* Every day brought new Porter victims. By mid-April, they numbered forty-eight.

Without question, it was the most serious crisis in the life of the American Catholic Church. Victims' advocates demanded to know why the church had not alerted authorities, and they answered lamely: *We didn't know about such things back then.* In one national poll of Catholics, only 50 percent said they thought children were safe in churches.

Under intense scrutiny by a public itching for an indictment, Massachusetts authorities took their time, aggravating Fitzpatrick and the other victims, who publicly assailed the DA in Bristol County, which encompassed the various towns of the Fall River diocese, for capitulating to the "hard-line, hard-core defenders of priests."

May 23, 1992
Roxbury, Massachusetts — On a steamy, uncomfortable morning, one of the hottest in memory, Cardinal Law was in a simmering rage. "The papers like to focus on the faults of a few," he complained, sliding furiously to the imperial plural: "We deplore that!"

Overnight, the media coverage had exploded from a sad story of a single predatory priest to an extraordinary tale of deception and betrayal. Porter, it turned out, had drawn complaints from as early as 1963. But rather than defrocking him, church leaders sent him either home to pray or to the Servants of the Paraclete, the religious order that ran a chain of clinics for troubled priests, or to psychiatric hospitals, one of which gave him electric shock therapy. Repeatedly they pronounced him cured, only to see him offend again. Porter's superiors began lending him out to other dioceses, in Minnesota and New Mexico, exporting their problem with cavalier disregard.

Four years passed before they caught on to their own errors and removed Porter from active ministry, in 1967; they defrocked him in 1974. But in the scant seven years of his ministry, he had scarred innumerable young lives. The small group of original claimants was well on its way to the 101 who would eventually come forward.

Legally, MacLeish had a major impediment. Thanks to his many taped and broadcast confessions, it would be easy to prove Porter was guilty—but difficult to collect a cash award. Enshrined in Massachusetts law was a provision called "charitable immunity," which capped the civil liabilities of any nonprofit at $20,000. Though this was unusual among states, the thinking behind it was noble: a group that delivered food to the elderly should not have to carry the same risk of lawsuits—and attendant insurance coverage—as McDonald's. Raping minors was never part of the church's nonprofit mission, and surely was not equivalent to inadvertently serving spoiled chicken to the homebound, but the law shielded the Fall River diocese nonetheless. MacLeish had figured he could do better in an out-of-court settlement. He told Fitzpatrick he would not file a formal lawsuit. Instead he worked as a negotiator on his clients' behalf to wheedle a cash offer in exchange for keeping the matter out of the courts.

How much he could hope to get was an open question. Fall River was one of the poorest dioceses in the nation. An assets search proved the diocese owned little more than its churches and schools—which the Porter victims didn't wish to liquidate. MacLeish had gone searching for a deeper pocketbook in the Boston archdiocese, arguing that the cardinal's role as metropolitan archbishop gave him supervisory responsibility for neighboring Fall River. The *Boston Globe,* feeling the expansion of liability was fair, questioned whether the church "in good conscience" could take refuge in the charitable immunity clause.

The overall tenor of media coverage had reached an all-time low,

Law felt. Rather than condemning the facts of Porter's abuse, he seized the opportunity at a rally against drug-related violence in Roxbury to lash out at the bad press the church was getting. Porter was a lone aberration, he declared; in Boston, there were only decent, pious priests. His remarks were angry, impulsive, and spontaneous. "The good and dedicated people who serve the church deserve better than what they have been getting day in and day out in the media," Law declared. "St. Paul spoke of the immeasurable power at work in those who believe. We call down God's power on our business leaders, and political leaders and community leaders. By all means, we call down God's power on the media, particularly the *Globe!*"

Then he announced he would not discuss Porter or his crimes again.

Ray Flynn, the popular mayor of Boston, grimaced when he caught Law's tirade on the evening news. He longed for the old church that exercised authority decisively, not defensively. Medeiros had squandered that power, and Law never showed any nostalgia for it. The church, in Flynn's view, had abdicated its role as the single most influential player in Boston politics. That designation now belonged to the *Globe.* "You don't have to be a prophet to see the growing power of the *Boston Globe* and the diminishing power of the rest of the media and other institutions in this city," he thought. "He's playing King of the Hill, and there's no way he can win. It would be better if Cardinal Law got on an airplane and went back to Mexico. He's finished."

July 22, 1992

VATICAN CITY — Responding to the proliferation of gay rights ordinances in fifty-four municipalities, seven states, and the District of Columbia, Cardinal Josef Ratzinger sent a letter to the U.S. bishops instructing them that it was not only morally right to discriminate against gays, but for Catholics it was a duty. His remarks came at a time in America when gays and lesbians were finally scoring some advances in the area of public opinion. A national CBS News/*New York Times* poll had showed that 80 percent of Americans favored equal employment rights for gays, even if they didn't consider homosexuality "right" or "acceptable."

"Sexual orientation does not constitute a quality comparable to race, ethnic background, etc. in respect to non-discrimination," Ratzinger wrote. "Unlike these, homosexual orientation is an objective disorder and evokes moral concern. There are areas in which it is not unjust discrimination to take sexual orientation into account, for example, in the placement of children for adoption or foster care, in employment of teachers or athletic coaches, and in military recruitment." Besides, he argued, if homosexuals couldn't be fired, this removed any incentive to keep them in their closets, which Ratzinger saw as the gravest danger to the family. Self-avowed homosexuals "tend to be precisely those who judge homosexual behavior or lifestyle to be 'either completely harmless, if not an entirely good thing,'" he wrote. Those were the least acceptable homosexuals—they represented a force outside the church, bent on challenging its most hidebound principles. As a result, he made plain, talking about one's gayness, even among celibates, was as objectionable as genital relations.

On the other hand, he noted that strictly closeted homosexuals—who lived in isolation from colleagues and neighbors, who lived in secret defiance of their true selves, who by definition were disallowed the possibility of conjugal love—would have no need for antidiscrimination protections, because nobody but them would know their affliction.

Gay priests knew what this meant for them: the thin crack in the window through which they had pulled air was now sealed shut again. From 1992 forward, homosexual pastors would not speak publicly about who they were, except for those who got caught, or charged, or outed through some other means. Gone from view now were those men in the church who comported themselves with ethical correctness, the examples of integrated sexual identity, the healthy homosexuals.

September 21, 1992

NEW BEDFORD, MASSACHUSETTS — Months had passed and Bristol County DA Walsh still hadn't indicted Porter, despite the overwhelm-

ing weight of the evidence itself. Walsh had even sent two investigators to Minnesota to question Porter the week the WBZ report aired,
and Porter had confessed yet again. They had it on videotape. It was a
prosecutor's dream case: credible witnesses, an unaltered pattern of
behavior, and repeated confessions.

But he was extremely disinclined to become the first DA in the
commonwealth to prosecute a priest.

Furious, the victims' group began meeting every Friday night to plot
offensive strategy. Among the first things they did was to start calling
themselves *survivors* of James Porter, rather than *victims*. They intended to never be victims again.

They formed committees to put pressure on lawmakers, police,
prosecutors, the church, and the media. They began getting reports
that Porter's crimes hadn't ended when he left Massachusetts. Survivors had come forward in every state Porter worked as a priest. This
information they released to the public during press conferences
timed for maximum pressure on DA Walsh. In turn, Walsh pleaded for
latitude. Through the summer he had offered various reasons why an
indictment was unwise. It was unclear what crimes to charge Porter
with, as child abuse laws from the sixties were vague and spotty. For
each of the victims he'd interviewed, a great effort was required to determine which acts of abuse fell within the statute of limitations. He
didn't want to bring a case he couldn't win, he said.

Finally on Monday morning, September 21, months after he had
gathered most of his evidence, Walsh went to a secret grand jury,
which indicted Porter on forty-six counts of sodomy and indecent assault involving thirty Massachusetts children, beginning in the mid-
1960s. Porter would soon face civil suits in New Mexico and
Minnesota, mostly from former altar boys.

"It's like a rendezvous with destiny," Dennis Gaboury, one of the
survivors, declared on the day Porter was arraigned. The era of cover-
up and secrecy was over.

Church leaders saw it differently. They painted Father Porter as
an aberration, an isolated incident, a bad apple. DA Walsh effectively
endorsed that perspective. "This is not an indictment against the
Catholic Church," he would say. "This is forty-six indictments against

one named individual. The behavior of one person is not the behavior of others."

October 1992

NEWTON, MASSACHUSETTS — The telephone rang relentlessly. MacLeish rolled over in his bed and saw on his clock that it was 3 A.M. He was not surprised. Since taking on the church, his whole life had become a battleground. Bomb threats at his office were commonplace. The police were providing security. They routinely ran mirrors under his car before letting him start the engine. His enemies had found where he lived. One caller even threatened to kidnap his daughter from day care if he didn't stand down. He hired a private bodyguard to protect her during the day and installed a security system at home for night. Then late one evening in the fall, as Eric and Margot were watching *Backdraft* on the television, someone snuck up to the back window and fired a weapon in the air with a blast that lit the whole house. Police had agreed to round-the-clock protection and now posted cruisers at the driveway.

Eric told Margot he would quit the case to protect the family, but she had been as galvanized as he by the threats and tactics.

Ironically, through their attorneys the church officials in Fall River and Boston seemed more sanguine about resolving the cases than these shadowy militants. They had proffered several offers for settlement, but each had been rejected by the Porter survivors' group as inadequate. "How much do *you* think being sodomized six times by a priest is worth?" asked one, a North Attleboro man named Dan Lyons. The Fall River diocese had pleaded for understanding. The company that held its insurance premiums refused coverage. There was almost no money in the accounts, as the diocese proved by showing balance sheets (or what were purported to be balance sheets—MacLeish was not taking anyone at his word). The demands threatened to put the church there out of business, the diocese said.

They were at a standoff. If the matter went to trial, all sides lost. The diocese couldn't withstand the public scandal, and MacLeish's clients, if they won, couldn't be satisfied with the $20,000 cap.

MacLeish fumbled in the dark with the telephone. The line had the tinny, delayed sound of a transatlantic call. The man's voice on the other end was heavily accented. He wished to see an end to the public pillorying of the church. Would it be possible, the caller asked, to settle the case for around $2 million? This figure was considerably higher than what had been offered so far.

MacLeish's second thought was that he was being drawn into some sort of trap. His first thought was that he should be asleep.

"Will you not call me at three in the morning?"

"It is daytime already here," came the reply.

The Vatican? Knights of Malta? Maybe, he thought. In his groggy state, he didn't ask. Rather, he said he thought the sum was still small, but agreed to put it to his clients.

After mulling over the mysterious offer, the survivors ultimately rejected it. MacLeish conveyed all this to the church's attorney, who seemed well briefed on the new line of negotiation, MacLeish thought. In a matter of days there came another telephone call, and another proposed figure, five times greater than the last. This time, MacLeish didn't mind being awakened. His 101 clients would get up to $100,000 each on average. "That would be sufficient," he said. A diocese with no money settled the myriad claims against it out of court in the coming weeks with a check drawn off an escrow account set up by the attorneys. MacLeish never knew where the funds came from, nor did he care. He was relieved merely to be out of the business of fighting the church and back to the business of raising a family in safety.

Within a few months, Porter would enter a guilty plea and be sentenced to eighteen to twenty years in the Massachusetts prison system. Televisions across the country carried footage of him being locked away, the first priest Massachusetts caught and prosecuted. And as swiftly as the subject of sex-abusing priests rose to the national stage, it sank off the front pages and evening news scrolls to become a problem of the past. Allegations were still arising, in some cases making brief appearances in the press, but the various crimes were viewed as old stories, individual tragedies, the stuff of whispers, one-liners, and shame, not the sign of a craven culture within the church itself.

October 17, 1992

ARLINGTON HEIGHTS, ILLINOIS — "My friends, welcome to Wittenberg!" Richard Sipe stood before an audience of three hundred men and women, many of them in tears or frozen in anger, huddled in a convention hall on the outskirts of Chicago. "This meeting is the first of its kind *ever* to be held within Catholic Christendom. This is the first time that a group of Catholic Christians has gathered to evaluate publicly the celibate/sexual function of its clergy."

A subject they knew too well. These were victims of sexual abuse and their advocates—the hidden, wounded, rejected Catholics, men and women who had managed to survive abusive clerics, only to face a second, perhaps harsher, assault, by a church hierarchy that threatened or punished them, and by fellow parishioners who disbelieved them, sometimes even by loving parents, tricked by the powerful church to turn their backs on their own children. They had never before come together as a national group. They did not know exactly what to expect.

"This is not a time for vengeance or vituperation," Sipe told them. "This is a time for truth and transformation. We stand on the brink of the most profound reformation of the Catholic clergy and the celibate/sexual system since the time when Martin Luther challenged clerical integrity on October 31, 1517."

Nobody wanted that to be true more than Father Tom Doyle, who had traveled from Grissom Air Force Base in Indiana to attend the meeting. In the years since he was suppressed at the Vatican embassy, Doyle had gone from a defend-the-church, high-handed cleric to a dedicated revolutionary. His only plank was the protection of children. How strange, he often thought, that this would cast him into exile and rebellion.

Now, if he heard of a lawyer bringing a sex abuse suit against any diocese in the country, he would volunteer his services. As an expert in canon law, he proved an especially valuable asset in a lawyer's efforts to subpoena documents from dioceses. He knew, for instance, that if a lawyer requested personnel files, which was their legal right in civil litigation, dioceses tended to interpret the request narrowly, and the records they produced were not especially candid. That's because canon 489, he knew, required bishops to remove extremely sensitive documents from ordinary storage cabinets and place them in something called "secret archive files," which by church law were kept in the bishop's residence in a locked safe. In addition, if a decision had been made to defrock a priest, those files were kept in a third place, thanks to yet another canon law. Technically, these rich troves were not "personnel files," and were therefore hidden away from prying eyes.

Speaking at a regional gathering of diocesan attorneys recently, Cleveland Auxiliary Bishop A. James Quinn had gone a step further, suggesting that certain incriminating records should be expunged from files and destroyed. More damning reports, he proposed, could be protected by sending them to the papal nunciature in Washington, which had the status of a foreign embassy and therefore enjoyed diplomatic privileges. In any event, he said, "standard personnel files should contain no documentation relating to possible criminal activity."

Armed with Doyle's knowledge, attorneys representing abuse victims had been able to anticipate their adversaries' moves. In response, church officials attempted to short-circuit Doyle. One archbishop flatly told him, "Stay out of this." Others had called his religious superior to complain. There was talk of a formal order barring him from giving testimony. "Tell them not to waste their breath," he replied, "because that's not something I would or could obey."

Not dissuaded, Doyle had offered his help in 125 separate litigations over the past five years, even going so far as to take the witness stand against the church that employed him. For his efforts, this year he won the Cavallo Prize for Moral Courage, given by a wealthy philanthropist to someone who chose "to speak out when it would have been far easier to remain silent."

Nobody was up to his neck in the battle more than Doyle. But he knew Arlington Heights was not Wittenberg, Germany, where Martin Luther, a professor of Catholic theology, nailed his ninety-five theses to the old church door. In 1517, the laity was already up in arms, rankled by a hypocritical priesthood that was literally commodifying the one thing every Catholic craved, absolution. Participating in a Crusade, or sending one of his servants as a stand-in, could earn a sinner forgiveness. When Pope Leo X found himself cash strapped in the midst of a renovation of St. Peter's Basilica in Rome, he started *selling* indulgences through a door-to-door network of indulgence priests. Inner struggles for piety were no longer rewarded, and moral traditions were in collapse. Wittenberg was a symbol of a people primed for rebellion.

But American Catholics today still bought into the clerical system, which presumed that their priests were somehow different and apart from ordinary humans. They obeyed priests to a fault, it seemed to Doyle. Unless they were abused themselves, they were not able to believe the worst about their church. "The laity continues to support a church that's corrupt," he thought. "They don't want to confront the evil because it's going to rock their little bit of religious security! They bear a significant amount of responsibility for this tragedy!"

December 17, 1992

JAMAICA PLAIN, MASSACHUSETTS — Phil Saviano's winter was like his summer, one week staggeringly identical to the next, an indistinct procession of pills and blood draws and news of the AIDS epidemic's march through America. Over two hundred thousand dead now, no cure in sight. He was a bit more robust now than in recent months, but he was a clear-eyed rationalist. He'd trained himself not to despair. Death, he felt, was just another burden of life. He took it on like an unfulfilling job. On good days, he meandered about town visiting funeral parlors, shopping for a venue for his final good-bye.

Today was a good day. Since it seemed plain he would make it till Christmas, he dressed and headed out to do a little shopping—very little, given the pittance of his social security disability checks.

He opened his door and bent for his newspaper. His eye fell on a name he had not thought of in twenty years. Father David Holley, his parish priest. Two New Mexico Catholics—one twenty-eight and the other thirty-two—had filed suit, alleging he abused them when they were small boys.

Saviano was incredulous. He had never forgotten Holley, who ar-

rived at the neighborhood parish in East Douglas, an hour west of
Boston, when Saviano was exactly eleven and three quarters years old.
Though in his thirties, Holley had the agreeable personality of an adolescent kid. Parents loved him. The boys in CCD class, which met
every Friday afternoon, thought he was extremely cool. He dropped
into class often. When he tapped at the shoulder of this boy or that one
and asked him to stop by the rectory afterward to help him lift boxes or
move the flower arrangements, they were quick to agree, usually in
twos and threes, and lingered afterward to laugh at his jokes and mar-
vel at his card tricks.

Saviano remembered thriving on Holley's attention. One day the
cards that made the tricks had pornographic pictures on them. The discussions would lead to questions about girlfriends, prying questions, inquiries about the boys' budding sexuality, inquiries made at first with
words and shortly with hands.

The boys had all struggled to escape, but were not allowed to until
their bodies had been pinched and sized up by the priest. Sometimes
he showed them his own penis, to their silent dismay. They shared this
shocking secret together, unspoken.

But one afternoon, in the cool, dank basement below the church,
Holley found Saviano apart from the others, gripped his small body, and
forced the twelve-year-old boy to perform oral sex on him. Holley was
a big man, with big hands gripped on Saviano's arms. The boy's mind
raced, but he could not find a solution to his quandary other than this:
if he just did what the priest wanted and got it over with, he could go
on his way.

Of the boys who had been groped, really of all the boys ever born, he
was sure he was the only one required to perform this act. He sometimes wondered why he returned to help the priest time and again,
abused each time, but he could not formulate an objection—a religious
duress compelled him to do what he was told.

After taking his liberties, which became his regular habit, Father
Holley never commanded young Saviano into secrecy. He did not
threaten to dispatch the boy to hell, or remind him who was more credible, or pretend their liaison had been a private sacrament, or any of the
other tricks other priests used. He didn't need to express his authority

except through the clothing he wore, which gave him the power to dominate and exonerated him all at once. Saviano knew that he, not Holley, was responsible for everything that happened between them, starting with the priest's raw drives and urges. On Saturday afternoons, he would kneel in the rich confines of the confessional to seek his absolution for having been abused, to plead for grace from the one who abused him.

"Forgive me, Father, I have sinned. I yelled at my mother. I lied to my brother. And you know the rest."

In 1965, between one Sunday and the next, eighteen months into Saviano's nightmare of abuse, Father Holley had vanished from his parish without a word. Their secret remained buried. In all these years, until he stumbled on the story about New Mexico and the two youngsters who like him were plunged into his world of darkness there, Saviano had not thought about Holley again.

He pored over their story. It blew Saviano's mind wide open. Of course, he wasn't the only one! Yes, there *must* have been others. Why had that not occurred to him before? Why had he thought he was the father's only boy? Why had he felt so darkly special, so singularly and pathetically vulnerable?

Desperate to reach the two young men, Saviano called the *Boston Globe* reporter who bylined the story, Stephen Kurkjian, who agreed to put the men in communication—though not without doing his best to pry the local-angle story out of Saviano. He would not budge. Going public was the last thing in the world he wanted.

He knew what he needed, and that was the camaraderie of another man who knew Holley as he did.

When Joseph Hafermann came to the phone, however, Saviano was blindsided by a surge of his own guilt. *If he had found a way to stop Father Holley, Hafermann would not be a victim today.*

"It happened to me, too," Saviano said.

Sharing their histories, both men saw that the similarities were sickening. The wrestling, the card tricks.

Except Hafermann was eight when the pornographic cards made their first appearance.

Saviano wanted to cry. "It was bad enough for me—eleven, twelve. But eight?"

"I called the Worcester diocese to tell them about Holley," the man from New Mexico said. "He's up in Denver right now. He's probably still doing it to little kids. It doesn't seem like anybody's keeping an eye on him."

"Did they tell you about his record here?"

They had not. "It just seemed the diocese was unwilling to take action at all."

"It's really important for people to understand that he started molesting kids here in Massachusetts in the sixties. Clearly he has a very, very long history. If it would help at all," Saviano said, catching even himself off guard, "I would consider going public with my story."

"That's a big decision," said Hafermann, "that's up to you. It's a very humiliating event. Would going public make it more humiliating, or less humiliating? For me, it was less."

As he hung up the phone, Saviano wondered how his life might change if he were to call Stephen Kurkjian back at the *Globe*. But before he could fully imagine it, the phone rang again. Robert Curtis, an Albuquerque attorney, had just heard from Hafermann. "He's my client," Curtis said, "but we have something else in common. Holley abused me, too."

Saviano could not speak.

"We have an obligation to other children to get Holley off the streets," Curtis continued. "We should have been protected from Holley as children. But we weren't. There are few people in life who are given the opportunity to make a difference. *You* have an opportunity."

Within a week, Phil Saviano told his story anonymously to Steve Kurkjian. Then the speed of events accelerated. Holley victims began to stream out of the woodwork. Police in Alamogordo, New Mexico, issued an arrest warrant, but were told the priest had gone east to St. Luke Institute, outside of Bethesda, Maryland. The local sheriff attempted to make an arrest. Twice, they were told Holley was not there. Finally a team of officers combed the campus anyway and found Father David Holley cowering in a stairwell.

After the arrest Saviano no longer felt afraid to allow his name to be known. He was a dying man with little to lose. He agreed to tell every intimate aspect of his abuse to *USA Today*. But there was one thing he did not mention: the fact that he had AIDS. He was sure the diocese would use that to discredit him: "Gay guy dying of AIDS? Who's going to believe this guy?"

And one thing he hadn't anticipated. They would want to photograph him. The problem was, he *looked* like a gay guy dying of AIDS. The only solution he could come up with was makeup. He slathered it all over his face. But when he crawled out of his car in East Douglas to greet the photographer, he knew it was no use. He leaned up against the façade of the old church, decrepit and out of breath, and ruined.

January 20, 1993

BRIGHTON, MASSACHUSETTS — Sister Catherine E. Mulkerrin, John McCormack's new secretary and top aide, took notes during a phone conversation with a sad woman who wished to report what she knew about Paul Shanley. Since he was a little boy, the mother said, her son had had trouble with self-esteem and depression. This stemmed from an older boy in the neighborhood who started terrorizing, and even molesting, her son when he was just three or four. When the child was around fifteen or sixteen, a psychologist referred him to Father Shanley. She was so pleased it would be a priest counseling him; that alone gave her hope.

It wasn't until recently that her son told her what really happened, that Shanley had molested him—"touching, fondling"—on a strange theory that it would somehow make him well. It did not. Rather, it caused him additional psychological distress and required extensive, though ultimately futile, therapy. He had begun to see his life as radiating a terrible sickness.

She was calling now because she had promised her son she would "do the right thing the right way." It was the last promise she made to him before he took his own life.

In the wake of the Father Porter abuse scandals, across the country dioceses had appointed individuals to field allegations of sexual abuse and handle them appropriately, according to a briefly worded policy adopted at the semiannual meeting of bishops. For the Boston archdiocese, Mulkerrin was that person. She wrote up detailed notes about the telephone conversation. However, nowhere did she note what she intended to do or what anybody else in the chancery advised. It was not apparent that any follow-up was planned. The allegation was not mentioned again. The archdiocesan administration had more perplexing concerns about Paul Shanley: whether to hold his monthly checks to $400 for housing allowance and $900 for his sick-leave stipend (raised from $800 the year before), or increase his housing allowance substantially, as he had requested, so that he might live in a private apartment. At the time, they assumed he was in residence once more at St. Anne's Rectory in San Bernardino, but even that assertion seemed less than clear. At the highest levels of the archdiocese, memos flew on these administrative topics.

February 15, 1993
CHICAGO, ILLINOIS — "Be *prepared* and *make restitution* as your coming face to face with Almighty God is coming *very soon! YOU* go to Church—my God! Your *hypocrisy* and *dastardly life will bring you the fires of hell!*"

This is the way crazy people express themselves, Barbara Blaine knew. She was a lawyer representing indigent, abused, and neglected children. Notes of this variety had found their way to her in-box before.

Only this time, the letter was addressed to her personally, and delivered not to her fusty offices in Chicago, but to her parents' home in Toledo, in the house where she grew up in a cozy bedroom, where she would go and pray after Father Chet Warren touched her, beginning one summer afternoon in 1969. "Jesus forgives everything," he had told her. She was not sure whether he meant his actions or hers.

The church was the axis of Barbara's family life. Her father was head of the parish council and coached the school baseball team; her mom served with enthusiasm on the Altar and Rosary Society. All eight children attended parochial school. But Father Warren had praised Barbara for being especially righteous. Then he touched her. He kissed her. Images of hellfire spun in her head. She recoiled, but he calmed her down reassuringly. "Jesus forgives anything," he said. "You are holier than the other girls."

She became his lover. She was thirteen. It was the summer before she began eighth grade. He was in his early forties. Their assignations continued for four lonesome years. He discouraged her from partaking in any after-school activity that might take her away from him. When she turned seventeen, she finally found her voice to tell him to stop. He became very angry, but did not return to touch her again.

Over the years that followed, when Chet Warren would materialize on the landscape of her memory, she would think of her helpless stupidity, and blame only herself. Regret was never more lasting. She reproved herself with selflessness. While her twin sister married and began a family, Barbara never rested. After college and graduate school, where she earned a master's in social work, she enrolled at Theological Union to steady her faith. After, she moved to Kingston, Jamaica, to work as a lay missionary, and then to Chicago to join a Catholic Worker community. There she committed herself to poverty and nonviolence in the pursuit of "hospitality for the homeless, exiled, hungry, and forsaken." She helped set up a shelter in a decommissioned convent in Edgewater, a dissolute neighborhood on the South Side.

It was in her austere quarters there one hot summer day that she had opened the *National Catholic Reporter* to discover a groundbreaking series on child abuse in the priesthood, the first ever published, inspired by the Gauthe case. Each devastating story had cast her mind back to Chet Warren. Her reaction was immediate and visceral. Sweat squeezed out of every pore; she began to pant. Could it be that her lamented past was not her fault? For the first time she imagined herself as the priest's *victim* instead of his secret child playbride. It was the last piece of the puzzle, and for once her childhood—really, her whole life—made sense.

She was not the only one. There was an epidemic and she had been stricken.

Father Chet Warren was still chaplain at the Catholic hospital in Toledo—she had bumped into him just recently, when a family member was being treated there. Everybody in her family remained close to him. No doubt other families held him above suspicion, too.

She contacted the superiors in the order that ordained Warren, the

Oblates of St. Francis de Sales, whose adherents live vows of chastity, poverty, and obedience. She pleaded with them to keep an eye on him at the hospital. "Monitor him, make him get treatment," she said, "because he obviously has a problem if he's perping on high school girls."

With a firmness she took as condescension, they dismissed her concerns, suggested she had "misinterpreted" the priest's intentions. "Nobody else has said anything negative to us about Father Warren," a representative told her. Primed for that sort of response, she called the Toledo diocese directly, as he was under the diocese's supervision while at the hospital. Then she called the hospital administrators, who were deferential and promised to keep him out of little girls' rooms. But they would not consider terminating him.

Furious, Barbara looked into bringing a civil suit, but was thwarted by Ohio's statute of limitations for prosecuting on sex crimes against children: six years from the accuser's eighteenth birthday. She went back to school, too, this time to study law. And she went to the press, often and loudly hounding Father Warren. The more she pressed, the further away from her church Barbara felt she was moving. For a woman who loved her faith, this was a devastating experience.

By 1989, she knew she could find peace only among those who understood how unhealed she was. With several other victims she knew in Chicago, she started a group called Survivors Network of Those Abused by Priests, or SNAP. She wanted a place for mutual support and strength, a place not unlike the church she grew up in, only this one in exile. Reaction from Catholics was startlingly hostile. It was as though she were trying to bring scandal upon the church, as though embracing truth was a worse sin than what was done to them all in the first place.

But she never got a letter as upsetting as this one. For one thing, it was written on stationery from the parish she grew up in, St. Pius X, the church where her mother still actively served.

> Hundreds in the parish are astounded that your "mother" can be a lay distributor of Christ. *She is as mentally ill as you are!* You are truly not God-fearing. Your friend, Gary, removed from life in a car accident—that should have been enough of a lesson!

All we can say is: *now is the time to make restitution for all your slanderous lies* because the *time on this earth is short for you. A just God will take care of you.* You will *never* be able to change people's beliefs of such a Christ-like man.

Be prepared to meet the Almighty!

The letter was signed, cryptically, "hundreds and thousands of Toledo people."

March 23, 1993

ALAMOGORDO, NEW MEXICO — Rather than stand trial, David Holley, looking as dusty and hunched as a nursing home denizen, threw himself on the mercy of the court, just as James Porter and Gilbert Gauthe had before. He admitted to selecting eight New Mexico boys in the 1970s, the good ones and the quiet ones and the especially holy ones, boys just like Phil Saviano. He admitted he warmed them up with card tricks, then fondled and kissed them while they wept and prayed.

Holley's confession covered only charges relating to assaults in New Mexico. None were filed in Denver or Worcester, because the statutes of limitation there had passed. Saviano was disappointed. Holley's attorney, however, was hopeful that the judge would show lenience as reward for his client's decision to avoid all the traumas the trial would bring the victims. "He admitted to God and to everybody else that he's committed these offenses," the lawyer said.

The judge was not moved. He knew what had happened in New Mexico was just the tip of the iceberg. By now, nearly a hundred of Holley's victims had come forward. The judge sentenced Father Holley to 275 years in prison. It was the longest sentence anybody could remember.

Across the country the sentencing was covered in only a small handful of newspapers. The *Los Angeles Times* ran the longest story. It was eighty-two words.

May 1993

WORCESTER, MASSACHUSETTS — Phil Saviano and the three other New England victims of Father David Holley's predations were in agreement. They wanted the Worcester diocese to provide them with whatever psychotherapy they might need, which, given their traumatic childhoods, might be considerable. And they wanted to know just how bad a guy this was—so they were asking that the diocese open up files on him to the public.

Eric MacLeish, who had done so well for the Porter victims in the Fall River diocese, agreed to represent them in negotiations with the diocese of Worcester. He interviewed the victims, detailed their allegations in letters to the bishop, and laid out their demands for financial restitution.

The Holley group discussed the possibility of suing rather than settling. Saviano especially favored formal litigation. A public trial and jury verdict, he thought, would harm the church more than the money. Despite the rising number of settlements, no one had ever actually filed a lawsuit against the church in Massachusetts before. Wanting to make no false steps, Saviano bought a book called *Everything You Wanted to Know About Civil Cases*. One by one, his fellow survivors joined him. Saviano knew it would be a difficult road. But he looked at the bottle of Seconals in his nightstand and thought, Thank God I didn't take those yet. He had work to do. He went on to form the New England chapter of SNAP.

MacLeish and his associate filed their lawsuit, naming the priest, Holley, and the Worcester bishop, Timothy Harrington, whom they alleged was managerially negligent, compounding the problem. Eventually, the number of Massachusetts plaintiffs grew to four.

Saviano knew the community he grew up in would close ranks. He didn't anticipate it would get violently confrontational once word of the suit got around. Anonymous phone callers warned him to drop the case. In a wildly scrawled fax, one parishioner wrote him, "You fucking pussies ought to let go of the past and the blow jobs you all enjoyed!"

Even his family—especially his family—disapproved. His godparents, his aunts and uncles, his siblings, none of them ever mentioned his public campaign, never offered their condolences for his abuse once it became known, or their support for his suffering. For him, the pain of their silent disavowal was excruciating. He felt ashamed. But Phil's seventy-four-year-old father didn't feel silence alone was enough to convey his rage. He and his wife, Phil's stepmother, were active in church affairs. Phil's homosexuality was a source of embarrassment for them. They could not stand by now and watch the church suffer the scandal of publicity surrounding their son's warfare.

"Leave the church alone," his father screamed. "You've got one foot in the grave and one foot on a banana peel! I can't imagine why you're doing this!"

June 17, 1993
NEW ORLEANS, LOUISIANA — Twice a year, American bishops converge on one city or another to coordinate activities in the areas of world affairs, domestic legislation, and national priorities. This year sexual misconduct was the main item on their agenda. Though it had been summarily dismissed along with the Doyle-Peterson-Mouton manual at their 1985 meeting, the subject was never entirely tabled. Committees had been formed to discuss whether or not a priest who abused minors should be barred from ministry (no conclusions were reached), and between 1986 and 1988, the top lawyer for the bishops' group compiled numerous catalogues of "liability theories" and proposed defenses for local dioceses to use in litigation, which many now faced. Estimates of the cost to dioceses in legal fees and payouts had already crossed the $300 million mark. Secretly two archdioceses, Chicago and Santa Fe, were contemplating bankruptcy as a result.

The bishops had another, more fundamental problem: according to polls conducted by religious and secular institutions alike, they had lost the trust of their parishioners. Attendance was down nearly 10 percent since the Porter case blew open. Knowing they had to make a show of their contrition, they dotted their June convention with public declarations of remorse and ended it by creating a new ad hoc subcommittee on sexual abuse. That subcommittee, made up entirely of bishops, had broad mandates, from asking Rome for the power to laicize notorious sex offenders to tending to low morale among bishops and priests "burdened with the terrible offenses of a few." In addition, the bishops adopted a brief, 372-word resolution establishing a new national, though voluntary, policy for dealing with individual allegations of abuse. Its key provisions were the prompt removal of clergy *where the charges were supported,* reporting to civil authorities *when required by law,* and informing the affected community *when appropriate.*

Before heading home, the bishops passed a broad resolution declaring that they had "reflected—once again and more deeply—upon the pain, anguish and sense of alienation felt by victims. . . . We pledge ourselves to one another to return to our dioceses and there to examine carefully and prayerfully our response to sexual abuse; to assure ourselves that our response is appropriate and effective; and to be certain that our people are aware of and confident in that response."

One opportunity to redeem that pledge was close at hand. Barbara Blaine from Toledo and nine other members of SNAP were also in New Orleans, in a rented boardroom in a hotel just a block away. They had asked bishops to attend a rap session, and they sat waiting to see who would join them.

The hour ticked by quietly. Nobody showed.

"We are not just sad about what happened years ago, we're sad about what's happening now," she said. "Church leaders beg us to come to them, yet they treat us like the enemy."

As time went on, SNAP took an increasingly polarizing public stance. Now Blaine was telling victims to ignore the diocesan review boards and the toll-free numbers that some dioceses were setting up. She believed they were a sham. Instead, she advised abuse victims to tell their therapist, to join a support group—and to go to the police.

"They implore us to keep quiet. Then they violate our confidentiality. They beg us to avoid litigation. Yet they punish us."

She was inconsolably furious about what they had done to her, and not just the menacing letter sent to her parents. "They lied to me," she spat. "They told me I was the only one who'd made sexual abuse allegations against the priest, when they *knew*—and I subsequently found out—about others. Then," she said, "they made slanderous statements against me and my family."

Wednesday, August 25, 1993

BOSTON, MASSACHUSETTS — The *Boston Globe*'s Sunday magazine was always printed and delivered in bundles to the newspaper's offices the Wednesday beforehand. As top editor on the magazine, Ande Zellman got her copies in the morning. The cover story of this week's offering was on James Porter, or more precisely, the impact the whole Porter scandal had on the hardscrabble, working-class Catholic town of North Attleboro. Zellman had asked a city-side reporter, Linda Matchan, to revisit the townspeople to see what the scandal had done to their faith, their families, and their community. What she got was a powerful portrait of a place penned in by its secrets, where many knew about the predator among them, but no one said a thing.

That the ebullient Father Porter seemed to prefer children's company to adults' was seen by many as a plus, a sign that the young curate had a "way with kids." Just how far overboard did he go when he supervised St. Mary's altar boys or coached North Attleboro's Little League All-Stars? The notion that a priest could have sexual designs on children was a concept most people could not fathom. "It was a sin even to have had the thought pass through your head," says Bea Gaboury, who sent her five children to St. Mary's School and has learned that her youngest son is among Porter's accusers.

And so while Porter was allegedly fondling, assaulting, and sodomizing scores of boys and girls in St. Mary's Parish between 1960 and 1963, there was little public speculation about his inclinations. A North Attleboro mother who says she found Porter fondling her 12-year-old son in his bedroom while the priest was visiting never spoke of what she saw, because, "My husband said, 'Who would believe you? It's his word against yours.'" Another who remembers telling "10 or 20" other mothers that Porter had touched her son improperly said not one would believe her. Boys who were sexually initiated by the priest say they kept it to themselves, because they were scared they'd be called homosexual. Girls who normally told their best friends all their secrets say they didn't divulge what Porter had done to them because they were sure it must have been their own fault.

It was a family secret on a grand scale, a sort of townwide "institutional denial."

This was the kind of story Zellman really loved, emotional and sweeping, but contained in a small time and place. As she stood behind her desk in her glass-walled office reviewing the text, across the building the newspaper's publisher, Bill Taylor, was in his office taking a telephone call from the archdiocese. Somehow the church had already gotten a copy of Sunday's magazine, and the chancery was outraged once again. Taylor had suffered these calls since the Porter story first broke, and he always gave them his full attention, as he was not merely the publisher but the owner. His family had owned and published the *Globe* since 1872.

From its first days, the *Globe* was a staunchly pro-Catholic paper, positioning itself as the daily read for the masses of Irish Catholic domestic workers. Early *Globe*s often ran priest homilies as front-page news. The tonier *Herald American* and other papers pandered to the Boston Brahmins and routinely published classified ads that baldly declared, "Irish Need Not Apply." Only the *Globe* refused them.

But with the arrival of the 1960s, along with much of old-line Boston, the paper let its hair down, and this angered the church and its faithful, especially Irish Catholics. In particular, the *Globe* had editorialized in favor of busing, which the Irish enclaves of South Boston, essentially white ghettos where ethnic and neighborhood solidarity was especially pronounced, opposed with energy. When antibusing riots erupted there in 1974, the Southies blamed the paper in particular for fomenting integration—for many years thereafter, protesters with placards spent every weekend on Morrissey Boulevard outside the newspaper's headquarters. The *Globe*'s editorial page meanwhile had gone liberal, endorsing reproductive choice for women and the antiwar movement, all of which rattled the church.

It was hardly conceivable, but relations had reached a new low around the Porter coverage.

Taylor was embarrassed to have to admit to the chancery that he was not aware of what was appearing in his magazine. He called his brand-new top editor, Matt Storin, whom he had handpicked for the job—and whose appointment was designed to help calm church-*Globe* relations. Storin was a Notre Dame graduate and a social conservative. He agreed that the paper had slid into the antichurch camp, and he pledged that the chancery would find an editorial environment more attentive to the church's point of view under his watch. "There is no way I can completely reverse years of bad feelings," he had said, "but I can make a good-faith effort."

Taylor demanded to know how a Porter story had slid through to publication without even a whisper of warning. But Storin too was in the dark. Although mention of the article had appeared on the daily circular, called the "story budget," for several weeks, he had failed to notice. Furthermore, Zellman had sought and received permission to borrow the writer from the Metro staff, a lengthy and formal—and transparent—negotiation. Probably because he was new on the job, he had not yet expanded his regular attentions to include the magazine. The fault was his own. But Storin blamed Zellman. He promised his publisher that no such surprises would happen again.

"Any editor worth his or her salt would say, 'No surprises—here comes a sensitive piece.' Obviously this was a sensitive piece," he said.

When Storin hung up the telephone he completely blew his top. His temper was already fabled. He screeched and bellowed, cursed, and banged about his office. Then he lit out to find Ande Zellman. By the time he arrived at her open office, the sound of his rampage had gathered up a nervous crowd of staffers. A large pane of glass separated her from the onlookers, and the door was left wide open. But even if they had been inside a bomb shelter, Storin's voice would have reached every ear on the floor.

"What's this doing in the magazine!" The Porter story was dead and buried, he said; it made no sense to resurrect it now. "Why?" he demanded. "This was overkill! It doesn't reveal anything new! It's too much, too late!"

He accused her of embarrassing the paper. He screamed about his own Catholic upbringing, in contrast to her being a Jew.

"How dare you blindside me like that!"

And then he hurled his copy of the magazine at Zellman, a small woman, knocking her back on her heels. She stood agape, wearing a look of pure panic. She was sure he was about to lunge across the desk and throttle her. But he turned and stormed out instead, with his clear message ringing in the air: write critically about the church at your own grave professional peril.

September 13, 1993
BRIGHTON, MASSACHUSETTS — The first clear memory of Father Paul Shanley that a man named Steven, now forty-five and unemployed, wanted to share with Sister Catherine Mulkerrin involved a perplexing incident in the parish baptistery of St. Patrick's in Stoneham many years ago. Steven was twelve, one of Shanley's altar boys. He did not recall why they were in that room. Out of the blue it seemed Shanley instructed one of the other boys to masturbate, and he was made to watch. In the ensuing months, Shanley would occasionally send for Steven, ostensibly for pastoral counseling. The boy's grandmother had died and in his grief, he said, he was going through "some sort of scrupulosity." These sessions sometimes developed into mutual genital fondling. They did not end when Shanley was transferred abruptly in 1967. Rather, wherever he was, the priest continued sending for Steven, frequently asking him to stop at a drugstore along the way to fetch one of many prescriptions.

"The sexual abuse took place in three main places," he said, "St. Patrick's Rectory in Stoneham, St. Francis in Braintree, and a cabin in the woods at Blue Hills. He would also take me to another confessor after the event and messed up my thoughts and feelings."

This was the man's first meeting with Mulkerrin, the archdiocese's point person for sexual abuse complaints, but the second time he'd told her his story. When he first called, she had asked him to write her a letter detailing what had happened to him and what exactly he wanted to receive from his church as a result. These steps, while overtly legalistic, were in keeping with the new policy the bishops had just announced; they were designed, as the media releases read, to "restore the trust." The needs he revealed were not insubstantial: $50 a week for health insurance, $50 a week for individual therapy; $50 a week for group counseling, to be disbursed to the various third-party entities. He was on a mission to calm his mind.

When they met at the chancery, Sister Mulkerrin explained that the archdiocese could pay for therapy sessions but not general medical insurance, and that a legal waiver letter must first be signed.

Steven's allegations met all the requirements necessary to trigger an investigation, in keeping with the new policy. Immediately, Paul Shanley was removed from his part-time job in San Bernardino and ordered back to Boston to appear before a new review board. There, Shanley acknowledged various transgressions. In fact, he said he had violated his chastity oath seven times in his lifetime, four of them with minors. The review board recommended the second-stiffest sanction contemplated in the new policy, a lifetime ban from wearing the Roman collar or performing any public function of a priest. The stiffest would be forced laicization.

He accepted this with courage, it seemed to Cardinal Law. The archdiocese then sent him to the Institute of Living in Hartford, Connecticut, to undergo intense counseling for his apparent illness. Among his many diagnoses were narcissism and clinical histrionics, but he was deemed unlikely to reoffend, based in part on his age, which was now sixty-two, and the unfortunate consequences of the efforts to cure his prostate ills. But one psychiatrist, Dr. Edwin H. Cassem of Massachusetts General Hospital, wasn't entirely convinced. "Father Shanley is so personally damaged that his pathology is beyond repair. It cannot be reversed," he told Father John McCormack, who had asked him to review the priest's file. "How do we protect others from him?"

Sister Mulkerrin had joined McCormack's staff in 1992 with a background of expertise in management and parish structures, religious education programs, and church sacraments. This gave her no preparation for counseling sex assault victims. The stories she heard were heartbreaking. But what most disturbed her was the scope of the problem. By the middle of 1994, to her disgust, she had chronicled credible allegations against more than a hundred Boston priests. No one knew better that there was a fundamental, festering, cancerous problem in her church. Yet it did not seem that McCormack, or the cardinal himself, was appropriately disturbed. She had strongly urged Law to take a proactive stance. She felt the church should actually go looking for victims of sexual abuse, by visiting each alleged perpetrator's past assignments and making formal announcements. At the very least, she said, notices should be placed in local parish bulletins where the priests had served—victims should be offered prayer and therapy without having to come and ask for it. This she felt was necessary to fulfill the spirit of the new policy, which called for the church to "deal as openly as possible with members of the community."

John McCormack could not have disagreed more passionately. He argued that it might actually discourage other victims from coming forward by drawing too much attention to each individual case. "And we also wanted to avoid scandalizing people about the sexual abuse committed by clergy," he explained.

In despair and frustration, she began secretly to refer callers to Eric MacLeish's office, reasoning that civil litigation and public exposure offered more healing than the archdiocese was prepared to volunteer. But her defiance did little to assuage her conscience, and in 1994, after only two years on the job, Sister Mulkerrin resigned.

July 26, 1994
DETROIT, MICHIGAN — The day had come that Sister Gramick and Father Nugent had to answer the questions put to them by the Vatican commission. Twenty-three years had elapsed since the two first began ministering to gay people. A revolution had occurred over that time. Most states in the country had repealed laws against gay sex. Openly gay people held office in the Congress and in hundreds of state and local legislatures and community panels, including the PTA. Actors played gay characters on television and in film, some winning Oscars for their performances.

A month earlier, a record-shattering 1.1 million gays and lesbians, with delegations from Europe, Africa, Asia, and the Middle East, marched to the United Nations in New York City to celebrate gay pride around the world. It was one of the biggest public demonstrations in the city's history, drawing gay parents and teachers, gay playwrights and firefighters, social workers, Buddhists, nudists, and cops—a massive, diverse, and peaceful parade, the central feature of which was a mile-long rainbow flag that weighed four tons and required thousands of people to carry.

The questions from the Vatican involved opinions the pair had laid out in lectures and a book they coauthored in 1992, *Building Bridges: Gay and Lesbian Reality and the Catholic Church*. Each point of inquiry aimed at establishing whether the nun and the priest believed a gay couple, even in the privacy of their homes, could make love and still be moral. A typical demand went, *"Do you teach that the Church ought to change its official teaching regarding homosexuality and homosexual acts?"*

The Catholic Church was a top-down operation. Its shepherds stepped out of line all the time, but once their transgressions drew the notice of Rome, they really had only two options: career suicide, or capitulation. Gramick and Nugent knew the stakes. They went for a third option: the semantically complex dodge.

"We do not teach that the Church ought to change its teaching on homosexuality and homogenital acts," they wrote. "But the question might also be asked if we teach that the Church ought to remain open to new data which would influence the development of a particular teaching. The Church's teaching ought to be the truth as seen at the present moment." In other words, they tell people that they *believe* that one day the church will change its teachings on homosexual sex. That's speculation, they protested, not dissent.

When they had finished researching and crafting their replies, they flew to Detroit for their hearing. Gramick and Nugent brought with them a sort of legal defense team, including their religious superiors, several bishops, and a half dozen experts in moral theology and canon law. Their interrogation consumed the whole of the day. In it, commission members revealed they had listened to tape recordings made during Gramick and Nugent speeches. It would be three months before a verdict was rendered.

When it came, it was not good. Both were found to be unfaithful to the magisterium.

It is the view of the Commission that a major issue centers on a matter that Sister Gramick and Father Nugent do not consider central to their ministry, i.e. the question of the morality of homogenital acts. While this matter may be secondary to their primary purpose, it is a crucial question for the moral choices that affect the human person, and, therefore, it cannot be considered incidental. While the Commission believes that it is not inappropriate to criticize the Church at times or to speculate about possible development of Church teaching, the Commission found some of the criticism of the Church and speculation in the work of Sister Jeannine Gramick and Father Robert Nugent to be inappropriate and misleading in a pastoral setting.

They're doing it again, Gramick thought when she read the report. They're completely fixated on the genitals!

In secret, recommendations were forwarded to Rome for how to censure the pair. For their punishment, they still had to wait.

In the meantime, Sister Jeannine Gramick and Father Robert Nugent continued their ministry to gays through the 1990s. Rumors and whispered confidences suggested that the Congregation for Institutes of Consecrated Life and Societies of Apostolic Life, the special curial office that had first launched the commission investigating them, had sent its report to the Congregation for the Doctrine of the Faith, the old Inquisition office, for rendering judgment. As was customary, the subjects of the probe were not asked for input and so they did what they could to ignore the whole thing.

But word came down on October 24, 1997, when what was known as a *contestatio* arrived by the formal route, from Rome to the offices of their religious superiors.

The CDF found Gramick and Nugent guilty of doctrinal offenses. "Their writings have been found to contain erroneous and dangerous positions, which because of their wide diffusion, have already caused grave harm to the faithful," the report read.

By labeling their beliefs "erroneous" the congregation stopped short of declaring the pair outright dissidents. This gave them an opportunity to correct their errors—to apologize and rededicate themselves to the clear promulgation of the Catholic message. Gramick did this the following February. Her supplication, however, read as though her fingers were crossed. Couching herself in the language of obedience, she offered a copiously footnoted defense and clarification.

A reply came in June 1998, in the form of a letter from Sister Rosemary Howarth, general superior of the School Sisters of Notre Dame, advising her that the Congregation for the Doctrine of the Faith had tired of her indirect obfuscation. Throughout the year, Cardinal Ratzinger had been battling what he considered to be a "worldwide crisis of faith," one of the chief deviations being the increasingly accepted view that "heterosexuality and homosexuality come to be seen as simply two morally equivalent variations." To him, at this moment no greater threat to the church existed than the view that defended homosexual love. He required a steadfast, profound obedience from Gramick. What, wondered Cardinal Ratzinger via Sister Rosemary, did the sister *believe* in regard to gay sex?

The question made her furious. She rocketed back a reply.

"In freedom, I choose not to publicly reveal my personal beliefs regarding any doctrinal positions on homogenital behavior and homosexual orientation."

She knew she was in trouble now, but what could she do? Gay and lesbian Catholics were increasingly unlikely to accept a theology that denied them fundamental human expression. Those who did were psychologically tormented; she saw the deleterious effects so often in her ministry. Healthy homosexuals were leaving the church in droves. Gay priests and religious were cowering in fear. For some of them, she knew, their sexual drives at times exploded in distorted sickness, in bestial spasms of lust. Sometimes priests abused their trust with minors, she knew. It did not seem to her to be possible to grow up as gay and Catholic without tremendous damaging struggles.

If anyone needed to apologize for this, she thought, it was the church itself, not her.

August 10, 1995

JAMAICA PLAIN, MASSACHUSETTS — Phil Saviano's case against the Worcester bishop, Timothy Harrington, progressed in frustrating increments. Two years had passed. Church lawyers fought the litigants at every turn. However, in time the litigants had forced the diocese to produce enough internal memos to make it plain how much they knew, but didn't address, about Father Holley. The memo trail was indefensible. Holley, who was hospitalized repeatedly and once ordered to undergo shock therapy, was the subject of repeated complaints dating from his first assignment in 1962. When his own diocese tired of his endless recidivism, rather than sending him to jail, the presiding bishop wrote of his efforts to find "a benevolent bishop who could use his services," and began peddling Holley to dioceses around the country. That's how he got assignments in New Mexico, Minnesota, and Texas, where Bishop Joseph A. Fiorenza noted in his own records that he knew of the priest's past, but gave him faculties anyway. "With our shortage of priests," he wrote, "I am willing to risk incardinating him."

In Saviano's mind, the civil liability extended to every parish and diocese where Holley served, and every church-run facility that purported to treat and cure his problems. But the whole thing suddenly became moot. Saviano's AIDS-related pneumonia had returned and nothing he and his doctors did over the summer could contain it. Finally, on a hot Thursday in August, his breathing became so labored that he could not avoid hospitalization. His condition was grave. Doctors discovered an additional problem, a rare fungal infection in the lungs; they put him on oxygen and antibiotics so powerful his kidneys rebelled. It was not looking good, his doctor said. But for the first time in the course of his disease, Saviano knew with a profound certainty that he was not ready to depart. His battle with the church was only half fought. He wasn't ready to take his secrets with him to the grave.

"Listen," he said. "Remember awhile ago I asked you for the means to check out? I know this is going to sound like a contradiction, but I don't want to do that anymore. I never did get around to doing my deposition. I really want to have an opportunity to get that all down in a legal document. I don't know how this is going to go here for me this time, with this pneumonia, but I'd like you to do everything you can to keep me alive. Despite what I may have said. At least until I finish the deposition."

His lawyers pulled for him to rally. "We're going to take this to the end," promised Joseph Boyland, the associate of Eric MacLeish who was handling his case. "I want you to call me every day—every single day—tell me how you're doing, and if it looks like you are getting any worse, we'll do the deposition right there in the hospital."

Luckily, he turned the corner and eventually was discharged into nursing care, where Saviano's lawyers presented him with the best offer they could get out of the church. As compensation for being sexually molested by his priest for two years, and a lifetime of anger that followed, Saviano would get $15,500. The church offered the same amount to each Holley litigant. Their lawyers gave a strong endorsement for them to sign—so strong, in fact, that Saviano felt they were being given an ultimatum: sign on the dotted line, or find yourself another law firm. Saviano never cared about the money. What he was after was full disclosure. But he was also a pragmatist. He knew his future was not promising.

He capitulated. "Okay," he said, "I'll sign." He would withdraw his suit in exchange for $15,500, enough after paying off his debts, he figured, for a very simple burial.

He had one proviso. He wanted the diocese to acknowledge the terrible errors it made. They won't do it, Boyland predicted. And they didn't.

On the day Saviano was supposed to sign his settlement agreement, he felt outflanked and revictimized by the whole legal ordeal, regretful that he had come forward in the first place. But as he was about to put his signature on the form, something else jumped off the page at him. In exchange for the check, he was asked to accept a strict confidentiality requirement. Not only was he enjoined from mentioning Holley again, but if he signed he would never be able to say or write anything *on any subject* that might bring "scandal, embarrassment, ridicule or the like" to the church. He would have to quit SNAP. One clause even made it impossible for him to discuss his sexual abuse history with his therapist unless she also joined the nondisclosure pact.

"I can't sign this," he told Boyland. "I'm not going to keep their secrets for them!"

"This is nothing unusual," Boyland argued. All the other clients had
accepted it.

"I don't care," Saviano said. "If need be I'll just walk away from it. I
filed this because I wanted to know the whole story of Father Holley.
To a certain degree, I got what I came for. I know what happened."

Despite knowing his chances were minimal, Boyland agreed to ask
the diocese to drop the confidentiality clause. They would not. "With
all due respect to your client," wrote Frank Puccio Jr., one of the
church's attorneys, "there is absolutely no possibility that I will agree to
what your client has requested."

Saviano didn't care. His answer was unchanged. "It's mean," he said.
"Mean-*spirited*. They just don't care about the victims. All they care
about is keeping this stuff a secret."

By rejecting the offer, he was told, he was putting the law firm in a
position to consider dumping him altogether. Their lawyers' fee was a
percentage of the restitution, not hourly rates. They were trial attorneys, not social workers or church militants. They did not work for free.
They would not go to trial.

Boyland stuck it out, however, exchanging ocassional letters with
church lawyers. It would be another two years before the diocese would
agree to drop the gag clause, perhaps assuaged by the litigant's precarious health. However, for this concession, they would demand that the
settlement offer be reduced from $15,500 to $12,500. Unable to find
a lawyer who would take his case to trial, Saviano accepted. His share,
after lawyers' fees and expenses, was $5,400.

And when he was stronger, Saviano wrote a lengthy memo to the
Boston Globe with samples of the damning documents he unearthed in
the Holley case, proof of cover-up at the highest level, a *system* of abuse
in dioceses across America.

He got his answer in time: "This is old news," he was told. "We're not
interested."

September 26, 1995

Brighton, Massachusetts — "Hello, Paul," Sister Rita McCarthy said. "Sit down."

"No, Sister, I'm gonna stand. I feel more comfortable standing." Paul Ciaramitaro did not wish to be polite. He wanted to tell somebody what it felt like to be forcibly masturbated by a priest, to go half crazy with confusion about your own sexual orientation—then to finally do something for yourself, going to a lawyer, only to have the bishop clamp down on your own mother and make her believe she had to choose between her church, which she loved, and her son. He withdrew his lawsuit four years ago. But now he knew his mother's love didn't belong to him. It belonged to the church, which had already taken his virginity, his innocence, and his peace.

So he came to the chancery to see Sister Rita, who had replaced Sister Catherine Mulkerrin as the delegate for Cardinal Law to Catholics who had been molested by priests.

"Fuck the Roman Catholic Church," he wanted to yell. "It's a fucking scam. I fucking hate you all. You went ahead and used your power against my family. That was *my* fucking family, and my fucking family fucking turned on me." But he stood in silence, politely. He was here with one goal—to tell the church to its face what it had done to him. He didn't want any money, therapy, or prayers—nothing in return.

Sister Rita crossed a dark, wood-paneled library in the chancery and reached one of two desks buried beneath file folders, perhaps eight or ten individual stacks, each rising up a foot or more. Circling behind the desk, she sank in the chair and disappeared completely behind the chaos. Paul could barely catch glimpses of her habit as it scuttled back and forth behind the manila bunker. "Shiramitaro, Shiramitaro. S-H . . ."

"No, Sister, it's *C-I-A-R-A-m-i-t-a-r-o*."

"Oh!" Sister Rita exclaimed. "Then I've got to go over here to this other desk." She appeared momentarily, then vanished again behind the western tower.

A number of realizations arose painfully in Paul Ciaramitaro's mind. Obviously the nun was searching for records of the formal report that he and his mother first made years ago, when he told her what Birmingham was doing to him. This must be the file system for clergy abuse victims. Look how many there were! There must be thousands, he thought. His mouth fell open. In his abject loneliness, it never occurred to him there might be a plague.

"You mean," he whispered, "I wasn't the only one?"

"Oh, here you are," said Sister Rita when she reappeared, scanning his folder sadly. When she had read it, she laid the documents down and threw out her arms and drew him into a big hug. "I'm so sorry," she said.

"Stacks of paper up to your fucking ears," he thought, squirming away from her. "There's so many fucking people. Forgotten fucking people. And you want to give me a hug?"

Late in 1995

Boston, Massachusetts — "Will you listen to my three children? Will you listen to them?"

The woman who stood at the door of the dingy conference room in Mitchell Garabedian's law office on State Street was soaked in her own tears. Her three boys clutched at her side. "What Father John Geoghan did to them?"

Emotions made Mitchell Garabedian uneasy, especially concerning children, who also made him uneasy. Personal injury was his niche. He liked turning over the smaller rocks and pebbles that other attorneys missed. Lately he had devised a way to cash in on the Americans with Disabilities Act, which was fairly new, by pitting it against residency requirements for civil servants. For instance, he got a half million dollars for the old blind man in the wheelchair after the city terminated him from his job at the information booth at City Hall because he'd recently moved to a wheelchair-accessible home in the suburbs. Nobody had brought another such case yet. He found a woman on dialysis and made a similar claim. Nobody else was in this practice. That's the way he liked it.

This woman had been a client of his in another matter, though for the life of him he couldn't remember what it had been. She was a single mother who lived in the projects in Waltham, a community of desperation and sadness. It might have been anything.

Since she had shown up at his door, he would hear her out. Shauna Tannenbaum, one of Garabedian's associates, sat in on the meeting.

A priest had knocked on her apartment door one afternoon, she recalled, introduced himself with a high-pitched voice, and volunteered to help out with the children. He said other women here and there in the complex could vouch for him. He was assigned to St. Julia's in Weston, just across the tracks. He was dressed like a priest. She had no reason to suspect anything. He seemed like pure generosity.

Soon, he was baby-sitting while she ran errands, driving her children down to the Brigham's ice cream shop while she cooked, tucking them in at night.

"He was touching their private parts and was talking dirty to them," the boys' angry mother said.

The boys spoke in sour harmony about the way Geoghan's hands pinched and pulled them in private places during those outings, trapping them against car doors, warning them to keep their secrets. Their grades plunged. They became unruly. Her oldest son, now a teenager, washed his hands over and over till they cracked and bled, yet he still could not satisfy his need to be cleansed.

Shauna Tannenbaum was revolted. Garabedian was too, of course. But he was also delighted. He had brought cases against the powerful Boston church before—something few Boston attorneys had the stomach for. The archdiocese was represented by a quasi-independent law firm run by Wilson Rogers Jr., a courtly old Catholic barrister, and his two sons Wilson III and Mark. They were brute adversaries, he knew, who made you fight for everything you were entitled to. But Garabedian also knew the church was secretive and almost pathologically averse to negative publicity, the kind of defendant that would avoid trial at any cost, that ultimately settled out of court.

He also knew they were an enormously wealthy organization, whose real estate assets surpassed $2 billion, by most estimates (it was not required to disclose any of that under American law). It was the second-largest social service agency in Massachusetts, behind only the state itself, with nearly $40 million in total funding. Nobody knew how much money the archdiocese brought in through tithing, as the chancery declined to offer specifics even to the very Catholics who were donating the money. But it was widely known that of all United States dioceses, which were required to send a portion of their take to the Vatican in Rome each year, Boston's yearly remittance was by far the largest.

He had no compunctions against claiming some of that money, certainly not out of a sense of religious propriety. He grew up in the Armenian Orthodox Catholic Church, an Eastern Rite branch of Christianity that does not take its direction from the Vatican. In an important way, Garabedian was always morally independent from the church.

Almost a year ago, the woman said, she went to the chancery to ask for help for her abused children. A sister there agreed to cover therapy costs for a time, but Geoghan continued to plague her children with filthy phone calls. He talked to them about all manner of sex, including the suggestion that they have sex with their mother. A few weeks ago, she had gone down to the magistrate court and lodged a formal complaint against Father Geoghan's calls. Rather than arrest the priest or even open an investigation, the court placed her complaint in abeyance for twelve months, with a promise to reactivate it if another complaint were lodged during that time frame. If not, the complaint would be expunged.

"Playing deference," Garabedian said. "After all, he's a priest."

She wept inconsolably as she spoke. Any good trial attorney has a reliable fraud meter, or so he said. He could see she would make a good witness. He didn't need any independent corroboration of her story.

Garabedian couldn't wait to file the notice of claim. He took the case then and there, for his standard $33^{1}/_{3}$ percent commission.

As almost an afterthought, it occurred to him that this priest may have knocked on other doors in the sprawling projects. If he abused three kids on one floor, how many could he have found elsewhere?

"Here's my cards," he said to the woman, pushing a stack into her palm, "in case you speak to somebody else in the projects."

She supposed, and he would later confirm, that there *were* others. Many others. In her building alone, almost too many to count. Within weeks, a dozen other victims of Father John Geoghan would stand in the same conference room and tell a nearly identical story. This priest, though he was an old man at the time, had a voracious appetite for small children. The church officials must have known. Yet he was still in ministry, assigned to Regina Cleri in South Boston, caring for senior priests.

Garabedian would ask each new client if they had complained to the church about the priest. He needed to show a malicious foreknowledge; he needed the leverage of being able to say, *You knew about this and did nothing.*

"How rotten is this?" he asked this parade of mothers, almost greedily. "How much decay is in there?"

Garabedian filed his first case, for the three Waltham John Does, on July 10, 1996. He alerted the press, but only the local tabloid, the *Boston Herald* (it had long since lost its tony tenor), paid any attention, playing the story deep in the paper, on page 12. He had expected a bigger detonation—how often did a priest get sued? But he was not deterred. He hoped to file his remaining cases one by one, spreading the news story out over the next few months. He wanted to keep the pressure on the church in the public arena. Legally, he knew there were considerable obstacles for his suits, the most onerous being the $20,000 cap. But Garabedian had an idea. Forget about suing the archdiocese at all, he thought. If the corporation can't be held accountable, then surely its officers could. So he sued everybody who ever supervised Geoghan and did nothing to stop him, fifteen ranking Roman Catholic officials, including Cardinal Bernard Law himself.

Law wasn't a rich man either, but that wasn't why Garabedian went after him. He reasoned that the church, officially a nonparty to the dispute, would regard the prospect of the most powerful cardinal in America standing trial for civil negligence as so utterly unacceptable that it would pay handsomely to make these cases go away.

However, there was no quick "ka-ching," as the courthouse expression went; the church was not about to roll over and hand out cash without a fight. In fact, Wilson Rogers Jr., the church attorney, was dogged and quite brilliantly rehearsed. The first petitions filed in re-

sponse were not standard denials but a motion to have the entire proceeding impounded. It was an unusual request, one usually reserved
for parties in a trade secrets dispute, so that, for example, Coke could
sue Pepsi over recipe infringements without revealing its secret recipes
to Royal Crown. Judge James McHugh granted the request. The shield
of secrecy protected all documents related to the case except for the
most routine procedural motions, and barred lawyers from discussing
any aspect of the suit in public. Garabedian's clients couldn't even see
their own files without first signing written statements swearing not to
disclose anything they saw.

Chapter 7

Into the Courts

November 29, 1995

Los Angeles, California — "Holy shit," Jim Falls said to himself. He was watching television when the familiar face of Father Ted Llanos appeared, videotaped in a perp walk as he was unfolded from a police cruiser and shuffled into a precinct, with his hands cuffed and a forlorn expression on his face.

Jim and his younger brother, Michael, grew up in the seventies in a highly structured, very Catholic Stockton family. Both were altar boys. Their mother worked in the catechism program. When they were fifteen and sixteen, a gregarious new priest entered the parish church, sending shocks of excitement through the community.

Father Ted was chummy and erudite and stunningly well-read. When he said Mass at St. Louise de Marillac, it was standing room only. Like everyone else in town, Jim had been extremely impressed. "You'd think he walked on water," Jim remembered. Father Ted thought the same of Jim and Mike, and paid them exquisite attention. He rented them boats to take out all day long, and threw them cans of beer when they returned to express their thanks. Jim would come home from school and find Father Ted waiting for him, and they'd go to see a movie, then have a beer at the rectory.

The first time Father Ted touched Jim in a sexual manner, in 1977, Jim swore it would never happen again. He was wrong. He thought he was the only one, and he was wrong about that, too. He had been convinced Father Ted was somehow obsessed with him, and somehow he turned that into a belief that he was responsible for this attraction. He knew that allowing a priest to give him oral sex was not right. He also knew that if he were going to seek oral sex it would be from a woman with long hair and ample shape, not a bald and bloated man twenty-five years older than he.

Michael had thought the same thing. Here are the things they never told anyone, not even each other:

"It was always done in the rectory, always in the guise of it being blessed by the church. I was told that this was a good thing, and that God would like what I'm doing, that's the message I got. He said, if I mention it to anybody, nobody would believe me, and God, I was truly blessed, because he was doing this to me. I was fifteen, sixteen, seventeen, nineteen. You start asking yourself, Jesus Christ, is this *still* happening to me?"

"It destroyed my belief in the church. It destroyed my belief in God and everything I was raised to believe is true. When you lose your Father, when you lose your God, you begin to wonder why you're on this earth."

"The man was a master at what he did."

The brothers were now in their thirties. Michael was homeless and irretrievably drawn to crack cocaine, methamphetamines, and marijuana. Jim was ruining yet another relationship—he refused to marry, as he did with every girlfriend. He was between jobs, another chronic state. He was simply not comfortable with attachments. Neither man suspected his sexual abuse was the cause.

In contrast, their older brother, Tom, had escaped Father Ted's attentions because he was already off in college when the new priest arrived. He was the family success story, a state superior court judge.

The news report said that Ted Llanos had been arrested on a charge that he molested one boy, known only as "Mark K.," in the early 1970s. Other victims were encouraged to call a number on the screen, and Jim snapped up the phone. He was crying uncontrollably, though he did not exactly know why. Something inside him was erupting and pouring out of him.

"I can give you the whole case," he told the officer. "Extensive abuse for a number of years."

Shortly, the Falls brothers joined with seven other men in a lawsuit. There was trouble from the start. The statute of limitations for sexual abuse in California was among the least generous—victims had just one year from their assault, or in the case of minors one year from attaining the age of majority, to file a suit. For every one of them, the statute had passed long ago.

Their attorney changed tactics and charged the church with general negligence, which carries a one-year statute of limitations. His approach was interesting. He argued that the church had a "duty to care" for the plaintiffs, and behaved negligently by not stopping the abuse. He further alleged that Jim and Michael Falls and the others did not realize that the church was behaving negligently until that television news report, so the statute's clock should start running only at that point. This was known as a "delayed discovery" argument, generally disallowed in California courts at the time. What is more, the attorney, Joe Dunn, unearthed in discovery evidence that the diocese of Stockton, at the time under the leadership of Bishop Roger Mahony, was first informed of the priest's errant behavior in 1973 when the parent of two boys alleged abuse. The statute of limitations clock for the complainants should begin upon the discovery of this document, he alleged. This document was proof of negligence.

The diocese fought this interpretation mightily. In essence, the church argued that the victims of abuse had a burden of recognizing their victim status at the time of the abuse, and should have imagined the church's institutional culpability at that very moment. Because of their naïveté and faith, the church argued, the young men had forfeited their rights to seek justice in civil courts. Ultimately the church prevailed. The trial court ruled that because the nine men were past their nineteenth birthdays, their claims were invalid.

The rejection in court didn't help Michael's brief courtship with sobriety, and by the following spring a series of tailspins would land him at Charter Oaks psychiatric hospital for what was known as a medication evaluation, "to get me on something to even me out." In one of his evaluation sessions, his anger at the church came up. He said he'd noticed in the papers that Roger Mahony, now cardinal archbishop of Los Angeles, had been diagnosed with cancer.

"He played as big a role in this abuse as the priest did. He knew years ahead the guy was a molester, and just bounced him from church to church," Michael said. "I'm looking forward to the day he dies."

Next thing he knew, police were escorting him to jail for "terrorist threats" against Mahony, then shipping him for involuntary psychiatric evaluation on what was known as a seventy-two-hour hold. When that expired, they sought another one, and another. All charges were dropped and he was released nine days later, after members of the local SNAP chapter followed Mahony to a posh Brentwood parish and staged a loud protest. "I just want to cry," Mary Grant thought as she circled the parking lot with her sign. "Of course he wanted to kill Mahony. We're *all* so mad we could kill."

February 21, 1997
BOSTON, MASSACHUSETTS — In an unkempt sixth-floor office on State Street, behind grimy windows, Mitchell Garabedian had remade his entire practice around the John J. Geoghan cases. In early February, he had twenty-eight clients; by the close of the month there were thirty-eight. Some days he did two intakes at a time. Most of Geoghan's victims had been schoolboys, but two women said he had exposed himself to them as girls. (He was unusual in another aspect as well: his victims were equally divided between young preadolescents and teenagers, placing him among a small minority of men who prey on both sides of the puberty divide.) In some instances, Garabedian signed up the parents or spouses of victims, whose companionship they lost due to depression and stress stemming from their abuse, and filed claims of "loss of consortium," some seeking compensation in the high six figures.

To an old-fashioned trial lawyer, this looked like pay dirt.

As the cases dragged on, Wilson Rogers Jr. and his sons fought Garabedian at every turn. Even the most mundane aspects of legal comportment were battlegrounds. They forced Garabedian to seek court orders to get the simplest discovery information, and then forced him to seek court orders to enforce the court orders. When Garabedian named Cardinal Law as a defendant, Rogers strenuously objected, then went to court in an effort to seal that fact specifically, because the publicity would taint his reputation. It seemed a ridiculous request, even to Judge McHugh, whose procedural rulings tended to favor the church. McHugh called Law's publicity concerns "neither groundless nor . . . illusory" but insufficient to merit such unique consideration.

Nonetheless, thousands of documents had been produced, sheet by sheet, which narrated Geoghan's sad and troubled life spent wreaking havoc in six greater-Boston parishes over a thirty-four-year career.

A dozen of the documents, dislodged from Geoghan's personnel files and grudgingly sent to Garabedian, were key to his case. Throughout Geoghan's lengthy career, devout families had routinely complained that he had molested their children, some in pleading handwritten letters. Many begged the church to remove him from ministry. When confronted, internal documents showed, he freely confessed to sexual abuse, quickly adding he "didn't feel it was a serious problem." Neither, apparently, did his bosses. Following brief suspensions, usually under the guise of "sick leave," in 1980, 1984, and 1989, and in the wake of "the usual transfers," as one internal memo remarked, fresh allegations hounded him. But against a mounting body of evidence, they were often dismissed in follow-up memoranda as "hearsay" or "unfounded" or "vague."

Garabedian had enough to implicate Cardinal Law, who arrived in Boston at a time when Geoghan was listed as "between assignments," living with his mother, and under the care of various professionals. Surely the priest's internal dossier would have been enough to ring deafening alarms. But in October 1984, after receiving a new formal complaint about Geoghan, Law appointed him parochial vicar at St. Julia's Parish in Weston.

The memorandum that Rogers must have hated handing over to Garabedian was dated a few months later. Written by Auxiliary Bishop John M. D'Arcy to Law, it challenged the wisdom of sending him back into a church. "If something happens, the parishioners, already divided and angry, will be convinced the Archdiocese has no concerns for their welfare and simply sends them priests with problems," he wrote. D'Arcy was right. Many of Garabedian's clients came from St. Julia's, and they were shocked to see that Law had been specifically forewarned about the dangers, yet acted with such disregard. This was the smoking gun. Even the church had to admit it.

Garabedian's reaction was visceral. "A pedophile is a pedophile," he thought, "but the supervisors, what is this nonsense? These people are insane!"

Without admitting any guilt or responsibility, the archdiocese in extreme secrecy began to settle cases with a handful of Garabedian's clients, on the condition that none of them ever reveal the content of their complaints, or the sum of their financial recovery. Their settlements eventually topped $10 million, to be split fifty ways—after Garabedian's one-third commission was taken off the top. Suddenly he was a wealthy man.

But for every Geoghan case he settled, another client materialized. "I'm shooting fish in a barrel," he said once. Wilson Rogers Jr. privately begged him to retire to Florida, and once said he would settle with Garabedian only if he promised never to sue the church again, Garabedian told associates. "I said to him, 'Look, you got three hundred more people out there. You know they're there!'" Why would he retire now?

Simultaneously, Garabedian was providing behind-the-scenes support to two state senators who authorized bills to require clergy members who hear of child abuse to report allegations to the police. Doctors, psychologists, teachers, and other professionals who regularly worked with children were already mandated reporters. In the past, every time a measure was debated to include priests, the archdiocese strenuously—and successfully—lobbied to be excluded on the grounds that such a law impinged on canon law, which forbade priests from violating the sanctity of the confessional. At a press conference on Friday, Mark Montigney, a Democrat from New Bedford, declared that the "right of secrecy is insignificant when compared to the welfare of children. . . . No one is designated by God or man to abuse children." Coverage of his efforts occasioned another reminder of the John Geoghan suits, and images of the blinking priest filled television screens around the city—and all news about Geoghan was good for business.

Sometime in February 1997

DORCHESTER, MASSACHUSETTS — Patrick McSorley, who had been in and out of psychiatric institutions and rehab tanks, was walking across a restaurant with his sister and brother-in-law when he glimpsed on the television screen above the bar the rubbery elfin face of John Geoghan. It was immediately familiar, but he could not recall why. The priest had been arrested and charged with criminal sexual assault of a minor, the news reporter explained. It all came back to Patrick with vivid suddenness.

He recalled with exquisite clarity the clearness of the blue sky and the slant of the noon sun over the projects in Hyde Park. He remembered being happy, a twelve-year-old in total unity with his universe. He was playing baseball in an empty lot when he heard his mother call his name out the second-floor window. He ran home. There was a priest he did not know. Father Geoghan, his mother explained, had been the family pastor before Patrick was born. He'd just heard about Patrick's father's death, though a number of years had passed, and he rushed over with his condolences.

"He wants to take you out for ice cream," she said.

Priests were a constant presence in the McSorley household, but ice cream was a genuine treat. Sure, he said with a blink of his bright black eyes, which were ringed with long, silken lashes.

They left almost immediately, driving the short distance to Brigham's ice cream parlor in Cleary Square. They talked about the youth's favorite television show, *Spencer for Hire,* and the star, Robert Urich. Patrick asked for a tall dip. In the car heading home, he noticed Geoghan scratching around conspicuously in his own lap. He might have paid no attention except that it was clear the car was heading off to a remote part of the neighborhood. Geoghan eventually drew it to a halt alongside a desolate stretch of road.

There Geoghan grasped his hand on the boy's bare knee. "I'm sorry to hear about your father's death. For a young boy like you that's an awful loss." By the time he uttered that last word, the priest's hands were inside the child's shorts. Struck mute with terror, he sat immobilized. If he had wanted to scream, he could not have, such was his blind terror.

He stared straight ahead for a very long time as ice cream melted out of his cone and down his elbow till nothing at all was left.

When Geoghan was done, he leaned across to open the boy's door for him.

"We keep secrets. We're good at keeping secrets," he said in a jolly voice. "Would you like me to make a return visit?"

Geoghan never returned. A decade later, McSorley had never told a soul. In fact, despite all his therapy and intense introspection, he never once thought back on that afternoon with suspicion. Remembering gave McSorley the same terror now as it did then. Tears flooded his eyes. His legs went weak.

"What's wrong?" his sister asked.

"Father Geoghan molested me, too," he said.

She was stunned. "All of these years, and I didn't know about it."

"You know what? I didn't either."

Sitting in his kitchen over supper with his wife, Anthony Muzzi was watching the same news clip, and had a similar reaction. It's not that he had forgotten what Geoghan did to him—on the contrary, every detail was vivid, right up to and including the day Geoghan was banished from his home. But to grow up afterward, to even sleep at night, he had to fold up his memory and place it in storage like the prayer cards from family funerals, and when he accidentally uncovered it even decades later while watching television with a woman who knew nothing about it, he recalled it all with clarity, and the memory ached more now than ever, ached and ached until he finally realized that the cold-storage routine had only made matters worse. Look at your life, he thought. You had failed at so many things. The woman was your *third* wife. Your children were strangers. Commitment scared you. Risk terrified you. At forty-three, driving your truck back and forth from work, you prayed for life to get easier. It never did, though.

October 11, 1997
VATICAN CITY — Thomas Plankensteiner, an Austrian theologian, stood in St. Peter's Square with a very large group of his supporters, singing

and praying. They had come to see the pope, though they had not received an official appointment despite numerous requests. The matter was pressing. A scandal engulfed the archbishop of Vienna, Cardinal Hans Hermann Groer. Accused in 1995 of demanding sexual favors from unwitting seminarians and schoolboys, which he didn't exactly deny, Groer responded by blasting the news accounts as "defamation" and then went on as if nothing had happened, quietly slipping into a comfortable old-age retirement. Newspapers exposed case after case of alleged abuse attributed to Groer. Meanwhile, he and his replacement refused any comment.

The faithful rejected the double standard of a church hierarchy that was rarely silent about the petty transgressions of parishioners. The Austrian church was in fact often brutally punitive. Women whose husbands divorced them were routinely denied sacraments. People who fell behind in their collection-plate donations actually found themselves slapped with lawsuits by the church under a pre–World War II law that established a 1.5 percent salary tax on registered Catholics. Gays and lesbians who wished to live openly without persecution were especially rankled. Pursuing age-appropriate gay relationships cost them a place in their church; cornering underage males in seminary showers cost Cardinal Groer nothing. Collectively, Vienna's Catholics saw the Groer scandal as proof that their church held the reputation and status of its cardinals in higher esteem than the welfare and benign comforts of its parishioners.

Plankensteiner, his wife, Isabella, and a handful of acquaintances formed a group to oppose the culture of secrecy, arrogance, sex negativity, and sexual hypocrisy. Called We Are Church, their organization quickly crossed the Austrian borders to the rest of Europe and beyond, finding fertile soil of frustration in twenty nations, including the United States. The timing was perfect. Antichurch frustrations ran extremely high across the board. Inspired by the aggiornamento of Vatican II, there were by now over 650 lay reform groups in America, many of them moved by the hope that the church's reconciliation with the modern world would continue. A group calling itself the Women's Ordination Conference pushed for female priests and threatened to begin ordaining them even without permission. (In 2002, they did just that.) Another group, called Corpus, militated for married priesthood modeled on the practice of the Episcopal Church. Affiliates included Celibacy Is the Issue and the Web site www.rentapriest.com, a referral service to married clergymen who left the priesthood but were available to preside over weddings and the like in parts of the country where traditional Roman Catholic priests were scarce. The priest shortage had left 2,843 Roman Catholic parishes in America without a resident cleric.

In U.S. polls, six in ten Catholics were in favor of married or female priests, while in a survey of Boston Catholics, 74 percent disagreed with the requirement of celibacy. The thousand-member Association for the Rights of Catholics in the Church and the twenty-five-thousand member Call to Action, the largest reform group in the United States, considered these changes essential if the church hoped to claim relevance in the lives of younger Catholics.

On the other side, a number of organizations had formed to defend church orthodoxy against change, opposing most reform groups as "heretics, apostates, feminists, militant homosexuals, pro-abortionists, and assorted left-wing dissidents who are trying to coerce the Roman Catholic Church (and especially our beloved Pope John Paul II) to 'open up' to 'new ideas' (their ideas, of course)," in the words of one doctrinal conservative. Calling itself We Are Catholic, a counter-protest group mounted by high school students in Manassas, Virginia, passed a petition calling for the church to remain exactly as it was. Roman Catholic Faithful, based in Petersburg, Illinois, was especially concerned with the presence of homosexuals in the priesthood. The founder, Stephen Brady, who ran the organization from the back office in his family pizza parlor, spent his days on the Internet ferreting out priests involved in "the homosexual lifestyle," broadly defined as anything from sexual expression to presence at a gay rights rally, and reporting them to their bishops for discipline or removal.

But of all the reform or counterreform efforts, none were as immediately successful as We Are Church. The group's manifesto struck many ordinary Catholics as self-evident. We Are Church circulated a petition calling for dramatic change in church culture. It read in whole:

1. We believe in a loving church where the equality of all the faithful is respected, the gulf between clergy and laity is bridged and the People of God participate in the process of selecting their bishops and pastors.
2. We believe in a church with equal rights for women, where women are full participants in all official decision-making and are welcomed in all ministries, including the diaconate and the ministerial priesthood.
3. We believe in a church where priests may choose either a celibate or non-celibate way of life, where the right of a congregation to the Eucharist and pastoral care is more important than a rule of canon law.
4. We believe in a church which affirms:
   - the goodness of sexuality,
   - the primacy of conscience in deciding issues of sexual morality (for example: birth control),
   - the human rights of all persons regardless of sexual orientation, and the importance and urgency of issues other than sexual morality (for example: peace and non-violence, social justice, preservation of the environment).
5. We believe in a church which:
   - affirms people rather than condemns them,
   - respects primacy of conscience in all moral decision-making,
   - embraces and welcomes those who are divorced and remarried, married priests, theologians and others who exercise freedom of speech.

Circulating this declaration to ordinary Catholics, We Are Church was staggered by their eagerness to assent. Within a few months, over five hundred thousand Austrian Catholics had signed on, nearly 10 percent of the faithful there. They circulated the manifest into Germany, and within eighteen months it had garnered 2.3 *million* signatures.

It was with a sense of hope and triumphalism that Thomas Plankensteiner came to St. Peter's Square. Five hundred We Are Church volunteers from Ireland, Spain, Belgium, Venezuela, and a dozen other countries joined him on the morning they intended to turn over the results of their labors. In the square, they were immediately confronted by Italian and Vatican police officials, who steered the delegation toward the propylaeum to the right of St. Peter's Basilica and instructed them to make their petition at the towering Bronze Door on the Vatican Palace.

The Bronze Door. For centuries, aggrieved Catholics had walked down the long colonnade to knock on the Bronze Door, only to be stopped cold there. Plankensteiner's party fared no better. They did not win an audience with the pope. Nor did they gain access to any curial official, or curial staffer, or middle-level Vatican administrator for that matter. The man who appeared at the Bronze Door was an employee of Vatican Radio, a semiautonomous entity based in Vatican City. Descending a few steps to listen to Plankensteiner, Elfriede Harth from Germany, and Maureen Fielder from the United States, he agreed to receive their millions of signatures. But they were not given any indication what he would do with them. They didn't even get his name.

Wednesday, December 17, 1997
WESTON, MASSACHUSETTS — Auxiliary Bishop Emilio Allue was deeply distressed. Cardinal Law's powerful representative in the Merrimack region of the Boston archdiocese opened and closed his mouth, searching for words that would not come. He looked out upon the seventy-five congregants at St. Julia's Church, where John Geoghan had served from 1984 to 1993, his last parish assignment and his home base for molesting most of Mitchell Garabedian's many clients. Geoghan stood accused of crimes against twenty-eight children from the parish. Allue finally spoke on behalf of the entire Roman Catholic archdiocese of Boston: "To any person who has suffered abuse from a minister of the church," he said, "we apologize for what has happened and ask for forgiveness."

In a highly unusual show of contrition, every parish in Boston was celebrating a Mass of healing for the many victims of abuse. Traditionally such prayer days were observed for victims of war or natural disaster. This was a tremendous watershed. No diocese in the country had offered up a night of prayers for clergy sex victims before. Most had done nothing to acknowledge there had been a problem. It was a difficult and important gesture for Allue to come here.

Despite the biting cold outside, Phil Saviano and twenty-five other members of SNAP stood vigil on the sidewalk. Saviano was too angry to ever go inside a Catholic church, least of all to offer up his forgiveness. "The healing Masses are indicative of what's still wrong," Saviano told a reporter. "They want to handle this with prayer, inside the church. But when abuse happens, the appropriate response is to call a cop."

John Sacco, another SNAP member, agreed. He and his four brothers were repeatedly molested by Father Geoghan. Saving Geoghan's soul was the last thing he would pray for.

After the last hymn was sung, Bishop Allue headed for the rearmost exit in the church. He had instructed his staff to steer him clear of the protesters. But a nun who had helped arrange the Mass prevailed upon him to speak to them. That, she said, is what healing was all about.

She brought Sacco around to the back door to introduce him to the prelate.

Sacco was forceful. "Bishop," he said, "the church needs to provide free therapy to victims and report all cases to the police. That's the bottom line."

Bishop Allue was steely. "I understand your point, but we have a procedure," he said. "We're doing everything in our power."

Allue lifted up Sacco's hand and shook it, in a gesture of closure, then turned and walked away. To a staff member standing next to him the bishop said, "What else can we do?"

"He doesn't understand yet," Sacco said bitterly. "The apology is the beginning, not the end, of the conversation."

January 13, 1998
Rome — Alfredo Ormando awoke early and timidly made his way through the narrow streets. The thirty-nine-year-old man with crooked eyes, a frustrated writer from Naples, had made the long trip up the peninsula to Rome by train. He had arrived the day before. Nobody knew he was here. He strode into the pigeon-filled St. Peter's Square at dawn, when St. Peter's Basilica and the enormous foreboding walls of Vatican City were at their most beautiful, when a gentle calmness filled the mind with the profound sense of the church's long history. He

thought about the letters he had addressed to his family and dropped in the mailbox before heading north. Perhaps they would arrive today.

By chance, Ormando entered the square just after an Italian gay rights group called ArciGay had finished an all-night candlelight protest there to draw attention to a spate of attacks on gays. They planned to return that night. They did not blame Vatican staffers for these assaults. But they argued that John Paul II's escalating rhetoric against homosexuality conceived and gestated the brutality. It was true that most religions looked upon homosexuality with judgment and proscription. The Presbyterian Church rejected ordaining homosexuals and blessing same-sex families, despite great reform pressures. The United Methodist Church, after a contentious battle, declared gay love "incompatible with Christian teaching." The topic threatened to subsume Christians in a sad fight between traditionalists and modernists—often, that is, between people who do not have known gays in their families and those who do.

No church had suffered on this knife edge more than the Episcopal Church in America. Every year through the nineties, a growing minority of members of the House of Bishops argued heatedly to embrace gay sex as human sex, and gay relationships as equal and normal. The majority always prevailed. Nonetheless, in 1994 over fifty-two Episcopal bishops in America, out of a total 291, signed a statement of dissent. Anglicans around the world were stunned by it. It said, "We believe that homosexuality and heterosexuality are morally neutral, that both can be lived out with beauty, honor, holiness, and integrity and that both are capable of being lived out destructively."

One of the signing bishops, Newark's Right Reverend Walter Righter, did more than just sign. In 1990, despite church teaching to the contrary, he ordained as a deacon a "practicing homosexual," as the jargon went (the man in question was in a lasting relationship). This sent the church into the most ominous crisis of its history. Righter's supporters and detractors were equally excited and evenly divided. Church leaders could not let such unilateralism go unanswered. In 1995 the church charged Righter with heresy, the second such charge in the American church's two-hundred-year history. (He was exonerated at trial.)

Though he was himself gay, Alfredo Ormando was not a gay cam-
paigner. He was an extremely unhappy and isolated man. He came to
the square not to protest, but to take his own life. Secrecy and shame
embalmed him. Few knew he was gay—or how miserable a life he led.
In the letters to his family, he finally scratched out the truth about his
life.

Ormando doffed and folded his coat, which he laid near his feet. In
its pocket, he had made sure, were his last farewells. In a quick gesture
others later were unable to adequately describe, he splashed the contents of a container upon himself. Almost without delay, flames engulfed him and he walked in great burning monster strides, then ran,
toward the entrance of the basilica. But he did not make it inside. As
he approached the doorway, in flames, gendarmes forced him to the
ground and attempted without success to extinguish him.

He became the first person in Vatican history to self-immolate at the
doorstep of the Catholic faith. The letters he left behind were operas
of despair. "Oh Lord, ignite me, burn me with the flames of your heart,"
he begged. "I ask forgiveness for coming into this world, for having poisoned the air I breathed, which now poisons you with my breath, for
having dared to think that I could behave like a free man, for not having accepted a difference in me that I could not feel, for having considered homosexuality as natural, for having felt equal to heterosexuals
and second to no one, for having striven to become a writer, for having
dreamed, for having laughed.

"Don't give me a tear-stained tombstone so that I can be vilified even
when I'm dead," his letters pleaded. "If the petrol didn't succeed in re-
ducing me to dust, cremate me and scatter my ashes around the Roman countryside. I'd like to be useful at least as manure."

July 13, 1999
VATICAN CITY — Ending its eleven-year investigation into the theological beliefs of Sister Jeannine Gramick and Father Robert Nugent, by
now the most prominent gay rights advocates within the global church,
the Congregation for the Doctrine of the Faith issued what it called a
"notification." Both were called to Rome to the headquarters of their re-

ligious orders to receive the ruling, written by Cardinal Ratzinger and personally approved by Pope John Paul II:

> Given the failure of the repeated attempts of the Church's legitimate authorities to resolve the problems presented by the writings and pastoral activities of the two authors, the Congregation for the Doctrine of the Faith is obliged to declare for the good of the Catholic faithful that the positions advanced by Sister Jeannine Gramick and Father Robert Nugent regarding the intrinsic evil of homosexual acts and the objective disorder of the homosexual inclination are doctrinally unacceptable because they do not faithfully convey the clear and constant teaching of the Catholic Church in this area. Father Nugent and Sister Gramick have often stated that they seek, in keeping with the Church's teaching, to treat homosexual persons "with respect, compassion and sensitivity." However, the promotion of errors and ambiguities is not consistent with a Christian attitude of true respect and compassion: persons who are struggling with homosexuality no less than any others have the right to receive the authentic teaching of the Church from those who minister to them.
>
> The ambiguities and errors of the approach of Father Nugent and Sister Gramick have caused confusion among the Catholic people and have harmed the community of the Church. For these reasons, Sister Jeannine Gramick, SSND, and Father Robert Nugent, SDS, are permanently prohibited from any pastoral work involving homosexual persons and are ineligible, for an undetermined period, for any office in their respective religious institutes.

Gramick sat in bitter silence as the verdict was read. The CDF ordered every church in America to publicize the text of the "notification," making a public example of her and Nugent. They became the first pastoral ministers in the United States formally silenced by the Vatican, and joined the theologian Father McNeill in the growing ranks of Catholics punished for their divergent views on gay life.

"I suppose there is no appeal," she joked.

August 19, 1999

BRIGHTON, MASSACHUSETTS — Steve Lynch, a stringy long-distance runner and aspiring writer, stepped out of his sister's car on the corner of Commonwealth Avenue and Lake Street. He had just turned forty. And in recognition of this he had decided to stage a forty-day silent vigil outside the stately stone fences that guarded the driveway leading to the two-story chancery building, the mammoth residence, and, down a steep and windy hill, the tree-shaded campus of St. John Seminary. He knew some people would assume that he chose the precise number of days to symbolize the forty days Jesus spent in the desert doing battle with the devil's temptations, or the forty days of self-sacrifice that mark Lent, or in simple acknowledgment that forty days was the traditional duration of testing in his faith. But that wasn't part of his thinking whatsoever. His fortieth year was the darkest of his life. It was the year he remembered being abused by Father Samuel Lombard at the age of nine.

One of the first things he did was call to complain about Lombard to the chancery. There was little they could do, he was told. Lombard was on his deathbed at that moment. They would not confront a man who had just a few days left on earth. This plunged Lynch into a tailspin of despair and suicidal thoughts. He retreated to a place in the mountains outside Seattle, where he was living at the time, and thought it over through endless tears. On Saturday, July 11, 1998, all alone except for his demons, he found a way to forgive Lombard. "If you need to go, I forgive you," he said with some bitterness. "If you want to get out of here, go ahead."

Back in Boston, Lombard died that very day.

Though officials at the archdiocese would not discomfort their brother priest in his final days, the church did invite Lynch to see a therapist at the church's expense. He returned to Boston to seek help for his biting depression. It did little good. His was a difficult case, part heartbreak, part post-traumatic stress, all amplified by a sense of total betrayal.

Six months later, the archdiocese told him the budget for his treatment had been exhausted, and they cut him off. That's when the idea for a vigil struck him as something he had to do for his "deeper soul."

After waving good-bye to his sister, he moved onto a narrow patch of lawn along Commonwealth Avenue and placed two placards conspicuously at his side, one of which was a poem he had written about the men who were, like him, poisoned with grief and shame.

Forty days would pass from August to September, heat to chill, green to rust. Often crying, he sat in uninterrupted silence. Not that his vow would ever seriously be challenged. No employee at the chancery would come to talk to him, including the cardinal, who whisked past each day and night in a dark limo. Nobody pulling into the driveway smiled at him, or nodded, or even looked meaningfully in his direction. The heavy traffic along Commonwealth Avenue, on the other hand, would scrutinize his campaign openly. With so many lonesome days on his hands, Steve Lynch was able to tally their reactions. The results were discouraging. Of the drivers who acknowledged him, nine in ten showed him their middle finger.

Throughout 1999
BOSTON, MASSACHUSETTS — Linda Matchan, the reporter whose *Boston Globe* magazine feature had drawn so much internal heat, couldn't stop thinking the story of abusive priests was much larger than it appeared. She had seen how, in horror and embarrassment, the whole small town of North Attleboro kept secrets; she believed the same was happening in Boston, and not just about Geoghan. It was her reporter's intuition. She had chased a couple of leads, but got nowhere. Once, while interviewing Cardinal Law at his residence on another subject, she slipped in a question: was there more of this stuff going on in Boston?

He was very nice and avuncular, and handed her a box of brownies to take home with her. "Oh no, no, no," he said, "that's not happening anywhere else."

"There's more going on here," she told the assistant managing editor for projects and investigations, Ben Bradlee Jr. "I want to keep going."

"Matt says enough already with the priests," he said, meaning the editor Matt Storin.

In his apartment in Jamaica Plain, Phil Saviano didn't have any idea why he couldn't raise a reporter's interest at the *Globe*. Several times in recent years, he had sent memos detailing abusive priests to reporters whose names he plucked out of the paper. He never got an answer.

On the eve of the church's third millennium, Cardinal Law was at the pinnacle of power in the world church. Selected by the pope to sit on a half dozen powerful curial commissions, he was the American prelate to whom Roman authorities most often turned for advice and insight. A prominent symbol of his influence was John Paul II's readiness to choose future church leaders from Law's own staff, selecting his most loyal auxiliary bishops to fill top jobs in significant dioceses around the nation. Bishop Banks was tapped to run Green Bay, Wisconsin; Bishop Daily, after a stint as bishop of Palm Beach, was given the Brooklyn diocese; Bishop D'Arcy headed to Fort Wayne–South Bend, in Indiana; and Bishop Murphy took over Rockville Centre, in Long Island. All four men had helped Law run interference between priests and their accusers.

Even John McCormack got a plum reward. He was named bishop of the diocese of Manchester, New Hampshire, in July 1998. McCormack's star was rising fast. The United States Conference of Catholic Bishops named him chairman of their Ad Hoc Committee on Sexual Abuse, a sign of great deference and respect.

PART II

✤

"Who Trespass Against Us"

Chapter 8

The *Globe* and the Church

January 29, 2001

Boston, Massachusetts — Mitchell Garabedian's law firm had come to resemble a walk-in mental health clinic more than a personal injury litigation practice. He now had eighty-six new Geoghan accusers, beyond the fifty cases he settled in 1997. He filed their suits against sixteen various church officials who at one time or another had been charged with supervising this priest. With so many people involved, prelitigation preparations were cumbersome and frenetic. Garabedian and his chief associate, William Gordon, flew around the country conducting depositions of the many bishops who had left Boston to run other dioceses. In Boston, the work continued day and night: expert witnesses were retained, records were subpoenaed, psychological counseling was arranged.

The mood at the chancery was completely different. Because it seemed he was dealing with a total mercenary, Wilson Rogers Jr. put the lid on any talk of settling the new cases. His policy was to take his time. Perhaps Garabedian would lower his financial demands if he ran out of money. Four years had passed since Garabedian deposited any appreciable money into his bank account, Rogers knew.

For the church, the Geoghan embarrassment was already out in the open anyway. With multiple criminal charges pending against Geoghan, the church risked exposure more damaging than anything

Garabedian might exact. In an effort to blunt the impact, Cardinal Law made an extraordinary trip to Rome to petition for the power to defrock Geoghan. Pope John Paul II, who rarely removed a man from the priesthood against his will, granted the emergency request. Garabedian's advantage, which had been threats of public disclosure, was dissipating; surely he would back down.

He did not. He was no longer driven by a thirst for financial gain, or at least not exclusively. He was telling people he genuinely felt sorry for these Geoghan victims. In a way, this was true. After hearing so many stories of damaged lives, something unexpected had happened to Garabedian: he developed a nearly saintly thirst for justice. He remembered his own experience with suffering—as a teenager, he was struck by a car while jogging along the roadside, and dragged by the bumper until he was gravely hurt. His faith helped him through an arduous recovery. In contrast, his clients—many of whom were homeless, disconsolate, and severely depressed—had gone to their church for comfort, and found an adversary there; they had sought out their cardinal, but instead found menacing, foot-dragging, bloodless Wilson Rogers Jr. In waging a defense meant only to defeat the lawsuits, Rogers had driven home the very point of why the suits existed in the first place.

"The church is supposed to be the ultimate helper organization," Garabedian would say. "It's not the Boy Scouts, not the Boys' Club, it's not a comic book store—you're cloaked in all this garb where you're adored as a priest and you can do no wrong and you're up on your pedestal and you have the First Amendment protecting you and no one can look into your affairs and no one's going to question you and every year you get a new group of kids. Kids! When they get older you discard them. I have little boys who told me they got old enough to tell the priest, *No, I don't want you to do this to me anymore,* and what did Geoghan do? He took their younger brothers for ice cream and left the older boy behind crying in the driveway. See what I'm saying? Never a shortage. And now the church has the *gall* to say, 'We don't have the money, this isn't right, we can't pay the victims.' Well *excuse me,* for decades if not for centuries you made money from these pedophiles by knowingly putting them up in the altar saying, 'Give me your families, give me your money.' That was okay, you see what I'm saying? *Do some good! Let's try to just do some good, you follow what I'm saying?*"

He wanted to say to Wilson Rogers and to Cardinal Law, "Come down to my office and do one intake with me." He wanted to see their faces as they listened to the weeping tragedies he heard every day, he wanted them to see the irreparable harm the betrayal had wrought. This wasn't just sexual abuse, this was religious duplicity. "These people feel as though they've been thrown out of their church, which they have," he said. The victims had the temerity to regret their abuse profoundly. They couldn't forgive, not without atonement. Their last shot was a cash settlement, not because of what the money meant to them financially, but because of what it symbolized. Justice. Penance. Resurrection. Peace.

He couldn't remember how many times he had to say to them, "It's not your fault, what are you feeling so guilty about?"

It wasn't until January 29, 2001, that a judge, ruling in Garabedian's favor, finally put an end to Rogers's efforts to throw Cardinal Law's name off the lawsuits. The ruling made the cover of the *Herald,* but was typically ignored by the *Globe.* At a press conference announcing his victory, Garabedian said he could not reveal more about the case, because of the judge's gag order. At his side was Patrick McSorley, now twenty-seven, an unemployed cable installer and father of a two-year-old boy. Brooding and troubled, McSorley scratched his head absently and searched for words to explain what he was thinking, but all he could admit to was a confusion as profound as anyone's.

"I wonder to myself sometimes why the church protected the priest and not the children," McSorley said.

Kristen Lombardi wondered the same thing. As one of four news reporters at the alternative weekly the *Boston Phoenix,* and as a lifelong Catholic, she was stunned to think the cardinal might knowingly have endangered children. After reading McSorley's quotes in the *Herald,* she decided to investigate. For most of the next two months she sequestered herself in the basement of the courthouse with Geoghan's dockets in her lap, reading what little was in the public domain. The juiciest records were kept in the back of the clerk's office shielded from view, but anything that was argued in open court was public, including all procedural motions. Scattered in them she found tantalizing quotes referencing the sealed files, including evidence of the 1973 complaints from Maryetta Dussourd and her sister Marge Gallant, and their heated warning to Law in 1984, two years before McSorley's unfortunate encounter with Geoghan.

It was the tip of a thousand icebergs, but it helped her understand the scope of the crimes as far back as the 1960s. Even without being able to look at the actual documentary evidence, Lombardi began developing a story for her newspaper laying out a case for Law's negligence. She interviewed Richard Sipe, the psychotherapist and former monk, who told her Geoghan's reputation was widely known among officials not just in Boston but around the country. "Oh, Father Geoghan," he said. "He is notorious because he has been treated by so many people, at nearly every psychiatric hospital in the country." This detail had never been reported—in fact, until now almost nothing was known about the church-run pedophile and ephebophile centers. Did the church knowingly transfer a pathological abuser around the archdiocese? Citing confidentiality, the hospitals would not confirm her findings. Nor would Mitchell Garabedian, who had arranged for her to interview a few of his clients.

"Kristen, I can't confirm or deny anything. There's a confidentiality seal," he told her. The Rogers law firm was scouring the media for evidence that Garabedian had been leaking sealed information, he told her. He dug around in a folder and showed her a sheaf of motions claiming he had violated the order on numerous occasions.

"Whenever this trial is over, we'll go out to lunch and I'll tell you everything you'll need to know," he said.

"I need a psychiatric history," she pleaded.

"You're on the right track. That's all I can say."

She never proved the hospitalizations, but she found enough to suspect gross negligence by church leaders, including the cardinal. In the days leading up to publication, Lombardi was plagued by kaleidoscopic nightmares of terror and damnation, of her standing guilty before medieval tribunals that condemned her for eternity. She could not sleep.

This had never happened to her before. She blamed her vestigial Catholicism, but her apprehension, even self-loathing, was enormous and real.

Called "Cardinal Sin," her article appeared on March 23 in the *Boston Phoenix*. It was a powerful, though not entirely dispositive, exposé of Law's role in covering up the Geoghan crimes. At a time when he was publicly saying there were no priests guilty of misconduct on the archdiocese's payroll, she asserted, he was reassigning Geoghan from parish to parish.

Among the first phone calls Lombardi got after the story hit the stands was one from her own mother. "How could you do this? What if it's not true? You're ruining a man's reputation. This is a cardinal!"

"Mom," she interrupted, "did you even read the story?"

"No, I'm not going to read it! You don't blaspheme God, and the cardinal is a manifestation of God," she continued. "You don't just *go after him*. This isn't one of your politicians, Kristen, this is the cardinal!"

She had little to worry about. The article, and seven more she published over the next twelve months, together with two *Phoenix* editorials on the subject, went largely unnoticed.

Friday, July 27, 2001

Brighton, Massachusetts — Cardinal Law and his administration had allowed the *Boston Phoenix* stories on John Geoghan to go uncontested. Kristen Lombardi routinely left messages for chancery spokesmen, frequently faxed over lists of questions, but never once heard back following her initial story. Unfortunately for her, she did not return to the courthouse to monitor new procedural filings in the Geoghan case. If she had, she would have noticed that buried deep in Law's formal response to one of the allegations—typically these documents were a litany of "I deny's" and "Never happend's"—was a single, damning "Yes." Law admitted to receiving Maryetta Dussourd's handwritten letter in 1984: "[Law] admits that in September of 1984, he was notified of allegations that defendant Father Geoghan had molested seven boys," church lawyers wrote for the cardinal's signature. "[Law] admits that he acknowledged receipt of the September 1984 letter to him referencing allegations of sexual misconduct by John Geoghan."

This was evidence that Patrick McSorley, when he later heard about it, found stunning. It jibed with Geoghan's removal from St. Brendan's in Dorchester and his placement, a month later, at St. Julia's in Weston, which is where he was when he heard the news that McSorley's father had died. The pastoral house call, which included McSorley's fondling, should never have happened.

However, also in his legal filing, the cardinal asserted that the abuse of McSorley, if it happened, was really nobody's fault but McSorley's. "The plaintiff was not in the exercise of due care," he declared, "but rather the negligence of the plaintiff contributed to cause the injury or damage complained of. . . ."

"I was just a twelve-year-old kid," McSorley thought. "I didn't know he was a pedophile. I didn't even *know* this man. I don't understand why I should be held responsible like I seduced the priest!"

The *Boston Herald* discovered the court papers in July 2001 and ran a cover story that shook up Law sufficiently to cause him to issue an explanation, his first direct remarks on the Geoghan case.

"Never was there an effort on my part to shift a problem from one place to the next," he declared forcefully in his weekly column for the *Pilot*, Boston's diocesan newspaper. "It has always been my contention that it is better to know a problem and to deal with it than to be kept in ignorance about it." Once he adopted strict guidelines in 1993, he said, he immediately removed Geoghan from ministry. "It seems so obvious, but this is something that we have learned along the way. I only wish that the knowledge that we have today had been available to us earlier. It is fair to say, however, that society has been on a learning curve with regard to the sexual abuse of minors. The Church, too, has been on a learning curve. We have learned, and we will continue to learn."

Over at the *Globe,* columnist Eileen McNamara read this with suspicious eyes. Why, if the cardinal favored revealing problems over burying them, had the court records to the Geoghan suits been sealed at the church's request? Why was he still endorsing secrecy? "Law has been lucky so far," she wrote. "Judicial concern for fairness has dovetailed nicely with his penchant for secrecy. Only the resolve of the plaintiffs to see this suit through to the end can shine a light into corners of the church that the cardinal would prefer to keep forever in shadow."

Her column appeared on Sunday, July 29, the last day of a long era.

Monday, July 30, 2001

Boston, Massachusetts — The slightly Semitic, boyish man with the funny accent who was presiding over the Monday morning editorial meeting at the *Boston Globe* was the paper's new editor, Marty Baron, on his very first day in the office. Baron's plans for the *Globe* were still unclear to his new staff. He would endorse general principles, saying, for instance, "The obligation is to report fairly, accurately, and objectively," something everybody thought they were already doing. Adding to his mystery, Baron was the only outsider ever to edit the *Globe* in its 126-year history. The *Globe* had always been a family-owned paper, edited by Taylor scions or trustees. But in 1993, the *New York Times* snapped up the broadsheet for a spectacular sum, $1.1 billion dollars. Sacking Matt Storin—officially, "accepting his retirement"—and hiring a new editor from outside was the last step in sealing the corporate takeover.

Baron was an overnight industry hotshot. Being executive editor at the *Miami Herald* for the previous eighteen months had given him plenty of material for proving his mettle. Two of the nation's biggest news stories had unfolded in his backyard: the Elián González soap opera, involving an international custody battle over an adorable Cuban child orphaned at sea, and the last stand of Al Gore, wherein the presidential aspirant's dreams were scotched in a bizarre election-night calamity of confusing ballots, lost precincts, charges of disenfranchisement, and Supreme Court intervention. In April Baron had been named Editor of the Year by the American Society of Newspaper Editors.

In the course of the editorial meeting he asked people to throw around a few ideas for priorities in future coverage. Somebody brought up McNamara's column on Geoghan, and Baron wondered what future coverage was being contemplated. The shaking heads told him: none. "There's a confidentiality order, Marty," one of them said.

"I don't know what the laws of Massachusetts are, but in Florida typically these things were more open. Can't we get beyond the he-said-she-said aspects of this, with the lawyer saying one thing and the church saying something else? Have we considered challenging the confidentiality order?"

Among journalists, Floridians seemed to have an almost religious appetite for public documents even when it seemed in bad taste, as when the *Ft. Lauderdale Sun Sentinel* and others sued for the autopsy photos of NASCAR star Dale Earnhardt, over his wife's teary objections. They argued it was in the public interest to test the validity of the medical examiner's findings, because future NASCAR safety regulations depended on them. Taking on the grieving widow of an icon was one thing. Suing the most powerful institution in the state was another. Baron's staff looked at him blankly. Nobody thought what he was proposing was especially perilous or foolhardy, just unthinkable.

"Look, why don't we take a look at that as a possibility?" Baron offered brightly. "Ben," he said to Ben Bradlee Jr., who happened to be the son and namesake of the legendary *Washington Post* executive editor who had brought down the Nixon administration, "do you think there's something there?"

Bradlee agreed to have the staff investigate.

Later, as Baron strode through the newsroom, one staffer kindly offered a bit of sotto voce advice. "Are you aware of the history between the *Globe* and the Catholic Church?"

"Uh, a little bit," he said. "I read *Common Ground.*"

"I just wanted to let you know what you were stepping into," his concerned employee said.

Baron appreciated the well-meaning warning. "But it seems kind of immaterial to me, because maybe it wouldn't be my first choice to be challenging the Catholic Church, but on the other hand, the story is right in front of us. We have no choice."

By the end of that week, the paper's lawyers rendered their opinion on the matter of challenging the confidentiality order: Baron had First Amendment grounds to review the records in any ongoing litigation, especially one involving an institution as prominent as this one. There was a fifty-fifty chance of success.

Before taking the risk, Baron put out feelers to Walter Robinson, who headed up the paper's investigative unit, called the Spotlight Team. His e-mail blinked onto Robinson's screen at 4:36 P.M. on August 1: "What do you think about this Cardinal Law story? Is it something we should go looking at?"

"That's a little *bold*," Robinson laughed. The notion of the investigative unit of the principal newspaper in town investigating the Catholic Church was definitely not part of the normal course of events. He was impressed. "That's a bold move by our new editor!"

Robinson was a respected figure at the paper, where he had toiled for thirty years in sixteen different positions. However, he had been at the helm of the Spotlight Team for only a few months, and the team of three reporters he had assembled to help him was for the most part just as fresh. He recruited Mike Rezendes, an intense veteran political reporter from the State House beat. Sacha Pfeiffer, who spoke in the staccato, economical style of silver-screen journalists, had been covering the courts. The only investigative veteran was Matt Carroll, who for five years had developed an expertise in computer-assisted reporting, building databases on whatever slid under the team's magnifying glass, whether fraud among housing contractors or municipal corruption.

All four were raised Catholic. So, like Kristen Lombardi before them, they had a deep-seated cultural sense of the risks they were undertaking.

To answer Baron's question, they reread the *Phoenix* pieces and called various attorneys specializing in priestly abuse cases, all of whom hinted broadly at cover-up and conspiracy.

"We can go deep," Robinson said confidently. "We don't know much more about Geoghan, but that's just the start of it. It's clear there's something big out there."

Baron set it all in motion.

For the next three weeks, the Spotlight Team followed a two-pronged game plan. One goal was to learn as much as possible about the life and crimes of Geoghan. The other was wider: to see if he was part of a broad pattern within the church. This latter inquiry proved the most tedious. Without much effort the reporters were able to compile the names of attorneys known to have filed suits against the church, but most said they couldn't talk about old cases because of confidentiality accords. So the reporters tapped into a public electronic database that allowed them to compile a tally of each of the lawyers' cases. They did the same for the Rogers firm, the archdiocese's only legal counsel. By cross-referencing these lists, they found more than a dozen suits in common—strongly suggesting abuse claims. Like the Geoghan case, they had all been impounded and sealed by court order. But from the records it was possible to ascertain the identities of a number of alleged perpetrators.

To prove that these suspects were priests, they compared their names with the annual directories the Boston archdiocese published listing all nine hundred priests and specifics about their assignments, like residential addresses and parish responsibilities. Their suspicions proved correct. Then they noticed something peculiar in the directories. Priests who had been accused in legal papers were likely to have had repeated periods when they were listed as "between assignments" or on "sick leave." Thumbing through the pages, they found this was a relatively common designation.

"Here's one that says 'emergency response'—what the fuck is that?" Robinson said.

"How about this one: 'lend-lease,' like they shipped him out of town."

"Peter J. Frost, 'health leave.' Lists a civilian address."

Matt Carroll went to work. Perusing directories dating back seventeen years, he built a broad database of priests' career trajectories. Most passed those years quite unremarkably. However, a significant minority were suddenly listed as "unassigned" or on "sick leave" for a period of time, then returned to ministry, then removed, then returned. Surely some of them suffered from chronic poor health. But perhaps for a few the diagnosis was child abuser.

More than a hundred names emerged from Carroll's database as having suspicious assignment patterns—including nearly every one of the names mentioned in court papers. Many were currently serving as ministers in some capacity.

"My God," Robinson thought as the numbers added up. "What if there really *are* more Geoghans? What if there were *twelve* more Geoghans? What if it came to *fifteen*?"

August 2001

JAMAICA PLAIN, MASSACHUSETTS — If Garabedian's office resembled a drop-in clinic, Phil Saviano's apartment—headquarters for the New England chapter of SNAP—was a Red Cross tent in a war zone. Every week brought new victims calling him with tales of secrets and sadness. Their needs were all similar: they wanted someone to believe them. At support group meetings they shared advice on good therapists and sharp lawyers (although most had not contemplated a lawsuit), and they talked endlessly about the specific ethical duties they felt as victims of priest sex abuse. Was it their responsibility to leaflet at church if their perpetrators were still in the pulpit? To wear a wire? To go public? To warn the others?

When Lombardi's articles began appearing, and with the Geoghan case obviously heading for trial, the volume of calls picked up dramatically. It seemed that each new revelation caused another wave of victims to come forward seeking help. Nothing surprised Saviano anymore. He made it a point to keep track of each offending priest, building a file system to chart who had been sued, by whom, and how many other victims there might be—he tried to help introduce everybody linked to the same perpetrator.

But then came a call he never expected: Walter Robinson. They spoke for an hour that afternoon and a few more that night. Robinson was initially interested in one specific priest and wondered what Saviano knew about his career, which seemed to span dozens of parishes, not only in Boston but throughout the country. Saviano considered it a relatively obscure case; there were so many others that were worth investigating, he explained. Robinson invited him to a meeting with the staff at the *Globe* offices.

That meeting went on for three hours. Saviano said he had contact information for several of the names on their suspect list, sometimes multiple victims for each one. He brought documents from some of their cases, evidentiary letters from long-squelched litigation. He agreed to introduce *Globe* staffers to scores of victims in Boston and many times more than that nationally, men and women who were hiding in plain sight.

He even told his own story about Father Holley and his ongoing battles with AIDS, in the middle of which he unexpectedly broke into sobs. Grief, an awful artifact of his childhood, recurred at the most startling times.

When he had composed himself he looked around and saw that his questioners were near tears, too.

Robinson knew that for people in Boston to believe the worst about their powerful cardinal, they would need to see actual internal church records. Saviano was in possession of his own case files, but they related to the neighboring diocese of Worcester and were of little interest to the Spotlight Team. What he could offer instead was an introduction to alleged victims from Boston.

After trying to get the *Globe* to listen to him for a decade, Saviano returned home that night exhausted and emotionally spent, but full of hope. He called one of his best friends and said, "Well, I just gave the most important interview of my life."

September 7, 2001
UNDISCLOSED LAW FIRM, BOSTON — "No names," the man on the phone had told Walter Robinson. "I'm absolutely serious about this—nobody can know I'm talking to you."

Robinson had agreed to the terms, and arrived at the designated meeting place hoping he had found a way into the church's inner sanctum. An investigative reporter didn't want to go in through the front door; he didn't want to alert his quarry prematurely. He wanted to know what the administrators knew *before* he talked to them. This couldn't be done simply by creating databases. Robinson needed an insider to pass him information, and for this he revisited the hundreds of sources who had helped him over his long career, asking for introductions, networking his way in. One source led to another, and eventually to this man.

He was extremely nervous. His preconditions also included that Robinson could never reveal where he worked, or how he came upon any information he might provide, or the exact location of their meeting place, or anything that might identify the third person who joined them.

It was an extremely warm, beautiful late-summer day.

"You need to understand the dimensions of the problem," the man told Robinson. "To help you understand, here are the names of some priests." He slid a pile of papers across a table. "All these were hushed up."

Robinson began reading. He didn't recognize any names from the court records the Spotlight Team had compiled. In all, there were thirty priests and two religious brothers—twice as many molesting priests as Robinson ever dreamed possible.

These were not legal actions that were settled out of court, the man explained. Rather, these were handled extralegally, *privately.* The church was so anxious to keep these matters quiet that it offered money at the hint of litigation. "They never hit the courts. There was no paper."

He let Robinson jot down the names—Father O'Sullivan, Father Gale, Father Matt—but would not allow him to make a photocopy of the documents. The pages he presented revealed very little else. Robinson couldn't determine the identity or even the gender of the complainants in each case, how many charges were leveled against each priest, or how much was paid to make the allegations disappear even before they were formally lodged. In fact, there was not enough data in the disclosures the man was making to justify writing an article. That wasn't his intent. He wanted Robinson to know he was on the right trail. Despite years of angry denials, the archdiocese secretly knew it had an enormous problem.

As he headed back to his office, Robinson marveled at the archdiocese's cunning cover-up. "Side deals," he thought. "That's how it all was kept under the radar screen. *There was no paper.*" The names on his list were the answer to the riddle; now the Spotlight Team had to learn the riddle itself. When he barged through the office door that afternoon, he announced, "You're not going to believe this!"

September 14, 2001

LOS ANGELES, CALIFORNIA — Like Phil Saviano, Mary Grant had sued her local diocese and in 1991 settled for a paltry $25,000 without so much as an apology. She demanded an admission from Father Lenihan that he molested her repeatedly as a teen, a crime, and he did admit his culpability. Inexplicably, the church did nothing to punish him. He was not even offered therapy before he was promoted to head up a major parish in Anaheim, St. Boniface Church. Her efforts to get Lenihan arrested also went nowhere. In 1993 and 1994, she sometimes stood outside his church with a stack of flyers warning parishioners their pastor was an admitted molester.

When he was transferred to St. Edward's Parish, a large and wealthy church in Dana Point, she alerted congregants there, too. They weren't especially grateful to her; one man threatened to sue her and another warned that he would return with a car full of people to neutralize her through physical means. Lenihan remained entrenched in his church despite her efforts.

But the issue of clerical abuse was gaining public attention lately. Along with the Geoghan case percolating in Boston courts, a similar one had developed here. Ryan DiMaria, who was thirty-one, sued dioceses of Orange and Los Angeles for the abuse he said he suffered as a high school student at Santa Margarita High School, in southern Orange County. Church officials already knew that the school's principal, Father Michael Harris, had a history of manipulating male teens into sexual situations, DiMaria's lawyer contended. Both dioceses denied previous knowledge, and Harris himself claimed innocence, despite a proliferation of teens testifying against him.

However, just a few weeks earlier, on August 20, 2001, church officials settled DiMaria's suit with a stunning $5.2 million, the largest publicly disclosed settlement ever paid by the Catholic Church to an individual claiming abuse. Further, they agreed to an eleven-point policy devised by Ryan DiMaria, who had just graduated law school, to protect children in the future. Dubbed "Ryan's Law," it included hiring monitors for all diocesan Catholic schools, establishing a toll-free number for victims to call, and prohibiting all priests from being alone in social settings with minors. Lastly, church authorities apologized—not only to DiMaria, but to the four other men who said Harris had groped them. "Sexual abuse is a serious sin. It devastates its victims physically, emotionally and spiritually," the archdiocese's spokesman Tod Tamberg said in a statement. "Such activity simply will not be tolerated in our church."

Publicity surrounding that case had brought a rash of new people to SNAP meetings in southern California, which Mary Grant ran as regional coordinator. They flooded her phone machine and e-mail. "It's like I'm on a battlefield pulling out the injured," she thought. "Like a bomb went off and every day there are more victims."

It also brought interest from reporters. When Steve Lopez, a city columnist for the *Los Angeles Times,* called her—after hearing of her case through another means—she agreed to talk, using only her first name. She was not ready for the entire city to know her past. Lopez wouldn't have had much of a story if Lenihan hadn't also agreed to talk to him, also anonymously. His comments were candid. He admitted to other relationships, three of them significant, at least one with an adult woman. "I think celibacy is the toughest thing in the priesthood," he said in the article, published on September 14. "I love being a priest. But I don't like being a celibate."

He believed God had forgiven him for what went on with Mary.

"I'd like to think I'm a good guy, and I'm clinging to my sense of self-worth. I'd like to stand before my creator and say there was no malice in me."

Despite his precautions, "Father X" was instantly recognizable to Mary Grant. More significantly, the diocese recognized him, too. Immediately following publication of the article, the bishop for the diocese of Orange, Tod D. Brown, forced Lenihan to resign from his post as pastor at St. Edward's Parish. "Father John's resignation does not negate any of the good that has been accomplished in the parish during his time as pastor," Brown wrote in a letter to St. Edward's parishioners, but "this self-revelation is a cause of scandal to many in the Church, and it is a cause of great concern to me."

Finally, Mary Grant's wish had come true—her perpetrator was no longer in a position to molest other young girls under the pretext of ministering to them. But the circumstances of his removal really irritated her. "Imagine that," she told a friend. "He was not removed for molesting kids, which the church knew about all along, but they removed him for talking about having 'affairs' with women. If he hadn't talked about it, do you think they would have done anything? No! What was more important than anything else was keeping the secret. That's the rule he broke."

Late October 2001

BOSTON, MASSACHUSETTS — Mitchell Garabedian had cleverly figured out a loophole in the confidentiality order, and began smuggling some of the damning secret records out into the open. This was perfectly legal and justifiable. If, for instance, he filed a motion seeking to depose Bishop Robert Banks, he was expected to lay out a case for why he considered Banks's testimony germane, and this motion was not subject to the impounding order. He could have stated this in broad strokes: "Banks, as Boston's vicar for administration, directly supervised Geoghan's psychotherapy, according to certain archdiocesan records." However, the law allowed him to be more specific. Cautiously at first and then more boldly, he began attaching specific exhibits from personnel files and lengthy deposition extracts as attachments to his motions—citing, for instance, an April 1989 memo in which Banks notes what a psychiatrist told him about Geoghan: "You better clip his wings before there is an explosion. You can't afford to have him in a parish."

In this way, Garabedian was able to sneak a significant trove of incriminating evidence into the public domain. Any reporter who revisited those huge boxes down at the county clerk's office could finally write the definitive story of Cardinal Law's reckless endangerment of children.

The problem was, nobody caught on. Being for the most part inexperienced with the press, Garabedian was terribly disappointed. He pictured the Spotlight Team scouring documents late into the night, over and over, till they found one that wasn't supposed to be there.

Especially in the aftermath of the 9/11 terror attacks, it didn't work that way. The Spotlight Team, like nearly everybody at the paper, and nearly every reporter at nearly every paper in America, had been reassigned to cover the most serious and deadly assault ever on American soil. This was a story with deep Boston roots. Ten of the terrorists had somehow managed to board two airliners at Logan Airport, headed for Los Angeles. Mike Rezendes was dispatched to Florida to investigate the flight schools where they had studied. Sacha Pfeiffer, Matt Carroll, and Walter Robinson were likewise deployed. For five weeks their church project was on total hold.

Finally Garabedian just told Mike Rezendes point-blank about his scheme. Even then the information remained elusive. Rezendes spent weeks pawing through the voluminous files, but he couldn't find the exhibits and excerpts Garabedian said were there. The records had been gone through by reporters so many times they were in complete disarray. He asked Judge Constance M. Sweeney's aide for help, but got nowhere. Finally he was forced to turn the *Globe* attorneys on the court before the judge admitted that the records in question were simply missing. The judge asked Mitchell Garabedian to file them again, and authorized him to pass along a copy to Rezendes.

The choicest gift Garabedian gave him was a letter that Auxiliary Bishop John D'Arcy wrote to Cardinal Law in 1984. D'Arcy expressed grave misgivings about assigning Geoghan to St. Julia's Parish in Weston. "There are two things that give me concern," he wrote. "1. Fr. Geoghan has a history of homosexual involvement with young boys. I understand his recent abrupt departure from St. Brendan's, Dorchester, may be related to this problem. 2. St. Julia's for some time has been a divided and troubled parish. . . . If something happens, the parishioners already angry and divided, will be convinced that the archdiocese has no concern for their welfare and simply sends them priests with problems."

"My God, this is amazing," Rezendes thought. "They *knew*. It wasn't a slipup. It wasn't a mistake. It wasn't an oversight. This was discussed among the top officials of the archdiocese. There was someone who objected and it was done anyway!"

Sometime in December 2001

BOSTON, MASSACHUSETTS — Eric MacLeish could see the clouds gathering around the Boston archdiocese, and he felt perhaps a twinge of nostalgia about his old warrior days fighting over Father Porter. There was a lot more money to be made in the field, he knew—even if the cases went to trial. In Dallas, eleven former altar boys alleged that Father Rudy Kos had attacked them hundreds of times. For some reason, local diocesan officials had rejected entreaties to settle a suit, instead arguing before a jury that Kos—and all priests, by extension—was actually an independent contractor, not an employee, and therefore responsible for his own actions. The jurors were swayed instead by Father Tom Doyle and others who gave expert testimony in the case, and found church leaders "grossly negligent." The judgment they handed down—a staggering $119.6 million—was more than ten times larger than the previous record for litigation against the church, according to Reuters.

But MacLeish was not eager to tempt more gun blasts and bomb threats. Many victims of priests still called him, but he now passed them over to Bob Sherman, his best friend from law school, whom he had hired as a kind of one-man church litigation unit at Greenberg Traurig, a huge international law firm with nine hundred attorneys, whose main office was in Miami. Since early 1993, Sherman had handled suits against forty-five priests in various dioceses in New England. He was no grandstander. Each case was settled in a quiet fashion, without going to trial, and with a capitulation to the church's demand that barred the litigant from mentioning the fiasco ever again.

Recently MacLeish had made himself over into an expert in trade secrets. He wouldn't have jumped back into the priest business if not for a call from Tom Fulchino, one of the Porter litigants he had represented, bearing terrible news. Tragedy, it turned out, had struck twice: Tom's son Christopher was abused by their old parish priest John J. Geoghan. The revelation sent the whole Fulchino family reeling. "The bottom fell out," Tom said. "Geoghan is a sick man. And he was a sick man on the loose. It was up to Cardinal Law and the people to control that person. But they did nothing."

What could he do? MacLeish agreed to file suit.

Shortly thereafter, MacLeish was approached by an old acquain-

tance of his from Newton, a kind of town busybody for whom he had a
fondness. Jackie Gauvreau told MacLeish the story she had told a million times over about Paul Shanley, a story nobody else believed.
MacLeish was different. His firm had represented the four people who
brought the charges that resulted in his being removed from ministry in
1993. Of course he believed Gauvreau.

Really, she thought? You really believe me? You believe that Shanley's
a child molester? . . . *Really?*

August 15, 2001–December 24, 2001

Boston, Massachusetts — The *Globe*'s legal challenge to see the Geoghan files slowly wended through the courts while drawing little attention to what the Spotlight Team was up to. A first hearing was held
in September. By luck of standard judicial rotation, it was assigned to
Suffolk Superior Court judge Constance M. Sweeney, who was also
overseeing the eighty-six lawsuits Garabedian had brought relating to
John Geoghan. Sweeney was a tough, independent jurist who was disinclined to give the church any deferential treatment—despite the fact
that all her formal education up to law school had been in Roman
Catholic institutions.

Wilson Rogers Jr. made his arguments strenuously. Any communication between a priest and his superiors was protected by the constitutional separation of church and state, he said. If these cases went to
trial, he understood that the obligations of a civil society demanded
that the case be argued in open court. But before that time, he felt the
church maintained its unique status and any ruling to the contrary
"would be highly prejudicial to the Constitutional protections afforded
these Defendants."

This didn't dissuade lawyers for the *Globe*, who had advocated a uniform approach to civil litigation—if pretrial materials like depositions,
medical reports, and personnel files were deemed sufficiently important to merit public attention in other cases, if we believed that an open
court system furthered the cause of democracy, the same rules should
apply in this suit.

Even if that were true, Rogers countered, the *Globe* had no standing
in the current litigation.

When it came to child welfare, *Globe* lawyers responded, the public had an overwhelming and abiding interesting in judicial transparency.

Sweeney, who took until November 20 to make her ruling, staggered the church lawyers by siding with the *Globe*. The public's right to know, she found, overrode the church's right to privacy. Rogers appealed immediately, staying her ruling, and reiterated his concerns before Massachusetts Appeals Court judge Cynthia Cohen. But on Christmas Eve, Cohen rejected Rogers's defense, setting in motion the ultimate release of a trove of more than ten thousand pages of internal records on January 23.

Rogers went back to Judge Sweeney and pleaded for a few extra weeks, but she was resolute. "We are not going to delay any longer in making them public," she snapped.

It was exactly as Father Tom Doyle predicted almost twenty years before in his dire manual for the bishops: "Our dependence in the past on Roman Catholic judges and attorneys protecting the Diocese and clerics is GONE."

But when word reached him at an air force base in Germany, where he was stationed as a chaplain, that a judge finally defied the powerful archdiocese of Boston, he simply would not believe it would make a bit of difference. "So what?" he said. "I heard this before. With the Kos case it was, 'If the verdict comes down, it's going to be earth shattering.' Well it was. But what happened? Nothing. Porter case, same thing. Business as usual."

Friday, January 4, 2002, 4:15 P.M.
BOSTON, MASSACHUSETTS — An intense calculus went into determining when the Spotlight Team would begin publishing its series. Their campaign to get to the trove of Geoghan documents had alerted their competitors across town at the *Boston Herald* that they were up to something big. The church had to make all documents available by January 28—in the meantime, church officials were reviewing each one to decide whether to appeal for protection of individual exhibits. But once the documents were public, they would become available to any publication, not just the *Globe*. Could the *Globe* risk waiting till then to pub-

lish its first major stories? In addition, the explosive Bishop D'Arcy letter hidden in the public sphere for Rezendes was still sitting there for
anybody else to stumble upon. If somebody stole the *Globe* reporters'
scoop, it could ruin the series into which they had already invested
months.

Then something else happened they hadn't anticipated. Although
their Christmas Eve court victory opening up the Geoghan suit gave
the church several weeks to review all the old records, it immediately
took the veil away from documents filed subsequent to the order. They
learned the church was under orders to produce a quantity of medical
and psychiatric files late Friday afternoon. If they contained what Walter Robinson believed they would, the Spotlight Team would be forced
to pull the trigger early.

Robinson tentatively reserved space in Sunday's paper and sent
Rezendes and Carroll to the county clerk to make copies. They arrived
forty-five minutes before closing time. Rezendes easily recognized the
pile of documents he needed in a tidy, tall stack right on the clerk's
countertop.

"Great," he told the clerk, pointing, "I'd like to take those documents
to the copy room."

"Oh, no, you can't take those documents," she said, spinning them
out of reach.

"Why not?"

"They're under seals," she said.

"Oh, you don't know about the court order! Really, there has been
this court ruling that opens them up." He never snapped at civil servants, because that never made anything better. He was trying to appear honest. It didn't help. She refused to release the pages.

The head clerk came up to the counter. She conceded that what
Rezendes was saying might indeed be the truth, but felt it was safer to
make a mistake by not releasing them than err in the other direction.
"I'm really uncomfortable about this," she said. "We have been doing it
this way for how many x-number of years; whenever these documents
come in, they never go out. I'm not going to do anything without going
before a judge."

A judge, Rezendes thought, was a perfect idea. It was now four-thirty. The supervisor and the two reporters dashed from one empty courtroom to another. Most judges had already left for the day. Finally a sitting judge was located, Vieri Volterra of the Massachusetts Superior Court. He grimaced as he perused the stack the *Globe* wished to copy.

"These are pretty sensitive documents," he said.

"Yeah," Rezendes agreed.

"What are these? Psychiatric records?"

"Yeah."

"Where is the editorial responsibility in publishing something like this?"

At a quarter to five, after everything he had learned about the church in Boston, the last thing Rezendes wanted to sit through was a lecture on journalistic ethics. "We have a court order opening the files," he said helpfully.

The judge asked to see a copy. Matt Carroll flipped out a cell phone and called Walter Robinson back at the office, who slapped a copy of the order into his fax machine. Meanwhile, Volterra pressed his ethics issue over and over to the point where Rezendes realized he was just toying with him. When a clerk brought him the fax, the judge said, "You can have 'em."

The two men flew out of the courtroom down to the copy center. But the clerk who ran the place was standing at the elevator with her coat on. They begged and cajoled. And somehow they turned her around. It was fair to say that never before in the history of civil service had somebody reopened a darkened office and delayed her return home to her children for a full hour, just so a few newspaper reporters could make a deadline.

Back at the *Globe* offices, Robinson was scrambling to finish the last major piece of reporting, which was to scare a comment out of the archdiocese. He had been seeking an interview with the cardinal since mid-December. He had called again two days ago. They were planning to publish over the weekend, he had said, so he needed to talk to Law by Saturday. That was a big heads-up. Still, no one called back. "It has to be worse than covering the Kremlin under Brezhnev," he complained.

Tonight, he finally reached Donna Morrissey, the cardinal's spokes-woman, and gave her a bit of a lecture. "This is not that hard. We need a comment. We've been waiting for weeks."

Unbeknownst to him, at about that moment, Law was on the tele-phone with Marty Baron, the editor. "I just wanted you to know I'm not going to give an interview to the Spotlight Team," he said.

"I respect your decision," Baron said. "That's your prerogative. I wish you had responded differently, but it's your decision to make."

Late in the evening, Donna Morrissey reiterated the news to Robin-son.

"Doesn't he even want to see the questions? I'll fax a copy of the questions," Robinson offered.

The cardinal, she said, is not interested in seeing the questions.

Not even about child abuse? Not even knowing it will go on the front page, the powerful *Globe* going against the powerful church?

"Correct," she said.

Chapter 9

Explosion

Saturday, January 5, 2002

Jamaica Plain, Massachusetts — Phil Saviano was, as usual, disappointed. This collaboration with the *Globe* was starting to feel like every other time he tried collaborating with reporters. Over the years he'd assisted a half dozen of them, but when they finally filed their articles, about this or that sexual assault and the terrible emotional fallout, they invariably missed the larger significance, that the church disguised a *culture* of abuse. He wasn't sure if this meant most reporters were lazy thinkers, or if the truth about the church was too jagged and incongruous to be captured in a newspaper article. Or maybe politically it was just too dangerous to publish the larger story. Maybe the reporters had grasped the essential truth but were not allowed to write what they knew. There did often seem to be a disconnect between what the reporter told him and what eventually appeared in print.

But Phil was not prone to conspiracy thinking. What he suspected, and what disheartened him most, was that the seemingly well-intentioned *Globe* reporters might simply miss the larger story altogether. Mike Rezendes had not phoned since before Christmas, and at the time the only thing that had seemed to preoccupy him was competitive pressures. He had heard the *Herald* was snooping around the story.

Rezendes told Phil that the series was not slotted until February. "Maybe we'll have to move it up," he said, "but we're really not ready."

To Saviano this meant they'd probably condense their massive research into a hasty report. The bottom line was, he had little faith that anything would ever change. He took himself to bed, unconvinced his efforts would amount to anything.

Sunday, January 6, 2002, Feast of the Epiphany, at Dawn
WELLESLEY, MASSACHUSETTS — The morning brought a thin but heavy snowfall that bent tree boughs downward and held them still against an unseasonable breeze, delivering a warm, springlike Sunday. By afternoon, temperatures would reach nearly fifty degrees.

Jim Muller stood at his door, feeling uneasy. He reached for the *Globe*. Silence engulfed his affluent neighborhood on Boston's far western flank. He worried about the strange warm climate.

Muller was a scientist—a cardiologist leading a research effort for Harvard and MIT in blending technological innovations with medical-intervention sciences. Since his college days, his interests tended toward the extreme big picture. Inspired by William Fulbright's book *The Arrogance of Power,* which he read in 1967, Muller became obsessed with the dangers of Cold War brinksmanship and threw himself into peace work. "The thought of nuclear war so completely captivated my mind that I had to force myself to think about anything else," he wrote in his journal at the time. "Only the problem of destruction of the human race seemed to matter."

He seized on a deceptively simple idea that changed the course of history. In 1978, he and two other doctors launched the global nonprofit International Physicians for the Prevention of Nuclear War, founded on the principle that as doctors they knew that following a nuclear strike there would be no medical way to stop the suffering. It would be the earth's final epidemic, the single most devastating threat to humanity. As for any incurable epidemic, IPPNW prescribed prevention: strategic arms limitation, testing bans, and disarmament campaigns.

The original three grew to five hundred, then to two hundred thousand medical professionals in more than forty countries. Eventually IPPNW was credited with galvanizing a global movement against nuclear war. By 1985 there were so many no-nukes groups that a *Newsweek* cover on the phenomenon didn't even mention IPPNW, to Muller's absolute astonishment. For its leadership and moral stewardship, that year the group was awarded the Nobel Peace Prize.

But by then Jim Muller was no longer integrally involved with IPPNW. His dedication to his extracurricular activities—he had been the IPPNW workhorse, its secretary and translator—had caused terrible pressures on his home life. Kathleen, his wife, accused him of virtual abandonment, which was not at all far from the truth. If he was not at Harvard or seeing patients, he was attending conferences in Brussels or Moscow or locked in endless conversation on the phone. He hardly saw his three children, who were all preteens. Even his career suffered. He withdrew from IPPNW reluctantly in 1984, knowing it was the right thing to do. Since then, he satisfied his larger aspirations by speaking out against war, dedicating himself to his laboratory work, and regularly attending St. John's in Wellesley, one of the largest and most active churches in the archdiocese.

He returned inside with the paper. He did not immediately notice the bold stacked headline: CHURCH ALLOWED ABUSE BY PRIEST FOR YEARS, it read. AWARE OF GEOGHAN RECORD, ARCHDIOCESE STILL SHUTTLED HIM FROM PARISH TO PARISH.

Muller had not paid any attention to the Geoghan case. He never saw the *Phoenix* articles, or the stories in the *Boston Herald*. He had not seen the priest paraded on the evening news nearly five years ago, the broadcast that rocked Anthony Muzzi, Patrick McSorley, and countless others who recalled his touches. When Muller snapped the newspaper open, the story assaulted him. More than 130 victims had come forward with awful stories of being molested by this slack-faced man reproduced in grotesquely colored pictures. A boy told his mother, "I don't want him doing that to my wee-wee, touching my wee-wee." A mom told a ranking pastor that Father Geoghan would awaken her boys by "playing with their penises." Muller could barely read it. Here was a criminal in a Roman collar, a man who would sneak into darkened rooms and whisper hypnotic prayers to the boys he was groping.

But the story was so much more than that. Written by the entire Spotlight Team, it revealed the system of abuse in which Geoghan thrived. A priest told a church official he'd seen Geoghan wrestling with youngsters in his rectory room. What did the official do? Threaten to reassign the whistle-blowing priest to South America for saying such a thing. Another priest told an uncontrollably morose mother that Geoghan will "never be a priest again." In truth? Geoghan remained a priest, one who was assigned over and over again despite the clear dangers, an endless orgy of abuse that might have been stopped, should have been stopped, at any time after 1962.

The complaints of irate parents had poured in almost continuously thereafter. Twice church supervisors sent Geoghan for medical treatment. Once they took his word when he admitted abusing several boys but didn't "feel it serious or a pastoral problem." Seven times the church sent him to an unsuspecting new parish, and the sickness continued its course.

Father Geoghan was not removed from his last assignment until 1995, and only then after generating a flood of lawsuits, some of which had been settled secretly for a total of $10 million, the report said. Other victims were suing in order to get money for their psychiatric care. A seamless web of defensiveness and cruelty seemed to surround the archdiocese. The article carried the question that had no answer: "Why did it take a succession of three cardinals and many bishops 34 years to place children out of Geoghan's reach?"

But the most damning parts were the sad, pleading, handwritten letters parents had sent to Law, which the *Globe* had found in the court files and reproduced on the page. These they contrasted to the incomprehensibly chirpy notes Law subsequently mailed to Geoghan, as though he didn't know a thing.

Jim Muller could not believe what he was reading. While he'd been dedicated to world peace, suffering spread in his own backyard. He felt idiotic, then sick. His hands began to shake. He sat numb at the breakfast nook when Kathleen appeared in the kitchen. He thought, This is the same hierarchy that brought us the Inquisition.

Sunday, January 6, 2002, 8:30 A.M.
JAMAICA PLAIN, MASSACHUSETTS — Without specific plans on this sparkly January morning, Phil Saviano headed out for the paper and a cup of coffee. On his doorstep, he discovered that the story had broken. He was both terrified and relieved. But he was also mad. Nobody was decent enough to give him a heads-up? At the very least, he would like to have warned his parents this was coming.

But then he read the story.

"Wow," he thought. "Finally somebody got it."

Monday, January 7, 2002, 8:00 A.M.
WELLESLEY, MASSACHUSETTS — Somehow, Mary Scanlon Calcaterra avoided learning of the scandal all day Sunday and into Monday, when she climbed into her car to head for work and flicked on NPR, as she always did. That morning, as every morning, she cherished the Roman Catholic Church with a brilliant dedication and passion undiminished since her days at Catholic grammar school and Catholic high school, and Regis College in Weston. Though she raised five children, studied nursing, held various jobs, and served on the school committee, she still found time for significant church obligations. She taught religious education and was a veteran of countless confirmation retreats. Even now, as she was trying to find a way, at age fifty-five, to switch from being a surgical nurse to a specialist in hospice care, she was a church lector at St. John's, sang in the choir, and sat on her parish council, a consultative governance institution.

Calcaterra supposed she might be considered something of a charismatic Catholic, liberal politically but as enthusiastic a worshiper as any Southern Baptist. She was a woman prone to shouting "Alleluia" and "Praise the Lord!" even in a nave filled with long-necked Boston Catholics. This could not be overstated: she absolutely, ebulliently adored her church. There had been only one period of darkness in her relationship with her church. Her first marriage ended in divorce. For a time thereafter she was not allowed Holy Communion.

Yet her faith never wavered. She had dutifully pursued her rights under church law. She hired a canon lawyer—they are usually priests who have studied the textbooks of church legislation accumulated over the centuries, and are licensed to appear before church tribunals on matters ranging from the hierarchy of church teachings to parish-pastor disputes and financial quarrels. Working with him, she formulated her argument for an annulment, namely that certain impediments existed prior to her marriage that invalidated the marriage itself. That and a few hundred dollars in legal fees had made her marriage a fiction. To non-Catholics, it seemed a bit silly to preach that marriage was for eternity, while at the same time carefully maintaining this gaping loophole. Why not just acknowledge divorce? Even Representative Joseph P. Kennedy II, who famously annulled his marriage, reportedly called the procedure "Catholic gobbledygook." Far from being offended by it, Calcaterra found the exercise to be very soul-searching and cathartic— "one of the wonderful things the church does for us."

Until the awful radio report invaded her car, she had thought the church was capable only of wonderful things. Her children, on the other hand—like most in their generation—were not so enthusiastic. It was a tremendous struggle to keep her children believing. She resented their strong misgivings about their church's relevance in their world. "The church is *extremely* relevant," she said. "You just have to pay attention to what the message is." She hated to think they would take this morning's radio broadcast as more evidence of an unsalvageable church. She could hear their questions, which were hers as well: What church would allow this darkness to flourish? Could faith survive this cataclysm?

Would they be paying attention today?

The taste of shame rose up in her mouth. She was ashamed to be Catholic, ashamed of the one thing she truly felt and believed was at the core of her very being, ashamed of her faith. She tasted the disgust of it, and that made her cry suddenly and profusely in her car, and that made her feel tremendously alone.

She pulled into the parking lot at the orthopedic surgeon's office, as she did every morning. The day was clear and unusually warm. She found it unbelievable that the sun would keep shining after such news. She remembered having the same thought twenty years ago, on the day her father died, and recalled the visceral sensation of grief. That is what this feeling was, she thought, the dumb numbness of grief.

Tuesday, January 8, 2002
VATICAN CITY — If any of the powerful denizens of the airy corridors here had learned of the bomb dropped in Boston, it was not apparent. Nonetheless, deep inside the labyrinth, preparations for handling a world-class child abuse scandal were well under way. Although almost nobody knew it, in 2001 John Paul II had issued two motu proprios on the subject. The Latin term indicates that the pontiff was motivated to issue the decree "by his own accord"; motu proprios generally treat the issues that matter most to popes. They define papacies. Therefore, they usually are not slipped out into the world without fanfare. But their obscurity in this case was intentional. The Vatican press corps was not alerted. The documents were not even published until the end of the year, and then only bound deeply in the dense yearly journal that records all the actions of the Holy See that year—in Latin.

In them, John Paul decried the abuse of minors by priests to be among the "graver offenses" against church law. And he announced that Cardinal Josef Ratzinger, one of the most polarizing figures in the Vatican Curia, was being given the responsibility for establishing guidelines for dealing with the problem. It was left to Ratzinger to inform the troops, and he did this in a letter to the more than forty-four hundred bishops worldwide, as well as the heads of religious orders, with a covering letter that demanded the document contents never be divulged, according to those who read it.

From now and into the future, Ratzinger ordered, even the vaguest claim against a priest, so long as the alleged incident occurred not more than ten years before the accusation, would trigger a church trial. However, that trial would be held in secret. Everybody taking part in it, from canon law defenders to prosecutors and jurors, would be ordained priests sworn to secrecy. Appeals would go directly to an ecclesiastical tribunal in Rome, under Ratzinger's authority.

It was plain that Ratzinger had wanted to bring a variety of standardized and timely justice procedures to the problem. He wrote,

"With this letter, we hope that not only will these serious crimes be avoided, but, above all, that the holiness of the clergy and the faithful be protected by the necessary sanctions and by the pastoral care offered by the bishops and others responsible." But the people reading the letter guessed he was motivated by a desire to contain a conflagration. Abuse scandals were flaring up in far-flung dioceses. Even before the Geoghan case, the church was facing a serious sex crisis of global proportions. Major civil and criminal cases were expanding in Ireland, France, Brazil, Italy, and parts of Africa—priests in at least twenty-three countries around the world had been implicated in sex crimes by the end of 2001. In one African diocese, the Vatican was forced to admit, priests who feared catching HIV from the locals instead pressed scores of nuns into sexual servitude; twenty-nine nuns became pregnant as a result, and one died after a botched abortion.

Out of necessity, Ratzinger was consolidating power centrally to come up with another way to deal with the problem. Above all else, it had to be done quietly.

Wednesday, January 9, 2002
BOSTON, MASSACHUSETTS — The *Globe* did what every paper does following a tremendous news exclusive. It fanned the flames. Several days in a row, the paper published a *Globe* hotline number for people to call with their own abuse stories. On Monday, it rang off the hook. On Tuesday, it jammed with calls again. By the end of the week, five hundred new victims would call from all over Boston. On the editorial page on Wednesday, the *Globe* called upon the cardinal to come clean: "It's time for the secrecy to end, both about the past and about whatever happens in the future. The cardinal owes Catholics an accounting of what really happened in the chancery when Geoghan's name came up and why the welfare of one tarnished priest, and of the church itself, outweighed the welfare of dozens of young members of Cardinal Law's flock."

Cardinal Law took the bait. That morning his press secretary, Donna Morrissey, called reporters to the chancery for an extraordinary press conference. The room overflowed with reporters, jammed in and jostling, surging toward Cardinal Law when he entered the room. Law radiated a stern sort of self-confidence. He was not an extemporaneous speaker, so he read from typed notes.

"The many acts that have been alleged against John Geoghan constitute a heart-rending pattern," he said in his familiar voice. "These acts have been reported in some detail in recent media stories. The horror of these acts speaks for itself. However much I regret having assigned him, it is important to recall that John Geoghan was never assigned by me to a parish without psychiatric or medical assessments indicating that such assignments were appropriate." He looked around the room, confident in his power to persuade. He was uncharacteristically noncombative, even contrite. His lengthy statement included an announcement that he was tightening the archdiocese's sex abuse policy—from now on there would be "zero tolerance" for child abusers. And he said his priests would now report all instances of abuse that come to their attention—outside of confession—to civil authorities, a policy he had openly fought for years as a violation of church-state separation.

"That some should criticize my earlier decisions I can easily understand. Before God, however, it was not then, nor is it my intent now, to protect a priest accused of misconduct against minors at the expense of those whom he is ordained to serve. Judgments were made regarding the assignment of John Geoghan which, in retrospect, were tragically incorrect. These judgments were, however, made in good faith and in reliance upon psychiatric assessments and medical opinions that such assignments were safe and reasonable."

When he opened himself up for questions, Margery Eagan, a columnist for the *Boston Herald,* chimed in: "I'm curious what kind of guidance you had regarding ex-Father Geoghan in terms of his psychiatric care and whether you now feel that was trustworthy advice."

"Well, you know, Miss Eagan," he said, "the difficulty is to try to put oneself back, in my case to put myself back, in 1984 when I got here, and to do so with the knowledge I have in 2002. I have been concerned about this issue and that is why I insisted on psychiatric evaluation. But I had confidence, and would have no reason not to have had con-

fidence, in those whose judgment I sought, psychiatrically and med-
ically. I'm no psychiatrist, but given the experience that I have had in
these ensuing years and with whatever reading I have done, I have
come to the conclusion that no matter what anybody says, that someone who is guilty of this kind of abuse simply cannot be placed in that
position of trust, which is the position of the priest."

He took a breath. "There is nobody, *nobody,* in an assignment in this
archdiocese now, no priest in an assignment in this archdiocese now,
that I'm aware of, who is guilty of sexually abusing a minor."

Walter Robinson couldn't have hoped for a better challenge. Back
at the Spotlight office, the database of suspects contained scores of
priests currently in good standing with the archdiocese even though
they had abused minors. Law had to know this. And he had to be
lying.

A Week Later
Wellesley, Massachusetts — Jim Muller had devoured every scrap of
the distasteful news. The *Globe* learned that the two doctors who examined Geoghan for the archdiocese and repeatedly gave him a clean
bill of health had no expertise whatsoever in predatory sexual abuse.
One was an old Geoghan family friend and neighbor. The other, a psychiatrist, had never treated sex offenders before and, in a twist, had
himself been sued for sexually molesting one of his patients. The whole
affair couldn't get more sordid. The state Senate responded unanimously, passing a bill on January 23 to make priests in Massachusetts
mandatory reporters of sexual crimes; the House followed a month
later. Before, the commonwealth was one of twenty states that specifically exempted clergy. Law promised future compliance, but Attorney
General Thomas F. Reilly and prosecutors in the five counties within
the archdiocese wanted the church to apply the law retroactively by
turning over records of all past allegations.

"When it comes to any evidence, they should report any priest or
member of the church. Let prosecutors make decisions on whether
they are actionable," Reilly told reporters. "Given what's happened
here, the church should err on the side of complete disclosure on the

issue of the abuse of children. There shouldn't be a free pass on anything when it comes to the sexual abuse of children."

Reached by reporters for comment, Donna Morrissey said it wouldn't
be possible to comply with Reilly's request.

Muller's stomach had remained as queasy as on that first day. Recently he asked a friend at church how he was feeling about it, forget-
ting for a moment that the man's son was a priest. "Jim, it's a horror,"
came the reply. Muller thought no other word existed to describe it. He
saw it on everybody's face at St. John's, among the wealthiest of
Boston's 362 parishes.

"I'm so discouraged," he confided in Kathleen. He was not sure how
he could just ignore it.

"Jim," Kathleen said, "we're Sunday Catholics. This isn't your job.
Stay out of it."

He remembered the first time he had received communion at St.
John's, as a young idealistic father. Back then, St. John's bristled with
kids and teenagers and young couples. The youth ministry was active.
It was not unusual to see over a thousand attend a Mass, even on non-
holidays. Now his own children, who had left home for college and independent lives, would attend Mass only if their father had them in a
paternal half nelson. At fifty-nine, Muller was still among the youngest
parishioners at St. John's.

The problem was, he thought, the Catholic Church was out of step
with young people's lives. They looked at church uncompromisingly.
For some time now, Jim Muller had felt that by practicing cafeteria
Catholicism—picking and choosing among the doctrines for the things
that made sense to him, and disregarding the rest—he was guilty of a
sort of lazy hypocrisy. His children rejected this as inauthentic, which
he knew it was. He and Kathleen both had made their compromises in
small, almost imperceptible stages. They continued using birth control
even after *Humanae Vitae* was handed down. They objected to the very
notion that a church hierarchy might attempt to govern such personal
matters as sexual love. But they kept their objections to themselves. As
a result, they confessed fewer and fewer things, less and less often, creating more and more psychic space between themselves and their
church.

In significant other ways Jim was nonetheless a church conservative, or at least a church nostalgic. He craved some of the fabulous aspects of the Mass that were done away with in the name of modernization. In his youth, Gregorian chant epitomized a church of miracles. He missed the Latin liturgy, its muffled mystery and transcendental force. He understood why these things were changed, and he even applauded the effort to make Catholicism accessible and significant in ordinary people's lives. But he felt as though the church had opened up the wrong things to the parishioners. They craved decency and democracy, and respect for their life decisions in a modern world—they craved a catechism of the here and the now; the church gave them tinny language instead.

Once he told his pastor, Father Tom Powers, that he feared for the future of a church rejected by his own offspring. "It made no sense to me," he said, "because they're extremely spiritual people. I asked my daughter, 'Where did your spirituality come from? Pop culture? Madonna?' And you know what she told me? *Star Wars.* *'May the force be with you.'* " He lifted his hand as if to joust. He laughed. He found something wonderful, and desolate, about the explanation.

"We have lost the next generation," Powers agreed. "We have pushed them away."

Muller knew it was true, and it disturbed him. It was the prophet Jeremiah who said, "Shame on the shepherds who let the sheep of my flock scatter and be lost."

He had asked Powers, "What's lost if you lose institutional religion?"

"Community," the priest answered.

At the time, Jim Muller shrugged. But since learning about Geoghan, he no longer felt he had the luxury of passivity. This was a Catholic Watergate. How could he not do something to harness his disgust?

"Maybe I could start small, like I did in the peace movement in sixty-seven. Start up a discussion group and write a 'My Turn' column for *Newsweek.* It's hard to be a Catholic and *not* try to change the church."

Kathleen knew what this meant. Remembering how the peace movement had disrupted their lives, she was not prepared to lend him out now, just as she was setting up her own office and psychotherapy practice. Jim had promised to help establish her billing systems. Meanwhile, their daughter was marrying in October.

"We don't need that," she said.

"I am afraid of a movement just as much as you are," he said, "and I'm certainly afraid of trying to lead a movement."

"It destroyed our family," she said.

He knew she thought this. "Yes," he said, "I know."

Tuesday, January 15, 2002
Boston, Massachusetts — The ten thousand pages of Geoghan records the church had protected for years were scheduled to be made public on January 23. On behalf of the archdiocese, the Rogers law firm appeared before Judge Constance Sweeney during a status conference and petitioned for a two-week delay. The lawyers had not had time to review each document to see what data were still protected by confidentiality agreements, Wilson Rogers III explained.

Rogers persisted in his entreaties, but Sweeney cut him off. "I am not going to engage in discussion with you. The order is my order. The order was issued in November. It is nearing the end of January. . . . I expect my order to be complied with," she said.

Walter Robinson, sitting in the courtroom, was stunned at Sweeney's steely demeanor. It was then that he and Ben Bradlee Jr., his editor, knew they were going to get to see those files.

Tuesday, January 22, 2002
Boston, Massachusetts — Because the *Boston Globe* had sued to gain access to the documents, it got copies the night before they were made public—they arrived in six heavy cartons at around 8 P.M. The Spotlight Team was still at work, and would stay and pore through the documents till well after midnight for two nights in a row. It was more than they had dreamed of. Medical reports, endless complaints, internal doubts, scrupulous debates on what to do with Geoghan, outpourings of concern for Geoghan, praiseful assignment letters sending him to

this church or that. But the most stunning aspect of this chronicle of a sad life wasn't what was in the files, but what wasn't. In all ten thousand pages, rich with concern for healing Geoghan, there was no acknowledgment of Geoghan's many, many victims, no gesture of concern for their well-being.

January 23, 2002
BOSTON, MASSACHUSETTS — Priests spun through the glass doors of the Boston Park Plaza Hotel in somber clusters, their heads down. Most were in civilian clothing. One priest, wearing clerical garb, snapped off his collar when he realized a camera crew was filming him, plainly ashamed. It was as though three weeks of revelatory bad press had turned the clock back two hundred years, and Roman Catholic priests in Boston were gathering clandestinely again.

Demands for Law's resignation were mounting, no longer just among radio shock jocks. Half of Boston's Catholics held him personally responsible, and thought he should go. Two *Wall Street Journal* columnists saw no other solution. Even some of the cardinal's staunchest defenders had wavered on his tenure. Ray Flynn, the former Boston mayor and onetime Vatican ambassador, now was a lone voice defending Law, slamming the *Boston Globe* for "blaming him for the despicable behavior of a sick former priest."

The cardinal had called this meeting to assure his priests that he was not going away. This scandal gave him the opportunity to lead the rest of society into a deeper understanding of the vulnerable child, he planned to tell them. "I want the Archdiocese to become a model for how this issue should be handled," he had written in his prepared remarks. "I have a responsibility as your archbishop to help that happen, and I want you to know that with every fiber of my being I am going to try and see that that happens."

Law's limo pulled up to the hotel after most priests had pushed inside. Owing to the darkly tinted windows, he could not be identified until he swung open the back door and unfolded his large frame from the backseat. The only man standing there ready to greet him was Steve Lynch from Danvers. He stood all alone, in the blustery cold, the sole protester. As usual, his eyes were stretched and dyed with his profound pain.

Law closed his door and moved away from his car but did not look Lynch in the eye. He walked around him nervously. He did not say a word but instead scrambled for the safety of the hotel lobby.

Lynch called after him. "I want the truth, Bernard Law."

January 28, 2002

BRIGHTON, MASSACHUSETTS — It wasn't until after Law knew the *Globe* was sniffing around that he began cleaning house. Father Jay Mullin, who had settled a suit for $60,000 and had twice been sent to treatment facilities, was removed from a job at a Catholic nursing home on December 1, 2001. And Law told Father Ronald Paquin, a man who admitted frequently molesting boys in the seventies and eighties and was unassigned to a parish, that he was no longer to receive payroll checks and his health insurance would lapse in a year's time. The morning's *Globe* carried a bulleted list of twenty-four names of area priests implicated in abuse; based on reviews of pending lawsuits, settled suits, criminal charges, and church sources, each man stood accused as a child molester. Their alleged victims were almost all teenage altar boys, of all the kids in church the ones with the most profound faith. Between the twenty-four priests there were perhaps 150 victims, maybe more. Many claims were settled by the church before ever becoming lawsuits, and officials would reveal nothing about the terms or conditions, or even a global figure for how much money was spent, or whether it came from the weekly collection plates—a point of great concern to area Catholics.

Nor would the archdiocese reveal what had become of these men. From public records the reporters learned that one priest was dead. Two had been arrested in recent weeks: a Gloucester priest, Father Frederick L. Guthrie of St. Ann's, and Father Kelvin Iguabita of All Saints Church in Haverhill, were both buckled into Flex-Cufs and carted off to jail. But the rest? Had they continued serving? Had they even been disciplined? What about the rest of Boston's priests?

January 31, 2002
Boston, Massachusetts — The Spotlight Team published five articles
on this date, bringing to sixty-five the number of stories about abusive
priests and corporate cover-up since the series began three weeks earlier. They knew this was only the beginning. Their database was now
complete. Stretching back forty years, it showed that 102 priests had
been abruptly removed from an assignment and put into one of the tell-
tale categories of suspension that suggested sexual impropriety. A thousand telephone calls from ordinary Boston Catholics since January 6
had provided confirmation for the reporters' suspicions. For almost
every suspect, they now matched wrenching stories of sexual misconduct.

By conservative estimate, the paper reported, over the past decade
legal claims were settled against seventy Boston-area priests, "under an
extraordinary cloak of secrecy." Eric MacLeish's firm alone had handled
suits against forty-five priests and five members of religious orders. The
cost, which the church would not reveal, was undoubtedly enormous,
but nobody would ever know. This fact angered Catholics almost as
much as the abuse itself—all these years, their charitable donations
had been used not for supporting the missions of the church, but for
covering up the rampant misdeeds of the clergy. Under constitutional
protections, religious institutions were not required to follow any accounting or disclosure standards, and most dioceses around the country gave only a broad picture of their financial standing. In Boston, it
was possible for tens of millions of dollars to feed the lawsuits without
ever showing up on a public report.

State and county prosecutors were less interested in the source of
funds than in the possibility that criminal charges might be brought
against individual perpetrators or the church itself for negligence. The
attorney general asked the church to open its records for inspection.
Throughout the month of January the cardinal, through his spokeswoman, refused repeatedly, but under withering public pressure—reportedly matched by the strong disapproval of members of the
archdiocese's lay-led Finance Council, made up of some of Boston's
most prominent and wealthy Catholics—he had buckled earlier in the

week. After 8:00 P.M. on January 30, lawyers for Law dropped off a tally with the attorney general, the five county district attorney offices that fall within the archdiocese, and a number of police departments. Law would not reveal publicly how many priests were part of his reports, but news accounts speculated it was thirty-eight, a fraction of the suspected number. However, he stressed emphatically that his list represented every allegation ever brought against a Boston priest—and reiterated his assertion that no priests accused of sexual abuse were currently in the church's employ.

Law enforcement officials were baffled by the contents of Law's reports, which dated back to the 1960s. "The information includes a rough description of the victims and their ages," David Procopio, a spokesman for the Suffolk County district attorney, complained. "The next step will be to see if the names of the victims will be provided to us." The chancery said it would not reveal additional information, because of confidentiality agreements with victims. In press reports, those victims said the only reason such agreements existed was that the church demanded them.

But the day's most striking story would also become one of the most enduring in the series. Written by Sacha Pfeiffer, it told a complex story of the laudable politics, heroic apostolates, serial violations, and voracious, dark sexual appetites of Paul Shanley.

> Boston's Catholics had never seen a priest quite like Paul Shanley.
>
> Handsome and charismatic, he wore his hair long, growing thick sideburns and shedding his Roman collar for plaid shirts and jeans. He openly questioned church teachings, particularly its condemnation of homosexuality, clashing often and publicly with his superiors, including then-Cardinal Humberto Medeiros. . . .
>
> But in the parishes and counseling rooms where desperate and troubled young people sought his help, the Rev. Paul R. Shanley was a sexual predator. In interviews with four people who said they were abused by Shanley, as well as their families and lawyers who have settled at least three sexual abuse claims against him

with the Archdiocese of Boston, the same stories repeatedly emerged: rape, molestation, and coerced sex in which Shanley used his power and authority to prey on those who came to him for guidance and support. . . .

Shanley's story is among the most insidious cases of clergy sex abuse found by the Spotlight Team. The number of his victims is unclear. But in four decades as a priest, he often worked exclusively with adolescents, and his much-publicized youth ministry attracted countless young people with its counterculture mission.

Saturday, February 2, 2002
BRIGHTON, MASSACHUSETTS — In a press release issued on Saturday morning, Donna Morrissey asserted that Law had not intended to mislead Boston Catholics or law enforcement officials, but the archdiocese now admitted that there were two active priests currently serving area churches about whom supervisors had received formal complaints. The men—Paul Finegan of St. Bernadette Church in Randolph, and Daniel M. Graham of St. Joseph Church in Quincy—were removed from their positions late on Friday.

Graham had enough time to rush a farewell statement into the parish bulletin, offering an alternative explanation for his hasty departure. He was taking medical leave to care for his diabetes and his elderly father, he offered. "I apologize for the abruptness of this change, but sometimes overwhelming needs must be dealt with immediately," he wrote. Morrissey made it clear that Graham, who in addition to his duties at St. Joseph was also a regional vicar charged with overseeing nineteen parishes south of Boston, had not told his parishioners the truth.

Sacha Pfeiffer wasn't surprised. "I've been lied to so many times by priests it's ridiculous," she said.

Morrissey offered no explanation for when church officials discovered the allegations, which dated back many years, or how it was that they had not been included in the reports to law enforcers. Five days later, she would craft another press release announcing six more removals of priests with long records of complaints. Four of those priests had been sued in the past, and the church had settled the cases out of court. Surely even a cursory glance of personnel files would have revealed this fact. But when reporters called for explanation, Morrissey let them ring off into voice mail, with no intention of calling them back. Her office was in chaos, as was much of the chancery. Ancient personnel files were turning up left and right, some in cardboard boxes in the basement, some across the street at the cardinal's residence. Meanwhile, every time she crafted a press release and sent it around for approval, it would touch off semantic debates over whether to say the old policies were "wrong" or a "mistake."

She grew impatient. "I'm getting bombarded with hundreds and hundreds of calls a day. My phones here, my cell phone, my home phone—they're all constantly jammed," she would complain bitterly. "I have to maintain a credibility out there. I need a good grasp of what's happening."

Nobody, it was clear, had any idea of the scope of the problem.

Sunday, February 3, 2002
ST. PATRICK CHURCH, LOWELL, MASSACHUSETTS — Dominic George Spagnolia was "throwing a nutty," as he would admit himself. He could not contain his rage about the abuse and cover-up. It distracted him through the Mass's opening procession and up to the collection. The gospel for the day was the Sermon on the Mount—"Blessed are the poor in spirit . . . blessed are the sorrowful . . . blessed are the meek"—which reached into his rage and made it into something he could not ignore. When it came time for his homily, he let it all loose, pacing furiously and red-faced up and down the aisle. Spags was a walker. He never preached from a pulpit. But nobody had ever seen him animated like this before, either. In a hail of anger, he marched from the narthex to the chancel, the transepts to the door, spewing invective against his deceptive, heartless church.

Reading the *Globe* stories every morning had thrown his mind back to Roxbury and his open warfare with arrogant leadership. After leaving Roxbury, and for the next twenty years, he and the Roman

Catholic Church had been perfect strangers. Except for an occasional christening or wedding, he never once attended Mass. For the first dozen years back in the lay state, he worked for the mother of a fellow seminarian who operated a string of suburban nursing homes and took him on as her personnel manager. He adored the work, especially when he was put in charge of opening the company's facility in Provincetown in the early eighties. It was during the town's renaissance as a center for culture and, especially, gay tourism. He loved the energy and excitement that defined gay men and women. Most of his staff had been gay. They knew he had been a priest, and that seemed not to bother them. One woman, his secretary, had even asked him to perform a commitment ceremony for her and her girlfriend, and after some soul-searching he had agreed, thinking simply, Why not? (He would not call it a marriage, though, thinking that would not be right.)

In 1985 he had gotten a chance to buy a rambling house in Yarmouthport, a Cape Cod town nearby, which he turned into a bed-and-breakfast, a dream come true. But as he realized almost from the start, the romantic notions he entertained had nothing to do with the reality of running an inn. The hours were punishing. Cooking chores began at dawn and ended when the last dish was washed after nine at night. In between: cleaning, shopping, serving, advertising, banking, answering phones. "It's not *Bob Newhart*," he complained. What was supposed to have been a time of great relaxation and personal enjoyment was in the end the least fulfilling thing he'd ever done. He was frequently seized by a wanderlust, a nostalgia for the real struggles of Roxbury, the war protests, the racial face-offs. He grieved for his lost life of meaning. In this way, Spagnolia was not unlike a lot of aging hippies who were settling down around him on the shore, dissatisfied, disaffected, dispirited. When the nineties dawned and the dot-com revolution gathered, he thought he had never been more unhappy.

There was no single trigger for deciding to go back to the church. He explained it this way: "The Lord just gave me a kick in the ass and told me to get back to what I was supposed to be doing." The kick was cruel. Despite his endless labors, his business was failing, and his efforts to bail out and sell it were fruitless. The bank took it all in fore-closure. Then doctors diagnosed him with cancer of the thyroid and throat—at the very time his mother back in Boston was getting extremely old and required his assistance. "Talk about friggin' Job," he thought.

In October 1991 he drafted a formal letter to Cardinal Law, whom he had never met, volunteering his services as a refurbished priest. The chancery had classified his resignation a "leave of absence," he reasoned, so why not return to work? "The shoe fit." After a brushup year in the seminary, he was soon assigned as associate pastor at St. Mary's, a comfortable parish in Franklin—not the sort of work he felt called to. But during his brief stay there, marked by the recurrence of his tumor, there came a mysterious intervention that would change his life. It happened during the Saturday evening Easter Vigil in 1994, during the Litany of the Saints. Spagnolia came around to the front of the altar and laid himself facedown on the floor, while the choir sang the invocations. His palms and cheek were pressed against the floor; his glasses were knocked askew on his big face.

> *All ye holy Virgins and Widows . . .*
> *All ye holy Saints of God,*
> > Make intercession for us.
> *Be merciful.*
> > Spare us, O Lord.
> *Be merciful.*
> > Graciously hear us, O Lord.
> From all evil, O Lord, deliver us!

When he climbed up off the floor he felt something strange, a transcendence, as if something had lifted his bulky frame upright. Being a dry-eyed Catholic, he did not give it any credence. But after the service, a woman in a wheelchair approached him. She had seen something during the prayer she thought he should know about. While Spags lay on the floor, Jesus appeared and told her that he had been healed, she said.

It was not within the realm of Spags's beliefs for Jesus to carry messages in such dramatic ways. However, the woman had no reason to know of his illness. Because it couldn't hurt, he submitted to an ultrasound and needle biopsy the Tuesday after Easter, and learned the impossible, that he was tumor-free. Alleluias spilled out his mouth. "I don't know what the hell is going on," he said, "but the power of God and the hand of God has been in every aspect of my life. There's got to be a reason."

The reason became clear when the delegate from the chancery offered him the pastor's job at St. Patrick's Church in Lowell, beginning in 1999. St. Patrick's stood in the center of Lowell's historic section known as the Acre, as beautiful and mysterious a colossus as the church Montgomery Clift served in Hitchcock's *I Confess,* and one of the poorest parishes in the archdiocese. Since the 1970s, it had increasingly become home to Vietnamese immigrants drawn here by the lure of high-tech industries. But the jobs vanished when Wang Laboratories collapsed into bankruptcy in 1992, pitching Lowell into some of its most difficult years.

The years had treated St. Patrick's with uncommon hostility. Spags's first thought as he approached its sidewalks was about the trash. It lay up against the crumbling entry steps and tangled in the roots of half-dead shrubs. The sign out front was broken. Behind the church, the 130-year-old cemetery, with historic shamrock monuments, sat in near ruin. Inside was not much better. The main nave had long been shuttered in favor of a smaller chapel. A persistent water leak had destroyed the grand plaster ceiling over the altar, and warped the hand-hewn trim. Debris and the smell of mold filled the room.

He still thought it was the most beautiful church he had ever seen. St. Patrick's gave him an opportunity to return to his roots as "a radical Christian," by which he meant a "back-to-the-gospel" priest. In his first official move, Spags increased the parish's food-voucher program and redoubled its ministry to the poor and the Asian community. But what made him a local savior—not just among St. Patrick's parishioners but for the entire tight-knit town—was his pledge to rescue the crumbling structure from decay. Spags reopened the church's doors and asked his small parish to meet there, instead of in the basement chapel. "Thank you for letting me come home," one parishioner wrote him in a letter. "To me that was worth whatever expense."

St. Patrick's was a beggar parish—rather than sending yearly offerings to the chancery in Brighton, for most of the past thirty years St. Patrick's had required a reverse flow of capital. In 1999, the year Spags arrived, the subsidy was substantial, though not enough to meet the basic infrastructural needs of the church, much less provide services to its many neighbors in need. So when Spags announced his intention to renovate and restore the old building, he encountered deep skepticism. But his leadership prevailed. By 2000, he had raised $230,000 from parishioners and the greater Lowell community. By the close of 2001, the fund had $750,000. Parishioners like thirty-six-year-old Thu Vu were almost disbelieving. "This is totally due to Father Spags," he knew. "He is the one that has encouraged us to make our church and our own lives better."

Down in Brighton, church leaders were astounded. One asked Spags if he'd consider heading up the development office for the whole archdiocese, but he declined with a crooked laugh. Then the administrator asked him if he'd be sharing any of the fund with the chancery this year. "Screw you," he said. "Not until we're done."

Then the scandal broke.

Spags had known John Geoghan in passing. He was in the class behind him at St. John's. When the news first spread about his predilections, Spags remembered clearly the images of him marching through the seminary grounds pumping out a wave and a soprano hello to all he passed, and he thought, "Oh God, one never knows what evil lurks in the hearts of men." He had never heard any rumors about Geoghan. All these years they'd traveled in different circles. Spags remembered bumping into Geoghan only once, at some official archdiocesan function. He had no reason to believe the man was innocent. The graphic news accounts had convinced him otherwise. How on earth could the church have let it go on like this?

Shanley was another story. On the rare occasions that Shanley felt he needed some time away from his ministry, he would show up at Spags's rectory in Roxbury to flop on the sofa. No priest was considered more pastorally committed, more Christlike, than Paul Shanley. But there was also a whisper of doubt about him, the way undercover officers, the especially successful ones, lived under a shroud of suspicion back at the station house. Shanley had gone "under." For years he had operated without church or rectory, sleeping through the day and stalking the Combat Zone nearly every night. What were the chances he had stayed celibate?

But Spags never expected such a litany of allegations. After reading the *Globe* account, Spags called up another priest from the Association of Urban Priests, to say, "Can you believe this?" to somebody whose incredulity would be, like his, imperfect. The old friend reminded him that when Cardinal Medeiros had removed Shanley from ministry, the association was convinced it was because of his radical beliefs, and that they might be next. "Remember how we all went down to complain to the cardinal? All the while Medeiros had all the information about why, and he never shared it," he said.

The secrets were so old and integral, so permanent, Spags thought, that they weren't just a stain on the fabric of the church; in fact they were the very fabric itself.

When he hung up the telephone, Spags began a fast, praying that Pope Innocent XI was right when he said that the evil spirit "fears us more when he knows we are prepared to fast."

Halfway up the aisle, Spags stood among his parishioners, like them deceived. It was Candlemas, celebrating the first day that Christ, then just forty days old, entered into the house of God aglow in the arms of his purified mother. In a distant corner at St. Patrick's, "Ave Maria" was sung and hundreds of candles proclaimed the light of the world. Spags was preaching against the darkness. He felt confused and betrayed by Cardinal Law, whose duplicity and obfuscation were so baldly apparent. How sad he was to serve a church whose pastors abuse children, not once or twice but hundreds of times. Predators in holy vestments; wolves, not shepherds. This was not a cardinal that could be trusted.

"This was a Nixon!" he said, when the music had drifted off.

"This was a cover-up!"

In other parishes such criticism would have sent parishioners into spirals of shame. But Spags's parish was familiar with his rants. He never called Law "Eminence." To him, he was flatly "Boss." Eileen Donoghue, Lowell's former mayor and a lifelong St. Patrick's member, chuckled every time she heard this. But she frequently warned him about the risks he was courting. He didn't care. "I've never cared for the cardinals," he said, "not when I was young and it mattered to my career, and certainly not now that I'm sixty."

He preached against the staggering settlements, the gag orders, the lawyers, and the spin doctors, paid for with *your* money. He told his church for the first time that he had been refusing to participate in any of Law's spring fund-raising appeals. For the Promises for Tomorrow capital campaign alone, St. Patrick's was expected to contribute $145,000. Three times the cardinal had sent representatives to Lowell in order to strongly encourage a change of heart, but he had held fast, he said.

"How much would eventually go to whitewash the rapes of children? How much in salary to the defilers? How much to shut up the victims?"

He was especially incredulous about Law's comments saying his decisions on Geoghan and the others were based on the appropriate thinking of the time. "Granted, we were all a bit naïve back then," Spags fulminated. "If somebody were to ask me what pedophilia was back then, I would have said a foot disease." But he had never heard the allegations. "I didn't have this mother's letter about her seven sons."

"Your mouth, Spags!" Sister Joanne Sullivan, the principal of St. Patrick's School, thought as the pastor railed. "Your mouth is going to get you in trouble."

He did not shy away from details. Did you read in the papers, he asked, how Geoghan had transferred his personal property out of his name, to protect it from civil judgment? What could the beach house be worth? How much therapy could that buy for the victims? This man had prayed to the Lord with these small children at the very moment he was abusing them! Pure depravity!

Red in the face, puffy with anger, Spags tore into a scripture passage of his own choosing, from Matthew: "At the same time came the disciples unto Jesus, saying, 'Who is the greatest in the kingdom of heaven?' And Jesus called a little child unto him and set him in the midst of them, and said, 'Verily I say unto you, except ye be converted, and become as little children, ye shall not enter into the kingdom of heaven.'"

He strode to the front of the church, turned, and faced the pews, which were unusually full and quiet. Some congregants were openly crying. He continued, speaking the gospel from memory, knotting his fists tightly at his sides.

"'Whoever therefore shall humble himself as this little child, the same is greatest in the kingdom of heaven. And whoso shall receive one such little child in my name receiveth me. But whoso shall offend one of these little ones which believe in me, it were better for him that a millstone were hanged around his neck, and that he were drowned in the depth of the sea.'"

He let that message spark and snap in the air.

WELLESLEY, MASSACHUSETTS — Kathleen Muller returned from celebrating her mother's ninetieth birthday in Indiana, where she was disappointed to find that people were not transfixed with the sexual abuse crisis back in Boston. Perhaps, she thought, the crisis wasn't as bad as it seemed at the epicenter. Maybe she and Jim had blown the problem out of proportion. But when she picked up the morning's *Globe,* that thought vanished from her mind. The main story was about the Fulchino family from St. Julia's, in Weston—Tom, the dad, who had been abused by the notorious Father James Porter in 1960, and his son Chris, one of the last young boys to be preyed upon by Geoghan, who shouted out this warning as the boy fled: "No one will ever believe you." The story brought her to tears.

Kathleen Muller was unable to accept the thought of a church-loving family being put through so much pain. "Jim, this is the final straw, it broke my heart. I can't go to church today," she said. "I'm just so sad! I can't go to a church that has some people running it responsible for that, who allowed that to happen." Her fear was that Father Tom Powers, their pastor, would say something to minimize the news, or worse, ignore it altogether. The thought of sitting in a pew surrounded by this silence filled her with a nauseated shame.

"You have to do something."

Jim knew his wife would come around. "Should I talk to Father Tom about a community meeting?

"I think Father Tom would actually encourage having parishioners talk; he wouldn't feel angered by that. It would give him the support and courage *he* needs, because I'm sure he's as deeply hurt by the whole thing as we are."

Father Powers wanted to say yes to Jim Muller, but knowing the political firestorm that was likely to erupt if the chancery found out, the pastor first polled his staff at St. John's. Several days passed before he telephoned Muller at his small Mass General office with the verdict. Until he heard Powers's voice on the line, Muller hadn't realized how huge he felt the stakes were. If Powers, whom he admired greatly, were to nix the idea, he was not convinced he could ever go back to Mass.

"Great idea," Powers said. He told Muller he would not direct the proceedings. It was to be lay led. This sort of open-mike event might have been commonplace in the houses of worship for other religions, but Muller knew it was nearly unheard of inside a Catholic church.

February 8, 2002
BRIGHTON, MASSACHUSETTS — Without comment, the archdiocese reported another forty-nine names of abusive priests to the civil authorities. Again, the authorities complained that a list of suspects' names stripped of any other information—no names of the alleged victims, no details of the alleged assaults—made it impossible for them to determine if a crime had been committed, and if so, against whom.

Monday, February 11, 2002
BASEMENT OF ST. JOHN'S IN WELLESLEY, MASSACHUSETTS — Of the twenty-five parishioners who arrived for the first community meeting Muller organized, he knew only a few by name. One of them was Mary Scanlon Calcaterra, a fiery presence, who had bought the Mullers' old house from them and become a close family friend.

Around the circle of chairs, a sad and angry energy buzzed. One of the first men who rose to speak decried the events with unique eloquence, comparing the sex scandal with everything from Watergate to Iran-Contra to Enron. "I believe Justice Brandeis was right when he said, 'Sunlight is the best disinfectant,' " he said to applause. "We need sunlight here. This is our archbishop. One of the churches where Geoghan served is in the next parish over! You know, in the history of the church, saints were people who lived in difficult, challenging times. We forget, but a lot of them were martyrs. Maybe this is the time when people like us have to stand up and take whatever comes."

This was Jim Post, a professor at Boston University with a law degree and a Ph.D. in management, and the chief academic theoretician of the famed Nestlé boycott of the seventies and eighties. Muller did not know this. "We are always telling young people to stand up in a situation where the outcome matters to them," Post concluded. "Well, here I am. This matters."

Then Peggy Thorp, a mother of three, spoke, followed by Svea Fraser, a chaplain associate at Wellesley College and one of only two women to earn master of divinity degrees from Blessed John XXIII National Seminary. She knew the significance of this event. A conversation among Catholics on matters of the church? It was literally unheard of. She recalled Jesus' biblical designation of Peter as the rock on which the church would be built. "We are the living stones that make up the church," she said. "The church is not just the leaders."

Hearing this put some of the members on edge. One person expressed concern about joining a splinter group. "Is this a St. John's group, or isn't it?"

"We'd better remain a little separate because we might do some things, or say some things, that Father Powers wouldn't do," Muller offered. He looked at Powers, who sat in a chair in the circle. "Which raises a point," Muller continued, "about whether we shouldn't meet on church property at all."

Powers did not hesitate. "You *are* the church," he said. "*You* are the church."

Chapter 10

The Unburdening

Early February 2002

NEWTON, MASSACHUSETTS — Paula Ford's heart stopped when she saw the picture of Paul Shanley in the *Globe*. Before his retirement, Shanley was her family's pastor at St. Jean's in Newton, a church her grandparents had helped build. She had liked Shanley, though she knew others who didn't. She recalled Jackie Gauvreau's epic campaigns to discredit him—like almost everyone else, she thought Gauvreau was a kook. But there he was now, accused of atrocities. Maybe she had been right.

Maybe this would explain it.

Her son Greg was the family's heartbreaking mystery. Just twenty-four years old, he had been hospitalized seventeen times for depression, liquor and drug abuse, and suicide attempts. He burned himself with cigarettes. He had a pathological temper and a penchant for setting fires. Medication and intensive therapy would lift him up slightly, but never enough. Almost nonstop from the time he was sixteen to nineteen, Greg had been in residence at state psychiatric facilities. Doctors diagnosed a personality disorder. There was no history of mental illness in either parent's family. It was perhaps the worst thing a parent would be forced to accept, a disabled child, a child who was so pathologically unhappy.

Psychiatrists were equally frustrated. Years ago, Greg had told a doctor that he had been molested by several older boys, including a cousin. This was a tantalizing clue. But it was given little credence because Greg soon edited the story to say that he meant they'd played strip poker with him, nothing more. A number of years after that, he once again claimed a rape history, but this time he was more vague about the identity of his assailants. Frequently, he also said that nothing untoward happened whatsoever.

Childhood rape could have been an external cause of Greg's functional deficits and disturbances. His manifest mental illness was consistent with severe neurosis following such a history. The French Canadian researcher Michel Dorais, in his book *Don't Tell: The Sexual Abuse of Boys,* described these symptoms as often including violence toward oneself and others, a distrust, or a feeling of being unloved or unable to love. Victims "have hardly any markers to guide their way on an emotional level and have no references to gauge their feelings or those of others," he wrote. "Their emotional disarray is enormous." Several studies seemed to suggest that these were the result of permanent neurological changes in the minds of abuse victims. Using an anatomical MRI brain scan, University of Pittsburgh researcher Michael De Bellis examined nineteen males and twenty-five females, whose mean age upon first abuse was 4.5 years (and whose abuse lasted on average 2.8 years). Most suffered from post-traumatic stress and all showed abnormal brain development, including smaller intercranial volumes overall and specific structural anomalies associated with major depression, anger management problems, anxiety, and difficulty managing interpersonal relationships. For boys, the brain changes were more acute than for girls, he found—leading De Bellis to hypothesize that boys experience more stress from such maltreatment than girls.

It went without saying that any number of factors could have contributed to Greg Ford's total lack of joy. Sexual trauma was but one possible explanation. Given a total absence of evidence, any other explanation was equally plausible.

Nevertheless, his therapists pursued the abuse theory relentlessly, but it produced no results. Greg's stories were shifting and unreliable, always vague, and sometimes punitive. A number of years ago, when

Paula's husband, Rodney, was restraining their son during an outburst of exceptional violence so wild the police were called and he was sent again to a psychiatric facility, Greg was ranting, "How would *you* feel if you were fucking raped?" His protestations were so loud the neighbors heard every word. In a later incident, he told his mother about a dream in which a man was molesting him but when he turned to see who the man was, he woke up.

At one point, one of his treatment clinicians even suspected the boy had been sexually abused at home by a family member. He penned his suspicions into Greg's patient chart: "Abuse at home?"

Whatever the origin of these traumas, Greg Ford was not improving. It would be natural for parents to have trouble accepting that. Standing in the kitchen of their home one evening, they handed a copy of the *Globe* exposé to their son. They wanted to know if Paul Shanley had assaulted him.

He looked at the article and studied the picture of Shanley, who had been his CCD teacher. He didn't read all of the text.

"Do you know who this is?" Greg's father, Rodney, asked.

Greg shook his head. "No," he said.

Rodney left Paula and Greg in the kitchen and rummaged through a trove of old photographs. He returned with a snapshot of Greg on his First Communion day. He was a tiny boy in a small blue suit, with his mouth cranked open like a small bird's. Paul Shanley stood over him with the consecrated host pinched between his fingers.

"Greg, who's that man there?" Rodney asked.

Nothing.

"Who is that little boy right there, Greg?"

Greg put down the photograph and stood up, then collapsed to the floor in tears. His brain was flooded with images. Religious education classes. Card games with the pastor. Bits of conversation. A sensation of being ripped wide open. Terror.

"It started when I was six," he remembered. "He'd say, 'If you ever tell anyone, they won't believe you.' He said something would happen to my parents!"

In horror and rage, the Fords began calling the parents of other troubled young men from Newton. It was Paul Shanley who had raped their son.

When news got around, many people—very few of them in the media—regarded the Ford boy's allegation with skepticism. For one thing,
Shanley did not have a history of interest in small children. In Shanley's
past was strong evidence that he violated celibacy and abused his
power with vulnerable youths, some below the legal age of consent. But
all had passed the threshold of puberty. He had been a kind of self-
styled sexual liberator, initiating young men in their teens and early
twenties in the realm of sexual hedonism, often to messy results. But
they were all *men,* that is, physically and hormonally masculine, not the
formless cherubs of a pedophile's lust life. Now young children? So late
in his life? Pedophiles first struck before age twenty, on average. If the
Ford charge were true, it meant that when Shanley hit his late fifties,
he moved his sexual crosshairs to prepubescent children.

There was the additional problem of Greg Ford's late recollection of
the abuse. In interviews with police and attorneys, he said the memory
presented itself only the moment he saw the communion photograph.
Before then, he said, he had no specific recall. Shanley's abuse had
been filed away so deeply that all those intervening years of therapeutic examination and parental prodding failed to reach it even when it
was put to him directly, over and over: *Were you abused? Who abused
you?*

His memory, Greg said, was repressed, and only now recovered.

Recovered memories were the subject of great suspicion and debate
going back to Sigmund Freud, who first postulated the dynamic a hundred years ago. He theorized that all cognition involved a degree of repression, described as the avoidance of frightening or uncomfortable
wishes, fantasies, emotions, or memories. Surmising that nothing was
more debilitating than childhood sexual assault, he postulated that the
history of such crimes was often obliterated in one's mind. He supposed this accounted for the sticky adult neurosis cases he saw in his
practice among well-to-do housewives, and diagnosed his patients as
sexual abuse victims.

Later, he repudiated his own theory. What he once called repressed
memories of sexual assaults were actually fantasies stemming from patients' own taboo desires, he concluded. This became the foundation
for his revolutionary psychoanalytic theories of infantile sexuality. But

the debate he started was never resolved. One landmark study from 1994, which involved women seventeen years after they were treated for known childhood sexual assault, found evidence that Freud was right the first time. The women had agreed to join the study without knowing why they were selected. Each was asked if she had been sexually abused as a child, and 38 percent—mostly women who were assaulted by a family member at a young age—said no. "Long periods with no memory of abuse should not be regarded as evidence that the abuse did not occur," the lead researcher wrote. Advocates as diverse as the National Organization for Women, members of the Christian right, and New Age believers embraced the view, which won endorsement by Hollywood celebrities and daytime television talk show hosts. Many social workers found it a plausible diagnosis. Trial attorneys especially jumped on the recovered-memory bandwagon, establishing its validity in courts across the country.

But psychiatrists, for their part, remained extremely wary. The American Psychiatric Association has said that a true "recovered memory" was extremely rare, if it existed at all, and manufactured, or "false," memories—the practice of adopting a vivid scenario so completely that it seems in all regards like a memory—were much more common. When listing "disassociative amnesia" in its *Diagnostic and Statistical Manual,* the APA stressed that for such a recovered memory to be reliable it must be matched with corroborative evidence. Sometimes, researchers posited, patients might accept as memory an untruth in order to gain some advantage, or because it plausibly explained some part of their history that had troubled them. Often, research suggested, the heartfelt interventions of a well-meaning therapist—or parent—"implanted" the false memory.

A principal body of data validating this thinking came from a 1994 study by two University of Washington researchers, Elizabeth Loftus and Jacqueline Pickrell. A small group of children and young adults was asked to provide detailed information on their early childhood experiences, based on a list of questions the researchers compiled after interviewing the subjects' siblings. Three of the items derived from their actual personal histories; the fourth involved a false scenario about a time they got lost at a mall at age five. By the end of the experiment, 25 percent had adopted the false event as part of their histories. In a similar study the following year, 18 percent of a sample group of college students were convinced either that they had spilled punch on guests at a wedding or were forced to evacuate a supermarket after the sprinkler system was triggered—false scenarios fed to them by researchers. Interestingly, they did not immediately adopt the false memories on first questioning and came to accept them as history only on second interview.

More recently, academics and clinical researchers had been staking out a middle ground. If the selective amnesia of trauma is a rare phenomenon, they wondered, perhaps there is a partial version. Perhaps some memory is "delayed," some "discontinuous." Experts agreed there was a "process" of memory, that the ability of a mind to vividly recollect an event ebbed and flowed. In one survey of undergraduate students, 18 percent of those reporting childhood sexual abuse said they had a period in which they lacked some memories of the abuse. Rather than experiencing amnesia, however, they seemed to be reporting periodic or selective lapses in recall. This might help explain the way Patrick McSorley's memory of fondling came to the fore only when he saw Geoghan's face on television, or how David Clohessy's mind was carried back to Father Whiteley when Barbra Streisand's character disclosed her experiences with incest. Their memories were apparently intact, but without a context they had faded, the way most memories do. Faded, but not vanished. Trauma is a hard thing to remember in crystalline detail, but it is even harder to forget altogether.

None of this necessarily bolstered the veracity of Greg Ford's claim, because the relevance of possible abuse had been stressed in his case so often. But other elements of his troubled life seemed to fall into a constellation around this "last piece of the puzzle," as his father, Rodney Ford, called the Shanley charge. It was at about the time he was six that Greg Ford's sunny childhood came mysteriously to an end. That year his parents were summoned to catechism class after he had "sat on a pencil." At least that's what they were told. Concerned, Paula had taken him to the hospital for treatment. How ridiculous she felt now. How could she have missed the warning signs—a pencil in the *rectum*?

Greg's memories came back in scraps. He was convinced the rapes lasted five years, until he was eleven. How much suffering might have been saved if only she had caught on! The Fords called MacLeish, whose name was prominently featured in the *Globe* story.

It didn't stop there. Paul Busa, who was a St. Jean's classmate of Greg Ford's and now worked as a military police officer at Peterson Air Force Base in Colorado, also recovered a terrible memory about Paul Shanley. They came after his girlfriend got wind of Greg Ford's charges and told him about them. At first, he thought it couldn't be true. But he began to have inexplicable physical sensations, like crying jags and panic attacks, which were so debilitating that for several days he called in sick for work. Feeling suicidal, he checked himself into Cedar Springs psychiatric hospital. Then came a narrative—Shanley calling him out of CCD classes, walking him to the rectory, or the bathroom, or the confessional, and penetrating him on a regular basis between 1983 and 1990, from age six to thirteen.

Even he didn't believe the memories at first. But the images came in clearer over time. "I thought, was I making this up? The way my body was reacting . . . I knew it had happened."

Busa called MacLeish, who sent him an airline ticket and signed him up as a client upon his return to Boston. He told MacLeish that he must have "started to repress memories of the abuse almost immediately from the time it began."

February 11, 2002
BOSTON, MASSACHUSETTS — John J. Geoghan shuffled into room 12 of Suffolk County Superior Court on a warm winter morning. He had not slept well the night before, perhaps he had not rested at all. His mind seemed utterly slack and childlike, but his face showed every day of his sixty-six years. After settling in a chair next to his lawyer, he raised a tremulous hand to shake a visitor's, then laughed elfinly upon remembering about the handcuffs that bound together his wrists. "Oh!" he said, "how silly!" He regarded his appendages with delight before letting them sink forlornly back into his lap. His voice grew disconsolate and he said it again, this time without the surprise. "How silly."

His ankles were cuffed as well, one to the other, although it would take a wild imagination to fear that he might make an escape. During previous court appearances, he had been allowed to go unaccompanied to the bathroom. But spectators had complained. They demanded that he be treated like any other suspect. They felt Geoghan had already been given enough special privileges. Special privileges had caused this problem in the first place.

So he sat, clamped down in this way, on one side of the wooden barrister's rail bisecting the courtroom. The judge and all the lawyers had strolled away for a brief recess. Meanwhile, his elderly sister, Catherine, leaned in to speak to him. "It is terrible, oh, so complicated," she said. Her rheumy-eyed and crooked face hung above a string of oversized pearls. But her voice sang like a jingle on her broad Boston pronunciations. Tugging on the collar of her sweater, she too seemed inappropriately jolly, though Geoghan took obvious comfort in her melodiousness.

"When all of this is over, the truth will come out. When all of this is over, we will say what really happened," she beamed.

Geoghan's eyes brimmed with a sort of rapture. "Yes," he said to her. "Then the truth will be out."

A reporter approached the pair cautiously. "Do you feel bad?" he asked Geoghan. "The slightest bit of remorse?"

He smiled and wagged his head. "Name, rank, and serial number," he said with a laugh.

He glanced around the room behind him, which was filling with observers, almost all of them men, some in their twenties, some graying and bald. They had come to see the man who taught them about shame. Did Geoghan recognize Anthony Muzzi Jr.? Probably not. Tony was stout and sturdy, his body thick from his decades as a construction worker; he was no longer the quiet, obedient boy whom Geoghan doted on between his thirteenth and sixteenth years. Was the face of Patrick McSorley familiar? Pacing nervously at the door, McSorley still gave the impression of being very young, though he was twenty-seven. Father Geoghan saw Patrick's dark eyes and rigid features only once, for less than an hour, on a gorgeous July afternoon in 1986.

If the men in this room were familiar to the priest, he kept his recog-

nition a secret. He smiled. On his judgment day, he preferred to let his
sister do the talking. She made her opinion plain. "He never met these
men," she said through a bright smile. "He doesn't even know their
names."

John Geoghan was about to stand trial for slipping a hand into the
bathing suit of a ten-year-old boy to steal a brief squeeze of his rear end.
In the annals of sex abuse, this was quite nearly benign. But the boy,
whose name had never been revealed though he was twenty now, testified that feeling Geoghan's fingers crawl over his flesh was as awful a
shock as if they had been razors. "I swam to the other side of the pool
as quickly as I could get away," he testified. To those who doubted lasting harm could follow such simple liberties, the young man pointed to
a litany of his distrusts and disorders that had stayed with him in the
many years since. He had no doubt they were related.

Deliberating briefly, the jury found Geoghan guilty of indecent sexual assault on a minor. A judge would sentence him to nine to ten years,
the maximum.

Mid-February 2002
LOWELL, MASSACHUSETTS — Each time Olan Horne had the dream, he
recognized it for what it was; even in the soupy fog of the dream itself,
he knew it was the one about peril without escape, the one he'd been
having since he was eleven. Racing up a wide flight of stairs. Chased.
Through a field. Pursuers who gained on him. The smell of must, an
old wool carpet, a stagnant pond, his feet ankle-deep in stretchy paste.
He swung his fists again and again, but he could not unfurl his arms to
land a punch, his elbows locked at useless angles, his fists missing always by inches, doomed.

Since the *Globe* series began, Horne had been studying the papers
the way a long-traveled seaman scans for shore, hoping to find some
reference to Father Joseph Birmingham. So far dozens of names had
appeared in the *Globe,* not one of them belonging to the man who molested his teenage body and invaded his mind even thirty years later, as
a forty-three-year-old butcher and father of two. He was not a religious
man—he had long ago lost a belief in God. His only tie to the church
was his bitter memory of Birmingham.

Olan Horne got his best friend from school, Dave Lyko, on the telephone. In twenty-five years, they had never talked about their shared past at St. Michael's in Lowell, except in euphemisms, not even when they were out for an afternoon of recreation in the trawler, when it was just the two of them shouting in the wind. It was enough to make childish reference to Father *Burning-hand,* or Father Q, "top of his class at the *semen*-ary." Implications sealed their solidarity, and it was comforting.

"Man, isn't this wild?" Lyko was just as surprised by the growing scandal, and just as disappointed that Birmingham still remained unmasked.

"Should we call the fucking papers?"

"Oh man, Olan, that's up to you. I'm no up-front guy. I'll be behind you, though. We should do something. I mean, this fucking guy got everybody in Lowell."

"Grabbed your dick the way other people fucking shook hands hello."

"I bet you that if I went through my old school pictures one by one, every one of them would say, 'Yup, Birmingham jumped me.' "

Shit, Olan thought, that's just what we should do. A few days later, the two men hunched over the class portraits. They began with the eighth grade, 1973.

"This one's *definitely* a hit—they went skiing once."

"He was an altar boy, I bet he's one."

"This one, I remember, he came to me all freaked out, 'Father put his hand in my pants!' What were we there, eleven?"

"This one did. This one did. This one *definitely* did."

"Made you believe he was your friend, and then sooner or later you realize you're fucking *dating* the guy."

"Take a look at these Lowell kids. Tall, slender, sandy blonds who are all pretty good-looking kids, all athletic kids, all in good shape."

"Him. Him. Him. These guys are now the backbone of Lowell, the lawyers, firemen, cops, Boy Scout leaders, pharmacists. He got us all."

Caught up in the spirit of truth telling that had seemed to grip Catholic Boston, Olan Horne and Dave Lyko resolved to call each one, a task that would take over a month. Digging up old secrets was uncomfortable work. Some men hung up on them. Some cried. Some referred them to their own brothers, saying, "It must have happened to them too."

From their eighth-grade class alone, thirty said Birmingham had abused them.

"That blows my mind," Dave's wife, Sheryl, said. As a young girl in Lowell, she also knew Father B. She saw how he doted on the boys. She watched his car head to the beach filled with them, saw him inviting them for ski weekends or for tennis matches while the girls, pushed to the periphery of the church's drop-in center, were barely addressed. "It's amazing to me that there wasn't one group of boys he liked over another—he wanted every boy in this whole Christian Hill area and every boy in lower Centralville. He wanted all of them. My God, how does something like that go on and no adults know about this man?"

News of Horne's and Lyko's efforts raced through Lowell—it got to the point where people knew why they were calling before they even said a word. With the church scandal in the papers, the reaction from the larger community was not as uniformly supportive as Olan expected. One woman spit at him. "I knew Birmingham," she said. "This didn't happen." At the butcher shop one morning, a colleague called to him: "Olan, you must be good at these." Olan turned to see a pork tenderloin spilling phallically over the man's belt.

The entire staff was laughing wildly.

"Let me explain something to you," Olan said. "You're grabbing an eleven-year-old kid. You pull him to the floor. You grab him by the back of the head and you take your cock, and you stick it down his fucking throat. Got him by the back of the head doing it. Kid's fucking having a panic attack. And then this guy puts me on the floor with his knee in my back, you know, the guy's ejaculating all over my back, he's beating the shit out of me because I'm trying to get away, but I'm like, still, 'Fuck you!' That's a blow job? Hell no, that ain't a blow job. That's *rape*. You need me to fill you in on any other sexual points? You want to hear some more? You tough enough? Because I can go places you've *never* been."

When Olan had succeeded in contacting everybody on his list, he began seeking out the people those men had referred him to, who in turn referred him to others. Still more people came out of the woodwork. A local mailman stopped him one wintry morning and said, "Good for you, Olan, keep it up." Then he grabbed his shoulder, conspiratorially steering him into a private conversation.

"Let me be honest with you, he turned me upside down and jerked me off half a dozen times, that's all. I'm okay. Don't get me involved. But I think what you're doing is great."

"Whoa, wait a minute," Olan said. "Let me ask you a question. Say the coach, he jacks off your kid half a dozen times. You're *okay* with that?"

"Fuck you, Olan," the mailman said. "Don't make me get involved."

"Just asking you."

"Oh, fuck you."

When he was done, when Olan had talked to everybody he could find from the town of Lowell who knew Father Joseph Birmingham, he built a master list of the boys who said they were molested during Birmingham's seven-year hitch at St. Michael's.

There were 128 of them.

Sunday, February 17, 2002
LOWELL, MASSACHUSETTS — An icy rain fell all around Boston. Though he was feeling as sour as at any time since the crisis blew open, Spagnolia had much to celebrate today. Today was the annual Rite of Election, a diocese-wide ceremony welcoming into the family of Catholics all newcomers, be they adults who would soon receive baptism or converts from other Christian traditions who would soon be confirmed. Spags had twenty-two such candidates. After Mass, he and St. Patrick's director of religious education were planning to accompany them to the cathedral for the annual welcoming celebration.

The New Testament readings for the day were from Paul's letter to the Romans and chapter 4 of the gospel of Matthew. Spags considered them wholly irrelevant and skipped over them altogether. This week, he was concerned about the cardinal's apparent tactical shift. Blame the priesthood, he seemed to be saying, burn the priests, and save the church. By now Law had turned over to authorities the names of at least eighty-seven priests. Surely among that number were men subjected to false allegations, long ago dismissed, Spags said. And Boston's Catholics weren't buying it. Nearly half now believed Law, not the priesthood in general, was the problem; they demanded his resignation.

"For the love of God," Spagnolia preached, "this seeming aberration is just that, an aberration! This isn't about all priests! It is about a few bad priests, and the cardinals who were too ashamed to stop them!"

It was his third homily in a row on the subject, and he ended it, as he intended to, on this final note of disgust. He felt the pains of his dejected parishioners, saw them weep and pray for their church, and he worried not about their devotion, but about their emotional health. "Obviously we can see this is getting worse than anyone expected," he told them. "So many people are getting so depressed about this that I've wondered whether to mention it again. I have decided not to. This scandal will not cross my lips again."

Meanwhile, at Mass at the Cathedral of the Holy Cross, in downtown Boston, Law referred only briefly to the scandal during his homily, which centered on Lent, the part of the Christian calendar prior to Easter that focuses on sacrifice and self-denial. "We enter this Lent very conscious of the frayed trust among us, very conscious of the pain among us, very conscious of the feelings of betrayal," Law said. He acknowledged that for many parishioners, his handling of the unfolding scandal had proved a "source of alienation from their bishop."

That was an understatement. Outside the residence back in Brighton, more than a hundred victims and their supporters braved the frigid rain. Lori Lambert, a theology student, came because she was scared her church was imploding. Anne Barrett Doyle, a devout Catholic and not a victim, stood in the drenching cold because she could not read another story about abuse without doing something herself to stop it. Arthur Austin, Paul Shanley's accuser, was not a rally-type of man, but he came, too. So did Phil Saviano. The theme of the day was Law's resignation. "It seems like he's intent on ignoring all of this," twenty-four-year-old Asa Gallagher told the *Globe*. "But the pressure's definitely rising."

Seeing them all arrive, Steve Lynch—who had spent forty days at these ramparts utterly alone—choked back tears of gratitude. "I want to thank you for standing here," he told them. "I don't want to be alone anymore and I can't fight the church alone anymore."

"This is just the beginning," Doyle assured him. "I'm sure of that."

A few hours later, Spags sat with one of the largest delegations of Catholic converts represented at the cardinal's special Mass. Pastors all sat along the aisle at the end of their row of candidates. Finishing his service, Cardinal Law walked down among them and offered his congratulations, one by one, to his energetic priests and the new flock. He shook the hand of the priest sitting in front of Spags, but skipped a row and issued his felicitations to the priest behind him.

Spags was dumbfounded. "Now, *that's* a *snub!*" his religious director whispered in his ear. Spags supposed the cardinal had read about his diatribes, which were reported in the *Lowell Sun*.

Tuesday, February 19, 2002
LOWELL, MASSACHUSETTS — A day after the Presidents Day holiday, all priests in the Merrimack Valley region of the Boston archdiocese were called to St. Theresa's Church near Lowell, part of Law's ongoing campaign to assure his priests.

All, that was, except George Spagnolia. Hours before the meeting was to take place, Spags received a telephone call from the secretary of Charles Higgins, Law's delegate for handling sex abuse allegations, telling him not to attend—and summoning him instead to a chancery meeting the following day. Immediately he knew what this meant; he knew—he *knew*—someone must have brought an allegation.

He became extremely angry. He challenged the secretary, but she did not know anything more. He slammed down the phone. He was frightened, and began to flip back the pages of his life, every church, every parishioner, every altar boy, every small girl in pleated uniform. Who might have invented such a scurrilous charge? Who might have imagined an assault or impropriety, or remembered the wrong man? Nothing popped up. He was sickened with anxiety and confusion.

Unable to wait till tomorrow, he called his regional bishop. He was in the dark too. Spags called Richard Craig, the area vicar, who was totally dismayed, to demand to be released from the tenterhooks. Craig promised to talk to Higgins at the regional gathering that afternoon.

Finally, at five-thirty the rectory phone rang. Higgins offered an apology for his awkward administration of this matter. But it was true, he said, that Spags was facing a matter of serious concern for the church. Higgins mentioned a man's name. "Does this name mean anything to you?"

It did. He was one of several brothers from Roxbury who had hung around the St. Francis de Sales Church when Spags was parochial vicar. He had been one of Spags's altar servers, a very quiet kid, essentially good. Spags thought, maybe this is not about sex at all—perhaps a long-forgotten dispute between the brothers, or a tragedy within the family. He relaxed. The boy and his brothers, and a dozen or so other neighborhood boys, all African-American, had maintained a clubhouse in the church basement. It kept them safely off the chaotic streets.

"Kind of a Caspar Milquetoast," Spags said. "Always put down by the older kids."

Well, Higgins said, he'd received a call from the young man, now forty-five, on Saturday. The man had indicated his belief that Spags molested him more than thirty years ago, in 1971.

"You're shitting me," Spags said.

Following the call, Higgins continued, he had invited the man to the chancery and interviewed him at length that day. He found his story to be credible.

Spags's mind raced. A memory blew open with the explosive force of a grenade. He shouted, "The tent!"

"Yes," Higgins said sadly. "The tent."

"When I was doing the sit-in on the cardinal's lawn, fasting for weeks, every night some people from Roxbury would come and sing and read scripture. One night it was this kid and his friends, two or three of them, I can't remember. Asked if they could stay in the tent. During the night, I have a strong recollection of this kid shaking me and he said, 'Don't do that.' I remember those words! 'Don't do that.' And I said, 'Oh, sorry,' and rolled back over."

"Yes, that's right."

"I must have rolled over and crushed him or something. That's not assault!"

Higgins had not intended to have this conversation over the phone. He had developed a successful formula for delivering the bad news to long-ago abusers. Eight times in the past weeks, he walked gray-haired priests—men he knew—into his muffled chancery office and spoke to them in pastoral tones, letting them know they had been caught, letting them know their victims still hurt after years and decades, and still demanded justice. Seven of the eight had confessed immediately, unburdening themselves in tearful finality.

Higgins told Spagnolia the youth provided details that only a victim of abuse would know.

"Horseshit," Spags snapped. "I mean, he's still in the sleeping bag! It's not like I'm in there on his penis, whacking him off! Mother of God! I was on the cardinal's front lawn!" He felt entirely numb.

"For anybody to take this misinterpretation of the incident and to lay the blame on me for all the unfortunate aspects of his life, I totally reject that," he said. No one had yet said if the complainant's life had taken unfortunate turns. But Spags figured that as a motive to dream up a false allegation.

At almost every juncture in the expanding crisis, Cardinal Law had done just as much as he thought was necessary to respond to the sexual abuse stories. He appointed a new panel to advise him on policy. He went to Geoghan's final parish and apologized to the angry congregants. He assured Catholics that he planned to take a national leadership role in the campaign against child abuse. Then he moved on to other chores, trying to maintain his executive poise. No matter what was being disclosed in the press, the cardinal would not address it. Even his spokeswoman, Donna Morrissey, was loath to be quoted.

If the cardinal felt his recalcitrant silence would allow the onslaught of news to wither and fade away, he was wrong. With every passing day, his administration seemed angrier, more petulant, less pastoral, increasingly contemptuous of the act of revelation, and, worse, wholly undisturbed by the crimes being revealed. Perhaps it made some sense to stay out of the denial game. But where was the ministry to the afflicted? Where was the care for the church itself? Victims were quoted saying they felt revictimized by every passing day. It was easy to see why.

Rank-and-file Catholics were growing increasingly upset. Even bishops elsewhere were horror-struck by the cardinal's entrenched inaction. "Apologies are vitally necessary, but themselves are insufficient," Cardinal Roger Mahony of Los Angeles said in a statement.

By not speaking, by not presenting a Catholic Church that grieved for each new victim, that lamented and repented each new allegation, by not appearing in any way to care now—any more than in the past—for the health of young children abused by their ministers, Cardinal Law personified the ogre caricatured in the storm of lawsuits hitting the courts. Richard Nixon at his worst seemed more genuinely human than Law did right now.

In an effort to counter this impression, this morning Law called to his residence fourteen of Boston's most influential Catholics, including William Bulger, president of the University of Massachusetts; John Drew, head of the World Trade Center in Boston; Robert Popeo, perhaps the city's most powerful lawyer; former lieutenant governor Tom O'Neill, whose father was the late Speaker of the House Tip O'Neill; and Jack Connors, the well-connected advertising executive and Law's most stalwart booster and defender. Only one, the local marketing entrepreneur Donna Latson Gittens, was a woman. If they assumed they were being called on to critique Law's behavior to date, they were mistaken. Instead, he put them through a twenty-minute speech that many considered overly defensive and drippingly arrogant. One by one, his invited guests spoke their minds. Though several said they stood behind him, most invited his departure. "If our young kids were looking for another reason to not go to church, you handed them one," O'Neill said in his turn. "Don't treat this like a public relations issue. It's not. It's much bigger than that."

Yet from a PR standpoint, the archdiocese was only making matters worse. It became popular among journalists to analyze Donna Morrissey's many mistakes. Reporters expected her to articulate a message of compassion for the victims, or spin the cloistered chancery in a positive light, but she did neither. For the five weeks since the crisis broke, reporters had been buffeting her large second-floor office on Commonwealth Avenue with pleas for a comment. Any comment. She or her assistant suggested reporters would have much better luck if they put their queries in writing—a classic stall. When they complied, they still got no response. As Walter Robinson put it, "You couldn't get somebody to talk to even on small questions, like how many priests are serving in the diocese. I kept saying to Donna, 'C'mon, this is not that hard.'"

Morrissey had joined the chancery a year before, at the age of thirty-two, with an idea that she was simplifying her life after a decade of late nights and ladder climbing. Despite being possessed of a face like Cameron Diaz's, impeccable taste in business suits, a pair of shoes for every new day, and hair that while ironed and highlighted looked natural in any wind pattern and lush in any light, she was an ambitious behind-the-scenes type with no passion for celebrity. Her first job after college was as an off-camera field producer for a local television news program. Later, as an account executive for the PR firm Regan Communications Group in Boston, she had developed a steady smile and charming though ridiculously muscular handshake that would help her land major accounts like the large Legal Sea Food restaurant chain, and even crisis assignments. She had been retained by the grown daughters of Stephen Fagan, the former Framingham man who made national headlines when he was charged with having kidnapped those daughters when they were young and raised them under aliases. This had been a difficult, and not altogether successful, assignment—the daughters exhibited an inexplicable loyalty to their father and refused to even meet the mother who had searched for them for decades.

When the cardinal hired her, the church's only lament was that it was generating no news whatsoever. The new spokeswoman began by brokering a number of advantageous stories about the cardinal: his trip to Peru to work with earthquake survivors, the addition of new lights around Holy Cross Cathedral, surrounded as it was by federal housing projects. Back then, the cardinal had doubtless wanted nothing more. He named her to his cabinet, a position of serious significance. She was the youngest ever to serve on the cabinet, and the first woman.

Then came what Jack Connors, who founded the advertising firm Hill, Holiday, Connors, Cosmopulos Inc., called "the Vietnam War on Commonwealth Avenue." Outmaneuvered by the unexpected crisis, Morrissey turned to outside consultants for help, hiring the PR firm Morrissey and Co., a well-respected outfit that happened to be owned by her first cousin Peter, someone she could trust. But his firm had scant experience in crisis containment, either. For that Peter retained a consultant named Ernie Corrigan, an old newspaper man who had worked for the church in the past doing media trainings. He had run the failed 1990 gubernatorial campaign of Democrat Francis X. Bellotti, and currently was representing the Massachusetts Extended Care Federation, the trade group for most of the state's nursing homes—at a time when reports of resident abuse were up 129 percent in the state.

But that only left more people with nothing to do inside the chancery's PR office. Corrigan took the incoming faxes, categorized and bundled them, and sent them across the driveway and up the sidewalk to the cardinal's residence, to be handed to Father John Connolly, the cardinal's personal secretary. What happened after that was anyone's guess. Corrigan suspected some were rerouted to the law offices of Wilson Rogers Jr. It didn't matter. Almost nothing was returned. The chancery was an informational black hole, giving off neither heat nor light.

Wednesday, February 20, 2002
BRIGHTON, MASSACHUSETTS — As he was instructed to, the next day Spags arrived at the chancery, down the hill from the cardinal's residence, where he had pitched that tent thirty-two years ago. As he turned off Commonwealth Avenue, he saw Higgins walking across the parking lot with Father Joe Welsh, a friend of Spags's from seminary. It would be a few more days before Spags read in the paper that Welsh had also been charged. But he suspected it immediately, seeing the contorted smile on his old friend's face. Welsh and Spags were the ninth and tenth priests respectively to be removed from their Boston-area parishes in the past three weeks.

Higgins greeted Spags stiffly and escorted him through the building into his office, where he offered him an uncomfortable upholstered armchair. Closing the door, he got right to the matter at hand. The young man had reported two incidents of unwanted groping, Higgins now said, one on the night inside the tent and the other inside the rectory.

"Out-and-out lie," Spags said. "That never happened."

He tried to mount a lawyerly rebuttal, but it came out as churlish. For one thing, he demanded to know in which order the assaults were said to have happened. Higgins couldn't say. He demanded to know what made the account "credible," and Higgins demurred, except to allude that the young man had given an anatomical clue. He didn't say what that clue was, or ask if it were accurate. Rather, he leaned forward and showed his impatient face deliberately to Spags. The young man did not intend to press charges or pursue a suit, Higgins said, "which is a relief to us." His Eminence had decided that the priest's salary would not be interrupted, and that his health insurance would continue, Higgins stated. He expected Spags to move out of the residence by the end of the day. And he wished for a letter of resignation to follow, bringing this matter to a close.

Spags fell mute. What an irony, he thought. Thirty years ago he had tried to quit the priesthood and the cardinal would not allow it, and instead gave him a leave of absence. Now, at sixty-four and near the end of a lifelong journey, the only thing on earth he wanted was the arduous but uncomplicated pastor's life. He may never have attained genuine heroism. But he changed some lives and found happiness and purpose in the church, a fulfillment that had eluded him everywhere else. He wanted to stay. And now that was impossible.

He knew one thing for certain, and that was that for as long as he lived as a priest there would be a roof over his head and a pillow under it, and just enough extra money to eat and drink well—in his case, $1,800 a month. He had made no contingency plans. Yet Spags had the distinct feeling the cardinal's delegate thought he was walking this wayward priest off into the sunset.

An intemperate man, Spags climbed out of the chair. A million retorts and boasts bounced through his mind, but nothing came out. He completely lacked a thing to say—no astringent wisecrack, no biting bon mot, no booming threat. He stood as confused and bewildered as a drunk who'd been sucker punched. In pained silence, Higgins walked Spags across a chilly morning to his car. The priest slid into the bucket seat and glared at his administrator. "Fuck you," he thought, but did not say. "Fuck you. Fuck this diocese. And a royal fuck you to the guy in red."

Monday, February 25, 2002

LOWELL, MASSACHUSETTS — St. Patrick's was still in disrepair. Only half the interior was painted. The windows rattled and fogged. On the roof, ladders and roofing material were strewn in disarray. Inside the rectory next door, Spagnolia was drinking his eighth or ninth cup of coffee. Eileen Donoghue, whom he had retained as his civil attorney, and Sister Joanne Sullivan tried to steady his resolve.

After the chancery meeting, he called together his small staff, which consisted only of his secretary and his maintenance engineer, and told them what had happened. "You know who you've had your pants off for, and as God is my witness, this never happened," he said. He repeated this declaration at the next morning's Mass, which drew the usual sparse midweek crowd of about twenty-five retirees, mostly women—the "hard core," he called them. Many cried. He swore his innocence and vowed to fight to remain in the pulpit at St. Patrick's. Then he called an old friend from seminary, Jack Finnegan. He needed advice. He planned to head to the Cape, where friends could put him up. "Jack, I want to fight this," he said.

Good for you, Finnegan encouraged, but you have to fight it from inside the rectory, you must not leave town.

He referred him to the section of church law that says a priest has two weeks to act when given an "invitation to respond." Then he recommended a canon lawyer.

Spags decided he would not move.

That afternoon, he sat at his keyboard and composed a tightly worded note to Cardinal Law demanding an investigation and the right to exonerate himself. While accepting the instruction to not say Mass or perform the sacraments until he was cleared, he was not budging from the rectory. "Please be advised that pursuant to canon law, I oppose the cause for which you have invited my resignation," he wrote. "I notify you that I am refusing your invitation to resign my office of pastor."

He walked across the lawn from the rectory and slipped through a side door into the church for a hastily called press conference, with Sister Joanne leading the procession. He was stunned at what he saw

inside. Dozens of television cameras were set up in a bank facing the
pulpit, which was heavy with microphones, wires, and tape. The
church was packed. There were faces he recognized from other
parishes he had served decades ago, people he knew must have driven
an hour or more to be there. The mayor of Lowell was sitting in a forward pew. The former mayor was there, too, as were firemen, policemen, and city councilors, many of them wearing purple ribbons on
their lapels. This was the Lowell of literary legend, as Kerouac wrote:
"Follow along to the center of the town, the Square, where at noon
everybody knows everybody else."

Above their heads was an undulation of hand-lettered signs: "Innocent Until Proven Guilty" and *"Con Luon o Ben Cha,"* which was
translated as "We Support You, Father." They spilled from the pews
all the way from the front of the church to the back, more than a
thousand people in all—more than were congregated on Christmas
Eve.

Spagnolia was floored. It never occurred to him he would find so
much support. Nor did he ever realize how much he was loved. People in Lowell stood with the underdog, and itched for a good fight. But
that's not why they had shown up in droves. They believed in the man
with the crooked teeth they call Spags. He had come here a stranger
to them, and he had given everything he had. It was more than they
had gotten in years.

He turned to Sister Joanne and said, "Despite my super ego and my
incredible self-esteem, this is the most humbling experience of my
life."

Trembling, he stepped up to a bank of microphones. He did not
know, nor did he have any reason to suspect, that his remarks were being broadcast live via satellite to tens of thousands of Boston homes on
New England Cable, and beamed around the nation on C-SPAN. Nor
was he aware that of the scores of priests removed from their pulpits
since January across the country, he was the only one to declare his innocence.

"I have done nothing wrong," he began. And the room erupted into
wild, sustained applause.

"When I was ordained in 1964, my embracing the joys, responsibilities, and burdens of the Catholic priesthood did not abrogate my rights as an American citizen," Spags said. "I demand due process!"

He condemned archdiocesan policies that he said presumed him guilty even as he tried to clear his name. He revealed that officials had given him the name of his accuser, and called upon the Suffolk County prosecutors to investigate swiftly—so that he might return to preaching by Easter. In the meantime, he vowed to battle what he called the "fraudulent" policy of removing priests based on allegations, not due process. "I and many others believe that this policy is unjust and inherently evil in its implementation—for not only does it deny the very foundation of the individual's relationship to society, namely innocent until proven guilty, but also this policy dismisses summarily the code of canon law as it pertains to priests and, more specifically, the removal of pastors.

"For my reputation, for my brother priests serving the people of God in the archdiocese, and for the people," he called over the din of thunderous applause, "I cannot stand by mute and allow this injustice to continue unchecked!"

And then Spags did the unthinkable. He took on the cardinal archbishop of Boston, Bernard Law. "He has no credibility among his priests," he shouted, pumping a fist in the air. "They don't feel as though they can trust him. They feel as though he'd give them up in a minute to save his ass."

Lowell's fire chief, William Desrosiers, shook his head in feigned shock. "That's Father Spags," he thought. "He says it as it is, he always has. He has every bit of independence. He believes in himself and he believes in his faith."

Already the dance of reporters and sources was in full swing. Carol Evans, who had attended Mass at St. Patrick's for fifty years, told a reporter from the *Globe* that Father Spagnolia had much to do in preparation for Irish Week and Easter, and ought to be allowed to get on with it. "This is not right. Not right," added Elly Torres, who immigrated to Lowell from Cuba in the 1960s to work in the mills. "He is a good man, a good man. You knock on his door—knock, knock, knock—anytime, and he helps you. A good man."

Spags floated down the aisle embracing people he hadn't seen in years, like Stephen Pointras, the pastor of St. Michael's Church in Hudson, who had grown up in St. Patrick's Parish and returned at this trying juncture to show his admiration. As Spags approached the door, he glimpsed the Reverend Timothy Kapsalis, pastor from Holy Trinity Greek Orthodox Church, across the street, standing in the back of the room. Kapsalis had rarely been inside St. Patrick's, but he felt his presence now was required. "It takes a whole life to build a career, build a reputation," he thought, "and it takes a second to destroy everything." He came to show solidarity. But the sight of the man touched a corner of Spags's heart that had resisted disturbance since the crisis broke. He collapsed into blubbering tears, tucking his smooth bald head into Kapsalis's shoulder and crying so hard, and so loud, his sobs filled the hall to the rafters.

A reporter interrupted, wanting to know his thoughts on why so many people seemed to support him. He wrestled for composure, and had it in hand in an instant.

"Must be my pretty face," he said.

Tuesday, February 26, 2002
BOSTON, MASSACHUSETTS — The Massachusetts House of Representatives voted unanimously to require church employees to report suspected cases of sexual abuse to authorities, closing what critics said were broad loopholes in an existing law. Bowing to Cardinal Law's pleas, they exempted allegations made during Catholic confessions. A similar measure had already passed the commonwealth's Senate. Acting Governor Jane Swift said she would sign the bill at once when it crossed her desk, making Massachusetts the thirtieth state in the country to require clergy to report.

The first mandatory reporting law appeared in California in 1963 on the recognition that certain professionals had greater civil responsibilities toward children. Physicians and schoolteachers, for instance, were uniquely positioned to recognize sexual abuse and as such had unique responsibilities to stop it. By classifying them "mandatory reporters," lawmakers in effect deputized them to be the first line of detection. Versions of this law have eventually been adopted in every state in the nation.

Massachusetts adopted its first mandatory reporting law in 1973, giving members of over twenty-five professions forty-eight hours to convey their suspicions to authorities. Spiritual leaders were specifically exempted. Every few years an amendment to add clergy was contemplated, but always faced fierce opposition from the Roman Catholic Church, which argued that the Constitution protected all priest-penitent conversations, not just inside the confessional. Leaders of the Church of Christ, Scientist—which has headquarters in Boston—had a similar tradition, mandating secrecy for any conversation between a member and a church leader. But last fall, at about the time he became aware that the Spotlight Team was investigating the church, Cardinal Law withdrew his opposition.

The Reverend Nancy S. Taylor, president of the Massachusetts Conference of the United Church of Christ, the state's largest Protestant denomination, was ecstatic. "This is a great piece of legislation," she announced. "This legislation will help to protect the children who, until now, have simply not had the protection they deserve from the Commonwealth of Massachusetts or, sadly, from its religious institutions."

Donna Morrissey chose not to issue a statement.

Wednesday, February 27, 2002
LOWELL, MASSACHUSETTS — Spags looked out the front window of his rectory with the studied nonchalance of an overnight celebrity. Television camera crews were staked out in his front yard, satellite trucks ringed the block. A black limousine, sent by ABC News, waited at the curb to drive him five hours to New York City. He had said yes to Bill O'Reilly, yes to *Good Morning America,* and yes to Paula Zahn, but no to Oprah and Montel Williams, on the haphazard advice of his lawyer. In the distance, a pitiless ringing telephone signaled the impatience of a network producer—or more likely, *Newsweek.* His campaign to restore his good name had captured the imagination of the nation. Spags was immeasurably cheered. He knew his celebrity was not guaranteed. He knew this could go either way, and that the media lights were sure to fade quickly. For the moment anyway, he was the new twist in this

incredible story and he was going to wrestle from that any political advantage he could.

"I'm a ham," he said when he returned to a lengthy interview with Tom Farragher, a *Globe* investigative reporter, in his parlor. He barked out a laugh like an excited terrier. "This will probably be the very first chapter in my book!"

In the days since his face-off with headquarters began, he had scored a significant rhetorical victory. The archdiocese of Boston was now calling his removal "temporary," and had promised to reinstate him if exonerated. Still, a messenger arrived that morning from the chancery carrying a formal eviction notice. When Spags handed it to his attorney, Eileen Donoghue, she went ballistic. "It's just outrageous," she said. "You don't just say, 'Here's your hat, get out now.' That's hardly Christian."

Farragher had proposed to write a profile of the priest at the eye of the storm, and Spags was game. He shared war stories from Roxbury, and detailed his 1971 hunger strike and protest on the chancery lawn. He told about his life during his lengthy sabbatical. He said that while he never went to church during that time, he maintained his strong faith and commitments. He remained celibate. "Celibacy was for me," he said. "I felt called to that." He recalled his battle with cancer, and the financial straits that forced him to lose the Yarmouthport inn. Listening to himself speak, he seriously entertained the idea of writing not one book but several, a volume for each juncture in his life. The darkest of them would be this period of allegation and flux, a time in which he stood accused but could not contest. His accuser had declined to sue, the authorities were unable to indict on such an old case even if they were eager to, which they weren't, so he would never get a day in civil or criminal court to confront his accuser. Wendy Murphy, an articulate former prosecutor and fixture on the talking-head circuit, acted as the accuser's proxy in the media. To her, Spags's denials were just additional evidence of his guilt. "I think people who do such things to children often respond characteristically by saying, 'I'm not the type. Look at me,'" she suggested. "The screaming is loud and the denial is staunch."

Spags spoke indignantly about the fourteen-year-old boy he knew in

1971. "For me, personally, it would be nice if he just slipped away, you know?" Spags said. "But I think it's too late for him to do that. . . . In order to save face, I would assume that he has to come forward; otherwise I have basically called him a liar."

But he reserved his harshest attacks for the way he was treated by his superiors. "They could care less where I live," he said. "They never said, 'Do you have a place to stay?' Nothing. Nothing! You'd treat your dog who licks your face better than that."

He took a breath.

"We've been betrayed by our brother priests who commit sexual abuse on children, and we've been betrayed by our bishop because of the way he has handled it and the secrecy," he declared.

Ray Flynn, the former mayor—in 1993 he stepped down to accept Bill Clinton's invitation to represent the United States as ambassador to the Vatican—had now become the most vocal defender of Cardinal Law in Boston. He believed that terrible crimes had happened to children inside their church. Some of his own friends confided in him about their own histories at the hands of priests. He was disgusted at what he heard. The priests who did this belonged in prison, he believed. But during his nine years as mayor and four years as ambassador, he had many opportunities to work closely with Law. Nothing he had seen to date had convinced him that this man had intentionally put children in harm's way.

He argued his case on television with Tim Russert, Ted Koppel, and Jim Lehrer, and relentlessly opposed calls for Law's resignation on his own radio call-in show. "Forget whether you like the guy or don't like the guy, he's an American cardinal—there's just a handful of them. He's very close to the pope, he's very influential, very well respected in the U.S. bishops' conference, and now, all of a sudden, you want him to re-sign so you can bring in some other bishop so you can deal with all this? Wait a minute! You already have somebody who's on the line, whose reputation is right on the line, who is under *extraordinary* pressure to get the job done. He's *got* to deliver! If he's going to save any part of his reputation, he's got to get this policy in place in Boston, in the United States, and it has to be approved by the Vatican. Who better can do that? Who better can do that? Somebody with clout!"

Flynn didn't mind being out front about the cardinal, even if it meant taking the heat from the newspaper columnists. But what did bother him was that nobody from Law's kitchen cabinet of advisers was out there taking the heat with him. Where was Peter Lynch, the former head of Fidelity Investments? Where were the ringing defenses of Jack Connors, Tom O'Neill, William Bulger, or the others whom Law frequently entertained in the residence? Flynn was never invited to Law's inner circle—because, he assumed, he wasn't the proper "pedigree." Born to a dockworker and a scrubwoman in South Boston, Flynn was always considered more shanty Irish than lace-curtain, despite his high achievements. In Boston, that class divide was as significant today as ever.

The most powerful and high-flying men and women of Catholic Boston had taken cover. Flynn viewed this abandonment through the norms of his old neighborhood, where he still lived. "Law was never one of the boys," he told a visitor one day. "Think about it. If you're one of the boys and you get into trouble, generally, the boys will stick with you, right? He got into trouble. Where were the boys? They went south on him. He didn't really have anybody backing him up or saying, 'A good man, give him a chance, he made a mistake, let's work with him.' No. Once they smelled blood in the water, that was it. They just want him out of there. Because they can't control him anyway. He isn't politically powerful enough to call the shots in this city anyway. I hope you understand that point because if you don't get that one from me, you're not going to hear it from anybody."

For all his hauteur, Cardinal Law was in trouble, even deeper than he or anyone else knew.

Thursday, February 28, 2002
BOSTON, MASSACHUSETTS — Winston Reed was already angry at Dominic George Spagnolia when he opened the morning's paper and discovered the profile of him as a funny, impassioned, and quixotic priest perhaps wrongly accused, the very scenario of the Hitchcock film of his childhood. They had been mostly out of touch for years. He did not know much about Spagnolia, he had to admit. But he knew one thing. The man was no celibate.

He knew this because for four years while Spags was running his nursing homes, the two had slept in the same bed. Their relationship had not ended well. But that didn't mean it never happened.

It wasn't just being scissored out of the Spags photo album that irked him. There was something entirely unacceptable, in 2002, for a gay man to crawl back into a closet. It reflected badly on all gays. It suggested shamefulness. It was damned hypocritical. Dante wrote Brutus and Cassius into the lowest circle of hell for choosing to betray their friend Julius Caesar instead of their country, Rome. Reed was betrayed to protect the fiction of a heterosexual, celibate priesthood.

In a sloppy fit of anger, Reed sat at his computer and furiously typed out an e-mail to Tom Farragher at the *Globe* calling Spags a liar.

"I'm somewhat disappointed in him as a person and a priest," Reed told Farragher, who telephoned for an interview. He said he held no grudge against his former lover, but "you don't lie about it either. . . . I have no idea if the charges against him are true or not. I hope they are not. I do know that he has openly lied and that disturbs me. I don't want someone to build a following and create a cause that is built on lies and omissions."

Farragher reached Spags on the telephone and told him the long story of his interview with Reed.

"Oh, fuck," Spags said.

Was it true, then? Had they been lovers?

"Yes," Spags said. "Yes, it's true."

Farragher had his scoop and he said good-bye quickly, and in the months to come, that would be the thing that would bother Spagnolia most, that he had not been asked for his side of the story. Of course, there was no side of the story to tell that would make sense to anybody. Spags had known he was gay since the time he was ten, decades before there were words to describe what he was feeling and dreaming. Before stalking away from Roxbury in 1973, he lived a perfectly celibate life. When he allowed himself finally to embrace his gayness, he was middle-aged. The affair with Reed disappointed him—not profoundly, but worse, it let him down in ordinary ways. He found it dull and a bit irritating. All the fancy dinner parties, appetizers passed on silver trays, dinners plated at 11 P.M., smothered in sauces. He called Reed—it was a folk epithet at the time—a PT, a *poor thing*. When he learned Reed had stepped out on him, Spags walked away without rancor. Without, in fact, much emotion whatsoever, totally detached and untouched. He had entered into one other previous physical relationship, but he never tried something so silly as love again.

Now, of course, he was furious at Reed. But it was God he railed against. "Shit! What are you doing to me? What more do you want?" But he felt God getting mad back, felt the message was for him to do what he had to do, which was face the humiliation he had brought upon himself.

He called Eileen Donoghue. She listened in silence. "I was so con-ditioned to keeping it a secret," he said, "I didn't even think about it not being true, honest to God. I had no concept of it being a lie. No con-cept at all. It's not the first time that I had said it, and it's almost like you say something enough times you begin to believe it yourself. There was no concept of my intentionally lying to this man. It just flowed out like normal conversation."

"Oh, Spags," she said sadly, a bit confused. "That's not good."

He knew he had lost all hope anybody would believe he didn't touch that child. He was now on record as a liar.

"During my priesthood I was celibate," he said. "That was something that I took on because I wanted to be a priest. And I wasn't going to do anything that was going to jeopardize that decision. As this revelation probably would. I mean, it *has*, obviously."

The next morning, Donoghue arranged another press conference at the church for Spagnolia to confess to his prevarication, and announce that he would be leaving St. Patrick's after all. Satellite trucks once again arrived in droves. He realized that he—a man who had never once called himself gay publicly—would be coming out live on C-SPAN. He thought he would die.

First, he apologized for lying. "I will not try to defend it, except to say that there was no conscious decision to deceive, but rather in my naïve effort to protect my own privacy and that of others, I made the decision that these were times which were private in nature and I saw no need to reveal them. . . . Being gay doesn't mean you're a pedophile, being gay does not mean you cross-dress. They're apples and oranges. I am saying, 'Yes, I've had gay relationships.' But I have never harmed a child."

That night and the rest of the weekend, he packed his things up at the rectory. On Sunday, he noticed a *Boston Globe* photographer sitting in his car outside his window, obviously waiting for the picture of the fallen priest dragging his threadbare armchair to the U-Haul. Spags poured a mug of coffee and carried it out to the car. He knocked on the window. Handing it to the driver, he said, "I'll be leaving around two."

Then, as an afterthought, really, he said, "Maybe you guys can follow me to the Vatican when I make my appeal."

"The whole press corps will be there," he was told.

Chapter 11

Inside, Outside

Late February 2002

BRIGHTON, MASSACHUSETTS — Most mornings now, church employees arrived at the chancery through a line of protesters, and they left for home most nights past a battery of television cameras beaming their images live for the evening news. Being the locus of such negativity was totally incongruous with the way they thought about their jobs, and had them all in a state of expanding distress. But the pressures were not just at the chancery gate. Staff members at all levels were ordered to comb their files for any evidence of abuse allegations. More kept surfacing, giving the lie to Donna Morrissey's repeated declarations to the contrary.

She complained bitterly about being so misinformed. "How could our hospitals have a very state-of-the-art computer system where they could look up every doctor's appointment I've ever had since I was born at St. Elizabeth's, but yet, with our files, we had them on pieces of paper? That's disappointing, very disappointing," she castigated. What struck her as especially disturbing was that many of the files being recovered in dusty boxes throughout the building bore memoranda from Wilson Rogers Jr. Why he allowed her to keep issuing inaccurate press releases was an enduring mystery to her.

Meanwhile, Rogers was conducting endless meetings with staff, preparing a parade of individuals for depositions in civil suits, grilling clerks on how and where personnel records were filed away, and preparing for a meeting March 1 with the attorney general, which he hoped would blunt talk of a grand jury investigation. To some, it appeared that Rogers, not Law, held the reins of the church.

Barbara Thorp, who for nearly twenty years headed up the pro-life office for the archdiocese, sat on the outside of the chaos. But as a trained social worker, it seemed to her that the church was making a grave error. One day she sat down and spelled out her thoughts in an unsolicited memo to Cardinal Law.

The only authentic response from a church is to acknowledge the outpouring of pain from Catholics, she wrote. Like it or not, their histories with the church were the unhappy history of the church itself, and had to be faced. "We can't have a lawsuit be a barrier to what we need to be doing as a church," she argued. "We have to make an affirmative response to the victims. There are a lot of people out there who are hurting. I think everyone is experiencing a deep sense of shame and pain. The whole notion of this crisis is hard to take in. But clearly, whether it was recent or thirty or forty years ago, it is our obligation to people who had suffered so grievously to reach out to them in the name of the church."

She proposed the chancery set up a hotline and an office with trained therapists to listen to the stories of these men and women without defensiveness, and offer whatever help and apology the victims were willing to receive.

Through Father Connolly, Law thanked her for her suggestions— and appointed her to establish the new Office of Healing and Assistance. She accepted, knowing how little faith most victims had that the church would do anything on their behalf. She was prepared, if nobody else would, to take the brunt of their ire.

Sunday, March 3, 2002
BOSTON, MASSACHUSETTS — The scent of incense hung thickly in the air of Holy Cross Cathedral, striated with columns of refracted sunlight. The large stained-glass panels high over the nave depicted the Exaltation of the Cross. "We should glory in the cross of our Lord Jesus Christ, for He is our salvation," read an inscription. On her knees

in prayer, Donna Morrissey realized she could hear the protesters outside in the frigid morning. They punctured her reverie, and that made
her angry.

"Prison for Law," they chanted. "Full disclosure! Complete accountability!" Television crews were stationed at the doors. A Swedish
film crew was making a documentary. The weekly protests were getting bigger and bigger, with demonstrators now coming from as far
away as New Hampshire. Parishioners were afraid to use the front
door anymore. Some were complaining about television cameras
traipsing through the sanctuary. Now they had a megaphone outside,
and nobody could pray.

Out of frustration, the night before a group of parishioners from
the projects across from the cathedral had staged their own vigil,
chanting and singing in defense of Law. Touched, the cardinal
thanked them in Spanish and English at the beginning of Mass. But
outside his doorway just steps away were men and women who had
been molested as children. That was what this crisis was about. He
did not mention them. For some reason, he could not bring himself to
go out there and talk to them. Rather, he now arrived at his various
appearances in the manner of a mafia kingpin. At the last possible
minute before Mass, his driver would race him up to the cathedral's
back door so Law could vanish pristinely inside. He would depart via
a similar method.

Law moved to the front of the altar in preparation for his homily,
motioning for people to take their seats. The anger of the protesters
colluded with the extreme cold weather to keep the congregation
small. As she was swooping toward her pew, Morrissey's eye caught a
flash of motion in the central aisle. Some deep instinct propelled her
into the aisle, and it wasn't until that instant she realized how tightly
wound she was, how sure there would be violence.

Morrissey came face-to-face with Steve Lynch, who was crying copiously as he walked toward Law. She recognized him immediately—
this was the man who had stood so stoically outside the chancery all
these months. She had taken to waving hello, the way you might greet
a trash collector or the guy at the gas station, a fixture in your life from
a segregated world. On four separate mornings this past week she had

spotted him on Commonwealth Avenue standing morosely in the hail and rain, hoisting a sign that read, "Will Anyone Speak Up?"

This morning's paper had finally given Lynch his voice. According to the *Globe,* Lynch's case was a difficult one. He said he was raped by a priest, Father Samuel Lombard, when he was nine. But he recalled this trauma only in 1998, when he was thirty-eight years old. It popped into his head one afternoon while he spoke on the telephone. "Psychologically, I guess you could classify it as a memory. Spiritually, it's a knowing," the paper quoted him saying.

Two lawyers refused to take his case. He had tried to bring suit on his own behalf, but the church rejected his request for $35,000 and a judge threw out his claim on grounds it was beyond the statute of limitations. Without confirmation, the archdiocese considered his charge as unfounded, and allowed Lombard to serve as a priest until his death, at seventy-eight, of happy old age.

Morrissey held up her arms to stop Lynch. Concerned for his communications director, Law moved down the chancel toward her. Lynch stopped his advance, his eyes flooding tears.

"I'm standing before you, Cardinal," he cried, "and I'm taking my power back that your church stole from me."

About a dozen male worshipers took hold of him. They passed him over to two plainclothes Boston police officers, who seized Lynch by the arms. He did not resist as the policemen carted him out of the church. Morrissey followed into the vestibule, as the cardinal began his homily in earnest.

"Steven?" she called.

"Hi, Donna," he said, "how have you been?" The police were handcuffing him.

"I just feel terrible. This can't happen. You can't disturb the Mass. Officer, do you have to cuff him? Won't you give the man his dignity?"

The cameras that had been covering the picket line now rushed up the stairs to record the arrest.

"There's certain boundaries you can't go over," she repeated to Lynch before ducking hastily back inside. The last thing Morrissey wanted was to be photographed overseeing a man's ejection from the cathedral.

Law, when his homily was through, whispered in her ear, wanting to know if Lynch was okay.

"Yes, Your Eminence, he's fine."

"Was he arrested?"

"Once they had to escort him out, they had to arrest him," she said. This was not true. But Morrissey felt it was important to draw a firm line with the protesters.

"Well, can't we get the charges dropped?"

"No," she said crisply, "we can't. I have a great deal of sympathy for him. But you have to be careful what precedents you set."

In a lengthy interview with the *New York Times* on the growing American crisis, papal spokesman Joaquín Navarro-Valls became the highest-level church official to endorse the belief that the presence of homosexuals in the priesthood was the root cause. "People with these inclinations just cannot be ordained," said Navarro-Valls. "That does not imply a final judgment on people with homosexuality. But you cannot be in this field."

Liberals were aghast. But ultraconservatives in the American church hierarchy were heartened by his declaration, people like Bishop Fabian Bruskewitz of Lincoln, Nebraska, and Philadelphia's Cardinal Anthony Bevilacqua, who believed in his heart that homosexuals were incapable of remaining chaste, though there were no data to back this up. He argued that the pull of homosexuality—"an aberration, a moral evil," in his view—was simply too great to be vanquished. "A person who is homosexually oriented is not a suitable candidate for the priesthood, even if he has never committed any homosexual act," he said. He compared gay priests to alcoholics. With the "tension of the priesthood there's a tendency at times to seek some kind of outlet," he said. "The risk is higher. That's all we can say."

First Week of March 2002

BRIGHTON, MASSACHUSETTS — "I just need to ask you something," Barbara Thorp's first caller said. "Do you work for the church? I mean, are you based at the church? Are you a church *official* as it were? Because that would make a big difference for me in terms of being comfortable."

In her years with the archdiocese, even though she had manned the politically controversial right-to-life office, she always felt that the church logo on her business card had at the very minimum given her a boost in the trust department. Now, on her first morning in her new job, on her first telephone call, she knew she was working *against* that logo, one quavering voice at a time.

"I understand," she told the man. "My hope is that I can prove myself trustworthy, and I will *have* to prove it. I hope that I can hold your story and I hope that I can respond in a way that can begin to restore some trust. And that's all I can do. I can't . . . it's all up to you. The final judge and determiner of whether trust is restored is the person who's injured, is the person who's been harmed."

She offered to meet him in his home, or at Starbucks or Dunkin' Donuts—anyplace that didn't have the fiendish, duplicitous, *felonious* reputation of the Catholic Church. And she immediately began looking for a secular office building where she could relocate the Office of Healing and Assistance.

March 9, 2002
SOUTH BOSTON, MASSACHUSETTS — Each year, the archdiocese of Boston selected nearly three thousand Catholics from among the faithful in each parish and called them to a formal Convocation of the Laity. They represented the most committed of the lay Eucharistic ministers, religious education teachers, deacons, or members of parish councils. This was the tenth convocation under Law's stewardship, and he had anticipated it would be unprecedented. He sensed the tension and anger in the pews. He discarded his original agenda, which had called for dozens of workshops, in favor of what he called "listening sessions," in which he would invite the lay leaders to express their feelings on the crisis. And he planned to end the daylong session with an apology.

By coincidence, many of the people meeting regularly now in the basement of St. John's were invited, including Mary Calcaterra and Jim Muller. Fourteen of them arrived together Saturday morning and filed past tight security into the cavernous World Trade Center on the city's waterfront. They all wore red. It was the color of their anger. It also invoked the Holy Spirit, which they believed was the mysterious hand of God's goodness, needed now more than ever.

Knowing this exchange would be frank, and perhaps aware that Catholic protocol would be breached by the spectacle of ordinary parishioners calling upon him to resign, Law declared most of the meeting off-limits to reporters. Newspaper photographers, television cameras, and audio recorders would not even be allowed during the open session. If any of the city's broadcast outlets wished to air reports on the meeting, they would have to use edited footage released by the television station or the newspaper owned by the archdiocese, BCTV and the *Pilot* respectively.

As a result, nobody outside the convention hall heard ordinary Catholics rise one by one to tell their cardinal what they thought of the church crisis. Some indeed demanded his resignation, while others were equally ardent that he stay and repair his church. But the one theme that kept coming through was the unchallenged belief that if just one mother had been in on the decision making at the chancery, none of this would have happened in the first place.

When it came time for Mary Calcaterra to speak, she told about their discussion group in the basement of St. John's—an entirely layled movement seeking to help the church reform. She passed out printed materials showing the theological justification for the group and listing its concerns. In a show of politeness, she threw out an invitation to the large room. "Anyone is welcome," she said. "Please, join us." She had no idea how badly people wanted to hear those words.

March 11, 2002
WASHINGTON, D.C. — As usual, fifty church leaders attended the annual Administrative Committee meeting of the United States Conference of Catholic Bishops: heads of various USCCB committees, staffers, and representatives of the American church's thirteen geographical regions. They gathered in the group's blocky headquarters on the capital's outskirts for four days of meetings. Conspicuous among them was Wilton Gregory, the affable head of the sprawling, rural

Belleville diocese in southern Illinois. At fifty-four, he was among the youngest. And in a sea of pale prelates, he was the only African-American. But he stood out in many other ways as well: telegenic and media savvy, soft-spoken and accessible, he was a bishop for the new generation. Just four months ago, his brother bishops had appointed him the USCCB's president.

From the first day of the *Boston Globe* exposé, Gregory knew this would be the test of his lifetime, but also in an interesting way his liberation, for he was suddenly no longer the token black prelate in a predominantly white church. What mattered now was his leadership, not his race.

In a peculiar way, Gregory's whole career had prepared him for this moment. Ordained in Chicago, Gregory helped his mentor Cardinal Joseph Bernardin develop one of the strongest policies against sexual abuse in the church in America in the late eighties. He also watched as a scandal swept through the archdiocese, including charges against Bernardin himself, which were later recanted as the unreliable product of a "recovered memory." Because it was handled generously and forgivingly, and all out in the open, Bernardin and the diocese prevailed unscathed. For his contributions, Gregory was elevated to auxiliary bishop at thirty-five, the youngest in American history.

By 1993, a similar scandal was brewing in Belleville, described by one reporter as "a rat's nest of baroque sexual corruption, highlighted by a burglary carried out at one priest's home by a male prostitute from whom the priest regularly received massages in the nude." The pope, with Bernardin's encouragement, dispatched Gregory to calm the flock. Again, he chose correction over containment. In weeks, he removed twelve priests from ministry—so many, so swiftly, that he cast his diocese into confusion. But decisive action was the cornerstone of the policy the bishops approved at the USCCB meeting in 1992. The policy was not mandatory. However, Gregory had no problem complying. He would go to any extreme to make the church a safe place for children. He recalled that a chancery worker once suggested that the church should protect "its own" when priests are accused of abuse. He fired back, "Well, aren't these children our own? Aren't the parents of these children our own?"

He had thought that bishops across the country were doing the same thing—that the lessons of Gauthe and Porter had taken hold uniformly. When the situation exploded in Boston, he was sad to learn that Law had unilaterally rejected the sterner new policy. When similar crises erupted in New Hampshire—and then Louisville, Phoenix, New Orleans, Albany, and elsewhere—he knew the whole hierarchy was in trouble. Angry calls from other bishops poured into his office, he confided one afternoon. "The bishops that spoke to me said, 'We put into practice the policies of '92. We have done what was recommended that we do and have handled the situation fairly well. Not perfectly, but well.' They had a review board, they had a victim-assistance minister. They had taken priests out of public ministry. They had a written policy, they had spoken about this with their people—I mean, they have followed all of the steps that had been recommended in '92. And now they are feeling that they are going to be . . . that we are all going to be judged by the Boston situation. All of us are going to be involved in this no matter what we had done. No matter how careful, how forthright, how honest we had been. We are all going to be judged by the worst-case scenario."

When Gregory addressed the Administrative Committee now, he underscored that the crisis was no longer confined to New England. It threatened to bring the whole American church down. He believed the church was in its worst crisis since Martin Luther. "A response of the Conference has to be crafted. All of us are in this together. The revelations about Geoghan and Shanley are just outrageous. Just unconscionable! We as a body of Bishops have to address the situation of the abuse of children. Because as deplorable as all misconduct is, deplorable in the sense that it is a scandal, a betrayal of trust, *a demeaning of the office of public pastor and Shepherd,* the abuse of children is singular in its horror. Because you are dealing with those who are most vulnerable."

A bitter discussion unfolded. Some bishops put responsibility for the recidivist priests squarely on the medical professionals who treated them and then pronounced them well. Others blamed a cannibalizing press and anti-Catholic sentiments for inflaming the situation, or felt that homosexuality itself was the cause and regretted ever having ordained gays. Some wondered if celibacy had crippled the priesthood. Consensus was equally elusive on how the national church should respond. "Wilton, what we need is a blue-ribbon committee to help us address this," one said; a dozen other bishops agreed. "You need to put together a group of prestigious Catholics who will help us review this matter—and by their own public integrity and their own provenance will lend an air of integrity and significance." Still others thought it was unwise for the bishops to employ stand-ins on such a morally pressing subject.

The views were so many and varied that the Administrative Committee decided then to scrap the broad agenda already adopted for the annual USCCB conference, scheduled for June in Dallas. Instead, there would be just one agenda item: sex abuse in the church.

Later in the week, as he headed back to Illinois to begin a lengthy tour of the farm country to bless the spring crops and livestock, Gregory thought back on the idealized priests portrayed in Spencer Tracy and Bing Crosby films, men in collars who could do no wrong. "Suddenly it is exactly the opposite," he thought. "Nothing the church does has any credibility anymore. Bishops are human. They make mistakes. Now even an honest mistake is seen as malicious." Forget what this meant for the individual bishops. His greatest worry was that faith itself might not survive these challenges.

March 12, 2002
BOSTON, MASSACHUSETTS — "What do you want to get out of this?" Attorney Eric MacLeish had heard about the organizing Olan Horne was doing up in Lowell. He had been expecting his visit for some time. He also knew most of those cases were likely to be considered beyond the statute of limitations. So far, he had filed only one Birmingham suit. "Have you talked among yourselves about what sort of outcome you're looking for?"

Olan and Dave Lyko, who was sitting at his side, had gone over this time and time again. When they started making the phone calls, their goal was to get the truth out into the open. They discussed the possibility of suing, mostly because it seemed that was the popular Boston pastime, but just about everybody they contacted agreed they didn't want to penalize the church. Their tight-knit families were still dedicated Catholics, even if they weren't. What they wanted was to make sure nothing like this would happen again.

"We want systemic change," Olan said. "We want fundamental change in the way these perps do business. We want to get rid of this special dispensation priests have been getting for years."

His easy eloquence impressed MacLeish. "Well, you're in a good position, then. I think you can get that." He signed up the men as clients and agreed to sue on their behalf, promising only that by doing this their voices would be heard. He would let a judge decide if their claims fell within statute. Depending on which way that went, they might not earn a red cent in compensation, but he was not worried about that. He had plenty of guaranteed wins. A huge payday seemed certain.

"Let me ask you guys something," MacLeish said. "I know you're pulling together a group of guys. I have some other guys I'd like you to meet. You mind if I have them call you?"

By the time Dave and Olan reached Lowell, twenty-five miles to the north, word was out to the others. One by one they began calling over the next few weeks. Tom Blanchette said he had a small group of victims from Birmingham's first parish in Sudbury, perhaps twenty-five in all. From Salem, Bernie McDaid called—there might be a hundred there, he guessed. There was even a younger generation of boys from Lowell whom Birmingham reached after Olan and David, perhaps seventy-five more in addition to the original 128—in all, more than three hundred men.

Until Paul Ciaramitaro called, Olan thought perhaps the abuse ceased in Lowell. Paul was seventeen years younger than Olan, and much more angry than anybody else Olan talked to. The night he telephoned, Paul was nearly incoherent in his rage, and spoke about blowing up churches and other wild revenge. Olan worried the kid might be a gun-toting anti-Catholic zealot, or an instigator from the church's right wing, or a plain nut. He was none of those. Rather, his story of entrapment by Birmingham was nearly identical to everybody else's, only fresher. He was the troubled young man the others had once been, consumed by hatred and doubt, the fresh by-product of betrayal. Olan nicknamed him the Kid.

In fact, everybody on Olan's growing list had a similar history of angry outbursts, and though none of them had suspected Birmingham's abuse for bringing on this trait, Olan was beginning to think that perhaps they should. There was some justification for this conclusion among experts. Dr. Martin Teicher, a biopsychiatry researcher at McLean Hospital, a Harvard affiliate, had found that the abuse of children permanently altered their brain structure. Among the physical alterations he isolated were EEG disturbances, occurring twice as often as among nonabused subjects. The EEG measures electrical currents in the brain's limbic system, which controls many of the most fundamental emotions, like anger.

However, in his data Teicher had not been able to disentangle sexual abuse histories from physical abuse histories, because both characteristics tend to coexist in households, ground zero for most sexual crimes against kids. For this reason, it was possible to assume that the bundle of behavior issues researchers had associated with sexual abuse stemmed instead from the use or threat of force, not sexual contact; this led some scientists to argue there was "insufficient evidence to confirm a relation between a history of childhood sexual abuse and a postsexual abuse syndrome and multiple or borderline personality disorder."

Olan Horne was no neurobiologist. But in his outreach to Birmingham's former altar boys, he was becoming something of a sociologist. He kept noticing the exact same symptoms among the men who had surfaced so far.

And he knew that wasn't the extent of Birmingham's reach. So far he had only penetrated pockets of the old neighborhoods, for the most part rounding up only the men who hadn't moved away. Olan wondered if the total number of teenage boys Birmingham fondled could reach well over five hundred, perhaps as high as a thousand, men with histories not unlike his own—more than for any priest in Boston, or any known child abuser in history.

And it wasn't just the men who were manhandled. Olan knew how many people in his life had suffered as a result of his terrible rages. Every member of his family. His colleagues at the market. Total strangers in bars whom he'd dragged outside and beaten bloody against the bumper of a car. If each of the men molested by Birmingham had somehow wounded ten others—a conservative number, judging by Olan's life—then the pyramid of damage could reach ten thousand.

Joseph Birmingham was one of the suspected priests on Sacha Pfeiffer's assignment sheet, but he kept slipping off the top tier. That was mostly because she learned he was dead, which made him a less juicy target. A journalist liked to expose an ongoing crime, liked to hammer away at an inequity until it got cured. There was no reportorial sport in a dead man's crime spree. Also, she was daunted. Long before it was clear which suspected priests were the big ones, and which were the huge ones, Walter Robinson had divvied up the suspects' names. By luck of the draw, Sacha got all the huge ones.

But of them all, Birmingham most fascinated her. According to her sources, he was by far the most *pathological* about his assaults, methodically moving from boy to boy like a champion at a pie-eating contest. With some of the priests she'd researched, their victim types were apparent—fatherless children, or drug-addled teens, or the meekest altar boys. Birmingham was indiscriminate. He was voracious. His type was the next one.

Robert Sherman, the Greenberg Traurig attorney working for MacLeish, was about to file suit for one of his Birmingham clients, giving Pfeiffer the news peg she needed. Unlike the many lawsuits filed so far, this one would carry a claim of cover-up naming John McCormack, who since 1998 had been bishop of the diocese of Manchester, New Hampshire—a development that would merit front-page placement.

She began her reporting by interviewing the named complainant, a gentle man named James Hogan, who currently lived in Delaware. He told her that for the four years of his adolescence in Salem, he was unable to escape the attentions of Birmingham, not even at home, where the priest was a regular guest. "I went upstairs to bed and he would come up and abuse me there," Hogan told her. Pfeiffer and her reporting partner, Thomas Farragher, also interviewed David P. Venne and

James Davin, who said they were masturbated by Birmingham beginning in 1962; Tom Blanchette, whose first encounter was in 1966; and Joseph A. Favalora, whose single assault took place in 1986. Though their stories spanned a quarter century, they all recounted similar tales of silently protested sex.

But as a woman, Pfeiffer found the whole notion of this sort of rape—forced masturbation—curious. Can ejaculation truly be unwanted? No woman would ever respond to an unwanted touch that way. She admitted her bewilderment to a prosecutor, and he just laughed. "Do you know what it takes to give a thirteen-year-old an erection? Absolutely nothing. An *algebra* class can give him an erection."

Saturday, March 16, 2002
MILTON, MASSACHUSETTS — The gentle twenty-six-year-old man sitting in the passenger seat of Walter Robinson's car pointed down a long, windswept drive that angled off Highland Street toward a Georgian-revival-style brick mansion tucked in a thicket of firs. A small shingle, whose paint was discolored and cracked, identified the facility as Our Lady's Hall. Rumors had swirled for years about this place. In whispers it was Pedophile Palace, the final home for priests who had cycled through psychiatric treatment without success and were considered beyond help, the worst of the worst, too dangerous even to cut loose from the priesthood for they would certainly strike over and over again. In a *Globe* column in 1997, Eileen McNamara risked angering the church (and her editor) by revealing its location and purpose, which came as a complete surprise to the local police chief but did little more than get her branded as anti-Catholic. "If they are here, it really would be none of your business," Father Robert Beale, a director at Our Lady's, told her before slamming the door.

According to the twenty-six-year-old, Father Ronald H. Paquin had spent the better part of a decade here. Sacha Pfeiffer, who sat in the backseat, was able to confirm this by conducting a search on the Our Lady's address through a comprehensive database called AutoTrack. To her surprise, she also found that perhaps a dozen other residents there dovetailed with the Spotlight Team's database of suspected abusers. Intrigued, Walter Robinson went to the Milton Town Hall for a tenancy history going back to 1970, and found an unbroken correlation. The archdiocese would say only that Our Lady's was "transitional housing" for priests with troubles, like alcoholism. The truth seemed much darker.

Pfeiffer had first spoken to their passenger almost a month ago after writing her first story about Paquin's past, which included a predawn accident in which he lost control of his car, causing the death of one of his passengers, James Francis, who was just sixteen. Paquin was never charged. But in the 1990s, the church settled at least six sex abuse suits against him for a total of about $500,000. He had lived here beginning in 1990. However, in 1998 Cardinal Law inexplicably returned Paquin to ministry, records had shown, only to remove him again following allegations, finally defrocking him in 2000.

For that story, Stephen Kurkjian, a top *Globe* investigative writer on loan to the Spotlight Team, had found Paquin in a small apartment in Malden, knocked on the door, and asked him point-blank about his abusive history.

"Sure, I fooled around. But I never raped anyone and I never felt gratified myself," he offered frankly. "I've gone twelve years and haven't abused anyone, so I'm not a pedophile because I'm not a predator."

Until the twenty-six-year-old read the article, he had thought he was the only one. Until that moment, he had never considered the sex play between them, which had begun when he was twelve and ended when he broke it off at seventeen, as abuse. Paquin had told him he was conducting a scientific study of sexuality. Of course, he scarcely believed that. But until his senior year, when he met the woman who would become his wife, he had thought of the masturbation and oral sex sessions as a normal and natural aspect of their tight friendship. He loved Paquin and considered him a father figure. Over the years since, they had remained platonic friends. He thought Paquin had loved him back. When he read that he was only one of many, he felt betrayed, and responded almost like a cuckolded husband. He had confronted his former mentor, and gotten the truth.

"That was the turning point for me," he told Pfeiffer. He hired a lawyer. And he wanted the *Globe* to write a story saying Paquin hadn't

stopped his peccadilloes twelve years ago—the priest was still masturbating him, even after he had been sent to treatment. Even while he
was *in* treatment, even at Our Lady's.

They drove the car to the crest of the hill and parked. To test his
claim, Robinson and Pfeiffer asked the man to lead them on a tour of
the grounds. They needed to see how familiar the source seemed with
the place. He did not equivocate. Mostly when he had visited Paquin,
he would sneak through a door to the basement, which he walked to
without hesitation, or climb through his bedroom window—the tall one
around the side of the house. In that bedroom on two occasions, he
said, the priest had performed oral sex on him. Once he spent the
night.

Suddenly a door high up on the side of the building swung open and
a priest came to the balcony to inquire after their presence. Though he
was wearing Bermuda shorts and a T-shirt, Robinson recognized him as
Father Edward T. Kelley, one of the men who had surfaced suspiciously
in their database. Several cases against Kelley had been settled out of
court. But for years, he had also been a counselor at Our Lady's. Kelley
was on their "to-do" list—a known molester assigned to counsel other
molesters. It couldn't get more twisted than that.

Yes it could. Behind Kelley in the doorway they saw what appeared
to be a small teenage boy.

"You're Father Kelley, aren't you?" Robinson said.

Kelley grew suspicious. "You'd better call downtown," he said, easing
the door closed.

The three stood on the lawn in stunned and scandalized amazement.

"Did we see what we thought we saw?" Robinson asked.

"It's almost jaw-dropping," Pfeiffer said. "You almost can't believe
your eyes."

Back at the office, Robinson called Donna Morrissey. He gave detailed descriptions of the late-afternoon encounter with Kelley and his
young friend. "You're a mandated reporter now," he said, referencing
the new law. "I'm telling you what we saw. You have to report it to the
police."

Morrissey called back shortly. "You're mistaken," she said. "That was

a thirty-year-old priest being treated for alcohol problems." She gave
the name. Robinson looked him up in one of the many archdiocesan directories piled on the floor of his office. The priest was six feet tall. He
looked nothing like the child they had seen.

"I'm shocked," he said. "I've never been so shocked in my life."

March 21, 2002
VATICAN CITY — Staff members working for Cardinal Darío Castrillón
Hoyos, the Vatican official heading the Congregation for the Clergy, a
powerful curial office, let it be known that during his press conference
revealing the annual Holy Thursday letter from the pope to the priests
of the world, the cardinal would be willing to address the sexual abuse
crisis. Castrillón Hoyos had been briefed on the sorts of things reporters might ask, an official told John Allen, the correspondent for the
National Catholic Reporter and a frequent Vatican commentator for
CNN. Allen expected an indirect papal observation might be forth-
coming.

The pope's letter turned out to be extremely indirect, having mostly
to do with the nature of sin and the circumstances under which it
could be forgiven. John Thavis of Catholic News Service jumped up
with the first question. Was there a direct response from the Vatican to
the crisis, he wanted to know.

Castrillón Hoyos wrote the question down on a tablet at his elbow,
then asked for another question. It came from Allen. Does the Vatican
support permanently removing priests from ministry after a credible allegation? Reporters from the *Tablet, Newsweek,* and elsewhere piled
their questions onto Castrillón Hoyos's pad as well. What about the
mandatory reporting laws? Are there discussions to bar homosexuals
from seminaries? Is Cardinal Law still held in high regard? When he
had exhausted the curiosity of his inquisitors, the cardinal closed his
notepad and pulled out a two-page typed statement, jovially explaining,
"I don't want to take more risks than are necessary."

His statement underscored that only a small percentage of priests
were guilty of sexual misconduct, which had long been outlawed and
condemned by canon law. The problem was not especially troublesome

because it seemed contained—or inflated?—in America. "Concerning the problem of sexual abuse and cases of pedophilia, I have only one answer. In today's culture of pansexualism and libertinism created in this world, several priests, being of this culture, have committed the most serious crime of sexual abuse. . . . It's already an X-ray of the problem that so many of the questions were in English."

With that, Castrillón Hoyos embarked on an unrelated topic, angering Robert Blair Kaiser, the longtime *Newsweek* correspondent. "Your Eminence," he shouted, "could you please answer our questions?"

"I listened to your questions," Castrillón Hoyos fired back, "and I would hope you'll listen when I'm speaking."

Afterward, *New York Times* reporter Melinda Henneberger asked a Vatican official why the pope hadn't offered comforting words to American Catholics caught up in scandal. Her source replied, "With all that is going on in the world, I'm just not sure it would be convenient for him to choose to speak on this."

CLEVELAND, OHIO — Sixteen years had passed since Neil Conway entered treatment at St. Luke's, largely consisting of talk therapy and group confessions. He focused first on his alcoholism, then on his sexual compulsions, his relationship to power, and his emotional immaturity. He also found a way to accept his homosexuality privately. Still, when he was free to leave after six months of therapy, he did not feel ready to rejoin the world. At his request he was granted another six months in residence, and at the end of that, though his doctors considered him on the road to integration, he was not confident he had learned the truths about himself. An ancient monk once advised, "Go and stay in your cell; your cell will teach you everything," and that's what Conway did. He asked his bishop to classify him permanently disabled, and moved to an isolated tract of wooded farmland halfway between Cleveland and Akron to live in the tradition of monastic hermits, with no one for company but a cat and a dog and an army of demons from his past, entirely alone for sixteen years.

The examination of his conscience consumed his days. He prayed every morning, and in the afternoons, no matter the season, he stood outside in rapt reverie before a shrine he built to St. John the Evangelist, patron saint of the poisoned. He prayed for knowledge. He begged for forgiveness from the eight men he had groped. But he could not forgive himself. He felt raw for what he'd done. He knew he had violated everything he ever believed in, caused suffering to the very people he wanted to serve the most.

Eventually, he called each of the young men he had molested and offered his apology. Five told him they accepted it. That was not enough penance, he believed. But days and nights in self-reflection had not given him any other outlet.

When the crisis broke and spread through the church, news of it reached him via television. He seized on an idea: he would open up his hermitage and end his silence to speak out publicly as a sexual predator in a Roman collar—to reveal the lessons he'd reached in his self-imposed cell. He hoped other perpetrator priests would follow his lead. Seminaries had produced a battalion of them. If they believed in their duty as ministers, now was their greatest opportunity. Intense candor was what the scandal called for, and what the family of Catholics deserved.

He invited a *Newsweek* reporter to hear his story. At the very least, he thought his atonements could help the men he molested. "I want the eight young men to know I've chosen a path that has caused me a great suffering—the exposure—and I've done that in hope I can make it good," he said.

On a gray, snowy afternoon, the reporter arrived at his home, hidden at the end of a long switchback road near the snow-filled nape of a ravine. In his hermitage, Conway had lost hold of a sense of his physical self—he was sixty-five, unshaven, and unclean, in ill-fitting clothes. His lips were a dark hue of brown, stained by the coffee he consumed neurotically, and his fingers were the color of the orange tobacco he compulsively shoveled into his pipe. His grotto was as discomfiting as his own physical presence. Floors and countertops were thick with dust and animal dander. Through loose windows and doors came frigid gusts and sporadic dustings of snow. The Conway family was still one of Cleveland's most prominent—his siblings were major philanthropists—but Neil Conway lived in filthy self-denigration.

"I committed an abomination," Conway explained. "I'm sitting here on the dunghill of my own shame and guilt."

That afternoon, by chance, he had opened his mailbox to find a notice that had been mailed to all his neighbors announcing his presence as a threat to children. He was not deterred. "I'm willing to have my neighbors think I'm a pervert," he said. "I'm ready for my family to say I betrayed them and dragged the family name through the mud. I'm willing to do that with great sorrow, but I've got to make up for this terrible thing that I did. I don't want to be a star. I don't want to be a freak. I don't want to be an angry old man cursing at life. I don't want people to be morbidly curious about me. So what do I want? What do I want? There's a famous Tosca aria where she's trapped and she goes, 'God, you know my life is art, my trade is art and love.' I want to say: I was ordained a priest as a young man who was still a young boy—fourteen years old—emotionally and sexually. And I learned how to get what I thought I needed in the priesthood, doing what a priest does. Tosca says, 'Look what has happened to me!' I was so in love with my life, and at the same time I was in trouble right away, as soon as I stepped off the box.

"I didn't know how to get the right thing the right way. These were romance and intimacy for me, as I saw it. These were relationships! In that perverse state when I became a perpetrator, I was sure I was giving a great deal of pleasure. I thought I was giving them the gift of love—a priest who really loved them. There's an old saying in Catholic theology: *Agere sequitur esse,* your actions come out of your being. I thought the way a fourteen-year-old does, so I reverted to the age of fourteen in my behavior. I don't want to overdramatize this, but in therapy they always ask: Did you feel part of you was hovering over the event? Yes! Yes! That was it! I was able most of the time to block it out. I lived in two worlds."

In the other world, the world of the body, he had a long history. A male relative first introduced him to sex when he was fourteen, though he thought of the events neither as abuse nor even as sex. He was that alienated from his own desires. Sex was an abstraction he couldn't recognize even in its midst. He spent much of these past sixteen years trying to understand what mechanisms kept him from knowing he was gay. He had accepted the church's belief that homosexuality was a mortal sin. No longer. Theology had kept him blind to his heart, and then commanded he wage a war against this thing he couldn't see. He felt his whole life had been a deception. Now he would put it all on display.

"I was a predator," he said. "I claim full responsibility. Whatever damage I've done to these men can't be undone by me now, but I am deeply regretful for what I did. How do you make up for something as awful as child abuse? You can make a resurrection out of any death. That is my goal."

Saturday, March 23, 2002
ACROSS AMERICA — It was the eve of Holy Week, a time for great sadness and exuberance, seventy-six difficult days since the *Globe* published its first story of priestly sex abuse. A torrent of accounts had followed—190 investigative articles in the *Globe* alone, and thousands more in every major newspaper and many minor ones, and successive evening news programs. Perhaps no single group was more dispirited than Law's own priests. Holy Week is the time every year when priests are called upon to renew their vows, rededicating themselves to the celibate, self-sacrificing service of their flocks. Father Robert Bullock, pastor of Our Lady of Sorrows in Sharon, Massachusetts, was not feeling very keen about the whole enterprise. Sitting in an airport waiting area recently, he had been accosted by somebody accusing *him* of child abuse. He felt filthy. Ever since then he vowed to "never again go around in clerical clothes."

Now, when interviewed by a *Christian Science Monitor* reporter, he was perfectly willing to say how angry he was at his own boss for doing nothing to counter this grotesque caricature of the priesthood. "This has nothing to do with faith or Catholicism, but with structures—the way we have been as a church, the way authority has been exercised. He must do something radical—the trust is so fractured. He needs to go parish to parish, Sunday after Sunday, not with his agenda but just to listen. Those great pastoral skills need to be emphasized. If he doesn't do that, the trust is not going to be rebuilt."

No priest had ever offered such a public rebuking of his cardinal. But he wasn't the only one who felt this. From Cleveland to Tucson, Charlotte to Los Angeles, it was apparent that the betrayal of trust and innocence was a pandemic. Perhaps two hundred American priests were now the subject of credible allegations. Minneapolis-based lawyer Jeffrey Anderson, the best-known attorney in the country when it came to suing the church, by now had over six hundred civil cases pending or in development in a dozen states across the country—including two he would soon file under RICO statutes, alleging that the Catholic Church met all the legal definitions of an organized criminal enterprise. "They're using the wires and the mail to defraud, to deceive, to commit and conceal criminal activity, and it is a long-standing pattern and practice," he said. "That's what mobsters do."

Even the pope, who had kept a careful silence, finally took notice in his annual pre-Easter letter to the world's priests. Rather than condemning the policies of bishops and cardinals, he laid the blame on a few bad apples who had succumbed to what he called "the most grievous forms of the *mysterium iniquitatis* (the mystery of evil)." He worried most what their weaknesses did to their fellow clerics. "Great scandal is caused, with the result that a dark shadow of suspicion is cast over all the other fine priests who perform their ministry with honesty and integrity and often with heroic self-sacrifice."

Still, the structures of silence were dissolving rapidly this week. In Michigan, former all-star pro baseball player Tom Paciorek summoned a reporter to reveal that as a strapping high school athlete at Hamtramck St. Ladislaus on Detroit's east side, well on his way to being a six-foot-four, 215-pound major league athlete, he had nonetheless fallen prey to a priest who regularly involved him in unwelcome masturbation. In Mendham, New Jersey, a young man named Mark Serrano risked sacrificing the $241,000 out-of-court settlement he won in 1987 from the local diocese by violating its gag-order clause. He held a press conference disclosing the abuse he endured from ages nine to sixteen, which included groping, forced masturbation, and penetration. He called on others bound by church-imposed secrecy to follow his lead. "These people, they've been able to survive through secrecy," said Serrano, who at thirty-seven was a well-connected government affairs and communications executive involved in Republican causes. "The truth is so important and secrecy is so damaging. Not just for the people who have experienced abuse, but everyone needs to see this horrific truth for what it truly is."

David Clohessy, who had known Serrano for a number of years through SNAP, watched his press conference in awe. He knew what audacity it took for this young man to defy the last facet of church control over his own life. Clohessy was now the national president of SNAP. He knew countless Catholics who had long ago agreed to settlements with the church but now yearned to reclaim their personal histories and take part in this sad national festival of revelation—whether in therapy sessions, confessions, candlelight vigils, mass rallies, or newspaper articles. They were desperate for somebody to take the first step. Serrano was showing the way.

"This day was bound to come," Clohessy thought. "What did Martin Luther King say? No lie lives forever."

With the floodgates opening, wounded Catholics were now coming forward in armies. SNAP chapters were forming at a stunning pace. Many victims turned to their churches for reconciliation. Many more went to trial attorneys, hoping for closure. In Minnesota, Jeffrey Anderson was working twelve-hour days, seven days a week. Same for Kathrine Freberg in Irvine, California; Lynne Cadigan in Tucson, Arizona; and the handful of independent lawyers around the country known to have taken on the church. Steve Rubino, a solo New Jersey practitioner, kept a tally of the messages he'd received from priest abuse victims in the past week and a half alone. "Two hundred callers," he said. "And not a single one under statute."

That didn't matter to them. They simply needed to tell their secret stories to somebody. Unable to sue, disregarded by their church, locked out of the corridors of truth telling and reconciliation, they wholesaled their stories to journalists, or paralegals, or receptionists—anybody willing to listen.

Nowhere was the parade of casualties more overwhelming than in Boston. Mitchell Garabedian's office teemed with clients. Attorneys at Greenberg Traurig, where five were now working exclusively on abuse cases, were collapsing under the emotional pressure. To help clients and nonclients alike, Eric MacLeish hired a full-time social worker on his staff, probably the only one in a law firm in America. Diane Nealon, a soft-spoken recent graduate in the field of forensic social work, expected she would monitor client intakes, help identify tortuous claims, and offer support during trying junctures like depositions and interrogatories. She was right. Only, the people who needed her help most were not the clients. They were the lawyers.

March 24, 2002, Palm Sunday
MARTHA'S VINEYARD, MASSACHUSETTS — Tom Blanchette picked up his Sunday paper. There, on page A1, was Sacha Pfeiffer's groundbreaking story about Father Joseph Birmingham, cowritten with Thomas Farragher.

> A former Salem man who alleges he was sexually molested hundreds of times by a parish priest in the 1960s said that Bishop John B. McCormack of Manchester, N.H., who was assigned to the same Salem parish at the time, saw the priest taking him to his rectory bedroom and did nothing to stop it.
>
> McCormack, who was an auxiliary bishop in Boston under Cardinal Bernard F. Law, said through a spokesman the allegation by James Hogan is false. But in response to Globe inquiries, he acknowledged that he was warned more than 30 years ago that the Rev. Joseph E. Birmingham was molesting children at St. James parish in Salem.
>
> Thomas Blanchette, another man who alleges that Birmingham molested him in the 1960s, said he approached Law at Birmingham's funeral in 1989 and told him about the abuse. Blanchette said Law silently prayed for him, but then instructed him to keep the information secret.
>
> "He laid his hands on my head for two or three minutes," Blanchette, who said his four brothers were also molested by Birmingham, said of Law. "And then he said this: 'I bind you by the power of the confessional never to speak about this to anyone else.'

And that just burned me big-time. . . . I didn't ask him to hear my confession. I went there to inform him."

A spokeswoman for the Archdiocese of Boston, Donna M. Morrissey, said yesterday that Law has "a vague recollection of such an encounter" but "no memory of the words exchanged." Morrissey added that "it is inconceivable to him, however, that he would ever have counseled someone never to speak of what they have suffered."

Law is willing to meet with Blanchette "to clarify any misunderstanding," Morrissey said.

Blanchette didn't need to be invited twice. An independent contractor on Martha's Vineyard, he picked up the telephone immediately to rearrange his week's obligations. He was going to see the elusive cardinal.

March 25, 2002

LOWELL, MASSACHUSETTS — News accounts of Birmingham's abusive career reached Lowell the way many things do, secondhand and late. The *Lowell Sun* ran an AP pickup of the *Globe* story a day later. Just the sight of Birmingham's photograph made Gary Bergeron's stomach turn. He knew Birmingham was dead. He'd come across his gravestone on the gray afternoon in 1992 when Gary buried his sister, just a few paces away. His kid brother Edward saw it first.

"Fucking Birmingham," he said.

Gary snapped to some long-forgotten part of his brain. He looked at his brother. That was the first time it had ever occurred to him that he was not the only one.

"You, too?"

"Yup."

Almost every day since the scandal broke in January he had hoped the moment of Birmingham's exposure would come. And now that it sat in his lap, in his large living room on this extremely cold and dark winter night, he had no idea what he was expected to do with it. Certainly he would have to tell his mother and father what Birmingham had done to him and his brother in the eighth grade. He was thirty-nine now. How he dreaded this. His parents' faith was the most prized Bergeron family heirloom, celebrated and protected like some antique porcelain figurine. He knew what damage this knowledge would wreak, knew personally that, as in Oz, once the curtain was pulled back on the church's wizards there was no way to draw it closed again. He hadn't been able to go to Mass in years.

He lit a cigarette and left phone messages for his brother Edward in Hilton Head, South Carolina, and for Bob Sherman, the Greenberg Traurig lawyer named in the paper. Edward was the first to return the call.

"Eddie," Gary said. "Birmingham's picture's in the paper."

"You're shitting me."

"Some guys have come forward. The news is out."

Edward's voice brimmed with excitement. He too had been expecting this moment. His mind swung back to that strange afternoon in ninth grade when the priest first circled behind him and plunged his hands into his underwear as if he were dousing a fire. "What do you want to do?"

"I don't know, but I got to do something. I think we should stand with them. It's just these guys—they could say it didn't happen or whatever. Let me think about it, let me think."

"Get me a soapbox and I'm there, I'm serious."

"Let's keep it cool, Eddie. You can have your soapbox but I just want to stand next to these guys, you know, to let everybody see these guys aren't lying, that it happened more than once."

It was not that Edward was more strident. He was more aggrieved. After fifteen years in therapy, on and off, and twenty years battling alcohol and cocaine, which had destroyed numerous relationships and wounded his kids, he had finally broken through to an understanding of what Birmingham's roaming hands had to do with his chaotic life of wreckage. "I might have been a drinker anyway, even without Birmingham. But all these years I kept trying AA and the basic premise of that is: You need a higher power. Well, I've got a little problem with God. Therein lies my biggest struggle in the past fifteen years: gaining this whole God connection."

He hadn't had a drink in four years, eight months, and a dozen or so days, thanks to his return to prayer. He finally said, "Okay, God, I'll believe in you." And by and by his life had become functional again—a decent job selling floor covering, a welcoming home, a reliable girlfriend, two bright children. But he couldn't help wondering how different it all might have been if he hadn't spent most of his adult years inside this "spiritual crisis syndrome," as he called it. If now was the time for truth telling about the Catholic Church's evil underbelly, Edward was keen to be the poster boy.

"I'll talk to anybody about that manipulative fucking bastard," he said. "I make no secret about it. I'm forced to look at this stuff all the time, because my life is always falling apart."

"This is not about money or publicity, it's about setting the record straight," Gary said, agreeing. "Letting people know the truth."

Edward thought about the only other time this subject had come up between them since that first time at the cemetery. A number of years ago when he had picked Gary up at the Savannah airport, he barely had a chance to mention how Birmingham had begun to figure into his psychotherapy sessions when Gary jumped all over him.

"What happened happened," he interrupted. "We got a good education, we put our lives together. The past is behind us. I don't want to talk about that."

Even now, Edward thought, Gary seemed reticent.

It was true. Gary was not prepared to display his freakish past for public consumption. By the time he hung up the phone, Gary couldn't even quite recall why he had dialed the attorney named in the paper. But immediately the phone rang with Bob Sherman's returned call.

Reciting his story in brief, Gary repeated his reasons for hesitancy.

"I don't want to stay as a victim," Gary said. His life wasn't perfect. Both his marriages had ended in divorce, but like his brother he was also now happily cohabiting with an adoring new girlfriend and talking about commitment again. His daughter and son were growing into amazing and responsible people. His carpentry business was thriving with steady and reliable referrals through word of mouth. He was living back in the house where he was born, which had been divided into apartments. His mother and father lived upstairs.

"I never, ever gave Birmingham the credit for what went on in my life. You know what, I always considered myself one of the lucky guys. My life was my life. I dealt with it as I dealt with it. It's the cards I was handed and I played it out."

Sherman accepted this as fact. He had spent the day fielding calls from people who had been accosted by Birmingham, he said. Some wore their lasting fury like a hideous tattoo; some, like Gary, wanted only to be counted in the sad census. He had also heard from some Salem parents who had gone to the chancery in the 1960s, and it was because of their complaints that Birmingham was sent to Lowell in the first place.

"Wait. They knew about him before I was abused?"

"Yes."

"Wait."

It was a small fact, this preknowledge, and not altogether surprising. He figured higher-ups were aware of the behavior; how could they not be? But now he flashed back to the very first time, that afternoon in the large shower room at the tennis club, and Gary now knew without a doubt that he had been placed in that mortifying circumstance pre-cisely *because* Birmingham was a notorious predator. They had moved Birmingham to Lowell when it got too hot in Salem! They never thought about the kids! Thinking this filled him with rage, more rage than he had ever felt about Birmingham before, an almost lunatic mad-ness, such as he had never known possible.

Still, he wasn't ready to go public. But he agreed to visit Sherman in his office to find out what more had been unearthed about Birming-ham.

Sherman had an opening on Friday, he said. "But that's probably not good for you because it's Good Friday, so what about the following Wednesday?"

"No, wait, you know what?" Gary said. "Good Friday is appropriate."

Tuesday, March 26, 2002
BRIGHTON, MASSACHUSETTS — It took Tom Blanchette half a morning to reach the chancery from his home in Martha's Vineyard, a trip involv-

ing a forty-five-minute ferry ride across winter-roiled Nantucket Sound. Traffic on the mainland was awful. Blanchette's nerves were frayed by the time he swung off Commonwealth Avenue, passed the "No Trespassing" sign, and finally extinguished his engine under a towering snow-heavy pine.

Inside, he stooped to shout his name through the thick bulletproof glass. "I'd like to speak to Donna Morrissey."

"Do you have an appointment?" the woman inquired in half pantomime.

"No," he said. "But she was trying to find me."

"You can't talk to her without an appointment."

"In that case, I'd like to make an appointment."

"You can't make an appointment *here*."

"My name was on the front page of the *Boston Globe* saying I was sexually abused as a child by Father Birmingham," he hollered. "Donna Morrissey was quoted saying that Cardinal Law would be happy to meet with me at any time."

"Oh," the woman said. She motioned for him to take a seat in the aseptic lobby.

He did, and thumbed through a stack of *Pilot* newspapers.

When the woman wanted to get his attention again, she had to rap heavily on the glass, which produced only muffled thumps. Her booth was so well armored that an invading army would have little impact.

"You want to speak with the Reverend John Connolly at the residence," she called, passing a slip of paper through a slot in the glass. "This is the number for his secretary."

Tom knew Connolly was the hulking personal secretary who appeared alongside the cardinal in most news photos these days. He also knew that the residence was just on the other end of the parking lot, so he headed there directly to try his chances in person.

The black Lincoln was in the driveway, so Blanchette assumed the cardinal was at home, and that meant Connolly would be, too. He gathered his breath before gripping the doorknob on the residence. To his surprise, it was double-bolted. He pressed the buzzer and by and by a nun worked the door open and addressed him through the crevice.

"I've just come from the chancery, and they told me to speak to John Connolly," he announced.

"Do you have an appointment?"

"No, I do not."

"You will need to make an appointment."

"That would be fine," he said, waiting.

"You must do that on the telephone."

She left and returned with a red slip of paper on which she had penned a number. But just as she handed this to Blanchette, he glimpsed Connolly over her shoulder.

"Father," he called out. "I've been looking for you!"

Though he had the physical characteristics of a pro wrestler, Connolly was an approachable sort with an easy humor. He didn't mind having to dispel the silly rumors. No, he had not once been a cop, nor did he carry a nine-millimeter in his priestly garb in defense of the cardinal. Though he stood over six feet tall and weighed 230 pounds (this was something that Boston Catholics weren't ashamed to ask him), he had never played college football, thank you, much less pro.

He returned Blanchette's greeting and once he understood why the man was wedging his shoe in the door, ushered him upstairs to a dining room on the second floor. The table, Blanchette thought, must seat thirty.

He gave the abbreviated story of his life, ranging easily from the abuse to his deathbed reconciliation with Birmingham and his encounter with Law at the funeral, the details of which he was not at all vague about. "He bound me to silence and told me to go see Bishop Daily, which I did do," he said. "I said to him, 'It is incumbent upon the archdiocese to seek out people who were sexually abused and help them. After all, isn't that the mandate of the gospel?' I never heard from him again."

"What are you here for?"

"Well, John? I want you to know what I said in the paper was true. It said the cardinal would be happy to meet with me, and if that's so, I'd be happy to meet with him."

Connolly would see what he could arrange. "But this is Holy Week," he said. "We have a lot of things scheduled. Today we're going to the cathedral and all the priests are going to renew their ordination vows. Then of course comes Easter Sunday."

"John, I understand. Many years have passed already. I can wait."

"I will call you tonight," Connolly promised, handing Blanchette his business card. "If by any chance I don't get back to you, call me at this number."

Blanchette never heard from Connolly again.

LOS ANGELES, CALIFORNIA — Meeting at St. Camillus Center for Pastoral Care, a Catholic facility affiliated with Los Angeles County/USC Medical Center, eight priests working for the archdiocese of Los Angeles and the diocese of Orange gathered in secret to discuss the crisis and what it meant for them, as gay clergy. Their invited guest was Bill Mochon, a recent seminary graduate who went into psychology rather than the priesthood upon his graduation. His patients were mostly gay priests, and as a gay man himself he advised Cardinal Mahony from time to time on policies relating to homosexuals.

Until relatively recently, the group had not paid much attention to the media storm except to recall the admonition they remembered being given in seminary: "Don't fuck the flock." So far, at least, Los Angeles had been mercifully spared the worst of it. No group member knew any of the twelve priests who had been named in public reports. Nor were they privy to any gossip about any of their acquaintances. But with each passing day they realized that as gays they could not ignore the significance of the crisis. Rumors were flying about a backlash against all gay priests, a prospect that terrified them. Only one of the eight was at all open about his sexual orientation; the rest were entirely clandestine.

"We keep hearing about a witch-hunt. What is the likelihood of that?"

"Have you heard anything from downtown?" another asked. "Are we just blowing smoke up each other's butts, or are we right?"

"Nothing," Mochon told them. "I haven't heard anything."

"What if it actually does happen? What if somebody in the Vatican says, 'All you homos, you're the cause of all of this, get out of here!' Is there anything we can do?"

Nothing seemed more absurd to Mochon. Still, he believed that as gay priests they would do themselves a huge political favor by being forthright about their lives. He had encouraged them to speak to reporters, but out of fear they had declined. Around the country, since the crisis broke there had not been a single gay parish priest—though there were perhaps twenty-five thousand of them—who would say publicly that he was gay. In recent years, only a dozen or so priests had come out of the closet, but most did so at the end of a scandal or in retirement, when they knew their career would not suffer. The rest, like these men—ranging in age from thirty-six to fifty-four—confined their secrets to small circles of friends.

"Roger wouldn't do that," Mochon said, meaning Cardinal Mahony.

"He's a bit of an asshole," one man said.

"True," said another. "But when it comes down to taking out gay priests, he'll take care of his own."

"Are you outing him?" Speculation about Mahony's sexual orientation was a Los Angeles parlor game. "I mean, did you ever see the way he wears his tool belt around the cabin? That's an *accessory!*"

"Not taking care of other gays, but taking care of his priests. He's very committed to his priests."

"Well, I wouldn't want him to be part of the tribe."

"But what if they're right?" one priest interjected. "What if this really *is* a gay problem?"

His query drew anger from his colleagues, but he persisted. "Maybe the way homosexuality is treated, it causes a snap in the mind of some sort. Maybe they're right and we're wrong."

"You mean, a different kind of gay panic—that the *gays* are panicking?"

That's exactly what he wondered. From a psychological perspective, it was, after all, unusual to have a profession in which members of a dominant culture felt like unwelcome infiltrators, forced to exist in a state of dishonesty. Or maybe the point was that gay priests, by internalizing the notion of their desires as evil—and then teaching that extremely negative perspective to generations of young gays—had done something dire to them. A retired priest from Cocoa Beach, Florida, named Father Don Whipple had authored over a hundred position papers denouncing the "Don't ask, don't tell" policies toward gay priests as psychologically damaging. "They let us in, and they allow us to be here, but they provide nothing for us as a gay community," Whipple said. "We're brought up to hate who we are. We're afraid when we go to confession to confess who we are. If we come out, that is a reason for dismissal. We learned a long time ago how to survive in a hostile environment, which is: we pass as being straight. And in doing so we do a lot of damage to our psyches. Because we're not the persons we are meant to be, we are not ourselves. We have to wear the mask for a lifetime of punishment."

Whipple, who belonged to the religious order of Holy Cross Fathers and spent his career teaching in all-boys schools, believed this created tremendous challenges that had never been acknowledged. "It has a way of coming out sideways because you don't deal with it straight on, you deal with it in weird and strange ways. It could be in the form of wrestling with boys. Immature behavior. Touching."

He came to know his own homosexuality only after a lengthy retreat—when he was sixty-seven.

This fit in with what Father John McNeill, author of the book *The Church and the Homosexual,* had been arguing for years. "From my viewpoint the most serious problem here is the call for all priests to be chaste," McNeill said. "This is not an equivalent demand for a heterosexual priest and a homosexual priest. Most people miss that, they seem to deal with the fact that chastity would be exactly the same thing for both groups. But a heterosexual priest's sexual desire to reach out to a woman is considered good in itself. And always a valid choice, if they chose to leave the priesthood. Whereas the homosexual priest is taught that his desire to reach out to another male is *evil*. And *never* an option. Therefore it's not a question of sacrificing a good as it is for a heterosexual, it's repressing an evil desire. The church wants gay priests to interiorize homophobia and self-hatred, and this leads to all sorts of neurotic stuff. It's a very different demand. There are many gay priests who receive the grace to live out a positive celibate life not based on self-hatred, but self-acceptance. But the majority, I think, find that impossible. What is bad psychology has to be bad theology." For making similar pronouncements, McNeill was expelled from his religious order, the Society of Jesus, in 1988 on the orders of Cardinal Ratzinger, making him a priest without portfolio. Only then did he come out of the closet.

Mochon was stunned that these priests would believe such a thing. He figured they must be extremely beaten down and dispirited, or spiritually exhausted, to think there was something inside them that would touch off a massive crime spree against young men and boys. "Forget it," he said. "This has nothing to do with being gay."

"Even so," one of the men said, "I'm signing up for social work school while they're still covering our tuition. That way when they kick us out of the priesthood, I'll have something to fall back on."

Good Friday, March 29, 2002
BOSTON, MASSACHUSETTS — "From the sixth hour until the ninth hour darkness came over all the land," Matthew wrote. "And when Jesus had cried out again in a loud voice, he gave up his spirit. At that moment the curtain in the temple was torn in two from top to bottom."

In the breeze outside Holy Cross Cathedral, a protester carried a sign reading, "Will children ever be safe in the church?" Another read: "House of Rape." Four hundred people gathered on the steps outside the cathedral. Most were dressed in purple to signify the suffering commemorated on Good Friday, the day Christ died on the cross. A small girl, moist in the morning air and gripping an umbrella beneath her chin, pinched the corners of a cardboard sign. "Law," it said in smeary ink, "You made a bad decision! Jesus is mad at you!" She stood porcelain still, as simple and vulnerable as the child she was, like the children before her whose faith was enormous, and then gone.

Other little girls stood inside wearing lavender frills, overawed and still on the day at the heart of their faith. As though the world were mirrored in perfect refraction, the church was inside and outside the cathedral equally, the rituals were observed on both sides of the towering doors. Moving among the makeshift Stations of the Cross erected along Washington Street's sidewalk, the protesters reenacted the traditional passion of Christ. Inside communicants did likewise, crisscrossing the red-carpeted ambulatory, four hundred other Catholics in somber synchronicity.

Cardinal Law lifted a heavy wooden cross, the weight of which tilted him unsteadily. Outside at precisely that moment, a woman raised up a palm-sized crucifix to the gathered, and they venerated it.

"We bring to the cross our collective sufferings as church," said the cardinal inside, "particularly in this challenging hour, as we seek the rec-onciling, healing love of Christ for those who have suffered sexual abuse as children by clergy, as we seek to strengthen the effectiveness of our resolve to protect children, as we seek the restoration of trust among the faithful." He pleaded sonorously for forgiveness and healing, he prayed for the church to come together at this holy time, more than ever now. "Even though we carry in our hearts those who bear the wounds of be-trayal through abuse inflicted by others, especially by clergy, even though we experience the pain of dissent within the church, we fix our gaze with unshakable hope on the risen Lord. He is our light."

On the sidewalk, the injured rose one by one, speaking the truths about their own pain, which was not brushed away by the cardinal's de-sires. Arthur Austin did not spare details. The touch, the smell, the rage. "Why is it too much for you to hear? No one in the church wor-ried that it might be too much for any victim to bear the abuse, over and over, in hopelessness. There is nothing polite about rape."

This was the largest protest ever on these steps. Perhaps there had never been as large a protest by Catholics *as Catholics* on a cathedral doorstep anywhere in the American church. For victims, the day was momentous. They had not expected so many nonvictims to accompany them on the picket lines. Even a dozen nuns had joined the vigil. Women representing the Sisters of Mercy, the Sisters of Notre Dame de Namur, and the Sisters of St. Anne were chanting and surging, pray-ing aloud, rosaries lacing their old fingers. "There aren't even words," Sister Jon Julie Sullivan said. "There aren't even words to tell you how many changes we need."

In a sepulchral voice, staggering at the altar, the cardinal rose up to the words of Christ at the last.

"'Now there was set a vessel full of vinegar: and they filled a sponge with vinegar, and put it upon hyssop, and put it to his mouth.

"'When Jesus therefore had received the vinegar, he said, It is finished: and he bowed his head, and gave up the ghost.'"

Tears slicing his cheeks, Steve Lynch took a place on the stone steps in the brightening spring day. A man had never felt such icy solitude as he had two years ago. He could not believe his eyes now. Seas of victims like himself and scores of nonvictims now began to link their hands together and slowly marched themselves into one long line and laced this human rope all the way around Holy Cross Cathedral until the energy inside was entirely engulfed in their arms.

"You are about to witness the greatest resurrection before your very eyes," he declared, sobbing, arms outstretched. "You will be swept away by the courage and strength of those who are wounded. Their resurrection will be in the beauty, health, and freedom that is theirs to claim."

March 31, 2002, Easter Sunday

ACROSS AMERICA — Many bishops around the country noted with alarm that Easter attendance, a bellwether of the health of greater Catholicism, was significantly affected by the scandals. Although some cathedrals and churches were full as ever—even Holy Cross Cathedral in Boston had a capacity crowd—others had unusually empty pews. This was particularly noticeable because in the aftermath of 9/11, Americans' attachments to their churches surged to the highest levels ever recorded. Just a scant few months later those gains were erased. The annual Gallup Index of Leading Religious Indicators would later confirm that faith in all organized religion had hit an all-time low in 2002, thanks to the Catholic clergy scandals.

More troubling were collection-plate receipts, off by double digits in churches in California, Wisconsin, Florida, and elsewhere. A national survey found that one in nine regular churchgoers had reduced giving on the parish level, and 19 percent said they stopped all support for their dioceses. In Boston, where Cardinal Law arrived at Mass surrounded by a retinue of bodyguards, some parishes were reporting 25 percent reductions in attendance, and an evaporation of tithing. Nationally, a severe financial crisis loomed, plunging into peril the 2.6 million students in Catholic parochial schools, 670,000 students at Catholic colleges and universities, and countless people who rely on

Catholic Charities and the national network of church-run hospitals, accounting for 17 percent of all admissions.

CLEVELAND, OHIO — Father Don Rooney presided over Easter Mass at St. Anthony's on Sunday, March 31. He was relaxed and upbeat. Helen Spirakus watched him cradle a couple's newborn after the service. It gave him such joy. "Father Don looked like our Lord looking down at that baby," she thought. "So radiant."

Rooney, who was forty-eight, joined his family for lunch at a West-lake restaurant that afternoon, then spent the rest of the day tending to church matters. Two days later, diocese officials reached him on the telephone. They had received a call from a woman who claimed Rooney kissed and groped her twenty-two years ago, when she was a teenager. He said he recalled the woman, but was shocked by her charge. No, he did not touch her, he said; yes, he would be glad to visit the chancery in the morning to discuss the matter.

When the appointed time arrived, he would not make an appearance. Officials called his rectory and left messages, but he was out running errands. In the afternoon, he would stop by his mother's house with four or five small boxes of financial and personal papers, books, and knickknacks. She was not around, so he jotted down a note:

Hi Mom—
It's just me. I dropped off a few boxes and put them in the garage.
Could you store them for me, for a little bit.
Thanks, Don
—I'll call you later.

Bishop Anthony Pilla had a reasonable reputation in the Cleveland diocese, known less for what he was than for what he wasn't: an ideologue for either the right or the left. He was no more prepared for the scandal than any of his peers. He had already been forced to admit that thirteen men under his direction had been removed following allegations, and in a week he would sideline another nine. One, Father Donald Brickman, served as vicar of justice in the church's own court for hearing abuse charges, though he himself had such charges pending. A

grand jury was investigating the entire structure for criminal wrongdoing, preparing a subpoena for internal church records. The district attorney's office had assigned four prosecutors full-time and twenty-five
more part-time to the church probe. Yet Pilla had not spoken publicly
about the scandal, despite the fact that Neil Conway, one of his own
priests, could not keep himself from scrupulously confessing his crimes
to whatever reporter caught him on the phone.

Feeling it was time to make a declaration, Pilla agreed to an interview with Ted Henry, a reporter for channel 5 who had covered the local church for more than twenty years. Henry had never seen the
bishop more tense.

"To your knowledge," he asked, "is there anything left unsaid that
we're all going to hear about soon?"

"Yes," he admitted. "People are coming forward, and I know we'll
have to be prepared to deal with them forthrightly."

"Will they involve possibly your men here in Greater Cleveland?"

"Yes."

"Are you aware of any such cases now?"

"Yes."

"What's being done with them?"

"We will apply the policy, as we said. We will apply the policy as we
have applied the policy."

"Part of your answer was to reply in the future tense; why are you not
applying it all equally now?"

"We are," he said, "We will."

When Father Don Rooney promised to go to the chancery on Wednesday, certainly he meant to keep his promise. But when he got in the
car, his mind mutinied. It was not the looming reprimand that frightened him, or even the face of disappointment from his superiors. He
knew he had had a history of groping the girls—a feel here or kiss there.
He had been called in about it before, and managed to live through the
humiliation. But then it was all kept in the circle.

These days were different. He would be humiliated publicly—he
surely knew it now—like a common criminal. The prospect burned in
him like illness. This was the feeling of culpable cowardice.

When he did not show, the vicar's office filed a missing persons report.

Rooney never returned to his rectory. Hours became a day. On a frigid and snowy Thursday morning, April 3, he parked his car in the parking lot beside a suburban Cleveland CVS. Shoppers weaved through the winds for their prescriptions and sundries. He took a pen and wrote down the names of his family members on a piece of paper, followed by a brief note, and placed it at his side. He knew what he was contemplating was wrong. Catholic teaching on suicide was crystal clear. God gave life in a kind of lease agreement: only God could take it back. Suicide was a grave injustice, a sin so malignant that, in the past, the sinner was denied a Christian burial. According to the Catechism of the Catholic Church, grave mental illness, anguish, or severe fear of hardship, suffering, or torture could diminish one's moral responsibility for suicide. "We should not despair of the eternal salvation of persons who have taken their own lives," it said. "By ways known to him alone, God can provide the opportunity for salutary repentance."

As he lifted a small handgun to his head and tickled the nine-millimeter bullet out of its chamber, the priest knew this loophole was his only hope. Blood colored the soft fabric on the ceiling and darkened the windows. A police officer found his slumped body just before noon. He was the first suicide by an American priest in the church crisis.

In the days that followed, the soul of Father Rooney would be prayed over by grieving parishioners who remembered all the good he had done. He had paid one family's school tuition when they were on hard times. His sagacity changed another woman's life entirely. "If anybody is sitting in heaven, he is," one of his mourners told a reporter. "I feel I have another saint to intercede for me." Even diocesan leaders bid farewell in poetic eulogies and promised a burial befitting a servant of the Lord.

It was enough to make Regina Scolaro sick. The Father Rooney she remembered burnt her cheeks with his lips and tore at her eleven-year-old breasts with hands so enormous they imprisoned her. She knew the people preparing to bury Rooney knew this, for she had reported it way back then. She had barely mentioned it since—she told her parents only a week earlier. And she would not have come forward now, except she knew the isolation and despair the anonymous woman who had brought the charge against him must feel. She did not want her to shoulder any responsibility for his death—he was escaping justice that was due Scolaro and others as well.

"I've tried to forget this for twenty years, and I hoped I never would have to talk about it," Scolaro told a *Plain Dealer* reporter between tears. "But I have to help this other woman."

Later, she would sue the diocese for $10 million, which was just the evidence Father Rooney's mother needed. "They're trying to get their hands in the Catholic till," she would say.

April 1, 2002

MARTHA'S VINEYARD, MASSACHUSETTS — "I'm Tom Blanchette, I'm calling from Martha's Vineyard, and he told me to call him please to make an appointment? That's what I'm doing." Because he hadn't heard anything back from the chancery about meeting Law, Tom Blanchette waited until the Monday or Tuesday after Easter to telephone Father John Connolly again. He got no further than the priest's assistant.

She thanked him and said she would pass along the message.

When Blanchette's phone rang a week later he was surprised to hear Bob Sherman, the attorney from Eric MacLeish's office, on the line. The two had never spoken. He was calling cold.

Sherman said he was pulling together a group of Birmingham litigants. He would love to represent Blanchette. But even more to the point, in order to bolster the other suits he was about to file, he needed to get the details of Blanchette's history. Birmingham had gotten to Blanchette early on. Blanchette's family had a history of alerting the archdiocese. Blanchette himself claimed to have informed the cardinal. Establishing these facts would be an essential first step in anybody else's suit. Sherman hoped he could convince Blanchette at the very least to give an affidavit in support of the other litigants.

"My goal," Blanchette averred, "is to fix this problem. I seem to have an inside track—the cardinal wants to see me and talk to me. I'd rather be seen as his friend than his enemy. I think I can do more good that way."

Sherman, who was ordinarily a temperate fellow, let loose a derisive chuckle. "We have handled dozens and dozens of these cases," he said. "They *always* say, 'We'll call you back,' and they never do. If you want a place at the table you will have to come with us. We are having a press conference on Thursday at one in the afternoon to announce twelve new Birmingham suits. Even if you don't file with us it would be great to have you there to speak to how much they knew."

Tom Blanchette left another message for Father Connolly. When he did not hear back he decided, with some trepidation, to make his way to the Greenberg Traurig offices, located in a towering office building on the edge of the oldest part of town, whose windows overlooked the endless Big Dig construction project and, in the distance, Boston Harbor, where the first great revolt against Old World paternalism began.

A Week or So Later

NEWTONVILLE, MASSACHUSETTS — Only because the lawyer Bob Sherman had recommended it, Gary Bergeron went to see Barbara Thorp at the Healing and Assistance Office, which had been relocated out of the chancery to an unmarked suburban office complex. Sherman recommended everybody seek out the help being offered by the church. He had no particular worries about Gary's emotional well-being, he just believed that if the church was willing to offer help, the church's opponents should consider accepting. In that way, he was a man of considerable faith himself.

Gary was skeptical. But as he filled out a background form at Sherman's office in order to give his support to the litigants, something caught the lawyer's eye.

"You've lived twenty-two places in twenty years," Sherman said. "You think that's normal?"

That right there bedeviled his mind. Of course he thought he was normal. On the afternoon he sat with Thorp in her darkened office he believed he was doing this for his church, not for himself. He believed church leaders were somehow blind to what it meant to be a victim. He was resolved to educate them, but in so doing he hoped to discover the reality for himself.

"I want to know your story," Thorp began by way of introduction. She saw herself as an ecclesiastical punching bag, prepared to take the worst that people could deliver. (One woman had been consumed by a need to see her priest's rectory bedroom again, and Barbara Thorp accompanied her to the place of her defilement.) "But I want to start with an apology. I am sorry for what happened to you. And I want you to know how grateful I am that you are here."

"I want to open a dialogue," Gary Bergeron said. "This isn't about money. This is about doing the right thing. I want you to know that."

She said she did, but he thought she might be trying to pacify him. Gary began his story anyway, from the beginning, in the tennis club shower, through all those times the priest's hand made his arms go rigid and scrambled his mind. After his whipsaw induction into the crisis over the past four weeks, the details were by now familiar on his lips.

So why was it more difficult and overwhelming now? To his own mortification, he cried. So did Thorp.

"I guess I do have some things to work out," he admitted. So did she.

Thorp gave him a list of therapists whom he was invited to see; the church would cover the cost, she said. He had never believed in therapy, but his crying jag so surprised him he took the list anyway and vowed to call.

Thorp had lost count of how many people had come to her office so far, but there must have been over a hundred. The telephone had been ringing nonstop since early March. On the one day since then she took off for personal reasons, twenty-eight people had left her messages, all of them first-time callers. She admired and respected each one of them. But Gary Bergeron, so gently handsome and self-possessed, so scared for the church of his parents, constructive and earthy in his anger, so genuine—Gary gave her an idea.

"Let me ask you something," she said. "When you came in here, you sat down and you said you were very angry and very frustrated. And I've spoken with you for two hours and I've heard your sincerity. And you are able to let me know how you feel even though you are angry and even though you are frustrated. The cardinal needs to hear this. The cardinal has a rare opportunity right now. Would you be willing to talk to him?"

Some small part of her thought, *Maybe this is the one His Eminence will hear.*

"Sure," he said, "I'd be willing to do that." What he wanted was to forgive the church of his childhood, to feel less personally responsible, to forgive himself. It was the right thing.

"Great, I will start making the arrangements now."

Monday, April 8, 2002
Boston, Massachusetts — It seemed that everybody in Boston was in a state of high anticipation (or deepest dread) about the press conference Eric MacLeish was publicizing like a Geraldo Rivera special. He had actually held a news conference on Saturday *announcing* that he would have a news conference on Monday to release a trove of documents from Paul Shanley's personnel files. Responding to a broad motion by MacLeish, Sweeney had ordered Rogers to turn over every record he could find. MacLeish knew he had something enormous in the stalls, something that would buck and snort and change the direction of this crisis for good as soon as he threw open the gate. History would record Paul Shanley as the worst of them, the epitome of clerical crime, beginning at 1:30 P.M. on Monday, April 8, at the ballroom of the Sheraton Boston Hotel and Towers.

A pall hung over the chancery and the residence. Right up to Friday night, Wilson Rogers Jr. had fought the public release of documents. He argued every angle in the books: First Amendment, privacy rights, fair trial. Not just unconvincible, Judge Sweeney was *harshly* unconvincible.

Morrissey knew how bad it would look. Law didn't have a chance— what could he say? "I should have looked in his file"? "I *never* look in files"? "I leave the file-looking to others"? Morrissey readied an ineffective press release. "Whatever may have occurred in the past, there were no deliberate decisions to put children at risk," it said.

Nobody's dread matched Theresa Shanley's. The priest's tightly wound niece was inconsolable. Uncle Paul had been her surrogate parent after her father died. This was the man who performed all her siblings' weddings, and whom she had selected to give her away at hers.

She had rejected every single allegation against her uncle, and he had encouraged her in that course.

When it became clear the documents were coming out, she knew she had to see them for herself. But to her lasting disbelief, the archdiocese wouldn't provide her with copies. Even her uncle said he wasn't able to get his hands on them. So this was it, this was what she was left with, sneaking into a media maelstrom at the Sheraton.

"I've got no choice," she told Paul Shanley on the telephone the night before.

Paul Shanley, when he learned of her plans, forbade it.

"Not only am I going, Uncle Paul," she protested, "I'm going to stand up and tell this guy to fuck off."

"Don't, Theresa, please promise me you won't," he said. He was calm. He saw this entire affair as a blood sport, a lion mauling—not the forum for justice, which would come, he believed.

"Then tell me, do you know another way to get a copy of your personnel file, Uncle Paul? Because I haven't gotten anywhere."

"Promise me?"

"I promise," she moaned.

When she slipped into the back of the Sheraton ballroom the next afternoon—with her husband in tow—she could see the stacks of documents, thick eight-hundred-page bricks, resting on a table to one side of the room. There must have been more than a hundred people jamming through the door. MacLeish clients. Parishioners from St. Jean's in Newton, where the Ford boy had worshiped. Police detectives. Officials representing the attorney general. Assorted weepers and shouters and curiosity seekers. Television cameras glared from the perimeter of the room—perhaps forty of them or more. Crouching down front was a mosh pit of still photographers, their shooting arms lifted at the ready, firing whenever they suspected a display of emotion—*chaka, chaka, chaka*.

To her frustration, the swarm of women guarding the document stacks were not releasing any until the presentation was through.

Trapped, she and her husband took a seat.

MacLeish had put the files on a PowerPoint presentation, highlighted and animated, and was projecting them page by page onto a huge screen. Wearing a wireless microphone, he strode around the front of the room like a motivational speaker, decrying each new page. He slapped his fist in his palm and threw his voice up and down the volume chart. His red face blistered, his eyes shot fire.

"We were lied to!" he bellowed, as to a jury. "We were deceived!"

The Medeiros letter ending Shanley's sexual-minorities ministry, the oath he refused to sign, the Bishop Banks letter clearing his return to ministry in California, calling him "a priest in good standing" despite everything.

"This is very difficult for me, and do I feel terrible? Yes," MacLeish shouted.

The Bishop Murphy letter placing him on restrictions again: no roommates, no working with teenagers, no living in neighborhoods frequented by homosexuals. The Law letter granting his retirement, warmly: "Without doubt over all of these years of generous and zealous care, the lives and hearts of many people have been touched by your sharing of the Lord's Spirit. You are truly appreciated for all you have done."

Then the terrifying word: NAMBLA.

A gasping sound punctuated the auditorium. How universally terrifying that acronym was—North American Man/Boy Love Association, the most unloved support group in the world. It unfolded that among the documents was a copy of an article from a publication called *Gaysweek*, a long-defunct New York–based newspaper. It detailed a 1978 political conference called by a gay rights group to discuss the appropriateness of age-of-consent laws and debate the ability of teenage boys to exercise agency over their sex lives. The organizers were responding to a round of arrests for sex with underage male prostitutes that were largely derided as police entrapments, a political stunt by a prosecutor up for reelection.

At earlier times, Gore Vidal had addressed the larger body, which for a number of politically arcane reasons was called the Boston/Boise Coalition. So had Allen Ginsberg. On this day, attendees had included representatives of major religious groups as well as leading academics, feminists, and gay radicals. A reverend representing the national office of the Unitarian Universalist Church, an Episcopal pastor from Christ

Church Cathedral in Hartford, and a homosexual Buddhist all spoke. So did the chairman of Boston University's Department of Psychiatry. Especially in Boston, they observed, the seventies youth culture had given teens a stronger sexual sense. Was the commonwealth right to hold the line at sixteen? Why not fourteen, like South Carolina, or eighteen, like North Dakota? Were the men and women arrested for crossing that boundary all doing harm? If so, what kind?

Immediately afterward, the article noted, a small caucus of "boy-lovers" and teenagers formed a group.

"This we believe was the start of the so-called NAMBLA organization," MacLeish said. He snapped a copy of the news account on the big screen, enhancing the paragraph attributed to Paul Shanley with a bright yellow wash.

> Father Paul Shanley, representative of Boston's Cardinal Medeiros for outreach to sexual minorities, told the story of a boy who was rejected by family and society, but helped by a boy-lover. When his parents found out about the relationship, however, the man was arrested, convicted, and sent to prison. "And there began the psychic demise of that kid," Shanley commented. "He had loved that man . . . it was only a brief and passing thing as far as the sex was concerned, but the love was deep and the gratitude to the man was deep, and when he realized that the indiscretion in the eyes of the society and the law had cost this man perhaps 20 years . . . the boy began to fall apart." Shanley concluded, "We have our convictions upside down if we are truly concerned with boys . . . the 'cure' does far more damage."

The cameras were scratching and exploding as MacLeish advanced to another image, a photograph of a six-year-old boy, exceptionally small and cute, merrily dangling from a metal rail in his backyard. Rodney Ford, who had been comforting his son Gregory on the dais, projected his voice into the room.

"That's my son at six years old," he said. "Look how happy he was. Shanley took his innocence. How would you feel? How do the people feel who still support Cardinal Law? *Look* at him. That could be your

child. But it happens to be mine." He searched out faces in the crowd
he recognized from St. Jean's. His pastor was there, in agony. Rodney
Ford sobbed angrily, and reached for his son. This small gesture cut at
the hearts of many in the audience, who no longer muffled their keening desperation. Even reporters were in tears.

"Cardinal Medeiros, with the full knowledge that he had, assigned
Father Shanley to St. Jean's parish with the knowledge of him being a
pedophile," Ford continued with difficulty. "Cardinal Law with that
knowledge elevated him to pastor. I put the question out there to you
people: If this was your child, what would you want done? And I put
this out to law enforcement agencies: If this was your child, what
would you want done? Am I wrong to think Father Shanley should be
put in jail? Am I wrong to think that Cardinal Law should resign immediately? Am I wrong to think that Cardinal Law should be prosecuted and put in jail? Am I wrong? I want you people to answer that. I
already know my answer."

Theresa Shanley was feeling woozy. All around her people seethed
with contempt for her uncle. If she were being honest, she would admit that much of what MacLeish said disgusted her, too. She was a
Catholic, too. And a mother. She was no defender of "boy love." But she
was doing something that nobody else in the room was doing: exercising skepticism. MacLeish showed only one document from the Shanley file about an allegation of abuse, dating from 1966, the Blue Hills
case involving a teenager whose claims the diocese considered unfounded. Let's say Uncle Paul had had sex, she thought. Did she be-
grudge him this? Absolutely not. That whole celibacy thing creeped her
out, anyway.

But was it child abuse? Or was it plain sex? Was the kid above the
age of consent, or below? Why was nobody even addressing this? Isn't
that the issue here?

Where were the dozens and scores of statutory rape allegations, the
ones that made Shanley "a depraved priest who knew few limits to his
sexual cravings," as the *Globe* reported so authoritatively?

She saw no smoking gun projected onto that screen. An article taken
out of context. A gay rights plank made to look sinister by old-line
church ladies writing letter after letter to their cardinal about him. A

clampdown by Rome, his refusal to sign an oath—that all fit into Paul's description of how his unpopular endorsement of gay rights was crushed and silenced. Her uncle was Galileo. This was the Inquisition.

MacLeish read through other memoranda purporting to narrate the church's knowledge. But they were all so oblique they could mean anything. For years Shanley was mysteriously on medical leave. One note made reference to his "malaise" and another lamented his "issues of the past." Could this be his prostate trouble? Another declared, "Paul Shanley is a sick person."

His allergies? she thought. High blood pressure? Heart arrhythmias? You bet he was sick.

The exposition dragged into a third hour. Before he was done, MacLeish walked his audience through eighty-seven documents. As she sat and waited for him to finish she fantasized about running her own PowerPoint presentation, highlighting different paragraphs, the exculpatory ones she assumed were there.

Now Arthur Austin was being introduced. How she detested this man, the poet laureate of the Shanley attackers. He was all over the television, as Shanley's main "victim." Even by his own admission he was *twenty years old* before going to bed with her uncle, which maybe never even happened, which is what Shanley told her. "He was in love with me," Shanley said, "a puppy dog crush."

That was the one thing about her uncle she couldn't comprehend, why he ever allowed this pathetic man to befriend him.

Austin rose and stood behind the podium.

"If the Catholic Church in America does not fit the definition of organized crime, then Americans seriously need to examine their concept of justice," he said. "Bernard Law and Wilson Rogers knew of, and countenanced, indeed abetted, the ongoing rape and sexual defilement of children and young men and women, by known sexual predators. There is not a spark of decency or goodness between the two of them. The stains they have on their hands now will never come off."

He struggled for composure. Tears filled his eyes. Greg Ford, who was sitting between his mother and father, left his seat and walked over to place a hand on Austin's shoulder. The oldest and youngest Shanley accusers. The pages on which Austin had written his words shook between fingers. Clearing his throat, he pressed on, his gentle hypnotic voice gathering strength as his homily mounted.

"I say to them today: You and your church have taken thirty-four years of my life from me, my anguish does not end, ever; like an incubus, Paul Shanley still haunts my dreams. And you, Bernard, my cardinal, my prince of the church, my shepherd, my father in Christ, how long have I hungered at your indifferent door for a crumb of compassion, justice, or mercy? Or even a crumb of simple honesty? You are a liar; your own documents condemn you. You are a criminal, a murderer of children; you degrade the office you hold in the church; you are an affront to Jesus Christ; and I call on Almighty God to bear witness to the foulness and treachery of your behavior, the evil you have nurtured and condoned, and the minds, hearts, and souls you have destroyed."

When it finally was time to collect the documents, another barrier presented itself. They were only for reporters. The minions guarding them were examining credentials. Theresa and her husband lined up anyway, and when they got to the front she smiled and mumbled mendaciously beneath her breath.

"Excuse me?" the woman said. "Could you repeat—"

She reached for one of the heavy piles and when it was pressed tightly against her torso, Theresa Shanley yelled, "I've got it! Run! *Run!*"

At home that night, Theresa locked herself in a room downstairs and read every last page. More than half involved his controversial beliefs about homosexuality, the kind of epic intellectual and spiritual struggles they make movies about. Mercurial, overheated, and dead right— this was the Uncle Paul of her adoration.

It was hard to deny the significance of the rest of the documents, though. Paul Shanley did not lead a pretty life. With his colleagues he was whiny, irascible, histrionic, snotty. With laypeople, he was often high-handed. Medeiros *hated* him; his deputies wanted nothing to do with him. He was a self-important, miserable pain in the ass.

She had always known he was gay, though she never asked him. Nobody did. It was generally agreed to relegate that fact to the realm of rumor. From the time when she was a little girl her parents would go back and forth about it. "He's gay." "He is not." "I'm sure of it." "So what?" And then he'd walk through the door, and the subject was dropped.

Here were all the unwelcome pieces of evidence. He was demonstratively gay. And sexually active. And sexually *promiscuous*. At one point he admitted to at least nine affairs. Four with "adolescents," all years ago. (Among the things she never cared to learn: since 1992, he had been unable to have sex due to his prostate troubles.) He had sex with people he was counseling. That was all inexcusable. That was wrong, unethical, and immoral. It was also disgusting.

And there was something that stopped her heart. MacLeish had sued her uncle before, in 1993.

The case had been settled in secret. But the information was all right there. He was given inpatient treatment at Institute of Living, the Connecticut facility for clergy who can't control their sexual impulses. There he was diagnosed with narcissistic personality disorder, with histrionic tendencies. He was given a strict outpatient regimen. *That's* what they had on him before wishing him well in California.

Alone in the room, Theresa cried and cried, but when she emerged, the crying was over.

"How bad was it?" her husband asked.

"It was awful. It was the worst. But I'm fine." She shrugged. "There's not a thing about pedophilia. This isn't about kids. I'm not saying my uncle was a saint. But it's about creeps like Arthur Austin. Uncle Paul is innocent."

April 9–13, 2002
ROME — As USCCB president, Bishop Gregory was expected to make two trips a year for a ceremonial lunch with the pope and in order to deliver news of the American church to the curial offices. He left his home for the airport with a mixture of trepidation and resolve. There was a war on in America, and the commander in chief had remained silent. Gregory hoped to convince him to seize a leadership role.

Around Vatican City, the crisis was perceived very differently. It had not gripped anybody's attention. Curial officials had dismissed it as a function of an untamed secular press corps. Specifically, the pope had not been extensively briefed on the scope of Catholic dissatisfaction. In fact, it appeared he had been assured that not much at all was happening in America. Although Gregory didn't know it, just the day before he arrived in Rome, the pope had lunched with members of the Papal Foundation, a nonprofit agency that helps fund the pope's many charitable activities, from fighting AIDS in Africa to establishing seminaries in the former Soviet Union. As historian and theologian George Weigel later pointed out, the American cardinals present—Philadelphia's Anthony Bevilacqua, Baltimore's William Keeler, and Washington's Theodore McCarrick—seemed to downplay the American goings-on as a time of "purification," not a world-class crisis in the least.

Gregory took his place at the pope's lunch table and bowed his head for his spiritual leader's prayer and blessing. With him was the USCCB vice president, Seattle's Bishop William Skylstad, and the USCCB's secretary general, Monsignor William Fay. Officially, the pope was in excellent health, but that fiction only gave meaning to the old expression "The pope is never sick until he's dead." Wild tremors in his hands and weakness in his legs, signs of advanced Parkinson's disease, made movement extremely difficult. Ushers wheeled him in and out of Mass on a sort of papal trolley or nearly levitated him by his armpits to move him up and down stairs. When he spoke, words came out in slurry whispers, making it difficult to know which of the eight languages in his arsenal he was attempting. Around the Vatican it was said he no longer chewed his own food.

When he was finished saying grace, John Paul turned to his guests. "What is the situation in the United States?"

Gregory was sure the worst had not yet been revealed, he said. He believed the scandal would permeate even the smallest diocese, and the sense of heartache and betrayal would rock the church at its foundation. The crisis of leadership was severe. Catholics believed that bishops had forsaken their children in order to protect the priests. It was imperative, he said, for Rome to understand how serious a challenge the hierarchy in America faced.

Bent with age and illness, the pope no longer broadcasted emotions on his face. But clearly this was shocking news to him. What, he wanted to know, could the Holy See do to help?

For their June meeting in Dallas, the bishops were preparing a firm new policy for dealing with priests who have assaulted children, Gregory told the pope. They no longer wanted to leave compliance up to the individual bishops. So they planned to submit their new policy to Rome and ask for the Holy See to impose the norms on the American church. This was highly unusual. Gregory said he hoped the pontiff would consider their request expeditiously.

The American delegation left the meeting confident that Pope John Paul had a clearer understanding of the crisis and had handed them his imprimatur and best wishes. But he was not planning direct intervention himself. Gregory and his entourage pressed their case in subsequent meetings with heads of the various curial offices, without apparent success. On his last day in Rome, April 13, he told reporters he had been encouraged to return home and resolve the problems. "We came away from these conversations with a strong sense of the Holy See's desire to listen and to support our efforts to respond effectively to the concerns we share with our people," he said.

April 11, 2002
Brighton, Massachusetts — Near midnight, after the last of the protesters was sure to have abandoned the encampment on Commonwealth Avenue and an extremely hot and humid darkness had settled in, Cardinal Law slipped out of the residence with a hastily packed suitcase. Most high-ranking members of his staff did not know he was leaving, and those who did were instructed not to inform others, especially Donna Morrissey. He did not want his spokeswoman to be in a position where she would have to lie. He was supposed to spend the night finishing an editorial for the *Pilot*—he wrote one every week—but he could not focus on that now. It would be the first time in his tenure that he missed a deadline. There was not even enough time to tell the editor, Antonio M. Enrique, to paste up the issue without him.

Due largely to the MacLeish press conference, Law's grip on the archbishop's office was at its most tenuous. Now most Boston Catholics felt his resignation was appropriate. In the past few days, the *Globe* and the *Manchester Union Leader* had also called for him to step aside. Every few hours, rumors bounced through the pack of reporters now covering the scandal full-time that Law had already resigned, and in their drive to be the first to cover the news they had begun calling church officials at home at all hours of the night. Gubernatorial candidates like former U.S. labor secretary Robert Reich put Law's ouster on their platforms.

Even Law's closest allies, like Jack Connors, had had enough. "They can keep their dresses and their titles, but they have lost their moral standing," Connors told an acquaintance. "If they are unable to tell the truth to their colleagues, their pastors, and the faithful, they may hold on to their titles, but they will not be our leaders."

Law may not have wanted to resign. But he felt he had to present this option to his boss, the pope—and he felt it was important to keep their discussion a secret. To avoid detection, he did not use his own Lincoln Town Car. It was too recognizable. A week earlier, as he was heading to a wake for the mother of one of his seminarians, a television crew spotted him and gave chase as if he were O. J. Simpson. He hired an unmarked car instead. He advised his driver against using Logan Airport, a twenty-minute trip from the residence. Instead, they drove to Newark International Airport, in New Jersey, five hours through the night. There, Law and his amanuensis, Father John Connolly, secretly caught a Continental Airlines flight to Rome, where the pope was waiting for him.

Although Vatican City is no larger than a college campus, Bishop Gregory had no clue that he and Law were both in Rome. In fact, on the Saturday that Gregory was talking to reporters and wrapping up his trip, Law was laying out his woes to the pope, his secretaries, and Cardinal Giovanni Battista Re, prefect for the Congregation for Bishops. Their combined presentations—and the fact that the pope was given his first official briefing on the American press coverage of the crisis that weekend—helped him understand how disastrous the situation was. It would never be revealed whether Law presented a resignation. However, the pope clearly intended for him to ride out the crisis. As a show of his continued support, and an acknowledgment of his concern for the crisis, John Paul resolved to call all his American cardinals to Rome for an extraordinary summit.

April 12, 2002

BRIGHTON, MASSACHUSETTS — In the fourteen months that Donna Morrissey had been working at the chancery, this was the first time she could recall when she didn't know where the cardinal was. It was her practice to dial over to the residence first thing each morning and talk to Connolly, if not Law, to confirm the day's wildly shifting priorities. Neither was in. And nobody was offering explanations. The more she pressed, the more cagey everyone became.

Bishop Walter Edyvean, who as vicar general and moderator of the curia was second in command, would say only that he was "in consultations" and praying and meditating on his tenure. She supposed that was good news. It meant he hadn't yet resigned.

Through the chancery grapevine she heard that a two-page letter from the cardinal was being blast-faxed to the brother priests of the archdiocese, a process that can take a couple of hours. Snagging a copy, she saw that it was Law's declaration that he would *not* resign under pressure. He intended to stay put and "serve this Archdiocese and the whole Church with every fiber of my being. This I will continue to do as long as God gives me the opportunity."

The letter went on to reiterate his flagging defenses. He relied on the experts, he was only following the church's policy on secrecy, and so on. But Law now called these measures mistaken, and vowed to reform them. Perhaps the most ill-advised sentence was about the Shanley revelations, still fresh in the memories of every person in Boston. "The case of Father Paul Shanley is particularly troubling for us," he wrote. "For me personally, it has brought home with painful clarity how inadequate our record keeping has been."

She knew what this would look like to the outside world. The cardinal fought tooth and nail to keep those records secret, and now that they were out, he was aligning himself with the same shock and horror that everybody else felt. Too pat. Nobody would buy it.

"As long as I am your Archbishop," he concluded, "I am determined to provide the strongest leadership possible in this area. I know that there are many who believe my resignation is part of the solution. It distresses me greatly to have become a lightning rod of division when mine should be a ministry of unity."

She was relieved. She knew many people in Boston would be, too. Already, though, she could see from her window that the press encampment along Commonwealth Avenue had swollen to perhaps fifty people, including the networks. They sensed something was amiss. Law, who had spoken out only twice about the crisis, had taken to hiding out in plain sight, that is, appearing places as usual but refusing questions from the press. But in recent days, as the clamor for his resignation mounted, he had not been seen at all.

Her desk telephone was ringing nonstop and her cell phone now was so jammed with incoming calls she could not dial out. Her assistant Karen might have devoted her entire time transcribing the messages. But Morrissey had no plans to return the calls. Instead, she had gotten a new cell phone and kept the number a secret.

It was midmorning. She figured somebody from the hierarchy would brief her shortly and by midafternoon she could release public remarks. In a way, she didn't mind not knowing where the cardinal was. The dark wasn't always a bad place to be. There were things she never wanted to know about church workings, things that belonged in the realm of the mysterious. Anyway, it gave her a plausible deniability. "Sorry, guys," she could say with a smile, "I have no idea where he is, either—you know, the cardinal archbishop of Boston doesn't have to report every little appointment to me!"

But for some reason she didn't understand, arrangements for a press conference had already been made by Father Christopher Coyne, the director of the archdiocese's office for worship and a professor of sacred liturgy at St. John's Seminary. Law's inner circle had begun calling on Coyne to handle certain communications issues. It was a closing of rank—he was, like them, a priest. Reporters liked him. His sound bites sounded compassionate, while Morrissey's were seeming more and more recalcitrant. She bit her tongue. Certainly, she could use the help.

Still, what did he know about crisis management? Very little, she thought, if this plan of his was any indication. He had already told reporters to expect a news release. That was mistake number one. They had put it out on the radio, which gave plenty of time for protesters to arrive and make a scene—a nightmare backdrop that she would never send a client into. Already she could see the protesters massing with their posters and flags. Simultaneously, passersby were blasting their car horns. Stretching her neck, she discovered why. "Honk if you want Law to resign," one of the banners said. The noise was deafening.

She called the cops for crowd control. She ran upstairs to the Capital Campaign office and recruited every woman that wasn't terrified to stand with her outside, a human shield. She cornered Edyvean and queried him on the detailed meaning of the letter—she would be grilled down there and needed some answers. He was exceedingly vague.

When her secret unlisted cell phone rang, she jumped a little.

"Hello?" she said tentatively.

"It's Kay," came the voice of the cardinal's secretary. "I've got His Eminence on the phone. He would like to speak with you."

"Thank *God!*" she exhaled, then sucked in her breath and waited for his familiar voice to crackle on the line.

"Hi, Donna," he said, sounding tired. "How are you?"

"Your Eminence, you're making for an interesting afternoon around here, thanks a lot. To be honest, I had planned to sneak away to do my taxes!"

He didn't laugh. She didn't mean him to, really. It was true. Her dad was going to draw up her return and then take her to a ball game.

"Okay, we're going to play a little Q&A here, Your Eminence, and you tell me what information you want out there. Where are you?"

"I am in consultation with advisers and contemplating what is in the best interest of the Roman Catholic archdiocese of Boston."

"Okay, good!" she cried, scribbling. "They're going to ask me where *exactly*."

"Just tell them that for now," he said.

Given the telephonic connection, which made him hard to hear over the bleating horns outside, she assumed Rome, but she kept that to herself.

"Will you be celebrating Mass at the cathedral on Sunday?"

"No, I will not."

That was all he was able to reveal now. Hanging up, Morrissey knew this was not going to go well. Out the window now she could see television cameras perched on the stone wall. That would mean they would be shooting her from overhead, which any public relations specialist knew was a treacherous disadvantage. It would make her look cornered and small.

Nancy, her secretary, poked her head in the door. "Donna, there's a Bill in the lobby to see you."

She'd nearly forgotten—her father was picking her up. "Tell him to *get up here*," she barked.

He ran up the stairway and through her door. "Dad," she said miserably, "I have to do this *press conference*. The honking, the noise, it's a time bomb, I don't know where he *is*. I just need five minutes. I look a *wreck*."

She looked beautiful. A dark navy suit coat over a boat-necked navy blouse. Skirt to the knees. White hose, dark, square-heeled, fashionable pumps.

"Will you come with me, please?" she begged, gripping his hand and pulling toward the door.

He followed her down the stairs, across the parking lot, and into the sea of turmoil, but unfortunately in juxtaposition to her physical perfection he wore a grim scowl that was misinterpreted by many as belonging to the ranks of church *opponents*.

Several of the cameras went live, uplinking her image to satellites and piercing into regularly scheduled broadcasts. Instantly Morrissey was in living rooms around the state. Although her name was by now familiar in newspaper and television reports, she had managed to stay behind the scenes for months. This was her first major television appearance, and it would mint her as a Catholic beauty, one of Boston's most eligible bachelorettes, the church's famous "spokesbabe."

In a semifragile voice, she read the cardinal's letter into the microphones. "I don't have much more to add," she added.

Where was the cardinal now?

"He is in private meetings and in prayer to find the best way to serve the archdiocese and the community at this troubled time," she replied.

Can you tell us where?

"No, I'm sorry," she said, "I don't know myself."

Is he leaving open the possibility of resigning in the future? Because the language does seem a bit ambiguous.

"All I can tell you is what is in the letter," she said.

Has he had any communication with the Vatican? Will he be available for comments? Will he celebrate Mass on Sunday? Where is the cardinal now? Where is he this minute? Do you even know where he is?

Chapter 12

Outside, Inside

Early April 2002

ST. LOUIS, MISSOURI — Late in the evening, David Clohessy was at his desk in his busy home when a reporter from the *Boston Globe* called for his comments about another priest. Such calls filled his days and nights now. As the president of SNAP, he had appeared on national television programs and was regularly quoted on the front pages of papers from Los Angeles to New York, to the ongoing consternation of his devout parents, Joseph and Mary. Without exception he spoke in defense of the victims and against the priests and bishops who had violated their trust. But this call was different. For the first time he was consumed by concern for the priest. The thought of his public disgrace made him ill. He knew the man had already left the church and through soul-searching and therapy was endeavoring to live a harmless life.

He knew something else. He and the priest shared a dark history. Decades ago both had worshiped with Father John Whiteley, and fended off his constant advances.

Going against all his instincts, Clohessy lifted the telephone and left a message for the priest. Ten minutes later, the call was returned.

Clohessy explained that the diocese of Jefferson City had publicly acknowledged receiving a credible allegation of sexual abuse against the priest. His name would appear in the papers in the morning. "I know this is going to make your life really hard," Clohessy said.

"Thanks for the heads-up," the man replied.

When he hung up the phone, David Clohessy realized this was the longest conversation he had had with his brother, Kevin, in many years.

Monday, April 15, 2002

WELLESLEY, MASSACHUSETTS — Looking out over the sea of bodies pressed together in the parish hall of St. John the Evangelist School, Jim Muller felt a surge of adrenaline run through his veins. Every week since Father Powers gave him permission to hold crisis discussions among the laity, his group doubled in size. Though there had never been a mention of their efforts in the media, four hundred men and women arrived this week to express anger at the church—and hunger for reform. They came not only from Wellesley and other affluent Boston suburbs, but in the case of Carolyn Disco, who was the mother of a seminarian, from as far away as Merrimack, New Hampshire. Paul Baier, a young father and one of the few Republicans in the group, set up an official Web site. It drew over five thousand visitors in the first weeks, and was signing up a hundred people every twelve hours from all across New England.

Muller marveled at how quickly the movement had taken off, when it had failed to ignite during the Porter scandal in 1993 or the Gauthe crisis in 1985, or any of the minor eruptions along the way. He used what he called "the space shuttle analogy" to understand it: the sex abuse scandal was a booster rocket that only now was large enough to launch an entire reform movement.

Their group now had a name, Voice of the Faithful, and a flower-power-era slogan, which had first tumbled off Muller's lips a few weeks ago: "Keep the Faith, Change the Church." A more difficult attainment had been the group's constitution, which was born after a tremendous syntactical labor in which this amorphous coalition had had to decide not just what it opposed, but what it favored. Unanimously the members had adopted three affirmative goals: supporting victims, defending "priests of integrity," and encouraging structural change within the church.

There was some concern about whether or not they had a right to organize in this fashion. Svea Fraser, a divinity school graduate who had cofounded the group, dug through her old Vatican II literature to find the citations that declared that the faithful had a right, and a responsibility, to take part in the running of their church—like having parishioners review the qualifications of new priests and electing lay members to church financial and pastoral councils, instead of allowing priests to select their members. Muller had called these things "the unfinished business of Vatican II." Some Catholics felt it was not their rightful role to run their church—Protestants hired and fired their clergy, not Catholics. But it was hard to argue that the old system had worked to anybody's advantage, besides the abusive priests'.

Muller blamed the passivity of the laity for letting bishops sweep the scandal under the rug. "Boston should not let that happen" again, he said. "The underlying disease is absolute power. The people of Boston know how to deal with absolute power!"

The reference was not lost on anybody in the room. April 15 in Boston was Patriots Day, the celebration of the battles of Lexington and Concord, and above all the Boston Tea Party, which touched off the Revolutionary War. "We have donation without representation," Muller said to wild applause, "and we have to change that!"

Tonight the membership was going to consider whether or not to call for Cardinal Law's resignation. It was a perilous course, as they knew. Catholics had even less say in the tenure of their cardinals or bishops than about who would serve in their parish churches. But following the hammering stream of revelations, the sentiment was overwhelmingly against Law. Sixty percent of Massachusetts Catholics wanted him to resign, according to a new Quinnipiac poll. Even longtime Law defenders lashed out against him. David F. D'Alessandro, chairman and CEO of John Hancock Financial Services, a powerful Catholic donor, publicly called for his ouster, as did the *Boston Herald,* a staunch church ally in recent years. "Sorrow does not make up for the sad fact that he has lost the trust of too many in his flock, some of them forever," the *Herald* said in an editorial. "It's time for Law to make his exit."

It was time, Muller and the steering committee felt, to put the question to the body.

Still, he was careful to introduce the problem in context. "We know the pedophilia scandal is not limited to Boston. It's in Dallas; it's in Chicago—in any big city. It's been in Ireland and Australia," he said. If Voice of the Faithful was going to take a position on one church leader, he said, it had to be reached by consensus. "You don't have to like it," he said, but "all must be willing to go forward with it." Then he and Jim Post presented a draft "consensus statement" demanding that Law step aside.

The discussion went to a white heat almost immediately. Most favored the declaration. But several felt it was well outside the rights of ordinary Catholics to interject their opinions into church governance. The tension between the camps was tremendous. But the gap never narrowed and Muller, sensing he was losing control of the room, feared the coalition would collapse. When he finally called for a poll of opinion, 219 voted in favor of the letter, and nine voted against. The measure failed to reach the necessary unanimity, but the point was clear: Law had lost the faith of the faithful.

Tuesday, April 16, 2002
BRIGHTON, MASSACHUSETTS — It was the herald of what would be a hot summer, one of the hottest in Boston in more than a century. Cardinal Law prepared a statement, which Donna Morrissey posted on the church's Web site for reporters to access. In it, he admitted for the first time that he had secretly gone to Rome. Rumors flew that he had formally offered his resignation but the pope rejected it. Law would not confirm this in so many words.

> The focus of my meetings was the impact of the Shanley and other sexual abuse cases upon public opinion in general and specifically upon the members of the Archdiocese. The fact that my resignation has been proposed as necessary was part of my presentation.
>
> I had the opportunity to meet with several officials of the Holy See. The Holy Father graciously received me.
>
> The pope and those others with whom I met are very conscious of the gravity of the situation. It is clear to me that the primary em-

phasis of the Holy See, like that of the Church in the Archdiocese, is upon the protection of children.

As a result of my stay in Rome, I return home encouraged in my efforts to provide the strongest possible leadership in ensuring, as far as is humanly possible, that no child is ever abused again by a priest of this Archdiocese.

It is my intent to address at length the record of the Archdiocese's handling of these cases by reviewing the past in as systematic and comprehensive [a] way as possible, so that legitimate questions which have been raised might be answered. The facilities of Boston Catholic Television and *The Pilot* will assist in making this record available.

April 19, 2002

MANCHESTER, NEW HAMPSHIRE — Because his fingerprints appeared so frequently on so many cases that were now the subject of damning headlines in Boston, Bishop John McCormack must have known his tenure as head of the Ad Hoc Committee on Sexual Abuse for the nation's bishops' conference was in jeopardy. The national office today announced McCormack was stepping down to accommodate "the press of diocesan business." McCormack himself made no announcement.

The new head of the ad hoc committee was Bishop Harry J. Flynn of St. Paul and Minneapolis. But as SNAP and other victims' groups quickly pointed out, the regime change did little to alter the overall perception that the ad hoc committee was essentially charged with defending the church, not expunging misconduct. Of the eight members on the committee, five had been exposed for moving sexually abusing priests from parish to parish in their own dioceses, or accused of promoting a policy of cover-up and obfuscation.

April 20, 2002

BRIGHTON, MASSACHUSETTS — In an effort to find records related to another errant priest one Saturday morning, a team of chancery workers had been scouring the rows of gray steel shelves in a basement storage room when they came across a series of boxes marked with Paul Shanley's name. They were shocked to discover that these contained more personnel records relating to Shanley's long and well-chronicled career. The court had ordered all Shanley records turned over weeks ago, and they now knew they were in contempt of court.

Bringing the boxes upstairs, church personnel looked through them and saw they added to the complex and troubled narrative of Shanley's long years in ministry. Most troublesome were Shanley's own journals, written in the 1970s and mailed to the many supporters of his street ministry. In them he had admitted to acts that sounded indefensible today: showing a young woman how to shoot up properly, registering at VD clinics so that prostitutes and runaways could use his name for testing, justifying underage prostitution as a means for emancipation.

They were turned over to Eric MacLeish's law office immediately, but that did little to repair the church's gathering reputation for incompetence or worse.

Father Christopher Coyne was forced to hold a press conference to express the archdiocese's embarrassment and frustrations about having misplaced the boxes. "Any of us who are reasonable people can look at this and say this case was not handled well. We did not oversee his ministry or life well. This just adds more evidence to support that fact."

MacLeish's clients weren't buying that excuse at all. They accused the archdiocese of withholding records in violation of a court order, trying to save one last ounce of credibility. "This is a conspiracy," said Rodney Ford. "This isn't the church that I know. This is organized crime."

His wife, Paula, added, "I think God has just about had it with these guys."

Sunday, April 21, 2002
AZUSA, CALIFORNIA — The Southern California SNAP chapter had drawn up a long list of churches where known molesters had worked or where SNAP members had complained of abuses and found no support. In their area alone, they identified fifty parishes. Every Sunday, one church at a time, they intended to show up in a picket line, with

leaflets telling parishioners who might have been abused how and where they could find help. Even if no new churches were added, the SNAP members knew where they would be every Sunday for the next year.

This week, they were to gather at St. Frances of Rome Church in Azusa, just days after Father David F. Granadino, the pastor there, was placed on administrative leave. The archdiocese had said he was being investigated for possible wrongdoing based on a single call placed to the sex-abuse hotline in March. But Mary Grant knew there were other alleged victims, including Jeff Griswold, who was a client of her attorney's. Grant knew that Griswold had talked to Granadino with a tape recorder supplied by the police department, the same way she had spoken to her own perpetrator. On tape, Granadino acknowledged molesting Griswold.

Mary arrived in Azusa just about 10:00 A.M., an hour before Mass. Jim Falls was there with a sign he made: "House of Rape." He knew there was nothing constructive about this message, and didn't care. Once his brother landed in psychiatric detention simply for suggesting to a therapist that he wished Cardinal Mahony would die, confrontation was all Jim Falls had on his mind. Rita Milla, another SNAP member, brought a sign that was only slightly less jarring: "Stop Crucifying the Children."

They divvied among them flyers that read, "Father Granadino has been removed for a good reason." The pamphlet included a message meant to show solidarity with other potential Granadino targets. "Would he buy you or your friend gifts? Ice cream? Would he take you or your friend on trips? Any overnight sleepovers?" The words were creepy and direct. They were Mary Grant's idea. "If somebody had stood outside my church when I was a kid with a leaflet like this," she reasoned, "I might have been able to say *no* to Father John Lenihan."

What the demonstrators did not know, and would have had no way of knowing, was that the Los Angeles Sheriff's Department had spent the past few weeks grilling a hundred children from the church, hoping to ascertain whether Granadino had continued abusing children at his latest parish. Already unnerved, the parishioners' moods were brittle.

Right away, Father Michael Sears asked the demonstrators to leave church property. They refused. When parishioners began trickling in for services, the atmosphere turned uncommonly hostile. One church member snatched flyers from a demonstrator, tore them in half, and hurled them back at her. Mary Grant was becoming accustomed to such anger. She had once watched a kindly-looking woman rip leaflets out of her daughter's hand with such force, it sent the girl twirling. The right response, Grant thought, was to not react, to just look through them.

She tried to address the parishioners as individuals. "We are here to let anyone know if they've been a victim, they are not alone," she said evenly. It did not calm the scene. Men and women lobbed obscenities down the church steps. One older woman cried bitterly, "You don't know our church. Just get out of here!"

Suddenly, a half dozen churchgoers closed in a tight circle around Rita Milla, whom they correctly identified as the sole Spanish speaker on the picket line. Speaking in Spanish, they pelted her with a fusillade of verbal abuse. Milla's eyes flooded with terror. They called her stupid and a liar, a self-interested oaf, a traitor, an idiot. Frightened, Milla tried to locate an escape route. She could not dash into the church. A cordon of parishioners had linked arms and barricaded off the steps. When Jim Falls, still circling with the other picketers, swept in front of the human fence, one parishioner, Norma Arisa, broke free from the group and crashed into his chest, striking him and grabbing for his "House of Rape" sign. Police surged into the crowd to arrest Arisa.

With the melee breaking around them, Mary Grant stood on the flat feet of her disbelief, staring blankly at the advancing officers. Just then a man leaned close to her ears. "I bet you enjoyed it, didn't you?" he whispered lewdly.

She fixed a trancelike expression on her face, the very one she had perfected as a child when, with Lenihan pinning her down and poking his fingers into her, she stared curiously at a light switch or an electrical socket on the wall as though they were mesmerizing works of art. She knew passive self-defense, she knew survival. She refused to show any response whatsoever to this bizarre scene, or the man taunting her so vilely.

But a reporter from the *Los Angeles Times* couldn't help but react. "What did you say?" Tina Dirmann demanded of the man. "I can't believe what you just said!"

Finally one of the parishioners acknowledged just how out of bounds the scene had gone. She approached the menacing circle around Milla and implored them to stand down. "We should be setting an example with our faith," her voice cracked, "not shouting inappropriate and vulgar things!" They did not stop. Milla was sobbing and afraid. She dropped her sign on the sidewalk and shoved through the crowd, and she ran through the heat until she was out of sight. Yet they kept howling after her, their Sunday shoes stomping on the plea she had nailed to the end of a long stick, "Stop Crucifying the Children."

April 23, 2002

APOSTOLIC PALACE, VATICAN CITY — "Dear Brothers," the pope began, addressing the delegation of American cardinals he had called to Rome. Eight in total, plus Bishop Wilton Gregory, had taken up chairs in a tight semicircle around him in the ornate receiving room inside his private apartment. His voice was hard to hear, and harder to comprehend, though he spoke in English. "Let me assure you first of all that I greatly appreciate the effort you are making to keep the Holy See, and me personally, informed regarding the complex and difficult situation which has arisen in your country in recent months. I am confident that your discussions here will bear much fruit for the good of the Catholic people of the United States. You have come to the house of the Successor of Peter, whose task it is to confirm his brother Bishops in faith and love, and to unite them around Christ in the service of God's People. The door of this house is always open to you. All the more so when your communities are in distress.

"I too have been deeply grieved by the fact that priests and religious, whose vocation it is to help people live holy lives in the sight of God, have themselves caused such suffering and scandal to the young. Because of the great harm done by some priests and religious, the Church herself is viewed with distrust, and many are offended at the way in which the Church's leaders are perceived to have acted in this matter.

The abuse which has caused this crisis is by every standard wrong and rightly considered a crime by society; it is also an appalling sin in the eyes of God. To the victims and their families, wherever they may be, I express my profound sense of solidarity and concern."

The gathering was perceived as a trip to the woodshed for leaders of the American church, but the pope, always oriented toward solutions, had arranged for the cardinals to spend two days with the heads of each of his curial offices examining the various aspects of the crisis in America, and devising answers. However, in his brief comments before convening those sessions, he made it clear that he saw the root cause as being outside the priesthood, in the dangerously lax mores of society: "The abuse of the young is a grave symptom of a crisis affecting not only the Church but society as a whole. It is a deep-seated crisis of sexual morality, even of human relationships, and its prime victims are the family and the young. In addressing the problem of abuse with clarity and determination, the Church will help society to understand and deal with the crisis in its midst."

Some of the cardinals had thought now would be the time to question the role of celibacy and Catholic sexual morality. Opinion writers hammered at this point (most sharply in *Slate,* beneath the memorable headline "Does Abstinence Make the Church Grow Fondlers?"), and 64 percent of Americans believed that forced celibacy contributed to the alleged behavior of the accused priests. Most American Catholics saw no reason for celibacy and favored allowing their priests to marry. Within the church, there were signs this requirement might be revisited. In fact, there already *were* married priests—after 1980, the pope extended a special favor to married former Episcopalian priests who converted to Catholicism, exempting them from the celibacy requirements. Currently there were perhaps a hundred such men in Roman Catholic pulpits. If their service to God was not impaired by wives and children, why would anybody else's?

Los Angeles's Cardinal Roger Mahony promised he would open the Rome meeting to all those issues. However, he was ruled out of order. Instead, the participants were encouraged to focus on a reaffirmation of what the pope called "the fullness of Catholic truth on matters of sexual morality." In John Paul's mind, the crisis was one of discipline, not doctrine.

Many took that to mean a frank discussion on the presence of gays in the priesthood, as Cardinal Bevilacqua of Philadelphia revealed on the eve of the meeting. "We feel that a person who is homosexually oriented is not a suitable candidate for the priesthood, even if he did not commit an act," he said, amplifying his earlier remarks. "There is a difference between heterosexual candidates and homosexual candidates. A heterosexual is taking on a good thing, becoming a priest, and giving up a very good thing, the desire to have a family. A gay seminarian, even a chaste one," he said, "by his orientation, is not giving up family and marriage. He is giving up what the church considers an abomination. It is possible we have homosexuals who are very chaste. But the risk is much higher that he will fail on celibacy."

The evidence was to the contrary: gays were slightly less likely to violate the rule of celibacy than straights, according to surveys. However, Wilton Gregory added his voice to Bevilacqua's when he met with reporters in Rome, suggesting a growing consensus among the cardinals. "It is most importantly a struggle to make sure that the Catholic priesthood is not dominated by homosexual men. Not only that it is not dominated by homosexual men, but that the candidates we receive are healthy in every possible way, psychologically, emotionally, spiritually, intellectually. . . . That is the ongoing concern of seminaries."

Theologians in America were quick to condemn both men's views as bigoted and prejudicial. Staff members at the bishops' conference, of which Gregory is president, repudiated them, and even conservatives found that kind of talk repugnant. "I don't think most Catholics would care if their priest is gay or straight, to tell you the truth," William Donohue, president of the Catholic League, an orthodox group, told a reporter. "I think the issue for them is whether he can live up to his vow of celibacy. I'd take a chaste gay priest any day over a promiscuous straight one."

But the bishops' antigay comments set a tone for the meeting, and steered the future discussion away from examining their own leadership. "They need to find something they can use as a scapegoat about this whole thing—they're saying gay priests are guilty until proven guiltier," Father Tom Doyle thought when he read the bishops' comments. "They are not willing to look at the institution! This crisis all along is about cover-up!"

The news conference to tell the world what plan the cardinals had devised was scheduled for noon Eastern Standard Time—dinnertime in Rome. Their deliberations had been productive. Thanks to the focused work of everybody involved, they now had a multipronged blueprint for tackling the crisis. They would call on Rome to conduct an inspection of seminary policies throughout America to determine if any changes in instructions or admissions standards were needed. They would commit themselves to a national day of prayer and penance. And they would promise to develop a set of "national standards" for responding to new allegations—which would include the quick removal of priests guilty of "notorious" crimes involving "the serial, predatory, sexual abuse of minors," and a separate procedure for dealing with nonnotorious or truly repentant priests.

They seemed to have no idea that this would be derided as "a couple of strikes and you're out." Indeed, their planned policy seemed once again to punish only those whose secret couldn't be contained and protect those who were less "notorious." It was not destined to satisfy anybody.

Making matters worse, the press conference did not go off as planned. Behind the scenes, the cardinals had difficulty drafting their final statement to the press—flummoxed in part by the need to translate the text into Latin, a formality. Reporters were kept waiting for two and a half hours.

At 2:30 P.M. EST, only two American cardinals—Washington's soft-spoken archbishop, Theodore McCarrick, and Francis Stafford, who was based at the Vatican—filed into a large blue room at the Vatican to take questions from the press. They sat in their red skullcaps at a long table that obviously had been arranged to accommodate the entire delegation. Bishop Gregory, accented in his magenta-trimmed cassock, took a microphone.

"The question of the reassignment of those who harmed children is certainly uppermost in our minds," he said. "However, the specific resolution to that particular question in the United States will be finalized when the bishops meet in June. There is a growing consensus, certainly among the faithful and bishops, that it is too great a risk to assign a priest who has abused a child to another ministry. That's clear. But it was not within the competence of this particular meeting to come up with a decision to that."

"The Holy Father is calling upon us to be people of light, and that's what we're going to try to be," McCarrick added.

"Where's Law?" a reporter demanded.

Gregory fielded the question. "Originally when we thought we would complete our work earlier, it was the intention of all of the cardinals to be present. However, presuming that the press conference would take place earlier, some of them made plans—presuming that the press conference would be completed by now. And some of them simply could not get out of those plans. I am not certain what the situation with Cardinal Law is."

The answer struck the reporters as absurd. "Will there be other meetings with Law?" one wondered. "Is he dodging us?" shouted another.

"I do not believe so," Gregory said. "But I could not tell you why he is not here."

April 24, 2002

LOWELL, MASSACHUSETTS — Gary Bergeron accompanied his parents through a frigid night to St. Michael's Church in Lowell, on the border of Christian Hill and lower Centralville. Sensing how deeply wounded Lowell was in this crisis, Father Albert Capone, the current pastor, had called together his community in prayer thirty-two years after Birmingham's lamented arrival. Unwrapping their scarves, the Bergerons bent and touched their knees to the floor and slid onto a long wooden pant-burnished pew. Joseph and Catherine Bergeron were in total shock about what had happened inside this building at the hands of a pastor whom they had loved. But their despair had been abstract. Until earlier this week, they still had had no idea that their two sons, Gary and Edward, had fallen prey. Neither man had had the courage to tell them, so certain were they of the harm their stories would cause. They knew this even as children, and in a half-conscious way they allowed themselves to be defiled over and over in silence to protect their parents' naïveté.

It was Gary who broke the news. It had not gone well. Joseph had always been overtly demonstrative with his emotions, and in his eighth decade he had become something of a weepy man. Now, knowing what his church had done, his eyes were swollen and torn. A devout Catholic, his life revolved around his church today as it did in his childhood, which unfolded in a Catholic orphanage. His expression of betrayal was severe. So Gary was not surprised when, as Father Capone rose to speak, his father knotted his scarf again, rose, and left the church in twisted distress to walk back home through the glacial night.

After the service, Gary drove his mother home and followed her up to their apartment on the second floor. He found Joseph alone in a darkened room.

"Dad, are you okay?"

"I couldn't sit there."

"Yeah, I know. I understand."

"No, you don't. You don't understand."

Gary looked at his father and saw he was weeping; perhaps he had never stopped.

"I might as well tell you now," Joseph burst out angrily, "because I never have told anybody. You kids need to know that I know you are suffering. I know you have suffered all of your life. *Because of my sins!* Because what you went through, *I* went through. You see? I went through this same thing. When I was eight years old."

Gary was floored, so floored he could barely hear the words his father was saying.

"Dad? You were abused too?"

"I never even told your mother. Never told nobody. And because I never said anything to anybody, it kept happening, don't you see? Those are my sins. And there's nothing I can do about it now, because it's too late! But you have to know. You have to know."

Holy shit, Gary thought. In his mind developed a picture of a demonic Catholic Church routinely defiling its young, a bizarre cult of men in robes reaching into children's pants backward into the ages.

How pervasive is this? he wondered. *How far back does this go?*

Immediately he turned to thoughts of Evan, his own six-year-old son. Was he next? *Was it already too late?* He knew he would be torn apart by guilt if anything happened to Evan, just as Gary's father sat before him in savage agony. He knew he had to step out of the shadows now.

"No Bergeron will ever have to live through this again," he announced.

Monday, April 29, 2002
WELLESLEY, MASSACHUSETTS — Phil Saviano sat nervously behind a low table on a raised stage in the basement of St. John the Evangelist Parish Hall. In the ten years he had been leading the New England SNAP chapter, he had never once been invited to address a group of Catholics who had not themselves been sexually abused. But here he was, looking out at the five hundred mournful faces who now made up Voice of the Faithful, and he realized as if for the first time how thoroughly shunned he and his fellow victims had been. To go a decade and never see a sympathetic Catholic face!

He began his address by mentioning this fact, and the audience stood and applauded for more than five minutes. He was surprised that this choked him up.

Slowly, tentatively—because he was afraid he would cry—Saviano told his own story in detail, the abuse, the internalization, the long years of self-blame; then the revelation, the relief, the pummeling legal skirmish, the war with his own family. "I think that you all have a better idea why sexual abuse victims here in Massachusetts have been so angry and so frustrated for so many years," he said.

But Voice and a number of other nonvictims' groups, including Coalition of Concerned Catholics, had rekindled his hope in humanity, if not his hope for his church. "I feel for the first time a sense of solidarity with the general public of Catholic parishioners," he told them truthfully. "It's a wonderful feeling."

April 30, 2002
BOSTON, MASSACHUSETTS — Gary Bergeron pushed off the elevator into the reception area of Greenberg Traurig, which was so clotted with people it looked like an airport terminal during a blizzard. Across the room he

could see Courtney Pillsbury, the associate attorney who was in charge of organizing the press conference to announce that the Birmingham litigant group now counted forty, including the Bergeron brothers. Haunted by their father's story of abuse, both men had signed legal complaints, and Gary invited Pillsbury, Sherman, Thomas, and MacLeish to make his story public, if they felt it would help expose this scandal.

"You know what? I know what it's like to be a victim," he had said, "and now I know what it's like to be the brother of a victim and the son of a victim. But I couldn't imagine what it's like to be the father of a victim. And if anything ever happened to my son, I don't know what I'd say. I don't know if I could control myself, I really don't. I'm doing this for my son."

Pillsbury was becoming adept at handling media. She believed the church battle would be won or lost on the evening news. The archdiocese was not prepared to let any of these cases go to a jury. Rather, they continued to do everything imaginable to tangle the cases in prelitigation obfuscation. The only tool proving effective in countering the church's legal intransigence was sustained, coordinated, well-timed exposure. For this particular press announcement Pillsbury wasn't expecting much attention, though. In the mathematics of newspaper inches, a long-dead priest like Birmingham, no matter how voraciously he hunted down young men, was not half as interesting as a squinting, churlish Paul Shanley, an inappropriately tittering John Geoghan, or a pulpit-pounding George Spagnolia, with his one vague and troubling allegation. Those had become the signature priest perpetrators in Boston headlines that rippled across the world. Birmingham's destructive swath had earned front-page attention for a day or two, in Boston and Lowell, and promptly sank back into the loud background noise of the scandal.

Nonetheless, Pillsbury had invited a few Birmingham litigants to attend. Gary accepted, with a nervous proviso: he did not want to be photographed. In anticipation of the media blitz, he had written a letter to his extended family the night before and told them his entire story of abuse. It was the hardest thing he had ever had to do. He told them his name would appear in the papers. He just wasn't ready to lend his face to the cause.

What he found in the swarming lobby frightened him: camera crews, sound technicians, photographers, cell phones sounding, vaguely familiar men and women in makeup and careful hair. Their clatter was deafening, the intensity of their focus numbed him. A receptionist pulled Gary through the bedlam and ushered him around an endless labyrinth of offices to a small conference room where Bob Sherman and Courtney Pillsbury were already sitting with Bernie McDaid and Dave Lyko, the other men scheduled to make appearances. Sherman made introductions.

Gary was distracted. "Bob, Courtney said there weren't going to be cameras."

"There's a ton of cameras," Bernie said, excitedly.

"She said what?"

"No cameras," she admitted.

"Well, then. It looks like things have changed."

"Don't worry about it, Gary," said Bernie, a housepainter who was already a veteran of the press conference. This was his second or third broadcast appearance, including a European TV news magazine. "It's like a camcorder, no different."

Gary was as nervous as he was at his First Communion.

"Look, we put out a press release about availability, and cameras started showing up," Sherman said. "But don't worry—if you don't want to talk, you don't have to."

When it was time, Sherman walked with his guests toward the main conference room. Even he was shocked by what he saw there. Over forty people scrambled for seats and camera angles, representing media outlets from CNN, MSNBC, AP—teams from as far away as Montreal, all jostling to cover what had become the biggest story of the year. Some of them actually had to leave the room to permit the litigants to squeeze in, which they did in a hailstorm of camera flashes.

This, Gary thought, must be what it's like to run for president.

Sherman made his presentation ably, calling Birmingham perhaps one of the most prolific perpetrators at the epicenter of the crisis. So far there were ten accusers from Sudbury, seventeen from Salem, twelve from Lowell, and at least one each from Brighton, Gloucester, and Lexington, he said. There might well be more than a hundred litigants before this was through. "This is the fastest-growing complaint against the archdiocese," he said. As Birmingham was dead, the suits named only supervisory defendants: Cardinal Law, Monsignor John

Jennings (now retired and living in nearby Framingham), and Bishop
John McCormack.

The reporters sprayed their questions at the panel of complainants,
and Gary, surprising himself, suavely laid out his opinions for the world
to witness.

"My brother and I are still absolutely shocked about the fact that the
church knew about the problems they were having with Father Birmingham and they sent him to St. Michael's, where they just gave him
a new batch of victims. And when he left Lowell they gave him another
batch of victims, and another batch of victims. And when he left *there,*
they gave him another batch of victims, and another batch of victims."

"Do you blame Cardinal Law?" a voice in the room asked. "Do you
want him to resign?"

"Personally? I personally want Cardinal Law here," he said. "I want
him to stay here, and I want him to clean this mess up. I want him to
restore my faith and more importantly I want him to restore the faith
of my parents, who don't have fifty years left to heal."

Gary was halfway home when he turned on his cell phone and found
eight messages from people who had already caught his appearance.
Neighbors, old friends from St. Michael's, former girlfriends he had not
heard from in years, some burbling congratulations almost as though they
had not paid attention to the substance of what he was talking about.

But some of the callers had paid very close attention. And they were
furious. He had braced for a tongue-lashing from knee-jerk defenders
of the church. He had girded his nerves for the onslaught from reac-
tionaries who might even accuse *him* of bringing scandal upon the
church, or inventing his story, or fomenting crisis for financial gain. He
was ready for the antigay jokes.

What he had not expected was a backlash from other victims. *How
dare you defend Cardinal Law,* they accused. *Be careful about standing
in our way.*

Late April 2002
BOSTON, MASSACHUSETTS — Paul Finn, the president of Commonwealth Mediation and Conciliation, had overseen the discussions be-

tween Garabedian and Wilson Rogers Jr. regarding the eighty-six plaintiffs against John Geoghan. It had been difficult going. Through most
of the previous year, the church had held to an offer of $10 million, re-
jected by Garabedian as paltry. But the minute Judge Sweeney had
ruled to lift the court seal on documents, the church's offer increased
dramatically. By March there was an agreement in principle. In a sliding range proposed by Finn, a complex mathematical formula would be
used to evaluate each individual's claims, depending on the nature of
his assault and the degree of his suffering. Eventually the church would
pay out between $15 million and $30 million. Finn would render the
determination for each plaintiff.

A victorious Garabedian brought each client into his office for his
signature, a cumbersome exercise given their numbers. Many were dis-
pleased. The papers were full of news about settlements elsewhere,
many of which had been considerably larger: a pair of brothers shared
$7 million in a quick settlement from the diocese of Stockton, and in
Minneapolis, a jury awarded one man $3.5 million.

Tony Muzzi was especially adamant. After lawyers' fees and expenses, under the formula he stood to take home a few hundred thousand dollars to compensate for years of smothering molestations that
cost him his religion and his easygoing nature. He'd rather go to trial.
Even if the group came up against the $20,000 cap, at least they would
have played every card they had. At least they exposed the church for
what it was. A guilty verdict, he reasoned, would hurt the church more
than any financial penalty. But Garabedian was single-minded. He had
bundled his cases together for negotiation, and as a result was forced
to settle them together, all or nothing. The others were signing. Under
pressure to consider their needs, Muzzi finally put his name on the document. With the stroke of a pen, the case that broke open the church
crisis came to a close. If there had even been one sentence of apology,
he thought, that would make this capitulation less painful.

Only it wasn't closed, as it turned out. Unbeknownst to most people,
the mediator's brother was Joe Finn, an influential Boston accountant
who had served on many powerful archdiocesan boards for years. These
days, in disgust, he was attending Voice meetings instead. When Joe

learned about the settlement agreement, he was outraged at the thought that parishioners' donations to the church would be spent to compensate for the crimes of individual clerics. Considering it another betrayal, he decried the settlements often in Voice meetings. "Where do you think this money is coming from?" he asked. "In rough numbers, published by chancellor David Smith in January or February, it costs roughly $18 million to run the archdiocese. And about $14 million of that comes from the cardinal's appeal, which we all know nobody is donating to this year. They're in steep decline. They're already cutting like crazy. Garabedian's got eighty-six claimants, for $30 million. Look around! There are five hundred other cases, *five hundred*. It's nuclear winter here in Boston!"

He would never interfere in his brother's work. But he could not just sit on the sidelines and watch his church court financial disaster without ever consulting with the faithful about how best to handle the overall crisis.

Acting entirely on his own, he hired a canon lawyer to see what his rights were as an ordinary baptized Catholic. He got a five-page memo that detailed the only way for lay Catholics to wrestle control of the cases away from church lawyers: through the Finance Council, a group of wealthy Boston business leaders who helped direct church spending. *They* could reject the settlement outright. Law would be bound by their decision.

Finn was surprised. He had always thought the Finance Council was strictly advisory. Polling the council members, he learned they were under the same misperception. He mailed each of them a copy of the lawyer's memo. "You guys have the power to say no," he told them. "You didn't even know about the previous payments! That was a violation of canon law. Oversight of the finances of the archdiocese is your right. But also your responsibility."

May 1, 2002
WELLESLEY, MASSACHUSETTS — This morning, for the first time, news of Voice of the Faithful appeared in the *Boston Globe*. The article was touching and powerful, and in every way pleased Jim Muller. The timing was perfect. Voice had gotten so large it was now establishing chapters in churches throughout the archdiocese.

The problem was the headline: "Catholics Drawn to Splinter Group in Wellesley."

Muller leapt to the phone and called Jim Post. "We have really got a problem now," he said. "That word 'splinter' is not going to do us any good with the chancery."

Post had drawn the same conclusion. So had most others in the group. Even the article's author, *Globe* religion writer Michael Paulson, was surprised by the headline, which he considered factually incorrect; for the paper's online edition, he had the headline changed to read, "Catholics Drawn to Lay Group in Wellesley." He knew that there were centuries' worth of baggage connected with the language of Catholic disunity. Martin Luther was a splinter. The whole of Protestantism was a splinter. Voice of the Faithful wanted to work *inside* the church, not form a new church. Their weapons were the doctrinal documents of Vatican II, not revolutionary proclamations by dissident theologians. In fact, the article quoted an expert who recently addressed Voice, Stephen J. Pope, the chairman of Boston College's theology department, specifically advising them on the dangers of appearing as "heretics, usurpers, or schismatics."

If Law and his administration branded Voice a splinter group, their chances of effecting change were nil.

"We'd better approach the vicar general, Bishop Edyvean, to explain ourselves," Muller told Post.

Edyvean consented to a meeting, which he scheduled for later in the month. In the meantime, though, the fallout was swift. Edyvean called priests around the archdiocese who had supported Voice and discouraged them sternly. Further, he wrote a letter on Law's behalf dissuading priests from helping the laity organize. One, Father Powers, the pastor at Muller's church, St. John the Evangelist, was so nervous after his warning that he asked Muller to refrain from endorsing other chapters. Instead, the group agreed to look for a new home to draw some of the pressure away from Powers.

May 2, 2002
SAN DIEGO, CALIFORNIA — Paul Shanley was in the bathroom when the telephone rang. He let it go off to the machine. But he was horrified to

hear the message, from a U.S. marshal. "We're looking for Paul Shanley," the man's voice said. "We understand you may know where he is. We have a warrant for his arrest."

His next thought was anger. Shanley had instructed his attorney to promise cooperation with the authorities. He was a *priest*, besides. It made him furious that they would stage such a showdown now.

He left a message for his attorney, and returned the officer's telephone call. He asked for five minutes to dress and get his things in order, which the officer granted. Then at 10:40 A.M. he was placed in handcuffs and walked out to the marshal's vehicle before the unblinking eye of a television camera. His arrest was carried live in Boston.

Meanwhile, back in a working-class neighborhood of Braintree, still living in the house he grew up in though he was fifty-three now, still occupying an aimless space between adolescence and functional adulthood, Arthur Austin watched the arrest on his television the way others watched boxing matches: on his feet, red in the face, screaming at the top of his lungs.

"Hey, Paul! I did this! I'm the one that lit the train of powder and it burned all the way to San Diego and blew up in your face. And you never thought this was going to happen! Your arrogance was *supreme*! I did it. *I* did it. When I die, put that on my tombstone. I will rest peacefully. Hey, Paul! I'm the one! Me. Me!"

Later, when Shanley landed at Logan Airport—he had waived an extradition hearing—he was told to wait in his seat until all other passengers deplaned. Then a team of officers boarded the craft and fixed around him a heavy bulletproof vest. A guard put handcuffs back on his wrists. They moved him defensively through the corridors of the airport and outside to the curb, where a phalanx of cruisers awaited, lights flashing. He felt a hand on his head pushing him into the second car, and then this convoy sped off toward the county jail.

May 3, 2002
BOSTON, MASSACHUSETTS — David Smith, the chancellor, and Cardinal Law walked into the morning meeting of the Finance Council without any reason to expect opposition to the settlement arrangements for the

Geoghan 86. In fact, the two—and Wilson Rogers Jr.—had visited the body previously, soliciting their support for the arrangement in principle. They believed they had secured it.

To their surprise, the council members spoke one by one against the agreement. Now there were over a hundred more cases pending, with more likely to follow, they argued. Until the archdiocese developed a global settlement scheme, they said, they would oppose any piecemeal approach. They gave a show of hands; it was nearly unanimous.

And they told him their decision was binding.

Law was stunned. He didn't believe they were right, and insisted that their role was merely advisory, but they produced the canonical decision that Finn had given them. Law left the room angrily. He consulted with his own canon lawyers. What he found amazed him. All these years, his Finance Council had been in a position to trump the cardinal archbishop of Boston, and nobody had any idea.

"Blindsided," David Smith fumed. He was as angry as Law about the rejection. But there was little he could do. He returned to his office and went to work crafting a press release announcing that the deal was undone. Law called Rogers, who in turn called Garabedian.

It was quarter to five on a Friday afternoon when Garabedian picked up the phone. He was apoplectic. "Thursday morning the deal was done," he screamed. "Thursday morning all necessary defendants would sign the papers. That's what you told me! It's just another sham. The Finance Council? I think it's just another sham. For eleven months I negotiated with you people, and you never once mentioned that you needed the approval of the Finance Council. You repeatedly told me it was only—that it could not prevent the cardinal from signing!"

No amount of shouting would do any good. Garabedian believed he had an enforceable deal. The parties had represented as much in open court. He vowed to bring a motion to enforce. Rogers vowed to fight it.

Finally, Garabedian asked for time to reach each of his eighty-six clients by phone—he would spend the weekend if necessary—so that he could break the news to them personally. Rogers said that would not be possible. A press release was already out to the media.

Garabedian slammed down the phone. "These are soulless individuals who lie, cheat, and steal. They enable rapists, they steal the souls of children, and they lie on top of all of it. How they can live with themselves is beyond me. I guess they just don't have mirrors to look into."

Garabedian was especially worried about Patrick McSorley, whom he tried to reach first. Because of his precarious living situation, which involved staying with his girlfriend on nights she wasn't mad at him, or on friends' sofas, Garabedian didn't reach him until Saturday. By Monday, McSorley had gone into a steep emotional tailspin. He returned to drugs and alcohol, which he had sworn to abjure, then in a panic checked himself into a rehab facility. "I thought it would be safer here," he explained. "My head just couldn't handle the ups and downs."

May 6, 2002

Wellesley, Massachusetts — The first available parking place Jim Muller found was six blocks away from St. John's, where the weekly Voice of the Faithful meeting was to take place. The streets were filled with circling cars and streaming masses of Catholic couples and families heading into the parish hall. Reporters and television cameras and satellite uplink trucks filled the sidewalks. He thought he would never see such an outpouring of concern and energy, and he felt that something good and important had come out of the crisis. Namely, community.

The group had gotten so large it now had to meet in two separate rooms at St. John's, and had spawned chapters in parishes across Boston. Or tried to. "Half of our new groups get shut down," Paul Baier complained. "It's always the same: First the pastor welcomes Voice of the Faithful and puts a notice in the bulletin welcoming the group. Then two weeks later he withdraws his support." Baier suspected the pastors were coming under coordinated pressure, but he couldn't prove it. The Voice leaders had discussed the possibility of civil disobedience. "These are our churches," Muller had said. "They were built by our parents and grandparents. I want to see them arrest us for holding a meeting in the basement!"

As he made his way to the door of St. John's, Muller stopped to introduce himself to a group of people he overheard speaking German. They turned out to be a television crew from Berlin, as excited about the scene as he was. "This reminds me of the night the wall fell in

Berlin," one of the men told him. "Something historic is happening at St. John's."

At that moment, Muller realized that the group he founded in sadness had the potential to become not only a national cause, but an uplifting global movement of Catholics to reclaim their church and affirm their faith.

"Look around," he told the reporter. "We have something here all these hundreds of people want. It doesn't have to be sold to them, just revealed!"

May 7, 2002
Lowell, Massachusetts — A searing dry heat receded with the sun, swept out on a blustery wind, and a day that had been summery plunged toward a stinging cold night. Olan Horne was among the first to arrive at the East End Club, a private-function hall two blocks from St. Michael's. Pushing through the restaurant on the first floor to the back stairway, he noticed that all eyes were on him. Familiar faces. Friends of his parents, men and women he went to school with. Word must have spread about the meeting he had arranged for the victims of Joseph Birmingham. He saw shame in their eyes, and judgment; he saw them shake their heads in disappointment. He wanted to fire back a look of defiance, but he could not. His humiliation was too great.

A few minutes later Bernie McDaid followed him through the gauntlet, and even though he did not know any of the people of Lowell, shame bent his eyes down toward his shoes as well.

Downstairs in the tight basement meeting hall nearly eighty people would shortly take their places around dinner tables, at Olan's invitation. Partly because he remembered so many of them from school and partly in honor of their lost innocence, Olan thought of them all as kids. In his opening remarks, that word kept slipping out. He had thought about revealing the specifics of his traumas, but he did not. Instead, he meandered into a discourse on what this group might accomplish together. Even Olan Horne was surprised to hear himself recommend accommodating the church's leadership. The church made this mess; the church had to clean it up.

"They fucked up big here," Olan was saying. "They hurt each and every one of us. If we embrace them, how can they hit us again? I'm not saying we should give them a second opportunity, but let's say we're going to give them a second chance. It's not like I want to come back to Catholicism. I'm not a little kid. But we should give them a chance to win us back."

In the far corner of the farthest row of chairs, Gary Bergeron sat with his arms folded, surveying the men whose childhoods so paralleled his own. One by one they rose and blubbered through their woeful histories, and this began to bother him. He thought, *We were masturbated by Father Birmingham, nobody's idea of a good time. But it's not like we were stabbed by the man!* What happened to him was absolutely wrong and demanded exposure. It had cost him his relationship to the church. But plenty of people had no relationship to a church—75 to 80 percent of Americans, according to studies, regularly avoided religious institutions and lived moral and ordinary lives nonetheless. In an unintended way, what Birmingham had taught him was that the institutional church wasn't essential to his life and his faith, which was profound and un- shaken; that the church was not the literal "Bride of Christ" he had been taught but a temporal network of buildings, good values, and well- meaning men who so badly wanted him to believe this mystical heaven- on-earth thing that they compounded one horrendous decision with another to keep him from glimpsing the first little flaw. The flaw of hubris. For destroying his relationship to the church, Gary held no grudge against Birmingham, no more than he hated the person who first told him there was no Santa Claus.

But none of this, he thought, had any lasting psychological impact. A man's hand on his genitals, a priest who wouldn't let him be—that's all it was.

When he heard Olan Horne call for the creation of a weekly support group meeting, he was literally disgusted. A men's support group? He wanted nothing to do with it.

Many of the other men in the room were similarly apprehensive. But Olan was a compellingly energetic figure and he got several to agree to return at least one more week. They would call themselves Survivors of Joseph Birmingham, or SOJB.

When the meeting came to an end and the survivors spilled out onto the sidewalk, Olan pulled Gary aside. Walking together, they seemed entirely incompatible. Olan was garrulous, Gary subdued. Olan bragged on himself, Gary never did. Olan didn't mind people not liking him, and this Gary obliged with a fierce enmity that glimmered in the evening air. Olan took it as a challenge.

"I think you misunderstand who I am," Olan said. "Let me tell you what I'm actually trying to do here because I know I've never told you this story. I want you to understand. *Gary, I have no fucking idea what I'm trying to do here.* But all I'm telling you is—I'm going to be honest here, I'm going to be straight up—this is a laboratory. What I think we should do in it is this: we need to start a dialogue. It is that simple. We need to get the people at the chancery talking to us. Anger's like curry. We say it all the time: anger's not its own spice. You break it down to each individual flavor and you work it, you find that everybody's on the same level here. When I first called down to Boston, I remember being angry. I used to have a more visceral response to what would be told to me: 'Well, we can't do that.' 'Well, you are *going* to do it.' We got to move it down the field like a football. What are we trying to get done here? Do you want to destroy the church? Or do you want to fix it? Because if you want to fix it, you've got to have a plan for how to do that."

The word that came to mind when Gary thought about Olan was "scary." He thought about how he had spent the last thirty years of his life trying to forget this. He wasn't about to make a hobby out of reliving it.

Gary followed Olan Horne over to St. Michael's, where a line of television cameras awaited them. Olan had called in the press. He lined up the survivors on the cascading steps of the church in chronological order of their profanation. Gary did not take his place, but instead walked alone back to his car.

Meanwhile, the number of Boston area priests suspected of child abuse now topped a hundred. Most had multiple accusations against them. According to church officials, on average each was transferred to at least two subsequent churches, perhaps exposing them to two-thirds of all Boston-area parishes.

Summer 2002

BRIGHTON, MASSACHUSETTS — On most of these summer nights, Donna Morrissey left her spare office exhausted and dispirited, sometimes requesting a police escort through the stone gateway at the end of the parking lot. She did not go home. Rather, she headed to her aunt's house just down the street, her port in the pitching storm.

But nothing was so simple. These days Elinor Cosgrove, who was Morrissey's maternal aunt, was engaged in a war against end-stage lung cancer—small-cell type, the gravest sort—and as her main caregiver, Morrissey was the one who held the pail for her when the chemo turned her stomach inside out each night. It was a difficult and heartbreaking chore for Morrissey, especially with the swollen weight of the crisis on her shoulders, but it helped to center her. *This* was who she had been before the crisis, staunchly family-focused, a devout young woman recognized for her generous heart.

The truth was, she was afraid to go home alone. Often at weekly cabinet meetings, someone predicted violence. For Morrissey, it seemed to lurk everywhere. One evening in May she pulled into her condo parking spot just as a strange man surged out of the bushes toward her car. Another man mailed her an unnerving ten-page marriage proposal; as a direct result of her exploding notoriety, now an old stalker had resurfaced after many years. Third parties were leaving messages of warning about him, things like "This guy's on a drunken tear" or "You better get someone to drive you home."

The police increased patrols around her neighborhood as a result.

Friends and relations openly wondered why she continued putting up with it, especially given how Sisyphean her task seemed. "The only way I would jump ship," she would promise, "is if I was ever put in a position that I knowingly was releasing misinformation or knew something was going on that shouldn't be going on. I'd walk out the door that day. Poor record keeping or trying to be here while we put a system in place, an unbelievable system in place, so that this doesn't happen again? That's different. But if someone ever asked me to lie or cover something up or what have you, that would be the day I would leave because I couldn't do that. And that day hasn't happened."

Elinor Cosgrove, who was sixty and wise in church affairs, gave Morrissey tremendous courage. Her faith, even in the jaws of death, was a leviathan. At her side she kept the rosary beads she was given in parochial school.

Some nights it was not clear who was holding the pail for whom.

Stay, her aunt insisted. *Horrible things happened there. They need to clean this mess up. As long as you can do good there, stay.*

"I want to do what I can to help, because it's my church, it's my community," she said. "To see this happen was awful, just awful. You know, I may be naïve and it's my own opinion, but what were we *all* thinking? Shame on *us.* Why did *I* not know that people in my community, young kids, were being raped? Why didn't *I* know that priests that I thought were infallible, individual priests, had been accused of this stuff? How come *I* couldn't pick up on the signs? Why didn't *I* know personally, or why didn't *any* of us know if a child is exhibiting signs of abuse that you got to take a second look? Shame on all of us."

May 8, 2002
Boston, Massachusetts — At a few minutes after 8 A.M., the elevator in Garabedian's office pinged open and Mark Keane appeared, bald and intense, clutching a twenty-ounce cup of coffee from Dunkin' Donuts.

"Hey, how you doing?" Garabedian called. "Come on in." For a man who was going to become the first attorney to depose the powerful cardinal, he seemed unexpectedly relaxed, though he was not. In a musty office littered with formless stacks of paper, he slid low into a leather chair at the conference table, elbows stabbing the armrests.

Through his lawyers, Law had tried everything imaginable to avoid being deposed. But once the settlements collapsed, Garabedian was single-minded about dragging him in for pretrial questioning. Appearing before Judge Sweeney, he sought a court order compelling Law to appear on May 14. Sweeney had read in the papers rumors that the pope might make him an ambassador and give him diplomatic immunity. Fearing that, or the possibility he might flee to Rome, she pushed it up a week. She even briefly contemplated confiscating his passport and demanding a $30 million bond, but in the end she did not. However, she ordered the deposition to be videotaped, usually something that is done when a witness has a fatal disease. In this case, she had no faith whatsoever that Law would be around or available at the time of trial.

Traditionally, a plaintiff is allowed to sit in on the deposition. Of his eighty-six clients, Garabedian had chosen Mark Keane to represent the Geoghan victims. Keane, now thirty-two, had been a slight and nervous fifteen-year-old when Geoghan cornered him at the Waltham Boys and Girls Club and forced him to perform oral sex.

Keane smoothed the front of his rumpled white shirt. "I wasn't sure what to wear," he said. He wore white jeans and no tie.

"You're fine," Garabedian waved.

"I didn't sleep too good last night," he said, still distracted by his attire.

"Just take notes, don't draw too much attention to yourself—they're looking for any excuse to not answer questions."

"I'll be quiet," he nodded.

"Keep your chin up," Garabedian said. "Look them square in the eye. If you see darkness or evil, just look right through it."

The two sunk into a tense silence. They jiggled their legs violently, unnoticed.

Ping. Shauna Tannenbaum, Garabedian's law associate, strode into the office wearing a plum-colored suit. She smiled at Keane, but Garabedian pulled her aside immediately with a muttered "Excuse me a minute" on his way out of the room. When the two returned, both appeared tense. "Okay, let's go," Garabedian commanded, and he and Keane dragged various valises and cartons of documents to the elevator and down to the street to wait for William Gordon, the associate whom Garabedian had chosen to do today's examination of Law.

Turning the corner in a three-piece chocolate suit and a Scottish driving cap, Gordon, an extremely short and eerily pale man, arrived with a bounce in his step. The lawyers whispered among themselves while Keane worried about his children and his finances. Three weeks ago his boss fired him. "Your mind is elsewhere," he had said. Keane had to agree.

Out of nowhere, Garabedian produced a hand dolly to help transport the multiplying cartons, which contained internal archdiocesan documents to present to Law for his verification. They did not have to travel far, just two blocks up State Street to Congress, across an uneven brick roadway in Boston's financial district. There, they would find Cardinal Law in a cordon of security guards. They would be frisked. All of them would feel quite intimidated.

Garabedian turned to his young client and looked squarely into his black eyes. "Let's do this," he said, offering a hand.

He turned to Tannenbaum and took her hand. "Let's do this." He turned to clasp Gordon's hand, saying, "Let's do this," then set off in earnest as Keane, Gordon, and Tannenbaum struggled with the dolly, occasionally stopping to restack the tower.

From somewhere in the bustling financial district crowds, a voice called out, "Good luck!"

"Who was that?" Gordon wondered.

"I don't know," said Garabedian, perplexed. But then another and another voice called out. "Go get 'em," and, "Good luck!"

For this brief moment, Garabedian was the hometown team.

"We're not the ones who need it!" he called back giddily.

Sometimes combative, sometimes morose, and occasionally funny during his four-hour deposition, Cardinal Law said he could recall nothing about the Geoghan problems. Not complaints about John Geoghan from mothers of abused kids. Not deciding to remove him from ministry or putting him back in a church months later, or receiving any warnings from his deputies that this was not the best course of action.

May 14, 2002
BALTIMORE, MARYLAND — Sunlight squinted into the bedroom of the apartment where Dontee Stokes lay in bed with his fiancée and their beautiful daughter, who was eighteen months old and particularly cuddly. Stokes felt in high spirits. In fact, his mood was one of unusually good cheer. When people remarked on this, Stokes—a twenty-six-year-old African-American barber at a clip shop called the KP—said he was hopeful now, after a long spell of sadness. Everyone knew the trigger was the crisis in the church.

Back in 1993, when Stokes was seventeen and sinking into his first serious depression, he told a therapist what his priest had been doing to him for three years at St. Edward's Church. He hadn't meant for his story to land on the television news. He hadn't even told his mother about the pesterings. But his therapist was a mandated reporter. Police showed up at his home and talked him through filing a report. Immediately Father Maurice Blackwell, one of the most prominent African-American clerics in Baltimore, was suspended. His myriad supporters decorated the church with yellow ribbons.

At the chancery's request, Stokes told his story to an independent lay panel appointed by the archdiocese of Baltimore, which found his accusations credible; he passed two lie-detector tests administered by the police. Still, nothing happened. The district attorney declined to prosecute because Stokes was sixteen—the age of consent—when the most serious encounters took place. Cardinal William Keeler overruled his advisory board and reinstated Blackwell, and on the day Blackwell celebrated his victorious homecoming Mass, television crews were on hand to capture Congressman Kweisi Mfume speaking to the cheering congregation on his behalf. Even members of Stokes's own family sided with Blackwell over him.

Being so spectacularly disregarded bothered Stokes even more than being molested. Nightmares haunted him. He turned to alcohol and marijuana, then fasting and prayer, but nothing stopped the dreams. He tried to submit himself totally to Christ, but it wasn't until he stopped attending Mass and instead found a home for himself in a storefront Christian church around the corner from St. Edward's that peace slowly returned.

When the church scandals broke across the country, Stokes's family feared the news would drag him back to that dark time. It seemed to have the opposite effect. He was elated by each new revelation.

Today was his day off. The family rose late. At midday, he drove his fiancée to work and took his little girl to his mother's house for a planned visit with his extended family. There he found his young cousins playing in his old bedroom. That's when he remembered the gun. Other barbers had told him he should carry one, but after purchasing a .357 Smith & Wesson on the black market a year or so ago, he felt immediately stupid, and stashed it in his old room. He thought he'd turn it in to the local precinct during the next gun buy-back program, usually held at Christmastime.

Worried the kids might find it and hurt themselves, he slid the large pistol into his gym bag.

When it was time to meet his fiancée for lunch, he strapped his daughter back into the car seat and flung his gym bag beside her. In a few blocks he turned down Reservoir Street, as usual. He spotted Father Blackwell standing in his front yard. This was not uncommon. Stokes had seen the man hundreds of times in the past decade. But this was the first time he saw him standing there with a small crowd. Stokes recognized several faces from the chancery, including his own cousin. Fueled by the daily news accounts of priests being taken from ministry, Stokes's mind leapt to a wishful conclusion: They have come to banish Maurice Blackwell once and for all, he surmised.

The thought thrilled him. He spun his car around to take another look—to gloat, really. He stopped the car a few feet from the gathering and rolled down the window. He smiled brightly. Blackwell did his best to ignore him, but his visitors repeatedly drew his attention to the handsome young man in the idling car. The priest turned around finally and snapped a dismissal. Stokes couldn't quite hear the words. He believed the priest was using obscenities, although at the same time he thought perhaps he was hearing things that weren't being said. He felt stupid— it was a dumb thing to stop. Blackwell turned away from the car. Stokes heard him say, "Fuck you," but he knew he may have been saying something altogether different. He was splintering.

"I didn't even get an apology," Stokes called after him bitterly. And as he said those words, he reached in the backseat, seized the pistol, and went blind with rage or fear. The loud *thun, thun, thun* terrified him as much as it did the people on the lawn, and sent Maurice Blackwell to the grass with one bullet in his hand and two in his hip.

Dontee Stokes knew he would turn himself in, but he gassed the car and headed for his fiancée's office to deliver the baby first. From there he made his way on foot up a long hill to the nearest police station. Along the route he came upon the Gillis Memorial Christian Community Church. An old woman with a walker was making her way inside.

He felt a need to pray. Following her, he discovered a revival was under way. Standing like the others, he commenced a profound series of prayers for Blackwell and his daughter—so teary and fervent that he didn't notice when the others had taken their seats and the room fell silent. He continued praying and crying until Pastor R. Lee Johnson interrupted his trance by calling him forward to recommit himself to God.

Sobbing and confused, Stokes stumbled to the front of the church. There he was surrounded by other church members who touched him and prayed aloud for his soul.

When the service was over, Pastor R. Lee Johnson put his arm over Stokes's shoulder and accompanied him the rest of the way up the hill to the police station.

May 18, 2002
BRIGHTON, MASSACHUSETTS — Despite entreaties from many parties, in flat disregard for the still-developing mushroom cloud of crisis, Cardinal Law had retreated again to the bunker on Commonwealth Avenue. He did not say a word about Shanley's arrest, had no comments when Eric MacLeish filed suit against Bernard Lane and exposed his nude therapy sessions at the Alpha Omega home for wayward kids, was mum when Middlesex district attorney Martha Coakley resigned from Law's Commission for the Protection of Children, saying that to remain on the panel would compromise her law enforcement duties. In the vacuum of his silence, Donna Morrissey was forced to admit that Law had routinely ignored his own abuse policies, the ones he kept trumpeting as revolutionary.

Law was not only keeping quiet, for the most part he had disappeared from public view. Facing the certainty of sharp protests, he declined to attend Boston College's commencement, where he had spoken six of the past ten years; he canceled a speech at Pontifical College Josephinum in Columbus, Ohio; he phoned in an eleventh-hour no-thanks to Hellenic College in Brookline, which had offered him an honorary degree. Meanwhile, aided by a poorly selected agenda at the chancery, Law's moral stature was actually plummeting even further. As if to say his ecclesiastical authority was undimmed, Law busied himself promulgating the kind of irksome tough-love policies that had defined his tenure. In response to a question from a young woman, for example, Law said it would be inappropriate to attend a relative's gay commitment ceremony. The harshest example had come on May 13 when, crushing the simple expectations of area Catholics, he decreed that family members would no longer be allowed to deliver eulogies at their loved ones' funerals, which were to focus on God in heaven, not the deceased.

The following day he sacked longtime *Pilot* editor Monsignor Peter Conley for coverage that was not deemed sufficiently positive. The local papers had had a heyday with that, likening it to Nixon's Saturday Night Massacre at the height of the Watergate investigation.

The man once considered more powerful than any governor now scraped around at the bottom of public opinion polls. The latest had found that three-quarters of American Catholics believed he was lying about what he knew. Now 64 percent demanded his resignation. At home the bell tolled even louder. Only 18 percent of Boston-area Catholics had a favorable opinion of Law, and over half had lost confidence in the church as an institution.

He ignored these sorry developments during his homily at the Cathedral of the Holy Cross on this Pentecost Sunday, marking the day when the Holy Spirit was said to have descended upon the apostles. Once again, Cardinal Law behaved as if nothing of significance were happening in his church. But something happened between morning and afternoon that showed him changing course: he released a letter containing his most detailed defense to date, and had it read from pulpits to every Catholic in the Roman Catholic archdiocese of Boston:

Dearly Beloved in Christ,

Today is Pentecost. With all my heart I pray that the Church in Boston might be given new life by a fresh outpouring of the Spirit's gifts. I would first like to thank you for maintaining your faith despite what you are seeing and reading about the current situation facing the Catholic Church. Difficult times come for each of us in different ways, and we need to draw on our faith in prayer in order to face these difficulties.

All of us are burdened by the seemingly never-ending repercussions of the sexual abuse of children by clergy. The scandalous and painful details which have emerged sear our hearts. The harm done to victims and their families is overwhelming. Bewilderment has given rise to anger and distrust. In the process, my credibility has been publicly questioned and I have become for some an object of contempt. I understand how this is so, and I am profoundly sorry that the inadequacy of past policies and flaws in past decisions have contributed to this situation. I wish I could undo the hurt and harm. . . . I am certain that as time goes on, fresh revelations concerning cases will necessitate some explanation on the part of the Archdiocese. Never, however, has there been an intent to put children at risk. . . .

As the newspapers immediately pointed out, his prayer for reconciliation did nothing to address the one central theme in the crisis, an unresponsive church. The church in Boston had an untold number of violated parishioners, some of whom had been trying to get meetings with the cardinal. Law had declared his willingness to talk to them, repeating, "I will meet as many victims as would want to meet with me [on] the timetable of their own choosing." Donna Morrissey was telling reporters he regularly received victims at the residence, offering an apology, a prayer, and assistance. She could not say how many he had seen or how many more were scheduled, however. "They're private meetings that are not part of the public schedule and it's not something we're going to get into the details about," Morrissey said.

This came as news to Gary Bergeron. Two months had passed since Barbara Thorp, the director of the Healing and Assistance Office, said she would arrange a meeting. Gary was calling every few days. So were several other members of the Birmingham support group. In fact, not one of the clients at Greenberg Traurig had scored an appointment all year. "It's just not happening," said lawyer Bob Sherman. "We have had dozens of people who have attempted to meet with the cardinal pre- and postlitigation, and they've been rebuffed."

Everybody with any knowledge of the situation assumed that Law and his spokeswoman were lying, out and out. Nobody was getting more frustrated by the double-speak than Tom Blanchette, who by now had made a half dozen trips to the chancery in the eight weeks since Donna Morrissey told reporters, "Cardinal Law is willing to meet with Mr. Blanchette." He had left business cards for Morrissey, Father John Connolly, and Cardinal Law himself, to no avail.

Fed up, he went to the press. "Despite Cardinal Bernard F. Law's public vow to meet victims of clergy sexual abuse, the Boston Archdiocese is routinely ignoring requests for those sessions, victims and their attorneys say," the story began.

Denying that the chancery had become an impenetrable bunker, Donna Morrissey told the reporter that Law was giving preference to abuse victims who had not retained attorneys. Asked why Blanchette, who had not sued, was never contacted, Morrissey said, "I just don't have a number for him."

"They probably put my number in the same place they put the Shanley records," Blanchette chafed. "They're still inept."

May 22, 2002
BOSTON, MASSACHUSETTS — Humiliated and chastened by the public revelation of his homosexuality, Father George Spagnolia had receded into anonymity. He furnished a temporary ground-floor apartment in Beacon Hill with a seriously off-kilter table and wobbly chairs that his sister had pulled from a pile in her garage. A friend gave him a toaster; another provided the coffeepot. The Dacron love seat in the bedroom was the only thing he brought with him from St. Patrick's in Lowell, and probably he shouldn't have. Technically, it belonged to the church. But he needed something to rest on as he read into the night, and besides, the day he put it in the moving van he was sure he was beginning a journey that would bring him and his love seat right back where they started.

That seemed increasingly remote now. Neither his civil lawyer nor his canon lawyer had heard a thing from the archdiocese in the three months since he was evicted from his rooms. He continued demanding his day before a church tribunal, but the weeks and months ticked by without any indication when that might come. So Spags persisted in this paralytic juncture, this purgatory, neither acquitted nor convicted.

A day or two earlier, Michael Ritty, his canon lawyer, had proposed taking the offensive. If Spags were to bring some sort of canonical lawsuit against the archdiocese—for violating the canon governing administration of a parish during a pastor's temporary suspension, for instance—perhaps he might provoke a tribunal hearing on the main charges. Ritty's theory was to argue that continuing Spags's exile indefinitely sowed confusion in the minds of parishioners and tended to suggest he was guilty even without a trial. Two other canonical experts he polled on the tactic were divided in opinion. But Spags felt he had little choice. "It's the only way to counter their strategy, which is to keep me in limbo so they won't have to bother with me again," he told him.

Otherwise, what else was there for him to do—a man of sixty-three, cast into the city without a penny to his name? The archdiocese was giving him a monthly housing allowance of $1,400, barely enough to cover his apartment, and was footing the bill for his two attorneys. Surely this could not go on forever.

While he awaited justice, Spags was spending most of his days in Boston Common talking to the homeless and downtrodden people perched on benches there, steering them to food and shelter. It was a self-styled ministry, one that reminded him of the purpose and meaning that lured him to the priesthood in the beginning. He did not feel sorry for himself, and spent almost no energy bemoaning his spectacularly public and stupid self-destruction. That's because something amazing had happened to him the minute his secret was out. He realized he'd spent his entire life afraid. The worst thing that could possibly happen to him, the one thing he dreaded, had come to pass. He was dragged out of the closet. And it wasn't that bad. Walking through the Common, eating at the local Italian joint, pushing quarters into the hands of grimy old men, he knew people recognized him from television as the bald-headed priest who lied about two boyfriends. And that made him feel thoroughly free for the first time in his life.

May 23, 2002

BRIGHTON, MASSACHUSETTS — For their delegation to the chancery to meet with Bishop Edyvean and push for their three affirmative aims, Voice of the Faithful was allowed to select three members. It was clear that Muller would be among them. Extremely bright, charismatic, a Nobel laureate, he was the brains of the group. Mary Scanlon Calcaterra, because she was its heart, was also selected. The third slot went to Steve Krueger, the group's executive director, who for the past several years had been serving on the pastoral council of the archdiocese and was already acquainted with Edyvean and Law as a result. Soft-spoken, with a slight stutter, quick to well up in tears, Krueger wore his disappointments out on the surface, not concealed behind the paint of eloquence or polish. Even if Edyvean did not already know him, he would see in a glance that his heart bled for his besieged church. By trade Krueger was an investment consultant for small and midsized companies. All his life he had been what he called a "major events Catholic," a man for whom religion was entirely encoded in his genes, but played little role in daily life. That changed a few years ago when AIDS had claimed a good friend, and then the friend's brother, in a matter of a few months. Krueger began finding nourishment in his church in a new way. He became active in church-based AIDS ministries through St. Ignatius Church in Brighton, and sat on his local parish council, which he also represented to the diocese-wide council. Though he was well into his thirties, he briefly considered entering the seminary before concluding that celibacy would never work for him, so instead he had been seeking a way to live and serve as an unordained minister, perhaps in AIDS work. Still, in gentle ways he had already experienced ideological disappointments, especially over the church's stubborn position against condom usage, even to prevent the spread of HIV. He understood the church teaching about the lesser of two evils— shouldn't spreading a deadly virus be considered a greater evil than encouraging people to use prophylactics? This dissonance once led him to ask Cardinal Law, "If I prayerfully contemplate a church teaching and find I disagree with it, what can I do?" To which the

cardinal answered, "If you pray long and hard enough, you will come
to agree."

On the afternoon of the scheduled meeting, Krueger was the most
nervous. He arrived early, in time to see Mary Calcaterra and Jim
Muller pull in off Commonwealth Avenue.

They were greeted by Bishop Edyvean and Father Mark O'Connell,
a canon lawyer who was Edyvean's adviser on canonical affairs.

Edyvean jumped right in. "We can agree with your first two goals,
'support priests of integrity' and 'support the victims.' But we have some
questions about the third, 'shaping structural change.' Let us agree
from the start that we support the documents of Vatican II."

All did. One by one they introduced themselves and shared their
great concerns for a church they loved. Mary Calcaterra was struck at
how well the churchmen listened to their presentations. But she was
not altogether trusting of their thoughts.

"We are a centrist group," Muller assured. "We didn't call for Law's
resignation, though many people wanted to."

The bishop put a hand on the table. "You had no business discussing
His Eminence's resignation."

"Holding that meeting together was one of the most difficult moments I have confronted in my life. It is really hurtful for me to hear
you say that," Muller replied.

"Well," interjected O'Connell, "it is hurtful to us to hear you saying
that the press forced you to call for the cardinal's resignation."

Muller knew what O'Connell was talking about—an erroneous line
in a news story for which he'd requested a correction. "I didn't say that,
Father," he said. "The press said the laity was calling for his resignation,
but we didn't—there was a very small minority that felt it was inappropriate to take a position on the cardinal's tenure, and because we operate on consensus, that left us unable to take a position."

Trying to grab back the initiative, Muller asked the bishop to issue a
statement affirming the right of Voice of the Faithful to form chapters,
but Edyvean declined.

"Are you trying to block or in any way inhibit the formation of chapters?" Muller and the others had broad suspicions Edyvean was or-
chestrating the backlash.

Bishop Edyvean did not answer directly, but instead said it was the chancery's job to oversee and coordinate what went on inside parishes. Unsatisfied, Muller asked again, and a third time.

"Sometimes a priest will call and ask me what they should do when laity wants to have a meeting," Edyvean said. "In one instance, I discouraged it."

Conversation moved on to an even more difficult matter. Voice of the Faithful, concerned by reports that the cardinal's annual fund-raising appeal was falling short, was contemplating establishing its own fund. Called "Voice of Compassion," the fund would promise contributors that not one cent would go toward lawyers to fight victims or PR consultants, or to feed secret multimillion-dollar slush funds. Instead, it would be earmarked directly for charity. "There are many people who want to give money right now but feel they can't in good conscience," one of them said. "Those are the people we are appealing to."

Edyvean said he was not sure how the church could accept those donations, which might be viewed as undermining the primary role of the archbishop in carrying out fund-raising. O'Connell raised a hand high over his head, as if holding aloft a flag. "The importance of the archbishop and his right relationship with the work of the church is here," he said. He dropped his other hand over the rail of his chair and reached down nearly to the ground. "The importance of funding the ministries and the programs of the archdiocese is down here."

The stunning coldness of such a declaration seized Steve Krueger. He could not breathe; he blinked away tears.

Jim Muller said, "The money is for the poor."

"The poor," O'Connell said, "will have to wait."

Before letting the bishop and the priest leave, Muller—with one eye perfectly focused on organization building—had a substantial conversation with Edyvean about how the meeting could be portrayed to reporters. Muller proposed a joint press release, but the bishop declined, though he felt comfortable portraying this meeting as "a conversation" that may continue into the future. They shook hands.

In the parking lot outside, just after Mary Calcaterra strapped herself back into her car, her telephone rang. She listened in shock as a reporter told her Edyvean had already issued a statement and faxed it to media outlets. It said, "Bishop Edyvean pointed to the right of all the faithful to form associations. He underscored the fact that associations in the church, from the point of view of both theology and canon law, are meant to aid the mission of the church and that mission is carried on necessarily with and under the bishop of the diocese. Likewise, it is the diocesan bishop's role to exercise vigilance with regard to the way in which Catholic associations perform the tasks they set for themselves."

"We went in there wanting to talk about victims and the poor," she fumed, "and all they wanted to talk about was obedience to the bishop. *That was their one theme.*"

MILWAUKEE, WISCONSIN — Archbishop Rembert Weakland, one of the most liberal voices in the church hierarchy, was well regarded among his peers and priests and praised by progressive Catholics around the country. A sign of his unimpeachability came a few years ago when he was selected by the bishops' conference to draft what would become one of the major documents from the American church, a profound re-stating of Catholic responsibility to the poor in a culture of affluence. Church conservatives assailed his various positions, which included quiet dissent against church teachings on homosexuality and support of women's ordination, and especially his overt endorsement of condoms to stem the spread of HIV.

He had not been better than others, however, in handling allegations against his priests, and in at least one instance when a young man sued the archdiocese claiming abuse by a pastor who had in fact been convicted and was serving time for molesting altar boys, he got the case thrown out on grounds it was beyond statute—and then vigorously countersued to recover $4,000 in court costs. That alone could account for some of the glee people across the country felt when they turned to *Good Morning America* on Thursday morning and heard Charles Gibson announce a "serious new allegation of sexual misconduct in the Catholic Church."

Gibson's guest was a slick and erratic fifty-three-year-old man named Paul Marcoux, who told in a deep and measured voice how he'd been serially date-raped by Weakland in 1979, beginning when the younger man was thirty. "He was sitting next to me and then started to try to kiss me and continued to force himself on me and pulled down my trousers, attempted to fondle me," he said. Weakland had paid him $450,000 to keep it a secret, he said.

The truth proved less salacious, but far weirder. Indeed, there had been a relationship. It lasted for months, and was characterized by mutual emotional neediness. When it was over Marcoux took great exception. Apparently unable to win back Weakland's attentions, he instead hectored him for the money, which he said he needed for a video project he had hatched for teaching Bible stories to children. Reluctantly, but in total secret, Weakland used church money to make the "investment," which involved signing a gag order about their encounters.

Unfortunately the archbishop had fallen deeply in love with Marcoux, who was nearly twenty years his junior. This was undeniable, as Weakland had committed his feelings to a lengthy, sad letter commemorating their breakup—which also was released by ABC and proved the most humiliating disclosure in the sad saga.

"My mother's sage advice when I lamented about the injustice of it all was to warn me that I should not put down on paper what I would not want the whole world to read—but here goes anyway," Weakland began. "During the last months I have come to know how strained I was, tense, pensive, without much joy. I couldn't pray at all. I just did not seem to be honest with God. I felt I was fleeing from Him, from facing Him. I know what the trouble was: I was letting your conscience take over for me and I couldn't live with it. I felt like the world's worst hypocrite. So gradually I came back to the importance of celibacy in my life—not just a physical celibacy but the freedom the celibate commitment gives. I knew I would have to face up to it and take seriously that commitment I first made thirty-four years ago. I found my task as priest-archbishop almost unbearable these months and I came to realize that I was at a crossroads—and I knew I had to get the courage to decide. There is no other way for me to live, Paul. Ridicule me if you must—I am expecting it. Say I am seeking escapes, but I must be me. . . . The amount of time at my disposal is so very limited. My function as bishop is all absorbing. There is no other way. I have to be free and unencumbered, if I want to give total service to His Church. . . . I cry as I write this: they are personally the greatest renunciations the Lord has asked me to make for His Kingdom."

He signed the letter, "Paul, God is good. I love you."

Humiliated and ashamed, immediately following the television broadcast Weakland fired off an urgent request asking the Vatican to allow him to retire. At a press conference announcing his failings, the men and women who stood by him wept loudly. His career was shattered.

Some conservative pundits rejoiced. "There is simply no defending Weakland in this matter," wrote Rod Dreher of the *National Review*. "His is a perfect example of what happens when a bishop puts his sexual gratification and own reputation over holiness, humility and the good of the Church." But most felt that he had fallen victim not only to his own confused heart, but to an intensely venal ex-lover and a hungry media maw. Many lamented the tendency to blur the nuances of his sad demise with the child abuse scandal inappropriately. He was a gay man in love, however pitifully. Even conservative commentator William Donohue, of the Catholic League, saw Weakland as the victim of a "sexual McCarthyism. . . . It's time everyone—on the left and on the right, straight as well as gay—chilled out. Enough is enough."

Chapter 13

Toward Holy Cross

Thursday, May 16, 2002

SILVER SPRINGS, MARYLAND — Nurses on the fourth floor of St. Luke Institute had not seen Father Alfred Bietighofer since breakfast. He had missed his morning therapy session—it would be his first since intake interviews were completed earlier in the week—and was not seen by anyone at lunch. Father Stephen Rossetti, the St. Luke's director, was a bit concerned. He dispatched a nurse to find out where he was.

Not that Bietighofer showed any signs of depression. A sixty-five-year-old parish priest, he had been assistant pastor at St. Andrew Church in Bridgeport, Connecticut, until ten days ago, when an attorney representing ten men accused him of serial sex crimes. Bietighofer had been accused before. He steadfastly declaimed his innocence. Not knowing whom to believe, Bridgeport bishop William Lori had sidelined him from his parish work, bringing to seven the number of Bridgeport priests removed since January, and made arrangements for him to be evaluated at St. Luke's. There, psychologists screened him for suicidal tendencies on admission and again at midweek, and found none.

Bietighofer had expressed eagerness to cooperate. He frequently prayed in the dark second-floor chapel, and people who spoke with him in the bright cafeteria thought he displayed a steady, if resolute, demeanor. They had not yet established what course of therapy, if any, was needed.

He was not the staff's only worry. St. Luke Institute was under tremendous pressure. When the scandals first broke, this was a sleepy sanatorium for a handful of troubled priests, only a quarter of whom were sex offenders. By March, all forty-three rooms and eight berths in an adjacent halfway house were full, and in April the waiting list stood at two months. Bishops, desperate to assure the faithful that they were responding appropriately, were exerting great pressure to jump their troubled priests to the top of the list. Behind the scenes, St. Luke's was a battleground. Rossetti saw it coming—two years earlier, he had told his staff, "Nobody knows how many priests have abused and are back in ministry—if people knew, they would flip out."

The nurse walked down a long, quiet hallway to room C217, the last door on the left. She knocked. No response came through the heavy door. Reticently, she turned the knob and leaned against the door, encountering resistance. She leaned harder. When the door finally budged, she heard a clunk as the body of the priest, which had been hanging from a length of bedsheet knotted and wedged in the door, fell to the aqua carpet.

Word of the suicide spread quickly through a community already overwhelmed by sadness. State regulatory authorities immediately shut down Rossetti's operation, claiming he had not done enough to anticipate such an eventuality. Touring the facility that afternoon, they wrote up citations for numerous violations, including the fact that each of the patients' rooms had glass mirrors that could be shattered and used for slitting wrists, and clothing hooks, fixed on the door beneath simple wooden crucifixes, that could serve as cleats for nooses fashioned from belts, shoelaces, sheets, or articles of clothing.

Back in Bridgeport, Catholics suffered a deep and complex grief, none more than Mario Jaiman, a thirty-six-year-old former altar boy who had met a week earlier with Bishop Lori. Under the guise of sex education, Bietighofer had fondled him repeatedly, he said. He was convinced every altar boy had had the same experience. "We wanted justice, we didn't want death," he told the *Hartford Courant*. "This is not what we were looking for."

Bishop Lori moved quickly to assure the accusers they were not responsible for the priest's suicide. "In the face of such overwhelming sorrow, what can we learn?" he said in a formal statement. "We learn once again that every person, without exception, has dignity and worth in God's eyes. We learn that it is best for all concerned when issues of abuse are dealt with immediately, as they happen, rather than years later." By implication, he was pointing a finger at his predecessor Edward Egan, who just a year ago was tapped to become the new archbishop of New York. Egan had left countless priests in ministry, despite allegations. In extreme secrecy, Egan settled twenty-six lawsuits for more than $12 million on his way out of town. As part of the settlement, he insisted on language that barred any party to the negotiation from mentioning details of the charges. As a safety measure, he also demanded that attorneys for the victims return to the diocese every copy of every letter, deposition, or document produced during the discovery phase of the suit.

During his tenure, there was no evidence that Egan had ever reported an allegation of abuse to civil authorities, as required by state law. Connecticut's attorney general was investigating possible criminal charges against the diocese, and Egan in particular. Similar criminal probes were under way in Massachusetts, Kentucky, and New Jersey, as well as in Cincinnati, Cleveland, Los Angeles, and Phoenix. The New Hampshire attorney general, Philip McLaughlin, was convinced Bishop McCormack had engaged in illegal conduct that led to the harming of countless children. "I think it is absolutely self-evident that that's the case," he told the *New Hampshire Sunday News*. "There's no ambiguity about it. The question is, can we get the kind of evidence to bring prosecutions within the statute of limitations?"

June 10, 2002
JAFFREY, NEW HAMPSHIRE — Bishop McCormack, who had been waging an aggressive defense against charges in New Hampshire as well as in Boston, where he was now named in dozens of suits, had removed his first priest from active ministry in mid-February, and since then another eighteen priests were removed from ministry or resigned volun-

tarily. This year's seminary class, however, produced only two ordained priests. The severe priest shortage exacerbated a snowballing financial crisis and forced McCormack to close parishes, which he had avoided up to now. More cuts were looming, though. Because of security concerns he was planning to cancel his annual summer reception, a champagne fund-raiser on the lawn of his grand residence that last year raised a record $415,000. Donations to individual churches were also off steeply, as Catholics stayed away from services.

Now on June 10, in a massive redeployment of personnel, McCormack changed the assignments of thirty-eight priests. Very few parishes enjoyed the luxury of a pastor and a curate; they were all one-man shows, if that—some priests were covering two or three parishes.

One of them, Father Roland P. Cote, was taking the helm at St. Patrick's in Jaffrey at a precarious time. The parish's long-term priest, James "Seamus" MacCormack, had been a whistle-blower of sorts. More than a year earlier, police had called him to a house to identify the body of a man whose wallet contained MacCormack's phone number. What he saw there scandalized him. His old friend, Father Richard Connors, lay dead of a heart attack, wearing only a leather accessory on his genitals. The medical examiner later determined that Viagra contributed to his heart failure. MacCormack had alerted his superiors to what he saw, but he was further mortified when they sent a team to the dead man's rectory and crated out a huge supply of pornographic magazines and videos.

Privately MacCormack and Bishop McCormack had exchanged harsh words over the campaign to sanitize news of the death. The priest's criticisms escalated once the sex abuse crisis engulfed the church. Concerned he might go public, diocesan leaders took his insolence as evidence of mental illness. They had referred him for psychological treatment. Father Edward Arsenault, chancellor of the Manchester diocese, told the clinic conducting the examination that MacCormack lacked "any prudent sense of with whom to share confidences." Tests confirmed his sanity. Nonetheless, Bishop McCormack placed him on administrative leave, upsetting his parishioners.

As a replacement, Father Cote was a fair homilist and well-liked pastor. However, Bishop McCormack did not tell parishioners that Cote had just been investigated by police and the diocese for a sexual arrangement he had with a man from Newport, beginning when the man was eighteen, or seventeen, or sixteen, according to various versions of the story. Cote admitted the affair, but said it was consensual and had nothing to do with church—the young man was not a parishioner and was unaware Cote was a priest. In New Hampshire, sixteen is the age of consent, so Cote had broken no law.

Even in the middle of a shattering scandal, John McCormack felt it was not important to mention this fact to the parish.

It would have been different if it had been a young man of faith that Cote had seduced, the bishop reasoned. It was quite another thing to take a non-Catholic teenager to bed. Surely the people of St. Patrick's would agree.

Tuesday Nights

LOWELL, MASSACHUSETTS — "You don't trust. You have anger issues. Forget about having any faith," Bernie McDaid was saying. Once a week, the Survivors of Joseph Birmingham slumped in leather chairs scattered around the large meeting room at the local campus of the University of Massachusetts, nodding in recognition. "I went into heavy alcohol and drug use. Heavy. It was quite fast. Literally, I met Birmingham when I was fourteen and a half, and by fifteen and a half I'm hanging out with these ex–Vietnam vets and they're all shooting me up with crystal methamphetamines and I'm doing Seconals, and all these ups and downs, and drinking around the clock. I went from class president to kicked out of school in a year. My family couldn't help me."

"Cocaine, mostly marijuana. Some pills, that was me," said Paul Ciaramitaro, a bundle of nervousness. "What's going on in your mind? Nobody likes you, that's what. Birmingham catches you in this isolation and locks you there. You're knocked down, all you can see are your weaknesses. You lash out."

Anger, Olan Horne agreed, was their common theme. "Like I say, the last guy you want knocking on your door if you owe me eight bucks is me."

What most surprised Gary Bergeron about the Survivors of Joseph Birmingham was how dissimilar their meetings were to the therapy sessions he had seen in movies—no Kleenex, no role-playing, no "Let's process this," just a bunch of guys who didn't know one another before who came to realize how humiliating pasts can leave identical marks. He was quick to rages, too, and turned his back on his studies at precisely the same time as these guys. He trusted nobody. Constant self-censorship was the only thing between him and chronic substance abuse, brutal rage, economic chaos, lovelessness.

"My relationships were horrendous, absolutely horrendous," Gary said. "I never, ever, like Bernie, lived up to my potential, I'm really realizing that now. I come from a family where everybody's a college graduate except for myself and my younger brother—the two Birmingham victims. Everybody has stable marriages except for myself and Eddie. My parents were married fifty years! I never, ever stopped to look in that mirror to realize, Oh, my God."

"Ever married?" he was asked.

"Twice. Major hostilities. Only time this ever came up was a one-minute conversation with my ex-wife, probably like five years ago when we were splitting up, the day we walked into court. She said she wanted to move back home to Virginia and take Evan with her. I said, 'No way. I live for my son.' And she said, 'You know what? Unless you tell that judge in there that you are going to get counseling for the abuse that you told me about from the priest, you're not getting custody.' "

"She saw that as a problem?"

"Majorly. That's how much denial I was in. I just didn't see it. The hardest thing in my life has been to look in the mirror at forty and realize, you know what? You've been living thirty years of lies because this is not the way normal people live. I mean, in my life for the last thirty years, I never had a black-and-white moment. It was all gray."

Olan Horne snorted. "We've had our fucking faces kicked in, our psyches kicked in," he said. "I mean, how do we get over that?"

"Something I keep thinking about," said Bernie McDaid, "was how when Birmingham would come to our class, your guts would be in your throat, and you were hoping, *hoping* he didn't see you, your head would be down, *no eye contact,* and you pray, 'Take Tommy So-and-so.'

He says, 'Tommy So-and-so,' and instantly you got this relief and you would start sniggering at little Tommy. Better him than you. We're all doing this, of course, because we all know what's about to happen. I'm not proud of this. But we did it. This is how boys acted. Tommy's walking all the way across the room to that door and he's going into an inferno and we're *laughing,* and it's all over for him, he knows it, he's beet red, scared shitless, he's looking at the floor and that door and he knows he doesn't have a chance. And now this year I see this in my mind's eye watching that play out, me snickering and the guys snickering and I get a real sick feeling. *Wait a minute,* you know? That was *your* face turning red, that was *your* inferno you were going into, that was *your* fear going down that lane, *you* were the one that didn't have a chance."

"That's the biggest problem for me is the living with the regrets," Gary said. "You know, I've been through the litany of the apologies. And the part that sucks, you know, is that people look at us, or at me, anyways, and say, 'You guys are so great, you've done so much, you're public-speaking on this constantly.' Everybody comes up to us and just pats you on the back, and I just think to myself, My God, what we could have done had this *not* happened? I look in this room with Bernie and Olan and the others and literally I see greatness. I wonder what this world would've been like for us had we been able to follow the paths we should've followed. We've wasted, my God, *I've* wasted thirty years wandering around, running away from something or running toward something and never realizing where I already was."

Nobody had more incontrovertible evidence of his own squandered potential than Bernie McDaid. "Let's start now," he said. "Let's use our talents on a higher level. If anybody can fix this crisis, look around—it's us."

How strange, McDaid thought. Not one of them doubted him.

Thursday, June 13, 2002
DALLAS, TEXAS — The three hundred members of the United States Conference of Catholic Bishops headed to their annual June meeting in an extreme state of anxiety. They had never been so scrutinized. Year after year they usually accredited a dozen or so reporters, mostly

from the nonsecular press, but now nearly a thousand journalists had requested credentials. Arbitrarily, organizers cut the list to 750. Fifty or so were invited to watch the proceedings live while the rest were sent to a bull pen on a different floor, outfitted with closed-circuit television screens—in a show of muscle, the bishops rejected *Boston Globe* reporters' pleas to attend the live session, flatly admitting it was in retaliation for the paper's aggressive coverage.

Still, they were eager to get out a message of responsiveness. The night before their meeting was to start, Archbishop Harry Flynn, head of the sexual abuse ad hoc committee, was on *Nightline* assuring the country that the body would pass an effective new policy to protect children. Catholics were hopeful. In an ABC News poll, 77 percent said they believed the Dallas meeting would produce meaningful change.

At the same time, however, 63 percent disapproved of the bishops' performance to date. So far this year, at least 250 priests had been ousted under the media's glare. Four U.S. bishops had resigned amid their own sex scandals, and many others stood accused of protecting abusive priests. On the front page of the *Dallas Morning News* today were the results of a national survey of the track records of 285 bishops. By scouring published articles and court documents, the paper concluded that two-thirds of them engaged in cover-ups, denials, or transfers of known sex abusers and child molesters.

Inside the conference center at the luxurious Fairmont Hotel, Maria Rullo Schinderle, who worked for the diocese of Orange County, in California, was glancing out the window. Cabs and limousines were pulling up in droves, dropping off the three hundred American bishops at the door. Across a wide boulevard in the punishing ninety-two-degree heat stood three or four victims with protest posters. Not one bishop had gone up to them.

"I really feel like we should go out there and talk to the victims," Maria said to her friend Meg Waters, also volunteering from Orange. "I want to welcome them, because it shouldn't be them versus us."

Meg joined her at the window. "You don't want to be seen as giving a dime to a beggar," she said.

"I don't want them to think it's a gesture for the cameras," Maria agreed.

Down below, Kristopher Galland was standing before a news crew from New Orleans, with small middle-school portraits of himself arrayed in his palm, an archipelago of his suffering. "I was abused between the ages of eleven and fourteen," he was saying.

Unlike the majority of Catholics, the victim-survivors were not anticipating a transformation of thought to come out of the conference. The bishops had already given a preview of their new policy. Pronouncing themselves totally against the sexual exploitation of children, they nonetheless explicitly declared that a priest who fondled just one child was not to be automatically removed from ministry, if his transgression was in the distant past. Catholicism, they argued, was predicated on the belief that through penance and "Catholic conversion" of sinners, all but the extreme cases could be rehabilitated. Critics called this a "two strikes" clause. "Only one freebie," joked Jay Leno. "I hope it was a cute one!"

Mostly in silence, members of the press corps stretched their necks as the three hundred bishops began to arrive in their tinted limos and black suits, walking heads down toward the hotel door without acknowledging the protests or the banks of television cameras from CNN, NBC, MSNBC, and Fox, which were broadcasting live.

"It's a perp walk," one of them said.

"Holy pedophilia!" called a protester, who had dressed as John Paul II.

When Law pulled up to the door, he waved self-consciously to the crowd. He did not answer the shouted questions from a press corps ramped into overdrive by a crisis that had lasted four mouths. "How do you feel, Cardinal?" "How was your trip?" "Do you feel besieged?"

"The cardinal is looking forward to meeting with his fellow bishops," Donna Morrissey said on his behalf. "I would not describe him as being under siege."

Despite Morrissey's remonstration, Cardinal Law's reception from fellow prelates in Dallas was tentative and chilly, in stark contrast to his dominance over the national body in past years. They turned their heads when he passed through crowded rooms, and in situations where it was not possible to avoid hellos, hello is what they left it at.

They were angry at Law for many reasons: for failing to adopt an effective policy against sexual abuse at a time when most other dioceses had; for exquisite mismanagement of the media; for attracting over seven hundred reporters to their conference, making them feel like hostages; for giving them no way out but this public display of contriteness, as Bishop Wilton Gregory acknowledged in his powerful presidential address.

"My brother Bishops, there is a lot of anger among us in this room—righteous anger," he began. "Since 1985—as a Conference and individually as Diocesan Bishops—we have been working on the problem of sexual abuse to ensure, as much as is humanly possible, that the Church would be a safe environment for our children. In 1992, after seven years of study and work that included listening sessions with victim-survivors and other members of the Church, consultations with experts, and experimentation with policies on the diocesan level, we together adopted *Five Principles to Follow in Dealing with Accusations of Sexual Abuse*. The vast majority of Bishops embraced these principles, made them the standard for policies on sexual abuse in their dioceses and, therefore, contributed effectively to the protection of children in the Church. These policies, however, were not implemented effectively in every diocese across this country.

"In a matter of a few months, this has become painfully clear. The very solid and good work that has been accomplished by the majority of Bishops in their dioceses has been completely overshadowed by the imprudent decisions of a small number of Bishops during the past ten years. It is as if the fabric of the good work that has been accomplished had never existed or had completely unraveled. The anger over this is very real and very understandable. I know. I feel it myself."

At his first opportunity, a session closed to the press on Friday morning, Law took the microphone in a large, darkened conference hall and offered his apology to all his brother bishops, but in particular to any bishop upon whom he foisted any priest, through transfer or lend-lease, with a known track record of sexual misconduct. Donna Morrissey had helped him find exactly the right words.

"Never in my wildest, worst nightmare could I have imagined" being at the hub of this enormous scandal, he told them. He spoke about what it was like for him personally: "the distrust, the anger, the sense of betrayal, the fact that for many, I've become an object of contempt." He begged their forgiveness for casting them all in a similar light.

His apology did not immediately warm the room to Law, and news of it only stoked the media frenzy. Under guidelines established by the national bishops' office, reporters, though allowed inside, had been warned not to approach any bishop as he strolled from meeting hall to meeting hall. Violators would lose their credentials and face immediate expulsion from the halls. The proper way to request an interview was through Sister Mary Ann Walsh, the reproving communications director for the conference who served as a conduit for all reporters. Scores of national reporters had requested time with Cardinal Law, though they never heard back from the sister again.

Isolated and sidelined, Law decided to do something he had not done since February: speak to the press. Through Morrissey, Law agreed to meet one-on-one with journalists from Boston. Sitting with Michael Paulson of the *Globe,* he argued that his disastrous experiences in Boston would be beneficial for the group's deliberation, and help them arrive at a policy that will surely protect children in the future. "Our focus really must be primarily the protection of children," he said. "Not that we are not to be concerned with the priests—we must be. Scandal—we must be. The good of the parish and the church—we must be. But the primary focus has got to be on children, and if it is, then the way you handle these other problems is going to be different, and it's that focus that has come to me with a new clarity."

The three-day meeting was unlike any bishops' conference meeting in the past. Bishop Gregory had invited leading Catholic intellectuals like R. Scott Appleby, the Notre Dame historian, to address the body. Their remarks were blistering. On two occasions, panels of victims gave another opportunity for the prelates to appear chastened. Accustomed to exquisite deference, the display made many bishops visibly uncomfortable, and the mood throughout the hotel was combative and tense.

Nevertheless, when their deliberations were through by the end of the week, the bishops adopted a complicated new policy for dealing with sexually abusing priests that, though stricter than the version they had previewed, still did not approximate policies that are in place for most Scout leaders, physicians, schoolteachers, or day care workers. A number of bishops argued strongly in favor of applying penalties only to repeat or "notorious" offenders, but they were overruled. The "Charter for the Protection of Children and Young People" promised that any priest accused of molesting children was to be removed immediately from ministry while a review panel largely made up of laity investigated the charges. If charges proved credible in the review panel's report, the priest would be permanently enjoined from public ministry. However, church leaders would allow him to remain within the community of Roman Catholic clergy, perhaps cloistered in a monastery.

The protesters were disgusted. "We already have a wonderful place in society for these people who are proven guilty," said Mike Emerton, a member of Voice of the Faithful. "It's called jail." For David Clohessy, who had spent most of the three-day conference in the lobby of the hotel with other SNAP members from around the country, making himself available to journalists and bishops alike, Dallas was more of the same. For one thing, as a victim and a survivor, he felt the bishops looked upon him with reproach, as though he and the others who had been preyed upon by priests were sworn enemies of the Catholic Church. "I long to see the day when a bishop stands up and says, 'We as a church are *grateful* to these survivors because they took a courageous step that has enabled us to clean up our own house and protect kids and give others the strength to come forward,' " he said.

One long afternoon as the bishops were meeting in closed session, Donna Morrissey had positioned herself on a sofa in the lobby and quite unexpectedly fell into an easy conversation with the SNAP people. The experience opened her eyes. Before, she had seen only their rage, which frightened and appalled her; now she saw their sadness. She mentioned this to Law as the two were readying to leave Dallas for Boston.

His curiosity seemed bottomless. "You talked to them? How long?"

"Three hours, maybe more," she said. "They were really interesting. I told them, there's going to be a lot of things we're going to disagree on, but I bet there's quite a few fundamental things we *do* agree on."

"How was it?" he wondered.

"We had a wonderful time. They were really good people."

Law was amazed.

June 19, 2002

LOS ANGELES, CALIFORNIA — The underground group of gay priests had been following the bishops' proceedings on C-SPAN. The Dallas charter did little to allay their fears. They remained convinced that gays were more vulnerable to an unjust allegation than straight priests, because the review boards would be more prone to believe the worst of a homosexual. By now all of them knew of someone who had been removed after charges were lodged. The veracity of the allegations had not yet been determined. But so far nobody had been cleared and sent back to a pulpit.

Bill Mochon convened a group meeting in his apartment at about 8 P.M. for a post-Dallas debriefing. At the invitation of the bishops' national headquarters, Mochon had addressed the conference on the subject of treatment risks and benefits for abusive priests. He favored a policy that would allow bishops discretion to return transgressive priests to ministry, if they demonstrated improvement. The American Psychological Association and the ACLU had made similar arguments. He was bitterly disappointed when the bishops overruled him, voting nearly unanimously for a flat one-strike rule. For this he blamed pressure from the victims, who made it impossible for any other outcome to be considered; the victims, in turn, blamed the bishops, whose comportment in the past was so uniformly disastrous that they could not be trusted to make individual judgment calls.

"I never saw such twisted, angry faces," Mochon said. "I thought the victims really exemplified the angry-equals-not-listening equation. I thought this would be a stronger, healthier, more focused group. They were just slamming the bishops out of rage. What they were promoting and advocating for is not entirely healthy. Because the issue is not so much zero-strikes versus one-strike or what have you, but the idea is, 'What is going on here? What is making this happen?' In psychology and in criminal law, we distinguish between sex with an adult or teenager over the age of consent and sex with a child under the age of consent. We distinguish all the time between fondling and penetration, consent and nonconsent, coerced and not coerced. Between proved and alleged. Not in the Dallas policy. There was no explanation, no education, no understanding being presented. I found that disheartening."

"That's it," said one of the priests, a soft, ordinarily cheery man in his sixties. "We better start on our contingency plans. Because all it takes is one phone call. We're all one phone call away from the ends of our careers."

Mochon wasn't buying it. "I'm having a hard time seeing how you would have a legitimate concern about being kicked out, frankly."

For the old priest, that almost was beside the point. He really wondered what any of them as gay men were doing in the priesthood in the first place.

"You know, if I were more aware of who I was in my twenties, I may never have gotten ordained in the first place. Certainly I would never encourage a gay guy to go into the seminary today. You'd have to be almost suicidal to apply. Look around! There are an awful lot of grumpy old priests in the Catholic Church. It is almost a caricature. Maybe Barry Fitzgerald was gay in *Going My Way* and Bing Crosby was straight or something, because Barry Fitzgerald was this grumpy old guy who, okay, maybe he had a heart of gold. But miserable! I wonder if these guys were *all* gay, if they had to put so much energy into clamping down on how they really felt or making sure that they talked about football, you know, all the things we do. And that ties into the drinking. You know the 'priest sitting alone in his room' idea, saying six-thirty Mass and that is all you see of Father all day. He is probably drinking himself sick. And I often wonder now, I mean everybody can't be gay, but I wonder if he *was* gay after all? Was he gay and just miserable? I don't think enough attention has been given to how we are oppressed or suppressed as gay priests, how we handle that. Because we have had some devils, some notoriously bad priests—every diocese, every city has some notoriously angry and upset priests that even the bishops are almost afraid of. Well what is behind all that? What is all that about?"

His fellow priests did not like to hear such talk. The gay priest wasn't always miserable—surely the sunniness in this room was proof of that.

But the old priest wasn't trying to say all gay priests were dour, cruel, or abusive, only that outside the priesthood there was a chance for self-realization, what he called "a healthy life," that didn't exist here. Factor in the murmurings from Rome about a possible purge of gays from the priesthood and, he said, "Why would a person want to take that on? I would question anybody's sanity today. I would certainly discourage a gay guy from going into the seminary today."

The old priest had given a great deal of thought to what he would do if forced out of the priesthood. In his own contingency plan, he would start attending services at the Methodist church across the road, where the minister was very welcoming. He would find volunteer work in West Hollywood, the gay neighborhood, perhaps helping distribute food to the hungry, and an apartment there, too. West Hollywood was where he intended to die.

"But the first thing I would do? That goes without saying. The first thing I would do is go and get a boyfriend."

June 23, 2002
BOSTON, MASSACHUSETTS — Phil Saviano spent the morning of his fiftieth birthday celebrating his lousy childhood at a solidarity walk for victims of sexual abuse. Since the day Father Holley first raped him, and certainly since the crisis exploded, he had never felt the kind of support and acceptance from Catholics he felt this morning. They gathered at the corner of Boston Common by the hundreds, grandparents and kids in strollers, teenagers carrying lawn chairs, their lapels bearing purple ribbons to symbolize suffering. Sixty held large blow-up photographs of sexual abuse victims, taken at the time of their abuse.

With music playing in the background, they paraded single-file to the cathedral, a procession that took over an hour. As he drifted along with the crowds, Saviano thought back on his supper the night before.

Out of the blue, an old boyfriend from New York had called. He had lost touch with Saviano in the late 1970s, but thought to call after coming across Saviano's name in the *New York Times*. He had traveled up to Boston to buy him a birthday dinner. These days he was married, with two children. His bisexual phase had not lasted long. But for him it had been memorable. He told Saviano that he had been the most beautiful man he had ever known, as gentle and striking as the statue of David. Saviano was surprised by this assessment. How could he have been so stunning and not have known it? Was this part of the Holley effect? Or was this because of his HIV infection? Was his HIV infection part of the Holley effect? Thinking back on it he realized that after their affair he became more of a recluse by the year, shying away from real or lasting intimacy.

For the past five years, the only thing he had done with any passion was organize his SNAP meetings.

He felt curiously free to ponder these things now, as he stood amid hundreds of supporters, people who didn't blame his abuse on him. Reinforcements. People who were ready now to take on the battle that had become the only thing in his life. He began to imagine returning to the workforce. He began to imagine putting it all behind him—the abuse, the AIDS, the rejection. Just then a reporter for the diocesan newspaper, the *Pilot,* approached and asked him how he felt about the event. "This was a very powerful event," he said. What he thought was, *This is a first step to healing.*

June 28, 2002
Brighton, Massachusetts — Having felt so foolishly outmaneuvered during their first meeting with Bishop Edyvean, the leaders of Voice of the Faithful prepared themselves much more thoroughly for their second meeting. They had divided up the topics to be discussed by themes. Jim Muller would once again ask for a public statement affirming the rights of lay Catholics to gather in Voice of the Faithful chapters, or—at the very least—a statement that the archdiocese does not oppose Voice. Steve Krueger was charged with talking about trust—suggesting that the hierarchy had to have enough faith in its laity to en-

trust them with a place at the table. Mary Scanlon Calcaterra's job, as always, was her passion, to speak for the victims.

"They're cordial as cordial can be," Steve Krueger warned the others, "but listen to what they're saying. And don't let them get away with anything. Our conversations here are being viewed by bishops across the country—we have to approach this very carefully."

But when they all sat down at the table (now with an additional canon lawyer representing the diocese and one other Voice member), Mary Calcaterra could not contain her anger, and excoriated them for issuing the sandbagging press release after the first meeting. That was unfair, she said baldly, and it would not be acceptable for that to happen again. Jim Muller then informed the delegation that the group would listen to what the priests had to say, and then would state their policy more forcefully than before.

"I view this as a negotiation," he said.

Priests and especially bishops were a sturdy bunch. Nobody in the room appeared to bristle at the castigation. Rather, their faces bore the expressions of patient disbelief, it seemed to Muller, as though such impertinences—especially those coming from a woman—would be answered in due time. Throughout the meeting, the clerics were measurably more arrogant and intolerant than at the previous meeting. Muller thought this meant they were also being more frankly honest. Krueger realized that the goals of Voice might benefit from a miracle or two. "How do we change the structure of the church within the structure of this church?" he thought.

The miracles did not happen at this session. Edyvean did not agree to endorse Voice of the Faithful, nor would he even commit to a further meeting, though Muller pleaded, "You're just getting to know us, why not declare a cease-fire?" Muller ended the meeting by giving a formal description of the upcoming Voice National Convention they had in the works, including their plan for a liturgy and Mass at the closing plenary. They nearly rushed through this last detail, fearful that Edyvean would declare the convention schismatic and proclaim the Mass unlawful. When he was done, Edyvean sat motionless. Then he smiled and turned to his fellow clerics. *"Silentium est assensio,"* he said. They all laughed smugly, Muller thought. He didn't know what it meant. It wasn't until they were down the stairs and in the parking lot that Mary, who recalled her Latin lessons, provided a translation.

"Silence is consent," she said angrily. To Muller that was good news. They would have their Mass.

Late June 2002
WELLESLEY, MASSACHUSETTS — Watching her husband lead Voice of the Faithful meetings, Kathleen Muller thought she had never really appreciated his laser intelligence before, or the brilliant way he could cut through complex problems with simple phrases and bring crowds of ordinarily taciturn Catholics to their cheering feet. She loved the mornings when NPR popped on the clock radio with Jim's voice and the evenings his name filled the papers. Her church needed him, and she could not have been prouder of his efforts.

But she needed him, too. For their daughter's October wedding, the bulk of the preparatory work was falling to Kathleen, who already felt overtaxed by her new psychotherapy practice. Meanwhile, her sister had fallen ill, and a half dozen other unexpected problems had confronted her. Yet most nights Jim would disappear into his study to answer hundreds of e-mail messages and hang on lengthy conference calls with the Voice leadership team, and she would find him there again in the mornings. In addition, she had developed a nagging worry for his security. At one huge Voice meeting, as he took the podium in the front of the room, Robert Kennedy's assassination came to her mind, and a kind of global anxiety seized her permanently. It was too much to bear.

"It's the peace movement all over again," she pleaded with her husband. "You have to pull back."

He knew she was right.

Sunday, June 30, 2002
DALLAS, TEXAS — Father Clifford Garner's postings on an Internet bulletin board known as St. Sebastian's Angels were mostly professional. Set up by a fresh-faced young priest from Maine, St. Sebastian's was

designed as a secured place for gay clergy to exchange views, fears, insights, and sometimes ribald jokes. Garner, who was thirty-six, was interested in tapping the collected wisdom of the community, especially as he prepared homilies on gay subjects for St. Pius X Catholic Church, a large and affluent parish in Dallas whose forty-six hundred regular parishioners tended to be quite conservative.

"I preached about how the Genesis story about Lot and Sodom is not about sexual sins or sexual issues (at least not in the foreground)," he wrote once. "But the story is about issues of inhospitality. In fact, that was the context of Jesus' use in the gospel—issues of hospitality. Well, this lady went ballistic, she told me that I was a priest in error and wrong to be teaching that this scripture was not about 'those homosexuals.' How do you handle these people?"

The most prolific contributor to St. Sebastian's, and the man that most of its members could count on to understand their pain as gay priests, was Reg Cawcutt, a prominent bishop from Cape Town, South Africa—and the president of that country's conference of bishops, Bishop Wilton Gregory's counterpart. Cawcutt made no secret of his homosexuality. But Cawcutt was also one of St. Sebastian's most wildly inappropriate contributors. He routinely petitioned others to post lewd photographs (which a few did do), persisted in juvenile double entendres, and incautiously flung invective at the antigay policies of the pope and Cardinal Ratzinger, whom he baptized "uncle asshole Ratz."

Others followed his lead. They admitted to sexual flings and love affairs. They speculated about one another's physical endowments. Their language devolved sharply. In this atmosphere, even Father Garner's sense of propriety slipped. One day he posted a lengthy appreciation for a lay minister he'd recently met. "He's no Ricky Martin, but he is Hispanic and we got along—wonderfully," he wrote. "I do have a very special place in my heart for those Latin blooded ones."

Though that was two years ago, it became an issue only in the past week because Stephen Brady, director of the orthodox group Roman Catholic Faithful, had infiltrated the chat room and drew reporters' attention to Garner's remarks. There was no implication that Garner had ever had sex with anybody. Parishioners were aghast nonetheless. At services on June 22 and again on June 23, Garner apologized for his in-

appropriate postings and distanced himself from the Web site, but the
laity remained angry. Several confronted him at Mass and demanded he
declare whether he was gay or straight. He declined. His pastor, Monsignor Lawrence Pichard, defended this stance, saying it was not germane to his ability to serve as a priest. Some called for his resignation,
which Pichard rejected.

That's when the anonymous bullying began. One unknown caller
threatened to beat him up if he returned to St. Pius X; a second also
threatened physical violence. Fearing for his own safety, Garner told his
pastor he would not return to preach. Pichard broke the news at Mass
on June 30. Many congregants were disturbed that their neighbors
might be menacing a priest. But not all. "That is not the kind of behavior you expect from a priest," David Weber, forty-one, told the *Dallas Morning News*. "He made his bed, now he has to deal with the
consequences."

July 10, 2002
BOSTON, MASSACHUSETTS — Two months in the county jail did nothing
to improve Paul Shanley's standing in the court of public opinion, and
even less in the eyes of the law. After his dramatic televised capture
and extradition, Shanley had been arraigned in a Cambridge courthouse on three counts of rape. He pleaded not guilty. Prosecutors
were able to convince the judge that Shanley posed a "tremendous risk
of flight." His bail was set at $750,000, a sum he had no hope of
matching on a yearly pension of $10,000, so he was remanded to a
Cambridge jail cell, placed in protective custody to shield him from
the judgments of other inmates, and on suicide watch to protect him
from himself.

The Greg Ford case was not his only concern. This afternoon, he was
to be arraigned on more counts. Middlesex district attorney Martha
Coakley had added charges that Shanley raped two other children from
Greg Ford's catechism classes, Paul Busa and Anthony Driscoll. "Almost on a weekly basis, Paul Shanley would come to take not only Paul
Busa but others from that class for 'talks,' " Coakley alleged. He would
scatter the three in various locations throughout the church, raping and

molesting them in the bathrooms or confessionals, before returning them to their teachers, she said.

Shanley remembered all three boys well. In fact, among the mementos he had boxed away back in his home was a picture of himself walking through a playground with all three, along with the warm letters they and their siblings scratched out on construction paper for him upon his retirement. "This is absurd," Shanley told his niece Theresa. "Those classes were run by laypeople. Mothers! You don't think mothers would notice me taking away a group of boys wholesale, and returning them raped and pillaged?"

Though she was quick to pass judgment against her uncle's accusers, Theresa didn't believe the young men—all twenty-four years old now—were lying. She thought they were wildly mistaken. They had probably been through some traumas in their lives, and now, she figured, in the glare of a media storm that branded Shanley the most dangerous priest in America, they fixed upon an explanation that comforted their minds. Like every other indication that her uncle molested children, she didn't believe a word of it.

Shanley's attorney, Frank Mondano, entered the courthouse in Cambridge at about one-thirty. His route required him to walk past a dozen protesters with bullhorns and signs: SHANLEY STOLE INNOCENT SOULS and THE REAL ISSUE: CHILD SEX ABUSE. Swarthy, muscular, flashy, Mondano strode into 6B, a windowless room that buzzed and glowed beneath a solid covering of fluorescent tubes. He did not offer a statement to the press; Theresa Shanley, the undisputed boss of this defense operation, forbade interviews. She did this more out of anger than any tactical plan. She begrudged the "enemies" and "opponents" and "fucking idiots" who had written about her uncle. Their crimes were varied. One woman was seen giving MacLeish a hello hug, so she was out; another had given too much airtime to Ford's vitriolic parents. Paul Shanley, who for so many years found allies in the media, did not override his niece's policy. He needed her enthusiasm. And if he ever hoped to get out of jail, he needed her money.

The courtroom was at capacity. Arthur Austin sat near the front. Next to him were the Ford parents—this had become their battle, not

Greg's. He had a civil suit and now this criminal action pending, but they also sued on their own behalf, claiming loss of consortium—because of Shanley's alleged cruelties, they lost the enjoyment and easy company of their son. They left their jobs to take on Shanley full-time.

Through a side door at precisely 2 P.M., uniformed court officers appeared with Paul Shanley and escorted him toward the defense table. Owing to the leg irons around his ankles, he advanced carefully and with vigilant eyes, searching out obstacles that might cause him to trip. Except for a blood red tie, he wore the colors of retreat: dust-colored hair, a gray jacket, gray eyeglasses and skin. Everything about him tried to vanish. His shoulders, eyelids, and mouth all rounded downward in slopes of resignation. He was powerless.

Judge Charles Hely read the charges—ten counts of child rape and six counts of indecent assault and battery—and Shanley said, "Not guilty," in a rehearsed tone time and again. When Hely entertained the issue of bail on these new charges, Mondano did not seek a reduction. Minutes after it began, the hearing was drawing to a close and Paul Shanley, who had been slumped forward in sagging discomfort, bent his neck slowly around to measure the scene. His eyes met with Austin. The kid whom he had counseled all those years ago had been vibrant with life, but now he was ghostly and pale, too, a fifty-four-year-old man dressed blowsily in shades of white.

Austin could not breathe. Feeling Shanley's eyes on him was like a knife on his throat. Despite the passage of these decades, he was as vulnerable to those eyes as ever. They were imperial, conquering eyes. Under their sway, he had allowed his body to be used for six years. The memory of them suspended everything in his life. The years had never allowed him to get over Shanley, and he hated him for his own vulnerability. His instinct was to look away, but he promised himself he would not. He stared back, projecting boiling rage. Only when Shanley was carted off by marshals was he able to move again, and he bolted out the door, bumping past Theresa Shanley, whom he did not know, to answer reporters' questions in cones of white light.

The timbre of his voice drove her nearly insane. "You were twenty years old," she called after him, mimicking his Shakespearean cadence. *"You were an adult!"*

Usually, DA Coakley would wait for extensive and detailed detectives' reports before bringing an indictment, but in the case of Busa and Driscoll, she acted on preliminary findings, mostly interviews with them. She did not have the luxury of waiting. Joe Bergantino from WBZ had learned where Shanley was living and broadcast a news account from the steps of his San Diego home; faced with the concern Shanley might flee, she placed him in custody the following morning, publicly thanking the reporter for the tip. As a result, much of the supporting detective work wasn't done until after the indictment. In the ensuing weeks, detectives interviewed dozens of potential witnesses, and their recollections were not encouraging for a successful prosecution. The women who taught catechism class to the three boys could not remember a single time they were taken out of the classroom, individually or in a group. Not once, much less every week for years. On this they were emphatic. If there had been an extensive pattern of "talks," they said, they would have noticed.

This was the problem with cases built on recovered memories. Like Greg Ford, the two newer plaintiffs had their memories return to them only after Shanley was named in the press. Details of their stories only came into focus over the following weeks. Paul Busa had trouble recalling aspects of his alleged abuse. Anthony Driscoll, who like the others was twenty-four years old, began having "flashbacks" after being called by Eric MacLeish as a potential witness, and in therapy came to believe he too was a victim.

But the strangest inconsistency came when the detectives reviewed Greg Ford's medical records. During his many psychiatric hospitalizations, he had a long history of discussing sexual abuse as a possible cause for his psychoses, substance abuse, violence, and incorrigibility. The records clearly showed him naming a cousin, then a neighbor, then a mysterious "man" as his perpetrators. Surely this undermined his claims against Shanley now.

The family had specifically recalled an event when Greg was eleven. They had gotten a telephone call from St. Jean's after a boy pulled a painful prank on their son, placing a sharpened pencil beneath him as he was about to sit down. In the criminal complaint against Shanley, the Fords said they suspected this was the first day their son was sodomized. Greg said he was sent to Paul Shanley's office after his injury. Shanley lowered his pants to treat the wound, but instead took advantage of the boy. The pain knocked him nearly unconscious, he said, but he remembered Shanley turning away from him when it was over and zippering up his pants. He didn't mention that when Paula Ford had raced to the church to collect him. Because he was crying and complained of bleeding, she took him directly to a hospital and he didn't mention it there, either. He said the memory came into focus only when he read about Shanley's other deeds in the *Globe* exposé.

However, he had submitted to an extensive examination in the emergency room, which was charted in his files. He was treated for a "laceration on rear end" very near his anus. So there would be no question about where this wound was, the treating physician had drawn a picture:

If he had been forcibly raped less than thirty minutes before presenting himself in this manner to medical experts, surely somebody would have picked up on his traumas, wouldn't they?

July 17, 2002

BRIGHTON, MASSACHUSETTS — Gary Bergeron was offered a cup of coffee at a dark and imposingly long dining room table inside the residence. He sat across from Barbara Thorp. As they awaited the cardinal's arrival, they barely spoke. Gary thought he would be nervous, but he was not. A week earlier, Barbara had called him triumphantly to announce Law's willingness finally to meet him—more than two months after she promised Gary she would make this happen. The delay irritated Gary. The cardinal had only gotten more recalcitrant, distant, and isolated; in the meantime, the scandal was continuing to explode like a cluster bomb. Gary thought this could have been avoided if the cardinal would agree to see the members of SOJB, the Survivors of Joseph Birmingham. The group's three most vocal leaders were stubbornly convinced that Law, who had proved himself to be deaf to any other advisers, would respond to them, working-class guys from Lowell, Salem, Sudbury, and Gloucester.

When Law arrived through a side door, he moved nonstop across the room to shake Gary's hand. Father John Connolly was with him.

"Thanks for coming to see me," Law said. "I'm sorry it's taken so long to arrange."

"So am I." Gary worried he sounded sardonic, which was not his intent. He was grateful he was not sweating noticeably.

"Let's get started, let's sit down."

"Okay. But let's get the ground rules out. Please call me Gary. And what should I call you? Because I am not going to call you Your Eminence. And I don't feel comfortable calling you Father."

Law's blue eyes frosted over. "Call me Bernie," he said, and showed his guest back into a chair.

Gary realized he had deluded himself; he was in fact very nervous, his almost paralyzed diaphragm caused his voice volume to modulate wildly. He felt out of breath.

"Bernie, I wanted to tell you about how Father Birmingham affected my family. There's eight of us kids in my family. Me and my brother Eddie were molested by Birmingham, and my two sisters are buried next to him in the same cemetery, so that's half of us who are somehow connected to Birmingham permanently. We're stuck with that for the rest of our lives. My parents are, too."

The cardinal nodded his understanding.

"Who this is really hurting is my parents," he said. His mother's faith was splintering, his father despaired all the time now.

He did not mean to show his anger, but suddenly it glinted through. "What the hell happened?" he demanded to know. "What the *hell* happened? I mean, how did you let this *happen*?" He thought he saw Connolly laughing.

"We never took the time to look at this collectively, Gary. We only saw it individually. We never laid out all of these files on one table.

And when you look at the church through the rose-colored glasses of preservation, you never get a clear picture."

"You know," Gary said, "I have a hard time believing you."

The cardinal shrugged.

"You know what? Don't let this become your legacy," Gary continued. "You have an opportunity here—we've all been given an opportunity here—to do the right thing. We have a chance to make right what has been made wrong. And for you to do that, you have to start engaging. You need to start meeting people like me, like my brother Eddie. You need to go to talk to our groups, to our parishes, you need to explain what happened. You need to go to confession. People can handle the truth. We're strong enough for that. Our religion is based on faith, and you have to have faith that the people can handle the truth."

Law thanked him profusely for the advice. Later, Barbara Thorp told Gary she thought the cardinal was moved by his words. But driving home that night, Gary was not at all certain he had much of an impact.

July 20, 2002

BOSTON, MASSACHUSETTS — The most difficult hurdle Voice of the Faithful encountered in organizing for their convention, scheduled for July 20, was not at all what any of them had anticipated. They thought they might receive grief from the peaks of Catholic academia, but they did not. Theologians from Weston Jesuit Theological School, Holy Cross College, and Boston College, the preeminent Catholic institutions in town, sent speakers—and sixty-six theologians signed a position paper declaring their conference licit. If they thought ordinary Catholics would shun their efforts, they were stunned when forty-two hundred people registered and traveled to Boston from every corner of the United States. If they thought Cardinal Law and Bishop Edyvean would ban their Mass, it never came to pass. If they feared the gathering would degenerate into a display of hand wringing and negativity, their fears were allayed when Father Tom Doyle, who flew in from his military base in Germany, accepted their "Priest of Integrity" award. In his emotional keynote address he acknowledged the "physical and emotional plundering" of his church by abusive priests and the "spiritual devastation" heartless bishops had visited upon all the faithful, including him. But being called in from the cold by a huge auditorium overflowing with ordinary Catholics moved him nearly to tears. "For years this sex abuse nightmare has caused so many of us to question everything we believed about our Church, and to even wonder if the Lord cared," he said. "Being here this weekend, bound up in faith and hope with the survivors and with all of you, has been for me and for so many an indescribable moment. God is alive and thriving in His church and *you* are the proof!"

Where they had trouble was finding a single conservative Catholic to speak to the group. The list of those who turned them down, or simply ignored them, was stellar: former drug czar William Bennett said he had a scheduling problem, papal biographer George Weigel declared he was booked a year in advance, journalist Rod Dreher never responded, and columnist Michael Novak was obligated to give a court deposition that day—unusual on a Saturday.

But the most surprising trouble was in drawing leaders of the victim-survivor groups, which proved even more difficult. Phil Saviano was supportive, but he was in the minority. Most of his peers were as suspicious of Voice of the Faithful as they were of the Catholic Church. Arthur Austin and the other members of the Coalition of Concerned Catholics and Survivors, the local network behind the regular demonstrations at the cathedral and the residence, suspected various reform efforts were taking advantage of the crisis to further their own agendas. Austin was regularly asked to speak to groups of priests or parishioners, and his addresses had become increasingly hostile. His low point came on the evening he sat before members of the Boston Priests' Forum, a well-meaning rebel group founded by Father Walter Cuenin and Father Robert Bullock to lobby for significant change in the way the archdiocese was managed. They wanted to learn from his experiences dealing with the church. What he detailed for them instead was the graphic physical geography of his violations, which disgusted them and made them angry.

Not knowing this, Mary Scanlon Calcaterra enthusiastically called to ask him to address the Voice convention. "I thought you'd like to read a poem," she said on his answering machine. She wanted to schedule him for a period of two or three minutes.

The call enraged him. He left her a message back refusing outright. The segment was insultingly small, he said, for shoehorning the voice of the victimized. This crisis was about the victims, nothing else—how dare they reduce that fact to a brief poetic interlude?

She was disappointed, but not heartbroken; Phil Saviano was already speaking. But about a week before the conference was to take place, the Coalition for Concerned Catholics and Survivors called her to a meeting at the home of Lori Lambert, a seminary student. Attending were Paula and Rodney Ford, Anne Barrett Doyle, Arthur Austin, and two other abuse survivors, Susan Renehan and Tom Buckley. Their purpose was to explain why they opposed the Voice conference altogether. They saw this new movement as piggybacking on the horrors of abuse, while staying out of the trenches where the survivor community dwelt. They detailed the realities of their lives: therapy, family hostilities, ongoing litigation, spiritual collapse, psychic despair. Where was Voice in all of this? Not at the weekly demonstrations outside the cathedral. Not at the court hearings or indictments or depositions. Not at the press conferences.

Mary walked away from the meeting with a better understanding of what it meant to be traumatized. But it wasn't until Austin called her at home the following Wednesday that she started being able to feel what she and her Voice colleagues were being asked to do: go to where the survivors were, rather than inviting them to the convention for feel-good cameo appearances. "You people want to have your convention, you want to think you're giving support to the survivors, but you won't do the one thing we need. You won't stand with us."

"What? Why wouldn't we stand with you?"

"Because you think you're going to get dirty if you come near us. Because you think we're unclean."

"What do you want us to do?"

"I had a dream last night," Austin said. "The people came out of the convention and walked to the cathedral to stand beside us there."

She thought it was a great idea to end the whole convention with a call to protest. "Okay," she said. "You have to be the person to bring it up, though. You have to speak."

He accepted. "But you're not going to like what I have to say."

"What?"

"Are you going to censor what I have to say?"

"You can diminish what people are doing, if you want. That will make me sad. But the only thing I ask is that you not incite violence."

On the day of the Voice conference, a steady picket line of victim-survivors handed out protest literature outside the doors, refusing to come inside. After a day of workshops and inspiring lectures, Austin was the last person introduced. He floated to the stage in an overflow auditorium slightly after 5 P.M.

"I want to address the issue of the angry survivors outside, who want nothing to do with you," he began. "For them, quite legitimately, your splendid conference is too little, too late, and too much about *you,* when it should always and urgently, and long since, have been about *them.* For them, this event is a shadow play, a thing without substance. And before you begin to grow indignant with me for saying this, let me ask you: How many of you took the time even to find out the name of one of those angry survivors? I am not a member of Voice of the Faithful. I don't stand here because I am one of you, or even because I particularly believe in you. I represent no one but myself, one man, one victim; but I say to every nonsurvivor in this hall, concerning those outside: You have no right to judge them, resent them, or feel Catholically smug and superior to them. You have never walked one step, one moment, of their agonizing, lonely, and hellishly terrifying journey. You do not live in a perpetual catastrophic moment. They do. So do I. You do not get to judge them, all you get is the right to beg their forgiveness."

The more he talked, the more frightened and sad Mary Calcaterra became. The conference had been a day of triumphs and hope, of momentum. To end on this discouraging note?

"There are forty-two hundred of you here today," he went on, "to honor your highly strategized, thoroughly debated and very, very quiet agenda; and yet on Sunday, June twenty-third at the Solidarity Walk to honor the humanity and courage of the priest-abused, both living and dead, your presence was noticeable only by its vast invisibility. The presence of your absence was everywhere. After prayer and reflection, I have been moved to ask you two questions today, in the name of every victim we remembered on that Sunday, including myself. First, where *were* you on that Sunday, as the dead were honored and the living comforted in the shadow of the very Church that had harmed them? And second, the simple, but fatigued and heartbroken question of Gethsemane: 'What, could you not keep watch even one hour with me?' The time has come for your answer. The time is now. And God is waiting. In God's name I challenge the members of Voice of the Faithful, after their liturgy, to walk from this convention hall with me to the Cathedral of the Holy Cross to stand in solidarity with each survivor victim who trusts you enough to let you walk with them. You have yet to prove yourselves to many, many people—including me— who live in the constant presence of their own violated bodies and souls. You can walk away from this. *You* can walk away from this. We cannot. Ever."

A stunned silence greeted the close of his speech, and he folded his remarks and left the stage before the glare of forty-two hundred chastised faces. Calcaterra broke into a sobbing cry. "I'm so mad at you," she said. "I know you did what you had to do, you said you were going to do it. But Arthur! These people came so far! We worked so hard! I don't want to see it all fall apart! What if it all falls apart? Why do you have to blame *them*?"

She didn't have to worry. When she and Austin spilled out onto the sidewalk to join up with the victim-survivors and stroll over to the cathedral, they were both blown away by what they saw: five hundred conference attendees holding lighted candles against the night, some singing, some crying, some trundling along in wheelchairs, pushing up the hill toward Holy Cross.

Sunday Morning, July 21, 2002
BOSTON, MASSACHUSETTS — A sparse parade of people, mostly Latinos and African-Americans in impeccable attire, headed inside Holy Cross

Cathedral for morning services, their ears full with the sound of bull-horns. "Attention all you Catholics in there! We are good Catholics from the parishes in Wellesley, Lynn, and Sudbury. The good Catholics are out *here*! Good Catholics are not in there. Think about it! Be educated. Don't believe the man in the red hat!"

The enormous raspy voice on the megaphone, the one that was frightening little kids and their moms, belonged to Steve Lewis, a short and intense middle-aged man from Lynn. Father Edward Kelley molested him as an eleven-year-old in 1968, and he described himself as being repeatedly retraumatized in the years since. When the Porter case hit the papers a decade ago, memories of his abuse recurred in powerful surges that were so destabilizing he was forced to take a leave from work at an area school. He sued that year and settled in 1995 for an undisclosed amount in an agreement that included a gag clause. When the *Globe* series reignited the whole issue, rage trapped Lewis once again. He broke his gag order February 26 to join the pro-testers, and hadn't been silent one moment since.

"It's a house of rape," he bellowed at the cathedral doors. "If you love your children, do not go in that cathedral!"

Mary Calcaterra from Voice of the Faithful visibly blanched. After joining in the candlelight procession at Austin's behest the night be-fore, she realized he was perfectly correct to chastise the ordinary Catholics. If she wanted to show her solidarity with the victims of priests, she had to be at the cathedral steps.

But she wasn't expecting the likes of Lewis. She knew how fright-ening his screeds were for the youngsters heading for Mass, especially on this Sunday. Each year, the cardinal called for a show of hands from boys contemplating the priesthood, invited girls to examine their hearts for signs they would be nuns. This was also the eve of Law's pil-grimage to Toronto to meet the pope for a week of celebrations lead-ing up to World Youth Day. A hundred teens were joining him at the cathedral, children whose innocence Mary prized, which was why she was protesting in the first place. She introduced herself to Lewis and then tried, whenever a new carload of parishioners approached Holy Cross, to engage him in a lengthy discourse and distract him from his angry reproofs.

Unconsciously rendered mute, Lewis howled only with his placard, which read on one side, "Pink slip for the priest in the red dress," and on the other, "Child rapists and their pimps belong in jail."

Same old same old, Arthur Austin thought. He meant this kindly. Dressed in a flowing white shirt and open sandals, he roamed airily through the parade of protesters, swaying left, then right, under a gorgeous cloudless sky. This had become his church, these were the laypeople of his imagination, cynical and hard like him, survivors. He was happy he had found them. He was comfortable. Without giving it much thought, in a peaceful reverie he slid out of line and snuck quietly inside the darkened nave. Eight years had lapsed since he was last in a church. From high atop marble pillars and flying buttresses, gilded angels and cherubs stared down at him, and the teenagers at the altar read in rounds from the book of Wisdom, flooding the cathedral with their young voices.

Presently Cardinal Law assumed the pulpit and unspooled a serpentine homily, first thanking the BCTV staff for manning the cameras that beamed these images to the sick and the elderly, then offering words on the kingdom of God, the utility of faith, and the terrible need for more clergy. He addressed himself specifically to the teenagers present. "To know God's will in our lives it is important to be watchful in prayer to see what it is that God is telling us," he said vehemently. This would be a high-pressure pitch. "Pray to know if you are given a vocation to the priesthood or the consecrated life. I invite you to take a moment of reflection: Is it *possible* God is calling you to a religious life? Is it *possible* God is calling on you to be a priest or a brother? It's a matter of letting God know we are *open* to know His will." He called to the choir director for a bit of soft music. "Remove from the hearts any fear, any anxiety, and let them know you are with us in peace and in happiness," he prayed.

When he was a boy, Arthur hadn't needed this arm twisting. His calling was powerful, and lasted up to the Friday night that Paul Shanley showed him how meaningless the priestly commitments were. In a way, he realized his vocation had never really died; in his dreams he still was a man of God. He had not left the church, he now knew. It had left him. When Law called his fourteen priests and dozen nuns to help him distribute communion, Arthur felt the pull to queue up on one of the many lines stretching to the back of the cathedral.

By coincidence, he had chosen the one that led directly to the cardinal. When he realized this, he said to himself, "Be careful when you evoke the radical grace of God. For that same power now has come to demand something of me." He offered a prayer for himself and inched forward, painfully aware that on his shirt was an enormous pin with the big red words "Reject Law."

Seeing him coming, Law stiffened. In six full months of crisis, this was the first protester to approach him in this way—not shouting or running, not openly malicious. Still, when Art raised his cupped hands, Law braced for a bath of lye. When they proved empty, Law placed a wafer there. Another bishop might have turned Arthur away empty-handed. But Law saw the moment as a step in reconciliation. He murmured a prayer, and Arthur placed the host in his mouth. Before turning to leave, he reached a hand out to the cardinal's recoiling shoulder.

"Pray for me, Your Eminence," he said.

"Thank you," Law said reflexively, in visible relief. "God bless you."

Arthur pivoted, but Law reached back and caught him by the arm. He knew what he meant to say.

"Pray for *me*," Law begged. "Please. Pray for *me*."

Tuesday, July 30, 2002

BRIGHTON, MASSACHUSETTS — Mile after mile, block by block, as he drove closer to his own meeting with Law, Olan's tension level rose. Barbara Thorp had set it up. She had a special feeling about the Survivors of Joseph Birmingham. She used whatever clout she had to get them to meet Law. Olan was granted an unprecedented three hours with the man behind the curtain. He wasn't sure how this was going to go. The one policy decision he made was to present everything in the form of a question—instinctively he figured that the Socratic method, being less confrontational, was more likely to produce change. Perhaps he could get the cardinal to see things differently.

These were some of the questions people suggested Olan should ask:

"Did you know Joseph Birmingham?"
"How could you forsake human suffering?"
"Do you think you can solve this problem without talking to the victims?"
"What's your PIN number?"

The last one came from Courtney Pillsbury, the trial attorney at Greenberg Traurig. She meant it as lawyer's humor. But sensing he needed an icebreaker, Olan had included it anyway. In all, he listed fifty-six questions on an old day planner, two per page, ordered by a Catholic schema: questions related to commission, then omission, then penance, and so on.

At the very last minute, to salve his jangled nerves, Olan imposed upon Dave Lyko to join him. When he swung by to pick him up, Dave was ironing a denim shirt. "Should I wear a tie?" he called out to Olan—then looked over to see his friend in shorts.

"Just do me one favor," Dave said. "Just don't build this guy another asshole in front of me. Because I don't want to be part of that."

The car pulled into the chancery driveway, then cut right toward the circular drive at the imposing mansion where Law lived, past the "No Trespassing" sign. From the knoll of a sloping hill, they could see heat stretching off endless parched lawns, sixty acres of bent and brown grasses that angled down through a grove of pines, twisted by the sun, and exploded in a white haze at St. John Seminary in the silent distance.

They rang the bell. Greeting them was Father Connolly, whom Olan took to be the bodyguard. He ushered them into a dining room. When the cardinal entered the room, Olan led off—he wanted the initiative to be his.

"Hi, how are you? I'm Olan Horne, and let me tell you a little bit about my story. This is my friend Dave. Listen, I have no idea which way this meeting is going to go."

Hands were shaken, and Olan slapped himself down in a chair and crossed his chunky pantless legs. He jabbed his thumb toward Connolly.

"I'm sure that big Frankenstein over there will want to pick me up and throw me on the fucking curbstone after three and a half minutes, but I have to tell you something. I'm here to ask you a lot of questions. I'm here to engage you and I'm hoping you step up to that opportunity."

Law knotted his long rubbery fingers in his lap, seemingly bemused. In these months of strife, he had come up with a studied expression to wear while being berated. There was something about Olan's working-class directness, though—a throwback to Law's days in rural Louisiana before anybody knew to be impressed by him—that was so immediately recognizable that it gave him a disturbing comfort.

"You know what, Olan? I think I will step up to that," he said.

"I'm not here for your affirmation. I know what happened. And you know what happened. And all I need to know is, well . . . I've got some questions and let me tell you what those questions are and where they came from."

The cardinal raised a hand in objection.

"Okay," Law said. "But before we get there, I want to say I'm sorry. *I'm sorry.* I'm sorry from the bottom of my heart. I cannot fathom what went wrong." He removed his glasses for emphasis. "In my youth, I was profoundly influenced by different priests. They represented all that was good to me. I placed great trust in them. You had a right to believe the same thing."

"People want to know," Olan said, "how could you do it, Bernie? How could you know about these men and then move them around?"

"I was trying to understand the pathology, I was trying to understand it through memos and letters from physicians and experts. My mistake was I never realized the effects of this pathology, I just never understood it."

"Well, fine, but how could you have missed that part? I mean, we were *kids*."

The cardinal looked exhausted.

"I was looking at this through the lens of preservation for my church," he admitted. "I was trying to concentrate on salvation for the priest, on the church's role. I was trying to think of the right thing to do, and that kept bringing me around to the church. I should have thought about you. I didn't get to meet Olan Horne ten years ago. I didn't know there were that many of you. I honestly didn't know it was this big."

"If you realize it now, what are you going to do about it? Are you going to embrace us? Are you going to let us in? I knocked on the door how many times trying to get in here, and you wouldn't let us. Half these court cases wouldn't be here today if we had been given the compassion and dignity of a returned telephone call."

"I know that," the cardinal said, whispering. "I know that now."

Olan stared at him the way you ogled a child with a profound disability, pity mixed with fascination. He could see that by doing the wrong thing Law was disappointing himself as much as he was everybody else, but he could not stop himself.

"Bernie, let me back up here. Let me introduce Dave. Dave's my best friend and he's traumatized by this whole thing. He's petrified, he's very nervous about this meeting. Dave's a cross between Cliffy Clavin and Pee-Wee Herman, a terrific guy. I hope I'm not embarrassing you, Dave. He's got pictures here he wants to show you."

"Please don't be nervous," Law offered. "This is just us talking."

"Yeah, I brought three pictures. This picture you don't probably remember, this is a picture of you," Dave said, producing a crinkled, faded photograph and extending it in his trembling hand. His voice was small and macerated by sadness. "And right there where you're standing, there's my church. There's me standing behind you. I'm waving. I'm the little guy right there."

He was a young man who believed.

"Now this picture, this is my wife. I've been going out with her since I was thirteen. And this. That's my first son. We had him baptized in that church. I was really proud of that day. We used to go to church every Sunday—

"And this." His voice caught and he went silent. Tears trailed down his cheeks. "This is a picture of my next son," he pushed out, placing his final photograph on the table. "The difference between my first son and my second son is, *he* made his First Communion, and *he* didn't. I don't trust the system. I brought these two pictures because this is my life before I understood what was going on, and I loved my church, and here's the second picture, and I don't even trust you guys enough to baptize my kid, have my kid make his First fucking Communion. Now that, my friend, is a sin. Think about where I sit. Think about what your actions have done to me."

Tears filled Olan's eyes, too. Law was miserable, his blue eyes ringed in pink.

"Why don't you trust the church," Law asked, still confused, "when it was Father Birmingham who did this to you?"

"I don't trust anybody anymore. I don't trust anything."

"Why don't you bring your child here and I will give him his First Communion, if you're afraid of people. Do you trust me?"

"Well, I don't know. I just . . ."

"I can tell you I will never touch your son."

Even more lasting than the memory of the abuse he had suffered, Dave now realized, was the rigid fury that defined his life. Could he trust Law, who had done nothing to end the abuses? Could he allow himself to accept an offer, allow Law to solve a problem, allow the *possibility* of trust? He did not know.

Taking his turn, Olan began pushing through his list of questions. Law fielded them gamely, but without much heart. Olan even tried the PIN number question, but Law had no idea what a PIN number was (he did not do his own banking). Out of frustration, Olan slammed shut his book of interrogatives.

"I fucking asked you enough questions," he said. "Let's just get this out on the table. What're you going to do? Who are you? This is who *I* am, a kid from Lowell who got raped by a priest. What do you want to know about me? What are you doing here? There's this wall around you. You've got 'Cardinal' in front of 'Bernard' like some sort of shield."

The look on Law's face was one of grave discomfort.

"You know, I call you Bernie Law all the time and people really take offense from that. And I don't understand it. I want to tell you that it's not done in disrespect. I came to meet Bernie Law. I didn't come to meet the cardinal. You want me to meet the cardinal and kiss your ring? Okay, but I'm here to meet Bernie Law. Take off the mask."

This was the moment Dave Lyko was not looking forward to. The cardinal offered some sort of riposte, but Olan moved to another idea.

"Bernie, what're you doing right now? I mean right this minute. Can you do me a favor and do something bold? Can you get in the car and drive up to Lowell and meet all my friends? We got a support group meeting for the Survivors of Joseph Birmingham tonight. You got to meet these guys."

"I can't," Law said. "I'm on my way to meet a group of seminarians." He glanced over to Connolly for confirmation.

"Well, when are you going to do it? Because if you want to know anything about this whole crisis, you got to know these guys."

The hard-sell routine caused the cardinal to laugh angrily.

"When can you come to a meeting where you'll engage the family members and when can you begin to understand and engage what this is all about? Because you have to do this, Bernie. I mean, it's simple. You don't even understand this *concept*. I mean, you have no *idea*. Neither did I. When are you going to grab this thing? When are you going to own this thing?"

"Well, I am trying," he complained.

"No, try harder. Reach out. Get curious. I can help you here. I mean, this is where it really comes together."

He laughed again. Something about Olan he trusted.

"All right," he said. "All right. I'll come."

He meant it. But four disastrous months would pass before he would make good on his word.

August 2, 2002

SUFFOLK COUNTY COURTHOUSE, BOSTON, MASSACHUSETTS — Rumpled and tightly wound, Mitchell Garabedian pushed open the swinging doors to Judge Sweeney's courtroom for Patrick McSorley and Mark Keane. The two clients wheeled in Garabedian's many boxes. It was the second day of a trial he had demanded to force the archdiocese of Boston to honor its $30 million agreement with the Geoghan 86. Coincidentally, all three men wore white. Their opponents, a battery of attorneys and clerics in navy and black suits, contrasted sharply.

You could see the edge of McSorley's nerves this morning. Taking his place beside the other litigants on the long bench behind the barrister's rail, he slithered around and pulled on his clothing as though mosquitoes ate at his skin. He extended his eyelid between pinched fingers and rummaged for a phantom lash. He drummed his heels on the carpet and clasped his chin in the vise of his hands, cranking it left and right, *snap-snap,* every few minutes.

"I'm not doing so well," he told Mark Keane.

"Me either," Mark said. "I don't think I slept last night."

"He didn't," whispered Mark's wife, Amy. "And out of nowhere, he started crying."

"Panic attacks," Mark said.

They fell into a messy silence as Garabedian called Cardinal Law to the stand—the first time a sitting cardinal had ever been sworn in as a witness in a trial.

"Cardinal, I'd like to show you a document," he said, approaching the witness box. He handed Law a newspaper. "Do you recognize the *Pilot*?"

"I do," he said, smiling. "A very good diocesan paper." He wiggled his head in a silent chuckle.

"Directing your attention to page four, I ask you to read the title of the article."

"The headline reads, SETTLEMENT REACHED WITH GEOGHAN VICTIMS."

"Thank you, sir," Garabedian said, returning to stand over his files. "Now, can you please read the first paragraph."

" 'After eleven months of litigation, the Archdiocese of Boston has reached a settlement with alleged victims of John J. Geoghan. "This settlement is an important step in reaching closure for these victims who have long endured the damage done to them by John Geoghan," Bernard Cardinal Law, Archbishop of Boston, said in a statement March twelfth.' "

Garabedian parked his glasses on his forehead. "Now. Do you recall making that statement?"

Law removed his eyeglasses. "I recall making that statement, and I also recall—"

"Thank you, Cardinal, you've answered the question," Garabedian interrupted. "Now, the first three words of this sentence, correct me if I'm wrong, are: 'This settlement is.' Correct?"

"Correct."

"It doesn't say this settlement *might* be, right?"

"No."

"Does it say this settlement *could* be?"

Law took a deep breath. "I read it as *is*," he said testily.

When the courtroom broke for the day, it seemed to lawyers observing the examination that Law had indeed declared the cases settled, and that his lawyers had committed the archdiocese to making the payments. They never predicated it on approval from the Finance Council. The agreement seemed enforceable. Judge Sweeney gave every indication she thought so, too, but promised it would be many weeks before she would make her decision known.

Law vanished through an unmarked door without issuing a comment to the reporters gathered near the elevator. They turned instead to Patrick McSorley, whose eyes went glassy. "To this day I feel as though my emotions have been scattered and stepped on and totally disregarded," he said in a fragile voice. "It's time for them to give us something we can believe in. They have to make good on this."

He turned toward the elevator, answering a call to smoke a cigarette. But he changed his mind and returned to the reporters' group, which was disbanding and packing up. "I have something more to say," he beckoned. Nobody heard him. "Excuse me, I have one more thing to say?" Out of politeness, one camera operator put his machine back on his shoulders and with a turn of a switch locked McSorley into a column of bright light.

He knotted and unknotted his fingers. "I pray," he said. "I pray—I just hope and I pray to God that this is over soon."

August 18, 2002

BOSTON, MASSACHUSETTS — More than two weeks had passed since the close of the hearings before Judge Sweeney, and her ruling had not yet materialized, but it was increasingly clear that no good could come of it, no matter which way her verdict fell. A victory for the church would be costly in a Pyrrhic sense, and would do nothing to resolve the matter of the Geoghan 86. What was more, there were by now hundreds of other cases pending, and there seemed to be no end to the rush of new litigants. The Finance Council had reached no decision yet about how to structure a global settlement fund. It was not at all clear to anybody in the archdiocese how much money would be available from insurance funds. There were countless policies, including ones from Aetna, Kemper, and National Catholic Risk Retention Group, each with on and off years, but some litigants alleged lengthy periods of abuse stretching over more than one policy—and in some cases during times when no policies at all were in place. The insurance was meant to protect the church, not individuals, and many had standard provisions exempting behavior that was intended or expected. Underwriters might argue that it was reasonable to expect that Geoghan would strike again, and therefore only his first violation would be covered. The situation was extremely fluid. Estimates of available coverage ranged from $10 million to $50 million.

If Sweeney were to rule in favor of Garabedian's clients, however, the church had made it very clear it would tie up the money in appeals, which could stretch on for years. Many could not wait that long for the money. Their epic war with the church had cost them greatly. Most had devoted tireless energy on a nearly daily basis for most of the past year; many had lost jobs as a result. Mark Keane, for instance, was still unemployed and uncertain how he was going to provide for his three children. The wait had not been easy on him. For his recurring panic attacks, his doctor prescribed Wellbutrin, Neurontin, and Ativan. Patrick McSorley was also well beyond his emotional threshold. Under the pressures of the trial, he had not been able to sleep, his elbows were cracked with a nerve-related case of psoriasis, and he sometimes prayed to God to end his miserable life. His fiancée had put him out on the street for good. "This is killing me," he said. "It's too much pain. I'd rather be all drugged down if I thought that would help."

Garabedian keenly felt the burden of their precarious grips. Financially, he was not much better off himself. He had not had a significant payday since 1997. Although he was not saying as much, his accounts must have been depleted by the extraordinary expenses this case had incurred, including crisscrossing the country to depose witnesses. He had staff that now included five full-time associates, plus support staff who could not wait till 2007 for a paycheck. Greenberg Traurig might have been able to subsidize a protracted appeal. Not Garabedian.

The archdiocese knew all this. At the onset of the trial Wilson Rogers Jr. reiterated the church's first offer, $10 million—the same sum Garabedian had rejected as paltry over a year ago. He hoped the offer would increase during the course of the trial but it had not. "Not a nickel more," he was told. "Anything higher, the Finance Council would reject." As the days ticked by, he was bitterly realizing how good any amount of money would look.

DOVER, MASSACHUSETTS — Arthur Austin carried a large bag toward the towering fieldstone portico of the St. Stephen Priory, a Georgian-style mansion on the banks of the Charles River. Built in the late nineteenth century, the priory was originally conceived as a facility for female religious, but as their numbers receded it was repurposed as a training facility for Dominican friars, and as a retreat facility for hire, providing silent retreats, guided retreats, and other kinds of R&R for the soul. Since summer, it had begun a special ministry to clergy abuse survivors, inviting them for periods of prayer and spiritual renewal.

Feeling himself inexorably pulled back toward his faith, Austin accepted the invitation in his belief that getting away would do him good. He had packed a bag of poetry supplies, and planned to write the epic, narrative tale of his affair with Shanley and his spiritual demise.

Walking through the doors, the first thing he noticed was the airy silence. Large meeting rooms, quaintly called "parlors," stood in regal stillness. In fact, throughout the compound, he saw very few postulants. Most apparently were in concentrated prayer.

A friar showed Austin to his room, which was enormous and wood paneled and cool in the hot summer's shade. He put his bag on the floor and closed the door. As he lay down on his bed he felt a profound sense of *arrival*. "I have been journeying to this room my whole life," he had thought.

This was no "getting away." This was his homecoming.

Austin's writing had come out in brilliant strokes, polished sentences in easy gestures. They surprised him not in their arrival but in their tone, which was *hopeful,* nothing like he had ever written before in his life. Throughout his retreat, he wrote every morning, following Mass and breakfast, and straight through till lunch. Afternoons, he walked in silence along the Charles, or sat poolside, or swam. His introspection was abysmal and challenging, and the more he searched the more he realized that what was inside him was the peace and the stillness of the place around him, a physical sensation, a *devouring* peace.

After a few days he realized as if by revelation that this introspection was not just that. It was prayer. He was praying. Just like that. Not "Dear God" praying, but something deeper and less conscious. A tremendous sense of the presence of . . . well, of *something.* And whatever that something was, it was also recognizing *his* presence: it listened, it counseled, it . . . it what? "How limp the language is for trying to describe it," he thought, "but every day has been a miracle for me in terms of healing."

On his last day, as he packed his bag in silence, he reviewed the poems he'd assembled here. They were not the Shanley pages he had expected. His self-imposed assignment was to scratch through those six unhappy years for something that would allow him to escape them, and the torture of them, which had lasted thirty years. The truth about that torture remained somewhat mysterious. How had one priest's lurid interventions destroyed him? It was true, he had been an adult when Paul Shanley first took after him during a counseling situation, which was highly inappropriate. He considered it a rape that lasted six years, but no law would view it that way. From the outside, it looked more like a regretted relationship, similar in character if not degree to stories most people could tell. Shanley would yell at him, would offer Austin's body to others for sex, or take it for himself whenever he needed; he was a lover without grace or generosity. But he was a priest, and that made all the difference to Austin back then.

Where did the rage still find nurturing? For one thing he wondered whether Shanley *made* him gay—how he hated that word, because gays were destined for such deep suffering, he was sure. He was certain

Shanley ran him from the church he loved and rendered him a pariah. Was he destined to be this forever—a victim?

As he offered thanks to the prior, he spoke of this one frustration during his healing stay, that he was still prisoner to his past.

"Forgiveness," the prior said. "That is the way to freedom."

Austin shook his head. "Forgiveness," he said. "I've always found it an impossible concept. I've never understood it."

"It's not a feeling," the prior said. "It's a moral *decision*."

"Oh, of course," he said, startled. "You *will* it. I never understood the presto-changeo-I-forgive-you crap. That never made sense to me."

"No, it's not that easy. It requires work. You've got to move yourself there, even reluctantly. There are people who may never want to do that."

"I can certainly understand that. There are limits. I don't know if I can ever forgive Paul Shanley. But the one thing I do know, I speak to a lot of people who say, 'I can't wait for him to get to prison, where they're going to do to him what he did to all his victims.' And I don't want that to happen to Paul Shanley. I don't want him to suffer the things I suffered. What is accomplished by that? It doesn't give Greg Ford back his lost childhood, or give me back my lost life; it's just more evil unleashed in the world. I do want him to stay in prison for the rest of his life, don't get me wrong. I want him to be accountable for everything he did to every person he touched in an evil way. But I don't want him to go through that, absolutely not."

The prior smiled. "It sounds to me as if you've already forgiven Paul Shanley."

Austin looked at him dismissively, almost angrily. He laughed.

"You don't ever have to feel good about Paul Shanley," the prior said. "That's not what this is about."

"I, um—I *don't*?"

The prior shook his head.

"Really? I don't . . . *Really*?"

August 19, 2002
St. Louis, Missouri — It was one of the hottest nights of one of the hottest years in St. Louis history, but David Clohessy hardly noticed.

Except for his frequent trips to the airports, and his sweat-drenched press conferences outside hotels SNAP couldn't afford, since the crisis broke he was almost never outside. While at home, he approached his advocacy work with intensifying zeal. He spent days and nights on his computer keyboard—even a casual scan of the Internet took half a morning now. Some days he answered two hundred e-mails and calls at a sitting, pouring in from reporters and television producers. But the ones that unhinged him, the ones that made him feel an intense burden of responsibility, were from the victims themselves, people who had never mentioned their abuse to a soul before seeing his face on television and thinking, *If not now, when?* Each of these messages, from Maine or Texas, was just as unnerving as the last. The emotions were so utterly raw and familiar that Clohessy often relived his own painful reckoning. He never cut a caller short. Sometimes their stories went on for an hour or more, and by opening up the doors to their past they came upon a litany of questions, never answers. How do they choose a therapist? Do they sue? Should they call their local church-scandal reporter (every city had one now)? How can they locate others abused by the same priest? Or should they even try?

Laura Barrett, his wife, was worried about the toll this was taking on him psychologically, and worried for their family financially. The school district of Riverview Gardens in northern St. Louis, where he was director of community services, had let him go two weeks ago. Officially they said it was because the school board had eliminated his $77,000-a-year position—and this was true. Back in the spring, by a vote of four to three, his position was done away with, allegedly because of budget shortfalls. But Clohessy suspected that wasn't the whole truth. Given how Catholic the city was and how uncomfortable his national exposure had seemed to make colleagues, he suspected he fell victim to a broad backlash.

It was true he had been conducting the business of SNAP from his office, and was immensely distracted. He figured nobody had noticed, which was flawed logic: everybody in the country was viewing his affecting television appearances; and if all the time he spent away from his Riverview responsibilities had gone unnoticed, how indispensable could his position have been anyway?

It was not as though the machinations of his ouster interested him in the least. In fact, he was far less worried about his unemployment than he should have been, given the fact that his wife worked just two-thirds time as a social worker and their bank accounts held nothing that might be called a nest egg, as the financial adviser they had consulted last year made plain. They had their two sons to worry about. Still, he considered this a huge blessing in disguise. If there ever was a moment to go full-time as a social reformer, now was it.

This morning, he began compiling a list of priests who were still in ministry but shouldn't be, in blatant violation of the Dallas Charter. It was not a difficult task. Clohessy did his research by parsing his morning e-mails, and used the Internet to gain easy access to clippings files of newspapers around the country. Within an hour he found eight examples of bishops who violated their own policies. Then something caught his eye. An acquaintance sent an e-mail about trying to start a new SNAP chapter in St. Louis, his hometown. On top of the e-mail were all of the individuals to whom the letter was addressed—the sender was not an e-mail wiz who could cloak such things. Clohessy noticed a name he recognized, a local priest who he knew was privately critical of the diocese. It interested him to think the man was going public. Wondering who else might be declaring their sympathies, he scanned for other recognizable names and old friends, the way alumni peruse class notes, and many brought back memories.

Then the very last name his eye rested on burned like acid. "Oh my God," he thought. "It can't be." An annoying terror sapped his body. He looked away and then back at the name, sneaking up on it. It was undeniable.

John Whiteley, the man he charged with abusing him and his younger brother, whom he had tried to sue years ago, was still alive.

Clohessy hadn't heard a thing about him since 1993, when his case was thrown out on statute of limitations grounds and the diocese told him the priest had "disappeared." Even after he became a national advocate for victims of clergy abuse, Clohessy never tried to track down his perpetrator. But in the back of his mind, he considered Whiteley his responsibility. Surely the church had washed their hands of him. It was the classic dilemma of all people who were molested by a priest. If the

perpetrator were still alive, if he was off molesting children as a secular high school teacher or a camp counselor, could they live with the
consequences of doing nothing to protect the community? On the
other hand, could they summon the strength to haunt the man for the
rest of his life?

Knowing that Whiteley was still alive, Clohessy knew he had to do
something. He called a reporter. "You once said you had some kind of
service that helped you find people. Do you think you could help?"

Keying details into a computer database, it took the reporter only a
few minutes to come up with an address and phone number. Whiteley
still lived in St. Louis.

Clohessy dialed quickly, afraid he'd lose his nerve. An answering machine picked up. But the voice was unmistakable. He hung up without
leaving a message. He was totally unprepared for this. By dedicating
himself to SNAP, he thought he was exorcising his own demons.
Maybe instead he was running away from them.

He called the reporter again. "Thanks a lot," he said. "Now I'm in-
credibly depressed."

August 26, 2002
CAMBRIDGE, MASSACHUSETTS — An automated metal door clanged shut
behind Sister Jeannine Gramick as another in front of her swept open,
revealing a small room deep inside the seventeenth floor of the county
jail. Two chairs faced a thick glass partition that framed Paul Shanley,
who stood and waved silently. In the many times she imagined this re-
union, she had never figured on a protective barrier. She wanted to take
Shanley in her arms and whisper, "Paul, don't worry."

Except for the many images of his face on the media, she had not
seen her old friend in twenty years. She was surprised at how he'd
aged. When the Shanley news first broke, Gramick's first thought was
of her own responsibility. How could she not have known her good
friend was so diseased? Then she fell to grief, for his soul and for the
children he touched. On the telephone with Brian McNaught, whom
she met through Shanley nearly thirty years ago, she found herself
near tears. But he chastised her bluntly. "You're assuming he's guilty,"

he said. "You should assume he's innocent." On the flight to Boston from Maryland, she wrestled with her own conscience about this. She came to the conclusion that, whether he was innocent or not, there had been an unacceptable race to demonize him without benefit of a trial. Even if he had done these things, she concluded, he was not the monster of his media portrait. He was not a venal man. If he were guilty, it would mean he was desperately ill, and deserved the compassion reserved for the infirm. She thought about St. Paul, who wrote mysteriously in one of his epistles of the thorn in his side, a thing to be overcome.

She took a seat and wrestled with the telephone handpiece hanging on the wall, but the grille in the glass was sufficient, and the acoustics reliable enough, that she would not need it. "You look well," she said, meaning the opposite.

He detailed his various maladies and complaints.

"Are they treating you well?"

"They've put me in a special section of the jail, for my own protection. They're protecting me from the other inmates, because this is the worst crime in the minds of people in jail." The second worst was murder, and the third was harming a senior citizen, he said. He chuckled about the hierarchy of ugliness, so opposite the church's. Luckily, he said, the men on his tier maintain his innocence.

She recalled the Paul Shanley she knew, an iconoclast and rebel, a man who led a movement for liberty, and it saddened her to see him so isolated, contained behind a wall of glass. She wondered who from the old days had come to see him, and was surprised when he answered that very few had. "I'm a pariah," he said. "Anyone who touches me faces the same fate of rejection and isolation."

This reminded her of a verse from St. Paul, in Romans 8:28, and she said it out loud, "For those who love God, all things work together unto good."

"Only two people from the archdiocese have come," he said. "One of them was a deacon from the chancery who brought laicization papers and asked me to sign. I hadn't requested them. They wanted to end it that way. I refused."

"Good," she said. She found this unconscionable. They should wait for a verdict before issuing a sentence, she thought. In the meantime, at the very least they should send a priest to pray with him.

"I don't know what I would do if somebody I knew were in this predicament," he said. "Would I distance myself? I probably would."

Gramick disagreed. "Your niece tells me you're going to be out by Christmas!" she said brightly.

She did not intend to ask him about his charges. He brought it up himself. "I never raped a child or forced anyone to engage in sexual acts," he told her. Earlier, his niece Theresa had given Gramick similar assurances. She detailed the many reasons she believed this, citing the police's evidence and the results of her own tireless investigation. "Recovered memories," she said, "*conveniently* recovered memories." She wasn't as sure about the civil suits, of which there were now over a dozen, except she believed her uncle's protestations that his alleged victims had been consenting. Gramick wanted to believe her, but wasn't certain until Shanley told her himself. Yes, he was saying, he'd had sex, but never with a child, and never criminally. She believed this.

A few weeks after her visit, Gramick accepted an invitation to return to Boston and address a small faith community there on the importance of her gay and lesbian ministry. Hoping to visit Paul Shanley again, she asked her sponsors to extend her stay by a day. But when they heard the reason for her request, they rescinded the invitation altogether. "We think it would be better if you don't come," one said to her.

It was just as Paul Shanley had said.

September 2, 2002
Los Angeles, California — The day Cardinal Roger Mahony had waited years for had finally come. He was going to go forward with the inauguration of his brand-new, modernist, towering Cathedral of Our Lady of Angels—the first new Catholic cathedral erected in the western United States in thirty years. His detractors considered the project a colossal monument to his ego—"Taj Mahony," the alternative paper *New Times* called it. It held special resonance now. Following the self-destruction of Cardinal Law and the bevy of church leaders he had helped anoint, Mahony was arguably the ranking American prelate.

With 4 million faithful, the Los Angeles archdiocese was the largest in the country. He would have a fitting church to show for it.

Situated on the shoulder of the Hollywood Freeway, the most amazing part of the building was the twenty-seven thousand square feet of alabaster, sliced as thin as membrane and incongruously used as stone windows. Inside, above the altar, was a fifty-foot-tall alabaster window in the shape of a cross, refracting sunlight throughout the day and beaming light outward from the cathedral at night. Sixty-thousand Spanish Jana limestone paving stones made up the floor, and a grand cherry-encased pipe organ stretched eighty-five feet high into the eleven-story space. The presbyterium, where priests gather with their bishop to celebrate Mass, was designed to hold four hundred clerics— a third of Mahony's clerical workforce—and the cavernous nave, uninterrupted by pillars and appointed with pews of a rare buttery wood, would accommodate three thousand.

The total cost came to $193 million, $150 million more than was budgeted. At the last minute, the cathedral design had been expanded after Mahony studied a comparison between his new home and St. Patrick's Cathedral in New York, and realized his was going to be smaller. In its final plan, Our Lady of Angels was thirty-two thousand square feet larger than Grace Cathedral in San Francisco, twenty-one feet higher than the Washington National Cathedral—and one foot longer than St. Patrick's. In 1999 at the groundbreaking ceremony, this one-upsmanship may have seemed "too much fun to avoid," as the archdiocese said on its Web site. But in 2002 it seemed almost tragic. At least sixty-one and perhaps as many as a hundred of Mahony's priests were under criminal investigation.

Mahony himself had drawn two allegations, both of which he staunchly denied, and neither of which seemed especially credible. One young man's father debunked every aspect of his story to the authorities, who charged him with extortion. A young woman with a history of emotional troubles alleged Mahony took advantage of her after she blacked out, but admitted she had no recollection of abuse, making it impossible for the police to pursue charges. But District Attorney Steve Cooley was intimating he would empanel a grand jury to investigate Mahony's role in the cover-up of clergy sexual abuse; two federal lawsuits accused him of running an organized crime syndicate not unlike the mob, only rather than illicit profits, the aims of his alleged racketeering scheme involved wholesale criminal sexual gratification with minors.

The crisis had left Mahony seriously short on cash. Donations to his annual appeal were off dramatically. His year-end operating deficit would reach $5.7 million. In addition, the year's bill for countering sex abuse allegations was $7.7 million, including a reported half million for public relations consultants, bringing total cash shortfall for the year to $13.4 million. He had been forced to eliminate 30 percent of diocesan programs, including specialized ministries to prisons and outreach to college campuses, minority groups, people with disabilities, and gay and lesbian Catholics. The budget for parochial education was slashed. Layoffs put at least sixty people out of work.

But that did not stop the lavish inauguration, on a day when malevolent breezes carried hundred-degree heat off the desert. Mahony's fellow cardinals and bishops showed up in phalanxes. Even Cardinal Law attended. This raised security concerns. Expecting protests, the archdiocese erected a chain-link fence around the entire perimeter of the cathedral and stationed security officers at the gate. Inside, where the stone building kept the prelates comfortably cool, Mahony gave a rousing homily that called the structure to a higher purpose. "Is all this splendor and architectural artistry enough for us? Can we rest content with the beauty arising from this spot? We must answer an emphatic 'No!' Not as a kind of cultural treasure was the cathedral built. As a vibrant symbol of God's habitat in our city, this outer form must find an echo in the inner graces of a people who listen intently to God's Word as it comes to us as challenge and consolation."

Outside in the burning sun, five hundred protesters circled the fence, denouncing a church whose priorities seemed backwards. A contingent from Catholic Worker carried signs reading "No Fat Cat Cathedral" and "Cardinal Mahony Must Go." A man wearing a giant papier-mâché cartoon head of Mahony, in defiance of the heat, told a reporter for *New Times*, "He's . . . been running a virtual underground railroad for pedophiles. Mahony's the Harriet Tubman of the predator-priest movement. Then he hires PR people. That's why I call him Cardinal Spin on my sign, which says, as you can see, 'Cardinal Spin: Lie, Deny, Get By.' "

Mary Grant, who carried a blow-up photograph of herself taken in the period she was being abused by Father Lenihan, looked up at the enormous structure, and she wondered how much it was going to cost to keep those windows clean.

September 5, 2002

LAKE ALBANO, ITALY — Inside the pope's summer residence at Castel Gandolfo, south of Rome on the breezy banks of Lake Albano, John Paul II received a delegation of Brazilian bishops making their yearly sojourn to see their boss. Dressed in gold and silver vestments, John Paul looked healthier than he had in months.

When he spoke, his subject was the crisis, a theme he had not addressed in public since his declarations of sorrow months before. For the first time, he laid the blame on homosexual priests, who he said had "deviations in their affections," suggesting they experienced great difficulty in honoring their commitment to celibacy. The view being expressed by certain vocal members of the Roman Curia was gaining influence and had won over the pope.

He told his audience—and by extension every bishop on the globe— that he considered it their "duty" to screen candidates for the priesthood "above all from the standpoint of morals and affections. . . . It would be lamentable if, out of a misunderstood tolerance, they ordained young men who are immature or have obvious signs of affective deviations that, as is sadly known, could cause serious abnormalities in the consciences of the faithful, with evident damage to the whole Church."

The remarks, delivered in Portuguese, were not widely reported in the secular press. But every gay priest in America heard them loud and clear. It was as they feared. The scapegoating was in full swing.

September 11, 2002

JAMAICA PLAIN, MASSACHUSETTS — A year had passed since the terror attacks that claimed 2,998 lives and turned the country on its head. On the anniversary, the nation's grief and confusion was no less difficult to bear, only different. From a dreadful, fiery moment in history, life was going on. There was a lesson in this for Phil Saviano. He had decided to reorient himself, to look forward from, not back upon, his own private terrors. For all of his adult life, his entire existence had been about darkness. Sexual abuse and viral death consumed him. They were his avocations. But if he were to be honest with himself, he would see how he had already won his wars. Physically he was well, thanks to medication and regular trips to the Y. And owing to his own personal diligence and tirelessness, the Catholic Church's systemic abuse of minors had finally been exposed. The news coverage would go on without his constant efforts, just as his life would go on. Now he was fifty. It was time to rejoin life.

Symbolically, he had disconnected his cell phone the day before, so he could enter the second post-9/11 year without the tether to SNAP. He had begun working as a freelance medical writer for pharmaceutical companies. All that remained was for him to tell his fellow group members.

But on his way out of his apartment he found, taped to his door, a thick envelope bearing his name. Peeling it open, he discovered a complex seven-part subpoena from the Worcester diocese. In connection with a lawsuit against Father Robert E. Kelley, who had admitted molesting fifty to a hundred girls and served a seven-year prison sentence in the nineties for sexual assault, Bishop Daniel P. Reilly's lawyers were demanding any information in SNAP files on the women who filed suit.

Saviano was furious. It was not as though there was any chance Kelley was innocent! Could his defenders really infiltrate a peer-led, all-volunteer self-help group? Did they have a right to his files? What could they hope to find there? Certainly nothing to exculpate Kelley, a convicted sex offender.

He read on. The diocese intended to depose him for any information he knew about these women's cases. The diocesan lawyer went on to demand every file or scrap of paper in Phil's apartment relating to any priest ordained in the Worcester diocese, whether or not a claim was made, and "the names of all persons who [say] they were sexually abused by any priests associated with Worcester."

To Saviano, this was a transparent attempt by the diocese to discourage victims from reaching out to one another for emotional support. "I guess," he thought, "I won't be retiring after all."

It took him two weeks of constant pressure, through lawyers and the media, to force Worcester's bishop, Daniel Reilly, to withdraw the subpoena. Reilly alleged he knew nothing about it, saying it had been filed by lawyers representing the church's insurance company, acting on their own. But admitting that lawyers, not church leaders, were the main architects of the diocese's response to the abuse crisis did little to reassure SNAP members.

September 18, 2002

BOSTON, MASSACHUSETTS — Two months had gone by since Mitchell Garabedian gave his closing arguments in his effort to enforce the $15–$30 million settlement he had reached on behalf of the Geoghan 86. For a reason she was not explaining, Judge Sweeney had still not issued her ruling. Time was not on Garabedian's side. He decided to present Wilson Rogers's final offer to his clients. Each would receive between $10,000 and $320,000, significantly below the earlier upper limit of nearly $1 million for people who were repeatedly molested or sodomized for many years. As before, all eighty-six would have to sign.

Lawyers around the country reacted harshly to the offer. "That's just shockingly low considering what's been paid in other dioceses," Lynne Cadigan, a Tucson attorney who had settled other clergy sexual abuse lawsuits, told the *Globe*. "Even the most minimal settlements that I've been involved with have amounted to more than that."

One at a time, in disappointment and need, the Geoghan 86 began to coalesce behind the smaller amount. But not all of them. Anthony Muzzi Jr., who now stood to receive just over $100,000, was so offended by the figure that he leapt down Garabedian's throat. "Closure? That's not closure! For the rest of my life I will think about how I was molested, how we were offered $30 million, and I could have lived with that, but they shove that up your you-know-what and say, 'We're going to give you a hundred grand.' I have to live with all of that? Getting revictimized and revictimized, saying this is all you're going to get? I can't get it out of my mind."

Muzzi wanted to know why Garabedian was even willing to entertain this paltry amount. He had started to imagine behind-the-scenes deals. One day on television, a lawyer for the church was quoted saying Garabedian had already accepted the offer. Garabedian quickly announced that wasn't true. But Muzzi and a number of Garabedian's clients remained puzzled. Several of them called Eric MacLeish and asked if he would take on their cases, but as much as he felt sorry for them, he could not poach their business. Garabedian had not collaborated with the other Boston attorneys suing the church. MacLeish was as baffled as Muzzi was about why Garabedian was buckling now.

Garabedian told Muzzi it was because the other clients needed the money and closure, especially McSorley. Muzzi felt the pressure to buckle intensely. He rolled it back and forth in his mind. Was this the best he could do? Would he be able to live with himself if he walked away, knowing the needs of the other clients? Would he be able to sleep at night if he signed?

"I'm almost losing faith, because it doesn't get you anywhere," Muzzi said. "Instead of any kind of positive advancements, all I get is negative advancements. Am I glad we did what we did? I like to feel that I'm part of the change that's taking over the church. Because I was one of the first. And look where it's gone from there. Me and two or three other people blew this thing wide open and brought the church down on their knees. I like to have credit for that, for cleaning up the church, because that's trash that shouldn't be there. You know what I mean? Do I get happiness out of that? Yeah. But aren't I letting them go free? Can I do that? There's no way you can beat them. They're scum. They don't care about the Catholic people. All they care about is money. And they're still trying to keep it."

Now, in mid-September, unable to hold out longer, Muzzi capitulated. He was among the last to sign. Garabedian carried eighty-six executed settlement agreements to court on September 19 and presented them to Sweeney, ending the battle that blew open the archdiocese of Boston and sparked the worst crisis in the history of the church in America. It was a hollow victory. Cardinal Law and the archdiocese would not admit culpability, as some Geoghan victims had asked. Church leaders even rejected a request by Garabedian to allow his clients to give victim-impact statements in the courtroom for the cardinal to hear. Instead it was left to Judge Sweeney to acknowledge the long journey of the Geoghan 86, many of whom had gathered in the courtroom.

"You made a fundamental difference in the way many people—including people who are secular authorities and religious authorities—look at the way institutions have to care for those they are bound to protect," she told them. "There is no question from the point of view of the civil side that Mr. Geoghan either raped or assaulted you or members of your family. Mr. Geoghan did in fact do what you said he did to you."

Chapter 14

The Backlash

September 20, 2002

PORTLAND, MAINE — Paul Kendrick, a fifty-three-year-old investment broker with a salesman's demeanor, stopped and ordered two cups of coffee to go, then headed to the chancery of the diocese of Portland. He didn't have an appointment. Though he'd been writing and e-mailing the bishop most of the year, he had barely gotten a response. All through his life, Kendrick had felt like a Catholic, but not especially a Christian—by which he meant that what rubbed off on him during his Jesuit education at Cheverus High School in Portland was a sense of culture and community, not God and Bible verse.

He would not be heading to the seat of his nominal faith now were it not for the case of a local youth, Michael Doherty, who accused his priest, teacher, coach, and family friend of routine molestation, forced masturbation, and sexual innuendo. That priest, Father James Talbot, had insinuated himself so thoroughly into the Doherty household that he was given his own room in the house, next door to his inamorato, who was fifteen and sixteen during the course of the sexual pesterings, which took place there, at the school, in motels, and at the rectory.

The case had first caught Kendrick's eye because Doherty had attended his alma mater, Cheverus High, where Talbot taught. But he was galvanized to action after reading that Doherty, who privately settled a lawsuit in 2001, and his family felt they'd been ostracized by the community, fellow parishioners, and Cheverus alumni for having come forward.

Kendrick had gone to the courthouse himself to read the legal files. What he found in Doherty's depositions disgusted him.

This could certainly meet some definition of evil, Kendrick had thought. He wanted to plead with church leaders to reach out to Doherty, to organize healing prayers, to actively solicit other victims of Talbot, to demand the removal of molesting priests, to promote transparency. He sent a moving letter to all thirty-five hundred fellow alumni and friends of Cheverus, and phoned and e-mailed Bishop Joseph Gerry and officials at the Jesuits' provincial offices. The diocese mostly ignored him. Father John Murray, the executive assistant at the Jesuits' offices, once wrote him a note saying, "I wanted to state that I believe that the Society of Jesus has taken appropriate action in regards to Fr. Talbot. Also, I do not feel it is appropriate to engage in further correspondence with you regarding the Society of Jesus' position on this matter."

If it weren't for Voice of the Faithful, which gave him an opportunity to vent his frustrations and find others who felt the same way, Kendrick was certain he would not have held firm. Several times in the spring he drove down to Boston to attend meetings. Then on May 29 he founded a chapter in Portland, and within weeks it was drawing nearly nine hundred people to meetings—in a tiny diocese with 115 priests. Sensing the momentum of the group, Bishop Gerry banned it from using church property "since that would imply endorsement," as a press secretary said. Nearly every day since then, Kendrick had sent a request for a meeting with Gerry. They went ignored.

His sense of spiritual panic skyrocketing, he headed for the chancery uninvited. The church, he knew, needed saving—and somehow he had come to believe he had a personal responsibility to save it. He could not wait another minute.

He had a coffee container in each hand as he walked through the front door of the chancery for the Portland diocese. The last thing he expected was to be afraid, but that's exactly what he was. His stomach growled. His hands shook so violently he worried about dropping the beverages. He was the cowardly lion, and this was Oz. "Look at me," he thought. "At the headquarters of my spiritual home, and instead of feeling inspired, I am terrified."

"Does the bishop have a minute? I brought him a cup of coffee—I thought we could sit and talk for a bit." He concentrated on steadying his hands.

The woman at the reception desk replied very kindly that the bishop was out of the office for the day.

"How about the co-chancellor, is he here? Either today or tomorrow? It's about Voice of the Faithful." He gave his name.

She rose and walked into the teeming center of the building to scavenge a reply. "No," she said sweetly on her return. "He will not see you today or tomorrow."

"Will he see me next week, or next month? Will he ever see me?"

Again, she made the long journey. "No," she said, taking her chair again, "he won't."

Kendrick was speechless. "Can I just digest this?" he said to the woman. "I am a Catholic. I volunteer for my church. I am having trouble digesting this."

She looked at him sympathetically, but mutely, incapable of helping him in any way whatsoever.

"Can I just digest this?"

She went about her work. Slowly he turned and slumped toward the door.

September 30, 2002

BOSTON, MASSACHUSETTS — Bishop Gerry in Portland was not the only prelate to declare Voice of the Faithful a threat. Bishop William F. Murphy of Rockville Centre told priests in the Long Island, New York, diocese that the group was not welcome in church-owned buildings, and Bishop William Lori outlawed the organization throughout Bridgeport, Connecticut. "I cannot support an organization like Voice of the Faithful which appears to promote dialogue and cooperation, but which in reality prosecutes a hidden agenda that is in conflict with the teachings of the Catholic faith," Lori said in August, without offering specifics. "I believe Voice of the Faithful is using the current crisis in the church to advance an agenda which neither I, nor the vast majority of Catholics, can embrace. For this reason, I cannot sanction Voice of the Faithful groups meeting in parishes or other church property in the Diocese of Bridgeport."

Newark's archbishop flatly branded the group "anti-Church and, ultimately, anti-Catholic." "Married clergy, ordination of women, abolition of the tradition of celibacy, altering Church teaching on sexual morality, and defiance of the apostolic authority that has guided the Church since its founding two thousand years ago by Our Lord Jesus Christ, have all found a place in the ranks of Voice of the Faithful," Archbishop John Myers said.

The group's national leaders vigorously countered these characterizations. Individual members might disagree with specific aspects of church teachings, they pointed out, just as individual Catholics did, but the group itself took no stand on doctrinal issues. This was by design. "We are mainstream Catholics," said Jim Post, who assumed the job of Voice president after Jim Muller curtailed his involvement to tend to his family obligations. "What they believe, we believe." The only thing about the church they attempted to change was the decision-making structure that allowed bishops to manage each diocese secretly, without lay participation. Wasn't this their post–Vatican II right?

They cited canon 215, which said, "Christ's faithful may freely establish and direct associations which serve charitable or pious purposes or which foster the Christian vocation in the world, and they may hold meetings to pursue these purposes by common effort." They even defended their right to give bishops a piece of their minds, quoting canon 212: "They have the right, indeed at times the duty, in keeping with their knowledge, competence and position, to manifest to the sacred Pastors"—that is, the bishops, archbishops, and cardinals— "their views on matters which concern the good of the Church."

Their protests did little good. Soon, Voice of the Faithful would find itself exiled from more Catholic churches, campuses, and meeting rooms in Brooklyn, New York; Camden, New Jersey; Baker, Oregon; and Dayton, Ohio.

In Boston, Voice leaders had noticed what seemed like banishments from churches, though every time they confronted pastors or Bishop Edyvean, the vicar general, they were told there was no orchestrated policy against them. But by late September, at least seventeen Boston-area churches had closed their doors to Voice chapters. Now on Monday, September 30, a regional auxiliary bishop, Emilio Allue, personally shut down a Boston chapter that had been meeting in St. Michael's Parish in North Andover. The pastor released Allue's written instructions to parish members and the press. It was the first proof that the archdiocese was behind the closures. "The activities and promotion of the [Voice of the Faithful] must be curtailed in order to avoid further scandal and polarity among our parishioners," Allue wrote to the pastor, Father Paul T. Keyes. "For the sake of unity and Catholic orthodoxy it is inappropriate to foster these meetings."

Despite the bannings, Voice of the Faithful chapters were now well established in forty Boston-area churches, and a hundred more Catholic churches nationwide—not to mention the dozens of branches meeting in exile in Congregationalist churches or nonaffiliated colleges. But Post sensed this was the beginning of the end, and in Boston, at least, he was correct. Within two weeks, Cardinal Law would announce that no new Voice chapters would be permitted in the Boston archdiocese until he could determine just how faithful Voice of the Faithful really was. Much had already been made about the group's coziness with the international group We Are Church, which the Vatican had cast as a bunch of apostates. A small but vocal group of church supporters turned against Voice of the Faithful. Calling themselves Faithful Voices, they infiltrated and disrupted Voice chapter meetings, pressing proposals to disband. In addition, they publicized the fact that an openly gay man sat on Voice's board of directors and a former Planned Parenthood officer had addressed the July convention.

"Voice of the Faithful wants the doctrine to come from the people and go up to God," said Carol McKinley, a founder of Faithful Voices. "No. Doctrine comes from God and you accept it."

Thursday, October 3, 2002

NEW YORK, NEW YORK — Monsignor William Varvaro, past president of the Canon Law Society of America, and currently the top canon law expert for the Brooklyn diocese, was an expert in defending priests against charges, unfounded or not. His advice to them was similar to the counsel police union lawyers give cops charged with crimes: Button up, and go to a lawyer. "A priest should say nothing," he said, noting that under the Dallas Charter anything an accused cleric revealed to his bishop could wind up in a police report. "Again, this is that old question of trust. It's that old question of the father-son relationship that's being destroyed."

About 150 priests had gathered inside Rosie O'Grady's Saloon, a midtown pub, to hear him give his address, sponsored by a new group of New York–area priests called Voice of the Ordained. This was the group's first meeting. But by inviting Varvaro as their inaugural speaker, rather than representatives of victims' rights groups, this group was setting a very different tone. Varvaro counseled priests to countersue their accusers. Across the country, a half dozen priests had taken his advice, charging the men and women who had accused them with slander and defamation. He even encouraged priests to sue their bishops for cooperating with civil authorities in violation of canon law.

Turning the other cheek was not one of his suggestions.

Nobody knew this better than Father John Bambrick, who had snuck into the midtown pub despite being from the Trenton diocese, in New Jersey, an hour's drive from the city. He was embroiled in litigation with Varvaro—as an opponent, not a client.

When Bambrick was a kid growing up in suburban New Jersey, all he dreamed of was becoming a priest. So he was thrilled when Father Anthony Eremito, who had performed a wedding in his church, took a keen interest in his vocation and began paying him regular visits. Even when Eremito held his hand through movies, even when the rubbing began, he felt lucky. He kept their secret until the eve of his own ordination, in the early 1990s, when he told New York's then archbishop, Cardinal John O'Connor. Bambrick wasn't the only one to complain. O'Connor promised him that Eremito would be removed from his parish and would not preach again.

Bambrick, now a dark-haired and boyish thirty-seven-year-old pastor at St. Thomas More Church in Manalapan, would have left it at that. But O'Connor did not keep his word. Not only did he allow Eremito to continue working as a priest, but from 1997 to 1998, he loaned him out to the diocese of Trenton, which posted him not far from Bambrick's own parish. When he learned this, Bambrick complained again, and Eremito's assignment was terminated.

Again, Bambrick had intended to let Eremito drift into memory. But in this year of revelation, he learned that Eremito was still wearing the Roman collar despite his many complaints—O'Connor had had him transferred even farther away, to Lubbock, Texas, where he worked as a chaplain at the Convent Medical Center.

No longer trusting his own church, Bambrick decided to go to the press. He flew to Dallas for the bishops' conference and peddled his story to reporters across the country fascinated by the priest-on-priest angle. The medical center staff removed Eremito and he refused comment, but the New York archdiocese confirmed Bambrick's story. Bambrick did not intend to sue. But he hoped that the media buzz would reach other victims, and that one of their cases would fall within the statute in New York, New Jersey, or Texas, so that a criminal charge could be brought. Bambrick talked about his experiences with the district attorney's office in Manhattan. Anthony Eremito, in turn, hired Varvaro as his canon lawyer and sued Bambrick in a church tribunal, charging him with "calumny" and seeking his removal from the priesthood.

Bambrick hid quietly in the crowd, which was three times as large as expected, comforted by the fact that nobody seemed to recognize him. Varvaro's opinions gushed on a flume of anger. The bishops who met in Dallas sold out their priests in order to please the piranha media, he declared. They defined abuse too broadly, and priestly privacy too narrowly, violating canon 220, an ancient precept guaranteeing every priest the right to *buona figura*, a good name and reputation. This violation was tremendous. *Buona figura* was a fundamental right, as inviolate as the Bill of Rights. It was the privilege of every man upon ordination. Whether or not his comportment was defensible, upright, or moral was between him and his confessor—not something for public consumption.

"You don't rush to burn everybody at the stake," Varvaro said.

A young man named Daniel Dugo, who had also slipped into Rosie O'Grady's though he was neither a priest nor a canon lawyer, could no longer contain himself. He rose to his feet. He had not planned to say anything. But his finger jabbed accusingly toward the dais.

"Pretty much I've heard enough," he bellowed. "What about due process for the victims? So if you rape a child once, it's okay?"

The crowd booed. Priests leapt to their feet, riotously. Three men seized Dugo and dragged him toward the door.

"If you have nothing to hide, let me speak," Dugo cried. "You're a bunch of animals and pedophiles!"

Though this was not the kind of discourse Father Bambrick had expected, he was not surprised that his brother priests had become a mob and turned on a victim. The whole institution was topsy-turvy, he thought. But in the melee that followed, he suddenly found himself face-to-face with the man he had accused, Anthony Eremito. They had not laid eyes on each other since 1998, when Bambrick briefly confronted him in the sacristy of St. Agnes Church in Atlantic Highlands, New Jersey, as he was preparing for Mass. Twenty-two years had passed since their alleged sexual tangle.

"Hello, Anthony," Bambrick said.

Eremito seemed startled. "Hello, John," he said.

A fraught silence followed.

Bambrick spoke next. "Do you want to talk?"

"No."

"Don't you think we should talk?"

"My lawyer told me to stay away from you."

Bambrick thought, *What on earth has happened to our church?*

October 4, 2002

HANSCOM AIR FORCE BASE, MASSACHUSETTS — When the American bishops met in June, there was one piece of business that they couldn't rightly address. Lay Catholics had called upon them to adopt a system of sanctions for bishops who failed to comply with the Charter. However, canon law didn't allow this. Bishops, being sovereign "princes," had no say over one another, but answered only to the pope. The pope, for his part, had already proved the unlimited scope of his forgiveness for clergy, much to the frustration of American Catholics. Father Tom Doyle put it most colorfully when he said, "The church in America is a dinosaur with a head the size of an ant, and the head thinks it's in charge. The bishops need to understand how precarious their position is."

Wilton Gregory alone seemed to get this. In his powerful opening statement in June he had chastised bishops for abetting perpetrating priests, much to the consternation of his peers. But in a stroke of political genius, just as the Dallas convention was winding down, Gregory had announced the formation of a church-sponsored watchdog group, headed by Oklahoma governor Frank Keating, a former FBI agent and federal prosecutor, and a self-described "solid, tough, no-nonsense Catholic." With financing from dioceses around the country, Gregory charged Keating and his thirteen-member commission with monitoring compliance with the new accord and holding bishops accountable with public pressure. It was a bold move, and not entirely well received among bishops unaccustomed to scrutiny. Some openly wondered if it violated canon law to let a layman scrutinize the bishops, and excoriated Gregory for the move; several privately vowed to foil the commission. But Gregory pressed on anyway, rounding out the commission with, among others, the Washington lawyer Robert Bennett and Leon Panetta, the former White House chief of staff.

Keating proved to be just the thorn in the bishops' side that Gregory had hoped, though even Gregory was pained by the harsh language Keating used in his first public statement after the appointment. "As a Catholic layman," he had said, "I am horrified and angry and shocked and puzzled and amazed that such criminal, such horrific, such sinful acts could occur within my faith community. It is a horrific and pitiful statement that people who have been ordained to the ministry would do such things. If someone obscures, absolves, obstructs, or hides that criminal act, arguably they are obstructing justice or are accessories to the crime." With Gregory sitting at his side, he vowed to expose bishops who moved errant clergymen "from child to child," and encouraged the faithful to walk out of church and stop making donations if their bishops didn't straighten up.

You could see the discomfort on Gregory's face. "I guess in the political arena, you shoot first and ask questions later," he thought. "Ecclesiastical language is by its very nature much more nuanced. But he is saying many of the things that people in the pews are thinking." Keating's own archbishop accused him of "mortal sin" for showing such disrespect.

All summer, his role had been mostly as a tough-talking figurehead, flying from diocese to diocese and meeting with bishops, victims' groups, and priests. He had not weighed in on the spreading policy to bar Voice of the Faithful from church-owned property.

Landing in Boston for the first time, he was greeted this afternoon at the Hanscom Air Force Base by Jim Post, who spent an hour imploring him to use his stature to counter the bannings. "We're not a bunch of nuts or radicals," Post told Keating. "We're Catholics who, number one, love our church, and, number two, are dedicated to finding a solution. Our message to bishops is, Don't lock doors, don't lock minds."

Shocked to hear about Voice's troubles, Keating vowed to bring it up whenever he could. He seized the first opportunity that evening at Regis College, the Catholic-affiliated school for women that had invited him to Boston to give a speech. In remarks that were equally harsh on Cardinal Law and angry at the entire system of church governance, he called on bishops to let Voice of the Faithful chapters back into their own churches. "Just because you wear a red hat does not necessarily mean that you have the knowledge of what is going on, and you need the input and advice of a wide variety of people," he told his audience of six hundred. "No one should be afraid of dialogue."

October 7, 2002
LOS ANGELES, CALIFORNIA — Cardinal Roger Mahony had finished his statement to the presbyteral assembly, his annual convocation for the twelve hundred priests from Santa Barbara, Ventura, and Los Angeles Counties. The usual fare at these meetings was news about health in-

surance changes and other archdiocesan housekeeping matters. The priests looked forward to the occasion as a rare opportunity to socialize with colleagues. Not this year. The tension was palpable. Mahony had chosen to meet in his new conference center, attached to the cathedral. The lavishness of the location alone inflamed tempers. So did the $15 parking fees.

Mahony advanced through a prepared speech. When he was finished, Monsignor Timothy Dyer, the pastor at Nativity Church in South L.A., rose from his pew and walked purposefully toward the microphone. Twelve priests followed him, a hostile black wall marching forward. Whatever it was intended to be, this shocking display was absolutely unheard of in church protocol. Priests just don't move in phalanxes.

Dyer unfolded a piece of paper. "It strains the credibility we have with our people when we dedicate a $189 million cathedral—rejoicing that it is fully funded—and, one week later, declare that sixty lay and religious employees must be let go because we have not planned wisely enough to raise the $4 million needed to fund their ministries."

Mahony reacted the way he had been taught to, with smoldering high-handedness. But it did not blunt the mutinous forces. Another organized group of priests who worked in prisons took the microphone and read a statement. Then another group, priests who had special outreach to the Latino community—encompassing fully 80 percent of the parishioners who pledged money to the church every Sunday morning. They demanded that funding be restored for the offices for Latino and African-American ministry and the establishment of a budgetary process that approximated multilateralism, if not democracy.

However, no priest rose to protest Mahony's defunding of the gay and lesbian ministry office, where Fran Ruth was at that very minute packing into boxes the flotsam of a historic sixteen-year experiment. Mahony had commissioned the office after the Vatican banned Dignity from meeting in Catholic churches. The office encouraged parish churches to extend "hospitality" to all gays and lesbians, and to preach in favor of sexual continence without condemning those who "act out," in the phrase of Father Peter Liuzzi, a past director. "As for the sin of homosexual activity, I think in our own city things like racial hatred and discrimination and deep-seated social injustice are far greater and more destructive," Liuzzi once said.

Ruth, a lesbian, wasn't surprised when she learned that nobody had jumped to her defense. "They're scared," she ruminated between her last few meetings before the office closed its doors for good. "Rome is looking to make gay priests the scapegoat for the scandal; they know this, so every priest is really taking ten steps backwards when it comes to ministering to gays and lesbians. And that is especially true for gay priests. Those that I do know, who are comfortable in their sexual orientation, are uncomfortable right now because of all the pressure, the outside pressure; the assumption is that if you're gay and you're a priest, you're not celibate. And not with adults. That's the problem right there. If you're gay you're a child molester. I've never seen anything like this. Priests who have been out for years are going way back into the closet. People are afraid to talk to me—they're calling me sometimes from pay phones! One priest who was going to help me set up some programs called me almost in *tears*. And said, 'It started. The persecution has started.' "

Week of October 7, 2002
ROCKVILLE CENTRE, NEW YORK — Bishop William Murphy, whose lawyers vigorously responded this week to the many cases pending against fifty-eight diocesan clerics, was preoccupied with other things. He never liked the suburban ranch house he was assigned when he took over the Rockville Centre diocese, in Long Island, in 2001: a nondescript brick structure with white flower boxes beneath small living room windows and a wicker love seat on the tiny porch. So he renovated an enormous, fifteen-thousand-square-foot, four-story marble convent whose slate roof and rolling lawns were reminiscent of the stately country homes of feudal Ireland. He outfitted his new quarters with a Sub-Zero refrigerator, a Viking stove, a high-tech wine cooler that kept reds and whites at different temperatures, three large Oriental rugs, an oak-manteled fireplace, and a newly constructed vaulted ceiling over the grandly appointed twelve-person dining room table.

This he had been able to finance by way of a special collection that had gone apace despite the sexual scandals. However, word eventually got out that Murphy had quietly evicted six aged nuns from their life-long home in order to claim the building as his, over their protests. The funding stopped.

Despite that, he was able to begin moving in this week, after es-corting journalists and Catholic high rollers on a tour through his new manse.

Simultaneously, the county DA was examining evidence of a cover-up scheme and presenting it to a grand jury first empaneled in May. Of particular interest were allegations that Murphy had set up a sex abuse hotline mainly for intimidating callers away from litigation—the priests manning it were trained attorneys who could track the allega-tions according to the church's liability. The absurdity of Murphy's timing in holding a lavish dedication of his new residence this week caused Jimmy Breslin, the *Newsday* columnist, to christen him "Man-sion Murphy" and speculate that perhaps the former Law crony had spent so much because he expected to house Law and Daily and other disgraced prelates once they went on the lam.

"You've got to be crazy to give the place any money," Breslin wrote. "When you go past St. Agnes, clutch your purse or keep your hands in your pockets."

October 8, 2002
VATICAN CITY — According to an article published by Catholic News Service, members of the Congregation for Catholic Education, the Cu-ria office charged with setting standards at Catholic seminaries and universities, were indeed moving to deny homosexuals admission to seminaries. It was the most formal salvo yet in the slow-brewing con-troversy about gay priests. "The Vatican has prepared a draft document containing directives against the admission of homosexuals to the priesthood," said the article by reporter John Thavis, citing informed Vatican sources. "The document takes the position that since the church considers the homosexual orientation as 'objectively disordered' such people should not be admitted to the seminary or ordained."

Nobody had seen the draft, which was said to have been written in collaboration with the Congregation for the Doctrine of the Faith and other Vatican agencies. Nor would it be made public in the coming year. But that didn't matter. The mere hint of its existence shot jolts of panic through priestly ranks in America.

"This is ludicrous," said Sister Jeannine Gramick. "Gay men will continue to feel called to ministerial life and the priesthood, but what will happen is they'll become closeted and secretive like they were in the fifties and sixties. We will be ordaining gay men who will be repressed, who will have an unhealthy self-concept, and their sexuality will come out in distorted ways. That's the breeding ground for sexual abuse. They're saying: Eliminate gay men and you'll eliminate the problem. But they have it completely backwards. When you put the whole weight of this institution against them, the pressure is tremendous."

Barring gays never kept gays out of ministry. The theologian Mark D. Jordan believed that was by design—the priesthood, he wrote in *Telling Truths in Church,* "solicits same-sex desire, depends on it, but also denounces it and punishes it," turning gay priests into partners in their own repression, and the repression of others. Sex was their feverish, and silent, obsession—he called it "chastity wrapped around obedience and so wrapped in turn with the cloak of 'discretion,' 'avoiding scandal to the Church.' The clerical culture that concealed repeated abuse is a culture of eroticized obedience. Since it is the obedience of men to men, the eros is homoerotic. Though not 'gay' in any ordinary sense. The sharpest challenge to this denied eros of clerical obedience is an out gay man."

It seemed true that the policy adopted by seminary formation directors in the 1980s to encourage sexually frank discussions between young men and their advisers about the challenges of celibacy had stemmed the problem of abusive priests. Those who trained as priests under the old rules engaged their psyches in warfare that produced no victories, only casualties.

"The answer is not to eliminate one orientation, but eliminate those individuals who are abusers," Gramick said. "And creating the climate where we talk about sexuality, all types, and discern who does have a call for celibacy and who doesn't. There are heterosexuals who don't have that call, and they abuse women. A lot of women have been victims, too."

October 14, 2002
VATICAN CITY — Bishop Wilton Gregory was called to Rome to receive the verdict from the Congregation of Bishops on the Dallas Charter for the Protection of Children and Young People. After lengthy deliberations involving many branches of the Vatican's government, it was determined that the Charter was not acceptable as written. Calling the plan a source of "confusion and ambiguity" and "difficult to reconcile with the universal law of the Church," Cardinal Giovanni Battista Re ruled that it must be reconsidered. For this, he established what he called a "mixed commission," made up of four American bishops chosen by Bishop Gregory and four Curia officials, instructing them to meet through the fall to develop revisions.

"The sexual abuse of minors is particularly abhorrent," Re wrote to Gregory. "Deeply moved by the sufferings of the victims and their families, the Holy See supports the American Bishops in their endeavor to respond firmly to the sexual misdeeds of the very small number of those who minister or labor in the service of the Church. But such a very small number cannot overshadow 'the immense spiritual, human and social good that the vast majority of priests and religious in the United States have done and are still doing,'" as Pope John Paul II had said.

Gregory was relieved. "They really are trying to work with us," he thought. "This is not going to be, you know, a slash-and-burn operation. They basically are going to take what we have done and modify it in some ways that can easily be accommodated." He was further heartened when Pope John Paul II invited him for a brief audience. The pope did not mention the Charter specifically, except to express his hope that Gregory would work with the Curia officials.

"How are the people in the United States?" the pope asked. "And how are the bishops? Take my pastoral solicitude and support to the bishops."

From these remarks, Gregory concluded that the pope was still monitoring the situation closely, and trusting that the revised Charter would meet the demands of the American crisis. Knowing the rejection would not play well in the press, Gregory was nonetheless relieved that in principle it had passed muster with the Vatican. When a member of his staff asked him when the revisions might be completed, he said, "Soon—certainly by our November meeting."

"Oh, Bishop," the employee said, "that would be a miracle."

"I believe in miracles," Gregory said.

October 16, 2002
BOSTON, MASSACHUSETTS — The financial committee of Voice of the Faithful had raised $55,800 in donations from area Catholics who wanted to support charities but could not bring themselves to mail the money in directly. In a bad economy and an endless scandal, it was an unexpectedly sizeable sum. On this crisp Wednesday morning, they dropped the check in the mail to Cardinal Law—with a stipulation. He was not to spend a cent on lawyers or fancy PR firms or other administration overhead, and the donors required an accounting of how it was used, an especially provocative provision. The archdiocese only ever released vague, aggregate financial figures.

They waited for an answer, not expecting it would go their way. When Law first learned they were collecting the money, he denounced the group for circumventing his authority. "The archdiocese cannot accept this initiative of Voice of the Faithful, or the monies collected in this manner because it undercuts that customary means of financial support to the mission of the church in this archdiocese, which is the Cardinal's Appeal. This approach of donating money to the mission of the church does not recognize the role of the archbishop and his responsibility in providing for the various programs and activities of the church," a statement said.

According to Voice's arrangement with its fiscal agent, the nonprofit National Catholic Community Foundation, if Law were to return the check, it would then be offered to Boston's Catholic Charities. Leaders there had said they were eager to accept it to finance more than

150 programs, including visiting nurses, job training, and food pantries that were suffering as a result of the scandal. Donation envelopes were coming back in the mail empty, scrawled with the word "No." This was not just a Boston phenomenon. A national survey found that almost 20 percent of the faithful had stopped donating to national Catholic causes, while 13 percent stopped contributing to diocesan collections and 6 percent were no longer tithing at their parish.

Some prominent Bostonians went the opposite direction, increasing their donations to help ease the burdens of the crisis on the poor. Fidelity Investments' Peter Lynch accelerated payouts on a pledge of $10 million he had previously made, so that the money would be on hand to help support programs. He also gave more than in previous years on the parish level and for support of inner-city parochial schools, his passionate commitment. "When there's a crisis, you have to say if you think the basic thing the Catholic Church does is a good thing or a great thing, and I think it is a great thing," he explained. "This was a very serious, egregious thing that was done by hundreds or thousands of people around the country. But the good work the church does is staggering."

It would not be enough. Boston's Catholic Charities had already been forced to lay off over 250 employees. The Cardinal's Appeal was faring worse. Last year it drew in $16 million; this year it was on track for about half that. Thirty percent of archdiocesan staffers had been laid off in recent weeks. There was talk of bankruptcy. The gesture of a $55,800 gift from Voice of the Faithful, a drop in the bucket, was nonetheless desperately needed.

But Law declared that the semiautonomous agency was not permitted to act unilaterally. And then he turned back the check.

In an effort to establish a broad pattern and practice of shuffling abusive priests, Eric MacLeish filed a daring motion seeking every record for every Boston priest ever accused of sexual improprieties. In theory, this would encompass substantially the same records the archdiocese had made available to prosecutors, some thirty thousand pages of memos covering nearly a hundred priests going back fifty years. MacLeish said he needed this comprehensive overview to prove his core allegation: that it was neither a judgment error nor a communications slipup that kept Paul Shanley in ministry, but a deliberate policy designed to limit liability and evade prosecution.

Despite vigorous opposition from the church, Judge Sweeney concluded that the law was on MacLeish's side. A new lawyer hired by the archdiocese to co-counsel the cases alongside the Rogers family—an aggressive former judge named J. Owen Todd—filed an appeal and sought an emergency stay. But on October 16, Appeals Court judge Kenneth Laurence upheld Sweeney's order. He gave the archdiocese just short of two months to turn over the documents to MacLeish.

At the time, MacLeish called this one of the most significant rulings so far in his various lawsuits. He had no idea just how significant it was.

October 29, 2002

DRACUT, MASSACHUSETTS — A steady stream of cars coasted into the parking lot behind St. Francis Parish at the crossroads of Wheeler and Parker roads, a simple New England structure planted amid acres of lush farmland, the elegiac meadows of Robert Frost's north-of-Boston muses. This was to be a top-secret gathering, specifically excluding media. This had been a point of some internal strife among the Survivors of Joseph Birmingham. Since his change of heart on going public, Gary Bergeron now believed that nothing should be kept in the shadows. He argued fiercely for throwing open the doors to the glare of the press. When he began telling people he wanted to meet the cardinal face-to-face, people told him he'd have a better chance getting on the appointment calendar of Jesus Christ. But they had met several times now. Law had received other Birmingham victims, too. In this process, Gary sensed, Law had begun to gain that human emotional response to the crisis that he'd long lacked. They'd broken through his defenses. And really, it wasn't that difficult at all. As the poet wrote, something there is that doesn't love a wall.

Law was finally meeting victims on their own turf. It was time to show this in public, to let Catholics know their cardinal's blood ran warm. This was the watershed in the crisis. Gary felt sure that every Roman Catholic in Boston and America had a stake in seeing how this came off.

Olan Horne's disagreement wasn't philosophical, but strategic. "I promised Bernie this was gonna be us and him, mano a mano," he said. "I can't go back on that."

Ultimately, they reached a compromise. The Law meeting would take place in an undisclosed location, that being St. Francis, and the media would be invited to wait at a nearby VFW hall to receive any members of SOJB or the church hierarchy who wished to speak their minds. Gary was elected to explain these rules to the press—he was on the phone for nearly an hour apologizing to Walter Robinson at the *Globe,* but asking for forbearance nonetheless. Reluctantly, Robinson agreed to the stipulation. At least, that was Gary's impression. But when the meeting was about to begin, Gary spotted an unmistakable golden coiffure slipping through the St. Francis door.

"Sacha Pfeiffer," he called out in a hurt voice. "What are you doing here?"

She had simply done her reportorial legwork: she called other likely invitees and innocently inquired, "How do I get to tonight's meeting?" Gary personally walked her back out the door. What he didn't know was that another reporter from the *Globe* had already gotten inside— Erica Noonan blended in easily with the large crowd. Her reporting would become the only record of this historic meeting.

The night's parameters were simple. Don't talk about the lawsuits or the legal issues; save that for the courtroom. Don't focus blame— the released documents were all the "gotcha" anybody needed; it was already plain who was at fault. Do talk about how Law's own decisions impacted your life. Show how vast the impact zone really was, beyond you to your parents, siblings, spouses, children. Show him *why* he needs to take responsibility. And keep it under three minutes.

When the cardinal arrived, in his long black cassock, he was en-folded by a fidgety entourage of priests and PR executives. By coinci-dence, it was the fortieth anniversary of Vatican II. It was appropriate, though entirely coincidental, that Cardinal Law took this day to leave his beautiful residence and come to see the other Catholics, the wounded and ostracized, the victims.

Stepping inside St. Francis and sitting at a long folding table, he began what people thought he should have started in 1984, a gesture of reconciliation. To be sure, most top church leaders elsewhere had also tried the above-the-fray posture, obviously aiming to appear princely and unsullied, rather than miserly and unyielding. Only two other bishops had met with survivors' groups—just a week earlier the new Milwaukee archbishop, Timothy M. Dolan, met publicly with victims, while Bishop Frank Rodimer of Paterson, New Jersey, had begun meeting with abuse survivors in April.

In some way, coming here was playing it safe. The Shanley and Geoghan claimants would peel off his skin, and the men who accused Bernie Lane or Ronald Paquin, and the members of the survivors' coalitions, would eat him alive. At least the way Bernie McDaid, Olan Horne, and the Bergeron brothers had explained it to him, the Birmingham group was unique in one key way. More than anything, they wanted the church to save itself. They felt the legacy of their abuse would be compounded a thousand times over if it led to the church's demise. They had enough to deal with without that on their heads. Some individual members had demanded Law's resignation, but the majority believed he must stay in office and solve the mess he helped create, not leave it to another generation. In Boston today, that was the warmest audience Law could hope to find.

"It crossed my mind that maybe he's doing this as a public relations move," Dave Lyko told the woman standing beside him. "But it's better than what he's been doing, which is not speaking, and ducking everybody. And even if it is a PR move, we don't care, because to have some dialogue is better than no dialogue."

Cardinal Law began a brief, unscripted atonement. "Apology is a weak thing, but I don't know how else to begin," he said. "I beg your forgiveness and I understand that can be a very difficult thing to give because the hurt is so deep, the memory so raw, and the wound so searing."

His eyes downcast, shoulders folded forward, he was overcome with contrition and remorse, crushed by the recognition of his legacy.

When he was done speaking, Bernie McDaid, who was running the meeting, opened the floor to comments. One by one the children of Boston rose on shaky legs to unfasten their secrets, their many past tragedies, like war veterans remembering the battles that claimed their limbs. It was a tableau of profound sorrow and grief spanning generations, seventy-five men and their families bound together by the serial crimes of a single priest, the compounding crimes of his superiors, united by a conviction that their sadness was avoidable, that anyone with a shred of sympathy could and would have spared the children.

Cardinal Law may have thought back on a line he wrote in the *Pilot* ten years earlier, in the wake of the Porter case, a line he clearly never truly understood until now. "From such evil acts, like a pebble dropped into a placid pool of water, there are ever-widening, concentric circles of betrayal and anguish."

There was no rancor. The speakers were fixed on a need to give words to woes, to stand in the light of this church basement and formulate a terrible truth, to lay their burdensome memories in the lap of this cardinal for him to feel the hideous weight and contour of them.

He could offer nothing in return but his ear. In places like South Africa and Sierra Leone, Guatemala and Chile, as truth and reconciliation commissions have built bridges between the wounded and the wounders, between the terrible past and a necessary future, so began a process of healing here, in a low-ceilinged hall on a desolate night.

When it was his turn to speak, even Paul Ciaramitaro, ordinarily so wound up and seething, was carried up in the spirit of truth telling. Looking into the crowded room, he said, "I want to ask for a moment of silence for the victims of Joseph Birmingham whose shame was so great they committed suicide." Six stood. Six bodies representing six others no longer here, friendly-fire casualties of the Catholic Church.

Law had known Birmingham. How could a man who appeared genial to his peers be for others a memory so dank they'd rather die? How could the touch of a hand do this? He had no answer. He lowered his head in silent prayer. Gail Sweeney's two brothers were abused by Birmingham; one took his life, and she stood for him. She would not allow Law to retreat from the sight of her.

"Don't close your eyes," she called out. "Look at us."

He did look up, agonized with knowledge, meeting one face after another after another throughout the quiet room.

When he spoke, he quavered. "I have the pain of someone who made terrible mistakes and caused you pain. It is a terrible, terrible, painful past."

Hearing that, Gary knew they had gotten through at last.

Sunday, November 3, 2002
BRIDGEPORT, CONNECTICUT — Simultaneously in each of the eighty-seven parishes that comprise this Roman Catholic diocese in western Connecticut, priests stood before their congregations and read aloud from a letter written by Bishop William Lori. It was highly unusual for him to make such a direct and coordinated appeal. But on this subject, he was tenacious. "I ask you to stand up for the truth about marriage and family in the Creator's plan," he wrote. "I urge you to join with fellow citizens in opposing legislation that would legalize same-sex unions in the State of Connecticut."

There was no bill wending through the Connecticut statehouse. There was no legislation whatsoever to comment on. An advocacy group called Love Makes a Family had promised to introduce two bills in the following year, one calling for extending marriage rights and re-sponsibilities to gays without limitation, and a less encompassing bill to establish "civil unions" along the model available in Vermont. This would establish a kind of parallel marriage track for same-sex couples (or offbeat straights—in New York City, which adopted a less official "domestic partnership" registration office, 55 percent of registrants were heterosexual couples). Neither bill was expected to gain much support. But the Bridgeport diocese—as well as the Norwich diocese and the archdiocese of Hartford—had agreed to circulate a petition today at the request of the Knights of Columbus. The all-male Catholic organization officially clung to a view of homosexuals as the product of absent fathers and coddling or domineering mothers, ar-rested in childhood, and treatable by prayerful intervention—they must be pulled *away* from their genital relationships, they argued, not given the benefits and false assurances conferred by marriage. "There is, moreover, a profound sterility in homosexual relationships," according to a Knights of Columbus publication, "because there are no transcendent goals and no family history. What the homosexual needs is to integrate one's bodily desires into a purpose beyond self-gratification. This means a conscious and free sublimation of sexual desire into some form of service for the community."

A team of Knights of Columbus volunteers stood in the back of each Connecticut church, clipboards and pens at the ready. They planned to come back Sunday after Sunday in an effort to reach all 1.3 million Catholics in Connecticut, about 40 percent of the state's population.

Bishop Lori's letter continued: "Current marriage law is not discriminatory. But same-sex legislation would violate our civil rights. For example, in Vermont, where same-sex civil unions have been legalized, the law penalizes justices of the peace who conscientiously refuse to participate in such ceremonies. Already the education of our children in public schools is being impacted. Some public school textbooks wrongly state that the Gospel does not prohibit homosexual activity. If marriage law in Connecticut is changed, your children will be taught distorted views concerning marriage and family that you may have little ability to change."

Of the thousand ordained priests throughout Connecticut, as many as half were themselves gay, if estimates were correct, and surely a portion of them were involved in secret relationships. Perhaps a few were in love, despite the risks. But they read Lori's words anyway. With the Knights of Columbus foot soldiers in the back of the room, it was almost impossible not to. This struck Anne Stanback, the president of Love Makes a Family, as perverse. "Makes you wonder what's going on in their minds," she said.

It also struck her as strange that Lori and the Knights of Columbus chose this topic to address amid the biggest crisis in the history of the American Catholic Church. But Robert Goosens, a chapter officer with the Knights, didn't see the incongruity. "This is about protecting marriage," he told a reporter. "It has nothing to do with what's going on with the priests and sexual abuse."

LOWELL, MASSACHUSETTS — Gary Bergeron had not been to Sunday
Mass for at least a decade. He had absolutely no explanation, then, for
why he fired up his enormous wall-sized television set this Sunday
morning, thumbing the remote till he got to BCTV, the official network of the Roman Catholic archdiocese of Boston. He did all this
just as cameras panned from nearly empty pews to capture the cardinal reaching the last steps of his procession, doffing his miter, and
passing his crosier to a handsome young altar server—an earnest
young woman (what a surprise). The cardinal carried himself to the lip
of the raised platform that held the altar, and lifted before him a
sheath of pages, which shivered in the long fingers of his unstill hand.

"Earlier this week, I was privileged and blessed to meet with a truly
inspiring group of people who had been sexually abused as children by
a priest," he read. "They had invited me to join them and their family
members and friends who gathered with them as they continued their
own efforts to deal with the devastating effects of the abuse they endured. That meeting, although difficult and painful at times, was truly
an occasion of grace for me and, I hope and pray, for all of those with
whom I gathered."

Gary called Bernie McDaid. "Turn on the TV, you're not going to
believe this," he said. In his home in Lynn, Bernie sat on a sofa with
his seven-year-old son, holding the telephone to his ear, listening with
Gary.

"It was suggested during our time together," Law continued, "that it
would be good for me to address, more publicly and frequently, a
number of issues which came up in the course of our time together.
After all, there are many other people who have been abused by other
priests. I told them that I would be willing to do just that. What follows now is a sincere attempt to honor the spirit of our meeting. I am
indeed indebted to all of those who contributed so much by their presence, words, and actions earlier this week.

"It almost seems like an eternity away, yet it was in January of this
year that the crisis of sexual abuse of children by clergy began to dominate our consciousness. Ten months later, I stand before you with a
far deeper awareness of this terrible evil than I had at that time.

"No one who has not experienced sexual abuse as a child can fully comprehend the devastating effects of this horrible sin. Nor is it possible for someone else to comprehend the degree of pain, of confusion, of self-doubt, and of anger that a mother or father feels with the knowledge that her child, that his child, has been sexually abused by a priest. Who can know the burden of a wife or husband of someone who was abused as a child?

"I do not pretend to fully comprehend the devastating consequences of the sexual abuse of children. Over these past ten months, however, I have been focused in a singular way on this evil and on what it has done to the lives of so many. As I have listened personally to the stories of men and women who have endured such abuse, I have learned that some of these consequences include lifelong struggles with alcohol and drug abuse, depression, difficulty in maintaining relationships, and, sadly, even suicide.

"It is impossible to think of an act of sexual abuse of a child in isolation. There is inevitably a ripple effect from this evil act which spreads out and touches the lives of all of us. Clearly, these evil acts have touched our life together as an Archdiocese. Our relationships have been damaged. Trust has been broken.

"When I was a young man I was profoundly influenced by different priests. They represented all that was good to me. During my high school years, Father Mark Knoll, a Redemptorist priest, was a great mentor. During my college years, Bishop Lawrence J. Riley and Father Joseph Collins made a lasting impact upon my life. Like countless others, I placed great trust in them.

"One of the insidious consequences of the sexual abuse of a child by a priest is the rupturing of that sacred trust. For some victim-survivors, not only is it difficult to trust priests again, but the Church herself is mistrusted. Many victim-survivors and their family members find it impossible to continue to live out their lives as Catholics, or even to enter a Catholic church building."

Saying this, his voice shattered. He attempted to look up at his flock, but could not. He was crying.

"With all my heart I apologize for this, once again," his voice cracked. "The forgiving love of God gives me the courage to beg forgiveness of those who have suffered because of what I did. As I beg your forgiveness, I pledge my unyielding efforts to insure that this never happens again."

For a long time, Bernie McDaid and Gary Bergeron hung on the line in silence. Then Bernie cleared the emotion from his throat.

"Jesus Christ," he said. "Look what we did. We made him understand."

November 4, 2002
ROME — Mary Ann Glendon, a Harvard Law School professor and influential opinion maker, addressed an audience gathered at the Regina Apostolorum Pontifical Athenaeum for an international conference. The theme of her speech was "reform, renewal, and the role of the laity in a time of turbulence." As a laywoman herself, she had a great deal to say about groups like Voice of the Faithful, none of it good.

"Now I need to say that it is understandable that many well-intentioned laypersons have been drawn into these movements. Many Catholics are deeply concerned about recent revelations of clerical sexual abuse; they want to do something about it, and they are grasping the slogans that are in the air. But slogans about structural reform and power sharing did not come from nowhere. They are the catchwords of what I call the generation of failed theories—theories about politics, economics and human sexuality that can now be seen to have taken a terrible human toll wherever they were put into practice. The die-hards who still cling to those ideas have seized on the crisis of 2002 as their last opportunity to transform American Catholicism into something more compatible with the spirit of the age of their youth."

In this, she said, they had a co-conspirator in the press. "I must part company with many of my fellow Catholics who have profusely thanked the media for bringing a serious problem to public attention. I could not disagree more. The fact that confusion reigns among the laity about what is to be done is due to the fact that the only narrative available to them—as they struggled to understand what was going on—was supplied by media accounts that were false in several crucial respects, of which I will name three:

"First: For months, the media played the story as though sexual abuse of minors by Catholic priests was breaking news, something that was happening right now. Later, they began to dribble out the information that nearly all the reported cases took place long ago—in the 1960s, '70s and '80s. Was it really news that a tiny minority of Catholic priests succumbed to the general sexual bacchanalia of those years? Yet, these old stories of clerical sexual abuse were the second most heavily reported story of 2002, second only to the war against terrorism.

"Second: falsehood. For months, the press created a climate of hysteria by describing the story as a pedophilia crisis, when in fact only a tiny minority of the reported cases involved pedophiles—abusers of prepubescent children—as distinct from homosexual relations with teen-aged boys.

"Third: For months, and to this day, the media has singled out the Catholic Church as a special locus of sexual abuse of minors, whereas all the studies indicate that the incidence of these types of misconduct is actually lower among Catholic priests than among other groups who have access to young children. . . .

"I often hear it said that the *Globe* will receive a Pulitzer Prize for its reporting on this matter. All I can say is that if fairness and accuracy have anything to do with it, awarding the Pulitzer Prize to the *Boston Globe* would be like giving the Nobel Peace Prize to Osama bin Laden."

Monday, November 11, 2002
WASHINGTON, D.C. — In the early hours of the morning, as the nation's bishops were stirring in their hotel rooms for two days of meetings to finally adopt their Charter to protect children, a warm breeze laced the capital district. Then a hot breeze. Suddenly came gale winds at sixty miles an hour, driven into Washington by a wall of frigid Canadian air racing across the Midwest and equal hot forces storming north from the Caribbean and the Gulf of Mexico. In the capital, where the fall foliage was at its colorful peak, enormous trees pirouetted in the rainy winds, slinging broken limbs like javelins through the

streets. It was not possible to see more than a few feet. The storm shrieked eerily past street signs and around building edges, but this did not daunt the protesters who had traveled to D.C. from across the United States. At dawn, they had begun assembling in the storm outside the Hyatt Regency on Capitol Hill, where the bishops were staying. They wore clear plastic tarps and in their sodden hands carried red octagonal signs that read, "Stop Spiritual Violence." There were fifty-four of them in a line stretching silently against the gray horizon. As reporters arrived in taxis and vans, and raced through the weather to the lobby, the protesters went largely unnoticed. "No bishop even looked at us," remarked Judy Osborne, who had traveled from Seattle, "much less said hello."

The group was called SoulForce, and represented gay, lesbian, bisexual, and transgender people of many faiths, not just Catholics. They had sent a letter to Bishop Gregory saying they planned to bring with them gifts intended for people with AIDS, and asked for an audience with him so that the parcels might receive his blessing. It was common for a bishop to bless such things, but this was a provocative request. If he refused the blessing, that would be seen as a sign of his hostility; if he granted it, it might show his acceptance for what the group stood for, which was full acceptance of gays, which was against church teaching. He chose to ignore the letter altogether, just as he had previous requests from the group.

They asked other bishops for blessings, too, but so far nobody had consented. Diana G. Westbrook, who had traveled here from Richmond, Virginia, wasn't expecting a visit from any of the men in black. "Bishops and priests will bless anything. They'll bless a soccer ball, if you asked them to. But they will never bless our gifts because we're gay, lesbian, bisexual, and transgender."

Much to the bishops' frustration, media interest in the crisis remained strong. Sister Mary Ann Walsh, the gruff-voiced spokeswoman for the United States Conference of Catholic Bishops, received applications from over three hundred reporters to cover the gathering. Arbitrarily she limited the number of credentials to a fraction of that. In icy silence, she heard out the many complaints from the journalists she rejected, but she was moved to reproach, not pity, and stood her ground.

Perhaps with this policy she hoped to limit the coverage of the scandal, but it had an unexpected countereffect. Scores of banished reporters came to Washington anyway, and set up shop in the Hyatt's lobby, where a choreography of dissent was being staged amid a sluggish stream of jazz music piped throughout the lobby and corridors.

Representatives of Voice of the Faithful were distributing position papers and reports on various bishops. In a back meeting room, representatives of twenty reform groups were meeting to see about coordinating offensives, according to organizers from Catholics for Free Choice, a pro-choice group, while a new advocacy effort called Survivors First introduced a Web site on which were posted the names of priests accused of sexual abuse, culled from court papers and news accounts—fifteen hundred names in all. David Clohessy stood at the foot of the escalator holding a continual press conference, answering the same questions over and over on behalf of SNAP, which now claimed more than four thousand members. In the lobby, an intense woman with heavy mascara named Maria Ferrara Pema, whose head was wrapped tightly in a turban, was promoting an autobiography she had written and self-published titled *Anatomy of a Life Possessed,* which according to her press release contained "The Shocking True Story of a Beautiful Actress Possessed and Tortured by a Catholic Priest!" (Her biography said she had made an appearance in Fellini's *Satyricon.*) "One thing is physically to be possessed, it is very harmful, but all the victim people, all who are here, first we were *spiritually* possessed," she told anyone who would listen. "That is the worst. Because you are lost. Betrayed. Your spirit is missing."

Their stories would figure prominently in the day's media coverage. Chagrined, Sister Walsh had signs placed around the lobby declaring it off limits to television and still cameras. Violators would be expelled from the premises. She also warned members of SNAP, Call to Action, Dignity, Catholics for Free Choice, Voice of the Faithful, and the other reform groups to stay out of the building or face trespassing charges. Private security guards began hustling offenders outdoors. They were not even permitted to speak to reporters under the hotel's large awning, but were pushed out to the sidewalk under a weeping sky.

"The bishops are still trying to circle the wagons, silence the victims, and keep our voices from being heard," Father Gary Hayes, an abuse survivor and activist from Kentucky, complained as he was being hustled out of the building.

"Their voices are heard all the time," Walsh snapped when queried by a reporter from the *New York Times*. "It's not possible to keep people's voices from being heard—and only a fool would try. We're simply trying to keep a sense of order here, and TV interviews in the lobby create a sense of chaos."

Not one person among the thousand or so who gathered for the conference believed her.

Amid this guerrilla struggle, there was neither optimism nor dread among the activists, only angry determination. Father Tom Doyle had grown concerned that the entire survivors' movement had locked itself into a self-perpetuating cosmology of rage. On the eve of the conference, he had sent out a mass e-mail to his old friends, gently encouraging them to search for an avenue of closure. It was not widely heeded. Father Hayes, for one, was put in poor humor by the suggestion, which lately he'd been hearing a lot. "One of my brother priests said to me, 'Some of the brothers are wondering when you're going to get over this.' I said, 'Tell my brothers to get over the fact that I am not over it. How am I supposed to get over it? What does that mean? *Get over it?*' " He looked through the rain-streaked window. "There's an old gospel saying, 'The gospel is meant to comfort the disturbed and disturb the comfortable.' So, I'm just glad they're disturbed."

The bishops had packed their agenda with many non-abuse-related items, from condemning war on Iraq and domestic violence to significant changes in liturgy to evangelical aims and goals. But the only subject anybody wanted to hear them pronounce on now was the revised Charter for the Protection of Children and Young People. As Bishop Gregory had predicted, the mixed commission mandated by Rome had completed its work more than a week before, following a two-day summit in Rome. In a PR blunder, the conference attempted to keep the findings secret. For several days news accounts speculated about what had been changed, relying upon leaks that were often wrong.

In fact, the Charter had been changed in significant ways, although

the zero-tolerance provision remained intact. Now, instead of giving allegations to a lay panel for formal review, the lay panels were specifically called "advisory." All evidence regarding a suspected abuser
would instead be forwarded to Rome's Congregation for the Doctrine
of the Faith, where a secret hearing might take place or, at the discretion of the congregation's staff, the matter might be remanded back to
ecclesiastic tribunals run by the diocese, also closed to the public.
This looked for all the world like a full retreat from transparency. But
Vatican officials were privately saying it was necessary for preventing
"kangaroo courts" and for guaranteeing due process to the accused
priests.

Further, the new document recommitted the church in its procedures to following a statute of limitations, either the canon law limit
(ten years from the victim's eighteenth birthday) or state law,
whichever is more generous. By this standard, most of the hundreds of
priests removed in 2002 would not be subject to church sanction. For
this reason there was a clause added giving American bishops the opportunity to request a waiver of the statute on a case-by-case basis.
But this gave discretion back to the very men Americans held liable for
the abuse crisis in the first place.

"The survivors I've spoken to in the last four or five days feel very,
very betrayed," David Clohessy told a reporter. "Pragmatically, this is a
huge retreat. Look at this: they keep using words like due process,
words that are applicable to criminal proceedings, but this isn't criminal court. This is like professional ethics and professional licensure review boards. If you're a therapist, and you admit you molested a kid
thirty years ago, the fellow therapists don't say, 'Well, that's beyond our
statute.' No. They yank a license. That's what this is about. If we were
going to lock people up or execute them, then a more rigorous sort of
due-process standard would be applicable."

A showdown seemed in the offing. Bishop Gregory, for one, was
dreading what he called "Dallas Two." Clohessy had left him several
telephone messages in the previous weeks, and he had not found the
emotional strength or diplomatic courage to return the calls. He made
no provisions for survivors to speak at the Washington meeting. Many
bishops left the Dallas meeting simmering mad at Gregory for sub-

jecting them to such a vitriolic public tongue-lashing. Even Gregory's touching displays of contriteness irked many of his brother bishops. But what most galvanized the country's bishops against him were his appointments to the lay commission designed to monitor compliance with the Charter, especially the tough-talking Governor Frank Keating. "The last thing that the Catholic bishops needed at that moment was leadership that was deferential," he explained in his defense. "People would say, 'Well of course they just appointed someone who will tell them everything they wanted to hear, never question them, never challenge them, never probe.'"

Now with his own leadership wounded, Gregory would back away from the fiery rhetoric that was so inspiring in Dallas. When he rose on Monday morning to address the assembly, he seemed tired and drawn.

"Brother Bishops, my Sisters and Brothers in Christ. In a few short weeks during the Season of Advent, we shall listen again to the opening words of the fortieth chapter of the Book of Isaiah. The prophet is speaking in the name of God to the people of Israel who have long been in exile in Babylon. The Israelites are broken and afraid; they are dispirited and uncertain of their future. They needed a word of hope. Isaiah steps into their midst and declares in God's name: *Comfort, give comfort to my people, says your God.*"

Bishop Gregory did not look up from his prepared remarks, but rather read them with detachment from the dais. He encouraged his fellow bishops to do more to spread comfort, especially in this difficult time. It was time to close ranks, to try to contain the discussion of abuse, cover-up, and scandal, and return to the work of the church. So he turned his rebukes outward.

"As bishops, we should have no illusions about the intent of some people who have shown more than a casual interest in the discord we have experienced within the Church this year," he said. "There are those outside the Church who are hostile to the very principles and teachings that the Church espouses, and have chosen this moment to advance the acceptance of practices and ways of life that the Church cannot and will never condone. Sadly, even among the baptized, there are those at extremes within the Church who have chosen to exploit the vulnerability of the bishops in this moment to advance their own agendas. One cannot fail to hear in the distance—and sometimes very nearby—the call of the false prophet, 'Let us strike the shepherd and scatter the flock.' We bishops need to recognize this call and to name it clearly for what it is."

Was he talking about the news media? Voice of the Faithful? SNAP and Linkup, the other national group for abuse survivors? He did not say, and would not clarify when asked by reporters. Rather, he then marched the bishops through two days of meetings, after which they adopted the revised Charter, 246 voting in favor and seven against, with six abstentions. By a similar plurality, they adopted a strongly worded resolution against the war the United States was preparing to wage on Iraq. In the frenzy around sex abuse by priests, this measure went unnoticed by most Americans, especially the president and his administration. Even conservative commentator and cradle Catholic Bill O'Reilly lamented the bishops' squandered moral imperative and corroded national stature. "Isn't it true there is no moral leadership in the American Catholic Church right now?" he asked his audience. "Isn't that a fact?"

It was the church's worst nightmare, and it had come to pass. As the flock knew, the shepherds had struck themselves.

Wednesday, November 27, 2002
BELLEVILLE, ILLINOIS — It was Thanksgiving week, and Bishop Wilton Gregory was driving to the far reaches of his diocese along unbending farm country roads to deliver his traditional Thanksgiving Mass, wondering what in the world there was to give thanks for this year.

He had tried to resume life as a simple shepherd in his church. He performed four weddings—more than in any summer in his nineteen years as a bishop. He blessed the crops, the herds, and the farm machinery, blessed statues of the Virgin Mary, prayed for the young, and visited the aged on their deathbeds. But always there were telephone calls from reporters to remind him of the church's troubles. The headlines were never-ending. He found some schadenfreude in the parallel revelations about other pillars of American life, especially the collapse of Enron and the self-destruction of its accounting firm, Arthur Andersen. Both cases helped convince him that in general moral stewardship was in short supply in America. In other words, people were sinful, as the church always taught. They would make mistakes, some even while wearing the Roman collar. But the institution—the Roman Catholic Church—remained blameless and pure.

"Obviously, we have been caught in a most compromised position— *most* compromised," he confided to his passenger. "I have given my life—and I don't regret this one bit—to the vision of life and creation of humanity that is to be found in the gospels and in the teachings and traditions of the church. No matter how many exposés may be brought to the public attention, I still believe that the vision of life and creation and the human person's destiny that has been proclaimed by the Catholic Church is noble and the right one. I say this with the same kind of intensity and conviction that we as Americans can say, 'Simply because we have a corrupt politician or corrupt public official, we don't stop believing in our country.'"

It gave him a measure of comfort, but casting priests in with the lot of corrupt accountants and corporate executives still weighed too heavily. "That is a hell of a position for society to be in," he said. "What do parents tell their children? Who do parents tell their children, 'Be like that person, here's somebody you can trust'? Who do we hold up as an ideal of integrity and trustworthiness," if not a priest?

No, he did not have much to be thankful for.

BOSTON, MASSACHUSETTS — The massive crates of church files Judge Sweeney ordered be turned over finally arrived at Greenberg Traurig late in the day. Eric MacLeish had not expected them to be so voluminous. Dozens and dozens of boxes contained the dense narratives of inappropriate and wounded lives. Over 150 complaints. Medical records, police records, draft press releases, forced retirement ceremonies, in total thousands of pages of detailed personnel files. Among the names were thirty-nine priests whose accusations had never before been made public. Connecting the dots to narrate these histories would be an enormous undertaking but potentially essential to the litigation. MacLeish gave his staff a week. We'll release these to the public in dribs as soon as we know what they are, he told them. He would call his first press conference for the following Wednesday.

For Courtney Pillsbury and David Thomas it would be a very long week. That afternoon they began their labors. After all they'd seen this year, they thought they were beyond the stage where they could be shocked. They were wrong.

James Foley was a curate at St. Joseph Parish in Salem. By some mix-up, his folder had been bundled together with another Father Foley, a long-dead pedophile. But the living Foley's file contained a far more intriguing narration. Beginning in the early sixties, psychiatrists labeled him "brittle, insecure and suspicious," and noted he struggled with "disordered thoughts." He was hospitalized for recurring breakdowns in 1964 and 1968 and 1996, the last time after a motor vehicle arrest when he argued that red lights were only for others.

His main problem seemed to be obsessional love affairs with teenage mothers. With one woman, he had fathered two children, all behind the back of her husband. There was no indication that the children, who today would be in their thirties, were aware of his paternity.

"He seemed capable of living a dual life," Courtney read from a confidential record.

Something else caught her eye. Written in a dry expository was the notation that the woman had been lobotomized. Diane Nealon looked over the files. "Lifelong battle with depression. That's what they did back then." The woman was perhaps no more able to consent to sex than if she were a toddler.

The file got more horrific by the page. A handwritten memo dated December 23, 1993, bore the initials BCL. The flowery handwriting was unmistakably Bernard Law's. These appeared to be the record of a meeting between Foley and the cardinal about an event that occurred sometime in the late 1960s.

"Relationship with married woman. Overdosed. He was present. He clothed. Left. Came back. Called 911. She died. A sister knows."

Holy shit, David Thomas thought. "This man was present at the death of a woman that he fathered children with. He confessed it to Law! Could it get more disgusting?"

Law's notes went on to itemize his three concerns. *Scandal*. Was
the sister likely to break her silence? *Spiritual welfare*. Was Foley right
with God? *Emotional and psychological well-being*. Could he use a
shrink? As he had promised he would, Law took the case to his much-
hyped review board. The records did not reveal details of the deliberations there. But several times over the next several years, according to
single-page verdict forms they produced, Foley was sent back to ministry, albeit with some limits (he was not to officiate at funerals or confessions, "because they could involve vulnerable women").

On another handwritten document, this one signed by John Mc-
Cormack, there was written one more concern, underscored twice:
"CRIMINAL ACTIVITY?"

Lacking was any suggestion that the archdiocese ever went to the
police. Worse, in page after page of damning records, there was not
one stroke mentioning the children who lost their mother.

Reading through to the last sheet, Diane Nealon was in distress.
Her anger was a fish line around her throat. "Can anybody get their
head around this? We're not suing a tobacco company or Enron. This
is the Catholic Church."

Friday, November 29, 2002
LOWELL, MASSACHUSETTS — "Barbara," Olan said through the telephone, "there's going to be something really bad coming out. We don't
think he can withstand this."

He reached Barbara Thorp on her cell phone in her car. Like everybody in the archdiocese, she was braced for whatever these new documents might include. She dreaded more chaos. She prayed
frequently for the healing that wasn't coming. Though no one on the
church payroll had been more of an advocate for honesty and truth
telling, she was tired of it and wished it would end—wished there
was no more ugly truth to tell. "I stepped into some kind of a Salvador
Dalí painting," she thought. She didn't know how to step back out
of it.

"What is it?"

"Really bad," Olan said. He, Gary, and Bernie had been briefed by
their attorneys on the new files. They were sickened. This, they knew,

was the final test for Law's leadership. If he didn't rise from his slumber now, he would be lost.

"There's going to be a big press conference Monday. Barbara, you got to get us in to see him. Now or never. Now's the time."

It was the first time she thought her boss might be finished. Her heart skipped.

"I'll try," she said.

Chapter 15

Faith and Morals

Sunday, December 1, 2002

Lowell, Massachusetts — Unable to sleep, Gary Bergeron slid out of bed at four-thirty in the morning. His dreams had been haunted by images of Law disappearing into a crowded blackness. He didn't understand why Law was not taking his or Bernie's or Olan's calls. He was more and more certain that Law was slipping away, becoming the imperial cardinal again, brittle and doomed. He was afraid that something he helped set in motion might undo the cardinal's career. Nobody had invested more in the cardinal's humanity than Gary. He believed all that stuff he was saying about Law piecing back together the church shards. But it was more than that. He feared for his parents' faith. Their moods sank with each passing day. They loved their church desperately, even after what it had done to two generations of Bergerons.

They had a right to their faith, Gary thought. The church had a responsibility to honor that, to shore it up, to live up to its promise.

He saw clearly what had to happen. The Survivors of Joseph Birmingham must go to find Bernie Law on his turf—inside the cathedral. That's where the Law of his nightmares had retreated. The crowded blackness was a defensive sea of his bishops and priests, and if they wanted to reach him they would have to do something they hadn't done in decades: they would have to go to Mass. He flicked on his computer and typed out an e-mail message:

"Dear Olan, hear me out. You're going to think I'm a retard. I got a message from God last night. He wants to see us at 11 today. Call me when you read this e-mail."

He pushed the button expecting it would be hours before he heard a reply. But almost immediately, the telephone rang.

"I can't fucking believe you," Olan said. "I had the same fucking thought."

They e-mailed Barbara Thorp, who as it turned out was also sleepless and at her keyboard, and the three agreed to converge on the 11 A.M. Mass. As soon as it was late enough, Gary called Bernie and a handful of others from Survivors of Joseph Birmingham, enjoining them to come. "Now or never," he told them. "Time is running out."

When he arrived at the cathedral, Gary was stunned at the number of protesters crowding the sidewalk. Old stalwarts like Stephen Lewis, Ann Webb, and Lori Lambert were there, as were dozens of semi-familiar faces. But they were joined by scores more, people who had never been part of the anti-Law carnival before. The morning papers, which Gary had not yet read, held the explanation. According to sources reached by the *Boston Globe,* Law had abandoned all faith in negotiated settlements and was preparing the archdiocese of Boston to file for bankruptcy:

> Seeking Chapter 11 bankruptcy protection would be an unprecedented and risk-laden step for the U.S. Catholic church. It would suspend action in civil lawsuits and bar the filing of new suits while the church reorganizes its finances.
>
> Legal specialists noted other advantages: It would force the 450 claimants into a single group in the federal court and set a time limit for the filing of new claims. And it would give the federal bankruptcy court wide latitude in overseeing a global settlement.

The chancery now admitted it had already hired top corporate attorneys to handle the filing, and a high-flying crisis-management public relations firm to help make this solution look unavoidable and just, and palatable to the Catholic family at large. How improbable it seemed. The church still had undiluted real estate holdings worth in excess of $1.3 billion against no more than $100 million in claims.

Watching the Catholic church seek refuge from its moral obligations to the faithful it harmed was a spectacle so hideous that ordinary Catholics across the city descended on the cathedral steps to express their outrage. The clergy sex scandal cried out for resolution, not legal mastery in what the *Globe* called "the bloodless domain of bankruptcy court."

"At the very least, it's rank intimidation," complained Jeffrey Newman, another lawyer at Greenberg Traurig.

How could Law have retreated to this stance? The article quoted insiders saying Law now had no faith in his chances of getting a fair trial before Judge Sweeney. A week earlier, in a ruling the church protested as wildly biased, she had merely stated what at this point seemed obvious to everybody in America: despite Law's assertions that he never transferred known risks around the archdiocese, she wrote, "records obtained through discovery reveal that some offending priests may well have been assigned to parishes, youth groups and the like, even though the cardinal or other archdiocesan personnel knew that the priests in question were at the least suspected of engaging in continuing sexual encounters with children."

Scruples did not keep Gary from crossing the picket line, and as this was his first trip to Holy Cross Cathedral since his boyhood, he slipped past many of the weathered activists unnoticed and unheckled. His would be a parallel tactic. The cardinal had responded well to him, Bernie, and Olan, coming in and out of reach like a weak radio signal. If anybody was going to make him hear the desperate word from the street, to wrestle him fully into focus on the human tragedy, it would be them.

Gary joined Olan, Bernie, and Barbara in the frontmost pew. The men fidgeted like altar boys, challenging one another to remember names for the altar appointments, sometimes giggling like the kids from Lowell and Salem they once were. Several times, Thorp was forced to hush them.

After the Mass was finished and only the din of protesters outside filled the hallowed nave, Cardinal Law doffed his crosier and headed right toward the first row of pews, with obvious relief.

"Hi, boys," he said. "What are you doing here?"

"We have to talk to you," Gary said. "We've been trying to call."

"You have to do something. You have to *say* something," Olan pleaded, "and it has to change everything. Or this is all going to fall apart. Bernie. Bernie! Say something *monumental,* Bernie."

Law's blue eyes looked right through them, all of his vision was inside his head now. He slid onto the pew next to them.

Gary felt queasy. Law was a patient on the critical lip of consciousness, giving no clue which way he would balance out. All the work they had done to make a man out of the cardinal seemed lost now.

"Take off the mask," Olan said. "We want to see Bernie."

Gary leaned in close enough that Law could smell the tobacco on him.

"You know," he said, "we're all to blame for getting to this point, every single one of us. The church is to blame because you didn't recognize the problem, you didn't see it as a problem. The laypeople, because we promoted these priests to the point where they were next to God and let them lead us around by blind faith. I think *I'm* to blame. I could've said something twenty years ago. Or ten years ago. Everybody's a player in this. We all have to do more."

Outside, Steve Lewis's bullhorn was bleating against the cold, this and that about rapes and penetrations.

"Cardinal, we need to sit down and talk. We're a barometer for you about what's going on out there. When these documents come out things are going to get crazy, and when they do we won't be able to put the genie back in the bottle," said Gary.

Law patted him on the knee. "I don't know if you're barometers, but you're good boys, you're really good boys," he said. He rose to leave.

"Thank you for coming," Law called sadly. "Please, come see me this week."

"When? Bernie, Monday?"

"Oh, Olan, I'm not sure. You'll have to work it out with Father Connolly." He gestured toward his personal secretary, always at his side.

"How about it, Connolly? Monday? Tuesday?"

"How about Wednesday?" Connolly said. "Wednesday afternoon."

They were agreed.

"Bernie," Olan said, "it's been a very long time for us to be inside a church. We have one question. What are those things hanging over the altar, the red things?"

"Those?" Law's voice took on a tone of studied awe, as though he were regarding a weathered reliquary, or Celtics championship banners. "Those are the hats that belonged to my cardinal predecessors. When I first came to Boston I had them put up there to remember their service to the archdiocese."

He stood still before the display. Then a thought occurred to him, which he inadvertently spoke out loud.

"I have always wondered what of mine they would put up there when I'm gone."

To Gary, this was an important and telling remark—it signaled that the cardinal had no intention of stepping aside. He was still planning to march the church out of its crisis, laboring until his dying day. As he said when he was first incardinated here, "Next stop, heaven."

"Sheesh, Bernie," Olan said without a beat. "You're standing here among a bunch of victim-survivors wondering what thing of yours they're going to hoist up over the altar? I'll give you one guess, Bernie, and it's not your friggin' hat!"

Connolly was mortified. Thorp, a hand to her lips, was so stunned she wanted to cry. But Law laughed as though he had never heard anything funnier in his life.

Monday, December 2, 2002
BOSTON, MASSACHUSETTS — Gary Bergeron told Bob Sherman he did not want to attend the "document release party," as he called it. "I don't know why you're bringing in all the activists," he said. "You don't even represent some of these guys. All they're doing is tearing everything apart."

"Got to," Sherman told him.

The Greenberg Traurig firm was hosting a private informational meeting for every player in the battle with the church, every advocate and activist, every victim and survivor—even Mitchell Garabedian (who now had a score of new cases) and all the other independent attorneys. It was absolutely essential that every single activist be up to speed before the documents hit the press. MacLeish was playing this like a final offensive. To keep the pressure up, he was going to release them in batches, a few each day over the next week or more. The nauseating stories of corporate indifference were guaranteed to detonate deep and loud. The first explosion would take place on Tuesday at a MacLeish press conference.

"It's a courtesy."

By now, Greenberg Traurig was the unrivaled leader in the specialized bar representing priestly sex abuse victims. Between Eric MacLeish, Bob Sherman, Courtney Pillsbury, David Thomas, Jeffrey Newman, and Diane Nealon, the firm was handling over half the Boston cases. With this new stack of documents, they now controlled personnel files on 135 priests against whom accusations had been made.

When he arrived at the law offices, Gary felt like he'd stumbled backstage at *Jesus Christ Superstar*. Every face that ever made the papers all year was there, people he'd never met. Representatives of SNAP, STTOP, VOTF, SOJB—like it or not, this was the alphabet of his faith now, his church in exile.

Courtney Pillsbury hushed the large room. "I want to start with a policy point," she said. "We are all individuals here, each with our own ability to decide what we think about the church. Some people are going to say, 'I'll never set foot inside a church again in my life.' That's fine. But some people *will* go to church, and that is up to them to decide."

"Wait a fucking minute," Steve Lewis exploded. "I know where this is fucking coming from. If you think I'm going to take advice from *you*, you're sadly mistaken."

"Hey," Gary shouted. "You can't talk like that to Courtney." Then he noticed that all eyes in the room were burning down on him and the other Birmingham survivors. Lewis must have spotted them going into the cathedral yesterday, he realized. He must have riled up the victim community about it. Incensed, Gary craned to his feet. Nobody was going to dictate what kind of victim he would be.

"You owe this woman an apology," he shouted. "Apologize to this woman. Apologize to this woman!"

Unyielding and bullheaded, Lewis kept hollering back. "Anybody

who gives legitimacy to this cardinal, this *criminal,* is aiding and abetting as far as I'm concerned in the crime of child rape!"

Tuesday, December 3, 2002
BOSTON, MASSACHUSETTS — After what she had listened to all year,
Sacha Pfeiffer felt incapable of being scandalized anymore. She was
wrong. When Eric MacLeish snapped through the files of eight new
priests, PowerPointing the evidence of their sexual hideousness on the
big screen at his firm's conference room, she was blown away by the
seediness of the entire bunch. In twenty-two hundred pages of documents, most names were unfamiliar to her. This was a whole new vein
of scandal.

There was Father Thomas P. Forry, who besides twice beating
bruises into his housekeeper, carried on a ten-year sexual affair with a
married woman who accused him of fondling her young son and threatening her husband with death if he spoke to authorities. Disturbed by
his multiple pathologies, psychiatric clinicians recommended commit-
ting Forry to a clergy treatment center for six months. But Law disagreed, instead returning Forry to his South Weymouth parish
forthwith without word of his troubles. Law had removed him only earlier this year after the crisis first broke, but until now he had kept the
file secret. For some reason, Law had concluded that the case did not
involve minors. Yet the church paid a cash settlement to the boy to keep
his claim quiet, according to the file.

There was Father Peter J. Frost, an admitted sex addict and child
abuser whose misdeeds got him removed from active ministry in
1992—to whom Law wrote an unsolicited note warmly extolling his potential for *returning* to ministry. And Father Richard A. Buntel, who in
1983 was accused of giving a fifteen-year-old boy cocaine in exchange
for sex and was described as having a reputation for drug abuse and sexual cavorting. For his dual indulgences, parishioners had given him a
nickname: the "blow king of Malden."

And there was Father Robert V. Meffan, who acknowledged that he
recruited three teenage girls into religious life in part by insisting they
play "brides of Christ," a game that included fondling and kissing his

genitals. He caressed their breasts, encouraged them to masturbate in front of him, and recommended they attach unique sexual feelings to various biblical passages, though he eschewed intercourse, saying that was for "the afterlife." Did Law remove him from ministry? Not even when a top aide warned he was not "balanced" and "could really harm us." Rather, upon his old-age retirement in 1996 Law wrote him an unctuous farewell: "You have worked over these years to bring God's work and His love to His people. We are truly grateful for your priestly care and ministry to all whom you have served during those years. Without doubt, over these years of generous care, the lives and hearts of many people have been touched by your sharing of the Lord's Spirit. We are truly grateful."

When Pfeiffer reached her *Globe* office again, she fumbled through her stacks of diocesan directories and found a telephone number for Meffan in rural Carver, Massachusetts. He answered with a ready voice, though he was seventy-three years old.

Yes, he said brightly, it was true; he had lured young women into sexual play. "I was trying to get them to love Christ even more intimately and even more closely," he said. "What I was trying to show them is that Christ is human and you should love Him as a human being. Don't think He's up there and He's spiritual and He's not human and physical. He's human, He's physical. That's what I was trying to point out to them. I felt that by having this little bit of intimacy with them that this is what it would be like with Christ. . . . To me they were just wonderful, wonderful young people. It was a very beautiful, I thought, beautiful, spiritual relationship that was physical and sexual."

She couldn't keep herself from reminding him of his commitment to celibacy.

"I didn't think that was destroyed because I always felt that to destroy celibacy you really had to have intercourse," he explained, "you'd have to be a father."

Wednesday, December 4, 2002
BRIGHTON, MASSACHUSETTS — In the dark dining room of the residence, Gary, Olan, Bernie, and Barbara Thorp had been waiting for the cardi-

nal in twitchy silence. Olan, especially unable to mask his dread, prowled the room with his eyes, recording the scene as if for the historians. He studied the lavender and gold archdiocesan coat of arms hanging on the wall, with its barry-wavy symbol for the great ocean harbor stitched over three golden hills, a reminder of the rolling terrain on which the city was founded. The walls were heavily draped with the flat oil portraits of the men who led the Boston see before him, from Jean-Louis Lefebvre de Cheverus through his successors, Fenwick, Fitzpatrick, Williams, O'Connell, Cushing, and the sour-faced Medeiros. Unwise role models, Olan thought.

When the cardinal finally appeared at a side door, he looked exhausted.

"How are you?" Olan Horne asked.

"I'm okay," he said, slumping into a chair at the long mahogany table.

"No, really," Olan said. "How *are* you?"

Law looked at Olan for a long time, then removed his glasses. "I'm lousy," he said.

Gary leapt to his feet. "I want to take you into that chapel down the hall," he said. "I think we all need a prayer. It's that important to me."

Olan Horne rolled his eyes. He no longer prayed, not even privately. He called himself an agnostic. Bernie McDaid prayed mostly the AA verses. Even Gary was surprised by his sudden need to appeal to the divine. Wearily, Law turned with his visitor toward the chapel. Barbara and Bernie followed. Even Olan joined. They were in there for several minutes.

Law's grip on the circumstances engulfing him was shakier now than ever. Nearly three-quarters of Americans, regardless of faith, who all year had been calling for his resignation, now believed the pope should fire him. Measured by leadership instinct, the past two days had been the cardinal's most ham-fisted, culminating this morning in a wild counterassault against Father Walter Cuenin that he unleashed during the morning cabinet meeting. Cuenin, pastor of the prominent Our Lady Help of Christians parish, had crossed Law many times over the past year—he testified at the statehouse in favor of gay marriage, sat for a lengthy and frank profile in the *New Yorker* detailing his criticism of the crisis, and helped found the rump group for disgruntled Boston clergy called the Priests' Forum, which as everybody in Boston now knew had scheduled a meeting of more than a hundred priests for later in the week to discuss whether Law should resign. Law lowered the hammer, ordering his staff to release the following statement to the press: "Until further notice, no Archdiocesan-sponsored or Archdiocesan-related meetings, programs, workshops, etc., are to be held on the grounds of Our Lady Help of Christians parish."

The outburst played badly even among Law's loyalists. "It's just amazing to me," said Ray Flynn. "When the pope gives these people the red hat, he doesn't give them the red hat because they're smart from a public relations point of view or they know politics or they're sophisticated in the political culture. They don't have the foggiest idea."

When they emerged from the chapel, Gary was still in an agitated state.

"Bankruptcy or no bankruptcy, I don't give a shit," he said. "Do what you guys think you need to do. But don't do this through the newspapers. It's got to go from your lips to our ears. You need to get out of this fucking museum! You need to get out here and come to where we are."

"Nothing is getting accomplished," Olan said. "This is a fire burning out of control."

Law was a baronial potentate, peering nervously out of his tower on the troubles. He looked exhausted.

"You've run out of time," Olan said. At that moment, though nobody knew it, Massachusetts attorney general Thomas Reilly was preparing subpoenas to force Law and his top aides to testify before a grand jury, a first in the history of the Catholic Church. Olan had been reading the tea leaves. "I'm worried about your safety," he said. "Police are getting reports, there's stuff on the Internet. Horrible, horrible stuff. About Mass next Sunday. Maybe you should not go."

"Oh, my God," Barbara blurted out. That somebody would so loathe the cardinal archbishop of Boston that they might storm into the cathedral and attack him? She couldn't fathom it.

"I want to tell you a story," Gary said. "I was talking to my daughter the other day. She's nine months pregnant—my first grandkid. I said, 'Where is the baptism?' Because that's what our family has always done. And she said, 'What are you talking about? Baptism? *You?*' Man, that upset me, Bernie. I mean, I want my grandchild baptized. In some religion, at least. And I want you to know I'm not going to stop until the day comes when that child *is* baptized. It's not that I really give so much as a fuck about the church. But so many people do. Good people. My parents! They're the ones that care. People in their sixties, seventies, eighties, they're the victims in this. Them and my grandchild. Forget about trying to get me back to the church. I'm a lost cause. My generation and my daughter's? We're gone. Work on keeping my parents. Work on my grandchildren. Work on the church."

When they left, if Cardinal Law had listened as closely as he seemed to, he knew what he could do and what he couldn't, and what was left to him as options. It was painfully clear that what Gary was saying was true. Law was not capable of holding on to even the most innocent in his flock, much less winning back the disenchanted. Everything he had done this past year inflamed the crisis. The church needed a savior and it was not him.

When the sun rose the next morning, he would tell a few of his closest advisers of his decision, and the following morning he was on a flight to Washington for a meeting with the papal nuncio, before booking passage to Rome. By chance, he left the residence in Brighton just hours before the marshals arrived with the attorney general's subpoenas.

Thursday, December 5, 2002
FOXBORO, MASSACHUSETTS — James Perry, a thirty-eight-year-old Knight of Columbus, could not describe the anger he felt after flicking on his television to find another story about another abusive priest. Over the eleven months of constant crisis, nobody had been more critical than he of the media's glee, the victims' greed, the lawyers' bloodless pursuits. More proof blinked on his TV. An overdressed Ally Bauder, a reporter for New England Cable Network, was knocking on the door of a priest's two-story brick split-level home like some sort of Publishers Clearing House official. She was accompanied by Stephen Kurkjian, the *Globe* reporter, and a television crew. The priest greeted her genially and as the camera rolled he invited her inside, poor guy.

The place was tidy and spare and James Foley, whose white eyebrows sat high on his forehead, brightly sank into an overstuffed armchair like a shut-in preparing with joyous anticipation to listen to a life-insurance pitch.

"We wonder if we could talk to you about a couple of things," Bauder said.

He nodded enthusiastically. "Of course!"

Bauder laid it all out, the files, the affairs, the overdose, the treatment facilities, all the gruesome facts that Courtney Pillsbury and David Thomas had found in the file folder, including his confessions to Law about the girl's fatal overdose, and the remark in McCormack's hand, "CRIMINAL ACTIVITY?" Foley was genuinely confused. "I'm just, uh, not comfortable, you know, *dealing with* . . . something . . . totally out of the blue, that I have no knowledge about, no inkling of what this is about."

Watching this on the television, James Perry thought, *Foley. Sounds so familiar.*

"You have any idea where they might have gotten this information?"

"No, I don't whatsoever," he said.

"And you have no children?"

"Absolutely not!"

"You don't have any idea of a woman having heart failure in your presence and you needing to call 911 but leaving before you did so?"

"Oh, no," he said.

The reporter read from the papers, which bore Law's initials: "Two children in '65, relationship with married woman, overdosed in his presence, started to faint."

Gently, he interrupted. "I think my record in the archdiocese is, well, beyond reproach! There's never been a single allegation. I have no idea where this kind of wild speculation comes from."

It went around like this for some time. Stephen Kurkjian, who was sitting nearby on a sofa, thumbed through the stack of photocopies he had just received at the chaotic MacLeish press conference. He peeled off a letter to John McCormack signed by Foley himself. In it, the priest said he would "regret to my dying day" all the events he was now denying while pleading for lenience.

"Is this your letter?" Kurkjian asked.

As he took hold of it, a reflexive flash of recognition crossed Foley's gentle blue eyes. Without changing demeanor, with no you-got-me shrug or Perry Mason sigh, he said simply, "Yes."

Foley let the hand with the letter drop to his side and began working his fingers across the document almost imperceptibly, slowly pulling it an inch at a time into the palm of his hand until it had disappeared into a wad in his fist. Meanwhile Bauder, in an affectless voice-over, recited its contents: "I cannot turn back the clock nor bring back the dead. How can the church suffer scandal from an episode that will never possibly be revealed? Who will reveal it? The Cardinal? Myself? A family member? Whoever knew the truth (and I'm not sure anyone ever did) would not wait twenty-seven years if there were any malicious intent to harm me or the church."

Watching this on television, James Perry thought he remembered hearing about Foley from his father, thought this was the priest who had helped his mother through her many depressions. Then he knew. He reached for the telephone and called his wife. "I think this is about my mom," he said. He was eight when she died alone in that room, naked, a belly full of pills. The gashing truth: She was not alone! A priest was with her. He might have saved her life, but he saved himself instead. A priest named James Foley—perhaps his namesake, good God, his own father.

Monday, December 9, 2002
BOSTON, MASSACHUSETTS — Breaking one of the bedrock rules of the priesthood, 10 percent of Boston's clerics gathering at Walter Cuenin's parish today rose up in mutiny against their cardinal, signing a petition for his resignation. "While this is obviously a difficult request, we believe in our hearts that this is a necessary step that must be taken if healing is to come to the archdiocese," their letter said. "The priests and people of Boston have lost confidence in you as their spiritual leader." No other cardinal or bishop in modern history had faced such an insurrection.

Friday, December 13, 2002

ROME — Law had arrived in Rome on Sunday in the company of Father Connolly. Through the week he met with Cardinal Giovanni Battista Re, prefect for the Congregation for Bishops, to discuss the snowballing legal issues in Boston, and with Cardinal Darío Castrillón Hoyos, prefect of the Congregation for the Clergy, which oversaw clerical discipline and financial troubles in dioceses. Just weeks ago Castrillón Hoyos had secretly approved Law's plan for contemplating bankruptcy as an option. Immediately, however, he encountered fierce objections from other American bishops, who said such a filing in Boston would impair their ability to raise funds elsewhere. Now Castrillón Hoyos expressed grave concerns that Law's financial situation not drag down the entire country.

The pope made Law wait till Friday for a brief meeting, which took place at eleven-thirty in the morning in the Apostolic Palace. Law offered his resignation. The pope had by now also received the extraordinary petition from Law's own priests as well as one from Voice of the Faithful, which had abandoned consensus and, by a vote of seventy-one to two, called a regime change urgent and described the leadership situation in Boston as chaotic and dire.

John Paul II accepted Law's resignation. The cardinal thanked him profusely. He bent to one knee and kissed the ring on John Paul's trembling hand. Thus ended the career of the most influential American cardinal, the prelate whose career gave hope and vision for a truly American Catholic Church—the man who fixed his eye on becoming the first American pope. Instead, he became the fourth head of a diocese in the United States to resign since the scandal broke nearly a year ago. Since 1990, twenty bishops worldwide had been swept out of their diocese under clouds of sexual scandal.

The crisis that began as a Boston phenomenon, sparked by the arrival of a new editor at the *Globe,* now reached nearly every American diocese and implicated more than twelve hundred priests, 432 of whom were still in active service and had been forced to resign, retire, or seek laicization. According to a record made by the *New York Times,* the number of people who had proclaimed their abuse in press remarks or lawsuits was 4,268. Eighty percent of them were male. Overall, the *Times* found that 1.8 percent of American priests ordained since 1950 had been accused of sexual crimes. However, the paper suggested that was only a partial picture. In the three dioceses that divulged complete lists of abusive priests, either voluntarily or under court order, the percentages were far higher. In Manchester, 7.7 percent of ordained clerics faced charges. In Baltimore, the number was 6.2. And in Boston, of the 1,774 priests ordained between 1950 and 2002, 5.3 percent drew complaints about sexual wrongdoing.

LOWELL, MASSACHUSETTS — "You better get up here."

It was Gary's mother, calling from upstairs. Her voice was heavy with dread.

Dashing into his parents' apartment, Gary found his father crying in front of the television as Donna Morrissey announced the cardinal's resignation. It was over. This made Joseph Bergeron afraid for his church, and for himself.

Gary was furious. "Fuck you," he thought.

January 1, 2003
RAMSTEIN AIR BASE, GERMANY — It was 5 A.M. on New Year's Day. Tom Doyle sat in his quarters, reflecting on the past year, which had brought him back from obscurity and scorn to sudden acclaim. To his surprise, he had just learned he was this year's selection to receive the prestigious Isaac Hecker Award for Social Justice, whose previous winners included Dorothy Day, who founded the Catholic Worker Movement, and Sister Jeannine Gramick. The news brought rounds of congratulations from victim-survivors like David Clohessy, who considered Doyle "the greatest unsung hero of this whole movement."

Though he was proud of the designation, he did not think it took exceptional heroism to advocate on behalf of child abuse victims. He was a priest; that was what priests did in the ordinary exercise of their duties, or so he thought. This was the subject of his New Year's message to abuse survivors, which he tapped out on e-mail before sunrise:

Some have asked me why I remain [a priest]. Others have asked how can I possibly remain and be honest. Others have heaped varying degrees of hostility on me simply because I am what I am. I understand all of these responses. I have never been more ashamed to be associated with the Catholic clerical structure or the institutional church. But, there is a difference between being a priest and being a priest/cleric. For some it takes quite a bit of inner struggle to see the difference and even more struggle to live the difference.

For me at least, the priesthood is no longer tied up with power, control, magic, pomp and ceremony. I don't own a Roman collar. I don't need one. Jesus didn't have one nor did the apostles nor did Mary or the other women who hung out with Jesus. It's all about the incredible power Jesus had when He showed compassion, understanding and acceptance of people. He reached out and loved the rejects of society. He didn't vaporize sinners, He embraced them. The only people He got really angry with were religious leaders and that was because they used people, hurt people and blasphemed in doing so.

Clericalism is a deadly disease. It's the virus that causes a priest's mind to become warped and twisted and truly believe that he is above others and has super powers, deserves special consideration and can get away with things others must answer for. Clericalism causes moral blindness. Clericalism causes addiction to power and control. Clericalism is basically why sex abuse victims were ignored and abusers covered up. Clericalism is why so many are still in denial. Some of the major carriers of this disease are laypeople who want to remain spiritual infants and have "father" tell them what to do and how to "be saved," whatever that means. These people are enablers. The only cure is reality and truth. . . .

It's a new year. The primary source of support for my faith in the Higher Power has been the steady courage of the survivors. The most important single source of meaning for what priesthood is for me has been walking with the survivors and trying to help them find justice.

A happy, successful and victorious 2003 to all. Tom

January 22, 2003

BOSTON, MASSACHUSETTS — It seemed entirely unlikely that Eric MacLeish's involvement in the crisis could get any more complex, but today, by a cruel confluence of events, he was hosting the simultaneous depositions of Bishop John McCormack and Cardinal Bernard Law, whose legal troubles did not end with his resignation. Both men had been deposed repeatedly in the past, including several times by MacLeish and his staff. McCormack was the man his junior associates most wanted to interrogate—in previous pretrial appearances, his arrogant and emotionless replies had terrifically offended their sense of morality, while flatly contradicting the testimony of many other witnesses, especially Sister Catherine Mulkerrin, his former deputy. Making matters worse, they'd heard rumors they tended to credit, that McCormack or someone else in the chancery had removed documents from the personnel files of Shanley, Birmingham, Lane, and other members of his 1960 seminary class. His loyalty to them seemed undying, even now more than a year into the crisis. MacLeish let Robert Sherman pick McCormack apart.

He was saving his own attentions for Law, who would be making his first return to Boston since his hasty departure. For the past month and a half, Law had been staying at a Benedictine monastery outside of Pittsburgh, in prayer and reflection. He had avoided the press and members of his old staff alike. When he arrived at the Greenberg Traurig offices, he was barely recognizable. Gone were the bodyguards and police escorts and various orbiting advance men who had once preceded his entrances, and served to underscore that nobody in Massachusetts, not even the governor, was as powerful as Boston's cardinal archbishop. He had lost a lot of weight. Shame, or penance, sloped his shoulders to the ground. The solitary man who picked his way from the elevator to the law firm's conference room, dressed in a simple black suit and Roman collar, was a portrait of ruin. His lawyers followed glumly behind.

MacLeish, whose law firm was now handling over 250 litigants against dozens of priests, decided to focus almost exclusively on Father James P. Foley, the priest whose scandalous tale of paternity and death was the final catalyst to Law's resignation. The four children of Rita J. Perry, whom he left to die of a drug overdose, were now suing the church for damages, the youngest two citing the priest as their biological father.

"Good morning, Cardinal," MacLeish began.

"Do you remember becoming generally familiar in 1993 that Father Foley had had a relationship with a woman who ultimately had a lobotomy and that he claimed to have had two children with this woman?"

"I'm not aware of the—I don't recollect anything about a lobotomy, but I do recollect hearing—having been told about the paternity and this relationship," Cardinal Law answered, in obvious discomfort. He seemed distracted and slightly addled, MacLeish thought.

"And you were outraged by it, is that correct?"

"Terribly outraged."

"In fact, your initial reaction was this man should be sent to a monastery for the rest of his life to do penance?"

"That's correct." Law had a nervous habit of removing his glasses and forming the bows into a triangle between the fingers of his left hand.

"Father Foley told you something about the death of this woman, did he not?"

"He told me something about the death of this woman."

"He told you in 1993 that the woman, who was married, was overdosed while he was present; that she started to faint, he clothed, put his clothes on, left, came back, called 911, she died, a sister knows. Did he tell you that?"

"I have a recollection of basically that information, yes."

"And this was certainly shocking information to you?"

"Absolutely. And I might say nothing like that have—had I ever heard or imagined before or since."

Then why, MacLeish wanted to know, had the man not been removed from ministry? Why didn't anybody call the police when the record showed concern for his legal culpability? Why hadn't Law or any other church official with this knowledge thought to find the children and express sympathy or support, or at the very least tell them the truth about their mother's death and their own paternity? MacLeish asked these questions in a dozen different ways, providing a dozen opportunities for the cardinal to equivocate and pass responsibility down his line of command.

"First of all, as I've indicated in other cases, Mr. MacLeish, in these issues I functioned through those delegated to follow through. That's why they were there, to do that. If you look at [my] calendar, you'll see that there are an awful lot of things that come across the desk on any one day. However important one issue is—and certainly this is a case all in its own category—it's precisely because of the importance of that, that it's important that someone is going to be responsible to follow through on that and it's not going to be put aside for something else that immediately is very pressing. So I handled this in a delegated way."

He never followed up with his delegates, nor did he ever wonder what became of the Perry family, he admitted. Like so many other cases, he somehow concluded that keeping the secret was the only acceptable response. It never crossed his mind again.

MacLeish knew he would never forget the horrible story of Father Foley, and couldn't accept that Law, Foley's spiritual leader and boss, might just let the subject drop.

"Was this perhaps the most serious matter involving a priest of the archdiocese that you recall dealing with, Cardinal, in your tenure here in Boston?" It was the rhetorical question of an angry man.

"Objection to the form," Law's attorney interrupted.

"You may answer," MacLeish told Law.

"How do you—you know, how do you . . ." A profound sadness washed down the cardinal's weary face. "How do you . . ." His shoulders sagged in resignation.

"I withdraw it," MacLeish offered, in pity and frustration.

"How do you judge these things?" Cardinal Law continued, nearly whispering.

When the deposition was interrupted for lunch, Law wandered sadly out of the conference room, a man alone. Bernie McDaid had been waiting in the reception area to talk to his old friend. When he saw the cardinal approach, he climbed to his feet.

"Bernie, hi," McDaid said, offering his hand. "I just wanted to come down here and see how you were getting by."

Law smiled weakly. "You're more Catholic than you think you are," he said, palming the back of McDaid's neck. "You're a good man. How are *you* holding up?"

"I'm tired, tell you the truth. It's a tough year on my end."

"I bet it has been. I bet it has."

January 28, 2003

Salem, Massachusetts — When John McCormack entered the Old Town Hall, he was a prodigal son, the long-ago parish priest who now ran a diocese of his own. He clasped hands up and down the aisles, that powerful ring in evidence, calling, *Hello! I recognize you! It must be thirty years!* Faces floated up in his memory, names formed anew on his tongue—McGee, Sweeney, Hogan, and McDaid, the once young men of Salem. Confused, the men took his hand and, not knowing what to do with it, allowed McCormack to swing on to the next hand and then the next.

"Look at that," Gary whispered to Olan. "The motherfucker doesn't get it one bit. He's greeting people like he's the friggin' president! They're gonna hang him, and he's got no idea."

There were eighty-five people in the room. Thirty of them were SOJB members. The rest were their parents, children, spouses, and siblings. After much internal, often sharp debate, the SOJB had invited McCormack to speak to them, just as they had Law. Gary, Olan, and Bernie anticipated this would be a much angrier gathering. Many held McCormack personally responsible for Birmingham's long uninterrupted career. Several had complained to him directly about Birmingham—this had been confirmed over and over in court papers. Inexplicably he never formally responded to their complaints. In depositions, he had said he believed it was not his place. There were even those, Bernie McDaid included, who felt McCormack had a personal knowledge about what Birmingham was doing, and to whom.

After Bernie called the assembly to order, McCormack made a brief opening address. Then one by one, members of the audience stood and called him everything from an enabler to a co-conspirator to a pimp. They demanded answers, and he offered none. They craved blood, and he would not shed a drop.

Bernie McDaid reserved the last three minutes for himself. He had not expected to be as angry as he felt now. A week earlier, in anticipation of this meeting, he had met with McCormack personally, cordially reacquainting himself with his boyhood priest. He told him in great detail about Birmingham's molestations and how in therapy he had realized the many ways his life was not what it could have been. After, he felt drained of his venom. But now, watching McCormack duck and parry and deny, his despair returned more powerfully than before.

He turned and faced McCormack, lifted his arm, and aimed a finger of accusation at him.

"I won't call you bishop anymore, John McCormack," he said. "You have become John McCormack to me now. I thought you were coming here to give us an apology, not more excuses. . . . I lived two doors from Catholic Charities when you worked there. I can remember having to get in Birmingham's car, which I never wanted to do, and him waving to you in your window, and I remember having this funny feeling: I wonder if McCormack knows what's going on. I know you saw us, I feel you've known all along about this stuff, and you've been hiding behind those cloaks and collars for years. Yeah, I'm upset. I want you to come forward and say you're sorry. Say you're sorry, so that we can heal. I want you to lay down your bishop title and come stand with us, in order for us to heal. You don't deserve that title. I'm not totally looking for malice here. I'll walk alongside you. We need you to understand what went on. Nobody's doing that yet. Nobody is saying this was a huge mistake, this cover-up."

Bernie scanned the audience, which included nuns and priests from the area. "It's not just the victims who are hurting. *These* people are hurting. The church—it's their church, not yours. Give them back their church. They need their church back, they need this whole mess cleaned up. My mother, a good Catholic, it's not her fault. She is a very quiet person. She and I met privately with Cardinal Law in August, and he gave her some beads blessed by the pope, and a Bible, and it helped her. See, I was pulled into this, I agreed to stand up and say what happened to me and take whatever came. But my mother felt ashamed to go to her own church because of all of this, like she couldn't pray there anymore because of what happened to her son! It is her church. It's our church. *We* built this church. You didn't. If you want this church to heal, and even if you want to heal yourself, John McCormack, quit. Step down and walk with us. We'll heal together."

As a rageful applause burst out around him, Bernie McDaid sat back down. He was not proud of what he had said, he did not intend to disrespect McCormack publicly. But he knew what he had said was true, that in order for anybody in the room including McCormack to put this matter behind them, the bishop had to acknowledge the pain that was caused by his inaction, and apologize in an effective way.

McCormack turned toward Gary, who was seated at his left. He kept his face innocent of expression. Gary was not sure what McCormack would do now. Would he defend himself once more? Would he remind these Catholics what kind of respect was owed a bishop? Would he parrot lines of contrition as Law had done at first, or beg for their forgiveness? He surely knew better than to raise his voice—he saw during the town meeting in Manchester how poorly that served his ends. But what, then, was his next step?

Nothing. He just kept looking at Gary, their faces inches apart. Time passed incrementally. In his pocket, he had a prepared script for his closing remarks. They constituted a kind of semiacknowledgment, but the words would seem hollow now. In fact, there was almost nothing he could say that would satisfy this crowd.

Gary stared back as though he were responding to a challenge. He had no idea what was happening. The silence filled a whole minute. Was the bishop waiting for him to say something? Let him off the hook? Thank him for coming? He stared right back into McCormack's dark eyes. Though he had lost all respect for his church, Gary realized with some disappointment that he still feared his church authorities. This made him angry. He allowed a shiver of disgust to flash on his face. Did McCormack notice? How could he not?

McCormack finally cranked his head toward the gathered room. "I can see that you are angry at me," he said. He rose and stood before them, the way Afrikaners had stood before the black citizens they repressed. He swept his eyes to the floor.

"I, uh . . . I hear the emotion, the pain, and I'm very sorry for that. It is painful for me. I want to feel your pain, I want to share in it. But . . . You see, I admit to you that I am not there yet."

Gary slipped Olan a note. "Nope."

Ginned up with anger and adrenaline, a couple of the fellows went out for drinks after the meeting broke up. As they entered the pub, Bernie walked past a man he knew from way back in Salem. He recalled immediately he had never liked the man, that in fact he and a bunch of the old gang had once beaten hell out of him when they were kids. The memory shivered through him. Why this memory, why now, he did not understand.

He snagged a ginger ale and returned to his friends in the back room. For the first time in his life, he felt guilty for his bullying youth. He thought, *Who am I to demand an apology from McCormack?* He knew he had to talk to the man. He returned to the bar.

"Hi," Bernie said, extending a hand.

The man begrudged him a sideways glance.

"You still with that group of guys?" he asked.

"You remember."

He didn't respond.

"I forgot about it till I saw you tonight," Bernie said. "I'm sorry for the events that happened. I was . . . I was a little punk. Full of anger. And I had no right to do that to you. I've been trying to work on my life lately, I'm nineteen years sober. And I hope you'll take my hand and shake it."

Bernie put his ginger ale on conspicuous display.

"I'm just very sorry," he continued. "And if you don't want to take my hand, I understand."

The man slid off his bar stool and took a full accounting of Bernie McDaid, dressed in his ironed khakis, his hair all gone to gray. He studied the ginger ale, and stared deeply into Bernie's eyes.

"I believe you," he said, taking his hand.

January 31, 2003
Boston, Massachusetts — Although Wilson Rogers Jr. had sworn in court that he had released every record of every priest in Boston accused of molesting children, MacLeish and his attorneys seriously doubted the claim. Clients continued to allege a history of reporting priests whose names had not yet appeared, despite repeated court or-

ders. When confronted, Rogers adamantly declared the archdiocese in compliance with court orders. The only records of sexual malfeasance that were not turned over, he insisted, involved allegations of sexual activity with adults—and they were therefore irrelevant to the litigation. If there was any doubt about these so-called adult-victim records, he added, MacLeish was welcome to review them in Rogers's office.

MacLeish arrived with a small army of lawyers. Dozens of boxes were arrayed around a conference table. The lawyers were left to comb through them. Courtney Pillsbury was not especially thrilled about poring through the correspondence of lonely-hearts widows or love-struck organists who had fallen for their kindly vicars. But there was a chance something useful might be hiding in there—if not for the lawsuits, then at least for their client who was writing a book. His working title was *I Met the Devil, His Name Is Father*. They peeled open the boxes and pulled out files one by one.

"Hey, wait a minute," said somebody. "This kid was a minor. And this one—what's this doing here?"

Somebody else found a minor too.

Remarkably, the allegations against these priests were not all brought by adults, as the Rogers law firm had sworn. In fact, on cursory first glance, two-thirds of the so-called adult-victim files contained charges of misconduct brought by minors. Apparently they had been classified as adult victims because these guys *also* fornicated with adults. But these were no tales of hidden love. Not one of the forty files contained a story of consensual sex that they could find. "These were coercive relationships," Thomas said. "These were rape!"

Father Paul J. McLaughlin was accused of accosting three youths in the Arlington suburb, one of whom was eleven or twelve. Father Victor C. LaVoie, while serving in Wilmington, was said to have fondled a fifteen-year-old boy. An accuser from Hull said that in 1967 or 1968 he was simultaneously molested by Father Leo Dwyer and Father John Dunn. Unbelievably, after a year of nonstop revelations, somehow the church had managed to keep the secrets of an additional twenty-four priests charged with molesting minors.

"These are egregious," Thomas said in amazement. "Hideous, heinous allegations!"

"It's almost like these are the ones they didn't want anybody to see," Pillsbury said.

The lawyers checked against church directories. Four of these guys were still in ministry.

Tuesday, February 12, 2003

University of Massachusetts, Lowell campus — Paul Ciaramitaro was sitting on the back of a leather library chair, digging the heels of his workboots into the armrests. "This is what I mean," he said to Bernie McDaid. He shook a copy of the *Lowell Sun* from last week. "It's *fucked*! I'd like to strangle the motherfucker."

Bernie McDaid waved off the article. He had already seen it. Last week a young reporter had attended the meeting of SOJB—under the specific proviso that *nothing* would be quoted. That's the way they all understood it, anyway. They agreed to have him there so he could get a feeling for what it was like to be them right now, at the beginning of year two in the trenches. It was Olan Horne's idea.

Here's how the article started:

> Everyone has a price, and Olan Horne wants to find out Bernie McDaid's.
>
> $50,000? No.
>
> $100,000? No.
>
> $200,000? Maybe, McDaid says, but he's not sure. He hasn't really thought about his price.
>
> Horne has his: $600 million.

"Makes us all look like whores," Bernie said.

"Guy never said anything about doing quotes," said Larry Sweeney, a pharmacist who was slumped in a chair across the room. "Took everything out of context, and the fucking context was: there's not enough money in the world to compensate for some priest putting his dick up a boy's ass." He looked accusingly at Olan.

"*I'm* the one in there saying I want to cripple the church and take home six hundred million," Olan said, hanging his head. He had had a few glasses of merlot before the meeting.

Paul Ciaramitaro slid off the chair and surged into the middle of the circle. "That's the fucking issue!" he shouted. "We can't be going through this shit when the press is around. What happens in this room stays in this fucking room."

"We got to start going back to the basics, guys," Olan agreed. "Because we're at a tough point in this whole thing. We've been going at this for three hundred and fucking sixty-five days. My life is in fucking *turmoil*. Bernie, say amen. Because I *know* your life's a wreck. And Gary, man, how's Julie doing with this?"

"Okay, everybody," Gary announced obligingly, "Julie and I had a big fucking blowout. But does anybody want to hear about my two-day fucking argument?"

The guys laughed, but Paul egged him on. "Back to basics," he said. "But let's go forward, too."

"She's on me about going to the movies. So I say, 'What's playing?' '*Do* you want to go?' 'What's playing?' '*Do you want to go?*' So what the fuck, right? Anyway, it ended with me going about four inches from her face and screaming, 'Cunt! Cunt! Cunt! Cunt!' "

"That's bad," Larry said.

"I called mine a whore," Bernie admitted sadly. "I've been twenty-eight years with my girl. Twenty-eight years. Two kids, fourteen and seven. And it's bad. It's brutal. I'll be honest, I'd like to say everything was fine and then this came along. Me and her were already going at it when I got the call to get involved in this."

Paul and his girlfriend were on the rocks too, he said, in a long and graphic aside that included hilarious details of their sexual exploits. But the more he unburdened himself about it, the more furious he got. Though he was now thirty-one, he still suffered from a teenager's uncertainty about his own sexuality, and for this he bitterly blamed Birmingham.

"I'll tell you what this is about," he exploded. "It's about sitting in the basement all through high school not knowing if I'm gay or straight. *Looking at videos trying to figure it out.* Yeah, once I had a homosexual experience in Montreal. But I was stoned out of my head, just about to lose my kidney. It was wrong, okay? For me. But who's going to say, am I normal? Let me ask you this, at what point do you feel comfortable in your life? Doing exactly what your parents wanted you to do? As a Catholic? Altar boy? CCD? When do you know you're normal? When do you do something just for you? When do you know what you want?"

The men slipped into a knowing silence. None of them had an answer.

"You don't think therapy helps? Therapy helps. Look at us," Gary said. He slid down on the sofa.

"Aren't we carrying way too much weight, though?" Olan asked. "Aren't we putting too much on this? Where's the jackpot in this for you?"

"You know what I want?" Bernie interjected. "I want the fucking pope. I want the pope to make atonement and change the system."

"Shit," Olan howled. "Well, they said we couldn't get to the cardinal."

"They're all shameless," Larry said. "Up to and including the pope."

"Bernie, think about it. The painter, the butcher, the carpenter: we're talking about going after the fucking *pope*. And you haven't learned that nothing is impossible?"

Bernie kind of shrugged. "I tell you what," he said. "I would rather go see the pope than go see my wife right now, because I *know* I won't get anywhere with her."

February 24, 2003
NEWTONVILLE, MASSACHUSETTS — "We're going to the Vatican," Gary announced, plowing into Barbara Thorp's office. She blinked at him with incomprehension. "Me and my brother, and Olan, Bernie, and my dad. I've got an in with the U.S. ambassador to the Holy See. Got some other insiders working on this, too. Olan's working the Law angle. We're going right to the Vatican with this. And we're getting in. We might not be invited, but we're getting in."

She knew that Gary and the others had not yet succeeded in establishing the sort of relationship with Auxiliary Bishop Richard G. Lennon, who had been named interim leader of the Boston archdiocese, that they had with Law. She had to agree with them that the silence from the chancery since December had been disheartening. But Rome?

"Barbara, I've come to realize for whatever reason, it's taken me a long time to figure out that the best ally the church has had through the years is time. Every crisis, they wait it out. They think if they wait it out long enough, a century will go by and it will all be forgotten. They're doing the same thing now! Look, we met with Lennon for two hours to open a dialogue. He hasn't gotten back to us now in *weeks*. Weeks become centuries. I don't have that time. You know what? My father? He doesn't have that kind of time to heal. It's time for this thing to get on. It's time for—"

At that very moment, to Gary's everlasting amazement, the large plain-faced electric clock that hung on the wall over the sofa in Barbara Thorp's office leapt off the wall and came crashing to the floor. Barbara screamed.

"God as my witness," Gary said to the rafters, "she got the message."

When Barbara had recovered, she said, "Do you mind if I make some calls? Because all I envision is the guys at the gate chasing you around St. Peter's Square with their ancient weapons."

When he got home that night, Gary's mother called him to convey a strange query. "Your father's got this question," she said, "about saving his soul?"

"What are you talking about, Mom?"

"Well, he hasn't been sleeping for three or four months. I finally asked him and he said he worries, literally worries, about going to hell. All he worries about now is saving his soul."

"Mom, what is this about?"

"Years ago, when Joe Birmingham first came here, we used to go to him for pastoral counseling, your father and I. Back then your father wasn't taking communion, because he had been divorced, and Joe said to him, 'You might want to think about going back to communion.' He said it was okay. And your father said, 'Okay, if you say so, because my conscience is clear. But this is on your soul now, not mine.'"

In past years, at a time when top theologians were reconsidering divorce and the sacraments, it was not uncommon for a priest to welcome divorced people back to communion. However, church teaching never changed, and those who "obstinately persist in manifest grave sin," as it was noted in canon 915, were not to be admitted to communion, a matter reiterated in June 2000 by the Pontifical Council for Legislative Texts. So the warning of St. Paul still stood: "Whoever eats the bread or drinks the cup of the Lord unworthily sins against the body and blood of the Lord [and] eats and drinks a judgment on himself."

"Now all he thinks about is the fact that he's been receiving communion for thirty years, all on the authority of a *non*authority," she told Gary. "He is convinced he's going to hell."

Being a rationalist, Gary gave heaven and hell no real attention. The final dispensation of the soul was not quite relevant in a modern world, he thought. Like most postboomers, his spirituality focused more on the morality of daily life than on the accretion of obedience to a particular dogma. If he had learned anything this past year it was that the Roman Catholic magisterium was no bulwark against immorality. Even if his father had been tricked into taking communion or shamed into silence about his own abused past, he had been a *decent* man, a *good* man, and if the nabobs on judgment day did not take that to mean he was a *moral* man, then this religion was even more harebrained than he thought.

He found his father sitting in the living room of his apartment upstairs, morose and frantic. "Dad, why don't you go down to St. Michael's and talk to Father Capone? I'm sure he'll clear this up."

That was the problem. Joseph Bergeron felt his predicament had been created by priests—the one who abused him when he was eight, the ones who taught him to keep his silence, the one who coaxed him into godly estrangement and then defiled his two sons. He no longer trusted priests. In fact, that was his most profound crisis.

"The only one, the only person that I would have talked to would have been the cardinal, and he's gone," he said.

"I'm going to call the cardinal, Dad. Do you want to sit with him? Because I'll set it up."

"I want him to save my soul. I want the cardinal to save my soul. I want to make a confession and tell him the whole story," he wept. "I want him to save my soul."

February 26, 2003
COVINGTON, KENTUCKY — Church lawyers fighting a lawsuit by a man who claimed he endured repeated molestations by his priest beginning when he was thirteen filed a stunning allegation suggesting that the boy, not the church or the priest, was culpable in his own victimization. "The plaintiff may have been comparatively negligent," the document filed on behalf of the Covington diocese stated. "The plaintiff may have assumed a known and obvious risk which acts as a complete bar to his recovery of any damages."

What had he done that might be considered negligent? He chose to enroll in the ninth grade at Newport Catholic High School. Maybe he *should* have known how perilous that decision was. There was no denying that such abusive behavior was commonplace. Only the proof came so much later. On this day alone, priests were arrested in Concord, New Hampshire; Dennis, Massachusetts; Brooksville, Florida; Fresno, California; and Flint, Michigan. Members of a grand jury empaneled by New Hampshire attorney general Peter Heed were readying a scathing report on the diocese there, part of a deal that allowed Bishop John McCormack to escape prosecution. The panel found the diocese was guilty of "flagrant indifference" to the suffering of children, and detailed its findings in a 154-page report available for downloading over the Internet. The state's Web site warned that it would be inappropriate for anyone under eighteen to read the report, owing to the graphic nature of the material.

Tuesday, March 4, 2003
BRIGHTON, MASSACHUSETTS — "You shouldn't be asking for this kind of thing right now, Gary," Father John Connolly said sternly. "There's too much going on you aren't aware of."

For months, Gary Bergeron had been begging Barbara Thorp to reach out to Cardinal Law for his help placating Gary's father, but she had made no headway. Gary also wanted to ask Law to call the pope and tell him they were coming. He would have settled for an audience with Law's interim replacement, Bishop Richard Lennon, but he had been even more cloistered. Frustrated, Gary called Law's old personal secretary. Rather than being solicitous as he had been in the past, Connolly was treating him like a bill collector again. He didn't return his phone calls. Gary called a half dozen times. His contempt was rising. The longer he awaited news from Law, the more worried he was for his father. He was seventy-eight. Healthy, yes, but at that age it was not a stretch to think that death could be at hand.

Gary called up an Associated Press reporter he had met and told her about his Rome expedition plans—and sent her to Connolly for comment. It worked like a charm. Finally, Connolly called him back. He was furious, though, and demanded Gary come to a meeting.

"It has to stop, Gary," he said. "This is not going to happen."

"All my father needs is a meeting with Law. That's all," he said. "Something convinced him he's going to hell, and he needs to make a confession. He's seventy-eight, John! To be going through it at his age? It's not bad enough he's got two kids that were abused, two other kids buried next to the priest that abused us. He was abused himself as an altar boy. Now at his age he's worried about saving his fucking soul. These are the issues, John, this is not a money issue. See what this is about? It is about believing in mankind or not. That's why we're going to Rome. They don't realize the damage they've done to thousands of people. My father's not an abnormality. My father literally is worried about going to hell at this point."

"What you should do is stop selling your father this magic pill. Going to the Vatican is not going to solve his problems."

Magic pill? Gary was stunned into silence. It was the Roman Catholic Church that taught his father to fear hell in the first place, to crave salvation, and now that he saw his own judgment looming, his faith was suddenly an Old World potion?

"This all started," Gary spit, "because of your refusing to do something for my dad, John. It's as simple as sitting down with my dad and explaining to him he's not doomed to hell. He wanted Law, but we can't get Law. So right now the only priest he trusts is at the Vatican. The church here has let him down."

"You know what, Gary? I'm part of the church, and I take offense at that."

"We already have tickets. I'm not looking for a coffee and a lunch

with the pope. I'd like a Mass with somebody over there, and a meeting with the Holy Father for my dad."

Connolly shook his massive head. This trip was worse than folly. It
threatened to make Boston appear to be spinning out of control in the
eyes of the Curia. If the Birmingham Survivors showed up over there
with their usual media circus in tow, it threatened all of their careers.

"John, I know that Lennon or Law just has to pick up the phone and
say, 'These guys are going over there, take care of them.' I know this is
how it's done."

"I'm telling you, Gary, if you think it's archaic over here, you're in for
a huge surprise."

"You know what I think? I think Rome doesn't have any idea of the
intensity of the feelings over here."

Connolly was no longer talking.

"Get me in to see Lennon. Get me on the phone with Law."

Nothing. It was the first time in the whole process that Gary was
pessimistic. "I hit the wall," he told a friend. "I finally found where the
big stone wall was, and I hit it head-on."

First Weeks of March 2003
Newtonville, Massachusetts — With Lent approaching, Bernie
McDaid was more frustrated than he had been at any time in the past
year. He could not believe he had not found anybody with enough
Catholic clout to pull strings at the Vatican. In the past week, he called
Ray Flynn; the former mayor and ambassador to the Vatican, it turned
out, had a published home telephone number. Flynn knew about the
Birmingham Survivors from their many media appearances, he said,
and he believed Bernie was trying to do the right thing. He promised to
make a few calls, but he was not encouraging. "What you're trying to do
is next to impossible," he explained.

Bernie was beginning to recognize that he felt some deep personal
responsibility for the crisis gripping the church. Coming forward as
powerfully as he did seemed to open an artery in the neck of his
church. The longer it went unbandaged, the more he panicked. Rec-
onciling the church and the faithful, he now believed, was a necessary

step for his own healing. Olan, though he felt similarly, had just announced he would not accompany them to Rome—an old hernia had
ruptured, and he was awaiting emergency surgery. Eddie Bergeron
bailed out, too; his recovery from alcoholism was too new and fragile to
be taking on the Vatican, he felt.

This seemed to intensify the burdens Bernie felt. He drove to Barbara Thorp's office in Newtonville.

"Barbara, you have to get me a phone number for Bernie Law. I need
to talk to him! He *has* to call the Vatican and get us in."

"I've tried, Bernie. But at the moment he's somewhere in Pennsylvania, and nobody seems to know exactly where."

He was disgusted. "Oh, c'mon, you don't know where he is? You can't
get him?" Sarcasm drenched his words. "Every time I go to you or John
Connolly directly or indirectly, you say 'I'm sorry, he's somewhere unreachable.' Gimme a break."

The provocation burned in Barbara's ears. "I can't tell you where he
is," she snapped. "I don't *know* where he is!"

"If you wanted to pursue Bernie Law, you could find him. I'm sorry.
That's the way I look at it. We're going to the Vatican either way!"

"Bernie, you can't do this!" she shouted. "You can't just go over there
and see the pope! It can't be done!"

For all these months, Barbara had been the lone voice of support inside the chancery for this Vatican trip. Now Bernie was losing her, too.
But he was undaunted.

"Believe me, anything can be done," he said. "I'm not taking no for
an answer."

March 5, 2003

LOWELL, MASSACHUSETTS — Gary Bergeron had written appeals for a
papal audience to Bishop Lennon and to various church officials in the
United States and Rome, including Cardinal Josef Ratzinger. In his letters, Gary presented his mission in desperately personal terms. "I have
begun to realize that my faith, not only in God and the Catholic
Church, but in mankind as well, will remain damaged unless steps are
taken to rebuild that trust." He also wrote to Ratzinger's counterparts

at the Congregation for the Clergy, the Congregation for Bishops, and the Congregation for Catholic Education, which, besides being the one Vatican office likely to be attuned to the needs of children, had as its prefect Cardinal Pio Laghi, who had been Vatican ambassador to the United States in 1985 when Father Tom Doyle was agitating to bring the abuse crisis out of darkness and secrecy.

In response to a dozen heartfelt plaints, Gary received absolutely nothing, not a note telling him not to go to Rome, not even a form letter wishing him luck. Dead silence.

But the snub that hurt the most came from Law. Over the Internet Bernie McDaid had scraped up an address for the Sisters of Mercy of Alma convent in Clinton, Maryland, the cardinal's new home. Gary wrote him a personal note, offering well wishes from an old friend, and he pleaded for help. But the letter went unanswered. Assuming there was a mix-up with the mail, Bernie placed several follow-up telephone calls, but he was impeded by an unfriendly receptionist who referred him back to the Boston chancery.

Frustrated, they devised a sort of last-ditch plan. Deep in the files for Father Birmingham they had found three documents they knew the church would not want out in the open. One showed that Bishop Lennon was no more innocent than the man he was replacing—he had been directly involved in transferring at least one known abuser. Another was an old memo they believed would force Bishop McCormack to resign in immediate disgrace should it ever gain wide distribution. Lastly, they had found what seemed to be a secret communiqué from the Vatican giving instructions to the Boston leadership on how to contain their growing scandal. These things had never been in the media before. Nobody in the church, including Bernie and Gary, would want to see them in the *Globe*. They weren't proposing blackmail exactly. But they thought that if nobody in Rome would agree to meet with them to discuss the scope of the American crisis, perhaps if they were to make a formal presentation of these letters to Vatican insiders, they would invite the delegation in to talk more about them.

But perhaps they wouldn't need their three smoking guns. In today's mail came an unexpected word of encouragement, however meager. Father Capone, the pastor at St. Michael's, where Gary's parents worship,

had suggested Gary write to Monsignor John Abruzzese, a Boston-
trained priest who was one of the most highly placed U.S. priests working at the Vatican. A midlevel functionary, he handled staff duties for
the Synod of Bishops.

With apologies, Capone said he could not give direct assistance in
arranging a papal meeting. However, he offered the advice that had
been given to disgruntled Catholics throughout the centuries.

"Shortly after your arrival," he wrote, "I would suggest that you contact the Prefecture of the Papal Household, at the Bronze Door in the
propylaeum at the end of the colonnade on the right, as you are looking at St. Peter's Basilica. The Holy Father usually has a general audience each Wednesday and sometimes at other times during the week.
The prefecture is the Vatican office which arranges such audiences."

The towering, unopenable Bronze Door, the wilting place for so
many expectations. That would be their only hope. That was where
they would go.

March 20, 2003
BOSTON, MASSACHUSETTS — Redoubling their hardball legal tactics,
lawyers representing the Boston archdiocese moved to have all 450
civil lawsuits thrown out as violations of the First Amendment protection of religion. Their novel and frustrating argument went like this:
Central to Catholic belief are the sacraments, especially the sacrament
of penance; Cardinal Law and his leadership team were exercising their
freedom of religion when they forgave abusive priests and transferred
them, rather than firing them; the litigants are treading all over that
right; they seek to "modify the church's understanding of forgiveness
and grace."

Judge Sweeney rejected the motion. The archdiocese appealed to
the state Appellate Division. During a court hearing in the case recently, attorney L. Martin Nussbaum, the First Amendment specialist
hired by the archdiocese, put it this way: "Some of the greatest leaders
in church history are, as the church would say, redeemed sinners, but
as our civil justice might say, former criminals."

Mark Chopko, general counsel to the United States Conference of

Catholic Bishops, was encouraging diocesan attorneys to test similar arguments around the country. No secular judge, he believed, would be equipped to rule on the teachings of a church. "How do you measure the reasonableness of a policy set in religious doctrines of forgiveness, of redemption, and so forth?" Some legal precedents to this argument were developing around the country. State courts in Wisconsin and Maine dismissed lawsuits brought by adults who said they were victimized by clergy members, specifically citing the constitutional rights of church officials to commit theologically based errors of judgment.

That, said lawyers for the plaintiffs and survivor group leaders, missed a fundamental point, that society's desire to protect children from harm was more powerful than any managerial policies of an organized religion. Criminal laws can't be broken, even by churches. "When it comes to the protection of kids, our courts have spoken," said Eric MacLeish. "The need to protect children supersedes fervently and deeply rooted religious beliefs."

March 22, 2003
LOWELL, MASSACHUSETTS — The front door on the Bergeron home was thrown open to a wildly hopeful, radiant morning—sixty-six degrees, colorful again, finally spring. This morning was a portent. A warming breeze carved away the gray snow piles and dried off last fall's scrabbled leaves.

"Dad, are you ready?" Katie breezed into her father's house, clutching up infant paraphernalia to her chest. *"Dad!"*

In his living room, Gary was folding seven ironed dress shirts into his suitcase, alongside his *Fodor's Guide to Italy* and an unread copy of *Inside the Vatican,* a primer of papal power dynamics that the author, Father Thomas Reese, had personally recommended in a recent e-mail exchange. Gary suspected he might not bring himself to read it. He feared it was a discouragement. In comments to the press, Reese had been asked to handicap Gary's chances of success, and he was melancholy. "It is very difficult to get an appointment with the pope, and to go to Rome without already having had an appointment arranged is really a waste of time. It just doesn't happen that way. Everybody in the world wants to meet with the pope and, especially now with his health reduced, he simply can't see everybody."

What was the use of that sort of pessimism? It did nothing to end the crisis, as Gary so strongly said in an e-mail he fired off to Reese after the article appeared: *Instead of shooting us down, why not try making helpful suggestions?* "Read the book," Reese suggested helpfully.

Appointment or not, wise or not, Joseph and Gary Bergeron and Bernie McDaid ("the Father, Son, and Holy Ghost," they jokingly dubbed themselves) were heading to Rome. Ultimately they had no choice, and no misgivings. *They believed* they would get in. In that way, their faith remained innocent and bold, perhaps foolishly bold, despite their many spiritual betrayals and in spite of the tribulations of the past few weeks. They clung to this faith, chose it over futility. Of the billion living Catholics on earth, *they* would get an appointment with the pope. They believed this. And man to man, each of the three would peer deep into those tiny eyes of his and find Karol Wojtyla rather than the Holy Father, the way they found Bernie Law in his cardinal's mien, and communicate to him the exact length and width and plunging depths of their violated humanity. So that he would know. They believed the church was a moral institution, or had been, or would become one again, because when Karol Wojtyla looked back into the eyes of the men from Lowell and Salem, he would see what he owed them, which was authenticity. Which was hope.

"I've just got a few more things to get in here," Gary replied. "Julie," he called, "have you seen my suit coat?"

It was in Julie's hand.

"Where's my dad?"

"I think he's already waiting in the van. You know your father."

Trying to remain calm—impossible on the eve of his first trip out of the country—Gary folded the suit coat on top of the folded shirts, and squashed and zippered the textile mass inside a big black nylon brick on wheels. "Okay," he said, "I'm just going to check my e-mail and then . . ." He looked around. On the coffee table was the last-resort file folder containing the three scandalous memos that he and Bernie had compiled, then nearly forgot. He forced the file inside a zippered pocket on the side of his suitcase.

As he walked down the hallway to the den, Julie quietly unzipped his bag, pulled out each item, and repacked the whole of it, turning his good dress shoes this way instead of that, refolding his shirts. She thought about how calm this next week at home would be for her, exactly one year after the weekend Joseph E. Birmingham was exposed in the *Globe,* exactly one hundred days since the cardinal left town, the priests, lawyers, and reporters, victim-survivors, the cell phones, and TV news all silenced for once.

From down the hallway came the explosion, what sounded like the computer flying off the desk and smashing on the floor, with Gary cursing bitterly.

With great caution, Julie methodically refastened the suitcase, rose, and crept down a long hallway to the den. "What is it?" she whispered.

"They canceled our friggin' reservations," he shouted. "The hotel in Rome just sent e-mail *canceling*! What if I hadn't just gotten the e-mail this second? What if we just showed up at the friggin' hotel?"

He entertained suspicion of a papal conspiracy. It was just one more obstacle, or one more sign. "That's just great. I'm taking my seventy-eight-year-old father to Italy to meet the supreme pontiff and we don't have an appointment and we don't have a hotel reservation."

Julie regarded his despair dubiously. "There are plenty of other hotels," she offered.

"Oh, Julie," he burst out impatiently, "we priced this one out to the penny, we budgeted everything around it." Gary's exhaustion was mythic, biblical.

Now Gary could hear his mother calling him from the front door, a bold Boston voice announcing that the caravan was about to leave.

"Fuck it," he said. "We've got a plane to catch." He buttoned a dress shirt over his skinny chest. "That's it. We're just going to show up at the hotel anyway and say we didn't get the e-mail. They'll find us a place. We're going to Rome!"

In the van on the way to Logan Airport, Gary debated whether or not to tell his father about the foul-up, and only when they nosed the vehicle into a parking spot outside Terminal B did he break the news. To his relief, his dad was not even slightly inclined to abort the mission, which he had adopted now as his own. "Look at this," Joseph Bergeron said, meaning the city around them, trapped in the vortex of crisis. "It goes as far back as it gets. It started in the *thirties,* at *least."*

Equally sanguine was Bernie McDaid, who rushed through the pneumatic terminal doorway a few minutes behind the Bergerons. "Oh, well, we're just going to have to pray," he joked. Or partly joked. He gathered close, with you're-not-going-to-believe-this news. "Last night, this lady who had been praying for me—actually she's one of the people who's been calling me and giving me encouragement, you know, which has been very helpful and I really appreciate it—anyway, she came by last night and did all this strange stuff with blessed oil from the shrine of Medjugorje and then she sprinkled holy water on my head, and check this out." He reached into his pocket and produced a string of deep red rosary beads. He held them up in his palm like a nest of hatchlings.

Gary touched them. So did his mother. "Very nice," she said.

Gary's dad slowly unzipped a pocket in his windbreaker, removed a folded leather pouch, and poured out a silver and mother-of-pearl rosary into the palm of his spotty hand. "Blessed by the pope," he said.

It was an impressive thing, to be blessed by the pope, Bernie had to admit. "Only thing is, I forgot how to do it. These are all Hail Marys, right?"

"These here," Gary's dad confirmed, segregating the smaller beads with his thumb.

"And these are, um, Apostles' Creed?"

"Oh, no," Joseph said, scandalized, "those are the Our Fathers." He rummaged through Bernie's palm, organizing the beads into clusters. "More Hail Marys. And a Glory Be."

Bernie laughed and shook his head in awkward befuddlement, the same as he had forty years ago when last he studied the rosary. For the first time in his life, he thought he might like to really understand it. "I guess I've got an eight-hour flight to figure it all out."

When it was their turn, the men threw their bags up on the US Air weigh station and sent their things off toward the plane. Circling around toward their gate, they fell into the bright column of light, beamed off a team of television cameras. Bernie McDaid had called in a few favors.

"I didn't want the guys over there in the Vatican saying they didn't know we was coming," he admitted.

A rookie field producer approached nervously, hoisting up a heavy microphone on the end of her sagging wrist like an extremely soiled diaper. "Can you, um," she started, "sorry, can you say, or explain or whatever, um, what you're about to . . . ?"

Gary looked into the camera, smiling easily. "We're on our way to the Vatican to hopefully gain an audience with the pope," he said. "As victims and survivors, we want to tell the pope how serious the problem is in this country. Here we are a year later, for us exactly a year later, and this archdiocese is still speaking through their attorneys, when they should be speaking through their priests and their leaders if they want to fix this crisis."

"I also believe," Bernie leaned in, "when they put a face on a victim or a survivor, they know how we're hurting. I think we can make a difference if the pontiff will in fact see us, just *see* us."

"We're hopeful," Gary said, honestly. "We're hopeful."

The camera operators snapped off their lights and slid their bulky machines from their shoulders, and began an origami with their cords while the field producers wandered off into cell phone chatter and new assignments. Beneath a canopy of broadcast flight information—the liturgy of an airport—Bernie McDaid, Gary Bergeron, and his dad, Joseph, headed to their gate, toward the ancient city, toward a primordial order, a place in their hearts. Only there, reconciliation. Only then, peace.

Postscript

Bishop Emilio Allue remains an auxiliary bishop in Boston, now in charge of the archdiocese's Merrimack region, which includes Lowell, Concord, and Haverhill.

The **archdiocese of Boston**, under the new leadership of Archbishop Sean O'Malley, settled most of the five hundred civil suits against it for $85 million in September 2003.

Arthur Austin has experienced a spiritual and religious reawakening, although he has not reconciled with his church. He continues on Social Security disability, at home with his mother.

Bishop Robert Banks remains as head of the Green Bay, Wisconsin, diocese. Massachusetts attorney general Thomas Reilly singled him out for harsh criticism for his role in "widespread cover-up that borders on the unbelievable," dating from his tenure in Boston as vicar general.

Gary Bergeron and his father, Joseph, spent a week with Bernie McDaid in Rome, where they called at the Bronze Door each morning, hoping for an audience with the pope. On their last day, Monsignor James Green, head of the English desk at the Vatican Secretariat of State and a high-ranking curial official, arrived at their hotel with a message from the pope: "The Holy Father realizes the seriousness of this problem, and is doing all he can. He will continue to do all he can to heal the church and to pray for the victims. He will see that this doesn't happen again." Through Green, they sent a message back, but have not yet gotten a reply.

Barbara Blaine, a Chicago attorney and advocate for abused and neglected children, was named a 2002 Woman of the Year by *Ms.* magazine for leadership of SNAP.

Tom Blanchette attends Episcopal services weekly. He and other SOJB members enjoy a good working relationship with their new archbishop.

The ***Boston Globe***'s Spotlight Team was awarded the 2003 George Polk Award for national reporting and the 2003 Pulitzer Prize for meritorious public service, two of journalism's highest honors.

Paul Ciaramitaro works with his father cooking and vending meals at construction sites. He hopes his share of the settlement will help him move out of his parents' home.

David Clohessy was named one of *People* magazine's 25 Most Intriguing People of 2002. He brought his children and wife to celebrate Thanksgiving 2002 at his parents' home, the first time in many years.

Father John Connolly serves as Archbishop O'Malley's personal secretary, the same position he held for Cardinal Bernard Law.

Father Neil Conway has not attended church services in many years. In November 2002, he went for a cup of coffee with a sixty-year-old man he met through the personals ads. It was Conway's first date. He was sixty-six at the time.

Patty Crowley celebrated her ninetieth birthday in August 2003. Her husband, Pat, died of cancer in 1974. The group they founded, the Christian Family Movement, declined sharply after the publication of *Humanae Vitae*.

Bishop Thomas Daily, whose negligence was detailed by the Massachusetts attorney general, resigned in August 2003 as head of the Brooklyn diocese. He cited his age, seventy-five, and not the scandal as his reason for stepping down.

Father Tom Doyle's superiors transferred him from Germany to Seymour Johnson Air Force Base, North Carolina, in October 2003, marking a homecoming after many years in foreign postings.

Bishop Walter Edyvean remains an auxiliary in Boston, now in charge of the archdiocese's western region.

Greg Ford was taken to a psychiatric hospital in restraints in September 2003 following a violent confrontation with his father. It was his eighteenth commitment. Meanwhile, he and his parents opted out of the global settlement agreement and were pursuing their case against the church in court.

Mitchell Garabedian was named Massachusetts Lawyer of the Year in 2002 and is recognized as the attorney who finally broke the church's code of silence.

Father Gilbert Gauthe was released from a Louisiana prison in 1995. Less than a year later, he was arrested in Texas for molesting a three-year-old boy and was sentenced to seven years' probation. In 1997, Louisiana jailed him again for raping a girl in 1982. He returned to Texas in 2000, where he was working as a bus driver for a Montgomery County senior center until recently, when his employer learned of his past.

Jackie Gauvreau tries not to say, "I told you so."

John Geoghan died in August 2003 after a premeditated attack by a fellow inmate. He was sixty-eight. His death, which sparked a statewide review of prison conditions, had an unintended consequence: because his case was on appeal at the time of his death, his conviction was automatically overturned.

Sister Jeannine Gramick received an order from the Vatican's Congregation for the Doctrine of the Faith in 1999 that permanently barred her from ministerial contact with homoscxuals. She continues speaking out against antigay prejudice nonetheless, now as a member of the Sisters of Loretto, an order dedicated to peace and justice. **Father Robert Nugent** was also silenced by the Vatican. Since the spring of 2000, he has been in compliance with his orders.

Mary Grant became SNAP's full-time regional director for the southwestern United States, and frequently spends her weekends protesting.

Bishop Wilton Gregory's three-year term as president of the United States Conference of Catholic Bishops ends in November 2004.

Father David Holley is serving a 275-year sentence in a western New Mexico prison for child abuse.

Olan Horne has recovered from minor surgery and remains involved in conversations with the Boston archdiocese on improving its response to abuse. He is still in touch with Cardinal Law.

Monsignor John J. Jennings is retired.

Cardinal Bernard Law is the chaplain for a convent in the suburbs of Washington, D.C. As a cardinal, he remains eligible to vote in papal elections until his eightieth birthday, in 2011.

Eric MacLeish, after spearheading the historic Boston settlements, plans to spend more time with his family.

Cardinal Roger Mahony remains the archbishop of Los Angeles. In May 2003 he dedicated a chapel within the new Cathedral of Our Lady of Angels in remembrance of sexual abuse survivors, none of whom were invited to the dedication.

Bishop John McCormack signed an agreement with the New Hampshire attorney general in December 2002 admitting the diocese of Manchester was guilty of failing to protect children. If he had not signed, Manchester would have been the first diocese in the nation to face criminal charges. He has not stepped down as bishop.

Bernie McDaid has separated from his wife. He suffered terrific financial pressures throughout the crisis, a result of meetings with church officials, lawyers, reporters, and survivors, which interfered with his house-painting business.

Patrick McSorley was found floating in the Neponset River in Massachusetts following a freak accident in June 2003 that resulted in a six-day coma. Shortly after his release from the hospital, police charged him with drug possession and arrested him a month later for failing to appear at a pretrial conference. "He's been through an awful lot," said his brother, William.

Donna Morrissey left her job as spokeswoman for the Boston archdiocese in April 2003. In September, she was named director of corporate affairs for the New England offices of the Red Cross.

Bishop John Mulcahy died in 1994, two years after resigning at age seventy as auxiliary bishop of Boston.

Bishop William Murphy remains bishop of the Rockville Centre, New York, diocese, having withstood demands for his resignation, a scathing 180-page grand jury report that called his abuse policy "a sham," and a district attorney who declared, "High-ranking prelates protected fifty-eight colleagues from disgrace rather than protecting children from these predator priests."

Father Ronald Paquin is serving a twelve-to-fifteen-year prison sentence in Massachusetts for child abuse.

Father James Porter is serving his eighteen-to-twenty-year sentence for child abuse in a Massachusetts psychiatric hospital. He waived a parole hearing in March 2002.

Bishop James S. Rausch died in 1981 while still serving as head of the Phoenix, Arizona, diocese, where his sexual activity was said to be widely known. He was succeeded by his vicar general, **Bishop Thomas J. O'Brien**, a tough administrator who used aggressive tactics to protect his priests from prosecution. To avoid a criminal indictment, in June 2003 O'Brien signed a deal with law enforcement officials relinquishing church authority over sexual abuse allegations. Two weeks later he stepped down following an unrelated indictment—for a hit-and-run accident in which a man died, a felony.

Wilson Rogers Jr. and his sons **Wilson Rogers III** and **Mark Rogers** were removed by Archbishop O'Malley in July 2003 from any involvement with the sexual abuse litigation.

Phil Saviano finally stepped down as coordinator of the New England SNAP chapter, and after a decade on disability started a business importing Mexican handicrafts, at Viva-Oaxaca.com. After the crisis broke, his father came to understand his struggles better, and in February 2002 told him he was proud of his efforts.

Father Paul Shanley posted $300,000 bail in December 2002 after spending seven months in a Cambridge jail. He awaits trial on ten counts of child rape and six counts of indecent assault and battery. Until then he cannot leave Massachusetts and cannot have contact with anyone under sixteen. His niece Theresa Shanley's support is undiminished.

Father Dominic George Spagnolia spent a year and a half demanding a hearing on the charge against him, without success. No trial date has been set. Meanwhile, Spags has begun buying and selling antiques, and considers going back to school to study antique appraising.

Dontee Stokes was acquitted in December 2002 of attempted murder, reckless endangerment, and assault for shooting and wounding **Father Maurice Blackwell**. On lesser gun charges, Stokes was sentenced to eighteen months of house arrest. Blackwell was indicted in May 2003 on four counts of child sexual abuse, including abuse of Stokes, and awaits trial.

Voice of the Faithful, now with formal affiliates in 188 American parishes, claims more than forty thousand members from forty states and twenty-one countries. It is still raising money for Boston-area charities.

Acknowledgments

When I began researching and writing this book, I saw before me a history of corporate crime and cover-up as unscrupulous as could be found in any industry. What I discovered instead was quite different—at once more profound and less clear-cut: the intensely trafficked crossroads of love and doubt, self-knowledge and faith, truth and abiding mystery. I found a church of individuals, many of them brokenhearted, all of them trying hard to look forward. My education in this came at the feet of many people who generously invited me into their lives and, for more than a year, allowed me clumsily to scrutinize them at their most intimate moments. For the faith they showed in me, my gratitude to them all is enormous.

Many agreed to help on deep background or off the record, and I thank them here—they know who they are. It is not possible to name all the others who shared their stories with me, but I want especially to recognize Gary Bergeron, Olan Horne, Bernie McDaid, and Paul Ciaramitaro; Father Neil Conway and Father Dominic George Spagnolia; Bishop Wilton Gregory, Father Stephen Rossetti, and Barbara Thorp; Mary Grant, David Clohessy, and Barbara Blaine; Patrick McSorley, Mark and Amy Keane, and Arthur Austin; Father Tom Doyle and Sister Jeannine Gramick; Jim Muller, Mary Calcaterra, Jim Post, Steven Krueger, and Mike Emerton. The history of the Roman Catholic Church in America is the history of their interior worlds.

No individual source was more helpful to me than Phil Saviano, whose enormous skills as a publicist are matched by his lasting patience and grace. He was my tour guide, interpreter, and friend throughout this enterprise.

If *Newsweek* had not cut short my vacation to send me to Boston, I would never have heard the first of the voices that came to populate this book. My thanks to all my colleagues there, especially Jonathan Alter, Jon Meacham, Marcus Mabry, and Ken Woodward, whose guidance—and examples—inform these pages.

It was both fortuitous and a curse that I was compiling this history from inside a crowded trench filled with seven hundred talented journalists from around the country. Because of their combined efforts in a year of truth telling, voices have been given to thousands of voiceless Catholics, allowing them to begin a healing journey. But their thoroughness was almost my undoing. A frustrating number of stones I encountered along the way were already overturned by them, and even when I managed to arrive there first, I was only just moments ahead of the pack. A journalist knows no greater disappointment than to lose a scoop. But my disadvantage became my advantage. By citing their extensive bodies of work here I was able to cover a lot more ground than humanly possible during this fast-breaking story. I am in their debt universally.

Among them, none more so than to the *Boston Globe*'s Spotlight Team, who produced a deep and broad record of this crisis on which I relied heavily. I also came to rely on the continual encouragement that the Spotlight staff showed me personally. Top investigative reporters were never known for their hearts; hereinafter, they will be. Their comportment throughout this crisis is the paradigm for a journalism of truth and compassion. My gratitude and pure admiration to Matt Carroll, Kevin Cullen, Thomas Farragher, Stephen Kurkjian, Michael Paulson, Sacha Pfeiffer, Michael Rezendes, and especially team editor Walter Robinson and *Globe* editor Marty Baron. In so many ways, this book would not have been possible without them.

I owe thanks to the lawyers handling the many cases around the country who took time to keep me informed, especially Mitchell Garabedian, Eric MacLeish, and Courtney Pillsbury in Boston, Eric Anderson in Minnesota, Lynne Cadigan in Tucson, Cindy Robinson in

Bridgeport, and Kathryn Freberg in Irvine. Their help was essential to finding and dissecting tens of thousands of courtroom records, around which much of this book is constructed. Through their forbearance, I met numerous rank-and-file Catholics who had been sexually victimized, or whose children or parents or siblings had. It was not possible to include all of their stories in one book. However, their lessons of strength and courage and trust inform every one of these pages.

I wish to thank Father Thomas Reese and Father James Martin at *America* magazine for their counsel, and Cindi Leive at *Glamour* for her extraordinary leniency and support. Special thanks also to Dan Curtis, David Kennedy, and Tom Donnelly for serving as my sounding boards when they thought it was the other way around.

I could not have completed this project without the able help of a tag team of editorial assistants, transcribers, and researchers: Brian Braiker, Mary Carmichael, Noah Derman, David Halperin, David Montero, and especially Tom Acitelli, whose days and nights spent laboring on this text were nearly as long as my own. His contributions to this book were enormous.

A word of thanks to Google, the Internet search engine. How a book was ever written before Google, I don't know.

For their thoughtful reading of parts or all of my manuscript, I thank Ande Zellman, Barry Yeoman, Debra Beard Bader, and Suki Kim; and for simple wisdom and uncommon support, my gratitude goes to Dorothy Maffei and David Burroughs, Domenico Rana and Richard Simms, Ellen Fanning, Bill Dobbs, Lisa Kessler, Steven Watt, Christopher Bader, Sally Chew, Kathleen Good, David Kirby, and Katrina Van Valkenburgh and Mike Newman.

Deepest gratitude goes to my agent and friend, Todd Shuster, who conceptualized the daunting enormity of this project and talked me into undertaking it, and to my Broadway Books family, especially Chuck Antony whose line edits saved me, and Gerry Howard, my terrific editor, whose invaluable advice tamed a sprawling manuscript.

Some years before the sexual abuse crisis erupted in the Catholic Church, my mother, Georgianne France, came upon similar dereliction within her Episcopal parish. For refusing to keep the church's secrets, she was sent into the exile of the uncooperative, separated from the faith that sustained her. The damage this cruelty did was visceral and permanent. Yet she never stood down, and ultimately prevailed. No hero in this book of heroes exceeds her in courage and moral bearing. For the many things she and my father, Gerald France, have taught me, my gratitude is immense.

Above all, I owe thanks to Jonathan Starch, my partner in all things, whose constancy and love impel me through each day and with luck will last forever.

New York
September 11, 2003

NOTES

My key resource for this book was tens of thousands of pages of court documents and hundreds of interviews I conducted around the country over a period of eighteen months, first in my role as a *Newsweek* senior editor and later exclusively for building the narrative that drives this book. Unfortunately, I was not able to speak to some principals in the crisis. Cardinal Bernard Law ignored a score of interview requests. Most members of his administration turned me down or ignored my calls and letters, a pattern repeated by heads of other dioceses around the country. Fathers John Geoghan and Paul Shanley declined interview requests, and Father Joseph Birmingham, whose short career in the priesthood caused so much sadness, was long dead. For their words and thoughts, I turned to the extensive record of court depositions available to me, as well as their contemporaneous notes found in various personnel files released by plaintiffs' attorneys, and interviews with their acquaintances. I believe I have accurately represented them here.

As in any work of history, it was my necessary challenge to re-create scenes, and for this I relied on long-ago published accounts of key events and the memories of those who witnessed them. To their exact recall I remained faithful. When the state of mind of an individual is presented—frequently as "she thought" or "he knew"—this is based on interviews with the individual, sworn depositions, or other published accounts, sometimes cast in quotation marks directly from the interviews, or else paraphrased in shorter form.

Where sources disagree, I have referenced the conflicts in the main text or the notes that follow. For the sake of continuity, some verb tenses have been changed. Events after January 2002 were witnessed or overheard by me, unless otherwise noted. What I have written is, I believe, all true.

CHAPTER 1. Before Orders

Late Summer 1953. Film dialogue: *I Confess,* 1953, by George Tabori and William Archibald, based on the play by Paul Anthelme. Spagnolia dialogue and thoughts: Interviews with Spagnolia.

Fall 1953. Bernard Francis Law background: *Boston Catholics* and interviews with the author, Thomas H. O'Connor, university historian and professor of history emeritus, Boston College; Jay Lindsay, "Once Hailed in Boston, Law Resigns in Disgrace," Associated Press, Dec. 13, 2002; "An Autobiographical Account, Written in '78," *Boston Globe,* Jan. 25, 1984; Anne Wyman, "Bernard Law's Early Years—Much Travel, Close-Knit Family," *Boston Globe,* Jan. 26, 1984; Jack Thomas, "Scandal Tarnishes Bright Career," *Boston Globe,* Apr. 14, 2002.

Spring 1954. Conway dialogue and thoughts: Interviews with Conway; interview with confidential source; parts of Conway's story first appeared in *Newsweek,* Apr. 1, 2002. Data from 1965 study: R. J. McAllister et al., "Psychiatric Illness in Hospitalized Catholic Religious," *American Journal of Psychiatry* (1965): 121, 881–84.

March 1954. Pius XII history: Joseph S. Brusher, *Popes Through The Ages* (Presidio Press, 1980); Robert Blair Kaiser, "Man of the Year," *Time,* Jan. 4, 1963. Septyckyj anecdote: Raul Hilberg, *Perpetrators Victims Bystanders: The Jewish Catastrophe, 1933–1945* (New York: HarperCollins, 1992). *Sacra Virginitas:* "Encyclical of Pope Pius XII on Consecrated Virginity," Mar. 25, 1954, Vatican electronic archives. Theological interpretations: Developed from interviews with various theologians, especially Lisa Cahill; J. Donald Monan, S.J., professor at Boston College; Mary Ann Hinsdale, director of the Institute for Religious Education and Pastoral Ministry at Boston College; James Keenan, moral theology professor at the Weston Jesuit School of Theology; Donald Cozzens, professor of religious studies, John Carroll University; R. Scott Appleby, professor of history, University of Notre Dame.

October 1954. Jennings anecdote: Eric Marcus, *Making History: The Struggle for Gay and Lesbian Equal Rights, 1945–1990: An Oral History* (HarperCollins, 1992). Assessment of the canon: Cory, *The Homosexual in America,* 160–69. McCarthy history: Donald A. Ritchie in his introduction to "Executive Sessions of the Senate Permanent Subcommittee on Investigations of the Committee on Government Operations," Vol. 1, Eighty-third Congress, First Session, 1953 (p. xxv). Eisenhower history: Kaiser, *Gay Metropolis,* 125. State laws: *The Homosexual in America; Gay Metropolis;* John Gerassi, *The Boys of Boise* (London: Macmillan, 1966), 98–99; *Laws of the Fifty-sixth General Assembly (1955),* quoted in "The Sensibility of Our Forefathers: The History of Sodomy Laws in the United States," self-published research by George Painter, 1991–2002. *One* article: "The Law of Mailable Material," *One: The Homosexual Viewpoint,* Oct. 1954, 6. Postmaster quote: Kenneth Pobo, "Journalism and Publishing," 2002, GLBTQ.com.

February 2, 1960. St. John history: Seminary archives; interviews with former seminarians; "The Role of the Church in the Causation, Treatment and Prevention of the Crisis in the Priesthood," unpublished study by Conrad Baars, delivered Nov. 1971 to all U.S. bishops. Blanchette anecdote: Interviews with Blanchette.

One Friday Afternoon, 1961. Miller anecdote: Andrew Wolfson, "A Priest's Troubled Path," *Courier-Journal,* Jun. 23, 2002; "The Rev. Louis E. Miller's Career and His Accusers," *Courier-Journal,* Jun. 23, 2002; Deborah Yetter, "Priest Indicted in Sex Cases," *Courier-Journal,* Jul. 27, 2002 (Miller pled guilty to charges involving more than twenty kids, and is serving a twenty-year sentence). School statistics: National Center for Education Statistics / Institute of Education Sciences, U.S. Dept. of Education; percentage derived from NCES data. Eighth-grader anecdote: Interview with subject; Br. Bernard F. Stratman, seminary department, NCEA. Nuns as percentage of workforce: Center for Applied Research in the Apostate (CARA), Georgetown University. Loneliness and alcohol data: ibid.

October 11, 1962. Color observations: Rynne, *Letters from Vatican City* (quotes) and interviews with Massimini. Pius XII and John XXIII histories: Allen, *Cardinal Ratzinger;* Bernstein and Politi, *His Holiness: John Paul II and the History of Our Time.* Adler anecdote: *Time,* Jan. 4, 1963. Momentous assessment: Interviews with Kaiser and Massimini. Leahy history: Anthony Massimini, "William K. Leahy: May 27, 1935–Jan. 2, 1999," Feb. 23, 1999, unpublished. Kaiser quote: *Time.* Pope quote: ibid. Assessment of curial dominance and Liénart quote: Bishop Charles Bushwell, "Vatican II, 40 Years Later," *National Catholic Reporter,* Oct. 4, 2002.

Summer 1962. Rogge and Swart anecdote: Interview with Swart; Laud Humphreys, *Tearoom Trade: Impersonal Sex in Public Places,* rev. ed. (Aldine de Gruyter, 1975). (Rogge was convicted of assaulting children in 1967 and 1985, but in April 2002 was still serving as a priest, according to Louis Rom, "Diocese Removes Two Priests Amid *Times* Investigation," *Times of Arcadiana,* Apr. 23, 2002.)

Spring 1963. Spagnolia anecdote: Interviews with Spagnolia. Celibacy: Abbott, *A History of Celibacy;* "Careful Selection and Training of Candidates for the States of Perfection and Sacred Orders," Vatican, Jan. 23, 1961. Boston archdiocese data: www.-Catholic-hierarchy.org. Minichiello quotes and seminary restrictions: Interview with Minichiello. "Jolly Johnny," "regular guy," and "never dated" quotes: Various interviews with St. John's alumni. Expulsion anecdote: Letter dated Jul. 31, 1954. Geoghan's uncle: Letter dated Jul. 9, 1955. Psychoanalysis as anathema: Interview with Minichiello; Gillespie, *Psychology and American Catholicism.* Sheen quote: *Psychology and American Catholicism,* 16. Moral textbooks: Various interviews.

May 18, 1963. Mothers of priests: Various interviews; Cozzens, *The Changing Face of the Priesthood.* Ordination quotes: Interviews with Conway. St. Thomas: Quoted in Vatican document, "The Relevance of Priestly Celibacy Today," Congregation for the Clergy, Jan. 1, 1993. John XXIII quote: Vatican document, *Sacerdotii Nostri Primordia,* Aug. 1, 1959, quoted in Thomas Doyle, "Roman Catholic Clericalism, Religious Duress, and Clerical Sexual Abuse," *Pastoral Psychology,* Jan. 2003. Cleveland priesthood figures: Interviews with Conway. Numbers and proportions of American Catholics and priests: CARA.

Late June 1966. Meeting background: Papers of John Marshall, at Notre Dame. Crowley involvement: McClory, *Turning Point,* 31, 62, 190. John XXIII's death: Luigi Sandri, "Blessed John XXIII's Remains Are Now on View at St. Peter's," *Christianity Today,* Jun. 11, 2001. Election anecdote: Peter Hebblethwaite, *Paul VI: The First Modern Pope* (Paulist Press, 1993) 330–31. *New Yorker* quote: in Wills, *Papal Sin,* 94. Quotes from Vatican II documents: Dogmatic Constitution on the Church, Nov. 21, 1964; Decree on the Apostolate of the Laity, Nov. 18, 1965, respectively, Vatican electronic archives. McBrien cite: Richard McBrien, "The Lay Apostolate," *Tidings,* Jan. 24, 2003. Apostles married: Peter, James, Jude, Judas, and Philip among them. History opposing contraception: Wills, *Papal Sin,* 75. Aquinas quote: *Papal Sin,* 76. Pius XI's view: *Casti Connubii:* Encyclical of Pope Pius XI on Christian Marriage, Dec. 31, 1930, Vatican electronic archives. Pius XII's view: *Turning Point,* 23. Efficacy rates: *Turning Point.* Letter to ACT: *Turning Point,* 53. Crowley speech: *Turning Point,* 104–5, emphasis added. Wills quote: *Papal Sin,* 91. Vote tally: *Papal Sin,* 93.

July 1966. Boy's anecdote: Unsigned handwritten memo in Shanley's personnel file, marked as evidence in court papers; Ralph Ranalli, "CEO Would Testify of Shanley Abuse, Diocese Neglect," *Boston Globe,* Jul. 22, 2003; "Plaintiffs' Memorandum of Law," *Gregory Ford et al. v. Bernard Cardinal Law et al.,* Jul. 21, 2003; Sally Jacobs, " 'If They Knew the Madness in Me,' " *Boston Globe,* Jul. 7, 2002.

Summer 1967. Muzzi anecdote: Various interviews with Anthony Muzzi Jr.; interviews with Garabedian; court complaint, "Deposition of Leonard Muzzi Jr.," Jan. 16, 2001; in interview, Geoghan denied all allegations against him; confirmed by deposition of Catherine Geoghan, Sept. 8, 2002.

June 24, 1967. Encyclical: *Sacerdotalis Caelibatus,* Encyclical of Pope Paul VI on the Celibacy of the Priest, Jun. 24, 1967, Vatican electronic archive. History of celibacy: "Priestly Celibacy and Problems of Inculturation," Cardinal Polycarp Pengo, Jan. 1, 1993, Vatican electronic archive. Popes' wives: J. N. D. Kelly, *Oxford Dictionary of Popes* (Oxford Press, 1986). Julius III: Richard McBrien, *Lives of the Popes,* 232, cited in *The Changing Face of the Priesthood,* 124. Gregory VII: Robert Blair Kaiser, "Resurrecting the Message of Jesus," *Newsweek,* Jul. 30, 2002. Martin Luther quote: *History of Celibacy,* 114. Paul VI encyclical: *Sacerdotalis Caelibatus.* Massimini and Leahy anecdotes: Various interviews with Massimini. "Judases": Ed Kohler, "Class Reunions Divide and Unite Priests," *National Catholic Reporter,* Mar. 21, 1997. Priests abdicating: Andrew Greeley, *The Catholic Priest in the United States: Sociological Investigations,* National Opinion Research Center study, 1971. National Conference: This entity changed its name in July 2001 to United States Conference of Catholic Bishops.

July 29, 1968. Crowley anecdote: Interview with Crowley; *Turning Point,* 35. Paul VI's text: In *Papal Sin,* 95, and *Turning Point,* 139. Backlash from bishops: *Papal Sin,* 86. Gallup poll: Aug. 7–12, 1968. Priests opposing: Megan Hartman, "*Humanae*

Vitae: Thirty Years of Discord and Dissent," *Conscience,* autumn 1998. Priests denying absolution and Catholics using contraception: Maurice J. Moore, *Death of a Dogma? The American Catholic Clergy's View of Contraception* (Community and Family Study Center, 1973), 35. Usage increased: C. Goldscheider and W. C. Mosher, "Patterns of Contraceptive Use in the United States: The Importance of Religious Factors," *Studies in Family Planning* 22, no. 2 (1991): 102–15. Among Protestants: Ibid. Paul complained: Hebblethwaite, *Paul VI,* 595. Attendance figures: *Turning Point,* 148. Conversation with Pat: Interview with Crowley; *Turning Point,* 137.

Fall 1968. McDaid anecdote: Interviews with McDaid; Bella English, "I Wanted to Run," *Boston Globe,* May 15, 2002; Birmingham is deceased. Wills quote: Wills, "Priests and Boys," *New York Review of Books,* Jun. 13, 2002.

Later in 1968. Austin anecdote: Interviews with Austin; through a family spokeswoman, Shanley acknowledges he knew Austin, but does not acknowledge the sexual relationship; Shanley declined interview requests. Deviations quote: *Diagnostic and Statistical Manual of Mental Disorders—I* (American Psychiatric Association, 1968). Beauty therapy: Arthur Guy Matthew, *Is Homosexuality a Menace?* (McBride, 1957), in Eric Marcus et al., eds., *Out in All Directions* (Warner Books, 1995).

Early 1969. Christmas collection plates: Interview with Coyne. Cushing quote: *Boston Catholics,* 275. Black clergy data: Contemporary figure from Rita McInerney, "Black Clergy Caucus Offers Prayer Support," *Georgia Bulletin,* May 9, 1988; 1930 figure from Timothy Meagher, university archivist and museum director, "Turning Toward a New Century," Catholic University of America electronic archives. Fichter quote: Joseph Fichter, *Organization Man in the Church* (Schenkman, 1974), cited in Barbara Balboni, "Through the 'Lens' of the Organizational Culture Perspective: A Descriptive Study of American Catholic Bishops' Understanding of Clergy Sexual Molestation and Abuse of Children and Adolescents," unpublished dissertation, Sept. 1998. Shanley background: "The 'Hippie Priest,'" *Vermont Sunday News,* Dec. 13, 1970. Doris Bland: for a history, see Rickie Solinger, *Beggars and Choosers: How the Politics of Choice Shapes Adoption, Abortion, and Welfare in the United States* (Hill & Wang, 2002).

June 28, 1969. Stonewall background: Teal, *The Gay Militants,* 17–27; Duberman, *Stonewall,* 194. Homosexual population: Based on accepted estimates from 3 to 10 percent. Suicide statistics: "Gay Male and Lesbian Youth Suicide," Report of the Secretary's Task Force on Youth Suicide, U.S. Department of Health and Human Services, 1989. Cross-dress statute: David France, *Bag of Toys* (Warner, 1992), 76. Philadelphia protests: Interview with Frank Kameny, seminal activist and first gay candidate for Congress.

Winter 1969. Aquinas quote: *Summa Theologica,* Question 154, 11. Vatican document: "Careful Selection and Training of Candidates for the States of Perfection and Sacred Orders," Sacred Congregation of Religious, Feb. 2, 1961, Vatican electronic archives. Dissociative disorder: Interview with Dr. Mel Allerhand.

CHAPTER 2. After the Summer of Love

Fall 1969. Birmingham's background: Various personnel records. McDaid background: Interviews with McDaid; Bella English, "I Wanted to Run," *Boston Globe*, May 15, 2002. Rediker quote: English, ibid. Survey of adult abuse survivors: Lois Timnick, "22 Percent in Survey Were Child Abuse Victims," *Los Angeles Times*, Aug. 25, 1985. Girls' abuse likelihood: Cathy Schoen, et al., "The Commonwealth Fund Survey of the Health of Adolescent Girls," The Commonwealth Fund, Nov. 1997 (of 6,748 students in grades five through twelve surveyed, 12 percent of girls reported they had been "sexually abused," versus 4 percent of boys). National Victim poll: "Rape in America: A Report to the Nation," National Victim Center and the Crime Victims Research and Treatment Center, 1992. Relationship to rapist: Bonnie S. Fisher et al., *The Sexual Victimization of College Women*, U.S. Department of Justice, National Institute of Justice and Bureau of Justice Statistics, Dec. 2000; "Sexual Assault of Young Children as Reported to Law Enforcement: Victim, Incident, and Offender Characteristics," U.S. Department of Justice, National Institute of Justice and Bureau of Justice Statistics, Jul. 2000. Fewer men report: Dorais, *Don't Tell,* 16. Priests targeting teens: Sipe, *Sex, Priests, and Power: Anatomy of a Crisis,* 13–15; Plante, *Bless Me Father For I Have Sinned,* 2, 89. Doyle study: "Roman Catholic Clericalism, Religious Duress, and Clerical Sexual Abuse." Pius V views: Pietro Cardinal Gasparri, ed., *Codicis Iuris Canonici Fontes,* vol. 1 (Typis Polyglottis Vaticanis, 1926). Code of Canon Law: Doyle study. Papal document: "Instruction on the Manner of Proceeding in Cases of Solicitation," Vatican Press, 1962, English translation of unknown origin, discovered by Doyle but acknowledged by Vatican. Jenkins data: Interview with Jenkins. Finkelhor data: Interview with David Finkelhor, director, Crimes Against Children Research Center, University of New Hampshire. Likelihood that gays will molest: Carole Jenny et al., "Are Children at Risk for Sexual Abuse by Homosexuals?" *Pediatrics* 94 (1994): 41–44. Authors reviewed records of 352 children admitted at Denver Children's Hospital and found that .07 percent of perpetrators were gay or lesbian. Also M. R. Stevenson, "Public Policy, Homosexuality, and the Sexual Coercion of Children," *Journal of Psychology and Human Sexuality* 12, no. 4 (2000): 1–19.

November 1969. McDaid background: Interviews with McDaid; Bobby Abraham did not wish to be interviewed; "Bobby" did not wish to have his last name known; "Michael" could not be located.

January 12, 1970. Anne McDaid history: Court records.

January 17, 1970. Jennings history: Jennings deposition, May 9, 2001. Archdiocesan data: Interview with Christopher Coyne, spokesman for Roman Catholic archdiocese of Boston; catholic-hierarchy.org; Andrew Bushell, "How the Church Went Wrong," *Slate,* Dec. 19, 2002. Jennings letter: Court documents. Massachusetts consent laws: Correspondence with Kate Trafaglia, Massachusetts District Attorneys Association. Chancery meeting with McCabe and Taylor: Globe Staff, *Betrayal,* 57;

contemporaneous notes signed "TJF," dated Nov. 4, 1964, in court documents. McCabe quotes: Sacha Pfeiffer, "Dozens More Allege Abuse by Late Priest," *Boston Globe*, Apr. 4, 2002. Sexton quote: *Betrayal*, 57. Birmingham quote: "TJF" notes. Massachusetts legal penalties: Correspondence with Hartwell, electronic resources librarian, Social Law Library, Massachusetts. Send-off party: Interview with Blanchette. McGee quote: Interview with McGee.

Mid-January 1970. Shanley anecdotes: Unless otherwise noted, see Paul Shanley, "Letter #3: The Hermit of Terrible Mountain or The Street Priest," undated manuscript received at cardinal's residence, Mar. 8, 1972; Don Clark, "Teen Exodus Predicted," *Boston Herald American*, Mar. 23, 1970. Combat Zone: *Crimson*, Nov. 30, 2000. Shanley's total acceptance of kids: Sally Jacobs, " 'If They Knew the Madness in Me,' " *Boston Globe*, Jul. 10, 2002. "Jesus" quote: Shanley, "Letter #11: Communes," manuscript, May 1, 1970. Holmes quote: *National Geographic Atlas of the World Revised*, 1995. Castro quote: Tom Hayden, "Two, Three Many Columbias," *Ramparts*, Jun. 15, 1968. Drug arrest data: FBI Uniform Crime Report, 2001; *Boston Globe*, Jun. 16, 1971, cited in Shanley's "Notes from the Road," unpublished manuscript, Jul. 1, 1972. O'Connor attribution: *Boston Catholics*, 254.

March 1970. McGee anecdote: Interviews with McGee and Bernie McDaid; Plaintiff's Memorandum of Law, *Ford v. Law*, Jul. 21, 2003. Her boy Matthew: A pseudonym at McGee's request. Sr. Grace quote: Interview with McGee.

April 3, 1970. Meeting anecdote: Interviews with McGee and Bernie McDaid; dialogue per McGee (Jennings, in a Dec. 2002 deposition, said he had no memory of this meeting.) McCormack meeting and dialogue: Interview with McGee; McCormack various depositions; dialogue per McGee.

August 1970. Campus high school project: Pam Bishop, "Roxbury Priest Starts Vigil for New School," *Boston Herald-Traveler*, date unknown for clip in court documents. Cushing retirement and Medeiros appointment: *Boston Catholics*, 287–89. New collection-plate policy: Correspondence with Coyne. New "appeal": Correspondence with O'Connor. Management structure: Bushell, "How the Church Went Wrong." Spags and Medeiros quotes: Bishop, "Roxbury Priest Starts Vigil for New School." "Oh, my brother" and "I'm doing *this*" quotes: Interview with Spagnolia.

Later in 1970. Lowell history: Courtesy Lowell National Historical Park Service. Kerouac quote: Catherine Watson, "If You Go to Lowell, Mass." *Minneapolis Star-Tribune*, Jan. 16, 2000. Horne anecdote and all dialogue: Interviews with Horne.

December 1970. Shanley anecdote and dialogue: "Boston Clergyman Jolts Audience in St. Albans," *Burlington Free-Press*, Dec. 8, 1970. *Vermont Sunday News*: Editorial, *Vermont Sunday News*, Dec. 3, 1970. Medeiros quote: Letter to Shanley, Mar. 5, 1970. "New Niggers" quote: Charley Lerrigo, "Priest Sees Bisexuals as New Niggers," *Boston Phoenix*, Jan. 16, 1973. Paralyzed campuses: *Pace [University] Press*, May 15, 1970. "These unfortunate" quote: Letter to Shanley, Mar. 5, 1970. Seminary admissions: *Boston Catholics*, 289–90.

November 1971. Baars study: "The Role of the Church in the Causation, Treatment and Prevention of the Crisis in the Priesthood." Terruwe anecdote: Correspondence with Sue Baars. Report distribution anecdote: Correspondence with Michael Baars. Kennedy study quotes: see Eugene Kennedy, *The Catholic Priest in the United States: Psychological Investigations*, United States Catholic Bishops Conference, 1972. Seper quote: Wills, "The Scourge of Celibacy," *Boston Globe Magazine,* Mar. 24, 2002. Data on sexual activity: Sipe, "Preliminary Expert Report," unpublished, 15–16.

Summer 1972. Ouija board, etc.: Shanley, "Notes from the Road"; George Weldmann, "Father Shanley Quits Streets, Sees Revolt," *Boston Globe,* undated. Stonewall anniversary and national assessment: D'Emilio, *Sexual Politics, Sexual Communities,* 238–45; D'Emilio quote: Ibid., 245. Boston-area assessment: Courtesy of the History Project, Boston, Mass. *Time* magazine: "Sex and the Teenager," *Time,* Aug. 21, 1972. Shanley quote: Charles Lerrigo, "Priest Says Alienated Youth Sexually Confused," *National Catholic Reporter,* Feb. 16, 1973. Seven biblical passages: For a study of these, see especially John Boswell, *Christianity, Social Tolerance, and Homosexuality* (University of Chicago Press, 1981). Pope orgiasts: Correspondence with Nelson H. Minnich, professor of history, Catholic University of America; Jordan, *The Silence of Sodom,* 117; Boswell, ibid. Shanley quote: Shanley, "Covering Letter," undated 39-page letter addressed to "friends," "Notes From the Road." Medeiros letter: Various drafts found among Shanley's personnel records. Shanley's reply: Dated Feb. 21, 1973.

Fall 1972. McDaid anecdotes: Interviews with McDaid.

Spring Semester 1973. Bergeron anecdotes: Interviews with Gary Bergeron, Edward Bergeron, and Joseph Bergeron.

June 5, 1973. School anecdote: Interviews with Spagnolia; correspondence between Medeiros and Spagnolia. Office of Black Catholics anecdote: Interview with Spagnolia; however, no such letter appears in Spagnolia's otherwise thorough personnel file released in court records, and the office is defunct and its officers could not be located. Office background: University of St. Thomas Archives and Special Collections, St. Paul, Minn., "National Office of Black Catholics."

Sunday, September 2, 1973. Conference history: Conference agenda and program, courtesy Dignity/USA electronic archives; interviews with John J. McNeill; text of McNeill speech courtesy of him.

October 1973. McLean anecdote: Interview with McLean.

1970s. Lane background and anecdote: Various court documents; Lane personnel files; MacLeish letter to Law, Sep. 27, 1993 (Lane, since retired, has not been charged with crimes but is named in pending suits.) DYS officials: Matt Carroll, "State Action on Priest Fell Short," *Boston Globe,* Mar. 25, 2002. Surette background: Tom Mashberg, "Priest Removed Amid Charges He Reassigned Others," *Boston Herald,* May 31, 2002 (the archdiocese settled a suit against him for $50,000).

June 1974. Mueller background and anecdote: Mueller deposition, Aug. 17, 2000; *Betrayal,* 19–21 (though she divorced in 1970, she was also still using her married name, McLean). All quotes: Mueller deposition, Aug. 17, 2000. Miceli anecdote: Ibid.; Miceli deposition, Sept. 9, 2000. Miceli quotes: McLean deposition, but specifically denied in Miceli deposition—in fact, Miceli testified that McLean had telephoned anonymously, rather than visited; that she was not in tears; that she never mentioned allegations of inappropriate touching, but complained that Geoghan was spending too much time at her home. Stokes et al. anecdote: Answers by Plaintiff Richard Stokes to Interrogatories Propounded by the Defendant Father Paul E. Miceli, Jul. 19, 2001; Answers by Plaintiff Ronald Oreto to Interrogatories Propounded by the Defendant Most Rev. Thomas V. Daily, Aug. 3, 2001; Answers by John McLean to Interrogatories Propounded by the Defendant Most Rev. Thomas V. Daily, Feb. 2, 2001.

Late Summer 1974. McGee anecdote and quotes: Interviews with McGee; interview with Ray McKeon. McKeon anecdote and quotes: Interview with McKeon.

CHAPTER 3. Gay Is Good

June 3, 1974. Conference anecdote: Interviews with McNaught and Gramick; Dignity/USA electronic archives; Brian McNaught, *A Disturbed Peace: Selected Writings of an Irish Catholic Homosexual* (Dignity Inc., 1981). Psychological research: See the studies of Evelyn Hooker, 1957–71. Freud quote: E. Jones, *Sigmund Freud: Life and Work* (1957), 208–9. APA designations: Kaiser, *The Gay Metropolis,* 235–40; correspondence with Robert Spitzer, Columbia College of Physicians and Surgeons. Bishops' guide: "Principles to Guide Confessors in Questions of Homosexuality," 1973. Priests' councils plank: "Civil Rights of Homosexual Persons," 1974. *Michigan* quote: McNaught, "Gay or Straight, Love Is the Goal," *Michigan Catholic,* 1974 (specific date unknown), from McNaught archives. McNaught employment problems: Interviews with McNaught and Gramick; Shanley diaries; Dignity/USA electronic archives. Gramick background: Interviews with Gramick; CBC broadcast, Jun. 24, 2001.

December 29, 1975. Magisterium background: McNeill, *The Church and the Homosexual,* 11–12. *Persona* quotes: *Persona Humana:* Declaration on Certain Questions Concerning Sexual Ethics, Dec. 29, 1975, text in Vatican electronic archive. "We can be birds" quote: CBC broadcast, Jun. 24, 2001. National seminary enrollment: "Catholic Ministry Formation Enrollments: Statistical Overview for 2001–2002," CARA, Mar. 2002; Richard Schoenherr et al., *Full Pews and Empty Altars* (University of Wisconsin Press, 1993). Boston seminary enrollment: Interview with Coyne. Medeiros quote: *Boston Catholics,* 290.

Sometime in 1976. Reticent priest anecdote: J. M. Hirsch, "Sources Say Documents Show McCormack Doubts Victims," Associated Press, Feb. 10, 2003.

September 23, 1977. Shanley quotes: Correspondence from Stevens to Sweeney, Oct. 4, 1977; correspondence from Sweeney to Medeiros, Nov. 17, 1977. Shanley tapes: Numerous leaflets in court records. Shanley opinions: "Notes from the Road." Becket Hall details: Diocese of Rochester internal memo, Sept. 13, 1977. Rochester diocese meeting: Sweeney memos, Nov. 2, 1977, and Nov. 17, 1977. Daily opinions: Daily deposition, Aug. 21, 2002. Daily quotes: Correspondence to Sweeney, Dec. 2, 1977.

October 14, 1978. Wojtyla handicapping and background: Allen, *Cardinal Ratzinger,* 120. Five hundred years: The last non-Roman was Adrian VI, elected in 1523. Balloting anecdote: *Cardinal Ratzinger,* 121–22; Bernstein and Politi, *His Holiness,* 165–71. Pope quote on abortion: "On Combatting Abortion and Euthanasia: Letter of Pope John Paul II to All the World's Bishops," May 19, 1991, Vatican electronic archives. Allen quote: *Cardinal Ratzinger,* 177.

Winter 1978. Kennedy anecdote: Joseph A. Reaves, "Priest Freed by Statute of Limitations," *Arizona Republic,* Jan. 8, 2003; Robert Nelson, "The Pain of Publicity," *Phoenix New Times,* Apr. 22, 2002; news release, Office of the Maricopa County Attorney, Richard M. Romley, Jan. 9, 2003.

November 14, 1978. Seper letter: Original in court documents. Medeiros treatment of Shanley complaints: Various court documents and Shanley's personnel file. Daily's replies to complaints: Various correspondence in personnel file, e.g., Daily's Dec. 27, 1977, correspondence to James Mang: "In the absence of His Eminence, The Cardinal, I write to acknowledge your letter to him of Dec. 19, 1977, regarding Father Paul Shanley's appearance in the Buffalo area. I shall be happy to convey your message to His Eminence and I know that he will deeply appreciate your interest." Medeiros's reply to the CDF: Correspondence to Seper, Feb. 12, 1979. Medeiros meeting with Shanley: Shanley correspondence to Medeiros, Feb. 9, 1979. Shanley quote in the *Globe:* James L. Franklin, "Priest Told to End His Ministry for Homosexuals," *Boston Globe,* Feb. 2, 1979; see also George Vescey, "Priest's Transfer Indicates Strife on Homosexuality," *New York Times,* Apr. 25, 1979. One mother quote: Franklin, ibid. Medeiros letter transferring Shanley: Correspondence to Shanley, Apr. 12, 1979. Shanley's angry reply: Michael Rezendes, "Files Show Shanley Tried Blackmail Letter," *Boston Globe,* Apr. 26, 2002. Medeiros's last word: Daily deposition, Aug. 21, 2002.

CHAPTER 4. Falling Apart

August 1979. Coveny anecdote: Daily deposition, Aug. 22, 2002.

August 17, 1979. Delaney letter: Filed in court record.

August 23, 1979. Daily response to letter: Daily deposition, Sept. 13, 2000. Quotes from letter: In court documents.

A Summer Night, 1979. O'Connell anecdote and quotes: Interview with O'Connell.

Christmastime 1979. Dussourd anecdote and dialogue: Dussourd deposition, Aug. 24, 2001; Matt Carroll, "A Revered Guest; a Family Left in Shreds," *Boston Globe,* Jan. 6, 2002; interview with Garabedian (Garabedian did not make Dussourd available for interview; her account of her husband's outburst has not been challenged or corroborated by her former husband). Netherlands study: C. W. G. Jasperse, "Self-Destruction and Religion," *Mental Health and Society* 3 (1976): 154–68 (case-control study of 9,189 suicides in Netherlands between 1961 and 1970 that compared suicide rates between Catholics and non-Catholics in each of those years; as Catholicism loses its hold, rates of suicide among Catholics rise to approximate rates in non-Catholics).

February 9, 1980. Dussourd anecdote and quotes: Dussourd depositions, Aug. 24 and 25, 2001. Thomas anecdote and quotes: Thomas deposition, Jan. 26, 2001; Daily deposition, Sept. 13, 2000. Geoghan quotes: Ibid. Daily letter: Court documents. Daily's plan: Daily deposition, Sept. 13, 2000. Thomas meeting with Dussourd and dialogue: Dussourd deposition, Apr. 24, 2001. Geoghan's next year: Brennan deposition, Sept. 21, 2000.

July 1981. Gauvreau background, anecdote with baby, and dialogue: Interviews with Gauvreau. Lagace background and Shanley's health: Internal memo referring to conversation with Shanley, signature illegible, Dec. 20, 1982. Shanley seeking transfer: Shanley letter to Fr. Gilbert Phinn, Sept. 28, 1979; Phinn to Shanley, Oct. 5, 1979. Quinn background, anecdote, and quotes: Interviews with Gauvreau; interviews with Quinn. However, Shanley's personnel file held Gauvreau's official 1983 complaint on this event, mentioning Shanley's comments to Quinn but not mentioning any alleged molestation; nor do subsequent official complaints (under the names Jacqueline Sagrera and "Jackie X") mention molestation. Gauvreau complaint sequence and quote: In Sacha Pfeiffer, "Woman Says Church Ignored Her Outcries," *Boston Globe,* Feb. 13, 2002. Gauvreau anecdote calling chancery: Interviews with Gauvreau; Daily letter to Shanley regarding his methods thwarting the likes of Gauvreau, in Daily deposition, Aug. 22, 2002. Gauvreau "sisters" quote: Interview with Gauvreau. Shanley barring her from Mass: Record of official complaint, Nov. 14, 1984. White quote: Interviews with Gauvreau. Shanley quote: Interviews with Gauvreau. Mother-daughter dialogue: Interviews with Gauvreau. Choir ban: Gauvreau's official 1983 complaint. Account of intervention and all dialogue: Interviews with Gauvreau.

July 24, 1982. Dussourd dialogue with son: Dussourd depositions, Aug. 24 and 25, 2001. Dussourd meeting with Daily: Kristen Lombardi, "Cardinal Sin," *Boston Phoenix,* Mar. 23, 2001; Noah Bierman, "Bishop Overlooked Allegations of Sexual Abuse," Cox News Service, Mar. 17, 2002; typed Daily notes, in court records. Gallant letter to Medeiros: Court records, date illegible, Aug. 1982. Medeiros reply letter: Court records, Aug. 20, 1982. Dussourd's temperature: Bierman, "Bishop Overlooked Allegations of Sexual Abuse."

December 14, 1982. Daily letter to Shanley: Aug. 22, 2002.

June 30, 1983. Gauthe anecdote and dialogue: Berry, *Lead Us Not into Temptation,* 14. Gauthe history: *Lead Us,* 61, 82–83. Mouton's approval of Gauthe: *Lead Us,* 52–55. Anonymous letter: *Lead Us,* 59. Gauthe's admission of "thirty-five": Janet Pume, "Child Molestation Trial Against Priest Opens," UPI, Oct. 13, 1985. Gauthe began to cry, anecdote, and quotes: *Lead Us,* 14. Sexual orientation correlation with abuse: *Sexual*

Preference, 98–104. Robichaux anecdote: *Lead Us*, 6–19 (name is pseudonym supplied by Berry). Sagrera anecdote and "evil" quotes: Michael Paulson, "Church Struggle Pains La. Region Stung by Abuse in '80s," *Boston Globe*, Jun. 12, 2002. Gauthe hotel arrangements: *Lead Us*, 15. House of Affirmation background: Servants of the Paraclete electronic archives. Gauthe's tenure: *Lead Us*, 38. Gauthe's tenure at Institute: *Lead Us*, 49.

Late 1983. Medeiros's death: O'Connor, *Boston Catholics*, 303. Shanley's promotion: Daily letter, Nov. 4, 1983. Shanley moves office: Maureen Orth, "Unholy Communion," *Vanity Fair*, Aug. 2002. Gauvreau thoughts: Interviews with Gauvreau. Shanley's quotes: Interviews with Gauvreau; interview with MacLeish. Gauvreau's quotes: Interviews with Gauvreau.

CHAPTER 5: Secret's Out

October 18, 1984. Gauthe indictment and scope of crimes: Barry Yeoman, "Is Nothing Sacred?," *Times of Acadiana*, Nov. 1, 1984; John Pope, "Church Knew of Abuses, Sex Case Depositions Show," *New Orleans Times-Picayune/States-Item*, Nov. 9, 1984. Robichaux reception in community: Berry, *Lead Us Not into Temptation*, 23–24. Legal trends against child abuse: See Levine, *Harmful to Minors*. Plethysmograph study: Gordon C. Nagayama Hall et al., "Sexual Arousal and Arousability to Pedophilic Stimuli in a Community Sample of Normal Men," *Behavior Therapy* 26 (1995): 681–94. Indifferent to gender: Interview with J. Michael Baily, chairman, department of psychology, Northwestern University. Cause of condition: A pedophile is a person with "recurrent intense sexual urges and arousing sexual fantasies involving sexual activity with a prepubescent child or children," according to the *Diagnostic and Statistical Manual for Mental Disorders IV—TR* (Washington: American Psychiatric Association, 2000). Presley and Zeus: Priscilla has said she did not have sex with Presley until their marriage, many years later; Zeus stole Ganymede and his many tutors and guards off to Olympia, indirectly touching off the Trojan War and angering his wife. Most teen attraction is simple lust: Interview with Baily. Brain scans: R. Langevin et al., "Neuropsychological Impairment in Incest Offenders," *Annals of Sex Research* 1 (1988): 401–16, cited in *Bless Me Father For I Have Sinned*, 63–64. Lothstein data: Interviews with Lothstein. Abused abuser hypothesis: Finkelhor correspondence; Lois Timnick, "22 Percent in Survey Were Child Abuse Victims," *Los Angeles Times*, Aug. 25, 1985; Randall J. Garland et al., "The Abused/Abuser Hypothesis of Child Sexual Abuse: A Critical Review of Theory and Research," in J. Feierman, ed., *Pedophilia: Biosocial Dimensions* (New York: Springer-Verlag, 1990), 488–509. Haywood study: Haywood et al., "Cycle of Abuse and Psychopathology in Cleric and Noncleric Molesters of Children and Adolescents," *Child Abuse and Neglect* 20, no. 12 (1966): 1233–43. Institute of Living data: Lothstein, "Neurological Findings in Clergy Who Sexually Abuse," in *Bless Me Father For I Have Sinned*, 63–78; and interviews with Lothstein. Not seen as violation of celibacy: Interviews with Lothstein.

January 25, 1985. Doyle's background and thoughts, and telephone dialogue with Paterson: Interviews and correspondence with Doyle. Johns Hopkins survey: Caryle Murphy, "For Gay Catholic Priests, New Scrutiny," *Washington Post,* Jun. 24, 2002. Proportions of gay and straight pedophiles/ephebophiles: C. Jenny, et al., "Are Children at Risk for Sexual Abuse by Homosexuals?," *Pediatrics* 94(1), 44–44 (1994); M. R. Stevenson, "Public Policy, Homosexuality, and the Sexual Coercion of Children," *Journal of Psychology and Human Sexuality* 12(4), 1–19 (2000). Opinion survey: James G. Wolf, *Gay Priests* (San Francisco: Harper and Row, 1989), 59–60. "The male body" survey: Paul Wilkes, "The Hands That Would Shape Our Souls," *Atlantic,* Dec. 1990 (in 1969, only 35 percent had the same response). Pedophiles no more gay than straight: Interview with Fred Berlin, founder of the sexual disorders clinic at Johns Hopkins University. Peterson's homosexuality: Thomas Fox, "What They Knew in 1995," *National Catholic Reporter,* May 17, 2002. Peterson quote: *Lead Us,* 77–78. Jan. 25 meeting: Correspondence with Doyle. O'Connell and Authenreith anecdotes: Bruni and Burkett, *A Gospel of Shame,* pp. 158–60. Galindo anecdote: *San Diego Union,* Dec. 29, 1985. Baltazar anecdote: "Church blamed in priest misconduct," news services, *Washington Post,* Jan. 24, 1985. Treinen anecdote: *A Gospel of Shame,* 157.

April 24, 1985. Law's elevation anecdote: James L. Franklin, "Bernard Law Receives Red Hat of Cardinal," *Boston Globe,* May 26, 1985. Law's career: O'Connor, *Boston Catholics,* 304–6. "After Boston" quote: Steve Marantz, "Many Praise Law's Work for Justice, Harmony," *Boston Globe,* Apr. 25, 1985. Pope's sweep of influence and Law's abortion views: James L. Franklin, "An Endorsement of His Leadership: Archbishop Law's Appointment Reflects Pope's Efforts to Shape Catholic Church," *Boston Globe,* Apr. 25, 1985. "Wise as serpents" quote: Franklin, "Bernard Law Receives Red Hat of Cardinal." Afternoon reception anecdote: Maria Karagianis, "Archbishop and Pilgrims Share an Occasion of Joy," *Boston Globe,* May 25, 1985; James L. Franklin, "Archbishop Law Arrives in Rome," *Boston Globe,* May 22, 1985.

June 1985. History of manual: Interviews and correspondence with Doyle; Thomas Doyle, "A Short History of the Manual," unpublished account, May 27, 2002. Citation from manual: F. Ray Mouton, Thomas P. Doyle, and Michael Peterson, "The Problem of Sexual Molestation by Roman Catholic Clergy: Meeting the Problem in a Comprehensive and Responsible Manner," unpublished, 1985. "Sometimes" quote: *Lead Us,* 112.

August 1985. Conway anecdote and dialogue: Interviews with Conway (efforts to reach Michael Doyle, who made his accusation public in a lawsuit, were not successful), substantially confirmed by diocese and clips. Allerhand anecdote: Interviews with Conway and Allerhand. Confession versus talk therapy: T. Postolache et al., letter in *Psychiatric Services* 48 (1997): 1592. Conway's treatment and diagnosis: Interviews with Conway; medical records; interview with Allerhand. First study: John Allan Loftus, "Sexuality in Priesthood: Noli Me Tangere," in Plante, *Bless Me Father For I Have Sinned,* 15. Second (McGlone) study: Robert Nugent, "Healthy Celibate Priests," *Vo-*

cations and Prayer, Apr.–Jun. 2002. Third (unpublished) study: An unpublished doctoral dissertation cited in Richard Sipe, "Preliminary Expert Report," unpublished, prepared for Dallas attorney Sylvia Demerest for plaintiffs in *John Doe I–XI v. Rudolph Kos et al.* and other actions.

October 1, 1986. Ratzinger anecdote and excerpts: "Letter to the Bishops of the Catholic Church on the Pastoral Care of Homosexual Persons," Oct. 1, 1986. Dignity history: Interviews with Marianne Duddy, executive director, Dignity/USA.

Sometime in 1986. Law's helicopter: James L. Franklin, "After a Turbulent Month, Cardinal Law Discusses Gains, Losses," *Boston Globe,* Nov. 11, 1986. Management structure: Interviews with Donna Morrissey. Nicaragua anecdote: See Bob Woodward, *The Veil: The Secret Wars of the CIA, 1981–1987* (New York: Simon & Schuster, 1990). Gauvreau anecdote: Interviews with Gauvreau.

Summer 1986. Doyle anecdote and thoughts: Interviews and correspondence with Doyle; copies of internal memoranda reproving his efforts. "Inquisition" quote: *Lead Us,* 325.

Early 1987. Birmingham anecdote: Handwritten notes from the meeting signed by Auxiliary Bishop John J. Mulcahy, dated Feb. 12, 1987.

March 25, 1987. Necochea anecdote: From her letter of Mar. 25, 1987, to McCormack. McCormack dialogue with Birmingham: McCormack depositions, Jun.–Nov. 2002. Law meeting with Birmingham: Law deposition, Aug. 13, 2002. Cleared for Gloucester: Personnel records. One St. Anne parishioner anecdote: Letter dated Apr. 4, 1987, to Law, name redacted. McCormack reply: Letter dated Apr. 14, 2002. Law's thoughts: Law deposition, Aug. 13, 2002.

Sometime in 1987. Gauvreau anecdote and dialogue with Law: Interviews with Gauvreau (Law has said he does not recall the event). Ciaramitaro anecdote, background, and dialogue: Interviews with Ciaramitaro; Gail McCarthy, "Local Man Among Victims of the Rev. Birmingham," *Gloucester Daily Times,* Jan. 20, 2003.

The Following Sunday, 3 P.M. Ciaramitaro anecdote: Interviews with Ciaramitaro; Birmingham personnel records signed by Mulcahy and Banks. Ciaramitaro's confusion: Interviews with him. ABC poll: Aug. 1987. Antigay violence: G. M. Herek, "Hate Crimes Against Lesbians and Gay Men: Issues for Research and Policy," *American Psychologist* 44, no. 6 (1989): 948–55. *Rolling Stone* poll: Peter D. Hart Research Associates, "The *Rolling Stone* Survey," Sept. 1987.

March 29, 1988. Gramick history with New Ways Ministry: Interviews with Gramick; "Gramick/Nugent Case, 1988–1999," *National Catholic Reporter,* undated. Hickey anecdote and Rome's reply: Letter from Archbishop Vincent Fagiolo, prefect of the Congregation for Religious and Secular Institutes, to Gramick, dated Jul. 23, 1988, repeats this history. Forced to withdraw: "Report of the Findings of the Commission Studying the Writings and Ministry of Sister Jeannine Gramick, SSND, and Father Robert Nugent, SDA," Oct. 4, 1994. Gramick barred from various dioceses: Press release, Roman Catholic Faithful, May 31, 1997. Meetings disrupted: Press release, ibid. Baltimore motherhouse anecdote: Letter from Archbishop Vincent Fagiolo, prefect of the Congregation for Religious and Secular Institutes, to Gramick, dated Jul. 23, 1988.

Late November 1988. Blanchette anecdote, thoughts, and dialogue: Interviews with Blanchette.

April 18, 1989. Blanchette anecdote, thoughts, and all dialogue: Interviews with Blanchette (efforts to reach Kelly were not successful). Birmingham's health data: Interviews with Courtney Pillsbury. Fuller suspicions: Interview with Fuller. Barone observations and quotes: Judy L. Thomas, "Catholic Priests Are Dying of AIDS, Often in Silence," *Kansas City Star,* Jan. 29, 2000. O'Sullivan background: He pled guilty to sex with altar boy, per Wendy Davis, "Priest Differs with Law Testimony," *Boston Globe*, Mar. 12, 2003. Percentage of the general population: Interview with Berlin. Funeral anecdote: Interviews with Blanchette; in depositions, Law allowed a vague memory of the encounter, but insisted he would not have tried to bind Blanchette to secrecy.

November 21, 1989. Shanley's maladies: Jun. 27, 1991, memo of a phone conversation with Shanley, by Frederick J. Ryan, Boston's vice chancellor. Technicolor quote: Shanley letter to McCormack, May 29, 1991. Loyalty oath: Gloria Negri, "Controversial Priest Leaves Newton Parish," *Boston Globe,* Dec. 6, 1989; "Priest Quits as Pastor over Oath," *St. Louis Post-Dispatch,* Dec. 9, 1989; John M. Swomley, "Infallibility in Ethical Perspective," *Christian Ethics Today,* Apr. 2003. Shanley letter to Law: Nov. 21, 1989. Clergy-to-lay ratio and reduced ordinations: Brad Knickerbocker, "A Calling in Crisis," *Christian Science Monitor,* Apr. 1, 2002; Wilkes, "The Hands That Would Shape our Souls." Decline in ordinations: Summaries provided by the Office of Vocation at the United States Conference of Catholic Bishops, comparing 1965 to 1995. Minor seminaries closing: Correspondence with Bernard Statman, National Catholic Education Association. United States Conference: This is the new name of the National Conference of Catholic Bishops, beginning Jul. 2001. Silva quote: Interview with Silva. Jordan quote: Correspondence with Mark D. Jordan, professor of religion, Emory University. Cozzens quote: Cozzens, *Changing Face of the Priesthood,* 109. Reports dropping off: "Portrait of the Accused," *New York Times,* Jan. 12, 2003.

Chapter 6. Confrontation

November 6, 1989. Dialogue: Author transcription of *Staggs v. Lenihan* recording; correspondence with Grant.

Fall 1990. Clohessy anecdote: Interviews with Clohessy and Barrett; Dawn Fallik, "Priest Scandal Puts Focus on Victims' Advocate," *St. Louis Post-Dispatch,* May 5, 2002 (Whiteley, who voluntarily left the priesthood in 1994, has never been charged or sued).

March 14, 1991. Jack White background: Globe Staff, *Betrayal,* p. 70. Shanley problems: Shanley letters to Boston archdiocese; Shanley letter to "Fred," Jul. 28, 1991. Oath quote: Shanley letter to McCormack, Mar. 14, 1991. Cabana Club Resort: "Shanley Co-Owned Gay Hotel in California," Associated Press, May 2, 2002.

November 9, 1991. Beatrice Ciaramitaro anecdote: Beatrice Ciaramitaro affidavit, quoted in "Plaintiff's Memorandum of Law in Support of Motion in Limine to Admit Evidence of Practices and Policies of the Roman Catholic Archbishop of Boston, A Corporation Sole, Concerning Sexually Abusive Priests Other Than Paul E. Shanley," *Ford v. Law,* Jul. 21, 2003. Dialogue: Interviews with Paul Ciaramitaro.

Summer 1992. Anecdotes and dialogue: Interviews and correspondence with Saviano.

May 1992. MacLeish anecdotes and dialogue: Interviews with MacLeish. Fitzpatrick anecdote: Ibid.; interviews with Anderson and Fitzpatrick; "Frank L. Fitzpatrick vs. Ex-Priest James R. Porter," Fitzpatrick's Web site; Bruni and Burkett, *Gospel of Shame,* 4, 11–13. Archibald MacLeish: Dirk Olin, "When Gregory Ford Told His Parents He Was Molested by a Priest, the Family Turned to a Pair of Greenberg Traurig Partners," *American Lawyer,* Jun. 2002. Fitzpatrick and Porter dialogue: Author transcription.

Thursday Evening, May 7, 1992. Anecdotes and dialogue: Author transcription of broadcast, WBZ-TV, May 7, 1992; interview with Bergantino; interview with Fitzpatrick; *Gospel of Shame,* 13–14. Family anecdote: Linda Matchan, "Thank God You Didn't Have to Live with Him," *Boston Globe,* Jun. 5, 2002. Porter cured: Transcript, WBZ-TV, May 7, 1992. Victim numbers: *Gospel of Shame,* 15. Poll: Ibid., 216. Fitzpatrick quote: Ibid., 23.

May 23, 1992. Law quote: Steve Marantz, "Law Raps Ex-Priest Coverage," *Boston Globe,* May 24, 1992. Porter coverage: Linda Matchan and Stephen Kurkjian, "Porter Personnel Files Show What Church Knew," *Boston Globe,* Oct. 21, 1992. Porter treatment: *Gospel of Shame,* 19–20. Porter defrocked and removed: Luz Delgado, "Two Defend Coverage of Ex-Priest," *Boston Globe,* May 25, 1992. Plaintiffs group: *Gospel of Shame,* 19. Liabilities cap: Alison Bass, "Law Limits Church Liability to $20,000," *Boston Globe,* May 13, 1992. Fall River finances: Interviews with MacLeish. *Globe* quote: "Responding to Porter's Victims," editorial, *Boston Globe,* Jul. 20, 1992. Law remarks: Kristen Lombardi, "Cardinal Sin," *Boston Phoenix,* Mar. 23, 2001; James L. Franklin, "The Cardinal and the News Media," *Boston Globe,* May 27, 1992; Marantz, *Boston Globe,* May 24, 1992. Flynn quote: Interviews with Flynn.

July 22, 1992. Ratzinger letter: "Some Considerations Concerning the Response to Legislative Proposals on the Non-Discrimination of Homosexual Persons," revised statement, Jul. 22, 1992, Congregation for the Doctrine of the Faith. Ordinance figures: Wayne van der Meide, "Legislating Equality: A Review of Laws Affecting Gay, Lesbian, Bisexual and Transgendered People in the United States," Policy Institute of the National Gay and Lesbian Task Force, 1999 (1992 year-end figures). Poll: Richard Morin, "American Attitudes Toward Gays Remain Steady," *Washington Post,* Feb. 15, 1993.

September 21, 1992. Porter confession: *Gospel of Shame,* 15. Porter sentence: John Larrabee, "Ex-Priest to Face Accusers in Court," *USA Today,* Sept. 23, 1992. Gaboury quote: *Gospel of Shame,* 25.

October 1992. MacLeish anecdotes: Interviews with MacLeish. Lyons quote: *Gospel of Shame,* 22. Porter sentence: James L. Franklin and Linda Matchan, "Porter Gets 18–20 Years," *Boston Globe,* Dec. 7, 1993.

October 17, 1992. Sipe quote: Richard Sipe, "Sexual Abuse by Priests . . . Why?" presented to the first national meeting of the Linkup, Oct. 17, 1992. Quinn quote: Michael Powell and Lois Romano, "Roman Catholic Church Shifts Legal Strategy," *Washington Post,* May 13, 2002. Doyle quotes and anecdotes: Correspondence and interviews with Doyle. Cavallo citation: Thomas Fox, "What They Knew in 1985," *National Catholic Reporter,* May 17, 2002.

December 17, 1992. New Mexico lawsuits: Interviews with Saviano. Saviano anecdotes: Ibid. Saviano quote: Margery Eagan, "One Survivor Tells a Tale of Triumph," *Boston Herald,* Oct. 17, 2002. Saviano and Hafermann dialogue: Interviews with Saviano and Hafermann. Saviano and Curtis dialogue: Interviews with Saviano; interviews and correspondence with Curtis.

January 20, 1993. Mother phone conversation: Mulkerrin memo, Jan. 20, 1993. Archdiocese inaction: Memos, Jan. 9; Jan. 23; Feb. 19, 1992.

February 15, 1993. Letter: Copy from Blaine. Blaine anecdotes and dialogue: Interviews and correspondence with Blaine. Warren quotes: Bonnie Miller Rubin, "Survivor Groups Gain Support Amid Priest Scandal," *Chicago Tribune,* Apr. 28, 2002 (Warren, still a priest, is contesting a lawsuit brought by another woman).

March 23, 1993. Holley sentencing: Paul Leavitt, "Desegregation Case Heard in La. Today," *USA Today,* Jun. 7, 1993.

May 1993. Anecdotes and quotes: Interviews and correspondence with Saviano. Fax: Copy from Saviano.

June 17, 1993. Liability theories: Brooks Egerton, "Documents Show Bishops Transferred Known Abuser," *Dallas Morning News,* Aug. 31, 1997. Cost to dioceses: James L. Franklin, "Catholics Struggle with Delay," *Boston Globe,* Nov. 22, 1992. Bankruptcy considerations: Sipe, *Sex, Priests, and Power,* 8. Polls and attendance data: *Gospel of Shame,* 216–18. Subcommittee background: Egerton, "Documents Show Bishops Transferred Known Abuser." Policy adopted: Franklin, "Catholics Struggle with Delay." Broad resolution: Egerton, "Documents Show Bishops Transferred Known Abuser." SNAP anecdotes and Blaine quotes: Interviews with Blaine; Michael Hirsley, "Don't Trust Catholic Officials with Abuse Cases," *Chicago Tribune,* Jun. 8, 1993.

Wednesday, August 25, 1993. Zellman anecdotes and dialogue: Interviews with Zellman, Matchan, Dan Golden, and Storin. Excerpt: Linda Matchan, "Sins of the Father," *Boston Globe Magazine,* Aug. 29, 1993. Chancery outrage: Interviews with Storin. *Globe* ownership: "Nieman Foundation Administers First Taylor Award," *Harvard Gazette,* May 2, 2002. Protest on Morrissey Boulevard: Interview with Golden and Dan Kennedy. New low: Interviews with Storin. Taylor, Storin, and Zellman dialogue: Interviews with Storin, Golden, and Zellman.

September 13, 1993. Steven and Mulkerrin dialogue: Letter from Steven to

Mulkerrin, Aug. 8, 1993 (no last name given). Shanley courage: Letter from Law to Shanley, Feb. 29, 1996. Cassem quote: Memo from Cassem to McCormack, Aug. 30, 1994. Mulkerrin background: Mulkerrin deposition in *Ford v. Law,* Dec. 19, 2002. New policy: Pam Belluck, "Boston Church Leaders Refused to Tell Parishioners of Abuse," *New York Times,* Jan. 9, 2003. McCormack quote: McCormack deposition, Jun. 4, 2002. Mulkerrin defiance: Interviews with MacLeish; Mulkerrin deposition; Michael Rezendes and Stephen Kurkjian, "Bishop Tells of Shielding Priests," *Boston Globe,* Jan. 9, 2003.

July 26, 1994. Parade: Janny Scott, "Gay Marchers Celebrate History in Two Parades," *New York Times,* Jun. 17, 1994. Answers and hearing: "Gramick/Nugent Case, 1988–1999," *National Catholic Reporter* electronic archives; interviews with Gramick and Nugent; Congregation for the Doctrine of the Faith, "Report of the Findings of the Commission Studying the Writings and Ministry of Sister Jeannine Gramick, SSND, and Father Robert Nugent, SDS," Oct. 4, 1997, *National Catholic Reporter* electronic archives. Gramick quote: Interviews with Gramick. *Contestatio* arrival: Interviews with Gramick; Congregation for the Doctrine of the Faith, "Erroneous and Dangerous Propositions in the Publications *Building Bridges* and *Voices of Hope* by Sister Jeannine Gramick, SSND, and Father Robert Nugent, SDS," Oct. 24, 1997, *National Catholic Reporter.* Gramick response: Jeannine Gramick, "Response of Sister Jeannine Gramick, SSND, to the Congregation for the Doctrine of the Faith Regarding 'Erroneous and Dangerous Propositions in the Publications *Building Bridges* and *Voices of Hope* by Sister Jeannine Gramick, SSND, and Father Robert Nugent, SDS,'" Feb. 5, 1998, *National Catholic Reporter.* Battle with Ratzinger: John L. Allen Jr., "Milestones in Campaign to Hold the Doctrinal Line," *National Catholic Reporter,* Dec. 1998. Gramick thoughts: Interviews with Gramick.

August 10, 1995. Holley background anecdotes: Brooks Egerton, "Documents Show Bishops Transferred Known Abuser," *Dallas Morning News,* Aug. 31, 1997. Saviano anecdotes and dialogue: Interviews and correspondence with Saviano; interviews with MacLeish. Puccio letter: Dated Nov. 1, 1995. Saviano anecdote: Correspondence with Saviano.

September 26, 1995. Garabedian background, anecdote, and dialogue: Interviews with Ciaramitaro; McCarthy notes from meeting.

Late in 1995. Garabedian background, anecdote, and dialogue: Interviews with Garabedian and with Tannenbaum; David Weber, "Mom Sues Priest for Alleged Sexual Abuse of Sons," *Boston Herald,* Jul. 11, 1996. Social service funding: Catholic Charities, 2002 annual report. Formal complaint: Weber, "Mom Sues Priest for Alleged Sexual Abuse of Sons." Motion to impound: Michael Rezendes and Walter V. Robinson, "Church Tries to Block Public Access to Files," *Boston Globe,* Nov. 23, 2002; Kathleen Burge, "Judge's Ruling Frees Documents in Geoghan Case," *Boston Globe,* Nov. 30, 2001.

CHAPTER 7. Into the Courts

November 29, 1995. Anecdotes and quotes: Interviews with Jim Falls, Michael Falls, and Mark K. Grant. Interviews with Dunn: "Court Refuses to Reinstate Suit Against Archdiocese," Associated Press, Jan. 28, 1999.

February 21, 1997. Geoghan cases: Mark Mueller, "Claims of Abuse by Priest Rise to 28," *Boston Herald,* Feb. 15, 1997; Mueller, "Senator's Bill Would Require Clergy to Report Suspicions of Child Abuse," *Boston Herald,* Feb. 22, 1997; interviews with Garabedian. Geoghan confession and various internal memos: Flatley deposition, Apr. 4, 2001. D'Arcy quote: Law deposition, Oct. 16, 2002. Garabedian quotes: Interviews with Garabedian. Settlement: Andrea Estes, "Church Settles Sex-Abuse Cases; Archdiocese Paid Millions to Geoghan's Alleged Victims," *Boston Herald,* Jun. 3, 1998. Montigney quote: Mark Mueller, "Senator's Bill Would Require Clergy to Report Suspicions of Child Abuse."

Sometime in February 1997. Anecdote and dialogue: Interviews with McSorley. Anecdote: Interviews with Anthony Muzzi Jr.

October 11, 1997. St. Peter's Square anecdote: Correspondence with Maureen Fiedler, Tobias Raschke, and Ingrid Thurner. Austrian church: John Pomfret, "Austrian Catholics Press for Changes in Church; Thousands Leave amid Scandal, Charges of Rigidity," *Washington Post,* Sept. 13, 1995. Groer background: "Austrian Bishops Label Cardinal a Paedophile," BBC News, Feb. 28, 1998. Lay reform groups: Per Call to Action USA. Priest shortage: David Briggs, "Women Still Seeking Equality in Churches," *Plain Dealer,* May 29, 2001. Married or female priests: ABC News/Washington Post/Beliefnet poll, Mar. 25–28, 2002. Celibacy: *Boston Globe*/WBZ-TV poll, Feb. 4–6, 2002. Association for the Rights of Catholics in the Church: Interview with Mary Louise Hartman. Call to Action: Interview with spokeswoman. We Are Catholic and Brady background: Interviews with Brady. Gathering signatures: Correspondence with Raschke and Thomas Arens. Rome anecdote: Correspondence with Raschke and Ingrid Thurner.

Wednesday, December 17, 1997. Mass for healing anecdotes: Joe Matthews, "Church Offers Masses in Apology for Abuse," *Baltimore Sun,* Dec. 18, 1997; interviews with Sacco and Saviano.

January 13, 1998. Methodist declaration: M. Garlinda Burton, "Hold Line on Homosexuality," *United Methodist Daily News,* Apr. 24, 1996. Episcopal bishops: Terry Mattingly, "Battle Lines Drawn in Latest Episcopalian Sex War," *Rocky Mountain News,* Sept. 10, 1994; David W. Dunlap, "Roll of Openly Gay Episcopalians Causes a Rift in the Church," *New York Times,* Mar. 21, 1996. Dissent quote: Greenbelt Interfaith News, online, Jun. 1, 1997. Omando anecdote: "Italian Gay Martyr Remembered," *PlanetOut News,* Jan. 14, 2000; International Lesbian and Gay Association electronic archives.

July 13, 1999. Excerpt: Congregation for the Doctrine of the Faith, "Notification of the Congregation for the Doctrine of the Faith Concerning Sr. Jeannine Gramick,

SSND, and Fr. Robert Nugent, SDS," May 31, 1999 (published in Jul. 1999). CDF order: Interviews with Gramick; Hanna Rosin, "Vatican Intervenes Against Gay Ministry," *Washington Post,* Jul. 14, 1999. First silenced: Interviews and correspondence with Gramick. Gramick quote: Ibid.

August 19, 1999. Anecdote and quote: Interviews with Lynch.

Throughout 1999. Anecdote and quotes: Interviews with Matchan.

CHAPTER 8. The *Globe* and the Church

January 29, 2001. Garabedian background: Interviews with Garabedian and Gordon. Law's Rome effort: John Ellement, "Defrocked Priest Charged with Rape," *Boston Globe,* Dec. 3, 1999. Garabedian perspective and quote: Interviews with Garabedian. McSorley quote: J. M. Lawrence, "Priest's Alleged Victims Cleared to Sue Cardinal," *Boston Herald,* Jan. 30, 2001. Lombardi anecdote and quotes: Interviews with Lombardi and Garabedian. Sipe quote: Lombardi, "Cardinal Sin." Dialogue with mother: Interview with Lombardi.

Friday, July 27, 2001. Law admitting Dussourd's warning: David Weber, "Law Admits to Receiving 1984 Warning on Geoghan," *Boston Herald,* Jul. 17, 2001. Law's assertions about McSorley's abuse: Ibid. McSorley quote: Interview with McSorley. Law's column: Bernard Law, "Restoring Hope to Broken Hearts and Lives," *Pilot,* Jul. 27, 2001. McNamara's column: Eileen McNamara, "Passing the Buck," *Boston Globe,* Jul. 29, 2001; interview with McNamara.

Monday, July 30, 2001. Baron principles: Dan Kennedy, "The Baron of Morrissey Boulevard," *Boston Phoenix,* Dec. 6, 2001. Baron as outsider: Kennedy, "Goodbye to All That," *Boston Phoenix,* Jul. 19, 2001. *Globe* sale to the *Times:* Ibid. Editorial meeting and dialogue: Interview with Baron. Earnhardt photos: Wire reports, "Earnhardt's Widow Pleads for Privacy," *St. Petersburg Times,* Mar. 5, 2001. Robinson's reaction to Baron's e-mail: Interview with Robinson. Spotlight background: Interviews with Robinson, Rezendes, Carroll, and Pfeiffer. Robinson quote: Interview with Robinson. Spotlight game plan and background: Michael Rezendes, "Scandal: The *Boston Globe* and Sexual Abuse in the Catholic Church," in Plante, *Sin Against the Innocents;* interviews with Robinson and Rezendes. Carroll's directory search: Interview with Carroll.

August 2001. Saviano efforts and conversations with *Globe:* Interviews with Saviano, Pfeiffer, and Robinson.

September 7, 2001. Robinson source meeting and anecdote: Correspondence and interviews with Robinson.

September 14, 2001. Grant settlement and Lenihan promotion: Correspondence with Grant and Tod Tamberg, spokesman for the Los Angeles archdiocese. Ryan DiMaria case: Interview with Katherine Freberg; Gustav Neibuhr, "Dioceses Settle Case of Man Accusing Priest of Molestation," *New York Times,* Aug. 8, 2001. Lopez column with Lenihan: Steve Lopez, "A Priest's Confession: 'Celibacy Is the Toughest

Thing,'" *Los Angeles Times,* Sept. 14, 2001. Lenihan resigning: Associated Press, "Popular Catholic Priest Who Admitted Sexual Relationships with Women Quits," Sept. 25, 2001 (Lenihan was charged with ten counts of felony sexual assault). Grant anecdote: Interview with Grant.

Late October 2001. Banks notes on Geoghan: Memo on Banks's letterhead, Apr. 28, 1989, from Brennan deposition. Spotlight Team work: Correspondence with Robinson. Garabedian conversation with Rezendes: Interview with Rezendes. D'Arcy letter: Dated Dec. 1984. Rezendes anecdote: Interview with Rezendes.

Sometime in December 2001. Kos allegations: Interviews with Sylvia Demerest and coverage from the *Dallas Morning News.* Fulchino case: Interviews with MacLeish (Greenberg Traurig would not allow contact with the Fulchino family); Walter V. Robinson, "For Father and Son, a Shared Anguish," *Boston Globe,* Feb. 3, 2002. Conversation between MacLeish and Gauvreau: Interviews with MacLeish and Gauvreau.

August 15, 2001–December 24, 2001. Sweeney hearing and ruling: Kathleen Burge, "Judge's Ruling Frees Documents in Geoghan Case," *Boston Globe,* Nov. 30, 2001. Cohen ruling: "Church Leaders' Depositions to Be Made Public," *Boston Globe,* Dec. 25, 2001. Sweeney quote to Rogers: Walter V. Robinson, "Judge Denies Delay for Church Papers," *Boston Globe,* Jan. 19, 2002. Doyle prediction: "The Problem of Sexual Molestation by Roman Catholic Clergy: Meeting the Problem in a Comprehensive and Responsible Manner." Doyle's reaction to judges' rulings: Interview with Doyle.

Friday, January 4, 2002. Rezendes and Carroll's anecdote: Interviews with Rezendes. Robinson Brezhnev quote: Interviews with Robinson. Baron's conversation with Law: Interview with Baron. Robinson dialogue with Morrissey: Interviews with Robinson and Morrissey. Morrissey final answer: Interview with Morrissey; Michael Rezendes, "Church Allowed Abuse by Priest for Years," *Boston Globe,* Jan. 6, 2002.

CHAPTER 9. Explosion

Saturday, January 5, 2002. Saviano anecdote and dialogue: Interview with Saviano.

Sunday, January 6, 2002. Muller background: Interviews with Muller. IPPNW statistics: Organization's electronic archives. Muller diaries: Irwin Abrams, "Origins of International Physicians for the Prevention of Nuclear War," Nov. 1994. Article in *Globe:* Michael Rezendes, "A Revered Guest; a Family Left in Shreds," *Boston Globe,* Jan. 6, 2002. Inquisition quote: Interview with Muller. Saviano anecdote: Interview with Saviano.

Monday, January 7, 2002. Calcaterra work: Interview with Calcaterra. Kennedy quote: Robert Royal, "Catholic Gobbledygook," *First Things,* Oct. 1997. Calcaterra anecdote: Interview with Calcaterra.

Tuesday, January 8, 2002. Pope's pronouncement: Philip Pullella, "Vatican Issues New Rules on Pedophile Priests," Reuters, Jan. 9, 2002. Sex crimes internationally:

"Vatican Admits Priests Raped Nuns, Forced Abortions," *National Post,* Mar. 21, 2001; Philip Willan, "Catholic Priests Abusing Nuns for Sex," *Guardian,* Mar. 21, 2001.

Wednesday, January 9, 2002. "It's time for the secrecy" quote: "A Shepherd and His Flock," editorial, *Boston Globe,* Jan. 9, 2002. Press conference: "My Apology . . . Comes from a Grieving Heart," transcript, *Boston Globe,* Jan. 10, 2002.

A Week Later. Geoghan therapists' histories: Michael Rezendes and Matt Carroll, "Doctors Who OK'd Geoghan Lacked Expertise, Review Shows," *Boston Globe,* Jan. 16, 2002. Legislative response: Leslie Miller, "Mass. House Approves Mandatory Child-Abuse Reporting for Clergy," Associated Press, Feb. 26, 2002. Reilly quote: Sacha Pfeiffer and Kevin Cullen, "AG Wants Church to Report Past Sex Abuse," *Boston Globe,* Jan. 17, 2002. Muller anecdotes and all dialogue: Interviews with Jim and Kathleen Muller. Number of parishes (as of 2001): Archdiocesan archives.

Tuesday, January 15, 2002. Status conference: Walter V. Robinson, "Judge Denies Delay for Church Papers," *Boston Globe*, Jan. 19, 2002. Robinson anecdote: Interviews with Robinson.

Tuesday, January 22, 2002. Documents: Walter V. Robinson and Matt Carroll, "Documents Show Church Long Supported Geoghan; Officials Gave Comfort Despite Abuse Charges," *Boston Globe,* Jan. 24, 2002.

January 23, 2002. Law not resigning: Michael Paulson, "Law Says He Won't Quit over Scandal," *Boston Globe,* Jan. 24, 2002. Law personally responsible: Michael Paulson, "Most Catholics in Poll Fault Law's Performance," *Boston Globe,* Feb. 8, 2002. Law clout and Flynn quote: Kristen Lombardi, "Cardinal Law Loses Clout," *Boston Phoenix,* Feb. 15, 2002. Law quote: Paulson, "Law Says He Won't Quit over Scandal." Law walking inside: Correspondence with Steven Lynch. Lynch quote: Paulson, "Law Says He Won't Quit over Scandal."

January 28, 2002. Mullin background: Thomas Farragher, "Church Cloaked in Culture of Silence," *Boston Globe,* Feb. 24, 2002. Paquin background: Michael Rezendes, "Priest Says Church Sought to Cover Up Suit Against Him," *Boston Globe,* Jan. 31, 2002. Guthrie and Iguabita: Globe Staff, "The Convicted and the Accused," *Boston Globe,* Jan. 28, 2002.

January 31, 2002. Legal claims: Walter V. Robinson, "Scores of Priests Involved in Sex Abuse Cases; Settlements Kept Scope of Issue Out of Public Eye," *Boston Globe,* Jan. 31, 2002; interviews with MacLeish and Garabedian. Secrecy quote: Ibid. Law hands names to prosecutors: Fred Bayles, "Disclosures Bring Questions of Church Responsibility," *USA Today,* Feb. 1, 2002. Procopio quote: Ibid. Article on Shanley: Sacha Pfeiffer, "Famed 'Street Priest' Preyed upon Boys," *Boston Globe,* Jan. 31, 2002.

Saturday, February 2, 2002. Press release: Interviews with Morrissey. Finegan and Graham background: Michael Rezendes and Walter V. Robinson, "Two Priests Ousted After Abuse Cited," *Boston Globe,* Feb. 3, 2002; Rezendes and Carroll, "Six More Priests Removed on Allegations of Abuse." Pfeiffer quote: Interview with Pfeiffer. Semantic debates: Jenn Abelson, "Law Spokeswoman Describes 'Nightmare'; Morrissey Says She Was Kept in the Dark About Scandal," *Boston Globe,* Mar. 21, 2003. Morrissey quote: Interviews with Morrissey.

Sunday, February 3, 2002. Spagnolia anecdotes and quotes: Interviews with Spagnolia; Matt Carroll, "Lowell Priest Quietly Removed," *Boston Globe,* Feb. 23, 2002; Thomas Farragher, "In the Eye of the Storm, Pastor Is Calm," *Boston Globe,* Feb. 28, 2002. Thu Vu quote: Thomas Farragher, "Accused Pastor Proclaims Innocence," *Boston Globe,* Feb. 26, 2002. Spagnolia anecdotes: Interviews with Spagnolia. Spagnolia quotes: Ibid. Sullivan quote: Ibid. Fulchino story: Walter V. Robinson, "For Father and Son, a Shared Anguish," *Boston Globe,* Feb. 3, 2002. Muller dialogue: Interviews with Jim and Kathleen Muller. Powers anecdote: Interviews with Muller. (Powers did not grant an interview.)

February 8, 2002. Another forty-nine names: Stephen Kurkjian, "DAs Given Names of 49 More Priests; Cardinal Says Records Are Being Combed," *Boston Globe,* Feb. 9, 2002.

Monday, February 11, 2002. Meeting anecdote and dialogue: Interviews with Jim Muller, Calcaterra, Post, and Frazer.

CHAPTER 10. The Unburdening

Early February 2002. Ford family background and anecdotes: Interviews with MacLeish and Pillsbury; Newton Police Department investigators report (MacLeish would not allow an interview with the Fords). Gauvreau: Sacha Pfeiffer, "Woman Says Church Ignored Her Outcries," *Boston Globe,* Feb. 13, 2002. Book quote: Dorais, *Don't Tell: The Sexual Abuse of Boys,* 87. Brain structure: Michael D. De Bellis et al., "Developmental Traumatology, Part II: Brain Development," *Biological Psychiatry* 45 (1999): 1271–84. Greg yells at father and his dream: Sacha Pfeiffer, "Woman Says Church Ignored Her Outcries." Abused at home: Interviews with MacLeish. Pedophiles' first strike: Jean G. Abel and Nora Harlow, *The Stop Child Molestation Book* (Xlibris: 2001). Freud background: See, among others, Jeffrey Masson, *The Assault on Truth: Freud's Suppression of the Seduction Theory* (New York: Farrar, Straus and Giroux, 1984). Study from 1994: L. M. Williams, "Recall of Childhood Trauma: A Prospective Study of Women's Memories of Child Sexual Abuse," *Journal of Consulting and Clinical Psychology* 6 (1994): 1167–76. "False" or "recovered" memories: "Position Statement on Therapies Focused on Memories of Childhood Physical and Sexual Abuse," American Psychiatric Association, Mar. 2000. 1994 study: Elizabeth Loftus, "Creating False Memories," *Scientific American,* Sept. 1997, 70–75. Delayed and discontinuous memory: Victoria L. Banyard, "Trauma and Memory," *PTSD Research Quarterly,* fall 2000. Study of undergraduates: T. P. Melchert, "Relationships Among Childhood Memory, a History of Abuse, Dissociation and Repression," *Journal of Interpersonal Violence* 14, 1172–92. Busa background and anecdote: Interviews with MacLeish (MacLeish did not make Busa available for interviews);

Michael Rezendes and Sacha Pfeiffer, "Shanley Is Arrested in California," *Boston Globe,* May 3, 2002.

February 11, 2002. Anecdote and dialogue: Noted by author. Trial and sentencing: Jay Lindsay, "Geoghan to Spend 9 to 10 Years in Prison," Associated Press, Feb. 22, 2002.

Mid-February 2002. Anecdote and dialogue: Interviews and correspondence with Olan Horne and Dave and Sheryl Lyko.

Sunday, February 17, 2002. Demanding Law resignation: Michael Paulson, "A Resolute Law Repeats He Won't Go," *Boston Globe,* Feb. 11, 2002. Spagnolia quotes: Interviews with Spagnolia. Law homily and scene at the residence: Scott Greenberger and Michele Kurtz, "Outside Cardinal's Headquarters, Protesters Multiply," *Boston Globe,* Feb. 18, 2002. Spagnolia snubbed: Interviews with Spagnolia.

Tuesday, February 19, 2002. Regional meeting anecdote: Interviews with Spagnolia; Robert Sullivan, "Faith in Their Father?" *Time,* Mar. 11, 2002. Priest's confession: Thomas Farragher and Caroline Louise Cole, "Accused Pastor Proclaims Innocence," *Boston Globe,* Feb. 26, 2002. Spagnolia quotes: Interviews with Spagnolia.

Bishops elsewhere: Interviews with Gregory; Bill Dedman, "Philadelphia Inquiry Finds Evidence of 50 Abuse Cases," *Boston Globe,* Feb. 23, 2002. Residence meeting: Interviews with Gittens and O'Neill; Globe Staff, *Betrayal,* 154–56. Robinson quote: Interviews with Robinson. Morrissey background and anecdotes: Interviews with Morrissey and Corrigan; Sally Jacobs, "Caught in the Crossfire, Boston Archdiocese Spokeswoman Donna Morrissey Has a Job No One Would Envy," *Boston Globe,* May 9, 2002. Resident abuse: Kay Lazar, "Nursing-Home Assaults Skyrocket in Mass.," *Boston Herald,* Mar. 17, 2002.

Wednesday, February 20, 2002. Ninth and tenth priests: Farragher and Cole, "Accused Pastor Proclaims Innocence" (Welsh has not been charged). All dialogue: Interviews with Spagnolia.

Monday, February 25, 2002. Anecdotes and dialogue: Interviews with Spagnolia; Michael Paulson, "Priest Emerges as Test for Church," *Boston Globe,* Feb. 26, 2002. Kerouac quote: Jack Kerouac, *The Town and the City* (New York: Harcourt, 1993), 4. Press conference: Interviews with Spagnolia; Paulson, "Priest Emerges as Test for the Church"; Michael Rosenwald, "A Loyal Flock, Accused Priest's Good Works, Straight Talk, Win Support," *Boston Globe,* Feb. 27, 2002; Eric Convey, "Holy War," *Boston Herald,* Feb. 26, 2002; Farragher and Cole, "Accused Pastor Proclaims Innocence."

Tuesday, February 26, 2002. Mandatory reporting background: National Clearinghouse on Child Abuse and Neglect. Massachusetts's first mandatory reporting: Massachusetts Attorney General Office; General Laws of Massachusetts, Part I, Title XVII, Chapter 119, section 51A. Law opposition and Taylor quote: Michael Paulson and Chris Tangney, "House Closes Loophole on Clergy," *Boston Globe,* Feb. 27, 2002.

Wednesday, February 27, 2002. Anecdote and dialogue: Interviews with Spagnolia; Thomas Farragher, "In the Eye of the Storm, Pastor Is Calm," *Boston Globe,* Feb.

28, 2002. Donoghue quote: Interviews with Donoghue. Murphy quote: Interviews with Murphy. Flynn anecdotes and quotes: Interviews with Flynn.

Thursday, February 28, 2002. Reed anecdote: Thomas Farragher, "Pastor Admits Lie on Celibacy," *Boston Globe*, Mar. 1, 2002 (Reed would not consent to an interview for this book). Spagnolia quotes: Interviews with Spagnolia. Press conference: Shelley Murphy and Caroline Louise Cole, "Lowell Pastor Agrees to Leave Rectory," *Boston Globe*, Mar. 2, 2002.

CHAPTER 11. Inside, Outside

Late February 2002. Morrissey quote: Interviews with Morrissey. Thorp background, anecdote, and quote: Interviews with Thorp (a copy of her memo could not be located; this is her re-creation).

Sunday, March 3, 2002. Cathedral anecdote: Interviews with Morrissey and Lynch; Scott Greenberger, "Alleged Abuse Victim Arrested at Church," *Boston Globe*, Mar. 4, 2002. Lynch and Lombard: Farah Stockman, "An Accuser's Quest for Recognition," *Boston Globe*, Mar. 3, 2002. Navarro-Valls: Melinda Henneberger, "Vatican Weighs Reaction to Accusations of Molesting by Clergy," *New York Times*, Mar. 3, 2002. Bevilacqua quotes: Rachel Zoll, "Abuse Scandal Leads to Church Debate on Homosexuality," Associated Press, May 25, 2002; Douglas W. Kmiec, "Can Gays Be Good Priests?" *Los Angeles Times*, May 2, 2002; Edward Walsh, "Cardinals Back 'Zero Tolerance,'" *Washington Post*, Apr. 27, 2002.

First Week of March 2002. Anecdote and dialogue: Interviews with Thorp.

March 9, 2002. Meeting anecdote: Interviews with Calcaterra.

March 11, 2002. Meeting description: Correspondence with David Spotanski; interviews with Gregory. Belleville scandal: Charles P. Pierce, "The Bishop's Quandary," *Boston Globe*, Jul. 21, 2002. Anecdotes and all dialogue: Interviews with Gregory.

March 12, 2002. MacLeish anecdotes and dialogue: Interviews with MacLeish, Horne, and Dave Lyko. Brain structure: Martin H. Teicher, "Wounds That Time Won't Heal: The Neurobiology of Child Abuse," *Cerebrum*, fall 2000, 50–67. "As yet" quote: J. H. Beitchman et al., "A Review of the Long-Term Effects of Child Sexual Abuse," *Child Abuse and Neglect*, 1992, 101–18. Horne speculative math: Interviews with Horne. Birmingham anecdotes: Interviews with Pfeiffer; Sacha Pfeiffer and Thomas Farragher, "Suit Names Archdiocese, N.H. Bishop," *Boston Globe*, Mar. 24, 2002. Pfeiffer curiosity: Interviews with Pfeiffer; see Michel Dorais, *Don't Tell: The Sexual Abuse of Boys*, 65.

Saturday, March 16, 2002. McNamara: Eileen McNamara, "Rights Collide on Milton Street," *Boston Globe*, Jan. 22, 1997. Tenancy history: Interviews with Robinson and Pfeiffer. Paquin accident and lawsuits: Sacha Pfeiffer, "Priest Pleads Guilty to Raping Altar Boy, Paquin Sentenced to 12–15 Years," *Boston Globe*, Jan. 1, 2003. Paquin removal: Stephen Kurkjian, "Records Show Law Reassigned Paquin After Settlements,"

Boston Globe, May 30, 2002. Paquin quotes: Sacha Pfeiffer and Stephen Kurkjian, "Priest Says He, Too, Molested Boys," *Boston Globe,* Jan. 26, 2002; Pfeiffer, "Priest Pleads Guilty to Raping Altar Boy." Quotes from twenty-six-year-old: Interview with Pfeiffer; Sacha Pfeiffer, "Treatment Center for Priests Called Site of Abuse," *Boston Globe,* Mar. 20, 2002. Kelley anecdote: Interviews with Robinson and Pfeiffer (the many allegations against Kelley include a 1977 arrest for being undressed in a car with a minor). Anecdote and dialogue: Interviews with Robinson and Morrissey. Kelley background: "The Accused," *USA Today,* Nov. 10, 2002; and Thomas Farragher, "Police Warned Archdiocese of Priest's Activities," *Boston Globe,* Feb. 5, 2003 (with Kelley facing neither civil nor criminal charges, his case remained in limbo).

March 21, 2002. Papal observation: John R. Allen Jr., "Cultural Gap: The Extra Hurdle in Covering the Vatican," *National Catholic Reporter,* Mar. 29, 2002. Pope's letter: John Paul II, "Letter of the Holy Father, Pope John Paul II, to Priests for Holy Thursday 2002," March 2002. Press conference and Kaiser quote: Allen, "Cultural Gap: The Extra Hurdle in Covering the Vatican." Hennberger dialogue: Maureen Dowd, "The Vatican Rag," *New York Times,* Mar. 24, 2002.

Monk quote: Peter France, *Hermits: The Insights of Solitude* (London: Chatto & Windus, 1996), 27. Conway anecdote and quotes: Noted by author.

Saturday, March 23, 2002. Bullock anecdote and quote: Interview with Bullock. Bullock quote to *Christian Science Monitor:* Jane Lampman, "Man at the Center of Catholics' Maelstrom," *Christian Science Monitor,* Mar. 22, 2002. Anderson quote: Interview with Anderson. Pope anecdote: "Pope Breaks Silence on Sex Scandal," CBS-News.com, Mar. 21, 2002. Paciorek anecdote: Jim Schaefer, Patricia Montemurri, and Alexa Capeloto, "Tom Paciorek Breaks Silence," *Detroit Free Press,* Mar. 22, 2002. Serrano anecdote: Correspondence with Serrano; Richard Lezin Jones, "Former Altar Boy Describes Years of Abuse, Then Years of Silence," *New York Times,* Mar. 18, 2002. Clohessy quote: Ibid. Rubino quote: Interview with Rubino. Nealon anecdote: Confirmed from transcripts of depositions.

March 24, 2002, Palm Sunday. Excerpt: Pfeiffer and Farragher, "Suit Names Archdiocese, N.H. Bishop." Blanchette anecdote: Interviews with Blanchette.

March 25, 2002. Bergeron anecdote and dialogue: Interviews with Gary Bergeron and Eddie Bergeron. Bergeron and Sherman dialogue: Interviews with Gary Bergeron and Bernie McDaid.

Tuesday, March 26, 2002. Anecdote and dialogue: Interviews with Blanchette. Meeting anecdote and all dialogue: Interviews with Mochon and unnamed priests. Twelve priests: Barbara Whitaker, "L.A. Cardinal Removes Priests Involved in Pedophilia Cases," *New York Times,* Mar. 3, 2002. Whipple quotes: Interview with Whipple. McNeill quote: Interview with McNeill.

Good Friday, March 29, 2002. Matthew quote: Matthew 27:45, 51. Protester sign: Michael Paulson, "Catholics Observe Good Friday with Protests, Prayer," *Boston Globe,* Mar. 30, 2002. Girl sign: Cover image, *Conscience,* summer 2002. Palm-sized crucifix: Paulson, "Catholics Observe Good Friday with Protests, Prayer." Law quotes: Ibid.; Chuck Colbert, "On Good Friday, Protesters Pray for Victims of Sex Abuse," *National Catholic Reporter,* Apr. 12, 2002. Austin: Ibid. Lynch quote: Ibid.

March 31, 2002, Easter Sunday. Survey of donors: "National Survey of Catholic Parishioners on Financial Accountability and Support," Oct. 2002, Gallup, commissioned by the Foundations and Donors Interested in Catholic Activities. Financial crisis: William C. Symonds, "The Economic Strain on the Church," *BusinessWeek,* Apr. 15, 2002. Rooney anecdote and quotes: Martin Kux, "Bless Me, Father," *Cleveland Scene,* Jul. 3, 2002; James F. McCarthy, "Panel Offers Bishop 1-Strike Policy," *Plain Dealer,* Aug. 9, 2002; Tom Breckenridge and David Briggs, "A Cross to Bear," *Plain Dealer,* Jun. 16, 2002. Thirteen men: Amanda Garrett, David Briggs, and Robert L. Smith, "Priest's Quick Suspension Signals a New Openness," *Plain Dealer,* Mar. 30, 2002 (Brickman, on administrative leave, has not been sued). Another nine: James M. McCarthy and David Briggs, "Diocese Suspends 9 More Priests," *Plain Dealer,* Apr. 9, 2002. Brickman: Ibid. Subpoena: Ibid. (subpoena issued Apr. 5, 2002). Pilla interview: Author's transcription. Missing persons report: David Briggs, Amanda Garrett, and Steve Luttner, "Priest to Get Full Catholic Burial," *Plain Dealer,* Apr. 6, 2002. Rooney suicide: Kaye Spector, "Priest Accused of Sex Abuse Is Found Dead," *Plain Dealer,* Apr. 5, 2002; Briggs, Garrett, and Luttner, "Priest to Get Full Catholic Burial." Scolaro: Ibid. Rooney mother quote: Kux, "Bless Me, Father."

April 1, 2002. Anecdotes and dialogue: Interviews with Blanchette.

A Week or So Later. Sherman and Bergeron dialogue: Interviews with Gary Bergeron. Thorp and Bergeron dialogue: Ibid.; interviews with Bergeron and Thorp; Thomas Farragher, "Many Victims Say They're Still Waiting to Meet Law," *Boston Globe,* May 23, 2002.

Monday, April 8, 2002. Morrissey anecdote: Interviews with Morrissey. Press conference: Author's transcriptions; Thomas Farragher, "Alleged Victims Detail Torment," *Boston Globe,* Apr. 9, 2002; Michael Paulson, "Heavy Blow to Cardinal's Credibility," *Boston Globe,* Apr. 9, 2002; Theo Emery, "Papers Show Archdiocese Knew of Allegations," Associated Press, Apr. 9, 2002; Brian McGrory, "The Cardinal Must Go," *Boston Globe,* Apr. 9, 2002. Shanley anecdotes and dialogue: Interviews with Theresa Shanley. Banks letter: Letter from Banks to Philip A. Behan, Jan. 16, 1990. The NAMBLA word: *GaysWeek,* Feb. 12, 1979. "A depraved priest" quote: "A Church Betrayed," editorial, *Boston Globe,* Apr. 9, 2002. Anecdote and dialogue: Interviews with Theresa Shanley; handwritten letter by Murphy, Mar. 3, 1994.

April 9–13, 2002. Papal Foundation: Weigel, *The Courage to Be Catholic,* 136–38. Pope's condition: "Ailing Pope Celebrates 82nd Birthday," Associated Press, May 5, 2002. Anecdotes and dialogue: Interviews with Gregory; *The Courage to Be Catholic,* 136–38; "Statement of Bishop Wilton D. Gregory to the Media in Rome," United States Conference of Catholic Bishops, Apr. 13, 2002.

April 11, 2002. Law departure: Interviews with Morrissey; interview with Thomas

O'Neill; Michael Paulson and Michael Rezendes, "Law Saw Pope, Discussed Quitting," *Boston Globe,* Apr. 17, 2002. Connors quote: Michael Paulson and Kevin Cullen, "More Are Calling for Cardinal to Resign," *Boston Globe,* Apr. 10, 2002. Pope called a meeting: *The Courage to Be Catholic,* 136–38.

April 12, 2002. Morrissey anecdotes and dialogue: Interviews with Morrissey. Cardinal's letter: "We Now Realize . . . That Secrecy Often Inhibits Healing," statement by Law, reprinted in *Boston Globe,* Apr. 13, 2002. Press conference quotes: Interviews with Morrissey; Michael Rezendes and Michael Paulson, "Law Decides to Stay," *Boston Globe,* Apr. 13, 2002.

CHAPTER 12. Outside, Inside

Early April 2002. Anecdote and dialogue: Interviews with David Clohessy; Frank Bruni, "Am I My Brother's Keeper?" *New York Times Magazine,* May 12, 2002.

Monday, April 15, 2002. Meeting: Interviews with Muller, Post, Calcaterra, and Emerton; Chuck Colbert, "New Groups Push for Change," *National Catholic Reporter,* Apr. 4, 2002. Poll of Massachusetts Catholics: Fred Kaplan, "Sixty Percent in Polls Say Law Should Resign as Archbishop," *Boston Globe,* Apr. 12, 2002. D'Alessandro anecdote: David F. D'Alessandro, "Church Can't Deal with Law at the Helm," *Boston Globe,* Mar. 19, 2002. *Herald* anecdote: "It's Time for Law to Make His Exit," editorial, *Boston Herald,* Mar. 13, 2002.

Tuesday, April 16, 2002. Law statement: Bernard Law, "I Return Home Encouraged," reprinted in *Boston Globe,* Apr. 17, 2002.

April 19, 2002. McCormack anecdote: Ray Henry, "Bishop Leaves Chair of Panel on Sex Abuse," *Boston Globe,* Apr. 20, 2002. Committee members: "Inside the American Bishops' Ad Hoc Committee," *Newsweek,* Jun. 17, 2002.

April 20, 2002. Anecdote and dialogue: Interviews with MacLeish. Ford's quotes: Michael Rezendes and Thomas Farragher, "Files Show Shanley Tried Blackmail," *Boston Globe,* Apr. 21, 2002.

Sunday, April 21, 2002. Granadino background: William Lobdell, Richard Winton, and Beth Shuster, "Recorder Used in Priest Probe," *Los Angeles Times,* May 2, 2002. Protest anecdote: Tina Dirmann, "Alleged Victims Picket Church," *Los Angeles Times,* Apr. 22, 2002; interviews and correspondence with Grant.

April 23, 2002. Cardinals meeting: "Analysis: Church in Crisis," interview with John Allen Jr., PBS.org; "Address of John Paul II to the Cardinals of the United States," Vatican electronic archives. Poll blames celibacy: "Poll: U.S. Catholics Angry at Church," CBS News, May 2, 2002. Episcopal priests: Kim Kozlowski, "Provision Gives Hope to Priests Who Married," *Detroit News,* Jul. 16, 2003. Bevilacqua quote: Ron Goldwyn, "Bevilacqua: Gays Can't Be Priests," *Philadelphia News,* Apr. 27, 2002. Gregory quote: "No Place in Religious Life for Child Abusers," South African Broadcasting Corporation, Apr. 23, 2002. Donohue quote: Interview with William Donohue. Doyle quote: Interview with Doyle. National standards: *The Courage to Be Catholic,* 142. Press conference: Transcribed by author.

April 24, 2002. Meeting at St. Michael's: Interviews with Gary Bergeron; Denise Lavoie, "SJC Dismisses Clergy Abuse Lawsuit on Statute of Limitations Grounds," Associated Press, Apr. 30, 2002. Family dialogue: Interviews with Bergeron.

Monday, April 29, 2002. Anecdote: Interviews with Saviano; Chuck Colbert, "Fueling Boston's Fires of Outrage," *National Catholic Reporter,* May 10, 2002.

April 30, 2002. Meeting at Greenberg Traurig: Interviews with Bergeron and McDaid. Sherman and Bergeron quotes at press conference: Jason Lefferts, "A Common and Horrific Bond," *Lowell Sun,* Feb. 6, 2003.

Late April 2002. Stockton settlement: Arthur Jones, "Church in Crisis—A Chronology of Sex Abuse in Southern California," *National Catholic Reporter,* Jan. 31, 2003. Minneapolis settlement: Fred Bayles, "Major Pedophilia Cases Within Church," *USA Today,* Feb. 25, 2002. Anecdotes: Interviews with Anthony Muzzi Jr. and Garabedian. Anecdote: Interview with Joe Finn, Krueger, and David Castaldi.

May 1, 2002. Anecdotes and dialogue: Interviews with Paulson, Muller, and Post; Michael Paulson, "Catholics Drawn to Splinter Group in Wellesley," *Boston Globe,* May 1, 2002. Edyvean and Powers: Pam Belluck, "Angry at Scandal, Lay Group Seeks Quiet Uprising in Pews," *New York Times,* May 30, 2002.

May 2, 2002. Shanley arrest: Michael Rezendes and Sacha Pfeiffer, "Shanley Is Arrested in Calif.," *Boston Globe,* May 3, 2002; interview with Theresa Shanley. Austin quote: Interview with Austin. Logan airport: Corey Dade, "Heavily Guarded Shanley Flown to Boston," *Boston Globe,* May 7, 2002.

May 3, 2002. Finance meeting: Interviews with Joe Finn and David Smith. Garabedian anecdote: Interviews with Garabedian. McSorley quote: Interview with McSorley.

May 6, 2002. Anecdotes and dialogue: Interviews with Muller. Baier quote: Interview with Paul Baier.

May 7, 2002. East End Club anecdotes and dialogue: Interviews and correspondence with Gary Bergeron, Horne, and McDaid. Studies of religiosity: Stanley Presser, director of the Survey Research Center and sociology professor at the University of Maryland, who studied thousands of personal diaries of Americans from the mid-1960s until 1990s, according to Bill Broadway, "Church Attendance Swells at Easter," *Washington Post,* Apr. 3, 1999. Perpetrators transferred at least twice: Michael Rezendes and Sacha Pfeiffer, "Cardinal Promoted Alleged Sex Abuser," *Boston Globe,* May 18, 2002.

Summer 2002. Anecdote and dialogue: Interviews with Morrissey.

May 8, 2002. Anecdote and dialogue: Noted by author. Sweeney worried Law might flee: Michael S. Rosenwald, "Judge Orders Questioning of Law," *Boston Globe,* May 7, 2002. Law performance: Walter V. Robinson and Michael Rezendes, "Law Recalls Little on Abuse Case," *Boston Globe,* May 9, 2002.

May 14, 2002. Anecdote and dialogue: Interview with Stokes; confirmed in police accounts.

May 18, 2002. New rules for eulogies: Brian McGrory, "Church Loses the Last Word," *Boston Globe,* May 14, 2002. Latest polls: "64 percent of Catholics Say Law Should Step Down," *Boston Globe,* May 16, 2002; Michael Paulson, "Most Catholics in Poll Want a Resignation," *Boston Globe,* Apr. 17, 2002. Law letter: "Cardinal Law's Letter to the Archdiocese of Boston," archdiocesan electronic archives. Law and Morrissey quotes: Farragher, "Many Victims Say They're Still Waiting to Meet Law." Sherman quote: Ibid. Press story: Ibid. Blanchette quote: Ibid.

May 22, 2002. Anecdotes: Noted by author. Allowance: Thomas Farragher, "Suffolk DA Opens Investigation of Charges Against Pastor," *Boston Globe*, Feb. 27, 2002.

May 23, 2002. Anecdotes and dialogue: Interviews and correspondence with Krueger, Calcaterra, and Muller (Edyvean and O'Connell declined to comment). Anecdotes: Interviews with Krueger, Calcaterra, and Muller. Edyvean statement: Michael Paulson, "Activist Group Told to Work 'with and Under' Law," *Boston Globe,* May 24, 2002. Calcaterra quote: Interviews with Calcaterra. Weakland background: Rod Dreher, "Weakland's Exit," *National Review,* May 24, 2002. Countersued a victim: Gill Donovan, "Documents in Milwaukee Abuse Case Unsealed," *National Catholic Reporter,* May 3, 2002. Gibson anecdote: Melissa McCord, "Wisconsin Bishop Settled Sex Abuse Claim," Associated Press, May 23, 2002. Marcoux quote: Margaret Spillane and Bruce Shapiro, "The Witchhunt Against Archbishop Weakland," *Salon,* May 25, 2002. Weakland "investment": Meg Kissinger, "Marcoux a Mix of Conflicting Emotions," *Journal-Sentinel,* May 23, 2002. Dreher quote: Dreher, "Weakland's Exit." Donohue quote: "The Case of Archbishop Weakland: Time for an Ethical Statute of Limitations," Catholic League press release, May 23, 2002.

CHAPTER 13. Toward Holy Cross

Thursday, May 16, 2002. St. Luke's anecdote: Interviews with Rossetti; Michael Kranish and Matt Carroll, "Accused Priest Hangs Self," *Boston Globe,* May 17, 2002; Stephen Manning, "Priest Accused of Abuse Found Hanged at Hospital," Associated Press, May 16, 2002. Rossetti quote: Interview with Rossetti. Jaiman quote: "Accused Priest Commits Suicide," United Press International, May 17, 2002. Lori statement: "Accused Priest an Apparent Suicide," CBS News, May 17, 2002. Egan background: Michael Kranish and Matt Carroll, "Accused Priest Hangs Self," *Boston Globe,* May 17, 2002.

June 10, 2002. Priest removals in New Hampshire and Boston: "What's Happened So Far in the Scandal in New Hampshire," *Union Leader,* Jun. 9, 2002. Only two new priests: "Diocese Gives Priests New Assignments Throughout the State," *Union Leader,* Jun. 11, 2002. Parish closings: Ibid. Fund-raiser canceled: Nancy Meersman, "Sex Scandal Won't Hurt Giving to Charities, Diocese says," *Union Leader,* Jul. 10, 2002.

Connors found dead: "Priest Alleges Porn Found at St. Pius X Rectory," *Union Leader,* Jul. 29, 2002. Arsenault quote: Kristen Zanin, "Bishop Sued for Keeping Salem Cleric's Porn Secret," *Eagle-Tribune,* Jul. 24, 2002.

Tuesday Nights. Anecdotes and dialogue: Interviews with Gary Bergeron, Horne, McDaid, Blanchette, Ciaramitaro, and Larry Sweeney.

Thursday, June 13, 2002. Retaliation against the *Globe:* Thomas Farragher, "Globe Is Denied Access as Punishment for Story," *Boston Globe,* Jun. 14, 2002. Latest poll: "ABC News Poll Finds Dropping Opinion of Church as Bishops Gather," ABC News, Jun. 12, 2002. Schinderle and Waters dialogue: Noted by author. Garland quote: Interview with Garland. Leno quote: Garry Wills, "The Bishops at Bay," *New York Review of Books,* Aug. 15, 2002. Reporter, protester, and Morrissey remarks: Noted by author. Gregory quotes: "A Catholic Response to Sexual Abuse: Confession, Contrition, Resolve," Wilton D. Gregory presidential address, Jun. 13, 2002. Law apology: Michael Paulson, "Law Says Painful Journey Led to Policy's Passage," *Boston Globe,* Jun. 15, 2002; interviews with Morrissey. Conference: Noted by author; interviews with Saviano and Morrissey. Emerton and Clohessy quotes: Noted by author. Morrissey anecdote and dialogue: Interviews with Morrissey.

June 19, 2002. Anecdotes and dialogue: Interviews with Mochon; interview with "the old priest."

June 23, 2002. March anecdote: Lisa Gentes, "Marching in Solidarity, Searching for Healing," *Pilot,* Jun. 28, 2002; interviews with Saviano.

June 28, 2002. Anecdotes and dialogue: Interviews with Krueger, Calcaterra, and Muller.

Late June 2002. Anecdotes: Interviews with Jim and Kathleen Muller.

Sunday, June 30, 2002. Garner anecdotes and dialogue: Interview with Brady; George Archibald, "Dallas Bishop Says Gay Priest Banned from Parish Work," *Washington Post,* Jul. 5, 2002; Susan Hogan, "St. Pius Priest Leaves After Threats," *Dallas Morning News,* Jul. 1, 2002. Cawcutt anecdote: His various postings.

July 10, 2002. Shanley makes bail: "Judge Mulls Bail Reduction Request from Ex-Priest's Attorney," CNN.com, May 9, 2002. Suicide watch: Interviews with Gramick. Shanley quotes: Interview with Theresa Shanley. Courtroom anecdote: Noted by author. Theresa Shanley quote: Interview with Theresa Shanley. Detective reports: Shared by confidential course. Busa background: Michael Rezendes, "Rev. Shanley Arrested on 3 Counts of Child Rape in San Diego," *Boston Globe,* May 2, 2002; and interview with MacLeish. Driscoll background: Interview with MacLeish. Pencil incident: Interview with Pillsbury; hospital records from confidential source, and confirmed with MacLeish and Pillsbury.

July 17, 2002. Anecdote and dialogue: Interviews with Bergeron and Thorp.

July 20, 2002. Conference anecdotes and dialogue: Noted by author. Lambert meeting: Interviews with Calcaterra, Lambert, and Austin. Conservative speakers: Correspondence with Caroline Disco. Cuenin and Bullock were angry: Interviews with

Cuenin and Bullock. Austin quotes: Noted by author. Calcaterra quotes: Noted by author. Conference anecdotes: Noted by author.

Sunday Morning, July 21, 2002. Anecdotes and quotes: Noted by author.

Tuesday, July 30, 2002. Anecdotes and dialogue: Interviews and correspondence with Horne, Dave Lyko, and Thorp; "Statement of His Eminence Bernard Cardinal Law," archdiocesan electronic archives, Nov. 3, 2002.

August 2, 2002. Anecdotes and dialogue: Noted by author.

August 18, 2002. Insurance issues: Edward Walsh, "Insurance a Worry for Catholic Church, Premiums Skyrocket," *Washington Post,* Jul. 10, 2002; interview with David Smith. Keane anecdote: Interview with Mark Keane. McSorley anecdote: Interview with McSorley. Garabedian anecdotes: Interviews with Garabedian. Austin retreat and dialogue: Interviews and correspondence with Austin.

August 19, 2002. Clohessy anecdotes: Noted by author.

August 26, 2002. Jail anecdote: Correspondence and interviews with Gramick.

September 2, 2002. Cathedral of Our Lady of Angels data: Archdiocesan Web site; Mahony e-mails; Robert Blair Kaiser, "Rome Diary," justgoodcompany.com. Mahony investigations: Ongoing. Cost to archdiocese: Rick Baars, "God and the L.A. Times Work in Mysterious Ways," *New Times,* Sept. 5, 2002; Larry Stammer, "More Layoffs, Cuts Possible in Archdiocese," *Los Angeles Times,* Jan. 24, 2003; Larry Stammer, "Diocese Denies Five Quit Because of Cuts," *Los Angeles Times,* Nov. 1, 2002. Mahony quotes: Archdiocese electronic archives. Protest anecdotes and quotes: Baars, "God and the L.A. Times Work in Mysterious Ways."

September 5, 2002. Pope speech: "Pope: Bar Deviants from Priesthood," CNN.com, Sept. 5, 2002.

September 11, 2002. Anecdote: Interviews and correspondence with Saviano. Subpoena quote: Tom Mashberg and Robin Washington, "Clergy Abuse Counselors to Fight Church Subpoena," *Washington Post,* Sept. 22, 2002. Reilly allegation: Kathleen A. Shaw, "Subpoena of Abuse Records Withdrawn by Bishop Reilly," *Worcester Telegram & Gazette,* Sept. 24, 2002.

September 18, 2002. Cadigan quote: Michael Rezendes, "$10m Geoghan Deal Is Dwarfed by Others," *Boston Globe,* Sept. 8, 2002. Settlement anecdote: Interviews with Anthony Muzzi Jr., McSorley, Garabedian, and Cadigan. Sweeney quote: Michael Rezendes, "Judge Accepts Geoghan Settlement," *Boston Globe,* Sept. 20, 2002.

Chapter 14. The Backlash

September 20, 2002. Kendrick background: Interview with Kendrick. Doherty background: Mechele Cooper, "Group Honors Sex Assault Witnesses," *Kennebec Journal,* Apr. 3, 2003 (after settling several cases, Talbot awaits trial for assault and rape charges). "This could certainly" quote: Letter to Bishop Gerry, Mar. 7, 2001. Murray letter: Dec. 4, 2001. Press secretary comments: Correspondence from Sue

Bernard to Kendrick, Sept. 4, 2002. "Look at me" quote and dialogue: Interview with Kendrick.

September 30, 2002. Gerry, Murphy, and Lori anecdotes: Michael Paulson, "Push Is On to Quell Voice of Faithful," *Boston Globe,* Aug. 17, 2002. Newark quotes: "VOTF Addressed by Boston, Newark Archdiocese," *Pilot,* Oct. 18, 2002; "A Voice Not Rooted in Faith," official communiqué from the archdiocese of Newark, Oct. 9, 2002. Post quotes: Interviews with Post. Canon laws: Thomas P. Doyle, "Voice of the Faithful: Its Right to Exist According to Canon Law," undated, published on the Voice of the Faithful Web site. Allue letter: "Catholic Lay Group Banned," Associated Press, Oct. 1, 2002. McKinley quote: Jay Lindsay, "New Group Counters Voice of the Faithful," Associated Press, Oct. 28, 2002.

Thursday, October 3, 2002. Varvaro quote: Daniel J. Wakin, "All Priests Seek to Assert Rights and Fight Church Abuse Policy," *New York Times,* Oct. 4, 2002. Saloon anecdote: Interview with Bambrick; interview with Dugo; Daniel J. Wakin, "Priests Seek to Assert Rights and Fight Church Abuse Policy," *New York Times,* Oct. 4, 2002. Countersuit trend: Sam Dillon, "Fighting Back, Accused Priests Charge Slander," *New York Times,* Aug. 25, 2002. Bambrick and Eremito background: Stephanie Saul, "A Priest's Burden," *Newsday,* Jun. 17, 2002; Richard Lezin, "Priest Who Saw Abuse from Other Side Becomes Watchdog," *New York Times,* Jul. 7, 2002 (Eremito is on administrative leave pending a review of this allegation). Bambrick testified: Interview with Bambrick. Bambrick and Eremito dialogue: Interview with Bambrick.

October 4, 2002. Doyle quote: Interview with Doyle. Keating background: Cathy Grossman, "Keating to Seek Resignation of Abusive Clergy," *USA Today,* Jun. 15, 2002. Keating remarks: Noted by author. Gregory's reaction: Interview with Gregory. Keating accused: Rachel Zoll, "Bishops' Reform Policy Keeps Meeting Resistance," Associated Press, Sept. 15, 2002. Hanscom anecdote: Interview with Post; interviews with Mike Emerton. Keating remarks to Regis College: Michael Paulson, "Keating Questions Banning of Lay Group," *Boston Globe,* Oct. 5, 2002.

October 7, 2002. Presbyteral assembly anecdote: Interview with Tod Tamberg, spokesman for Mahony; Larry B. Stammer, "Priests Stand Up to Cardinal on Budget," *Los Angeles Times,* Oct. 8, 2002. Fran Ruth background, anecdote, and quotes: Interview with Ruth; Larry B. Stammer, "Catholics Are Reaching Out to Gays While Standing Firm on Abstinence," *Los Angeles Times,* Aug. 30, 1997.

Week of October 7, 2002. Murphy anecdote: Jimmy Breslin, "Royal Stench of Arrogance," *Newsday,* Jun. 12, 2003; Jimmy Breslin, "Biggest Waste of Money, Bar Nun," *Newsday,* Oct. 8, 2003. Suffolk grand jury: Rosanne Bonventre, foreperson, Suffolk County Supreme Court Special Grand Jury, May 6, 2002, "Grand Jury Report," Jan. 17, 2003.

October 8, 2002. Thavis article: John Thavis, "Vatican Prepares Draft Directives Against Admitting Gays as Priests," Catholic News Service, Oct. 8, 2002. Gramick quotes: Interview with Gramick. Jordan quote: Correspondence with Jordan.

October 14, 2002. Gregory anecdote: Interviews with Gregory; Re letter to Gregory, Oct. 14, 2002.

October 16, 2002. Financial Committee anecdote: Interviews with Emerton and Krueger. Law statement: Gill Donovan, "Catholic Charities Board Members Reject Law's Ban on Donations from Lay Fund," *National Catholic Reporter,* Aug. 2, 2002. Donation envelopes anecdote: Justin Pope, "Catholic Charities of Eastern Massachusetts Report Drop-Off in Donations," Associated Press, Apr. 13, 2002. National poll: Agostino Bono, "Sex Abuse Crisis Threatens to Cut Church Funds," Catholic News Service, Nov. 13, 2002. Lynch quote: Interview with Peter Lynch. MacLeish motion anecdote: Interviews with MacLeish; Ralph Ranalli, "Court Tells Diocese to Release Abuse Files," *Boston Globe,* Sept. 26, 2002; Michael Rezendes, "Tension Grows in Shanley Case," *Boston Globe,* Oct. 12, 2002; Ralph Ranalli and Matt Carroll, "Archdiocese Loses Appeal on Documents," *Boston Globe,* Oct. 17, 2002.

October 29, 2002. SOJB meeting anecdote: Interviews with Ciaramitaro, Bergeron, Horne, McDaid, Morrissey, Pfeiffer, Robinson, Larry Sweeney, and Thorp; Erica Noonan and Sacha Pfeiffer, "In Meeting with Victims, Law Begs Forgiveness," *Boston Globe,* Oct. 30, 2002. Dave Lyko quote: Ibid. *Pilot* article: James L. Franklin, "Cardinal Calls Sex Abuse by Priests an 'Evil Act,'" *Boston Globe,* Sept. 25, 1992.

Sunday, November 3, 2002. Lori letter: Addressed to "Dear Friend in Christ," dated Nov. 2–3, 2002. Love Makes a Family background: Interview with Anne Stanback, president of the group. New York City data: "Report of Alfred C. Cerullo III, Commission of Finance, City of New York," undated, using 1998 figures. Knights of Columbus: Interview with Robert Goosens, Connecticut chapter officer; "CT Catholics Circulate Petition Opposing Gay Marriage," Associated Press, *Hartford Courant,* Nov. 1, 2002. Law television anecdote: Transcription by author; interviews with Bergeron and McDaid.

November 4, 2002. Glendon speech: "Where They Took a Wrong Turn—and Where There's Hope," Zenit News Agency, Nov. 4, 2002.

Monday, November 11, 2002. Washington anecdote and quotes: Noted by author, unless cited otherwise. Welsh snapped: Sam Dillon, "No Welcome Mat for Victims' Groups," *New York Times,* Nov. 12, 2002. Charter changes: Noted by author; interviews with Gregory and Clohessy. O'Reilly quote: Official transcript, *The O'Reilly Factor,* Feb. 12, 2003.

Wednesday, November 27, 2002. Gregory anecdote and dialogue with passenger: Noted by author. New personnel files: Interviews with Pillsbury, Thomas, Nealon, and MacLeish. Foley background: Various documents in Foley personnel file, especially letters from Paul J. O'Bryne, May 23, 1968, and Jun. 1, 1968; memo from Daily, Jul. 16, 1993; Law memo, Dec. 23, 1993; undated McCormack memo; letter from Foley to McCormack, Mar. 20, 1994.

Friday, November 29, 2002. Telephone anecdote: Interviews with Horne and Thorp.

Chapter 15. Faith and Morals

Sunday, December 1, 2002. Going to Mass anecdote: Interviews with Bergeron, Horne, McDaid, and Thorp. Bankruptcy article: Walter V. Robinson and Stephen Kurkjian, "Archdiocese Weighs Bankruptcy Filing," *Boston Globe*, Dec. 1, 2002. Real estate holdings: "A Bankrupt Archdiocese?" editorial, *Boston Globe*, Dec. 3, 2002. *Globe* "bloodless domain" quote: Ibid. Newman quote: Ibid. Sweeney ruling: Michael Rezendes and Sacha Pfeiffer, "Law's Attorney Blasts Judge for Remarks," *Boston Globe*, Jan. 29, 2003. Picket line: Interview with Lewis. Law dialogue: Interviews with Bergeron, Horne, McDaid, and Thorp.

Monday, December 2, 2002. Bergeron and Sherman dialogue: Interview with Bergeron. Meeting anecdote: Interviews with Bergeron, Pillsbury, and confidential source.

Tuesday, December 3, 2002. Press conference anecdote: Interviews with Pfeiffer, MacLeish, and Pillsbury. Forry background: Various personnel records; J. M. Hirsch, "McCormack's Responses to Abuse Mixed, *Concord Monitor*, Dec. 4, 2002 (Forry is on administrative leave pending investigation). Frost background: Various personnel records. Buntel background: Various personnel records (Buntel remains on administrative leave pending investigation). Meffan background: Various personnel records, especially letter from Law to Meffan, Jun. 17, 1996; Sacha Pfeiffer, "He Invoked Religion for Sexual Acts," *Boston Globe*, Dec. 4, 2002. Meffan quotes: Ibid.

Wednesday, December 4, 2002. Residence meeting anecdote and dialogue: Interviews with Bergeron, Horne, McDaid, and Thorp. Survey of American opinions of Law's tenure: Dec. 12, 2002, CNN/USA Today, conducted by Roper Center at University of Connecticut. Cuenin anecdote: Interview with Morrissey; Michael Paulson, "Curb Imposed on Newton Parish," *Boston Globe*, Dec. 5, 2002. Flynn quote: Interview with Flynn. Law's decision to quit: Interviews with Morrissey, Thorp, and confidential source; Kevin Cullen and Charles M. Sennott, "In the End, Cardinal Couldn't Outlast Scandal," *Boston Globe*, Dec. 15, 2002.

Thursday, December 5, 2002. Perry anecdote: Interviews with Perry and MacLeish; Natalie Jacobson, WCVB-TV, Feb. 4, 2003, author's transcript. Broadcast of Foley interview: NECN, Dec. 5, 2002, author's transcript.

Monday, December 9, 2002. Priests' petition: "Letter from Priests to Cardinal Law," Dec. 9, 2002.

Friday, December 13, 2002. Law goes to Rome: Various clips, especially Kevin Cullen and Charles M. Sennott, "A Respite, Then Firestorm Ignites," *Boston Globe*, Dec. 14, 2002. Voice of the Faithful vote: Interview with Krueger and Emerton. Bishop resignation data: "Worldwide, 21 Roman Catholic Bishops Have Resigned amid Church Sex Scandals Since 1990," Associated Press, Jun. 18, 2003. National data on accused priests: Laurie Goodstein, "Trail of Pain in Church Crisis Leads to Nearly Every Diocese," *New York Times*, Jan. 12, 2003.

January 1, 2003. Doyle reflections: Time-stamped by e-mail server.

January 22, 2003. Dual depositions: Interviews with MacLeish, Thomas, Pillsbury, and McDaid; Law deposition, Jan. 22, 2003. Law dialogue with McDaid: Interview with McDaid.

January 28, 2003. Old Town Hall anecdote: Interviews with Bergeron, Blanchette, Ciaramitaro, Horne, McDaid, and Larry Sweeney; J. M. Hirsch, "Bishop McCormack Meets Birmingham Victims," Associated Press, Jan. 29, 2003. Pub meeting anecdote and dialogue: Interview with McDaid.

January 31, 2003. Rogers sworn in court: Interviews with MacLeish, Pillsbury, and Thomas. McLaughlin, LaVoie, Dwyer, and Dunn anecdotes: Tom Mashberg and Robin Washington, "Files Add 24 Priests to Accused Sex Abusers List," *Boston Herald,* Feb. 1, 2003 (each faced one allegation of abuse—McLaughlin and LaVoie status, administrative leave pending investigation; Dwyer status, deceased; Dunn status, defrocked).

Tuesday, February 12, 2003. SOJB meeting anecdote: Noted by author. Article quoted: Jason Lefferts, "A Common and Horrific Bond," *Lowell Sun,* Feb. 6, 2003.

February 24, 2003. Bergeron and Thorp dialogue: Interviews with Bergeron and Thorp. Bergeron dialogue with mother: Interview with Bergeron, and with Catherine and Joseph Bergeron. Canon 915: "Declaration by the Pontifical Council for Legislative Texts," Jun. 24, 2000. St. Paul quote: Ibid.

February 26, 2003. Kentucky anecdote: "Covington Diocese Claims Victims Negligent in Abuse Case," 9News transcript, Feb. 27, 2002. Arrests elsewhere: Poynter Institute electronic database. New Hampshire grand jury: Peter W. Heed, "Report on the Investigation of the Diocese of Manchester," Mar. 3, 2003.

Tuesday, March 4, 2003. Bergeron and Connolly dialogue: Interviews with Bergeron; Connolly declined requests for comment.

First Weeks of March 2003. McDaid's frustration: Interviews with McDaid, Flynn, and Thorp.

March 5, 2003. Bergeron correspondence: Various letters. Lennon's memo: Dated October 1995, showing his role in handling allegations; Michael Rezendes and Stephen Kurkjian, "Lennon Gave Advice on Reassigned Priest," *Boston Globe,* Feb. 25, 2003. Abruzzese letter to Bergeron: Dated the previous week.

March 20, 2003. Legal tactics in Boston and elsewhere, including Chopko quote: Wendy Davis, "Redemption Key to Church Defense," *Boston Globe,* Mar. 24, 2003. Nussbaum quote: Kathleen Burge, "Lawyer Argues for Dismissal of Suits," *Boston Globe,* Jan. 18, 2003. MacLeish quote: Interview with MacLeish.

March 22, 2003. Travel anecdote: Noted by author.

BIBLIOGRAPHY

Abbott, Elizabeth. *A History of Celibacy: From Athena to Elizabeth I, Leonardo da Vinci, Florence Nightingale, Gandhi, and Cher.* New York: Scribner, 2000.

Allen, John L. Jr. *Cardinal Ratzinger: The Vatican's Enforcer of the Faith.* New York: Continuum, 2000.

Bell, Alan, Martin S. Weinberg, and Sue Kiefer Hammersmith. *Sexual Preference: Its Development in Men and Women.* Bloomington: Indiana University Press, 1981.

Bernstein, Carl, and Marco Politi. *His Holiness: John Paul II and the History of Our Time.* New York: Penguin Books, 1997.

Berry, Jason. *Lead Us Not into Temptation: Catholic Priests and the Sexual Abuse of Children.* Urbana and Chicago: University of Illinois Press, 2000.

Bruni, Frank, and Elinor Burkett. *A Gospel of Shame: Children, Sexual Abuse, and the Catholic Church.* New York: Perennial, 2002.

Catholic Theological Society of America. *Human Sexuality: New Directions in American Catholic Thought.* New York: Paulist Press, 1977.

Cory, Donald Webster. *The Homosexual in America.* New York: Paperback Library, 1951.

Cozzens, Donald B. *The Changing Face of the Priesthood.* Collegeville, Minn.: Liturgical Press, 2000.

———. *Sacred Silence: Denial and the Crisis in the Church.* Collegeville: Liturgical Press, 2002.

D'Emilio, John. *Sexual Politics, Sexual Communities: The Making of a Homosexual Minority in the United States, 1940–1970.* Chicago: University of Chicago Press, 1983.

Dorais, Michel. *Don't Tell: The Sexual Abuse of Boys.* Translated by Isabel Denholm Meyer. Montreal: McGill–Queen's University Press, 2002.

Duberman, Martin. *Stonewall.* New York: Plume, 1993.

Gillespie, C. Kevin, S.J. *Psychology and American Catholicism: From Confession to Therapy?* New York: Crossroad, 2001.

Goergen, Donald. *The Sexual Celibate.* New York: Seabury, 1974.

Hendrickson, Paul. *Seminary: A Search.* New York: Summit Books, 1983.

Investigative Staff of the Boston Globe. *Betrayal: The Crisis in the Catholic Church.* Boston: Little, Brown and Company, 2002.

Jenkins, Philip. *Pedophiles and Priests: Anatomy of a Contemporary Crisis.* Oxford: Oxford University Press, 1996.

Jordan, Mark D. *The Silence of Sodom: Homosexuality in Modern Catholicism.* Chicago: University of Chicago Press, 2002.

Kaiser, Charles. *The Gay Metropolis.* San Diego: Harcourt Brace & Co., 1997.

Kaiser, Robert Blair. *The Politics of Sex and Religion: A Case History in the Development of Doctrine, 1962–1984.* Franklin, Wisc.: Sheed & Ward, 1985.

———. *The Encyclical That Never Was: The Story of the Commission on Population, Family, and Birth, 1964–1966.* New York: Continuum, 1987.

Kennedy, Eugene. *The Unhealed Wound: The Church and Human Sexuality.* New York: St. Martin's/Griffin, 2001.

King, Eleace, IHM, and Jim Castelli. *Culture of Recovery, Culture of Denial: Alcoholism Among Men and Women Religious.* Washington: Center for Applied Research in the Apostolate, 1995.

Levine, Judith. *Harmful to Minors: The Perils of Protecting Children from Sex.* Minneapolis: University of Minnesota Press, 2002.

McClory, Robert. *Turning Point: The Inside Story of the Papal Birth Control Commission, and How* Humanae Vitae *Changed the Life of Patty Crowley and the Future of the Church.* New York: Crossroad, 1997.

McDonough, Peter, and Eugene C. Bianchi. *Passionate Uncertainty: Inside the American Jesuits.* Berkeley and Los Angeles: University of California Press, 2002.

McNeill, John J. *The Church and the Homosexual.* Boston: Beacon Press, 1976.

O'Connor, Thomas H. *Boston Catholics: A History of the Church and Its People.* Boston: Northeastern University Press, 1998.

Plante, Thomas G. *Bless Me Father For I Have Sinned: Perspectives on Sexual Abuse Committed by Roman Catholic Priests.* Westport, Conn.: Praeger, 1999.

———. *Sin Against the Innocents: Sexual Abuse by Priests and the Role of the Catholic Church.* Westport, Conn.: Greenwood, 2004.

Quinn, John R. *The Reform of the Papacy: The Costly Call to Christian Unity.* New York: Crossroad, 1999.

Rossetti, Stephen J. *Slayer of the Soul: Child Sexual Abuse and the Catholic Church.* Mystic, Conn.: Twenty-Third Publications, 1990.

———. *A Tragic Grace: The Catholic Church and Child Sexual Abuse.* Collegeville, Minn.: Liturgical Press, 1996.

Rynne, Xavier. *Letters from Vatican City.* New York: Farrar, Straus & Co., 1963.

Sipe, Richard A. W. *Sex, Priests and Power: Anatomy of a Crisis.* New York: Brunner/Mazel, 1995.

Smith, Karen Sue, ed. *Priesthood in the Modern World: A Reader.* Franklin, Wisc.: Sheed & Ward, 1999.

Teal, Donn. *The Gay Militants.* New York: Stein and Day, 1971.

Weigel, George. *The Truth of Catholicism: Ten Controversies Explored.* New York: Cliff Street, 2001.

———. *The Courage to Be Catholic: Crisis, Reform, and the Future of the Church.* New York: Basic, 2002.

Wills, Garry. *Papal Sin: Structures of Deceit.* New York: Image Books, 2000.

———. *Why I Am a Catholic.* Boston and New York: Houghton Mifflin Company, 2002.

INDEX

About the Author

David France covered the church crisis as a senior editor at *Newsweek.* He is the author of the bestselling *Bag of Toys,* and his feature writing has appeared in the *New York Times Magazine, The New Yorker, Esquire, Glamour,* and *New York.* He is the recipient of the National Headliner, Unity, and New York Press Club awards. France lives in New York City.